VISUAL QUICKPRO GUIDE

PHP
AND MySQL

FOR DYNAMIC WEB SITES

Second Edition

Larry Ullman

 Peachpit Press

Visual QuickPro Guide
PHP and MySQL for Dynamic Web Sites, Second Edition
Larry Ullman

Peachpit Press

1249 Eighth Street
Berkeley, CA 94710
510/524-2178
800/283-9444
510/524-2221 (fax)

Find us on the Web at www.peachpit.com.
To report errors, please send a note to errata@peachpit.com.
Peachpit Press is a division of Pearson Education.

Editor: Rebecca Gulick
Production Coordinator: Andrei Pasternak
Copyeditor: Robert Campbell
Proofreader: Alison Kelley
Compositor: Danielle Foster
Indexer: Karin Arrigoni
Cover Design: Peachpit Press
Interior Design: George Mattingly / GMD

ISBN 0-321-33657-7

9 8 7 6 5 4 3 2

Printed and bound in the United States of America

Dedication:

Dedicated to the fine faculty at my alma mater, Northeast Missouri State University. In particular, I would like to thank: Dr. Monica Barron, Dr. Dennis Leavens, Dr. Ed Tyler, and Dr. Cole Woodcox. I would not be who I am as a writer, as a student, as a teacher, or as a person if it were not for the magnanimous, affecting, and brilliant instruction I received from these educators.

Special Thanks to:

My heartfelt thanks to everyone at Peachpit Press, as always. Special mention goes out to Nancy Ruenzel, Nancy Davis, and Marjorie Baer, for their support; Andrei Pasternak, for turning files into chapters; Lisi Baldwin, for sending translated copies on to me; Whitney Walker, who edited the first edition; and the other dozen or so people at Peachpit and Pearson whose names and titles I don't know but should.

My gratitude to editor extraordinaire Rebecca Gulick, who makes my job so much easier. And thanks to Bob Campbell for his hard work, helpful suggestions, and impressive attention to detail. Thanks also to Karin Arrigoni for indexing, Alison Kelley for proofreading, and Danielle Foster for laying out the book.

Kudos to the good people working on PHP and MySQL, and a hearty "cheers" to the denizens of the various newsgroups, mailing lists, support forums, etc., who offer assistance and advice to those in need.

Thanks, as always, to the readers, whose support gives my job relevance.

Finally, I would not be able to get through a single book if it weren't for the love and support of my wife, Jessica. It's all downhill from here, I promise.

TABLE OF CONTENTS

TABLE OF CONTENTS

TABLE OF CONTENTS

INTRODUCTION

The age of static Web pages is over. For many years the Web survived as a domain where several simple HTML pages linked together constituted a site. But today's users expect exciting pages that are updated frequently and provide a customized experience. At the same time, Web site administrators want sites that are easier to update and maintain. For these reasons and more, building a site with just static HTML files is no longer acceptable. The Web is now a place for dynamic, frequently database-driven, Web applications.

This book represents the culmination of my many years of Web development experience coupled with the value of having written several previous books on the technologies discussed herein. The focus of this book is on covering the most important knowledge in the most efficient manner. It will teach you how to begin developing dynamic Web sites and give you plenty of example code to get you started. All you need to provide is an eagerness to learn.

Well, that and a computer....

What Are Dynamic Web Sites?

Dynamic Web sites are flexible and potent creatures, more accurately described as *applications* than merely sites. Dynamic Web sites

◆ Respond to different parameters (for example, the time of day or the version of the visitor's Web browser)

◆ Have a "memory," allowing for user registration and login, e-commerce, and similar processes

◆ Normally involve HTML forms, so that people can perform searches, provide feedback, and so forth

◆ Often have interfaces where administrators can manage the site's content

◆ Are easier to maintain, upgrade, and build upon

There are many technologies available for creating dynamic Web sites. The most common are ASP.NET (Active Server Pages, a Microsoft construct), JSP (Java Server Pages), ColdFusion, and PHP. Dynamic Web sites do not necessarily rely on a database, but more and more of them do, particularly as database applications like MySQL are available at little to no cost.

What's New in PHP 5

PHP 5, like PHP 4 before it, is a major new development of this popular programming language. The most critical changes in PHP 5—from a developer's standpoint—involve object-oriented programming (OOP). PHP has supported objects for a long time, but now it does so in a way that's more in keeping with true OOP thinking.

Besides the OOP alterations, PHP 5 uses a new version of the Zend Engine (the driving force in PHP), resulting in better performance. PHP 5 also has extended capabilities, a smattering of new functions, and a different set of supported extensions out of the box.

What Is PHP?

PHP originally stood for "Personal Home Page" as it was created in 1994 by Rasmus Lerdorf to track the visitors to his online résumé. As its usefulness and capabilities grew (and as it started being used in more professional situations), it came to mean "PHP: Hypertext Preprocessor."

According to the official PHP Web site, found at `www.php.net` (**Figure i.1**), PHP is "an HTML embedded scripting language." It's a complex but descriptive definition, whose meaning I'll explain.

To say that PHP is HTML embedded means that PHP can be interspersed within HTML, which makes developing dynamic Web sites much easier. Also, PHP is a scripting language, as opposed to a programming language: PHP was to designed to write Web scripts, not stand-alone applications. The scripts run only after an event occurs—for example, when a user submits a form or goes to a URL.

I should add to this definition by stating that PHP is a *server-side*, *cross-platform* technology, both descriptions being important. Server-side refers to the fact that everything PHP does occurs on the server (as opposed to on the client, which is the Web site viewer's computer). Its cross-platform nature means that PHP runs on most operating systems, including Windows, Unix (and its many variants), and Macintosh. More important, the PHP scripts written on one server will normally work on another with little or no modification.

At the time the book was written, PHP was at version 5 (5.0.4, technically), with version 4.3 still being maintained and commonly found on servers. This book will use PHP 5 specifically (see the sidebar), but you should not have problems if you are using a slightly older version. Obviously, it would be preferable to work on a server using the latest version of PHP, but since you cannot always control these things, this book promotes version-indifferent code as much as possible. In cases where recently added functions or variables are being used, notes are made indicating alternative solutions.

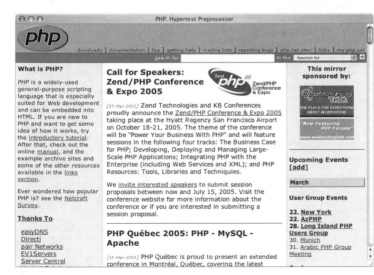

Figure i.1 The home page for PHP.

Why use PHP

Put simply, when it comes to developing dynamic Web sites, PHP is better, faster, and easier to learn than the alternatives. What you get with PHP is excellent performance, a tight integration with nearly every database available, stability, portability, and a nearly limitless feature set due to its extendibility. All of this comes at no cost (PHP is open source) and with a very manageable learning curve. PHP is one of the best marriages I've ever seen between the ease with which beginning programmers can begin using it and the ability for more advanced programmers to do everything they require.

Finally, the proof is in the pudding: PHP has seen an exponential growth in use since its inception (**Figure i.2**), overtaking ASP as the most popular scripting language being used today. It's the most requested module for Apache (the most-used Web server), and by the time this book hits the shelves, PHP will be on about 20 million domains.

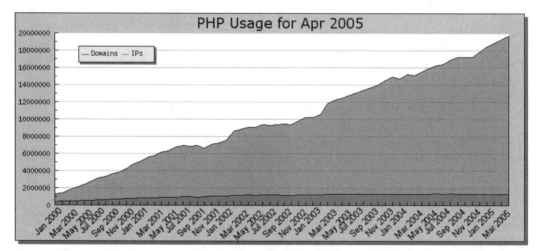

Figure i.2 This chart from Netcraft (www.netcraft.com) shows PHP's phenomenal growth over the past few years.

How PHP works

As previously stated, PHP is a server-side language. This means that the code you write in PHP resides on a host computer called a *server*. The server sends Web pages to the requesting visitors (you, the client, with your Web browser).

When a visitor goes to a Web site written in PHP, the server reads the PHP code and then processes it according to its scripted directions. In the example shown in **Figure i.3**, the PHP code tells the server to send the appropriate data—HTML code—to the Web browser, which treats the received code as it would a standard HTML page.

This differs from a static HTML site where, when a request is made, the server merely sends the HTML data to the Web browser and there is no server-side interpretation occurring (**Figure i.4**). Hence, to the end user and the Web browser there is no perceptible difference between what home.html and home.php may look like, but how that page's content was created will be significantly different.

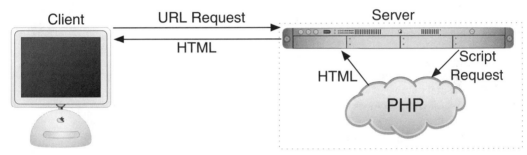

Figure i.3 How PHP fits into the client/server model when a user requests a Web page.

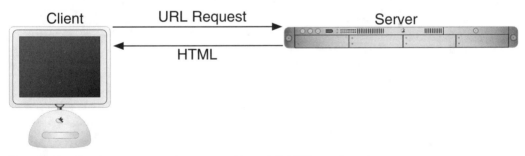

Figure i.4 The client/server process when a request for a static HTML page is made.

What Is MySQL?

MySQL (www.mysql.com, **Figure i.5**) is the world's most popular, and some might argue best, open source database. In fact, particularly as versions 4 and 5 add new features, MySQL is a viable competitor to the pricey goliaths such as Oracle and Microsoft's SQL Server. Like PHP, MySQL offers excellent performance, portability, and reliability, with a moderate learning curve and little to no cost.

MySQL is a database management system (DBMS) for relational databases (therefore, MySQL is an RDBMS). A database, in the simplest terms, is a collection of interrelated data, be it text, numbers, or binary files, that are stored and kept organized by the DBMS.

There are many types of databases, from the simple flat-file to relational and object-oriented. A relational database uses multiple tables to store information in its most discernable parts. Prior to the early 1970s (when this concept was developed), databases

Pronunciation Guide

Trivial as it may be, I should clarify up front that MySQL is technically pronounced "My Ess Que Ell," just as SQL should be said "Ess Que Ell." This is a question many people have when first working with these technologies. While not a critical issue, it's always best to pronounce acronyms correctly.

Figure i.5 The home page for the MySQL database application.

looked more like spreadsheets with single, vast tables storing everything. While relational databases may involve more thought in the designing and programming stages, they offer an improvement to reliability and data integrity that more than makes up for the extra effort required. Further, relational databases are more searchable and allow for concurrent users.

By incorporating a database into a Web application, some of the data generated by PHP can be retrieved from MySQL (**Figure i.6**). This further moves the site's content from a static (hard-coded) basis to a flexible one, flexibility being the key to a dynamic Web site.

MySQL is an open source application, like PHP, meaning that it is free to use or even modify (the source code itself is downloadable). There are occasions in which you should pay for a MySQL license, especially if you are making money from the sales or incorporation of the MySQL product. Check MySQL's licensing policy for more information on this.

The MySQL software consists of several pieces, including the MySQL server (*mysqld*, which runs and manages the databases), the MySQL client (*mysql*, which gives you an interface to the server), and numerous utilities for maintenance and other purposes. PHP has always had good support for MySQL, and that is even more true in the most recent versions of the language.

MySQL has been known to handle databases as large as 60,000 tables with more than five billion rows. MySQL can work with tables as large as eight million terabytes on some operating systems, generally a healthy 4 GB otherwise.

At the time of this writing, MySQL is on version 4.1.12, with version 5 in development. As the version of MySQL you have affects what features you can use (see the sidebar), it's important that you know what you're working with. For this book, MySQL 4.1 was used, and comments are included in the text where a feature is version-specific.

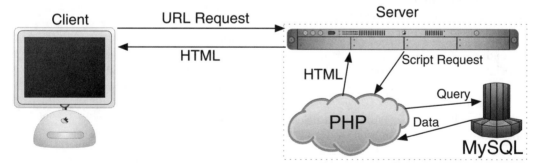

Figure i.6 How most of the dynamic Web applications in this book will work, using both PHP and MySQL.

What You'll Need

To follow the examples in this book, you'll need the following tools:

◆ A Web server application (for example, Apache, Xitami, or IIS)

◆ PHP

◆ MySQL

◆ A Web browser (Microsoft's Internet Explorer, Mozilla's Firefox, Apple's Safari, etc.)

◆ A text editor, PHP-capable WYSIWYG application (Macromedia's Dreamweaver qualifies), or IDE (integrated development environment)

◆ An FTP application, if using a remote server

One of the great aspects of developing dynamic Web sites with PHP and MySQL is that all of the requirements can be met at no cost whatsoever, regardless of your operating system! Apache, PHP, and MySQL are each free; most Web browsers can be had without cost (except for OmniWeb, Opera, and a couple others); and many good text editors are available for nothing.

Appendix A, "Installation," discusses the installation process on Windows and Mac OS X operating systems. If you have a computer, you are only a couple of downloads away from being able to create dynamic Web sites (in that case, your computer would represent both the client and the server in Figures i.3 and i.6). Conversely, you could purchase Web hosting for only dollars per month that will provide you with a PHP- and MySQL-enabled environment already online. (There are free PHP and MySQL hosting companies around, but they often leave much to be desired.)

The MySQL Versions

Versions 4.0, 4.1, and 5 are all major releases of MySQL, adding and changing the feature set. MySQL 4.0 added support for the InnoDB table type, which in turn allows for transactions and foreign key constraints. Version 4 also improved upon FULLTEXT searches and added the UNION SQL command.

The major addition in version 4.1 is support for subqueries, a handy concept present in most high-powered database applications. Version 4.1 also changed the way the PASSWORD() function was used, causing problems for many users (the OLD_PASSWORD() function replicates its old behavior).

Version 5 of MySQL will bring about three major features: stored procedures, cursors, and views. While these are all useful, they are outside the scope of creating basic Web applications.

Later on down the line, MySQL will release version 5.1, where it plans to add foreign key constraints for all table types as well as column-level permissions.

About This Book

This book teaches how to develop dynamic Web sites with PHP and MySQL, covering the knowledge that most developers might require. In keeping with the format of the Visual QuickPro series, the information is discussed using a step-by-step approach with corresponding images. The focus has been kept on real-world, practical examples, avoiding "here's something you could do but never would" scenarios. As a Web developer myself, I wrote about the information that I use and avoided those topics immaterial to the task at hand.

The structure of the book is very linear. It begins with three chapters covering the fundamentals of PHP (by the second chapter, you will have already developed your first dynamic Web page). After that, there are two chapters on SQL (Structured Query Language, which is used to interact with all databases) and MySQL. Both chapters address the basics of SQL, database design, and the MySQL application in particular. Then there's one chapter on debugging and error management, followed by another specifically on using PHP and MySQL together, a remarkably easy thing to do.

The following three chapters teach more application techniques to round out your knowledge. Chapter 11, "Extended Topics," will show you some extra ideas worth consideration but not required by all applications. Finally, I've included three example chapters, in which the heart of different Web applications are developed, with instructions. The appendices discuss installation and provide references and resources for more information.

Is this book for you?

This book was written for a wide range of people within the beginner-to-intermediate range. The book makes use of XHTML for future compatibility, so solid experience with XHTML, or its forebear HTML, is a must. Although this book covers many things, it does not formally teach HTML or Web page design.

Second, this book expects that you have one of the following:

◆ The drive and ability to learn without being guided by the nose, or...

◆ Familiarity with another programming language (even solid JavaScript skills would qualify), or...

◆ A cursory knowledge of PHP

Make no mistake: This book covers PHP and MySQL from A to Z, teaching everything you'll need to know to develop real-world Web sites, but particularly the early chapters cover PHP at a quick pace. For this reason I recommend either some programming experience or a curious and independent spirit when it comes to learning new things. If you find that the material goes too quickly, you should probably start off with the latest edition of my *PHP for the World Wide Web: Visual QuickStart Guide*, which goes at a more tempered pace.

No database experience is required, since SQL and MySQL are discussed starting at a more basic level.

What's new in this edition

The first edition of this book has been very popular, and I've received a lot of positive feedback on it (thanks!). In writing this new edition, I wanted to do more than just update the material for the latest versions of PHP and MySQL, although that is an overriding consideration throughout the book. Other new features you'll find are:

◆ Expanded and updated installation and configuration instructions

◆ Many new, advanced MySQL and SQL examples

◆ An entire chapter dedicated to error management and debugging

◆ New examples demonstrating techniques frequently requested by readers

◆ A broader range of extended topics

For those of you that also own the first edition (thanks!), I believe that these new features will also make this edition a required fixture on your desk or bookshelf.

How this book compares to my other books

This is my fourth PHP and/or MySQL title, after (in order)

◆ *PHP for the World Wide Web: Visual QuickStart Guide*

◆ *PHP Advanced for the World Wide Web: Visual QuickPro Guide*

◆ *MySQL: Visual QuickStart Guide*

I hope this résumé implies a certain level of qualification to write this book, but how do you, as a reader standing in a bookstore, decide which title is for you? You are more than welcome to splurge and buy the whole set, earning my eternal gratitude, but if you had to choose just one....

First, see the "Is this book for you?" section and see if the requirements apply. If you have no programming experience at all and would prefer to be led more gingerly, my first book would be better. If you are already very comfortable with PHP and want to learn more of its advanced capabilities, pick up the second. If you are most interested in MySQL and are not concerned with learning much about PHP, check out the third (it has a single chapter on MySQL and PHP).

That being said, if you want to learn everything you need to know to begin developing dynamic Web sites with PHP and MySQL today, then this is the book for you! It references the most current versions of both technologies, uses techniques not previously discussed in other books, and contains its own unique examples.

INTRODUCTION

Companion Web Site

I have developed a companion Web site specifically for this book, which you may reach at www.DMCinsights.com/phpmysql2 (**Figure i.7**). There you will find every script from this book, a text file containing lengthy SQL commands, and a list of errata that occurred during publication. (If you have problem with a command or script, and are following the book exactly, check the errata to ensure there is not a printing error before driving yourself absolutely mad.) At this Web site you will also find useful Web links, a highly popular forum where readers can ask and answer each other's questions (I answer many of them myself), and more!

Questions, comments, or suggestions?

If you have any questions on PHP or MySQL, you should turn to one of the many Web sites, mailing lists, newsgroups, and FAQ repositories already in existence. Appendix C, "Resources," lists the most popular of these options. If you need an immediate answer, those sources or a quick Web search will most assuredly serve your needs (in all likelihood, someone else has already seen and solved your exact problem).

You can also direct your questions, comments, and suggestions to me directly, via email, at: phpmysql2@DMCinsights.com. I do try to answer every email I receive, although I cannot guarantee a quick reply. Preference and more detailed responses will be given to emails directly pertaining to the content of the book itself; more prompt and thoughtful replies on other issues are best sought out through the mailing lists or the book's online reader forum.

Figure i.7 The companion Web site for this book.

INTRODUCTION TO PHP

To use an old chestnut, every journey starts with one small step, and the first step in developing dynamic Web applications with PHP and MySQL is to learn the fundamentals of the scripting language itself.

Although this book focuses on using MySQL and PHP in combination, you'll do a vast majority of your dynamic Web site legwork using PHP alone. In this and the following chapter, you'll learn its basics, from syntax to variables, operators, and language constructs (conditionals, loops, and whatnots). At the same time you are picking up these fundamentals, you'll also begin developing usable code that you'll integrate into larger applications later in the book.

In this introductory chapter, I'll cruise through most of the basics of the PHP Web scripting language. You'll learn the syntax for coding PHP, how to send data to the Web browser, and how to use two kinds of variables (strings and numbers) plus constants. Some of the examples may seem inconsequential, but they'll demonstrate ideas you'll have to master in order to write more advanced scripts further down the line. Once you comprehend the rules explained over the next 30 or so pages, you'll be ready to start creating your own dynamic Web sites.

Basic Syntax

As I mentioned in the book's introduction, PHP is an HTML-embedded scripting language. What *HTML-embedded* means is that you can intermingle PHP and HTML code within the same script.

To begin programming with PHP, start with a simple Web page. **Script 1.1** gives an example of a no-frills XHTML Transitional document, which I'll be using as the foundation for every Web page in the book (see Appendix C, "Resources," for information on XHTML).

To place PHP code within this document, you surround the code with PHP tags, either the formal and preferred

```
<?php

?>
```

or the informal

```
<?

?>
```

Anything placed within these tags will be treated by the Web server as PHP (meaning the PHP interpreter will process the code; text outside of the PHP tags is immediately sent to the Web browser).

A final consideration for your PHP scripts is that the file must use the proper extension. The extension tells the server to treat the script as a PHP page. Most Web servers will use .html or .htm for standard HTML pages, and normally, .php is preferred for your PHP scripts.

Script 1.1 A basic XHTML 1.0 Transitional Web document.

```
1   <!DOCTYPE html PUBLIC "-//W3C//DTD XHTML
    1.0 Transitional//EN"
2        "http://www.w3.org/TR/xhtml1/DTD/
         xhtml1-transitional.dtd">
3   <html xmlns="http://www.w3.org/1999/
    xhtml" xml:lang="en" lang="en">
4   <head>
5       <meta http-equiv="content-type" content=
        "text/html; charset=iso-8859-1" />
6       <title>Page Title</title>
7   </head>
8   <body>
9   </body>
10  </html>
```

Script 1.2 This first PHP script doesn't do anything, per se, but does demonstrate the syntax to be used.

```
1   <!DOCTYPE html PUBLIC "-//W3C//DTD XHTML
    1.0 Transitional//EN"
2         "http://www.w3.org/TR/xhtml1/DTD/
          xhtml1-transitional.dtd">
3   <html xmlns="http://www.w3.org/1999/
    xhtml" xml:lang="en" lang="en">
4   <head>
5       <meta http-equiv="content-type" content=
        "text/html; charset=iso-8859-1" />
6       <title>Basic PHP Page</title>
7   </head>
8   <body>
9   <p>This is standard HTML.</p>
10  <?php
11  ?>
12  </body>
13  </html>
```

To make a basic PHP script:

1. Create a new document in your text editor (**Script 1.2**).

It generally does not matter what text editor you use, be it BBEdit on the Macintosh, the very basic Notepad or more advanced Dreamweaver on Windows, or vi on Linux.

2. Start with your HTML document.

```
<!DOCTYPE html PUBLIC "-//W3C//
→ DTD XHTML 1.0 Transitional//EN"
"http://www.w3.org/TR/xhtml1/DTD/
→ xhtml1-transitional.dtd">
<html xmlns="http://www.w3.org/1999/
→ xhtml" xml:lang="en" lang="en">
<head>
    <meta http-equiv="content-type"
    → content="text/html;
    → charset=iso-8859-1" />
    <title>Basic PHP Page</title>
</head>
<body>
<p>This is standard HTML.</p>
</body>
</html>
```

Although this is the syntax I'll be using throughout the book, you can change the HTML to match whichever standard you intend to use (e.g., HTML 4.0 Strict).

3. Before the closing body tag, insert your PHP tags.

```
<?php
?>
```

It is highly recommended that PHP developers use the formal PHP tags, and I'll do so in this book. These are also known as XML-style tags.

continues on next page

BASIC SYNTAX

4. Save the file as `first.php`.

Remember that if you don't save the file using an appropriate PHP extension, the script will not execute properly.

5. Place the file in the proper directory of your Web server.

If you are running PHP on your own computer (presumably after following the installation directions in Appendix A, "Installation"), you just need to move, copy, or save the file to a specific folder on your computer. You can check the documentation for your particular Web server application to find this directory. Common options are `C:\inetpub\wwwroot` (IIS on Windows), `C:\Program Files\Apache Group\Apache\htdocs` (Apache on Windows), or `~/Sites` (Mac OS X with Apache, where ~ refers to your Home directory).

If you are running PHP on a hosted server (on a remote computer), you'll need to use an FTP application to upload the file to the proper directory. Your hosting company will provide you with access and the other necessary information.

6. Run `first.php` in your Web browser (**Figure 1.1**).

Again, if you are running PHP on your own computer, you'll need to go to `http://localhost/first.php` or `http://localhost/~<username>/first.php` (on Mac OS X, inserting your actual username). If you are using a Web host for your domain name, you'll need to use `http://your-domain-name/first.php`.

You should see a simple, but perfectly valid, Web page. If you see the PHP code (the tags), then either you did not use the proper extension or PHP is not enabled on your server.

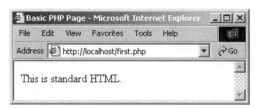

Figure 1.1 While it seems like any other (simple) HTML page, this is in fact a PHP script and the basis for the rest of the examples in the book.

✔ Tips

- To find more information about HTML and XHTML, see Appendix C, "Resources," or check out Elizabeth Castro's excellent book *HTML for the World Wide Web with XHTML and CSS: Visual QuickStart Guide* (ISBN 0-321-13007-3).

- One of the problems with using Notepad on Windows—which is frankly not a very good text editor—is that it will try to add `.txt` to the file's name when you save it. You can avoid this by saving the file as `"first.php"` (using the quotes) or by setting the Text Documents drop-down menu to All Files before saving.

- There are actually four different pairs of PHP tags. Besides the two I've already mentioned, there are the ASP (`<%` and `%>`) and script styles (`<script language="php">` and `</script>`), but these are far less commonly used.

- If you are uncertain about the status of PHP on your Web server, you should run the `phpinfo()` example demonstrated in Appendix A, "Installation," before continuing through this chapter.

- Because I am running Apache on my own computer within a small network, you will sometimes see URLs like `http://192.168.0.101/ch01/first.php` in this book, where *192.168.0.101* is the address of my server within this network. You'll see this in the occasional image, so don't let that confuse you.

- You can embed multiple sections of PHP code within a single HTML document (i.e., you can go in and out of the two languages). You'll see examples of this throughout the book.

- Because PHP scripts need to be parsed by the server, you *absolutely must* access PHP scripts via the URL (`http://localhost/first.php` or `http://www.dmcinsights.com/first.php`). You cannot simply open them in your Web browser as you would a file in other applications (in which case the address would start with `file://`).

BASIC SYNTAX

Sending Data to the Web Browser

To build dynamic Web sites with PHP, you must know how to send data to the Web browser. PHP has a number of built-in functions for this purpose, the most common being echo() and print().

```
echo 'Hello, world!';
```

```
print "It's nice to see you.";
```

As you can see from this example, either single or double quotation marks will work with either function (the distinction between the two types of quotation marks will be made clear by the chapter's end). Also note that in PHP all statements (a line of executed code, in layman's terms) must end with a semicolon.

Looking for an Escape

As you might discover, one of the complications with sending data to the Web involves printing single and double quotation marks. Either of the following will cause errors (**Figure 1.2**):

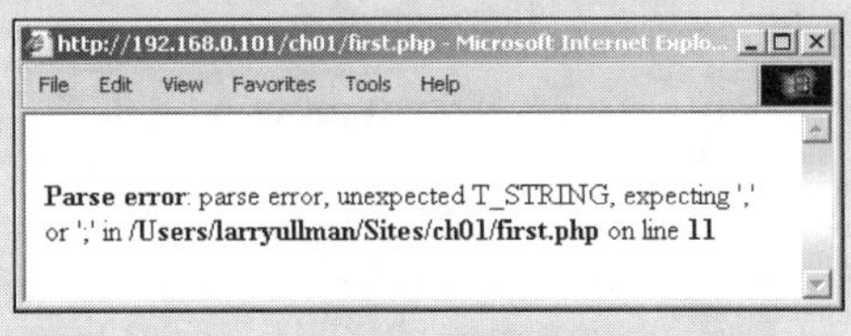

Figure 1.2 This may be the first of many parse errors you see as a PHP programmer (this one is caused by an un-escaped quotation mark).

```
echo "She said, "How are you?"";
```

```
print 'I'm just ducky.';
```

There are two solutions to this problem. First, use single quotation marks when printing a double quotation mark and vice versa:

```
echo 'She said, "How are you?"';
```

```
print "I'm just ducky.";
```

Or, you can *escape* the problematic character by preceding it with a backslash:

```
echo "She said, \"How are you?\"";
```

```
print 'I\'m just ducky.';
```

Understanding how to use the backslash to escape a character is an important concept, and one I'll cover in more depth at the end of the chapter.

Script 1.3 Using print() or echo(), PHP can send data to the Web browser (see Figure 1.3).

```
script
1    <!DOCTYPE html PUBLIC "-//W3C//DTD XHTML
     1.0 Transitional//EN"
2            "http://www.w3.org/TR/xhtml1/DTD/
             xhtml1-transitional.dtd">
3    <html xmlns="http://www.w3.org/1999/
     xhtml" xml:lang="en" lang="en">
4    <head>
5        <meta http-equiv="content-type" content=
         "text/html; charset=iso-8859-1" />
6        <title>Using Echo()</title>
7    </head>
8    <body>
9    <p>This is standard HTML.</p>
10   <?php
11   echo 'This was generated using PHP!';
12   ?>
13   </body>
14   </html>
```

To send data to the Web browser:

1. Open first.php (refer to Script 1.2) in your text editor.

2. Between the PHP tags (lines 10 and 11), add a simple message (**Script 1.3**).

echo 'This was generated using PHP!';

It truly doesn't matter what message you type here, which function you use (echo() or print()), or which quotation marks, for that matter—just be careful if you are printing a single or double quotation mark as part of your message (see the sidebar "Looking for an Escape").

3. If you want, change the page title (line 6).

<title>Using Echo()</title>

This is an optional and purely cosmetic change.

continues on next page

SENDING DATA TO THE WEB BROWSER

4. Save the file as second.php, upload to your Web server, and test in your Web browser (**Figure 1.3**).

If you see a parse error instead of your message (see Figure 1.2), check that you have both opened and closed your quotation marks and escaped any problematic characters. Also be certain to conclude each statement with a semicolon.

If you see an entirely blank page, this is probably for one of two reasons:

▲ There is a problem with your HTML. Test this by viewing the source of your page and looking for HTML problems there (**Figure 1.4**). If you don't know how to view the source, see the instructions at the end of the next set of steps.

▲ An error occurred, but *display_errors* is turned off in your PHP configuration, so nothing is shown. In this case, see the section in Appendix A on how to configure PHP so that you can turn *display_errors* back on.

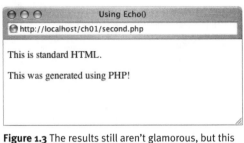

Figure 1.3 The results still aren't glamorous, but this page was in part dynamically generated by PHP.

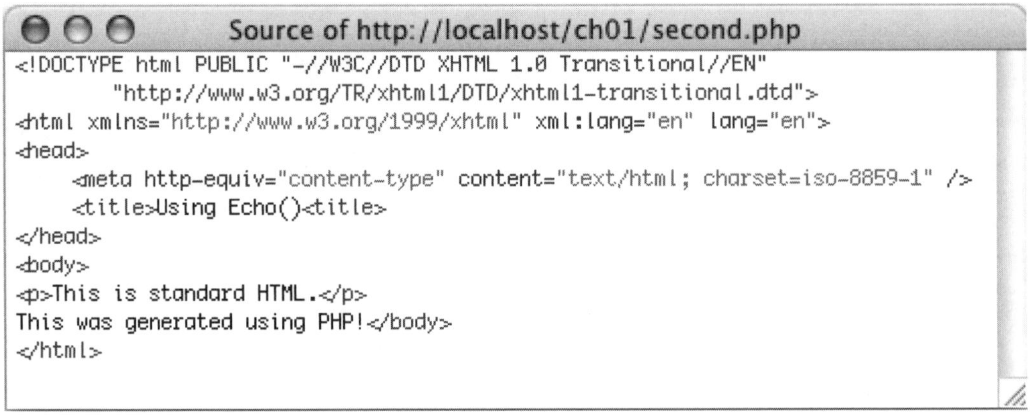

```
<!DOCTYPE html PUBLIC "-//W3C//DTD XHTML 1.0 Transitional//EN"
        "http://www.w3.org/TR/xhtml1/DTD/xhtml1-transitional.dtd">
<html xmlns="http://www.w3.org/1999/xhtml" xml:lang="en" lang="en">
<head>
    <meta http-equiv="content-type" content="text/html; charset=iso-8859-1" />
    <title>Using Echo()<title>
</head>
<body>
<p>This is standard HTML.</p>
This was generated using PHP!</body>
</html>
```

Figure 1.4 One common cause for seeing a blank PHP page is a simple HTML error, like the closing title tag here (it's missing the slash).

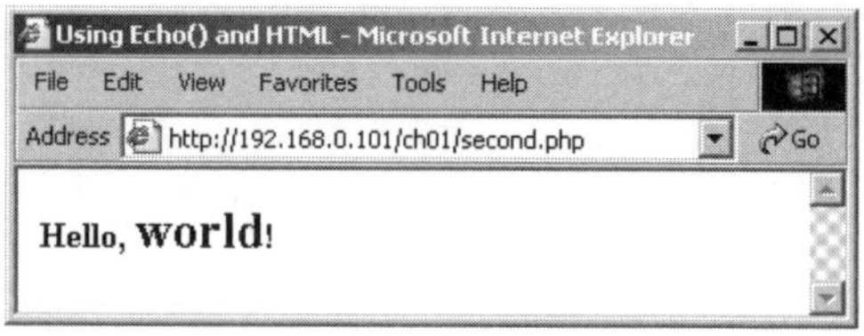

Figure 1.5 PHP can send HTML code (like the formatting here) as well as simple text (see Figure 1.3) to the Web browser.

✔ Tips

- Technically, echo() and print() are language constructs, not functions. That being said, don't be surprised as I continue to call them "functions" for convenience. Also, I include the parentheses when referring to functions to help distinguish them from variables and other parts of PHP. This is just my own little convention.

- You can also use echo() and print() to send HTML code to the Web browser, like so (**Figure 1.5**):

  ```
  echo '<b>Hello, <font size="+2">
  → world</font>!</b>';
  ```

- PHP is case-insensitive when it comes to function names, so ECHO(), echo(), eCHo(), and so forth will all work.

- With echo() but not print(), you can send multiple, separate chunks of data to the Web browser using commas:

  ```
  echo 'Hello, ', 'world!';
  ```

- Echo() and print() can both be used to print text over multiple lines, as you'll see.

- I prefer to use echo() over print(), for no particular reason. If you prefer print(), you can replace any reference I make to echo() with print() without a problem.

Understanding PHP, HTML, and White Space

Before I get any further into the depths of using PHP to send HTML and other data to the Web browser, it's important to fully comprehend the PHP process. With PHP you can send data (a combination of HTML tags and text) to the Web browser, which will, in turn, display it as the Web page the end user sees. Thus, what you are doing with PHP is creating the *HTML source* of a Web page. Pictorially, this means PHP is generating the HTML in **Figure 1.6** (accessed by choosing View > Source or View > Page Source in your browser), which the Web browser will turn into **Figure 1.7**.

With this in mind, there are essentially three areas where you can affect spacing: in your PHP scripts, in your HTML source, and in the rendered Web page. The extra spaces, tabs, and blank lines you create are generically known as *white space*.

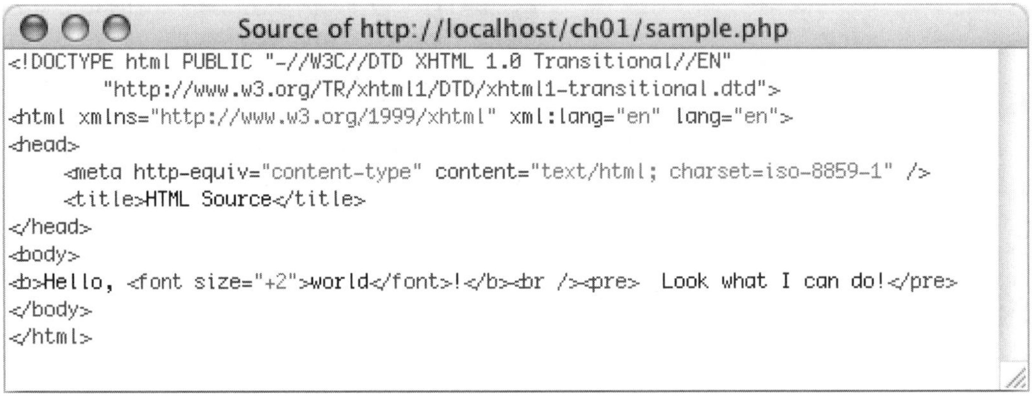

```
⬤ ⬤ ⬤          Source of http://localhost/ch01/sample.php
<!DOCTYPE html PUBLIC "-//W3C//DTD XHTML 1.0 Transitional//EN"
        "http://www.w3.org/TR/xhtml1/DTD/xhtml1-transitional.dtd">
<html xmlns="http://www.w3.org/1999/xhtml" xml:lang="en" lang="en">
<head>
    <meta http-equiv="content-type" content="text/html; charset=iso-8859-1" />
    <title>HTML Source</title>
</head>
<body>
<b>Hello, <font size="+2">world</font>!</b><br /><pre>  Look what I can do!</pre>
</body>
</html>
```

Figure 1.6 You'll use PHP to generate the HTML source of a Web page (like this)...

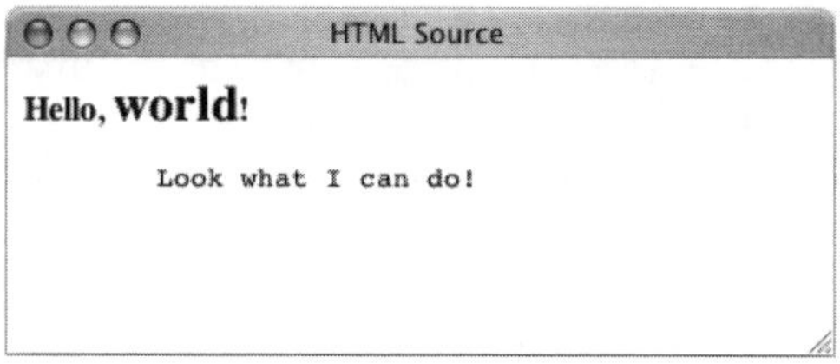

Figure 1.7 ...which the Web browser then turns into a nicely formatted display.

PHP is generally white space insensitive, meaning that you can space out your code however you want to make your scripts more legible. HTML is also generally white space insensitive. Specifically, the only white space in HTML that affects the rendered page is a single space (multiple spaces still get rendered as one). Consequently, the HTML in **Figure 1.8** will make the same page (see Figure 1.7) as the HTML in Figure 1.6.

To alter the spacing of the finished Web page, use the HTML tags `<br />` (line break, `<br>` in older HTML standards) and `<p></p>` (paragraph). To alter the spacing of the HTML source created with PHP, you can

- Use `echo()` or `print()` over the course of several lines.

  or

- Use the newline character (`\n`) within double quotation marks.

I'll demonstrate both of these techniques in the following script.

Source of http://localhost/ch01/sample.php

```
<!DOCTYPE html PUBLIC "-//W3C//DTD XHTML 1.0 Transitional//EN"
        "http://www.w3.org/TR/xhtml1/DTD/xhtml1-transitional.dtd">
<html xmlns="http://www.w3.org/1999/xhtml" xml:lang="en" lang="en">
<head>
    <meta http-equiv="content-type" content="text/html; charset=iso-8859-1" />
    <title>HTML Source</title>
</head>
<body>



            <b>Hello, <font size="+2">world</font>!</b>
            <br />

    <pre>    Look what I can do!</pre>

</body>
</html>
```

Figure 1.8 Extraneous white spacing in the HTML source will not affect the look of a page (see Figure 1.7) but can make the source easier to review.

To create white space:

1. Open `second.php` (refer to Script 1.3) in your text editor.

2. If desired, change the page's title (**Script 1.4**).

   `<title>White Space</title>`

3. If desired, delete the hard-coded HTML line: `<p>This is standard HTML.</p>` (line 9).

4. After the initial PHP tag, press Return or Enter.

   The blank line created by the Return/Enter key will not affect the PHP script, the HTML source, or the rendered HTML page, but it will begin to make the PHP script more legible (less congested).

5. Change the existing `echo()` statement so that it runs over multiple lines.

   ```
   echo 'This echo() statement runs
   over the course of two lines!';
   ```

   As you'll see once this script is executed, the Return/Enter key pressed in mid-sentence (so that *over* begins on the next line) generates HTML source over two lines. This works because the `echo()` statement continues until it hits the concluding single quotation mark.

Script 1.4 This script demonstrates the various types of white space created within the PHP code, the HTML source, and the rendered Web page.

```
1   <!DOCTYPE html PUBLIC "-//W3C//
    DTD XHTML 1.0 Transitional//EN"
2       "http://www.w3.org/TR/xhtml1/DTD/
    xhtml1-transitional.dtd">
3   <html xmlns="http://www.w3.org/1999/
    xhtml" xml:lang="en" lang="en">
4   <head>
5       <meta http-equiv="content-type" content=
    "text/html; charset=iso-8859-1" />
6       <title>White Space</title>
7   </head>
8   <body>
9   <?php
10
11  echo 'This echo() statement runs
12  over the course of two lines!';
13
14  echo "<br />This line should appear
    separately in the Web page.\n\n";
15
16  echo 'Now I\'m done.';
17
18  ?>
19  </body>
20  </html>
```

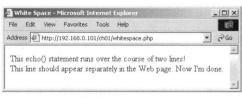

Figure 1.9 The only way to alter the spacing of a displayed Web page is to use HTML tags like
 (see Figure 1.10).

6. Type another echo() statement that uses the line break and newline characters.

echo "
This line should appear separately in the Web page.\n\n";

In this statement I am accomplishing two goals. First, I am sending a break character so that the Web browser displays this sentence on its own line. Second, I conclude the statement with two newlines to affect the HTML source (for the newline to work, you must use double quotation marks).

7. Add one last echo() statement.

echo 'Now I\'m done.';

Here I've used single quotation marks, but to print the single quotation mark (or apostrophe) in *I'm*, I have to escape the character.

8. Save the file as whitespace.php, upload to your Web server, and test in your Web browser (**Figure 1.9**).

You should see that the only spacing created in the final Web page by this script was accomplished by the <br />, which is printed between *lines!* and *This line*.

continues on next page

UNDERSTANDING PHP, HTML, AND WHITE SPACE

9. View the HTML source of the page (**Figure 1.10**).

Depending upon your browser, you can achieve this by

▲ Going to the View menu and choosing Source or Page Source.

or

▲ Right-clicking in the Web page and choosing View Source or View Page Source (Windows).

or

▲ Control-clicking in the Web page and choosing View Source or View Page Source (Macintosh).

In the HTML source you can see how the extra spacing in the PHP code is not transmitted. Using the newline character (refer to Script 1.4, line 14) or continuing a statement over multiple lines (lines 11 and 12) does have an effect on the HTML source but not on the rendered Web page.

✔ Tips

■ Use white spacing liberally in your PHP scripts to make them easier to code and edit.

■ When using PHP to generate HTML, you should try to make the most readable HTML source possible, in case you need to peruse and debug the raw HTML source.

■ That being said, in the interest of saving space in the book, the scripts written herein will not be as liberal with white space as those I would write normally (or as I would recommend you write them).

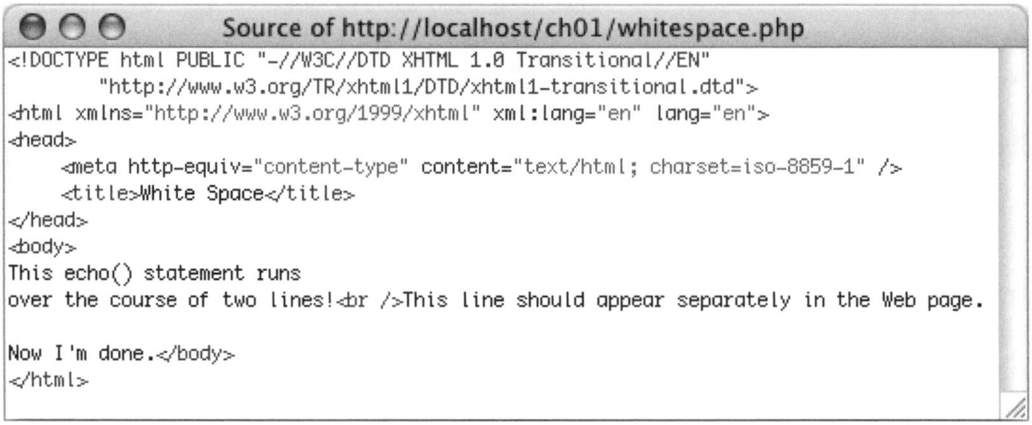

```
Source of http://localhost/ch01/whitespace.php
<!DOCTYPE html PUBLIC "-//W3C//DTD XHTML 1.0 Transitional//EN"
        "http://www.w3.org/TR/xhtml1/DTD/xhtml1-transitional.dtd">
<html xmlns="http://www.w3.org/1999/xhtml" xml:lang="en" lang="en">
<head>
    <meta http-equiv="content-type" content="text/html; charset=iso-8859-1" />
    <title>White Space</title>
</head>
<body>
This echo() statement runs
over the course of two lines!<br />This line should appear separately in the Web page.

Now I'm done.</body>
</html>
```

Figure 1.10 The PHP script creates some of this HTML code, which the browser then displays according to common formatting rules (see Figure 1.9).

WRITING COMMENTS

Writing the executed PHP code itself is only a part of the programming process. A secondary but still crucial aspect to dynamic Web site development involves documenting your code.

In HTML you can add comments using

```
<!-- Comment goes here. -->
```

HTML comments are viewable in the source (**Figure 1.11**) but do not appear in the rendered page.

PHP comments are different in that they aren't sent to the Web browser at all, meaning they won't be viewable to the end user, even when looking at the HTML source.

PHP supports three comment types. The first uses the pound or number symbol (#).

```
# This is a comment.
```

The second uses two slashes.

```
// This is also a comment.
```

Both of these cause PHP to ignore everything that follows until the end of the line (when you press Return or Enter). Thus, these two comments are for single lines only. They are also commonly used to add a comment on the same line as some PHP code.

```
print 'Hello!'; // Say hello.
```

A third style allows comments to run over multiple lines.

```
/* This is a longer comment

that spans two lines. */
```

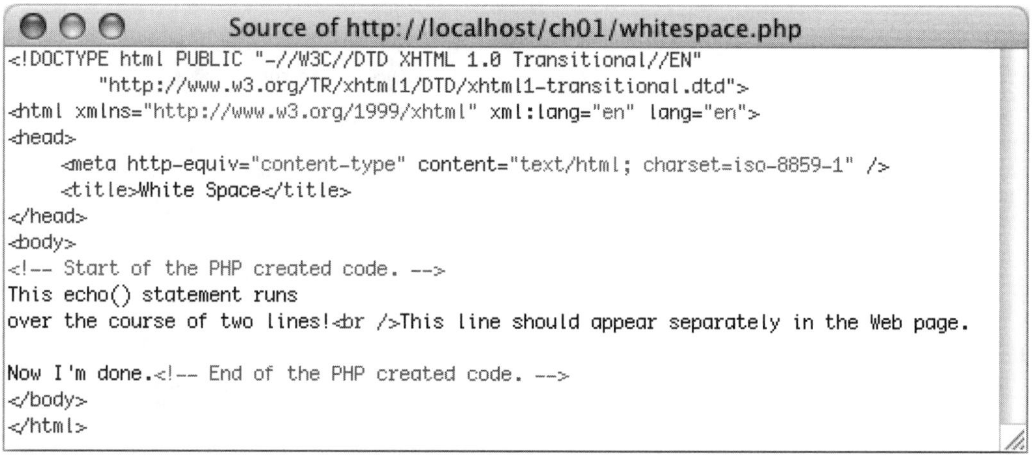

```
 ● ● ●          Source of http://localhost/ch01/whitespace.php
<!DOCTYPE html PUBLIC "-//W3C//DTD XHTML 1.0 Transitional//EN"
        "http://www.w3.org/TR/xhtml1/DTD/xhtml1-transitional.dtd">
<html xmlns="http://www.w3.org/1999/xhtml" xml:lang="en" lang="en">
<head>
    <meta http-equiv="content-type" content="text/html; charset=iso-8859-1" />
    <title>White Space</title>
</head>
<body>
<!-- Start of the PHP created code. -->
This echo() statement runs
over the course of two lines!<br />This line should appear separately in the Web page.

Now I'm done.<!-- End of the PHP created code. -->
</body>
</html>
```

Figure 1.11 HTML COMMENTS APPEAR IN THE SOURCE CODE BUT NOT IN THE WEB PAGE ITSELF.

To comment your scripts:

1. Open `whitespace.php` (refer to Script 1.4) in your text editor.

2. After the initial PHP tag, write your first comment (**Script 1.5**).

```
# Created February 2, 2005
# Created by Larry E. Ullman
# This script does nothing much.
```

One of the first comments each script should contain is an introductory block that lists creation date, modification date, creator, creator's contact information, purpose of the script, and so on. Some people suggest that the shell-style comments (#) stand out more in a script and are therefore best for this kind of notation.

3. Use the multiline comments to comment out the second `echo()` statement.

```
/*
echo "<br />This line should appear
→ separately in the Web page.\n\n";
*/
```

By surrounding any block of PHP code with /* and */, you can render that code inert without having to delete it from your script. By later removing the comment tags, you can reactivate that section of PHP code.

Script 1.5 These basic comments demonstrate the three syntaxes you can use in PHP.

```
1    <!DOCTYPE html PUBLIC "-//W3C//DTD XHTML
     1.0 Transitional//EN"
2          "http://www.w3.org/TR/xhtml1/DTD/
           xhtml1-transitional.dtd">
3    <html xmlns="http://www.w3.org/1999/
     xhtml" xml:lang="en" lang="en">
4    <head>
5        <meta http-equiv="content-type" content=
         "text/html; charset=iso-8859-1" />
6        <title>Comments</title>
7    </head>
8    <body>
9    <?php
10
11   # Created February 2, 2005
12   # Created by Larry E. Ullman
13   # This script does nothing much.
14
15   echo 'This echo() statement runs
16   over the course of two lines!';
17
18   /*
19   echo "<br />This line should appear
     separately in the Web page.\n\n";
20   */
21
22   echo 'Now I\'m done.'; // End of PHP code.
23
24   ?>
25   </body>
26   </html>
```

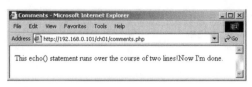

Figure 1.12 The PHP comments in Script 1.5 don't appear in the Web page, but they did have the effect of omitting a sentence (compare with Figure 1.9).

4. Add a final comment after the last echo() statement.

```
echo 'Now I\'m done.'; //
→ End of PHP code.
```

This last (superfluous) comment shows how to place one at the end of a line, a common practice.

5. If you want, change the HTML page's title.

6. Save the file as comments.php, upload to your Web server, and test in your Web browser (**Figure 1.12**).

✔ Tips

■ You shouldn't nest (place one comment within another) multiline comments (/* */), as it will cause problems.

■ Any of the PHP comments can be used at the end of a line (say, after a function call):

```
echo 'Howdy.'; /* Say 'Howdy' */
```

Although this is allowed, it's far less common.

■ It's nearly impossible to over-comment your scripts. Always err on the side of writing too many comments as you code. That being said, in the interest of saving space, the scripts in this book will not be as commented as I would suggest they should be.

What Are Variables?

Variables, in short, are containers used to temporarily store values. These values can be numbers, text, or much more complex arrangements. Variables exist at the heart of any programming language, and comprehending them is key to using PHP.

According to the PHP manual, there are eight types of variables in the language. These include four scalar (single-valued) types—*Boolean* (TRUE or FALSE), *integer*, *floating point* (decimals), and *strings* (text); two nonscalar (multivalued)—*arrays* and *objects*; plus *resources* (which you'll see when interacting with databases) and *NULL* (which is a special type that has no value).

Regardless of what type you are creating, all variables in PHP follow certain syntactical rules:

◆ A variable's name—also called its *identifier*—must start with a dollar sign ($), for example, $name.

◆ The variable's name can contain a combination of strings, numbers, and the underscore, for example, $my_report1.

◆ The first character after the dollar sign must be either a letter or an underscore (it cannot be a number).

◆ Variable names in PHP are case-sensitive. This is a *very* important fact. It means that $name and $Name are entirely different variables.

◆ Variables can be assigned values using the equals sign (=), also called the *assignment operator*.

This is just a cursory introduction to variables. You'll learn more about specific types (strings and numbers) as well as manipulating them later in this chapter.

To begin working with variables, I'll make use of several predefined variables whose values are automatically set when a PHP script is run.

To print out PHP's predefined variables:

1. Create a new HTML document in your text editor (**Script 1.6**).

```
<!DOCTYPE html PUBLIC "-//W3C//
→ DTD XHTML 1.0 Transitional//EN"
"http://www.w3.org/TR/xhtml1/DTD/
→ xhtml1-transitional.dtd">
<html xmlns="http://www.w3.org/1999/
→ xhtml" xml:lang="en" lang="en">
<head>
    <meta http-equiv="content-type"
    → content="text/html;
    → charset=iso-8859-1" />
    <title>Predefined Variables</
    → title>
</head>
<body>
</body>
</html>
```

2. Within the body tags, add your PHP tags and your first comment.

```
<?php # Script 1.6 - predefined.php
?>
```

From here on out, my scripts will no longer comment on the creator, creation date, and so forth, although you should continue to do so. I will, however, make a comment listing the script number and filename for ease of cross-referencing (both in the book and when you download them from the book's supporting Web site, www.DMCInsights.com/phpmysql2).

Script 1.6 This script prints three of PHP's predefined variables.

```
script
1    <!DOCTYPE html PUBLIC "-//W3C//DTD XHTML
     1.0 Transitional//EN"
2          "http://www.w3.org/TR/xhtml1/DTD/
     xhtml1-transitional.dtd">
3    <html xmlns="http://www.w3.org/1999/xhtml"
     xml:lang="en" lang="en">
4    <head>
5      <meta http-equiv="content-type" content=
     "text/html; charset=iso-8859-1" />
6      <title>Predefined Variables</title>
7    </head>
8    <body>
9    <?php # Script 1.6 - predefined.php
10
11   // Create a shorthand version of the
     variable names.
12   $file = $_SERVER['PHP_SELF'];
13   $user = $_SERVER['HTTP_USER_AGENT'];
14   $address = $_SERVER['REMOTE_ADDR'];
15
16   // Print the name of this script.
17   echo "<p>You are running the file <b>$file
     </b>.</p>\n";
18
19   // Print the user's information.
20   echo "<p>You are viewing this page
     using:<br /><b>$user</b><br />from the IP
     address:<br /><b>$address</b></p>\n";
21
22   ?>
23   </body>
24   </html>
```

3. Create a shorthand version of the variables to be used in this script.

```
$file = $_SERVER['PHP_SELF'];
$user = $_SERVER['HTTP_USER_AGENT'];
$address = $_SERVER['REMOTE_ADDR'];
```

This script will use three variables, each of which comes from the larger and predefined $_SERVER variable. $_SERVER refers to a mass of server-related information, like the name of the script being run ($_SERVER['PHP_SELF']), the Web browser and operating system of the user accessing the script ($_SERVER['HTTP_USER_AGENT']), and the IP address of the user accessing the script ($_SERVER['REMOTE_ADDR']).

Creating new variables with shorter names and then assigning them values from $_SERVER will make it easier to refer to the variables when printing them. (It also gets around some other issues you'll learn about in due time.)

4. Print out the name of the script being run.

```
echo "<p>You are running the file
↪<b>$file</b>.</p>\n";
```

The first variable I'll use is $file, which has the same value as $_SERVER['PHP_SELF']. Again, this particular variable always refers to the current script being executed. Depending upon the server, this could be anything from just *scriptname*.php to */path/to/scriptname*.php. Notice that this variable must be printed out within double quotation marks and that I also make use of the PHP newline (\n), which will add a line break in the generated HTML source. Some basic HTML tags—paragraph and bold—are added to give the generated page some flair.

continues on next page

5. Print out the information of the user accessing the script.

```
echo "<p>You are viewing this page
→ using:<br /><b>$user</b><br />from
→ the IP address:<br /><b>$address</
→ b></p>\n";
```

Here I've used two more variables. To repeat what I said in the third step, $user correlates to $_SERVER['HTTP_USER_AGENT'] and refers to the operating system, browser type, and browser version being used to access the Web page. The second variable—$address—matches up with $_SERVER['REMOTE_ADDR'] and refers to the IP address of the user accessing the page.

Again, PHP newlines are used, and I've also thrown in some HTML breaks so that the resulting Web page has extra lines to it.

6. Save your file as predefined.php, upload to your Web server, and test in your Web browser (**Figure 1.13**).

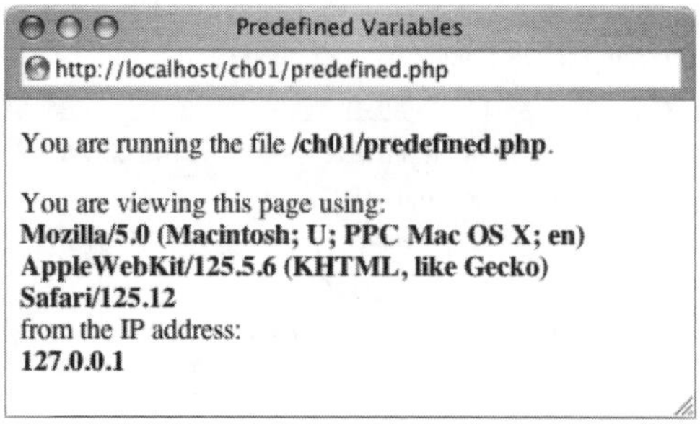

✔ Tips

■ If possible, run this script using a different Web browser (**Figure 1.14**).

■ The most important consideration when creating variables is to use a consistent naming scheme. In this book you'll see that I use all lowercase letters for my variable names, with underscores separating words ($first_name). Some programmers prefer to use capitalization instead: $FirstName.

■ PHP is very casual in how it treats variables, meaning that you don't need to initialize them (set an immediate value) or declare them (set a specific type), and you can convert a variable among the many types without problem.

Figure 1.13 The predefined.php script reports back to the viewer information about the script and the Web browser being used to view it.

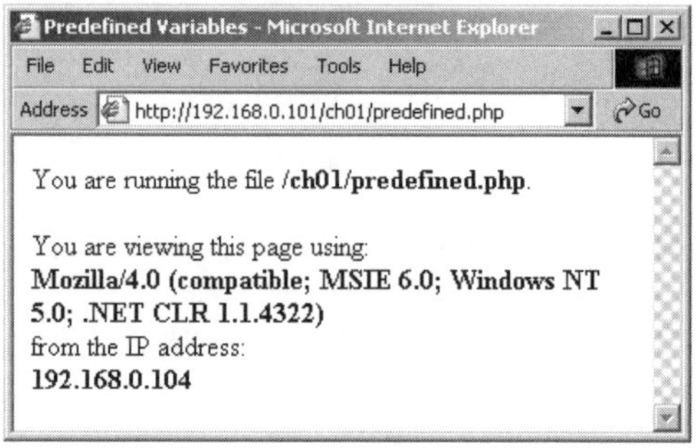

Figure 1.14 This is the book's first truly dynamic script, in that the Web page changes depending upon the person viewing it (compare with Figure 1.13).

About Strings

The first—arguably most important—variable type I'll go into is strings. A *string* is merely a quoted chunk of letters, numbers, spaces, punctuation, and so forth. These are all strings:

◆ 'Tobias'

◆ "In watermelon sugar"

◆ '1,000'

◆ 'February 3, 2005'

To make a string variable, assign a string value to a valid variable name:

```
$first_name = 'Tobias';

$today = 'February 3, 2005';
```

To print out the value of a string, use either echo() or print():

```
echo $first_name;
```

To print the value of string within a context, use double quotation marks:

```
echo "Hello, $first_name";
```

In a way, you've already worked with strings once—when using the predefined variables in the preceding section.

To use strings:

1. Create a new HTML document in your text editor, along with the PHP tags (**Script 1.7**).

```
<!DOCTYPE html PUBLIC "-//W3C//
→ DTD XHTML 1.0 Transitional//EN"
"http://www.w3.org/TR/xhtml1/DTD/
→ xhtml1-transitional.dtd">
<html xmlns="http://www.w3.org/1999/
→ xhtml" xml:lang="en" lang="en">
<head>
    <meta http-equiv="content-type"
    → content="text/html;
    → charset=iso-8859-1" />
    <title>Strings</title>
</head>
<body>
<?php # Script 1.7 - strings.php
?>
</body>
</html>
```

2. Within the PHP tags, create three variables.

```
$first_name = 'Nick';

$last_name = 'Hornby';

$book = 'High Fidelity';
```

In this rudimentary example, I'm going to create $first_name, $last_name, and $book variables that will then be printed out in a message.

continues on next page

3. Create the echo() statement.

```
echo "The book <i>$book</i> was
→written by $first_name
→ $last_name.";
```

All this script does is to print a statement of authorship based upon three established variables. A little HTML formatting (the italics) is thrown in to make it more attractive. Remember to use double quotation marks here for the variable values to be printed out appropriately (more on the importance of double quotation marks at the chapter's end).

4. Save your file as strings.php, upload to your Web server, and test in your Web browser (**Figure 1.15**).

5. If desired, change the values of your three variables and run the script again (**Figure 1.16**).

✔ Tips

■ If you assign another value to an existing variable (say $book), the new value will overwrite the old one. For example:

```
$book = 'High Fidelity';
$book = 'The Corrections';
/* $book now has a value of
'The Corrections'. */
```

■ PHP has no set limits on how big a string can be. It's theoretically possible that you'll be limited by the resources of the server, but it's doubtful that you'll ever encounter such a problem.

Script 1.7 String variables are created and their values sent to the Web browser in this introductory script.

```
1   <!DOCTYPE html PUBLIC "-//W3C//DTD XHTML
    1.0 Transitional//EN"
2       "http://www.w3.org/TR/xhtml1/DTD/
        xhtml1-transitional.dtd">
3   <html xmlns="http://www.w3.org/1999/xhtml"
    xml:lang="en" lang="en">
4   <head>
5       <meta http-equiv="content-type" content=
        "text/html; charset=iso-8859-1" />
6       <title>Strings</title>
7   </head>
8   <body>
9   <?php # Script 1.7 - strings.php
10
11  // Create the variables.
12  $first_name = 'Nick';
13  $last_name = 'Hornby';
14  $book = 'High Fidelity';
15
16  //Print the values.
17  echo "The book <i>$book</i> was written by
    $first_name $last_name.";
18
19  ?>
20  </body>
21  </html>
```

Figure 1.15 The resulting Web page is based upon printing out the values of three variables.

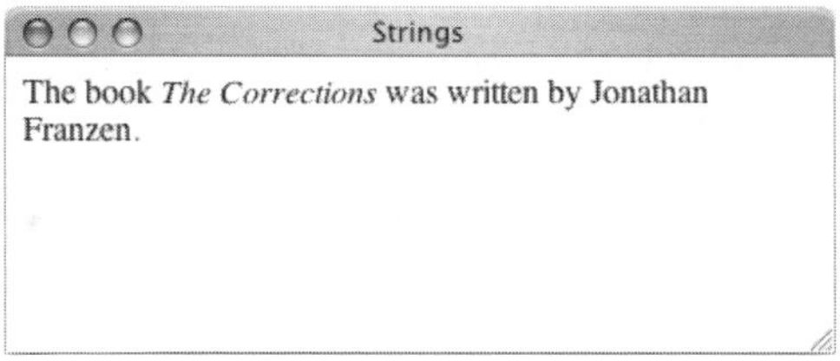

The book *High Fidelity* was written by Nick Hornby.

Figure 1.16 The output of the script is changed by altering the variables in it.

The book *The Corrections* was written by Jonathan Franzen.

ABOUT STRINGS

Script 1.8 CONCATENATION GIVES YOU THE ABILITY TO EASILY MANIPULATE STRINGS, LIKE CREATING AN AUTHOR'S NAME FROM THE COMBINATION OF THEIR FIRST AND LAST NAMES.

```
1   <!DOCTYPE html PUBLIC "-//W3C//DTD XHTML
    1.0 Transitional//EN"
2        "http://www.w3.org/TR/xhtml1/DTD/
         xhtml1-transitional.dtd">
3   <html xmlns="http://www.w3.org/1999/xhtml"
    xml:lang="en" lang="en">
4   <head>
5       <meta http-equiv="content-type" content=
    "text/html; charset=iso-8859-1" />
6       <title>Concatenation</title>
7   </head>
8   <body>
9   <?php # Script 1.8 - concat.php
10
11  // Create the variables.
12  $first_name = 'Melissa';
13  $last_name = 'Bank';
14  $author = $first_name . ' ' . $last_name;
15
16  $book = 'The Girls\' Guide to Hunting and
    Fishing';
17
18  //Print the values.
19  echo "The book <i>$book</i> was written by
    $author.";
20
21  ?>
22  </body>
23  </html>
```

CONCATENATING STRINGS

Concatenation—an important tool when creating dynamic Web sites—is like addition for strings and is performed using the *concatenation operator*: the period (.).

```
$city= 'Seattle';
$state = 'Washington';
$address = $city . $state;
```

The $address variable now has the value *SeattleWashington*, which almost achieves the desired result (*Seattle, Washington*). To improve upon this, I could write

```
$address = $city . ', ' . $state;
```

so that a comma and a space is added to the mix.

Concatenation also works with strings or numbers. Either of these statements will produce the same result (*Seattle, Washington 98101*):

```
$address = $city . ', ' . $state .
→ ' 98101';
$address = $city . ', ' . $state .
→ ' ' . 98101;
```

Concatenation is commonly used with string variables and will be used extensively when building database queries in later chapters. In the meantime, I'll modify the strings.php script to use this new tool.

TO USE CONCATENATION:

1. Open strings.php (refer to Script 1.7) in your text editor.

2. After you've established the $first_name and $last_name variables (lines 12 and 13), add (**Script 1.8**).

```
$author = $first_name . ' ' .
→ $last_name;
```

continues on next page

As a demonstration of concatenation, a new variable—$author—will be created as the concatenation of two existing strings and a space in between.

3. Change the echo() statement to use this new variable.

```
echo "The book <i>$book</i> was
→ written by $author.";
```

Since the two variables have been turned into one, the echo() statement should be altered accordingly.

4. If desired, change the HTML page title and the values of the first name, last name, and book variables.

5. Save your file as concat.php, upload to your Web server, and test in your Web browser (**Figure 1.17**).

✔ Tips

■ PHP has a slew of useful string-specific functions, which you'll see over the course of this book. For example, to calculate how long a string is (how many characters it contains), use strlen():

```
$num = strlen($string);
```

■ You can have PHP convert the case of your strings with: strtolower(), which makes it entirely lowercase; strtoupper(), which makes it entirely uppercase; ucfirst(), which capitalizes the first character; and ucwords(), which capitalizes the first character of every word.

■ If you are merely concatenating one value to another, you can use the *concatenation assignment operator* (.=). The following are equivalent:

```
$title = $title . $subtitle;
$title .= $subtitle;
```

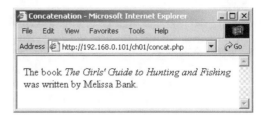

Figure 1.17 The end result of concatenation may never be apparent to the user (compare with Figures 1.15 and 1.16).

■ The initial example in this section could be rewritten using either

```
$address = "$city, $state";
```

or

```
$address = $city;
$address .= ', ';
$address .= $state;
```

■ The concatenation operator can be used when calling functions, like so:

```
$num = strlen ($first_name .
→ $last_name);
```

About Numbers

When I began discussing variables, I was explicit in stating that PHP has both integer and floating-point (decimal) number types. In my experience, though, these two types can be classified under the generic title *numbers* without losing any valuable distinction (for the most part). Valid number-type variables in PHP can be anything like

◆ 8

◆ 3.14

◆ 10980843985

◆ -4.2398508

◆ 4.4e2

Notice that these values are never quoted—in which case they'd be strings with numeric values—nor do they include commas to indicate thousands. Also, a number is assumed to be positive unless it is preceded by the minus sign (-).

Arithmetic Operators	
Operator	Meaning
+	Addition
-	Subtraction
*	Multiplication
/	Division
%	Modulus
++	Increment
--	Decrement

Table 1.1 The standard mathematical operators.

Along with the standard arithmetic operators you can use on numbers (**Table 1.1**), there are dozens of functions. Two I'll introduce here are `round()` and `number_format()`. The former rounds a decimal either to the nearest integer

```
$n = 3.14;
```

```
$n = round ($n); // 3
```

or to a specified number of decimal places

```
$n = 3.142857;
```

```
$n = round ($n, 3); // 3.143
```

The `number_format()` function turns a number into the more commonly written version, grouped into thousands using commas. For example:

```
$n = 20943;
```

```
$n = number_format ($n); // 20,943
```

This function can also set a specified number of decimal points

```
$n = 20943;
```

```
$n = number_format ($n, 2); // 20,943.00
```

To practice with numbers, I'll write a mock-up script that performs the calculations one might use in an e-commerce shopping cart.

To use numbers:

1. Create a new PHP document in your text editor (**Script 1.9**).

```
<!DOCTYPE html PUBLIC "-//W3C//
→ DTD XHTML 1.0 Transitional//EN"
"http://www.w3.org/TR/xhtml1/DTD/
→ xhtml1-transitional.dtd">
<html xmlns="http://www.w3.org/1999/
→ xhtml" xml:lang="en" lang="en">
<head>
    <meta http-equiv="content-type"
    → content="text/html;
    → charset=iso-8859-1" />
    <title>Numbers</title>
</head>
<body>
<?php # Script 1.9 - numbers.php
```

2. Establish the requisite variables.

```
$quantity = 30;
$price = 119.95;
$taxrate = .05;
```

This script will use three hard-coded variables upon which calculations will be made. Throughout the rest of the book, you'll see how these values can be dynamically determined (i.e., by user interaction with an HTML form).

3. Perform the calculations.

```
$total = $quantity * $price;
$total = $total + ($total * $taxrate);
```

The first line establishes the order total as the number of widgets purchased multiplied by the price of each widget. The second line then adds the amount of tax to the total (calculated by multiplying the tax rate by the total).

Script 1.9 The numbers.php script demonstrates the basics of an e-commerce calculator.

```
1   <!DOCTYPE html PUBLIC "-//W3C//DTD XHTML
    1.0 Transitional//EN"
2        "http://www.w3.org/TR/xhtml1/DTD/
         xhtml1-transitional.dtd">
3   <html xmlns="http://www.w3.org/1999/xhtml"
    xml:lang="en" lang="en">
4   <head>
5       <meta http-equiv="content-type" content=
        "text/html; charset=iso-8859-1" />
6       <title>Numbers</title>
7   </head>
8   <body>
9   <?php # Script 1.9 - numbers.php
10
11  // Set the variables.
12  $quantity = 30; // Buying 30 widgets.
13  $price = 119.95;
14  $taxrate = .05; // 5% sales tax.
15
16  // Calculate the total.
17  $total = $quantity * $price;
18  $total = $total + ($total * $taxrate); //
    Calculate and add the tax.
19  $total = number_format ($total, 2);
20
21  // Print the results.
22  echo 'You are purchasing <b>' . $quantity .
    '</b> widget(s) at a cost of <b>$' . $price .
    '</b> each. With tax, the total comes to
    <b>$' . $total . '</b>.';
23
24  ?>
25  </body>
26  </html>
```

ABOUT NUMBERS

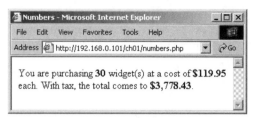

Figure 1.18 The numbers script performs calculations based upon set values.

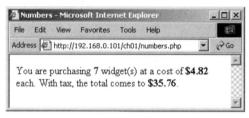

Figure 1.19 To change the generated Web page, alter any or all of the three variables (compare with Figure 1.18).

4. Format the total.

```
$total = number_format ($total, 2);
```

The `number_format()` function will group the total into thousands and round it to two decimal places. This will make the display more appropriate to the end user.

5. Print the results.

```
echo 'You are purchasing <b>' .
→ $quantity . '</b> widget(s) at a
→ cost of <b>$' . $price . '</b>
→ each. With tax, the total comes to
→ <b>$' . $total . '</b>.';
```

The last step in the script is to print out the results. To use a combination of HTML, printed dollar signs, and variables, I feed the code to the `echo()` statement using a combination of single-quoted text and concatenated variables.

You could also put this all within a double-quoted string (as in previous examples), but when PHP encounters, for example, `at a cost of $$price` in the `echo()` statement, the double dollar sign would cause problems. You'll see an alternative solution in the last example of this chapter.

6. Complete the PHP code and the HTML page.

```
?>
</body>
</html>
```

7. Save the file as `numbers.php`, upload to your Web server, and test in your Web browser (**Figure 1.18**).

8. If desired, change the initial three variables and rerun the script (**Figure 1.19**).

✔ Tips

- PHP supports a maximum integer of around two billion on most platforms. With numbers larger than that, PHP will automatically use a floating-point type.

- When dealing with arithmetic, the issue of precedence arises (the order in which complex calculations are made). While the PHP manual and other sources tend to list out the hierarchy of precedence, I find programming to be safer and more legible when I group clauses in parentheses to force the execution order (see line 18).

- Computers are notoriously poor at dealing with decimals. For example, the number *2.0* may actually be stored as *1.99999*. Most of the time this won't be a problem, but in cases where mathematical precision is paramount, rely on integers, not decimals. The PHP manual has information on this subject, as well as alternative functions for improving computational accuracy.

- Many of the mathematical operators also have a corresponding assignment operator, letting you create a shorthand for assigning values. This line

  ```
  $total = $total + ($total * $taxrate);
  ```

  could be rewritten as

  ```
  $total += ($total * $taxrate);
  ```

- If you set a `$price` value without using two decimals (e.g., *119.9* or *34*), you may want to apply `number_format()` to `$price` before printing it.

- If you use concatenation, the `number_format()`—or any other—function can be used inline with an `echo()` statement:

  ```
  echo 'You are purchasing <b>' .
  → $quantity . '</b> widget(s)
  → at a cost of <b>$' . number_
  → format($price) . '</b> each. With
  → tax, the total comes to <b>$' .
  → number_format($total) . '</b>.';
  ```

About Constants

Constants are a specific data type in PHP that, unlike variables, retain their initial value throughout the course of a script. In fact, you cannot change the value of a constant once it has been set. Constants can be assigned any single value—a number or a string of characters.

To create a constant, you use the `define()` function instead of the assignment operator (=) used for variables.

```
define ('NAME', 'value');
```

Notice that, as a rule of thumb, constants are named using all capitals, although this is not required. Most importantly, constants do not use the initial dollar sign as variables do (because, technically, constants are not variables).

Printing constants requires special syntax as well:

```
define ('USERNAME', 'trout');

echo 'Hello, ' . USERNAME;
```

You cannot print constants using `echo` "`Hello, USERNAME`", as PHP would just print *Hello, USERNAME* and not the value of the `USERNAME` constant (because there's no dollar sign telling PHP that `USERNAME` is anything other than literal text).

PHP runs with several predefined constants, much like the predefined variables used earlier in the chapter. These include `PHP_VERSION` (the version of PHP running) and `PHP_OS` (the operating system of the server).

To use constants:

1. Create a new PHP document in your text editor (**Script 1.10**).

```
<!DOCTYPE html PUBLIC "-//W3C//
→ DTD XHTML 1.0 Transitional//EN"
"http://www.w3.org/TR/xhtml1/DTD/
→ xhtml1-transitional.dtd">
<html xmlns="http://www.w3.org/1999/
→ xhtml" xml:lang="en" lang="en">
<head>
   <meta http-equiv="content-type"
   → content="text/html;
   → charset=iso-8859-1" />
   <title>Constants</title>
</head>
<body>
<?php # Script 1.10 - constants.php
```

2. Create a new date constant.

```
define ('TODAY', 'February 3, 2005');
```

An admittedly trivial use of constants, but this example will illustrate the point. In Chapter 7, "Using PHP with MySQL," you'll see how to use constants to store your database access information.

3. Print out the date, the PHP version, and operating system information.

```
echo 'Today is ' . TODAY . '.<br
→ />This server is running version
→ <b>' . PHP_VERSION . '</b> of PHP
→ on the <b>' . PHP_OS . '</b>
→ operating system.';
```

Since constants cannot be printed within quotation marks (the lack of a dollar sign causes them to be treated as capitalized text), I use the concatenation operator to create my echo() statement.

Script 1.10 Constants are another data type you can use in PHP, distinct from variables.

```
1    <!DOCTYPE html PUBLIC "-//W3C//DTD XHTML
     1.0 Transitional//EN"
2          "http://www.w3.org/TR/xhtml1/DTD/
           xhtml1-transitional.dtd">
3    <html xmlns="http://www.w3.org/1999/xhtml"
     xml:lang="en" lang="en">
4    <head>
5       <meta http-equiv="content-type" content=
        "text/html; charset=iso-8859-1" />
6       <title>Constants</title>
7    </head>
8    <body>
9    <?php # Script 1.10 - constants.php
10
11   // Set today's date as a constant.
12   define ('TODAY', 'February 3, 2005');
13
14   // Print the message, using predefined
     constants and the TODAY constant.
15   echo 'Today is ' . TODAY . '.<br />This
     server is running version <b>' .
     PHP_VERSION . '</b> of PHP on the <b>' .
     PHP_OS . '</b> operating system.';
16
17   ?>
18   </body>
19   </html>
```

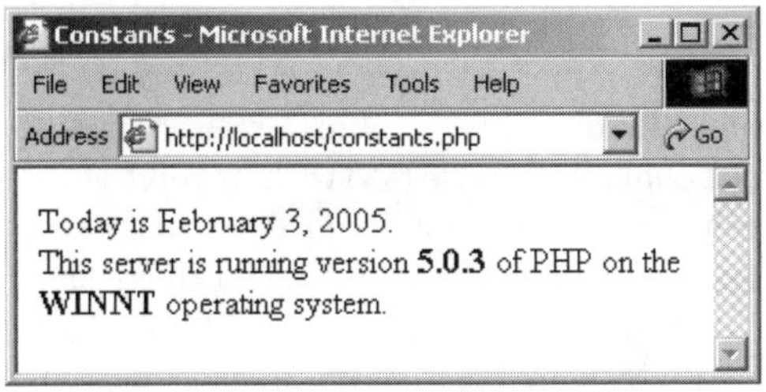

Figure 1.20 By making use of PHP's constants, you can learn more about your PHP setup.

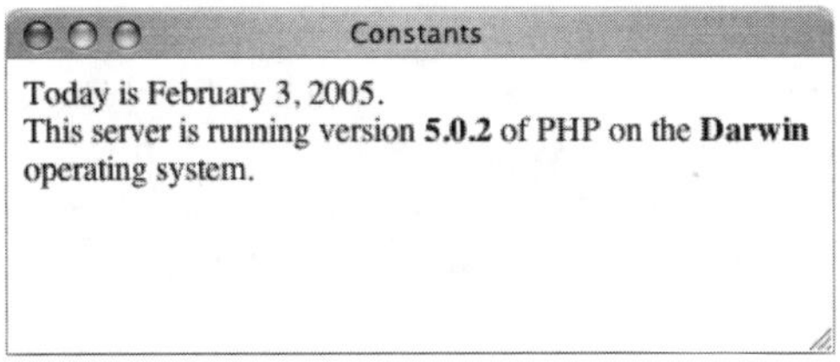

Figure 1.21 Running the same script (refer to Script 1.10) on different servers garners different results.

4. Complete the PHP code and the HTML page.

```
?>
</body>
</html>
```

5. Save the file as `constants.php`, upload to your Web server, and test in your Web browser (**Figure 1.20**).

Tips

■ If possible, run this script on another PHP-enabled server (**Figure 1.21**).

■ In Chapter 9, "Cookies and Sessions," you'll learn about another constant, SID (which stands for *session ID*).

Single vs. Double Quotation Marks

In PHP it's important to understand how single quotation marks differ from double quotation marks. With the `echo()` and `print()` statements you can use either, as in the examples in this chapter. But there is a key difference between the two and why you might use them. So far I've specified when you should use which, but now it's time to define the pattern more explicitly.

In PHP, values enclosed within single quotation marks will be treated literally, whereas those within double quotation marks will be interpreted. In other words, placing variables and special characters (**Table 1.2**) within double quotes will result in their represented values printed, not their literal values. For example, assume that you have

```
$var = 'test';
```

The code `echo "var is equal to $var";` will print out *var is equal to test*, whereas the code `echo 'var is equal to $var';` will print out *var is equal to $var*. Using an escaped dollar sign, the code `echo "\$var is equal to $var";` will print out *$var is equal to test*, whereas the code `echo '\$var is equal to $var';` will print out *\$var is equal to $var*.

As these examples should illustrate, double quotation marks will replace a variable's name (`$var`) with its value (*test*) and a special character's code (`\$`) with its represented value (*$*). Single quotes will always display exactly what you type, except for the escaped single quote (`\'`) and the escaped backslash (`\\`), which are printed as a single quotation mark and a single backslash, respectively.

The preceding rule applies to any use of quotation marks, be it in an `echo()` or `print()` statement, when assigning a value to a variable, or sending data to a function as an argument. As another example of how the two quotation marks differ, I'll modify the `numbers.php` script as an experiment.

Escaped Characters

CODE	MEANING
\"	Double quotation mark
\'	Single quotation mark
\\	Backslash
\n	Newline
\r	Carriage return
\t	Tab
\$	Dollar sign

Table 1.2 These characters have special meanings when used within double quotation marks.

Script 1.11 THIS FINAL SCRIPT DEMONSTRATES THE DIFFERENCES BETWEEN USING SINGLE AND DOUBLE QUOTATION MARKS.

```
1    <!DOCTYPE html PUBLIC "-//W3C//DTD XHTML
     1.0 Transitional//EN"
2        "http://www.w3.org/TR/xhtml1/DTD/
         xhtml1-transitional.dtd">
3    <html xmlns="http://www.w3.org/1999/xhtml"
     xml:lang="en" lang="en">
4    <head>
5        <meta http-equiv="content-type" content=
         "text/html; charset=iso-8859-1" />
6        <title>Quotation Marks</title>
7    </head>
8    <body>
9    <?php # Script 1.11 - quotes.php
10
11   // Set the variables.
12   $quantity = 30; // Buying 30 widgets.
13   $price = 119.95;
14   $taxrate = .05; // 5% sales tax.
15
16   // Calculate the total.
17   $total = $quantity * $price;
18   $total = $total + ($total * $taxrate); //
     Calculate and add the tax.
19   $total = number_format ($total, 2);
20
21   // Print the results.
22   echo 'Using double quotation marks:<br />';
23   echo "You are purchasing <b>$quantity</b>
     widget(s) at a cost of <b>\$$price</b>
     each. With tax, the total comes to <b>
     \$$total</b>.\n";
24
25   echo '<p><hr /></p>Using single quotation
     marks:<br />';
26   echo 'You are purchasing <b>$quantity</b>
     widget(s) at a cost of <b>\$$price</b>
     each. With tax, the total comes to <b>
     \$$total</b>.\n';
27   ?>
28   </body>
29   </html>
```

TO USE SINGLE AND DOUBLE QUOTATION MARKS:

1. Open numbers.php (refer to Script 1.9) in your text editor.

2. Delete the existing echo() statement (**Script 1.11**).

3. Print a caption and then rewrite the original echo() statement using double quotation marks.

```
echo 'Using double quotation marks:
→ <br />';
echo "You are purchasing
→ <b>$quantity</b> widget(s) at
→ a cost of <b>\$$price</b> each.
→ With tax, the total comes to
→ <b>\$$total</b>.\n";
```

The same intended result of this script—printing the quantity of widgets purchased, at what price, and what the total amount is with tax—can be achieved by using double quotation marks instead of single quotation marks and the concatenation operator, as it had originally. Notice that I've also used the \$$variable technique to generate results like *$3778.43* (the first dollar sign is printed and the second is the start of the variable name).

continues on next page

SINGLE VS. DOUBLE QUOTATION MARKS

4. Repeat the first echo() statement, this time using single quotation marks.

```
echo '<p><hr /></p>Using single
→ quotation marks:<br />';
echo 'You are purchasing
→ <b>$quantity</b> widget(s) at
→ a cost of <b>\$$price</b> each.
→ With tax, the total comes to
→ <b>\$$total</b>.\n';
```

The first line adds some spacing and a horizontal rule, followed by a caption. The second echo() statement is used to highlight the difference between using single or double quotation marks.

5. If you want, change the page's title.

6. Save the file as quotes.php, upload to your Web server, and test in your Web browser (**Figure 1.22**).

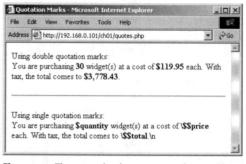

Figure 1.22 These results demonstrate when and how you'd use one type of quotation mark as opposed to the other.

✔ Tips

■ Because PHP will attempt to find variables whose values need to be inserted within double quotation marks, using single quotation marks is theoretically faster. If you need to print the value of a variable, though, you *must* use double quotation marks.

■ As valid HTML often includes a lot of double-quoted attributes, it's often easiest to use single quotation marks when printing HTML with PHP.

```
echo '<table width="80%" border="0"
→ cellspacing="2" cellpadding="3"
→ align="center">';
```

If you were to print out this HTML using double quotation marks, you would have to escape all of the double quotation marks in the string.

```
echo "<table width=\"80%\"
→ border=\"0\" cellspacing=\"2\"
→ cellpadding=\"3\" align=
→ \"center\">";
```

■ PHP also supports the *heredoc* method of quoting text. If you are already familiar with the concept or are curious about alternative methods, check the PHP manual for the proper syntax.

PROGRAMMING WITH PHP

Now that you have the fundamentals of the PHP scripting language down, it's time to build on those basics and start truly programming. In this chapter you'll begin creating more elaborate scripts while still learning some of the standard terms and syntax of the language.

I'll begin by writing HTML forms and showing how you can use PHP to handle the submitted values. Afterward, I'll cover conditionals and the remaining operators, arrays (another variable type), and one last language construct (loops).

Creating an HTML Form

Managing HTML forms with PHP is a two-step process. First you create the HTML form itself, using any text or WYSIWYG editor you choose. Then, you create the corresponding PHP script that will receive and process the form data.

It would be outside the realm of this book to go into HTML forms in any detail, but I will lead you through one quick example so that it may be used throughout the chapter.

An HTML form is created using the `form` tags and various input types. The `form` tags look like

```
<form action="script.php" method="post">
```

```
</form>
```

The most important attribute of your `form` tag is `action`, which dictates to which page the form data will be sent. The second attribute—`method`—has its own issues (see the "Choosing a Method" sidebar), but `post` is the value you'll use most frequently.

Within the opening and closing `form` tags you place the different inputs, be they text boxes, radio buttons, select menus, check boxes, etc. As you'll see in the next section, what kinds of inputs your form has makes little difference to the PHP script handling it. You should, however, pay attention to the names you give your form inputs, as they'll be of critical importance when it comes to your PHP code.

Choosing a Method

The `method` attribute of a form dictates how the data is sent to the handling page. The two options—`get` and `post`—refer to the HTTP (Hypertext Transfer Protocol) method to be used. In short, the `get` method sends the submitted data to the receiving page as a series of *name-value* pairs appended to the URL. For example,

```
www.dmcinsights.com/script.
→ php?name=Homer&gender=M
```

The benefit of using the `get` method is that the resulting page can be bookmarked in the user's Web browser (since it's a URL). For that matter, you can also click Back in your Web browser to return to a `get` page, or reload it without problem (neither of which is true for `post`). Unfortunately, you are limited to how much data can be transmitted via `get` and it's less secure (since the data is visible).

For these reasons I will generally use `post` throughout this book, with noted exceptions. There's a slightly technical discussion of when you should use which available at `www.w3.org/2001/tag/doc/whenToUseGet.html`.

Script 2.1 This simple HTML form will be used for several of the examples in this chapter.

```
script
1   <!DOCTYPE html PUBLIC "-//W3C//DTD XHTML
    1.0 Transitional//EN"
2           "http://www.w3.org/TR/xhtml1/DTD/
            xhtml1-transitional.dtd">
3   <html xmlns="http://www.w3.org/1999/xhtml"
    xml:lang="en" lang="en">
4   <head>
5       <meta http-equiv="content-type" content=
        "text/html; charset=iso-8859-1" />
6       <title>Simple HTML Form</title>
7   </head>
8   <body>
9   <!-- Script 2.1 - form.html -->
10
11  <form action="handle_form.php" method=
    "post">
12
13      <fieldset><legend>Enter your
information
        in the form below:</legend>
14
15      <p><b>Name:</b> <input type="text"
        name="name" size="20" maxlength="40"
        /></p>
16
17      <p><b>Email Address:</b> <input
        type="text" name="email" size="40"
        maxlength="60" /></p>
18
19      <p><b>Gender:</b> <input type="radio"
        name="gender" value="M" /> Male <input
        type="radio" name="gender" value="F"
        /> Female</p>
20
21      <p><b>Age:</b></p>
22      <select name="age">
23          <option value="0-29">Under 30</
            option>
24          <option value="30-60">Between 30 and
            60</option>
25          <option value="60+">Over 60</option>
26      </select></p>
```

To create an HTML form:

1. Begin a new HTML document in your text editor (**Script 2.1**).

   ```
   <!DOCTYPE html PUBLIC "-//W3C//
   → DTD XHTML 1.0 Transitional//EN"
   "http://www.w3.org/TR/xhtml1/DTD/
   → xhtml1-transitional.dtd">
   <html xmlns="http://www.w3.org/1999/
   → xhtml" xml:lang="en" lang="en">
   <head>
       <meta http-equiv="content-type"
       → content="text/html;
       → charset=iso-8859-1" />
       <title>Simple HTML Form</title>
   </head>
   <body>
   <!-- Script 2.1 - form.html -->
   ```

   There's nothing terribly new here—I'm still using the same basic syntax for the HTML page as I have in the previous chapter—but I have added an HTML comment indicating the file's name and number.

2. Insert the initial form tag.

   ```
   <form action="handle_form.php"
   → method="post">
   ```

   Since the action attribute dictates to which script the form data will go, you should give it an appropriate name (*handle_form* to correspond with this script: form.html) and the .php extension (since a PHP page will handle this form's data).

   continues on next page

3. Begin the HTML form.

```
<fieldset><legend>Enter your
→ information in the form
→ below:</legend>
```

I'm using the `fieldset` and `legend` HTML tags because I like the way they make the HTML form look (they add a box around the form with a title at top). This isn't pertinent to the form itself, though.

4. Add two text inputs.

```
<p><b>Name:</b> <input type="text"
→ name="name" size="20"
→ maxlength="40" /></p>

<p><b>Email Address:</b> <input
→ type="text" name="email" size="40"
→ maxlength="60" /></p>
```

These are just simple text inputs, allowing the user to enter their name and email address. In case you are wondering, the extra space and slash at the end of each input's tag is valid XHTML. With standard HTML, these tags would conclude, for instance, with `maxlength="40">` or `maxlength="60">` instead.

5. Add a pair of radio buttons.

```
<p><b>Gender:</b> <input
→ type="radio" name="gender"
→ value="M" /> Male <input
→ type="radio" name="gender"
→ value="F" /> Female</p>
```

The radio buttons both have the same name, meaning that only one of the two can be selected. They have different values, though.

Script 2.1 *continued*

(script continues on next page)

```
27
28      <p><b>Comments:</b> <textarea name=
        "comments" rows="3" cols="40">
        </textarea></p>
29
30      </fieldset>
31
32      <div align="center"><input type="submit"
        name="submit" value="Submit My
        Information" /></div>
33
34   </form>
35
36   </body>
37   </html>
```

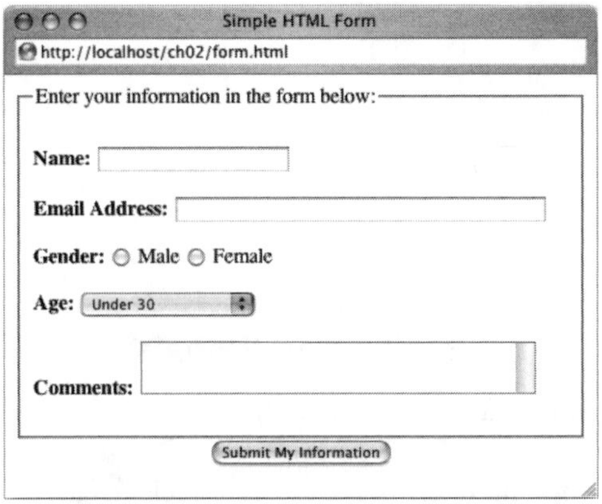

Figure 2.1 This form takes some basic information from the user.

✔ Tips

■ Since this page contains just HTML, I used the .html extension, but I could have also used .php without harm (since code outside of the PHP tags is treated as HTML).

■ For more information on HTML, XHTML, and forms, check out any of the resources listed in Appendix C, "Resources."

6. Add a pull-down menu.

```
<p><b>Age:</b>
<select name="age">
    <option value="0-29">Under
    → 30</option>
    <option value="30-60">Between 30
    → and 60</option>
    <option value="60+">Over
    → 60</option>
</select></p>
```

The select tag starts the pull-down menu, and then each option tag will create another line in the list of choices.

7. Add a text box for comments.

```
<p><b>Comments:</b> <textarea
→ name="comments" rows="3"
→ cols="40"></textarea></p>
```

Textareas are different from text inputs; they are presented as a box, not as a single line. They allow for much more information to be typed and are useful for taking user comments.

8. Complete the form.

```
</fieldset>
<div align="center"><input
→ type="submit" name="submit"
→ value="Submit My Information"
→ /></div>
</form>
```

The first tag closes the fieldset that was opened in Step 3. Then a submit button is created and centered using a div tag. Finally the form is closed.

9. Complete the HTML page.

```
</body>
</html>
```

10. Save the file as form.html, upload to your Web server, and view in your Web browser (**Figure 2.1**).

Handling an HTML Form

Now that I have an HTML form, I'll write a bare-bones PHP script to handle it. When I say that this script will be *handling* the form, I mean that it will do something with the data it receives. In this chapter, the scripts will reiterate the data back to the Web browser, but in later examples, it will be stored in a MySQL database, checked against previously stored values, sent in emails, and more.

The beauty of PHP—and what makes it so easy to learn and use—is how well it interacts with HTML forms.

Rather than requiring a parsing routine—as CGI scripts do—to access form data, your PHP scripts store the information in special variables. For example, say you have a form with an input defined like so:

```
<input type="text" name="weight"
→ size="20" />
```

The PHP page that receives the form data will assign what the user entered into this form element to a special variable called $_REQUEST['weight']. It is very important that the spelling and capitalization match *exactly*, as PHP is case-sensitive when it comes to variable names! $_REQUEST['weight'] can then be used like any other variable: printed, used in mathematical computations, concatenated, and so on.

In this example, I'll use a shorthand to refer to these variables (see the "Registering Globals" sidebar for an explanation of why the shorthand is required) and then print out their values.

Registering Globals

In earlier versions of PHP, the *register_globals* setting was turned on by default. This feature gave PHP an ease of use by automatically turning form inputs into similarly named variables, like $name or $email (as opposed to having to refer to $_REQUEST['name'] and $_REQUEST['email'] first).

As of version 4.2 of PHP, the developers behind PHP opted to turn this setting off by default because not relying on this feature improves the security of your scripts. Unfortunately, this also had the side effect that a lot of existing scripts no longer worked and many beginning programmers were stymied when they saw: blank values in their form results, error messages, or just blank pages.

To work around this, there are two options. First, you could turn *register_globals* back on, assuming that you have administrative control over your PHP installation (see Appendix A, "Installation"). Second, you could start using the *superglobal* variables, such as $_REQUEST, $_GET, and $_POST, as you do in the first handle_form. php example. These variables will be more formally discussed in the "What Are Arrays?" section later in this chapter. In the meantime, rest assured that all the scripts in this book have been written with the assumption that *register_globals* is off in order to ensure maximum compatibility and security.

Script 2.2 This script receives and prints out the information entered into an HTML form (Script 2.1).

```
script

1    <!DOCTYPE html PUBLIC "-//W3C//DTD XHTML
     1.0 Transitional//EN"
2           "http://www.w3.org/TR/xhtml1/DTD/
            xhtml1-transitional.dtd">
3    <html xmlns="http://www.w3.org/1999/xhtml"
     xml:lang="en" lang="en">
4    <head>
5        <meta http-equiv="content-type" content=
         "text/html; charset=iso-8859-1" />
6        <title>Form Feedback</title>
7    </head>
8    <body>
9    <?php # Script 2.2 - handle_form.php
10
11   // Create a shorthand for the form data.
12   $name = $_REQUEST['name'];
13   $email = $_REQUEST['email'];
14   $comments = $_REQUEST['comments'];
15   // Not used: $_REQUEST['age'],
     $_REQUEST['gender'], and
     $_REQUEST['submit'].
16
17   // Print the submitted information.
18   echo "<p>Thank you, <b>$name</b>, for the
     following comments:<br />
19   <tt>$comments</tt></p>
20   <p>We will reply to you at <i>$email</i>.
     </p>\n";
21
22   ?>
23   </body>
24   </html>
```

To handle an HTML form:

1. Create a new PHP document in your text editor, beginning with the HTML (**Script 2.2**).

   ```
   <!DOCTYPE html PUBLIC "-//W3C//
   → DTD XHTML 1.0 Transitional//EN"
   "http://www.w3.org/TR/xhtml1/DTD/
   → xhtml1-transitional.dtd">
   <html xmlns="http://www.w3.org/1999/
   → xhtml" xml:lang="en" lang="en">
   <head>
       <meta http-equiv="content-type"
       → content="text/html;
       → charset=iso-8859-1" />
       <title>Form Feedback</title>
   </head>
   <body>
   ```

2. Add the opening PHP tag and create a shorthand version of the form data variables.

   ```
   <?php # Script 2.2 - handle_form.php
   $name = $_REQUEST['name'];
   $email = $_REQUEST['email'];
   $comments = $_REQUEST['comments'];
   ```

   Following the rules outlined before, the data entered into the name form input, which has a name value of *name*, will be accessible through the variable $_REQUEST['name']. The data entered into the email form input, which has a name value of *email*, will be accessible through $_REQUEST['email']. The same applies to the entered comments data. Again, the spelling and capitalization of your variables here must exactly match the corresponding name values in the HTML form.

continues on next page

HANDLING AN HTML FORM

3. Print out the received name, email, and comments values.

```
echo "<p>Thank you, <b>$name</b>,
→ for the following comments:<br />
<tt>$comments</tt></p>

<p>We will reply to you at
→ <i>$email</i>.</p>\n";
```

The submitted values are simply printed out using the `echo()` statement, double quotation marks, and a wee bit of HTML formatting.

4. Complete the HTML page.

```
</body>
</html>
```

5. Save the file as `handle_form.php`, upload to your Web server in the same directory as `form.html`, and test both documents in your Web browser (**Figures 2.2** and **2.3**).

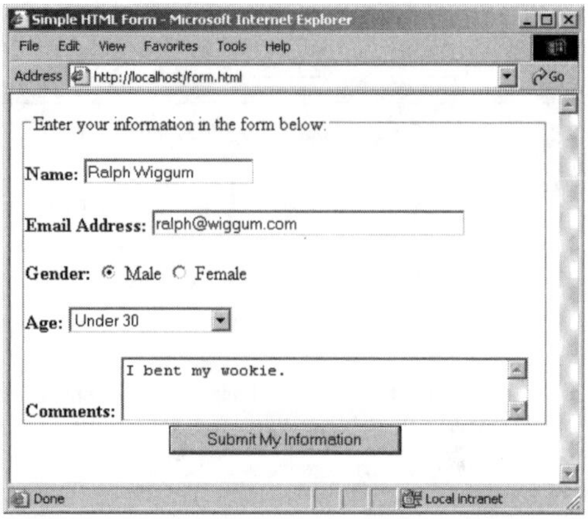

Figure 2.2 To test `handle_form.php`, you must begin by filling out the form.

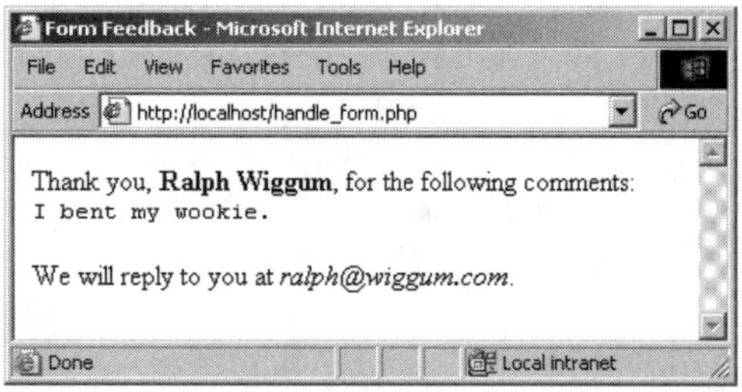

Figure 2.3 Your script should display results like this.

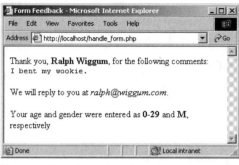

Figure 2.4 The values of *gender* and *age* correspond to those defined in the form's HTML.

✔ Tips

■ $_REQUEST is a special variable type in PHP, available since version 4.1. It stores all of the data sent to a PHP page through either the GET or POST methods, as well as data accessible in cookies.

■ If you see a blank page after submitting the form, first check the HTML source to look for HTML errors, and then confirm that *display_errors* is on in your PHP configuration (see Appendix A, "Installation").

■ If the PHP script shows blank spaces where the variables should have printed out, it means that the variables have no values. Likely causes are: you failed to enter a value in the form; you misspelled or mis-capitalized the variable names; or $_REQUEST is not available because you're using an outdated version of PHP.

■ If you see any *Undefined variable: variablename* errors, this is because the variables you refer to have no value and PHP is set on the highest level of error reporting. See the previous Tip about why variables wouldn't have a value, and then either change the level of *error_reporting* for your server (see Appendix A) or change it for a particular script (see Chapter 6, "Error Handling and Debugging") to stop such errors in the future.

■ For a comparison of how PHP handles the different form input types, print out the $_REQUEST['age'] and $_REQUEST['gender'] values (**Figure 2.4**).

Managing Magic Quotes

Built into PHP is a handy feature referred to as *Magic Quotes*. Magic Quotes—when enabled—will automatically escape single and double quotation marks in the values of variables. This can help prevent problems when working with databases or HTML. But, if I enter into a form some text that includes an apostrophe (**Figure 2.5**), the resulting page looks strange when the text is reprinted (**Figure 2.6**).

In PHP there are two main types of Magic Quotes: *magic_quotes_gpc*, which applies to form, URL, and cookie data (*gpc* stands for *get*, *post*, *cookie*); and *magic_quotes_runtime*, which applies to data retrieved from external files and databases.

If Magic Quotes is enabled on your server, you can undo its effect using the stripslashes() function.

```
$var = stripslashes($var);
```

This function will remove any backslashes found in $var. In the form example, this will have the effect of turning an escaped submitted string back to its original, non-escaped value.

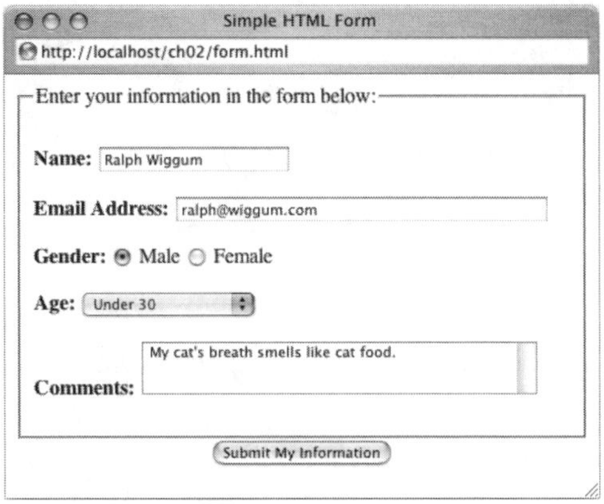

Figure 2.5 Quotation marks entered into form values can be disruptive in your Web applications (see Figure 2.6).

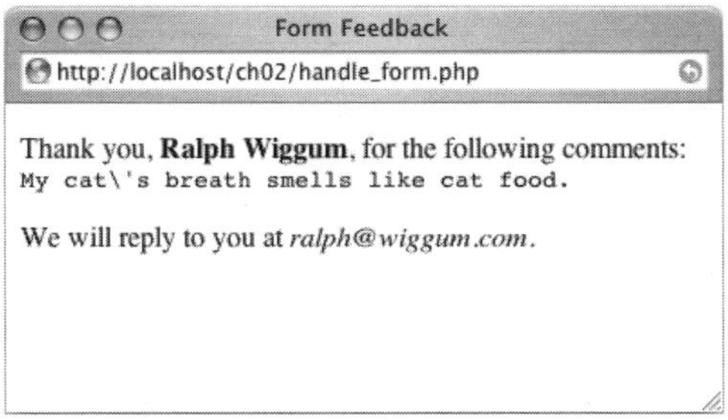

Figure 2.6 The apostrophe entered in the form was escaped automatically by PHP, generating unseemly results.

Script 2.3 The `stripslashes()` function will counteract the effects of Magic Quotes, removing unnecessary backslashes.

```
1    <!DOCTYPE html PUBLIC "-//W3C//DTD XHTML
     1.0 Transitional//EN"
2          "http://www.w3.org/TR/xhtml1/DTD/
           xhtml1-transitional.dtd">
3    <html xmlns="http://www.w3.org/1999/xhtml"
     xml:lang="en" lang="en">
4    <head>
5       <meta http-equiv="content-type" content=
        "text/html; charset=iso-8859-1" />
6       <title>Form Feedback</title>
7    </head>
8    <body>
9    <?php # Script 2.3 - handle_form.php
     (2nd version after Script 2.2)
10
11   // Create a shorthand for the form data.
12   // Use stripslashes() to combat Magic
     Quotes, if necessary.
13   $name = stripslashes($_REQUEST['name']);
14   $email = $_REQUEST['email'];
15   $comments = stripslashes($_REQUEST
     ['comments']);
16   // Not used: $_REQUEST['age'], $_REQUEST
     ['gender'], and $_REQUEST['submit'].
17
18   // Print the submitted information.
19   echo "<p>Thank you, <b>$name</b>, for the
     following comments:<br />
20   <tt>$comments</tt></p>
21   <p>We will reply to you at <i>$email</i>.
     </p>\n";
22
23   ?>
24   </body>
25   </html>
```

To adjust for Magic Quotes:

1. Open `handle_form.php` (refer to Script 2.2) in your text editor.

2. Change the first and third variable assignment lines to read (**Script 2.3**)

   ```
   $name = stripslashes($_REQUEST
   → ['name']);
   $comments = stripslashes($_REQUEST
   → ['comments']);
   ```

   Now the `$name` and `$comments` variables will be assigned the values of their associated `$_REQUEST` variables, but with any backslashes removed. These are currently the only two variables that must be cleansed of backslashes. Presumably the email address will not contain one (or else it would be invalid) and the age and gender inputs have preset values.

   continues on next page

3. Save the file, upload to your Web server, and test in your Web browser (**Figure 2.7**).

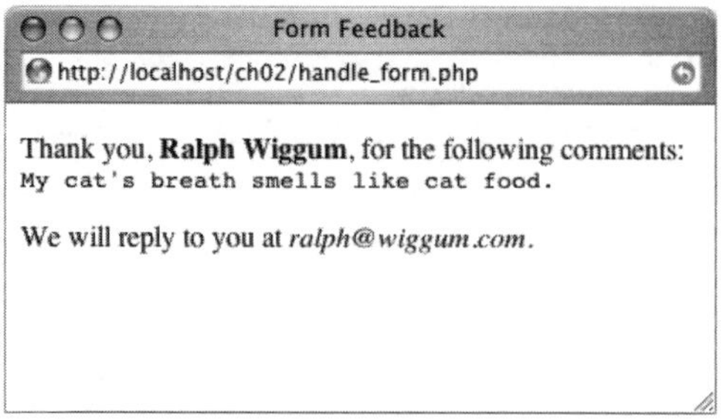

✔ Tips

- PHP includes a third form of Magic Quotes—*magic_quotes_sybase*—which has its own peculiarities and is less often used.

- A double backlash (\\) will be turned into a single backslash by the `stripslashes()` function.

- When form data is being used with a database—as you'll see in Chapter 7, "Using PHP with MySQL"—Magic Quotes (or a similar security measure) are important, as they prevent problematic characters from breaking the database query.

- In Chapter 7, you'll also learn a trick for automatically using the `stripslashes()` function if *magic_quotes_gpc* is enabled on your server.

- You can emulate what Magic Quotes does if it's disabled by using the opposite of the `stripslashes()` function, `addslashes()`.

- When working with strings stemming from forms, it's also a good idea to use the `trim()` function, which removes excess white spaces from both ends of the value.

  `$name = trim($name);`

Figure 2.7 Applying the `stripslashes()` function to the form values will undo the effects of Magic Quotes (compare with Figure 2.6).

Conditionals and Operators

Conditionals, like variables, are integral to programming, and most people are familiar with them in some form or another. Dynamic Web pages, as you might imagine, frequently require the use of conditionals to alter a script's behavior according to set criteria.

PHP's three primary terms for creating conditionals are if, else, and elseif (which can also be written as two words, else if).

Every conditional includes an if clause:

```
if (condition) {
    // Do something!
}
```

This in turn can become

```
if (condition) {
    // Do something!
} else {
    // Do something else!
}
```

and

```
if (condition1) {
    // Do something!
} elseif (condition2) {
    // Do something else!
} else {
    // Do something different!
}
```

If a condition is true, the code in the following curly braces ({}) will be executed. If not, PHP will continue on. If there is a second condition (after an elseif), that will be checked for truth. The process will continue—you can use as many elseif clauses as you want—until PHP hits an else, which will be automatically executed at that point, or until the conditional terminates without an else.

For this reason, it's important that the else always come last and be treated as the default action unless specific criteria (the conditions) are met.

A condition can be true in PHP for any number of reasons. These are common true conditions:

◆ $var, if $var has a value other than *0*, an empty string, or *NULL*

◆ isset($var), if $var has any value other than *NULL*, including *0* or an empty string

◆ TRUE, true, True, etc.

In the second example, a new function, isset(), is introduced. This function checks if a variable is set, meaning that it has a value other than NULL. You can also use the comparative and logical operators (**Table 2.1**) in conjunction with parentheses to make more complicated expressions.

Comparative and Logical Operators			
SYMBOL	MEANING	TYPE	EXAMPLE
==	is equal to	comparison	$x == $y
!=	is not equal to	comparison	$x != $y
<	less than	comparison	$x < $y
>	greater than	comparison	$x > $y
<=	less than or equal to	comparison	$x <= $y
>=	greater than or equal to	comparison	$x >= $y
!	not	logical	!$x
&&	and	logical	$x && $y
||	or	logical	$x || $y
XOR	and not	logical	$x XOR $y

Table 2.1 These operators are frequently used when writing conditionals.

To use conditionals:

1. Open handle_form.php (refer to Script 2.3) in your text editor.

2. Before the echo() statement, add a conditional to create the $gender variable (**Script 2.4**).

```
if (isset($_REQUEST['gender'])) {
   $gender = $_REQUEST['gender'];
} else {
   $gender = NULL;
}
```

This is a simple and effective way to validate a form input (particularly a radio button, check box, or select). If the user checks either gender radio button, then $_REQUEST['gender'] will have a value, meaning that the condition isset($_REQUEST['gender']) is true. In such a case, the shorthand version of this variable—$gender—is assigned the value of $_REQUEST['gender'], repeating the technique used with $name, $email, and $comments. If the condition is not true, then $gender is assigned the value of NULL, indicating that it has no value. Notice that NULL is not in quotes.

Script 2.4 Conditionals in your code allow you to modify behavior according to specific criteria.

```
1   <!DOCTYPE html PUBLIC "-//W3C//DTD XHTML
    1.0 Transitional//EN"
2        "http://www.w3.org/TR/xhtml1/DTD/
         xhtml1-transitional.dtd">
3   <html xmlns="http://www.w3.org/1999/xhtml"
    xml:lang="en" lang="en">
4   <head>
5       <meta http-equiv="content-type" content=
        "text/html; charset=iso-8859-1" />
6       <title>Form Feedback</title>
7   </head>
8   <body>
9   <?php # Script 2.4 - handle_form.php (3rd
    version after Scripts 2.2 & 2.3)
10
11  // Create a shorthand for the form data.
12  // Use stripslashes() to combat Magic
    Quotes, if necessary.
13  $name = stripslashes($_REQUEST['name']);
14  $email = $_REQUEST['email'];
15  $comments = stripslashes($_REQUEST
    ['comments']);
16
17  // Create the $gender variable.
18  if (isset($_REQUEST['gender'])) {
19      $gender = $_REQUEST['gender'];
20  } else {
21      $gender = NULL;
22  }
23
24  // Print the submitted information.
25  echo "<p>Thank you, <b>$name</b>, for the
    following comments:<br />
26  <tt>$comments</tt></p>
27  <p>We will reply to you at <i>$email</i>.
    </p>\n";
28
29  // Print a message based upon the gender
    value.
30  if ($gender == 'M') {
31      echo '<p><b>Good day, Sir!</b></p>';
32  } elseif ($gender == 'F') {
```

(script continues on next page)

Script 2.4 *continued.*

```
33      echo '<p><b>Good day, Madam!</b></p>';
34  } else { // No gender selected.
35      echo '<p><b>You forgot to enter your
        gender!</b></p>';
36  }
37
38  ?>
39  </body>
40  </html>
```

3. After the echo() statement, add another conditional that prints a message based upon $gender's value.

```
if ($gender == 'M') {
    echo '<p><b>Good day,
    → Sir!</b></p>';
} elseif ($gender == 'F') {
    echo '<p><b>Good day,
    → Madam!</b></p>';
} else {
    echo '<p><b>You forgot to enter
    → your gender!</b></p>';
}
```

This if-elseif-else conditional looks at the value of the $gender variable and prints a different message for each possibility. It's very important to remember that the double equals sign (==) means equals, whereas a single equals sign (=) assigns a value. The distinction is important because the condition $gender == 'M' may or may not be true, but $gender = 'M' will always be true.

continues on next page

CONDITIONALS AND OPERATORS

4. Save the file, upload to your Web server, and test in your Web browser (**Figures 2.8**, **2.9**, and **2.10**).

✔ Tips

■ It's standard procedure and good programming form to format your conditionals in such a way that it's clear that certain code is a subset of a conditional. In this script I've indented code one tab stop (or four spaces) from the line that governs it.

■ You can—and frequently will—nest conditionals (place one inside another).

■ The first conditional in this script (the isset()) is a perfect example of how to use a default value. The assumption (the else) is that $gender has a NULL value unless the one condition is met: that $_REQUEST['gender'] is set.

■ The curly braces used to indicate the beginning and end of a conditional are not required if you are executing only one statement. I would recommend that you almost always use them, though, as a matter of clarity.

■ Because it's very easy to mistakenly type $gender = 'M' instead of $gender == 'M', some people advocate rewriting such a condition as 'M' == $gender, which will create error messages if mistakenly typed as 'M' = $gender.

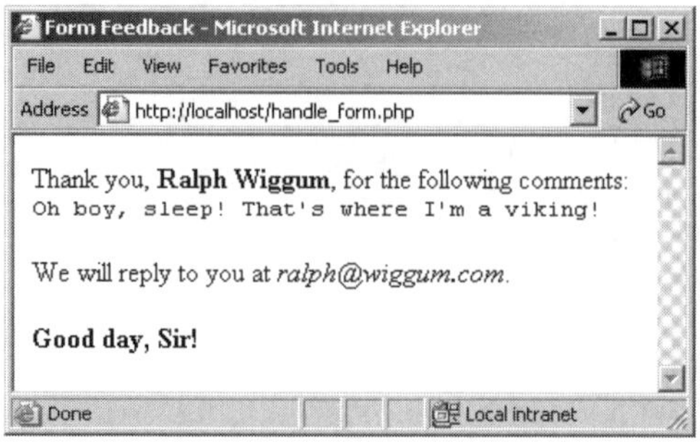

Figure 2.8 The gender-based conditional prints a different message for each choice in the form.

Figure 2.9 The same script will produce different results (compare with Figure 2.8) when the form values change.

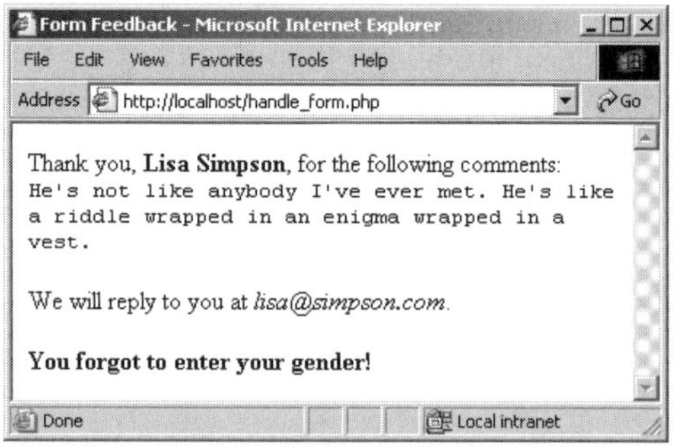

Figure 2.10 If no gender was selected, a message is printed indicating to the user their oversight.

Switch

PHP has another type of conditional, called the `switch`, best used in place of a long `if-elseif-else` conditional. The syntax of `switch` is

```php
switch ($variable) {

    case 'value1':

        // Do this.

        break;

    case 'value2':

        // Do this instead.

        break;

    default:

        // Do this then.

        break;

}
```

The `switch` conditional compares the value of `$variable` to the different *cases*. When it finds a match, the following code is executed, up until the `break`. If no match is found, the *default* is executed, assuming it exists (it's optional).

Hence, the conditional from Script 2.4 could be rewritten as

```php
switch ($gender) {

    case 'M':

        echo '<p><b>Good day, Sir!</b></p>';

        break;

    case 'F':

        echo '<p><b>Good day, Madam!</b></p>';

        break;

    default:

        echo '<p><b>You forgot to enter your gender!</b></p>';

        break;

}
```

The `switch` conditional is limited in its usage in that it can only check a variable's value for equality against certain cases; more complex conditions cannot be easily checked.

Validating Form Data

A critical concept related to handling HTML forms is that of validating form data. In terms of both error management and security, you should absolutely never trust the data being entered in an HTML form. Whether erroneous data is purposefully malicious or just unintentionally inappropriate, it's up to you—the Web architect—to test it against expectations.

Validating form data requires the use of conditionals and any number of functions, operators, and expressions. One common function to be used is isset(), which tests if a variable has a value (including 0, FALSE, or an empty string, but not NULL).

```
if (isset($var)) {

    // $var has a value.

} else {

    // $var does not have a value.

}
```

You saw an example of this in the preceding script.

One problem with the isset() function is that an empty string tests as TRUE, meaning that it's not an effective way to validate text inputs and text boxes from an HTML form. To check that a user typed something into textual elements like name, email, and comments, you can use the empty() function. It checks if a variable has an *empty* value: an empty string, *0*, NULL, or FALSE.

The first aim of form validation is ensuring that *something* was entered or selected in form elements. The second goal is to ensure that submitted data is of the right type (numeric, string, etc.), of the right format (like an email address), or a specific acceptable value (like $gender being equal to either *M* or *F*). As handling forms is a main use of PHP, validating form data is a point that will be re-emphasized time and again in subsequent chapters.. At this point, I'll write a new handle_form.php script that makes sure variables have values before they're referenced.

To validate your forms:

1. Begin a new PHP script in your text editor (**Script 2.5**).

```
<!DOCTYPE html PUBLIC "-//W3C//
→ DTD XHTML 1.0 Transitional//EN"
"http://www.w3.org/TR/xhtml1/DTD/
→ xhtml1-transitional.dtd">
<html xmlns="http://www.w3.org/1999/
→ xhtml" xml:lang="en" lang="en">
<head>
    <meta http-equiv="content-type"
    → content="text/html;
    → charset=iso-8859-1" />
    <title>Form Feedback</title>
</head>
<body>
<?php # Script 2.5 - handle_form.php
→ (4th version after Scripts 2.2,
→ 2.3, & 2.4)
```

continues on page 54

Script 2.5 Validating HTML form data before you use it is critical to Web security and achieving professional results.

```
                              script
1    <!DOCTYPE html PUBLIC "-//W3C//DTD XHTML 1.0 Transitional//EN"
2        "http://www.w3.org/TR/xhtml1/DTD/xhtml1-transitional.dtd">
3    <html xmlns="http://www.w3.org/1999/xhtml" xml:lang="en" lang="en">
4    <head>
5        <meta http-equiv="content-type" content="text/html; charset=iso-8859-1" />
6        <title>Form Feedback</title>
7    </head>
8    <body>
9    <?php # Script 2.5 - handle_form.php (4th version after Scripts 2.2, 2.3, & 2.4)
10
11   // Validate the name and combat Magic Quotes, if necessary.
12   if (!empty($_REQUEST['name'])) {
13       $name = stripslashes($_REQUEST['name']);
14   } else {
15       $name = NULL;
16       echo '<p><font color="red">You forgot to enter your name!</font></p>';
17   }
18
19   // Validate the email and combat Magic Quotes, if necessary.
20   if (!empty($_REQUEST['email'])) {
21       $email = $_REQUEST['email'];
22   } else {
23       $email = NULL;
24       echo '<p><font color="red">You forgot to enter your email address!</font></p>';
25   }
26
27   // Validate the comments and combat Magic Quotes, if necessary.
28   if (!empty($_REQUEST['comments'])) {
29       $comments = stripslashes($_REQUEST['comments']);
30   } else {
31       $comments = NULL;
32       echo '<p><font color="red">You forgot to enter your comments!</font></p>';
33   }
34
35   // Validate gender.
36   if (isset($_REQUEST['gender'])) {
37
38       $gender = $_REQUEST['gender'];
39
40       if ($gender == 'M') {
41           $message = '<p><b>Good day, Sir!</b></p>';
```

(script continues on next page)

2. Check if the name was entered.

```
if (!empty($_REQUEST['name'])) {
    $name = stripslashes($_REQUEST
    → ['name']);
} else {
    $name = NULL;

    echo '<p><font color="red">You
    → forgot to enter your
    → name!</font></p>';
}
```

A simple way to check that a form text input was filled out is to use the empty() function. If $_REQUEST['name'] has a value other than an empty string, *0*, NULL, or FALSE, I'll assume that their name was entered. If so, I'll strip the slashes from it as before to combat Magic Quotes. If the variable is empty, I'll set the $name variable to NULL and print an error message.

3. Repeat the same process for the email address and comments.

```
if (!empty($_REQUEST['email'])) {
    $email = $_REQUEST['email'];
} else {
    $email = NULL;

    echo '<p><font color="red">You
    → forgot to enter your email
    → address!</font></p>';
}

if (!empty($_REQUEST['comments'])) {
    $comments = stripslashes($_REQUEST
    → ['comments']);
} else {
    $comments = NULL;

    echo '<p><font color="red">You
    → forgot to enter your comments!</
    → font></p>';
}
```

The $comments variable receives the same treatment as $name in Step 2, while $email differs slightly, because I'm not applying the stripslashes() function to it.

Script 2.5 *continued*

```
42      } elseif ($gender == 'F') {
43          $message = '<p><b>Good day, Madam!</
        b></p>';
44      } else { // Unacceptable value.
45          $message = NULL;
46          echo '<p><font color="red">Gender
            should be either "M" or "F"!</font>
            </p>';
47      }
48
49  } else { // $_REQUEST['gender'] is not set.
50      $gender = NULL;
51      echo '<p><font color="red">You forgot to
        select your gender!</font></p>';
52  }
53
54  // If everything is okay, print the message.
55  if ($name && $email && $gender &&
    $comments) {
56
57      echo "<p>Thank you, <b>$name</b>, for
        the following comments:<br />
58      <tt>$comments</tt></p>
59      <p>We will reply to you at <i>$email
        </i>.</p>\n";
60      echo $message; // From the $gender
        conditional.
61
62  } else { // One form element was not filled
    out properly.
63      echo '<p><font color="red">Please go
        back and fill out the form again.
        </font></p>';
64  }
65
66  ?>
67  </body>
68  </html>
```

4. Check the status of the gender.

```
if (isset($_REQUEST['gender'])) {
    $gender = $_REQUEST['gender'];
    if ($gender == 'M') {
        $message = '<p><b>Good day,
        → Sir!</b></p>';
    } elseif ($gender == 'F') {
        $message = '<p><b>Good day,
        → Madam!</b></p>';
    } else {
        $message = NULL;
        echo '<p><font
color="red">Gender should be either
→ "M" or "F"!</font></p>';
    }
} else {
    $gender = NULL;
    echo '<p><font color="red">You
    → forgot to select your gender!</
    → font></p>';
}
```

The validation of the gender is a two-step process. First, I check if it has a value or not, using `isset()`. This is the main `if-else` conditional, which otherwise behaves like those for the name, email address, and comments. Within the `if` clause is some extra code that performs a validation on gender, testing it against the acceptable values. If gender does not end up being equal to either *M* or *F*, a problem occurred and an error message is printed. The `$gender` variable is also set to `NULL` in such cases, because it has an unacceptable value.

In previous scripts (refer to Script 2.4 and Figures 2.8, 2.9, and 2.10), I printed out a gender-specific message at the bottom of the page. Since I haven't yet printed out the initial *Thank you* message at this point in the script, I'll create a `$message` variable instead, which will be printed later.

5. Print the messages if all of the tests have been passed.

```
if ($name && $email && $gender &&
→ $comments) {
    echo "<p>Thank you, <b>$name</b>,
    → for the following comments:<br />
    <tt>$comments</tt></p>
    <p>We will reply to you at
    → <i>$email</i>.</p>\n";
    echo $message;
} else {
    echo '<p><font color="red">Please
    → go back and fill out the form
    → again.</font></p>';
}
```

This main condition is true if every listed variable has a non-`NULL` value. Each variable will have a value if it passed its test but have a value of `NULL` if it didn't. If every variable has a value, the form was completed, so the *Thank you* and gender-specific messages will be printed. If any of the variables are `NULL`, the second message will be printed.

6. Close the PHP section and complete the HTML code.

```
?>
</body>
</html>
```

continues on next page

VALIDATING FORM DATA

7. Save the file as `handle_form.php`, upload to your Web server in the same directory as `form.html`, and test in your Web browser (**Figures 2.11**, **2.12**, and **2.13**). Fill out the form to different levels of completeness to test the new script.

✔ Tips

■ To test if a submitted value is a number, use the `is_numeric()` function.

■ In Chapter 10, "Web Application Security," you'll see how to validate form data using JavaScript on the client side as well as regular expressions on the server side.

■ The `$age` variable is still not used or validated for the sake of saving book space. To validate it, repeat the `$gender` validation routine, referring to `$_REQUEST['age']` instead. To test `$age`'s specific value, use an `if-elseif-elseif-else`, checking against the corresponding pull-down options (*0-29*, *30-60*, *60+*).

■ It's considered good form (pun intended) to let a user know which fields are required when they're filling out the form, and where applicable, the format of that field (like a date or a phone number).

■ Another way of validating text inputs is to use the `strlen()` function to see if more than zero characters were typed.

```
if (strlen($var) > 0) {
    // $var has a value.
} else {
    // $var does not have a value.
}
```

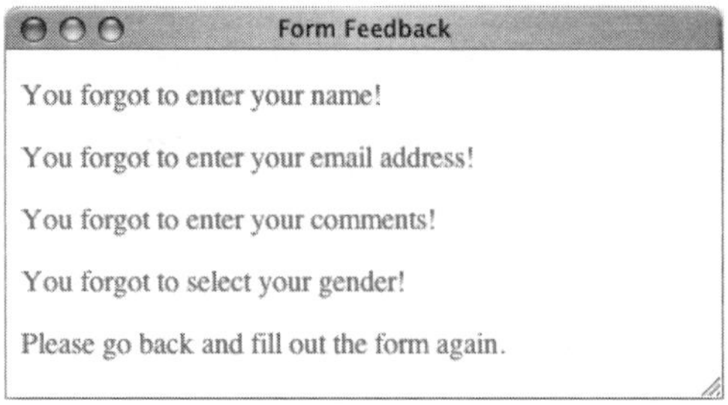

Figure 2.11 The script now checks that every form element was filled out (except the age) and reports on those that weren't.

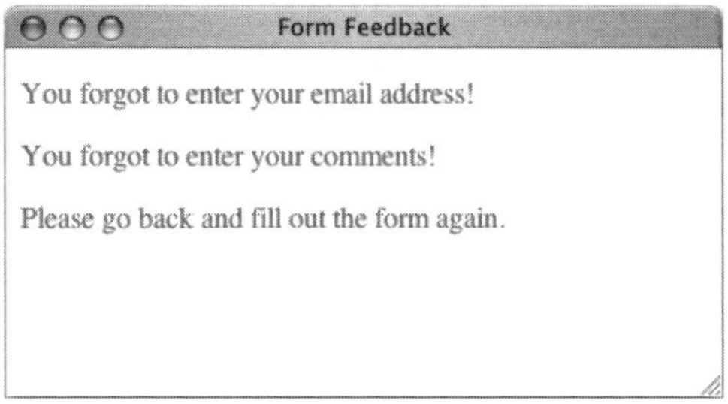

Figure 2.12 If even one or two fields were skipped, the *Thank you* message is not printed...

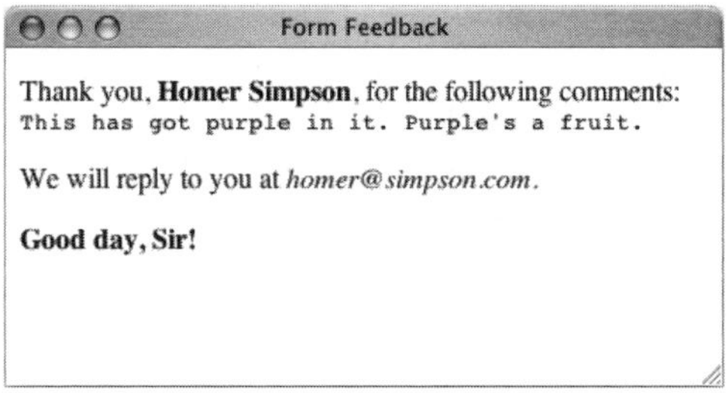

Figure 2.13 ...but if everything was entered properly, the script behaves as it previously had.

Array Example 1: $artists	
KEY	**VALUE**
0	Low
1	Aimee Mann
2	Ani DiFranco
3	Spiritualized
4	Air

Table 2.2 The $artists array uses numbers for its keys.

Array Example 2: $states	
KEY	**VALUE**
MD	Maryland
PA	Pennsylvania
IL	Illinois
MO	Missouri
IA	Iowa

Table 2.3 The $states array uses strings (specifically the state abbreviation) for its keys.

What Are Arrays?

The final variable type I'll introduce in this book is the array. Unlike strings and numbers (which are scalar variables, meaning they can store only a single value at a time), an *array* can hold multiple, separate pieces of information. An array is therefore like a list of values, each value being a string or a number or even another array.

Arrays are structured as a series of *key-value* pairs, where one pair is an item or *element* of that array. For each item in the list, there is a *key* (or *index*) associated with it. The resulting structure is not unlike a spreadsheet or database table (**Table 2.2**).

PHP supports two kinds of arrays: *indexed*, which use numbers as the keys (as in Table 2.2), and *associative*, which use strings as keys (**Table 2.3**). As in most programming languages, with indexed arrays, your arrays will begin with the first index at 0, unless you specify the keys explicitly.

As you can see, an array follows the same naming rules as any other variable. So offhand, you might not be able to tell that $var is an array as opposed to a string or number. The important syntactical difference has to do with accessing individual array elements.

To retrieve a specific value from an array, you refer to the array name first, followed by the key, in square brackets:

```
echo $artists[2]; // Ani DiFranco
```

```
echo $states['MD']; // Maryland
```

You can see that the array keys are used like other values in PHP: numbers (e.g., *2*) are never quoted, whereas strings (*MD*) must be.

continues on next page

Because arrays use a different syntax than other variables, printing them can be trickier. First, since an array can contain multiple values, you cannot simple code:

```
echo "Here is my list of states:
→ $states.";
```

Second, the keys in associative arrays complicate printing them. The following code will cause a parse error:

```
echo "IL is the abbreviation for
→ $states['IL'].";
```

To work around this, wrap your array name and key in curly braces when your array uses strings for its keys:

```
echo "IL is the abbreviation for
→ {$states['IL']}.";
```

Numerically indexed arrays don't have this problem, though:

```
echo "The artist with an index of 4 is
→ $artists[4].";
```

If arrays seem slightly familiar to you already, that's because you've already worked with a couple: $_SERVER and $_REQUEST (see the sidebar on "Superglobal Arrays"). To acquaint you with another array and how to print array values directly, a modified version of the basic handle_form.php page (refer to Script 2.3) will be created using the more specific $_POST array.

WHAT ARE ARRAYS?

Superglobal Arrays

PHP includes several predefined arrays by default. I am speaking of the *superglobal* variables: $_GET, $_POST, $_SESSION, $_REQUEST, $_SERVER, $_COOKIE, and so forth (added to PHP as of version 4.1).

The $_GET variable is where PHP stores all of the variables and values sent to a PHP script via the get method (presumably but not necessarily from an HTML form). $_POST stores all of the data sent to a PHP script from an HTML form that uses the post method. Both of these—along with $_COOKIE—are subsets of $_REQUEST, which you've been using.

The superglobals have two benefits over registered global variables (see the earlier sidebar "Registering Globals"). First, they are more secure because they are more precise (they indicate where the variable came from). Second, they are global in scope (hence the name), which will mean more to you after Chapter 3, "Creating Dynamic Web Sites." For this reason, I'll continue to directly use the superglobals for the remainder of the book. If you find the syntax of these variables to be confusing, you can use the shorthand technique at the top of your scripts as you have been: $name = $_POST['name'];

Script 2.6 The superglobal variables, like $_POST here, are just one type of array you'll use in PHP.

```
1    <!DOCTYPE html PUBLIC "-//W3C//DTD XHTML
     1.0 Transitional//EN"
2           "http://www.w3.org/TR/xhtml1/DTD/
            xhtml1-transitional.dtd">
3    <html xmlns="http://www.w3.org/1999/xhtml"
     xml:lang="en" lang="en">
4    <head>
5        <meta http-equiv="content-type" content=
         "text/html; charset=iso-8859-1" />
6        <title>Form Feedback</title>
7    </head>
8    <body>
9    <?php # Script 2.6 - handle_form.php
     (rewrite of Script 2.3)
10
11   // Create a shorthand for the form data.
12   // Use stripslashes() to combat Magic
     Quotes, if necessary.
13   $name = stripslashes($_POST['name']);
14   $comments = stripslashes($_POST
     ['comments']);
15   // Not used: $_POST['age'], $_POST
     ['gender'], and $_POST['submit'].
16
17   // Print the submitted information.
18   echo "<p>Thank you, <b>$name</b>, for the
     following comments:<br />
19   <tt>$comments</tt></p>
20   <p>We will reply to you at <i>{$_POST
     ['email']}</i>.</p>\n";
21
22   ?>
23   </body>
24   </html>
```

To use arrays:

1. Open handle_form.php (refer to Script 2.3) in your text editor.

2. Change the assignment of the $name and $comments variables to (**Script 2.6**).

   $name = stripslashes($_POST
   → ['name']);

   $comments = stripslashes($_POST
   → ['comments']);

   In the previous version of this script, the values of $name and $comments were assigned by referring to the $_REQUEST array, which will work. But since these variables come from a form that uses the post method (see Script 2.1), $_POST would be a more exact, and therefore more secure, reference.

3. Delete the line that creates the $email variable.

   Previously a shorthand version of $_REQUEST['email'] was created as $email. Since this script will now refer to $_POST['email'] directly within an echo() statement, this line is no longer needed.

   continues on next page

WHAT ARE ARRAYS?

4. Alter the echo() statement to directly print the $_POST['email'] value.

```
echo "<p>Thank you, <b>$name</b>,
→ for the following comments:<br />
<tt>$comments</tt></p>

<p>We will reply to you at <i>
→ {$_POST['email']}</i>.</p>\n";
```

Once you comprehend the concept of an array, you still need to master the syntax involved in printing it. When printing an array element that uses a string for its key, use the curly braces (as in {$_POST['email']} here) to avoid parse errors.

5. Save the file, upload to your Web server, and test in your Web browser (**Figure 2.14**).

✔ Tips

■ Because PHP is lax with its variable structures, an array can even use a combination of numbers and strings as its keys. The only important rule is that the keys of an array must each be unique.

■ The superglobals are new to PHP as of version 4.1. If you are using an earlier version of the language, use $HTTP_POST_VARS instead of $_POST and $HTTP_GET_VARS instead of $_GET.

■ In case you are the curious type, the parse error resulting from not using curly braces when printing arrays with string keys is daunting (**Figure 2.15**).

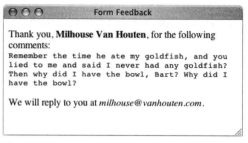

Thank you, **Milhouse Van Houten**, for the following comments:
```
Remember the time he ate my goldfish, and you
lied to me and said I never had any goldfish?
Then why did I have the bowl, Bart? Why did I
have the bowl?
```
We will reply to you at *milhouse@vanhouten.com*.

Figure 2.14 Using the superglobal variables won't affect the operation of your script, but it does make it more secure.

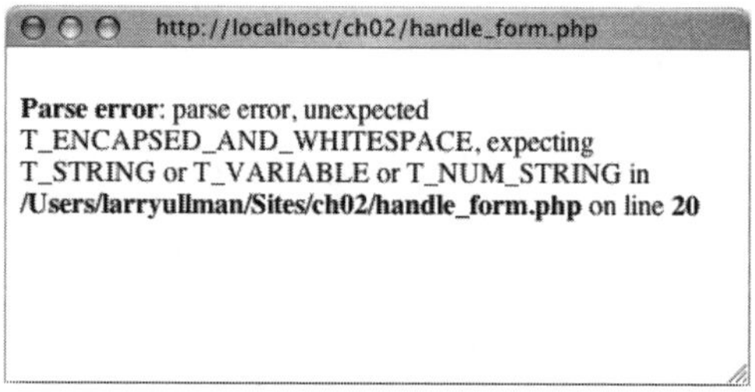

http://localhost/ch02/handle_form.php

Parse error: parse error, unexpected T_ENCAPSED_AND_WHITESPACE, expecting T_STRING or T_VARIABLE or T_NUM_STRING in **/Users/larryullman/Sites/ch02/handle_form.php** on line 20

Figure 2.15 The added complexity of the array syntax can easily lead to parse errors.

WHAT ARE ARRAYS?

Creating arrays

In the previous example, I used a PHP-generated array, but there will frequently be times when you want to create your own. There are two primary ways to define your own array. First, you could add an element at a time to build one:

```
$array[] = 'Tobias';

$array[] = 'Maeby';

$array['wife'] = 'Lindsay';
```

It's important to understand that if you specify a key and a value already exists indexed with that same key, the new value will overwrite the existing one. For example,

```
$array['son'] = 'Buster';

$array['son'] = 'Michael';

$array[2] = 'apple';

$array[2] = 'orange';
```

Instead of adding one element at a time, you can use the array() function to build an entire array in one step:

```
$states = array ('IA' => 'Iowa', 'MD' =>
→ 'Maryland');
```

This function can be used whether or not you explicitly set the key:

```
$artists = array ('Ani DiFranco', 'Air',
→ 'Wilco');
```

Or, if you set the first numeric key value, the added values will be keyed incrementally thereafter:

```
$days = array (1 => 'Sunday','Monday',
→ 'Tuesday');

echo $days[3]; // Tuesday
```

Finally, if you want to create an array of sequential numbers, you can use the range() function:

```
$ten = range (1, 10);
```

Accessing arrays

You've already seen how to access individual array elements by key (e.g., $_POST ['email']). This works when you know exactly what the keys are or if you want to refer to only a single element. To access every array element, use the foreach loop:

```
foreach ($array as $value) {

    // Do something with $value.

}
```

The foreach loop will iterate through every element in $array, assigning each element's value to the $value variable. To access both the keys and values, use

```
foreach ($array as $key => $value) {

    echo "The array value at $key is
    → $value.";

}
```

Using arrays, I'll show how easy it is to make a set of form pull-down menus to select a date.

To create and access arrays:

1. Create a new PHP document in your text
editor (**Script 2.7**).

```
<!DOCTYPE html PUBLIC "-//W3C//
→ DTD XHTML 1.0 Transitional//EN"
"http://www.w3.org/TR/xhtml1/DTD/
→ xhtml1-transitional.dtd">
<html xmlns="http://www.w3.org/1999/
→ xhtml" xml:lang="en" lang="en">
<head>
  <meta http-equiv="content-type"
  → content="text/html;
  → charset=iso-8859-1" />
  <title>Calendar</title>
</head>
<body>
<form action="calendar.php"
→ method="post">
<?php # Script 2.7 - calendar.php
```

One particular thing to note here is that
the HTML form tag is required to create
the pull-downs. Since it doesn't matter
where or when you embed PHP, I include
the form tag *before* going into PHP.

2. Create an array for the months.

```
$months = array (1 => 'January',
→ 'February', 'March', 'April',
→ 'May', 'June', 'July', 'August',
→ 'September', 'October',
→ 'November', 'December');
```

This first array will use numbers for the
keys, from 1 to 12. Since I specified the
first key, the following values will be
indexed incrementally.

Script 2.7 Arrays are used to dynamically create three
pull-down menus (refer to Figure 2.16).

```
1   <!DOCTYPE html PUBLIC "-//W3C//DTD XHTML
    1.0 Transitional//EN"
2        "http://www.w3.org/TR/xhtml1/DTD/
         xhtml1-transitional.dtd">
3   <html xmlns="http://www.w3.org/1999/xhtml"
    xml:lang="en" lang="en">
4   <head>
5       <meta http-equiv="content-type" content=
        "text/html; charset=iso-8859-1" />
6       <title>Calendar</title>
7   </head>
8   <body>
9   <form action="calendar.php" method="post">
10  <?php # Script 2.7 - calendar.php
11  // This script makes three pull-down menus
    for an HTML form: months, days, years.
12
13  // Make the months array.
14  $months = array (1 => 'January',
    'February', 'March', 'April', 'May',
    'June', 'July', 'August', 'September',
    'October', 'November', 'December');
15
16  // Make the days and years arrays.
17  $days = range (1, 31);
18  $years = range (2005, 2015);
19
20  // Make the months pull-down menu.
21  echo '<select name="month">';
22  foreach ($months as $key => $value) {
23      echo "<option value=\"$key\">$value</
        option>\n";
24  }
25  echo '</select>';
26
27  // Make the days pull-down menu.
28  echo '<select name="day">';
29  foreach ($days as $value) {
30      echo "<option value=\"$value\">$value</
        option>\n";
31  }
```

(script continues on next page)

Script 2.7 *continued*

```
┌────────────────────────────────────────┐
│ ▦▦▦▦▦▦▦▦▦▦▦▦ script ▦▦▦▦▦▦▦▦▦▦▦ ▦ │
├────────────────────────────────────────┤
32   echo '</select>';
33
34   // Make the years pull-down menu.
35   echo '<select name="year">';
36   foreach ($years as $value) {
37      echo "<option value=\"$value\">$value</
        option>\n";
38   }
39   echo '</select>';
40
41   ?>
42   </form>
43   </body>
44   </html>
```

3. Create the arrays for the days of the month and the years.

```
$days = range (1, 31);
$years = range (2005, 2015);
```

Using the range() function, I can easily make an array of numbers.

4. Generate the months pull-down menu.

```
echo '<select name="month">';
foreach ($months as $key => $value) {
    echo "<option value=\"$key\">
    → $value</option>\n";
}
echo '</select>';
```

With the foreach loop I can quickly generate all of the HTML code for the month pull-down menu. Each execution of the loop will create a line of code like <option value="1">January</option>.

5. Generate the days and years pull-down menus.

```
echo '<select name="day">';
foreach ($days as $value) {
    echo "<option value=\"$value\">
    → $value</option>\n";
}
echo '</select>';
echo '<select name="year">';
foreach ($years as $value) {
    echo "<option value=\"$value\">
    → $value</option>\n";
}
echo '</select>';
```

Unlike the months example, both the day and year pull-down menus will use the same thing for both the option's value and label (a number). This is why I didn't need to specify keys when making these arrays.

continues on next page

6. Close the PHP, the form tag, and the HTML page.

```
?>
</form>
</body>
</html>
```

7. Save the file as `calendar.php`, upload to your Web server, and test in your Web browser (**Figure 2.16**).

8. If desired, view the source code in your browser by choosing View > Source or View > Page Source (**Figure 2.17**).

Figure 2.16 These pull-down menus were created using arrays and the `foreach` loop.

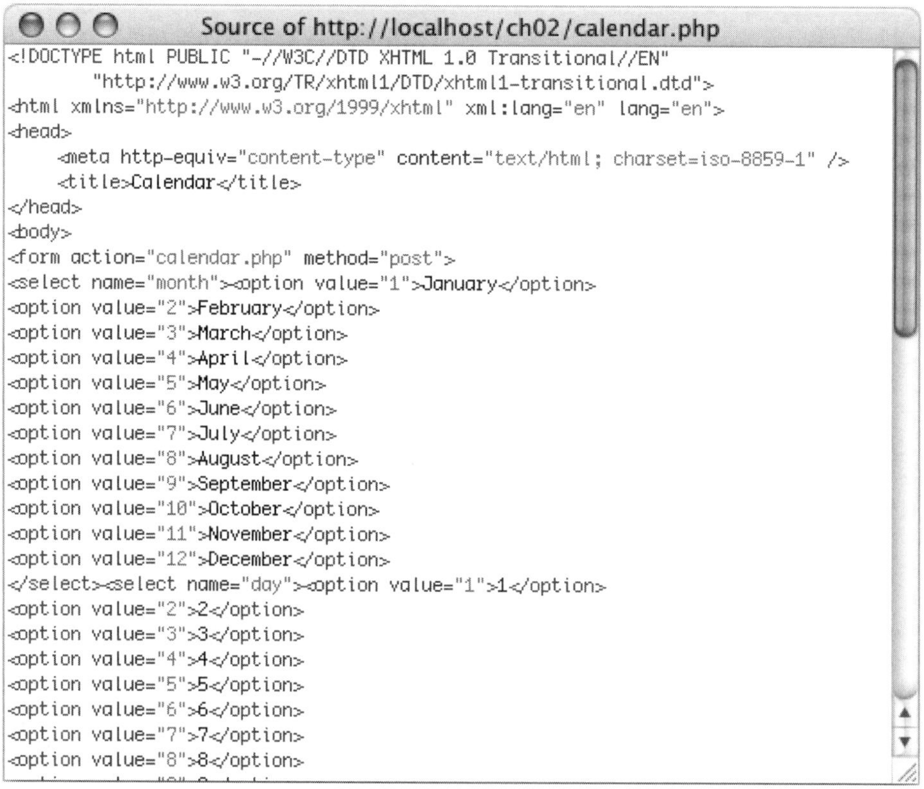

```
<!DOCTYPE html PUBLIC "-//W3C//DTD XHTML 1.0 Transitional//EN"
        "http://www.w3.org/TR/xhtml1/DTD/xhtml1-transitional.dtd">
<html xmlns="http://www.w3.org/1999/xhtml" xml:lang="en" lang="en">
<head>
        <meta http-equiv="content-type" content="text/html; charset=iso-8859-1" />
        <title>Calendar</title>
</head>
<body>
<form action="calendar.php" method="post">
<select name="month"><option value="1">January</option>
<option value="2">February</option>
<option value="3">March</option>
<option value="4">April</option>
<option value="5">May</option>
<option value="6">June</option>
<option value="7">July</option>
<option value="8">August</option>
<option value="9">September</option>
<option value="10">October</option>
<option value="11">November</option>
<option value="12">December</option>
</select><select name="day"><option value="1">1</option>
<option value="2">2</option>
<option value="3">3</option>
<option value="4">4</option>
<option value="5">5</option>
<option value="6">6</option>
<option value="7">7</option>
<option value="8">8</option>
```

Figure 2.17 Most of the source code was generated by just a few lines of PHP

✔ Tips

- To determine the number of elements in an array, use the `count()` or `sizeof()` function (the two are synonymous).

  `$num = count($array);`

- The `range()` function can also create an array of sequential letters as of PHP 4.1:

  `$alphabet = range ('a', 'z');`

- An array's keys can be multiple-worded strings, such as *first name* or *phone number*.

- The `is_array()` function confirms that a variable is of the array type.

- You don't have to use the names `$key` and `$value` in your `foreach` loop, but those are logical choices (some programmers abbreviate them as `$k` and `$v`).

- If you see an *Invalid argument supplied for foreach()* error message, that means you are trying to use a `foreach` loop on a variable that is not an array.

Multidimensional arrays

When first introducing arrays, I mentioned that an array's values could be any combination of numbers, strings, and even other arrays. This last option—an array consisting of other arrays—creates a multidimensional array.

Multidimensional arrays are much more common than you might expect (especially if you use the superglobals) but remarkably easy to work with. As an example, Table 2.3 displayed an array called `$states`, which would have been created by

```
$states = array ('MD' => 'Maryland',
→ 'IL' => 'Illinois', ...);
```

If you had another similar array for Canada

```
$provinces = array ('QC' => 'Quebec',
→ 'AB' => 'Alberta', ...);
```

then these two arrays could be combined into one multidimensional array like so:

```
$abbr = array ('US' => $states, 'Canada'
→ => $provinces);
```

Now, `$abbr` is a multidimensional array. To access the `$states` array, you refer to `$abbr['US']`. To access Maryland, use `$abbr['US']['MD']`. Simply use the name of the multidimensional array, followed by the key of the first array in square brackets (this key would happen to be the name of the inner array), followed by the key of the second, inner array (also in square brackets). To print out one of these values, surround the whole construct in curly braces:

```
echo "The US state whose abbreviation is
→ MD is {$abbr['US']['MD']}.";
```

Of course, you can still access multidimensional arrays using the `foreach` loop, nesting one inside another if necessary.

In this next example, `$_POST` will be a multidimensional array as the HTML form will create an array for one set of inputs.

To use multidimensional arrays:

1. Create a new HTML document in your text editor (**Script 2.8**).

```
<!DOCTYPE html PUBLIC "-//W3C//
→ DTD XHTML 1.0 Transitional//EN"
"http://www.w3.org/TR/xhtml1/DTD/
→ xhtml1-transitional.dtd">
<html xmlns="http://www.w3.org/1999/
→ xhtml" xml:lang="en" lang="en">
<head>
    <meta http-equiv="content-type"
    → content="text/html;
    → charset=iso-8859-1" />
    <title>Tell Us About Yourself</
    → title>
</head>
<body>
<!-- Script 2.8 - about.html -->
```

2. Begin the HTML form.

```
<form action="handle_about.php"
→ method="post">
    <fieldset><legend>Enter your
    → information in the form
    → below:</legend>
    <p><b>Name:</b> <input type="text"
    → name="name" size="20"
    → maxlength="40" /></p>
```

The form will send all its data to the handle_about.php script, using the post method. The first input is the user's name.

Script 2.8 This form has a series of check boxes the user can select. That particular input will create a $_POST['interests'] variable that is itself an array.

```
1   <!DOCTYPE html PUBLIC "-//W3C//DTD XHTML
    1.0 Transitional//EN"
2       "http://www.w3.org/TR/xhtml1/DTD/
        xhtml1-transitional.dtd">
3   <html xmlns="http://www.w3.org/1999/xhtml"
    xml:lang="en" lang="en">
4   <head>
5       <meta http-equiv="content-type" content=
        "text/html; charset=iso-8859-1" />
6       <title>Tell Us About Yourself</title>
7   </head>
8   <body>
9
10  <!-- Script 2.8 - about.html -->
11
12  <form action="handle_about.php"
    method="post">
13
14      <fieldset><legend>Enter your
information
        in the form below:</legend>
15
16      <p><b>Name:</b> <input type="text"
        name="name" size="20" maxlength="40"
        /></p>
17
18      <p><b>Interests:</b>
19          <input type="checkbox" name=
            "interests[]" value="Music"
            /> Music
20          <input type="checkbox" name=
            "interests[]" value="Movies"
            /> Movies
21          <input type="checkbox" name=
            "interests[]" value="Books"
            /> Books
22          <input type="checkbox" name=
            "interests[]" value="Skiing"
            /> Skiing
23          <input type="checkbox" name=
            "interests[]" value="Napping"
            /> Napping
24      </p>
25
```

Script 2.8 *continued*

```
                    script

              (script continues on next page)
26      </fieldset>
27
28      <div align="center"><input type="submit"
        name="submit" value="Submit My
        Information" /></div>
29
30    </form>
31    </body>
32    </html>
```

3. Create a series of check boxes so that users can select their interests.

```
<p><b>Interests:</b>
    <input type="checkbox" name=
    → "interests[]" value=
    → "Music" /> Music
    <input type="checkbox" name=
    → "interests[]" value=
    → "Movies" /> Movies
    <input type="checkbox" name=
    → "interests[]" value=
    → "Books" /> Books
    <input type="checkbox" name=
    → "interests[]" value=
    → "Skiing" /> Skiing
    <input type="checkbox" name=
    → "interests[]" value=
    → "Napping" /> Napping
</p>
```

The interests section of the form will give the user the option of selecting multiple choices. There are two naming schemes you could use for the various inputs in such a case: Either give them a name that matches their value (*Music, Movies,* etc.) or use an array. Here I've used *interests[]* as the name, which will, in the handling PHP script, create an array at $_POST['interests'] that stores all of the boxes the user checked.

4. Complete the page.

```
    </fieldset>
    <div align="center"><input type=
    → "submit" name="submit" value=
    → "Submit My Information" /></div>
    </form>
    </body>
    </html>
```

5. Save the file as about.html.

Now I'll create handle_about.php to make use of the $_POST['interests'] multidimensional array.

WHAT ARE ARRAYS?

To handle the form:

1. Create a new PHP document in your text editor (**Script 2.9**).

```
<!DOCTYPE html PUBLIC "-//W3C//
→ DTD XHTML 1.0 Transitional//EN"
"http://www.w3.org/TR/xhtml1/DTD/
→ xhtml1-transitional.dtd">
<html xmlns="http://www.w3.org/1999/
→ xhtml" xml:lang="en" lang="en">
<head>
  <meta http-equiv="content-type"
  → content="text/html;
  → charset=iso-8859-1" />
  <title>About You Form Feedback</
  → title>
</head>
<body>
<?php # Script 2.9 - handle_about.php
```

2. Validate that a name was entered.

```
if (!empty($_POST['name'])) {
  $name = stripslashes($_POST
  → ['name']);
} else {
  $name = NULL;
  echo '<p><font color="red">You
  → forgot to enter your name!</
  → font></p>';
}
```

The code here is almost exactly like that in earlier scripts (refer to Script 2.5), although it now uses the **$_POST** superglobal, which is more specific than **$_REQUEST**.

Script 2.9 This script prints out the values of $_POST['interests'], which is part of the multidimensional $_POST array.

```
1    <!DOCTYPE html PUBLIC "-//W3C//DTD XHTML
     1.0 Transitional//EN"
2        "http://www.w3.org/TR/xhtml1/DTD/
         xhtml1-transitional.dtd">
3    <html xmlns="http://www.w3.org/1999/xhtml"
     xml:lang="en" lang="en">
4    <head>
5        <meta http-equiv="content-type" content=
         "text/html; charset=iso-8859-1" />
6        <title>About You Form Feedback</title>
7    </head>
8    <body>
9    <?php # Script 2.9 - handle_about.php
10
11   // Check $_POST['name'] and strip any
     slashes.
12   if (!empty($_POST['name'])) {
13       $name = stripslashes($_POST['name']);
14   } else {
15       $name = NULL;
16       echo '<p><font color="red">You forgot to
         enter your name!</font></p>';
17   }
18
19   // Check the interests.
20   if (isset($_POST['interests'])) {
21       $interests = TRUE;
22   } else {
23       $interests = NULL;
24       echo '<p><font color="red">You forgot to
         enter your interests!</font></p>';
25   }
26
27   // If everything was filled out, print the
     message.
28   if ($name && $interests) {
29
30       echo "Thank you, <b>$name</b>. You
         entered your interests as:<ul>";
31
```

(script continues on next page)

WHAT ARE ARRAYS?

Script 2.9 *continued*

```
        ▣▣▣▣▣▣▣▣     script     ▣▣▣▣▣▣▣
32      // Print each interest.
33      foreach ($_POST['interests'] as $value)
        { // Loop through each.
34          echo "<li>$value</li>\n";
35      }
36
37      echo '</ul>'; // Close the list.
38
39  } else { // One form element was not filled
    out properly.
40      echo '<p><font color="red">Please go
        back and fill out the form again.
        </font></p>';
41  }
42  ?>
43  </body>
44  </html>
```

3. Add the lines for validating the interests.

```
if (isset($_POST['interests'])) {
    $interests = TRUE;
} else {
    $interests = NULL;
    echo '<p><font color="red">You
    → forgot to enter your
    → interests!</font></p>';
}
```

This conditional validates that `$_POST['interests']` has a value. If so, `$interests` is set to TRUE. Otherwise, `$interests` is set to NULL and an error message is printed.

4. Begin the final conditional.

```
if ($name && $interests) {
    echo "Thank you, <b>$name</b>. You
    → entered your interests as:<ul>";
```

If the form was filled out properly, both `$name` and `$interests` will have values, making this condition true. In that case, the user's name is printed as part of a message. Next, the submitted interests will be reprinted. Because I want the interests to be displayed as an HTML list, I print the initial unordered list tag (`<ul>`) here.

5. Print out all the selected interests.

```
foreach ($_POST['interests'] as
→ $value) {
    echo "<li>$value</li>\n";
}
```

Following the syntax outlined earlier, this loop will access every element of `$_POST['interests']`. Due to the nature of form check boxes, only those boxes that were selected will have a value in the `$_POST['interests']` array. Within the loop itself each value is printed within HTML list tags.

continues on next page

WHAT ARE ARRAYS?

6. Complete the final conditional.

```
  echo '</ul>';
} else {
  echo '<p><font color="red">Please
→ go back and fill out the form
→ again.</font></p>';
}
```

The first echo() statement closes the HTML list. The second is printed if either $name or $interests does not have a value, meaning that the form wasn't properly filled out.

7. Complete the PHP and HTML.

```
?>
</body>
</html>
```

8. Save the file as handle_about.php, upload to your Web server along with about. html, and test both in your Web browser (**Figures 2.18**, **2.19**, and **2.20**).

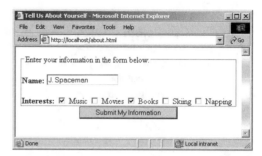

Figure 2.18 This HTML form makes use of check boxes.

Figure 2.19 The selected interests are repeated back to the user as an HTML list.

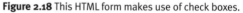

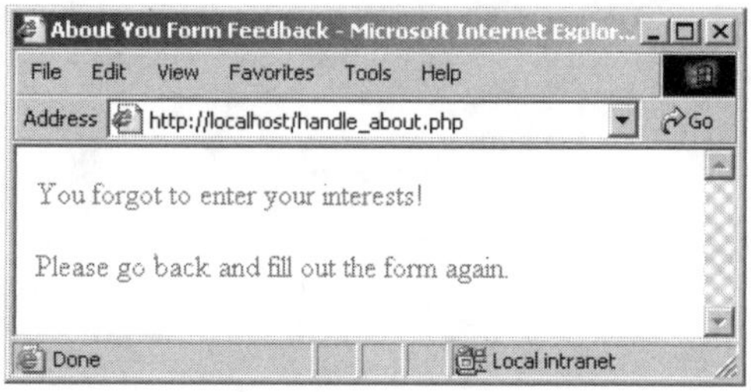

Figure 2.20 If a name was not entered or no interests were selected, error messages are generated.

WHAT ARE ARRAYS?

✔ Tips

- Even if the user selects only one inter-est, `$_POST['interests']` will still be an array because the HTML name for the corresponding input is `interests[]` (the square brackets make it an array).

- You can also end up with a multidimensional array by having an HTML form's select menu allow for multiple selections:

```
<select name="interests[]"
multiple="multiple">
    <option value="Music">Music</
    → option>
    <option value="Movies">Movies</
    → option>
    <option value="Books">Books</
    → option>
    <option value="Skiing">Skiing</
    → option>
    <option value="Napping">Napping</
    → option>
</select>
```

Arrays and strings

Because these two variable types are so commonly used, PHP has two functions for converting between strings and arrays.

```
$array = explode (separator, $string);
```

```
$string = implode (glue, $array);
```

The key to using and understanding these two functions is the *separator* and *glue* relationships. When turning an array into a string, you set the glue—the characters or code that will be inserted between the array values in the generated string. Conversely, when turning a string into an array, you specify the separator, which is the code that delineates between the different elements in the generated array.

```
$string1 = 'Mon - Tue - Wed - Thur - Fri';
```

```
$days_array = explode (' - ', $string1);
```

The `$days_array` variable is now a five-element array, with *Mon* indexed at 0, *Tue* indexed at 1, etc.

```
$string2 = implode (', ', $days_array);
```

The `$string2` variable is now a comma-separated list of days: *Mon, Tue, Wed, Thur, Fri*.

WHAT ARE ARRAYS?

To convert an array to a string:

1. Open handle_about.php (refer to Script 2.9) in your text editor.

2. Replace the definition of the $interests variable with (**Script 2.10**)

   $interests = implode (', ', $_POST
   → ['interests']);

   Instead of setting $interests to be equal to TRUE, it'll now be a string of comma-separated values.

3. Remove the foreach loop and the echo() statement from the main conditional.

   Since $interests is now an easily printable string, I'll do away with the loop and the use of the HTML list.

4. Change the first main conditional echo() statement to read

   echo "Thank you, $name.
   → You entered your interests
   → as:
$interests";

5. Save the file as handle_about.php, upload to your Web server, and test in your Web browser (**Figure 2.21**).

✔ Tips

- The function join() is a synonym for implode().

- For some reason I have an impossible time remembering when to use explode() and when to use implode(). As a mnemonic device, I try to remember that explode() blows things (a string) into little bits (an array).

- The explode() function takes a third, optional parameter, which is a number limiting how many array elements are created.

Script 2.10 The implode() function greatly facilitates conversions between arrays and strings.

```
1   <!DOCTYPE html PUBLIC "-//W3C//DTD XHTML
    1.0 Transitional//EN"
2       "http://www.w3.org/TR/xhtml1/DTD/
        xhtml1-transitional.dtd">
3   <html xmlns="http://www.w3.org/1999/xhtml"
    xml:lang="en" lang="en">
4   <head>
5       <meta http-equiv="content-type" content=
        "text/html; charset=iso-8859-1" />
6       <title>About You Form Feedback</title>
7   </head>
8   <body>
9   <?php # Script 2.10 - handle_about.php (2nd
    version after Script 2.9)
10
11  // Check $_POST['name'] and strip any
    slashes.
12  if (!empty($_POST['name'])) {
13      $name = stripslashes($_POST['name']);
14  } else {
15      $name = NULL;
16      echo '<p><font color="red">You forgot to
        enter your name!</font></p>';
17  }
18
19  // Check the interests.
20  if (isset($_POST['interests'])) {
```

(script continues on next page)

About You Form Feedback

http://localhost/ch02/handle_about.php

Thank you, **Jason Pierce**. You entered your interests as: Movies, Books, Skiing

Figure 2.21 Although this script works more or less the same as it had before (see Figure 2.20), the code is shorter and easier to comprehend (refer to Script 2.10).

WHAT ARE ARRAYS?

Script 2.10 *continued*

```
█  ▤            script            ▤ █
21    $interests = implode (', ', $_POST
      ['interests']);
22    } else {
23        $interests = NULL;
24        echo '<p><font color="red">You forgot to
      enter your interests!</font></p>';
25    }
26
27    // If everything was filled out, print the
      message.
28    if ($name && $interests) {
29
30        echo "Thank you, <b>$name</b>. You
          entered your interests as:<br />
          $interests";
31
32    } else { // One form element was not filled
      out properly.
33        echo '<p><font color="red">Please go
          back and fill out the form again.
          </font></p>';
34    }
35    ?>
36    </body>
37    </html>
```

Sorting arrays

One of the many advantages arrays have over the other variable types is the ability to sort them. PHP includes several functions you can use for sorting arrays, all simple in syntax:

```
$names = array ('George Michael', 'Ann',
→ 'Buster');

sort($names);
```

The sorting functions perform three kinds of sorts. First, you can sort an array by value, discarding the original keys, using `sort()`. It's important to understand that the array's keys will be reset after the sorting process, so if the key-value relationship is important, you should *not* use this function.

Second, you can sort an array by value while maintaining the keys, using `asort()`. Third, you can sort an array by key, using `ksort()`. Each of these can sort in reverse order if you change them to `rsort()`, `arsort()`, and `krsort()` respectively.

To demonstrate the effect sorting arrays will have, I'll create an array of movie titles and ratings (how much I liked them on a scale of 1 to 10) and then display this list in different ways.

WHAT ARE ARRAYS?

To sort arrays:

1. Create a new PHP document in your text editor (**Script 2.11**).

```
<!DOCTYPE html PUBLIC "-//W3C//
→ DTD XHTML 1.0 Transitional//EN"
"http://www.w3.org/TR/xhtml1/DTD/
→ xhtml1-transitional.dtd">
<html xmlns="http://www.w3.org/1999/
→ xhtml" xml:lang="en" lang="en">
<head>
    <meta http-equiv="content-type"
    → content="text/html;
    → charset=iso-8859-1" />
    <title>Sorting Arrays</title>
</head>
<body>
<?php # Script 2.11 - sorting.php
```

2. Create a new array.

```
$movies = array (
10 => 'Casablanca',
9 => 'To Kill a Mockingbird',
2 => 'The English Patient',
8 => 'Sideways',
7 => 'Donnie Darko'
);
```

This array uses movie titles as the values and their respective ratings as their key. This structure will open up several possibilities for sorting the whole list. Feel free to change the movie listings and rankings as you see fit (just don't chastise me for my taste in films).

Script 2.11 Arrays can be sorted in numerous ways.

```
1   <!DOCTYPE html PUBLIC "-//W3C//DTD XHTML
    1.0 Transitional//EN"
2         "http://www.w3.org/TR/xhtml1/DTD/
          xhtml1-transitional.dtd">
3   <html xmlns="http://www.w3.org/1999/xhtml"
    xml:lang="en" lang="en">
4   <head>
5       <meta http-equiv="content-type" content=
        "text/html; charset=iso-8859-1" />
6       <title>Sorting Arrays</title>
7   </head>
8   <body>
9   <?php # Script 2.11 - sorting.php
10
11  // Create the array.
12  $movies = array (
13  10 => 'Casablanca',
14  9 => 'To Kill a Mockingbird',
15  2 => 'The English Patient',
16  8 => 'Sideways',
17  7 => 'Donnie Darko'
18  );
19
20  // Display the movies in their original
    order.
21  echo '<p>In their original order:
    <br /><pre>Rating    Title
22  ';
23  foreach ($movies as $key => $value) {
24      echo "$key\t$value\n";
25  }
26  echo '</pre></p>';
27
28  // Display the movies sorted by title.
29  echo '<p>Sorted by title:<br /><pre>
    Rating Title
30  ';
31  asort($movies);
32  foreach ($movies as $key => $value) {
33      echo "$key\t$value\n";
34  }
```

(script continues on next page)

Script 2.11 *continued*

```
 35   echo '</pre></p>';
 36
 37   // Display the movies sorted by rating.
 38   echo '<p>Sorted by rating:<br /><pre>
      Rating Title
 39   ';
 40   krsort($movies);
 41   foreach ($movies as $key => $value) {
 42       echo "$key\t$value\n";
 43   }
 44   echo '</pre></p>';
 45   ?>
 46   </body>
 47   </html>
```

3. Print out the array as is.

```
echo '<p>In their original order:
→ <br /><pre>Rating  Title
';
foreach ($movies as $key => $value) {
    echo "$key\t$value\n";
}
echo '</pre></p>';
```

At this point in the script, the array is in the order it was created. To verify this, I'll print it out. I'm using the pre tags (for *preformatted*) to create a simple table in the resulting HTML. Within the foreach loop, the key is printed, followed by a tab, followed by the value, and then a newline.

4. Sort the array alphabetically by title and print it again.

```
echo '<p>Sorted by title:<br />
→ <pre>Rating   Title
';
asort($movies);
foreach ($movies as $key => $value) {
    echo "$key\t$value\n";
}
echo '</pre></p>';
```

The asort() function sorts an array by value while maintaining the key-value relationship. The rest of the code is a repetition of Step 3.

continues on next page

WHAT ARE ARRAYS?

5. Sort the array numerically by descending rating and print again.

```
echo '<p>Sorted by rating:<br />
→ <pre>Rating    Title
';
krsort($movies);
foreach ($movies as $key => $value) {
   echo "$key\t$value\n";
}
echo '</pre></p>';
```

The ksort() function will sort an array by key, but in ascending order. Since I want that reversed (highest score first), I use krsort(). This function, like asort(), maintains the key-value relationships.

6. Complete the PHP and HTML.

```
?>
</body>
</html>
```

7. Save the file as sorting.php, upload to your Web server, and test in your Web browser (**Figure 2.22**).

✔ Tips

- If you want to use decimal ratings for the movies, the rating numbers must be quoted or else PHP would drop the decimal points (numeric keys are always integers).

- To randomize the order of an array, use shuffle().

- PHP's natsort() function can be used to sort arrays in a more natural order (primarily handling numbers in strings better).

- PHP can also sort arrays using a user-defined sorting function. See the PHP manual for more information on the usort() function.

```
In their original order:

Rating    Title
10        Casablanca
9         To Kill a Mockingbird
2         The English Patient
8         Sideways
7         Donnie Darko

Sorted by title:

Rating    Title
10        Casablanca
7         Donnie Darko
8         Sideways
2         The English Patient
9         To Kill a Mockingbird

Sorted by rating:

Rating    Title
10        Casablanca
9         To Kill a Mockingbird
8         Sideways
7         Donnie Darko
2         The English Patient
```

Figure 2.22 This page demonstrates the different ways arrays can be sorted.

- PHP will sort arrays as if they were in English by default. If you need to sort an array in another language, use PHP's setlocale() function to change the language setting.

- Technically the <pre> tag is not allowed in XHTML Transitional documents, but I wanted to save you having to create all the requisite table HTML.

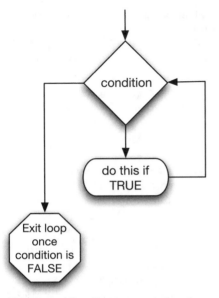

Figure 2.23 A flowchart representation of how PHP handles a while loop.

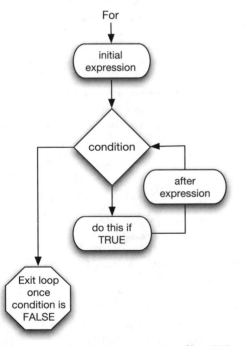

Figure 2.24 A flowchart representation of how PHP handles the more complex for loop.

For and While Loops

The last language construct I'll discuss is loops. You've already used one, foreach, when managing arrays. The next two types of loops you'll use are for and while.

The while loop looks like this:

```
while (condition) {

    // Do something.

}
```

As long as the *condition* part of the loop is true, the loop will be executed. Once it becomes false, the loop is stopped (**Figure 2.23**). If the condition is never true, the loop will never be executed. The while loop will most frequently be used when retrieving results from a database, as you'll see in Chapter 7, "Using PHP with MySQL."

The for loop has a more complicated syntax:

```
for (initial expression; condition;
→ closing expression) {

    // Do something.

}
```

Upon first executing the loop, the initial expression is run. Then the condition is checked and, if true, the contents of the loop are executed. After execution, the closing expression is run and the condition is checked again. This process continues until the condition is false (**Figure 2.24**). As an example,

```
for ($i = 1; $i <= 10; $i++) {

    echo $i;

}
```

continues on next page

FOR AND WHILE LOOPS

The first time this loop is run, the $i variable is set to the value of 1. Then the condition is checked (*is 1 less than or equal to 10?*). Since this is true, 1 is printed out (echo $i). Then, $i is incremented to 2 ($i++), the condition is checked, and so forth. The result of this script will be the numbers 1 through 10 printed out.

In this chapter's last example, the calendar script created earlier will be rewritten using while and for loops in place of foreach loops.

To use loops:

1. Open calendar.php (refer to Script 2.7) in your text editor.

2. Delete the creation of the $days and $years arrays (lines 17–18).

   Using loops, I can achieve the same result of the two pull-down menus without the extra code and memory overhead involved with an array.

3. Rewrite the $days foreach loop as a for loop (**Script 2.12**).

   ```
   for ($day = 1; $day <= 31; $day++) {
       echo "<option value=\"$day\">
        → $day</option>\n";
   }
   ```

   This standard for loop begins by initializing the $day variable as 1. It will continue the loop until $day is greater than 31, and upon each iteration, $day will be incremented by 1. The content of the loop itself (which is executed 31 times) is an echo() statement.

(script continues on next page)

Script 2.12 Loops are often used in conjunction with or in lieu of an array.

```
1   <!DOCTYPE html PUBLIC "-//W3C//DTD XHTML
    1.0 Transitional//EN"
2        "http://www.w3.org/TR/xhtml1/DTD/
         xhtml1-transitional.dtd">
3   <html xmlns="http://www.w3.org/1999/xhtml"
    xml:lang="en" lang="en">
4   <head>
5       <meta http-equiv="content-type" content=
        "text/html; charset=iso-8859-1" />
6       <title>Calendar</title>
7   </head>
8   <body>
9   <form action="calendar.php" method="post">
10  <?php # Script 2.12 - calendar.php
    (2nd version after Script 2.7)
11  // This script makes three pull-down menus
    for an HTML form: months, days, years.
12
13  // Make the months array.
14  $months = array (1 => 'January',
    'February', 'March', 'April', 'May',
    'June', 'July', 'August', 'September',
    'October', 'November', 'December');
15
16  // Make the months pull-down menu.
17  echo '<select name="month">';
18  foreach ($months as $key => $value) {
19      echo "<option value=\"$key\">$value</
        option>\n";
20  }
21  echo '</select>';
22
23  // Make the days pull-down menu.
24  echo '<select name="day">';
25  for ($day = 1; $day <= 31; $day++) {
26      echo "<option value=\"$day\">$day</
        option>\n";
27  }
28  echo '</select>';
29
30  // Make the years pull-down menu.
31  echo '<select name="year">';
```

Script 2.12 *continued*

```
                     script
32   $year = 2005;
33   while ($year <= 2015) {
34       echo "<option value=\"$year\">$year</
         option>\n";
35       $year++;
36   }
37   echo '</select>';
38
39   ?>
40   </form>
41   </body>
42   </html>
```

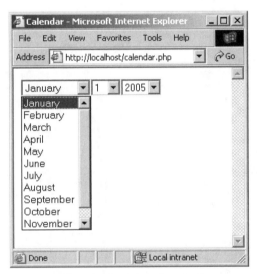

Figure 2.25 The calendar form looks quite the same as it had previously (see Figure 2.16) but was created with two fewer arrays (refer to Script 2.12).

4. Rewrite the $years foreach loop as a while loop.

```
$year = 2005;
while ($year <= 2015) {
    echo "<option value=\"$year\">
    → $year</option>\n";
    $year++;
}
```

The structure of this loop is fundamentally the same as the previous for loop, but rewritten as a while. The $year variable is initially set, and as long as it is less than or equal to 2015, the loop will be executed. Within the loop, the echo() statement is run and then the $year variable is incremented.

5. Save the file, upload to your Web server, and test in your Web browser (**Figure 2.25**).

✔ Tips

- PHP also has a do…while loop with a slightly different syntax (check the manual). This loop will always be executed at least once.

- The syntax and functionality are similar enough that the for and while loops can often be used interchangeably as I did here. Still, experience will reveal when the for loop is a better choice (when doing something a set number of times) versus when you'd use while (doing something as long as a condition is true).

- When using loops, watch your parameters and conditions to avoid the dreaded infinite loop, which occurs when the loop's condition is never going to be false.

FOR AND WHILE LOOPS

CREATING
DYNAMIC
WEB SITES

With the fundamentals of PHP under your belt, it's time to begin building truly dynamic Web sites. Dynamic Web sites, as opposed to the static ones on which the Web was first built, are easier to maintain, are more responsive to users, and can alter their content in response to differing situations.

In this chapter, I'll be covering a hodgepodge of ideas, all used to create dynamic Web applications. These include incorporating external files, handling forms and form data in new ways, writing and using your own functions, using PHP's date() function, and sending email. What all of these concepts have in common is that more sophisticated Web applications almost always use them.

Including Multiple Files

To this point, every script in the book has consisted of a single file that contains all of the required HTML and PHP code. But as you develop more complex Web sites, you'll see that this methodology has many limitations. PHP can readily make use of external files, a capability that allows you to divide your scripts into their distinct parts. Frequently you will use external files to extract your HTML from your PHP or to separate out commonly used processes.

PHP has four functions for using external files: include(), include_once(), require(), and require_once(). To use them, your PHP script would have a line like

```
include_once('filename.php');
```

```
require('/path/to/filename.html');
```

Using any one of these functions has the end result of taking all the content of the included file and dropping it in the parent script (the one calling the function) at that juncture. An important attribute of included files is that PHP will treat the included code as HTML (i.e., send it directly to the browser) unless it contains code within the PHP tags.

Previous versions of PHP had a different distinction between when you'd use include() and when you'd use require(). Now the functions are exactly the same when working properly but behave differently when they fail. If an include() function doesn't work (it cannot include the file for some reason), a warning will be printed to the Web browser (**Figure 3.1**), but the script will continue to run. If require() fails, an error is printed and the script is halted (**Figure 3.2**).

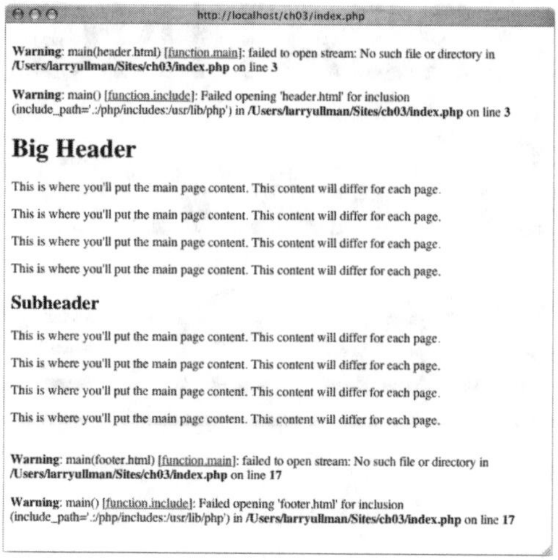

Figure 3.1 Two failed include() calls.

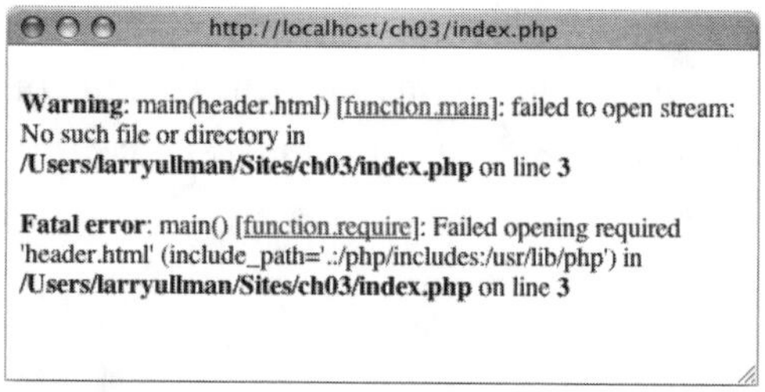

Figure 3.2 The first failure of a require() function will print an error and terminate the execution of the script.

Script 3.1 THE HTML TEMPLATE FOR THIS CHAPTER'S WEB PAGES. DOWNLOAD THE layout.css FILE IT USES FROM THE BOOK'S SUPPORTING WEB SITE.

```
1   <!DOCTYPE html PUBLIC "-//W3C//DTD XHTML
    1.0 Transitional//EN"
2       "http://www.w3.org/TR/xhtml1/DTD/
        xhtml1-transitional.dtd">
3   <html xmlns="http://www.w3.org/1999/xhtml"
    xml:lang="en" lang="en">
4   <head>
5       <meta http-equiv="content-type" content=
        "text/html; charset=iso-8859-1" />
6       <title>Welcome to this Site!</title>
7       <style type="text/css"
        media="all">@import "./includes/layout.
        css";</style>
8   </head>
9   <body>
10  <div id="wrapper"><!-- Goes with the CSS
    layout. -->
11
12      <div id="content"><!-- Goes with the CSS
        layout. -->
13
```

(script continues on next page)

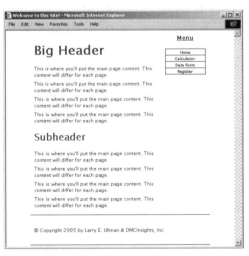

Figure 3.3 THE HTML AND CSS DESIGN AS IT APPEARS IN THE WEB BROWSER (WITHOUT USING ANY PHP).

Both functions also have a *_once() version, which guarantees that the file in question is included only once regardless of how many times a script may (presumably inadvertently) attempt to include it.

```
require_once('filename.php');

include_once('filename.php');
```

In this first example, I'll use included files to separate my HTML formatting from my PHP code. Then, the rest of the examples in this chapter will be able to have the same appearance without the need to rewrite the HTML every time. The concept results in a template system, an easy way to make large applications consistent and manageable. The focus in these examples is on the PHP code itself; you should also read the sidebar on "Site Structure" so that you understand the organization scheme of the files, and if you have any questions about the CSS (Cascading Style Sheets) or (X)HTML used in the example, see the references in Appendix C, "Resources."

TO INCLUDE MULTIPLE FILES:

1. Design an HTML page in your text or WYSIWYG editor (**Script 3.1** and **Figure 3.3**).

   To start creating a template for a Web site, design the layout like a standard HTML page, independent of any PHP code. The section of the layout that will change from page to page is enclosed within HTML comments indicating such.

   Note: in order to save space, the CSS file for this example (which controls the layout) is not included in the book. You can download the file through the book's supporting Web site (see the site's Extras page) or do without it (the template will still work, it just won't look as nice).

continues on page 85

Script 3.1 *continued*

```
                                       script
14        <div id="nav"><!-- Links section -->
15            <h3>Menu</h3>
16            <ul>
17            <li class="navtop"><a href="index.php" title="Go to the Home Page">Home</a></li>
18            <li><a href="calculator.php" title="Use the Sales Calculator">Calculator</a></li>
19            <li><a href="dateform.php" title="Check out the Date Form">Date Form</a></li>
20            <li><a href="register.php" title="Register">Register</a></li>
21            </ul>
22        </div>
23
24        <!-- Start of page-specific content. -->
25        <h1 id="mainhead">Big Header</h1>
26        <p>This is where you'll put the main page content. This content will differ for each page.</p>
27        <p>This is where you'll put the main page content. This content will differ for each page.</p>
28        <p>This is where you'll put the main page content. This content will differ for each page.</p>
29        <p>This is where you'll put the main page content. This content will differ for each page.</p>
30        <h2>Subheader</h2>
31        <p>This is where you'll put the main page content. This content will differ for each page.</p>
32        <p>This is where you'll put the main page content. This content will differ for each page.</p>
33        <p>This is where you'll put the main page content. This content will differ for each page.</p>
34        <p>This is where you'll put the main page content. This content will differ for each page.</p>
35        <!-- End of page-specific content. -->
36
37    </div><!-- End of "content" DIV. -->
38
39    <div id="footer"><p>&copy; Copyright 2005 by Larry E. Ullman &amp; DMCInsights, Inc.</p></div>
40
41 </div><!-- End of "wrapper" DIV. -->
42 </body>
43 </html>
```

Script 3.2 The initial HTML for each Web page will be stored in a header file.

```
                        script

1    <!DOCTYPE html PUBLIC "-//W3C//DTD XHTML
     1.0 Transitional//EN"

2            "http://www.w3.org/TR/xhtml1/DTD/
             xhtml1-transitional.dtd">

3    <html xmlns="http://www.w3.org/1999/xhtml"
     xml:lang="en" lang="en">

4    <head>

5        <meta http-equiv="content-type" content=
         "text/html; charset=iso-8859-1" />

6        <title><?php echo $page_title;
         ?></title>

7        <style type="text/css" media="all">
         @import "./includes/layout.css";
         </style>

8    </head>

9    <body>

10   <div id="wrapper"><!-- Goes with the CSS
     layout. -->

11

12       <div id="content"><!-- Goes with the CSS
         layout. -->

13

14           <div id="nav"><!-- Links section -->

15               <h3>Menu</h3>

16               <ul>

17               <li class="navtop"><a href=
                 "index.php" title="Go to the Home
                 Page">Home</a></li>

18               <li><a href="calculator.php"
                 title="Use the Sales Calculator">
                 Calculator</a></li>

19               <li><a href="dateform.php" title=
                 "Check out the Date Form">Date
                 Form</a></li>

20               <li><a href="register.php" title=
                 "Register">Register</a></li>

21               </ul>

22           </div>

23       <!-- Script 3.2 - header.html -->

24       <!-- Start of page-specific
         content. -->
```

2. Copy everything from the first line of the layout's source to just before the page-specific content and paste it in a new document (**Script 3.2**).

```
<!DOCTYPE html PUBLIC "-//W3C//
→ DTD XHTML 1.0 Transitional//EN"
"http://www.w3.org/TR/xhtml1/DTD/
→ xhtml1-transitional.dtd">
<html xmlns="http://www.w3.org/1999/
→ xhtml" xml:lang="en" lang="en">
<head>
    <meta http-equiv="content-type"
    → content="text/html;
    → charset=iso-8859-1" />
    <title>Welcome to this
    → Site!</title>
    <style type="text/css" media=
    → "all">@import "./includes/
    → layout.css";</style>
</head>
<body>
<div id="wrapper">
  <div id="content">
      <div id="nav">
          <h3>Menu</h3>
          <ul>
          <li class="navtop"><a href=
          → "index.php" title="Go to
          → the Home Page">Home</a>
          → </li>
          <li><a href="calculator.
          → php" title="Use the Sales
          → Calculator">Calculator</a>
          → </li>
          <li><a href="dateform.php"
          → title="Check out the Date
          → Form">Date Form</a></li>
          <li><a href="register.php"
          → title="Register">Register<
          → /a></li>
```

continues on next page

```
        </ul>
    </div>
    <!-- Script 3.2 - header.html
-->
```

This first file will contain the initial HTML tags (from DOCTYPE through the head and into the beginning of the page body). It also has the code that makes the column of links on the right side of the browser window (see Figure 3.3).

3. Change the page's title line to read

```
<title><?php echo $page_title; ?>
→ </title>
```

I'll want the page title (which appears at the top of the Web browser; see Figure 3.3) to be changeable on a page-by-page basis. To do so, I set this as a variable that will be printed out by PHP.

4. Save the file as header.html.

Included files can use just about any extension for the filename. Some programmers like to use .inc to indicate that a file is used as an include. In this case, you could also use .inc.html, which would indicate that it's both an include and an HTML file (to distinguish it from includes full of PHP code).

5. Copy everything in the original template from the end of the page-specific content to the end of the page and paste it in a new file (**Script 3.3**).

```
        <!-- Script 3.3 - footer.html -->
    </div>
    <div id="footer"><p>&copy;
Copyright 2005 by Larry E. Ullman
→ &amp; DMCInsights, Inc.</p></div>
</div>
</body>
</html>
```

Script 3.3 THE CONCLUDING HTML FOR EACH WEB PAGE WILL BE STORED IN THIS FOOTER FILE.

```
                    script
1          <!-- End of page-specific content.
-->
2          <!-- Script 3.3 - footer.html -->
3     </div><!-- End of "content" DIV. -->
4
5     <div id="footer"><p>&copy; Copyright
      2005 by Larry E. Ullman &amp;
      DMCInsights, Inc.</p></div>
6
7     </div><!-- End of "wrapper" DIV. -->
8     </body>
9     </html>
```

Script 3.4 This script generates a complete Web page using a template stored in external files.

```
1    <?php # Script 3.4 - index.php
2    $page_title = 'Welcome to this Site!';
3    include ('./includes/header.html');
4    ?>
5    <h1 id="mainhead">Big Header</h1>
6    <p>This is where you'll put the main page
     content. This content will differ for each
     page.</p>
7    <p>This is where you'll put the main page
     content. This content will differ for each
     page.</p>
8    <p>This is where you'll put the main page
     content. This content will differ for each
     page.</p>
9    <p>This is where you'll put the main page
     content. This content will differ for each
     page.</p>
10   <h2>Subheader</h2>
11   <p>This is where you'll put the main page
     content. This content will differ for each
     page.</p>
12   <p>This is where you'll put the main page
     content. This content will differ for each
     page.</p>
13   <p>This is where you'll put the main page
     content. This content will differ for each
     page.</p>
14   <p>This is where you'll put the main page
     content. This content will differ for each
     page.</p>
15   <?php
16   include ('./includes/footer.html');
17   ?>
```

The footer file contains the remaining formatting for the page body, including the page's footer, and then closes the HTML document.

6. Save the file as footer.html.

7. Create a new PHP document in your text editor (**Script 3.4**).

```
<?php # Script 3.4 - index.php
```

Since this script will use the included files for most of its HTML formatting, I can begin and end with the PHP tags rather than HTML.

8. Set the $page_title variable and include the HTML header.

```
$page_title = 'Welcome to this Site!';
include ('./includes/header.html');
```

The $page_title will allow me to set a new title for each page that uses this template system. Since I establish the variable before I include the header file, the header file will have access to that variable. Remember that this include() line has the effect of dropping the contents of the included file into this page at this spot.

continues on next page

9. Close the PHP tags and copy over the page-specific content from the template.

```
?>
<h1 id="mainhead">Big Header</h1>
<p>This is where you'll put the main
→ page content. This content will
→ differ for each page.</p>
<p>This is where you'll put the main
→ page content. This content will
→ differ for each page.</p>
<p>This is where you'll put the main
→ page content. This content will
→ differ for each page.</p>
<p>This is where you'll put the main
→ page content. This content will
→ differ for each page.</p>
<h2>Subheader</h2>
<p>This is where you'll put the main
→ page content. This content will
→ differ for each page.</p>
<p>This is where you'll put the main
→ page content. This content will
→ differ for each page.</p>
<p>This is where you'll put the main
→ page content. This content will
→ differ for each page.</p>
<p>This is where you'll put the main
→ page content. This content will
→ differ for each page.</p>
```

This information could be sent to the browser using echo(), but since there's no dynamic content here, it'll be easier and more efficient to exit the PHP tags temporarily.

10. Create a final PHP section and include the footer file.

```
<?php
include ('./includes/footer.html');
?>
```

11. Save the file as index.php and upload to your Web server.

Site Structure

When you begin using multiple files in your Web applications, the overall site structure becomes more important. When laying out your site, there are three considerations:

◆ Ease of maintenance

◆ Security

◆ Ease of user navigation

Using external files for holding standard procedures (i.e., PHP code), CSS, JavaScript, and the HTML design will greatly improve the ease of maintaining your site because commonly edited code is placed in one central location. I'll frequently make an *includes* or *templates* directory to store these files apart from the main scripts.

I recommend using the .inc or .html file extension for documents where security is not an issue (such as HTML templates) and .php for those that contain more sensitive data (such as database access information). You can also use both .inc and .html or .php so that a file is clearly indicated as an include of a certain type: functions.inc.php or header.inc.html.

Finally, try to structure your sites so that they are easy for your users to navigate, both by clicking links and by manually typing a URL. Try to avoid creating too many nested folders or using hard-to-type directory names and filenames containing upper- and lowercase letters and all manner of punctuation.

Figure 3.4 Now THE SAME LAYOUT (SEE FIGURE 3.3) HAS BEEN CREATED USING EXTERNAL FILES IN PHP.

12. Create an `includes` directory in the same folder as `index.php`. Then place `header.html`, `footer.html`, and `layout.css` (downloaded from www.DMCInsights.com/phpmysql2), into this `includes` directory.

13. Test the template system by going to the `index.php` page in your Web browser (**Figure 3.4**).

The `index.php` page is the final result of this template system. You do not need to access any of the included files directly, as `index.php` will take care of incorporating their contents.

14. If desired, view the HTML source of the page (**Figure 3.5**).

```
000               Source of http://localhost/ch03/index.php
<!DOCTYPE html PUBLIC "-//W3C//DTD XHTML 1.0 Transitional//EN"
     "http://www.w3.org/TR/xhtml1/DTD/xhtml1-transitional.dtd">
<html xmlns="http://www.w3.org/1999/xhtml" xml:lang="en" lang="en">
<head>
     <meta http-equiv="content-type" content="text/html; charset=iso-8859-1" />
     <title>Welcome to this Site!</title>
     <style type="text/css" media="all">@import "./includes/layout.css";</style>
</head>
<body>
<div id="wrapper"><!-- Goes with the CSS layout. -->

     <div id="content"><!-- Goes with the CSS layout. -->

          <div id="nav"><!-- Links section -->
               <h3>Menu</h3>
               <ul>
               <li class="navtop"><a href="index.php" title="Go to the Home Page">Home</a></li>
               <li><a href="calculator.php" title="Use the Sales Calculator">Calculator</a></li>
               <li><a href="dateform.php" title="Check out the Date Form">Date Form</a></li>
               <li><a href="register.php" title="Register">Register</a></li>
               </ul>
          </div>

          <!-- Start of page-specific content. -->
<h1 id="mainhead">Big Header</h1>
<p>This is where you'll put the main page content. This content will differ for each page.</p>
<p>This is where you'll put the main page content. This content will differ for each page.</p>
<p>This is where you'll put the main page content. This content will differ for each page.</p>
<p>This is where you'll put the main page content. This content will differ for each page.</p>
<h2>Subheader</h2>
<p>This is where you'll put the main page content. This content will differ for each page.</p>
<p>This is where you'll put the main page content. This content will differ for each page.</p>
<p>This is where you'll put the main page content. This content will differ for each page.</p>
<p>This is where you'll put the main page content. This content will differ for each page.</p>
          <!-- End of page-specific content. -->

     </div><!-- End of "content" DIV. -->

     <div id="footer"><p>&copy; Copyright 2005 by Larry E. Ullman &amp; DMCInsights, Inc.</p></div>

</div><!-- End of "wrapper" DIV. -->
</body>
</html>
```

Figure 3.5 THE GENERATED HTML SOURCE OF THE WEB PAGE SHOULD REPLICATE THE CODE IN THE ORIGINAL TEMPLATE (REFER TO SCRIPT 3.1).

✔ Tips

■ In the php.ini file, you can adjust the include_path setting, which dictates where PHP is and is not allowed to retrieve included files.

■ As you'll see in Chapter 7, "Using PHP with MySQL," any included file that contains sensitive information (like database access) should be stored outside of the Web document directory.

■ As a best practice, use the ./filename syntax when referring to files within the same directory as the parent (including) file, as I've done here. A file stored in a directory above the parent file would be included using the path ../filename, and a file stored in a directory below the parent file would use ./directory/filename.

■ You can include your files using relative paths—as I have here—or absolute paths:

include ('/path/to/filename');

■ Since require() has more impact on a script when it fails, I recommend using it for mission-critical includes (like those that connect to a database) and use include() for cosmetic ones. The *_once() versions provide for nice redundancy checking in complex applications, but they may be unnecessary in simple sites.

■ Because of the way CSS works, if you don't use the CSS file or if the browser doesn't read the CSS, the generated result is still functional, just not aesthetically as pleasing (see **Figure 3.6**).

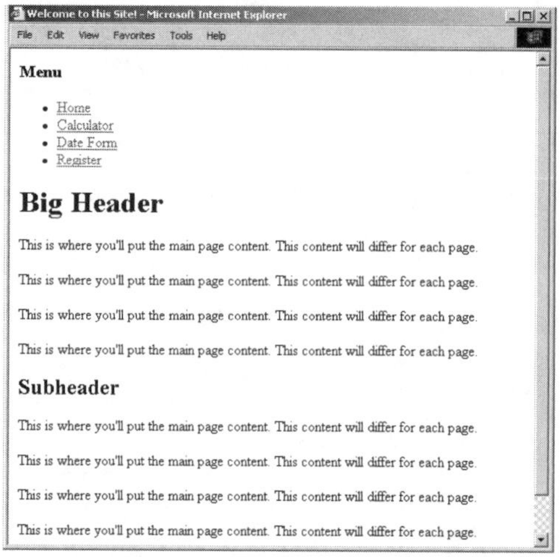

Figure 3.6 This is the HTML layout without using the corresponding CSS file (compare with Figure 3.4).

Handling HTML Forms with PHP Redux

All of the examples in this chapter and the preceding one used two separate scripts for handling HTML forms: one that displayed the form and another that received it. While there's certainly nothing wrong with this method, there are advantages to having the entire process in one script. To have one page both display and handle a form, use a conditional.

```
if (/* form has been submitted */) {

    // Handle it.

} else {

    // Display it.

}
```

To determine if the form has been submitted, I normally check that a $_POST variable is set (assuming that the form uses the POST method, of course). For example, you can check $_POST['submitted'], assuming that's the name of a hidden input type in the form.

```
if (isset($_POST['submitted'])) {

    // Handle it.

} else {

    // Display it.

}
```

If you want a page to handle a form and then display it again (e.g., to add a record to a database and then give an option to add another), use

```
if (isset($_POST['submitted'])) {

    // Handle it.

}
// Display the form.
```

Using the preceding code, a script will handle a form if it has been submitted and display the form every time the page is loaded.

To demonstrate this important technique, I'll start by creating a sales calculator. Later in this chapter this same method will be used with a registration page.

To handle HTML forms:

1. Create a new PHP document in your text editor (**Script 3.5**).

   ```
   <?php # Script 3.5 - calculator.php
   $page_title = 'Widget Cost
   → Calculator';
   include ('./includes/header.html');
   ```

   This, and all the remaining examples in the chapter, will use the same templating system as the index.php page. The beginning syntax of each page will therefore be the same, but the page titles will differ.

2. Write the conditional for handling the form.

   ```
   if (isset($_POST['submitted'])) {
   ```

   As I mentioned previously, if the $_POST ['submitted'] variable is set, I know that the form has been submitted and I can process it. This variable will be created by a hidden input in the form that will act as a submission indicator.

continues on page 93

Script 3.5 The calculator.php script both displays a simple form and handles the form data, performing the calculations.

```php
1    <?php # Script 3.5 - calculator.php
2    $page_title = 'Widget Cost Calculator';
3    include ('./includes/header.html');
4
5    // Check if the form has been submitted.
6    if (isset($_POST['submitted'])) {
7
8        // Minimal form validation.
9        if ( is_numeric($_POST['quantity']) && is_numeric($_POST['price']) && is_numeric($_POST['tax']) ) {
10
11           // Calculate the results.
12           $taxrate = $_POST['tax'] / 100; // Turn 5% into .05.
13           $total = ($_POST['quantity'] * $_POST['price']) * ($taxrate + 1);
14
15           // Print the results.
16           echo '<h1 id="mainhead">Total Cost</h1>
17    <p>The total cost of purchasing ' . $_POST['quantity'] . ' widget(s) at $' . number_format
      ($_POST['price'], 2) . ' each, including a tax rate of ' . $_POST['tax'] . '%, is $' .
      number_format ($total, 2) . '.</p><p><br /></p>';
18
19       } else { // Invalid submitted values.
20           echo '<h1 id="mainhead">Error!</h1>
21    <p class="error">Please enter a valid quantity, price, and tax.</p><p><br /></p>';
22       }
23
24    } // End of main isset() IF.
25
26    // Leave the PHP section and create the HTML form.
27    ?>
28    <h2>Widget Cost Calculator</h2>
29    <form action="calculator.php" method="post">
30        <p>Quantity: <input type="text" name="quantity" size="5" maxlength="10" /></p>
31        <p>Price: <input type="text" name="price" size="5" maxlength="10" /></p>
32        <p>Tax (%): <input type="text" name="tax" size="5" maxlength="10" /></p>
33        <p><input type="submit" name="submit" value="Calculate!" /></p>
34        <input type="hidden" name="submitted" value="TRUE" />
35    </form>
36    <?php
37    include ('./includes/footer.html');
38    ?>
```

3. Validate the form.

```
if ( is_numeric($_POST['quantity'])
→ && is_numeric($_POST['price']) &&
→ is_numeric($_POST['tax']) ) {
```

The validation here is very simple: it merely checks that three submitted variables are all numeric types. You can certainly elaborate on this, perhaps checking that the quantity is an integer (in fact, in Chapter 10, "Web Application Security," you'll find a variation on this script that does just that).

If the validation passes all of the tests, the calculations will be made; otherwise, the user will be asked to try again.

4. Perform the calculations.

```
$taxrate = $_POST['tax'] / 100;
$total = ($_POST['quantity'] *
→ $_POST['price']) * ($taxrate + 1);
```

The first line changes the tax value from a percentage (say, 5%) to a decimal (.05), which will be needed in the subsequent calculation. The second line starts by multiplying the quantity times the price. This is then multiplied by the tax rate (.05) plus 1 (1.05). This last little trick is a quick way to calculate the total cost of something with tax (instead of multiplying the tax rate times the total and then adding this amount to the total).

5. Print the results.

```
echo '<h1 id="mainhead">Total Cost</
h1>
<p>The total cost of purchasing ' .
→ $_POST['quantity'] . ' widget(s)
→ at $' . number_format ($_POST
→ ['price'], 2) . ' each, including
→ a tax rate of ' . $_POST['tax'] .
→ '%, is $' . number_format ($total,
→ 2) . '.</p><p><br /></p>';
```

All of the values are printed out, formatting the price and total with the number_format() function.

6. Complete the conditionals and close the PHP tag.

```
   } else {
      echo '<h1
id="mainhead">Error!</h1>
      <p class="error">Please enter
      → a valid quantity, price, and
      → tax.</p><p><br /></p>';
   }
}
?>
```

The else clause completes the validation conditional, printing an error if the three submitted values aren't all numeric. The final closing curly brace closes the isset($_POST['submitted']) conditional. Finally, the PHP section is closed so that the form can be created without using print() or echo().

7. Display the HTML form.

```
<h2>Widget Cost Calculator</h2>
<form action="calculator.php"
→ method="post">
   <p>Quantity: <input type="text"
   → name="quantity" size="5"
   → maxlength="10" /></p>
   <p>Price: <input type="text"
   → name="price" size="5"
   → maxlength="10" /></p>
   <p>Tax (%): <input type="text"
   → name="tax" size="5"
   → maxlength="10" /></p>
   <p><input type="submit"
   → name="submit" value="Calculate!"
/></p>
   <input type="hidden"
   → name="submitted" value="TRUE" />
</form>
```

continues on next page

The form itself is fairly obvious, containing only two new tricks. First, the `action` attribute uses this script's name, so that the form submits back to this page instead of to another. Second, there is a `hidden` input called `submitted` with a value of *TRUE*. This is the flag variable whose existence will be checked to determine whether or not to handle the form (see the main condition).

8. Include the footer file.

```php
<?php
include ('./includes/footer.html');
?>
```

9. Save the file as `calculator.php`, upload to your Web server, and test in your Web browser (**Figures 3.7**, **3.8**, and **3.9**).

✔ Tips

■ Another common method for checking if a form has been submitted is to see if the submit button's variable—`$_POST['submit']` here—is set. The only downside to this method is that it won't work if the user submits the form by pressing Return or Enter.

■ If you use an image for your submit button, you'll also want to use a hidden input to test for the form's submission.

■ You can also have a form submit back to itself by having PHP print the name of the current script—stored in `$_SERVER['PHP_SELF']`—as the action attribute.

```php
<form action="<?php echo
$_SERVER['PHP_SELF']; ?>"
method="post">
```

By doing so, the form will always submit back to this same page, even if you later change the name of the script.

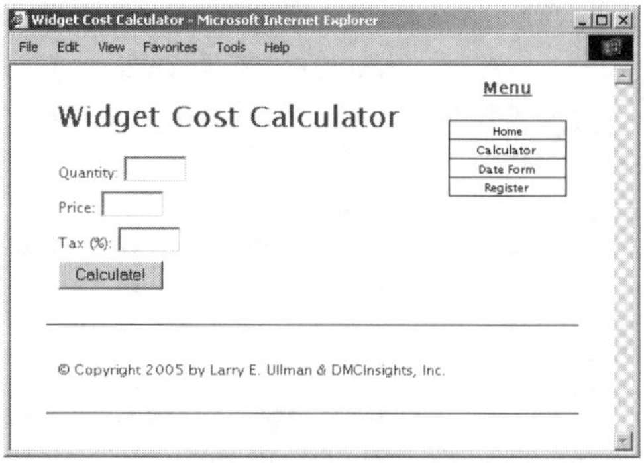

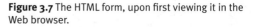

Figure 3.7 The HTML form, upon first viewing it in the Web browser.

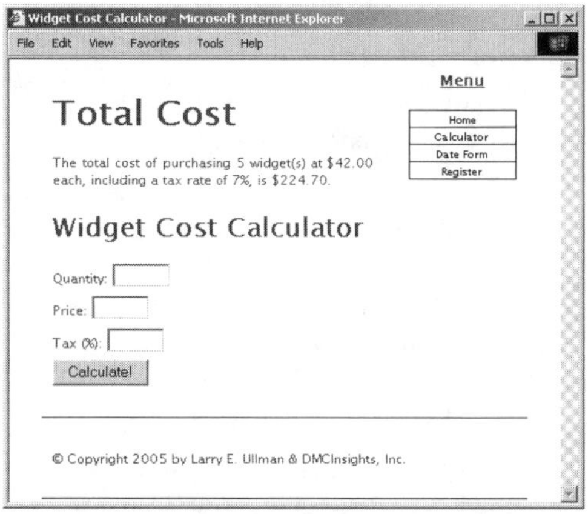

Figure 3.8 The page performs the calculations, reports on the results, and then redisplays the form.

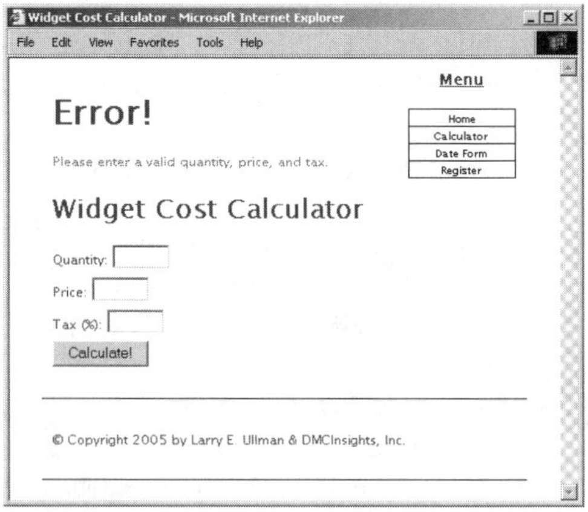

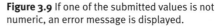

Figure 3.9 If one of the submitted values is not numeric, an error message is displayed.

Making Sticky Forms

You've certainly come across sticky forms, even if you didn't know that's what they were called. A *sticky form* is simply a standard HTML form that remembers how you filled it out. This is a particularly nice feature for end users, especially if you are requiring them to resubmit a form (for instance, after filling it out incorrectly in the first place).

To preset what's entered in a text box, use its `value` attribute:

```
<input type="text" name="city" size="20"
→ value="Innsbruck" />
```

To have PHP preset that value, print the appropriate variable:

```
<input type="text" name="city" size="20"
→ value="<?php echo $city; ?>" />
```

With this in mind, I'll rewrite `calculator.php` so that it's sticky.

To make a sticky form:

1. Open `calculator.php` (refer to Script 3.5) in your text editor.

2. Change the quantity input to read (**Script 3.6**)

   ```
   <p>Quantity: <input type="text"
   → name="quantity" size="5"
   → maxlength="10" value="<?php if
   → (isset($_POST['quantity'])) echo
   → $_POST['quantity']; ?>" /></p>
   ```

   The first thing I've done here is to add the `value` attribute to the input. Then, I print out the value of the submitted quantity variable (`$_POST['quantity']`). But first I want to make sure it has a value, so I check that the variable is set. The end result for the input's value is the PHP code

   ```
   <?php
   if (isset($_POST['quantity'])) {
       echo $_POST['quantity'];
   }
   ?>
   ```

   which I've condensed to its most minimal form (you can omit the curly braces if you have only one statement within a conditional block).

3. Repeat the process for the price and tax.

   ```
   <p>Price: <input type="text"
   → name="price" size="5"
   → maxlength="10" value="<?php if
   → (isset($_POST['price'])) echo
   → $_POST['price']; ?>" /></p>
   <p>Tax (%): <input type="text"
   → name="tax" size="5" maxlength="10"
   → value="<?php if (isset($_POST
   → ['tax'])) echo $_POST['tax'];
   → ?>" /></p>
   ```

continues on next page

Script 3.6 The calculator's form now recalls the previously entered values.

```
1    <?php # Script 3.6 - calculator.php (2nd version after Script 3.5)
2    $page_title = 'Widget Cost Calculator';
3    include ('./includes/header.html');
4
5    // Check if the form has been submitted.
6    if (isset($_POST['submitted'])) {
7
8        // Minimal form validation.
9        if ( is_numeric($_POST['quantity']) && is_numeric($_POST['price']) && is_numeric($_POST['tax']) ) {
10
11           // Calculate the results.
12           $taxrate = $_POST['tax'] / 100; // Turn 5% into .05.
13           $total = ($_POST['quantity'] * $_POST['price']) * ($taxrate + 1);
14
15           // Print the results.
16           echo '<h1 id="mainhead">Total Cost</h1>
17     <p>The total cost of purchasing ' . $_POST['quantity'] . ' widget(s) at $' . number_format
       ($_POST['price'], 2) . ' each, including a tax rate of ' . $_POST['tax'] . '%, is $' . number_
       format ($total, 2) . '.</p><p><br /></p>';
18
19       } else { // Invalid submitted values.
20           echo '<h1 id="mainhead">Error!</h1>
21     <p class="error">Please enter a valid quantity, price, and tax.</p><p><br /></p>';
22       }
23
24   } // End of main isset() IF.
25
26   // Leave the PHP section and create the HTML form.
27   ?>
28   <h2>Widget Cost Calculator</h2>
29   <form action="calculator.php" method="post">
30       <p>Quantity: <input type="text" name="quantity" size="5" maxlength="10" value="<?php if
       (isset($_POST['quantity'])) echo $_POST['quantity']; ?>" /></p>
31       <p>Price: <input type="text" name="price" size="5" maxlength="10" value="<?php if
       (isset($_POST['price'])) echo $_POST['price']; ?>" /></p>
32       <p>Tax (%): <input type="text" name="tax" size="5" maxlength="10" value="<?php if
       (isset($_POST['tax'])) echo $_POST['tax']; ?>" /></p>
33       <p><input type="submit" name="submit" value="Calculate!" /></p>
34       <input type="hidden" name="submitted" value="TRUE" />
35   </form>
36   <?php
37   include ('./includes/footer.html');
38   ?>
```

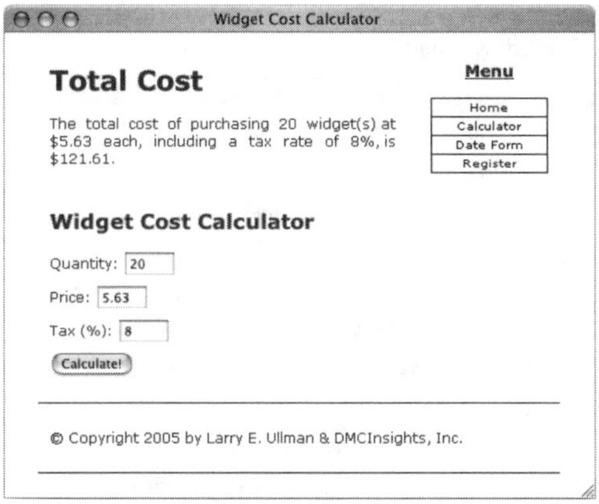

Figure 3.10 The form now recalls the previously submitted values...

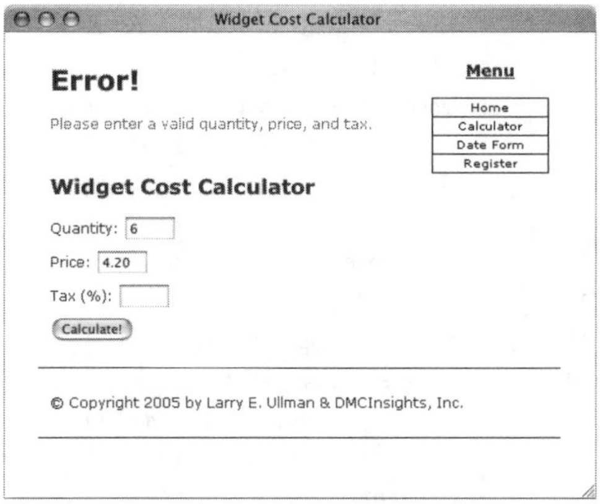

Figure 3.11 ...whether or not the form was completely filled out.

- To preselect a pull-down menu, use selected="selected":

  ```
  <select name="year">
  <option value="2005">2005</option>
  <option value="2006" selected=
  → "selected">2006</option>
  </select>
  ```

  You'll see an example of this toward the end of the chapter.

4. Save the file as calculator.php, upload to your Web server, and test in your Web browser (**Figures 3.10** and **3.11**).

✔ Tips

- Because some PHP code in this example exists inside of the HTML form value attributes, error messages may not be obvious. If problems occur, check the HTML source of the page to see if PHP errors are printed within the value attributes.

- You should always double-quote HTML attributes, particularly the value attribute of a form input. If you don't, multi-word values like *Elliott Smith* will appear as just *Elliott* in the Web browser.

- If Magic Quotes are on in your server, you'll need to apply stripslashes() before printing string variables as a form input's value:

  ```
  <input type="text" name="last_name"
  → size="20" value="<?php if (isset
  → ($_POST['last_name'])) echo
  → stripslashes($_POST['last_name']);
  → ?>" />
  ```

- On account of a limitation in how HTML works, you cannot preset the value of a password input type.

- To preset the status of radio buttons or check boxes as checked, add the code checked="checked" to their input tag.

  ```
  <input type="checkbox"
  → name="interests" value="Reading"
  → checked="checked" />

  <input type="radio" name="gender"
  → value="Female" checked="checked" />
  ```

- To preset the value of a textarea, place the value between the textarea tags:

  ```
  <textarea name="comments"
  → rows="10" cols="50"><?php echo
  → $_POST['comments']; ?></textarea>
  ```

MAKING STICKY FORMS

Creating and Calling Your Own Functions

As you've already seen, PHP has a lot of built-in functions, addressing almost every need. More importantly, though, it has the capability for you to define and use your own functions for whatever purpose. The syntax for making your own function is

```
function function_name () {

    // Function code.

}
```

The name of your function can be any combination of letters, numbers, and the underscore, but it must begin with either a letter or the underscore. The main restriction is that you cannot use an existing function name for your function (*print*, *echo*, *isset*, and so on).

In PHP, as I mentioned in the first chapter, function names are case-insensitive (unlike variable names), so you could call that function using function_name() or FUNCTION_NAME() or function_Name(), etc.

The code within the function can do nearly anything, from generating HTML to performing calculations. In this chapter, I'll demonstrate many different uses.

To create your own function:

1. Create a new PHP document in your text editor (**Script 3.7**).
   ```
   <?php # Script 3.7 - dateform.php
   $page_title = 'Calendar Form';
   include ('./includes/header.html');
   ```
   This page will use the same HTML template as the previous two.

Script 3.7 This function is useful for creating a series of pull-down menus.

```
1   <?php # Script 3.7 - dateform.php
2   $page_title = 'Calendar Form';
3   include ('./includes/header.html');
4
5   // This function makes three pull-down
    menus for the months, days, and years.
6   function make_calendar_pulldowns() {
7
8       // Make the months array.
9       $months = array (1 => 'January',
        'February', 'March', 'April', 'May',
        'June', 'July', 'August', 'September',
        'October', 'November', 'December');
10
11      // Make the months pull-down menu.
12      echo '<select name="month">';
13      foreach ($months as $key => $value) {
14          echo "<option value=\"$key\">
            $value</option>\n";
15      }
16      echo '</select>';
17
18      // Make the days pull-down menu.
19      echo '<select name="day">';
20      for ($day = 1; $day <= 31; $day++) {
21          echo "<option value=\"$day\">$day
            </option>\n";
22      }
23      echo '</select>';
24
25      // Make the years pull-down menu.
26      echo '<select name="year">';
27      for ($year = 2005; $year <= 2015;
        $year++) {
28          echo "<option value=\"$year\">
            $year</option>\n";
29      }
30      echo '</select>';
31
32  } // End of the function definition.
33
```

(script continues on next page)

Script 3.7 *continued*

```
         script
34    // Create the form tags.
35    echo '<h1 id="mainhead">Select a Date:</h1>
36    <p><br /></p><form action="dateform.php"
      method="post">';
37
38    // Call the function.
39    make_calendar_pulldowns();
40
41    echo '</form><p><br /></p>'; // End of form.
42
43    include ('./includes/footer.html');
44    ?>
```

2. Begin defining a new function.

```
function make_calendar_pulldowns() {
```

The function I'll write here will generate the form pull-down menus for months, days, and years as in calendar.php (refer to Script 2.12). The name I give the function clearly states its purpose.

Although it's not required, it's normal to place your function definitions toward the top of a script (or in a separate file).

3. Generate the pull-down menus.

```
$months = array (1 => 'January',
→ 'February', 'March', 'April',
→ 'May', 'June', 'July', 'August',
→ 'September', 'October',
→ 'November', 'December');
echo '<select name="month">';
foreach ($months as $key => $value) {
   echo "<option value=\"$key\">
   → $value</option>\n";
}
echo '</select>';
echo '<select name="day">';
for ($day = 1; $day <= 31; $day++) {
   echo "<option value=\"$day\">
   → $day</option>\n";
}
echo '</select>';
echo '<select name="year">';
for ($year = 2005; $year <= 2015;
→ $year++) {
   echo "<option value=\"$year\">
   → $year</option>\n";
}
echo '</select>';
```

This code is almost exactly as it was in the original script, only it's now stored within a function. One minor change is that a for loop is used to create the years pull-down menu (previously it was a while loop).

continues on next page

CREATING AND CALLING YOUR OWN FUNCTIONS

4. Close the function definition.

```
} // End of the function definition.
```

In complicated code, it's a useful tool to place a comment at the end of the function definition so that you know where a definition starts and stops.

5. Create the form and call the function.

```
echo '<h1 id="mainhead">Select a
Date:</h1>';

<p><br /></p><form action="dateform.
→ php" method="post">';

make_calendar_pulldowns();

echo '</form><p><br /></p>';
```

This code will create a header tag, plus the tags for the form (some extra HTML spacing has been added to fill up the resulting page). The call to the make_cal-endar_pulldowns() function will have the end result of creating the code for the three pull-down menus.

6. Complete the PHP script by including the HTML footer.

```
include ('./includes/footer.html');
?>
```

7. Save the file as dateform.php, upload to your Web server (in the same folder as index.php), and test in your Web browser (**Figure 3.12**).

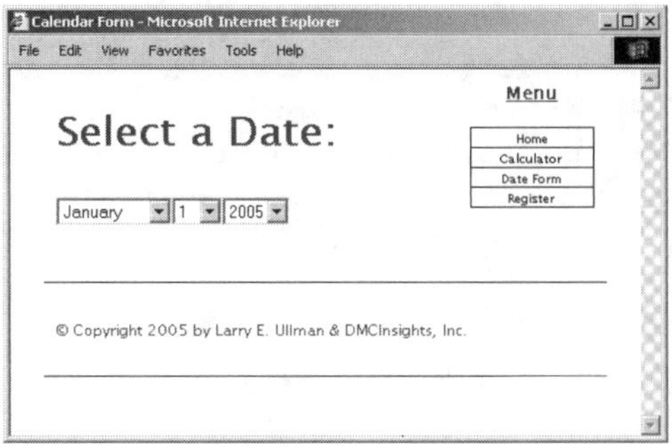

✔ Tips

■ If you ever see a *call to undefined function function_name* error, this means that you are calling a function that hasn't been defined. This can happen if you misspell the function's name (either when defining or calling it) or if you fail to include the file where the function is defined.

Figure 3.12 The pull-down menus are generated by a user-defined function.

■ Because a user-defined function takes up some memory, you should be prudent about when to use one. As a general rule, functions are best used for chunks of code that may be executed in several places in a script or Web site.

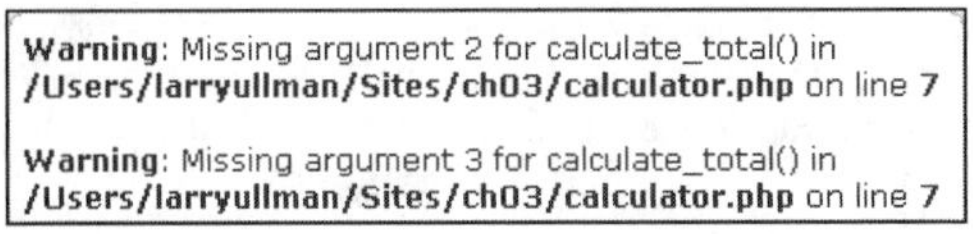

Warning: Missing argument 2 for calculate_total() in
/Users/larryullman/Sites/ch03/calculator.php on line 7

Warning: Missing argument 3 for calculate_total() in
/Users/larryullman/Sites/ch03/calculator.php on line 7

Figure 3.13 Failure to send a function the proper number or type of arguments is a common error.

Creating a function that takes arguments

Just like PHP's built-in functions, those you write can take *arguments* (also called *parameters*). For example, the print() function takes what you want sent to the browser as an argument and strlen() takes a string whose character length will be determined.

A function can take any number of arguments that you choose, but the order in which you put them is critical. To allow for arguments, add variables to your function's definition:

```
function print_hello ($first, $last) {

    // Function code.

}
```

You can then call the function as you would any other function in PHP, sending literal values or variables to it:

```
print_hello ('Jimmy', 'Stewart');

$surname = 'Stewart';

print_hello ('Jimmy', $surname);
```

As with any function in PHP, failure to send the right number of arguments results in an error (**Figure 3.13**). Also, the variable names you use for your arguments are irrelevant to the rest of the script (as you'll discover in the "Variable Scope" section of this chapter), but try to use valid, meaningful names.

To demonstrate this, I'll rewrite the calculator process as a function.

To write functions that take arguments:

1. Open calculator.php (Script 3.6) in your text editor.

2. After including the header file, define the calculate_total() function (**Script 3.8**).

   ```php
   function calculate_total ($qty,
   → $cost, $tax) {
     $taxrate = $tax / 100;
     $total = ($qty * $cost) *
   → ($taxrate + 1);
     echo '<p>The total cost of
   → purchasing ' . $qty . '
   → widget(s) at $' . number_format
   → ($cost, 2) . ' each, including
   → a tax rate of ' . $tax . '%, is
   → $' . number_format ($total, 2) .
   → '.</p>';
   }
   ```

   This function performs the same calculations as it did before and then prints out the result. It takes three arguments: the quantity being ordered, the price, and the tax rate. Notice that the variables being defined are not $_POST['quantity'], $_POST['price'], and $_POST['tax']. The function's argument variables are particular to this function and have their own names.

Script 3.8 The calculator.php script now uses a function to perform its calculations. Unlike the previous function you defined, this one takes arguments.

```php
1   <?php # Script 3.8 - calculator.php
    (3rd version after Scripts 3.5 & 3.6)
2   $page_title = 'Widget Cost Calculator';
3   include ('./includes/header.html');
4
5   /* This function calculates a total
6   and then prints the results. */
7   function calculate_total ($qty, $cost,
    $tax) {
8
9       $taxrate = $tax / 100; // Turn 5% into
        .05.
10      $total = ($qty * $cost) * ($taxrate + 1);
11      echo '<p>The total cost of purchasing
        ' . $qty . ' widget(s) at $' . number_
        format ($cost, 2) . ' each, including a
        tax rate of ' . $tax . '%, is $' .
        number_format ($total, 2) . '.</p>';
12
13  } // End of function.
14
15  // Check if the form has been submitted.
16  if (isset($_POST['submitted'])) {
17
18      // Minimal form validation.
19      if ( is_numeric($_POST['quantity']) &&
        is_numeric($_POST['price']) && is_
        numeric($_POST['tax']) ) {
20
21          // Print the heading.
22          echo '<h1 id="mainhead">Total Cost
            </h1>';
23
24          // Call the function.
25          calculate_total ($_POST
            ['quantity'], $_POST['price'],
            $_POST['tax']);
26
27          // Print some spacing.
28          echo '<p><br /></p>';
29
```

(script continues on next page)

Script 3.8 *continued*

```
          script

30     } else { // Invalid submitted values.
31         echo '<h1 id="mainhead">Error!</h1>
32         <p class="error">Please enter a
           valid quantity, price, and tax.</p>
           <p><br /></p>';
33     }
34
35 } // End of main isset() IF.
36
37 // Leave the PHP section and create the
   HTML form.
38 ?>
39 <h2>Widget Cost Calculator</h2>
40 <form action="calculator.php"
   method="post">
41     <p>Quantity: <input type="text"
       name="quantity" size="5" maxlength="10"
       value="<?php if (isset($_POST
       ['quantity'])) echo $_POST['quantity'];
       ?>" /></p>
42     <p>Price: <input type="text"
       name="price" size="5" maxlength="10"
       value="<?php if (isset($_POST['price']))
       echo $_POST['price']; ?>" /></p>
43     <p>Tax (%): <input type="text"
       name="tax" size="5" maxlength="10"
       value="<?php if (isset($_POST['tax']))
       echo $_POST['tax']; ?>" /></p>
44     <p><input type="submit" name="submit"
       value="Calculate!" /></p>
45     <input type="hidden" name="submitted"
       value="TRUE" />
46 </form>
47 <?php
48 include ('./includes/footer.html');
49 ?>
```

3. Change the contents of the validation conditional (where the calculations were previously made) to read

echo '<h1 id="mainhead">Total
→ Cost</h1>';

calculate_total ($_POST['quantity'],
→ $_POST['price'], $_POST['tax']);

echo '<p>
</p>';

Again, this is just a minor rewrite of the way the script worked before. Assuming that all of the submitted values are numeric, a heading is printed (this is not done within the function), the function is called (which will calculate and print the total), and a little spacing is added.

When calling the function, three arguments are passed, each of which is a $_POST variable. The value of $_POST['quantity'] will be assigned to the function's $qty variable; the value of $_POST['price'] will be assigned to the function's $cost variable; and the value of $_POST['tax'] will be assigned to the function's $tax variable.

4. Save the file as calculator.php, upload to your Web server, and test in your Web browser (**Figure 3.14**).

Figure 3.14 Calculations are now made by a user-defined function, which also prints the results.

Setting default argument values

Another variant on defining your own functions is to preset an argument's value. To do so, assign the argument a value in the function's definition:

```
function greet ($name, $greeting =
→ 'Hello') {

    echo "$greeting, $name!";

}
```

The end result of setting a default argument value is that that particular argument becomes optional when calling the function. If a value is passed to it, the passed value is used; otherwise, the default value is used.

You can set default values for as many of the arguments as you want, as long as those arguments come last in the function definition. In other words, the required arguments should always be first.

With the example function just defined, any of these will work:

```
greet ($surname, $message);

greet ('Roberts');

greet ('Grant', 'Good evening');
```

However, greet() will not work, and there's no way to pass $greeting a value without passing one to $name as well.

To set default argument values:

1. Open calculator.php (refer to Script 3.8) in your text editor.

2. Change the function definition line (line 7) so that only the quantity and cost are required arguments (**Script 3.9**).

   ```
   function calculate_total ($qty,
   $cost, $tax = 5) {
   ```

   The value of the $tax variable is now hard-coded in the function, making it optional.

Script 3.9 The `calculate_total()` function now assumes a set tax rate unless one is specified when the function is called.

```
1   <?php # Script 3.9 - calculator.php (4th
        version after Scripts 3.5, 3.6 & 3.8)
2   $page_title = 'Widget Cost Calculator';
3   include ('./includes/header.html');
4
5   /* This function calculates a total
6   and then prints the results. */
7   function calculate_total ($qty, $cost,
        $tax = 5) {
8
9       $taxrate = $tax / 100; // Turn 5% into
        .05.
10      $total = ($qty * $cost) * ($taxrate + 1);
11      echo '<p>The total cost of purchasing
        ' . $qty . ' widget(s) at $' . number_
        format ($cost, 2) . ' each, including a
        tax rate of ' . $tax . '%, is $' .
        number_format ($total, 2) . '. </p>';
12
13  } // End of function.
14
15  // Check if the form has been submitted.
16  if (isset($_POST['submitted'])) {
17
18      if (is_numeric($_POST['quantity']) &&
        is_numeric($_POST['price'])) {
19
20          // Print the heading.
21          echo '<h1 id="mainhead">Total Cost
            </h1>';
22
23          if (is_numeric($_POST['tax'])) {
24              calculate_total ($_POST
                ['quantity'], $_POST['price'],
                $_POST['tax']);
25          } else {
26              calculate_total ($_POST
                ['quantity'], $_POST['price']);
27          }
28
29          // Print some spacing.
30          echo '<p><br /></p>';
```

(script continues on next page)

Script 3.9 *continued*

```
                    script
31
32       } else { // Invalid submitted values.
33          echo '<h1 id="mainhead">Error!</h1>
34          <p class="error">Please enter a
            valid quantity and price.</p><p>
            <br /></p>';
35       }
36
37    } // End of main isset() IF.
38
39    // Leave the PHP section and create the
      HTML form.
40    ?>
41    <h2>Widget Cost Calculator</h2>
42    <form action="calculator.php"
      method="post">
43       <p>Quantity: <input type="text"
         name="quantity" size="5" maxlength="10"
         value="<?php if (isset($_POST
         ['quantity'])) echo $_POST['quantity'];
         ?>" /></p>
44       <p>Price: <input type="text"
         name="price" size="5" maxlength="10"
         value="<?php if (isset($_POST['price']))
         echo $_POST['price']; ?>" /></p>
45       <p>Tax (%): <input type="text"
         name="tax" size="5" maxlength="10"
         value="<?php if (isset($_POST['tax']))
         echo $_POST['tax']; ?>" /> (optional)
         </p>
46       <p><input type="submit" name="submit"
         value="Calculate!" /></p>
47       <input type="hidden" name="submitted"
         value="TRUE" />
48    </form>
49    <?php
50    include ('./includes/footer.html');
51    ?>
```

3. Change the form validation to read

```
if (is_numeric($_POST['quantity'])
→ && is_numeric($_POST['price'])) {
```

Because the tax value will be optional, I'll only validate the first two variables here.

4. Change the function call line to

```
if (is_numeric($_POST['tax'])) {
   calculate_total ($_POST
   → ['quantity'], $_POST['price'],
$_POST['tax']);
} else {
   calculate_total ($_POST
   → ['quantity'], $_POST['price']);
}
```

If the tax value has also been submitted (and is numeric), then the function will be called as before. Otherwise, the function is called providing the two arguments, meaning that the default value will be used for the tax rate.

5. Change the error message to only report on the quantity and price.

```
echo '<h1 id="mainhead">Error!</h1>
<p class="error">Please enter a
→ valid quantity and price.</p>
→ <p><br /></p>';
```

Since the tax will now be optional, the error message is changed accordingly.

6. If you want, mark the tax value in the form as optional.

```
<p>Tax (%): <input type="text"
→ name="tax" size="5" maxlength="10"
→ value="<?php if (isset($_POST
→ ['tax'])) echo $_POST['tax']; ?>"
→ /> (optional)</p>
```

A parenthetical is added to the tax input, indicating to the user that this value is optional.

continues on next page

CREATING AND CALLING YOUR OWN FUNCTIONS

7. Save the file, upload to your server, and test in your Web browser (**Figures 3.15** and **3.16**).

✔ Tips

■ To pass a function no value for an argument, use either an empty string (' '), NULL, or FALSE.

■ In the PHP manual, square brackets ([]) are used to indicate a function's optional parameters.

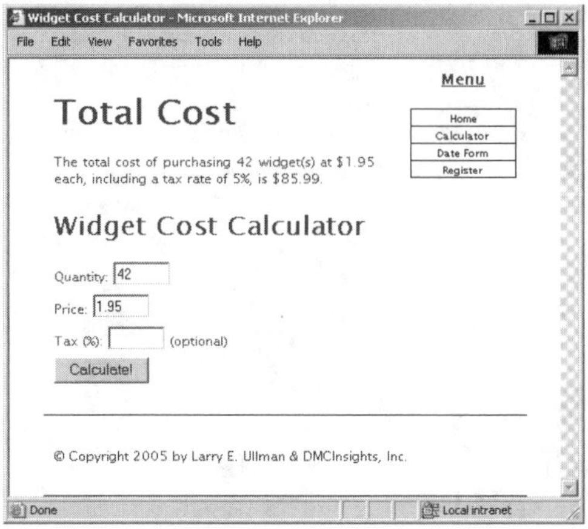

Figure 3.15 If no tax value is entered, the default value of 5% will be used in the calculation.

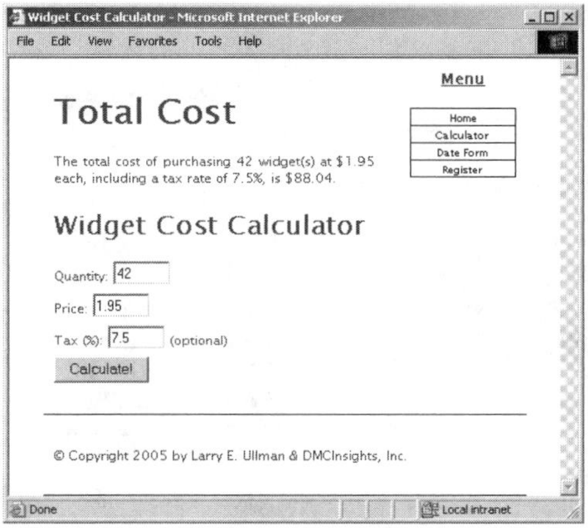

Figure 3.16 If the user enters a tax value, it will be used instead of the default value.

CREATING AND CALLING YOUR OWN FUNCTIONS

Script 3.10 The `calculate_total()` function now takes up to three arguments and returns the calculated result.

```
script
1    <?php # Script 3.10 - calculator.php (5th
     version after Scripts 3.5, 3.6, 3.8 & 3.9)
2    $page_title = 'Widget Cost Calculator';
3    include ('./includes/header.html');
4
5    /* This function calculates a total
6    and then prints the results.
7    This function returns the calculated
     total. */
8    function calculate_total ($qty, $cost, $tax
     = 5) {
9
10       $taxrate = $tax / 100; // Turn 5% into
         .05.
11       $total = ($qty * $cost) * ($taxrate + 1);
12       return number_format ($total, 2);
13
14   } // End of function.
15
16   // Check if the form has been submitted.
17   if (isset($_POST['submitted'])) {
18
19       if (is_numeric($_POST['quantity']) &&
         is_numeric($_POST['price'])) {
20
21           // Print the heading.
22           echo '<h1 id="mainhead">Total Cost
             </h1>';
23
24           if (is_numeric($_POST['tax'])) {
25               $total_cost = calculate_total
                 ($_POST['quantity'], $_POST
                 ['price'], $_POST['tax']);
26           } else {
27               $total_cost = calculate_total
                 ($_POST['quantity'], $_POST
                 ['price']);
28           }
29
```

(script continues on next page)

Returning values from a function

The final attribute of a usable function that I should mention is that of returning values. Some, but not all, functions do this. For example, `print()` will return either a 1 or a 0 indicating its success, whereas `echo()` will not. As another example, the `strlen()` function returns a number correlating to the number of characters in a string.

To have your function return a value, use the `return` statement.

```
function find_sign ($month, $day) {

    // Function code.

    return $sign;

}
```

The function can return a value (say a string or a number) or a variable whose value has been created by the function. When calling this function, you can assign the returned value to a variable:

```
$my_sign = find_sign ('October', 23);
```

or use it as a parameter to another function:

```
print find_sign ('October', 23);
```

To have a function return a value:

1. Open `calculator.php` (refer to Script 3.9) in your text editor.

2. Change the function definition to (**Script 3.10**)

```
function calculate_total ($qty,
→ $cost, $tax = 5) {
    $taxrate = $tax / 100;
    $total = ($qty * $cost) *
    → ($taxrate + 1);
    return number_format ($total, 2);
}
```

continues on next page

This version of the function will return just the calculated total without any HTML or sending anything to the Web browser.

3. Change the function call lines to

```php
if (is_numeric($_POST['tax'])) {
    $total_cost = calculate_total
    → ($_POST['quantity'], $_POST
    → ['price'], $_POST['tax']);
} else {
    $total_cost = calculate_total
    → ($_POST['quantity'], $_POST
    → ['price']);
}
```

Now the $total_cost variable will be assigned a value (returned by the function) with either function call.

4. Add a new echo() statement that prints the results.

```php
echo '<p>The total cost of
→ purchasing ' . $_POST['quantity']
→ . ' widget(s) at $' . number_format
→ ($_POST['price'], 2) . ' each is $'
→ . $total_cost . '.</p>';
```

Since the function just returns a value, a new echo() statement must be added to the main code.

Script 3.10 *continued*

```
script
30      echo '<p>The total cost of
        purchasing ' . $_POST['quantity']
        . ' widget(s) at $' . number_format
        ($_POST['price'], 2) . ' each is $'
        . $total_cost . '.</p>';
31
32      // Print some spacing.
33      echo '<p><br /></p>';
34
35    } else { // Invalid submitted values.
36      echo '<h1 id="mainhead">Error!</h1>
37      <p class="error">Please enter a
        valid quantity and price.</p><p>
        <br /></p>';
38    }
39
40  } // End of main isset() IF.
41
42  // Leave the PHP section and create the
    HTML form.
43  ?>
44  <h2>Widget Cost Calculator</h2>
45  <form action="calculator.php"
    method="post">
46    <p>Quantity: <input type="text"
      name="quantity" size="5" maxlength="10"
      value="<?php if (isset($_POST
      ['quantity'])) echo $_POST['quantity'];
      ?>" /></p>
47    <p>Price: <input type="text"
      name="price" size="5" maxlength="10"
      value="<?php if (isset($_POST['price']))
      echo $_POST['price']; ?>" /></p>
48    <p>Tax (%): <input type="text"
      name="tax" size="5" maxlength="10"
      value="<?php if (isset($_POST['tax']))
      echo $_POST['tax']; ?>" /> (optional)</p>
49    <p><input type="submit" name="submit"
      value="Calculate!" /></p>
50    <input type="hidden" name="submitted"
      value="TRUE" />
51  </form>
52  <?php
53  include ('./includes/footer.html');
54  ?>
```

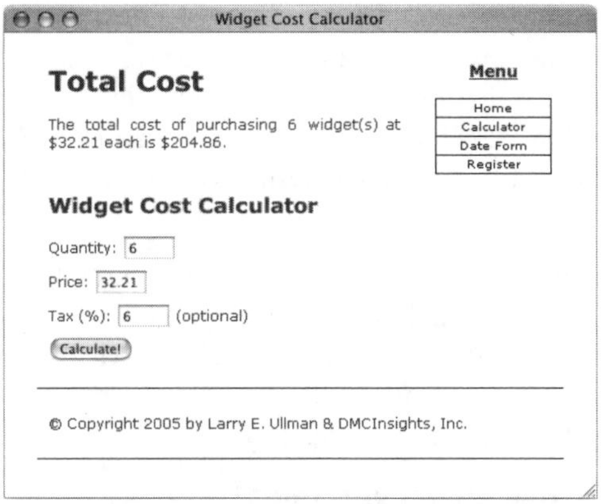

Figure 3.17 The calculator has a redefined function, but that has no impact on the end result (what the user sees).

5. Save the file, upload to your server, and test in your Web browser (**Figure 3.17**).

✔ Tips

■ Although this last example may seem more complex (with the function performing a calculation and the main code printing the results), it actually demonstrates better programming style. Ideally, functions should perform universal, obvious tasks (like a calculation) and be independent of page-specific factors like HTML formatting.

■ The `return` statement terminates the code execution at that point, so any code within a function after an executed `return` will never run.

■ A function can have multiple `return` statements (e.g., in a `switch` statement or conditional) but only one will ever be invoked. For example, functions commonly do something like this:.

```
function some_function () {
    if (condition) {
        return TRUE;
    } else {
        return FALSE;
    }
}
```

■ To have a function return multiple values, use an array and the `list()` function.

```
function calculate_total ($qty,
→ $cost, $tax = 5) {
    $taxrate = $tax / 100;
    $total = ($qty * $cost) *
    → ($taxrate + 1);
    $total = number_format ($total, 2);
    return array ($total, $tax);
}
// Normal page code.
list ($total_cost, $taxrate) =
→ calculate_total ($_POST
→ ['quantity'], $_POST['price'])
```

Variable Scope

Variable scope is a tricky but important concept. Every variable in PHP has a *scope* to it, which is to say a realm in which the variable (and therefore its value) can be accessed. For starters, variables have the scope of the page in which they reside. So if you define $var, the rest of the page can access $var, but other pages generally cannot (unless you use special variables).

Since included files act as if they were part of the original (including) script, variables defined before the include() line are available to the included file (as you've already seen with $page_title and header. html). Further, variables defined within the included file are available to the parent (including) script after the include() line.

All of this becomes murkier when using your own defined functions. These functions have their own scope, which means that variables used within a function are not available outside of it, and variables defined outside of a function are not available within it. For this reason, a variable inside of a function can have the same name as one outside of it and still be an entirely different variable with a different value. This is a confusing concept for most beginning programmers.

To alter the variable scope within a function, you can use the global statement.

```
function function_name() {

    global $var;

}

$var = 20;

function_name(); // Function call.
```

In this example, $var inside of the function is now the same as $var outside of it. This means that the function $var already has a value of *20*, and if that value changes inside of the function, the external $var's value will also change.

Another option for circumventing variable scope is to make use of the superglobals: $_GET, $_POST, $_REQUEST, etc. These variables are automatically accessible within your functions (hence, they are *super*global).

To use global variables:

1. Open calculator.php (refer to Script 3.10) in your text editor.

2. Change the function definition to (**Script 3.11**)

```
function calculate_total ($tax = 5) {
    global $total;
    $taxrate = $tax / 100;
    $total = ($_POST['quantity'] *
    → $_POST['price']) *
    → ($taxrate + 1);
    $total = number_format ($total, 2);
}
```

Since I've been using the superglobals anyway, I can rewrite the function so that it automatically uses these variables, ($_POST['quantity'] and $_POST['price']), instead of passing variables to it. Similarly, instead of returning the $total value, I can give it global scope.

continues on page 112

VARIABLE SCOPE

Script 3.11 Since $_POST is a superglobal variable, its values can be accessed within functions. The $total variable is made global within the function using the global keyword.

```
1    <?php # Script 3.11 - calculator.php (6th version after Scripts 3.5, 3.6, 3.8, 3.9 & 3.10)
2    $page_title = 'Widget Cost Calculator';
3    include ('./includes/header.html');
4
5    /* This function calculates a total
6    and then prints the results. */
7    function calculate_total ($tax = 5) {
8        global $total;
9        $taxrate = $tax / 100; // Turn 5% into .05.
10       $total = ($_POST['quantity'] * $_POST['price']) * ($taxrate + 1);
11       $total = number_format ($total, 2);
12   } // End of function.
13
14   // Check if the form has been submitted.
15   if (isset($_POST['submitted'])) {
16
17       if (is_numeric($_POST['quantity']) && is_numeric($_POST['price'])) {
18
19           // Print the heading.
20           echo '<h1 id="mainhead">Total Cost</h1>';
21
22           $total = NULL; // Initialize $total.
23
24           if (is_numeric($_POST['tax'])) {
25               calculate_total ($_POST['tax']);
26           } else {
27               calculate_total ();
28           }
29
30           echo '<p>The total cost of purchasing ' . $_POST['quantity'] . ' widget(s) at $' .
             number_format ($_POST['price'], 2) . ' each is $' . $total . '.</p>';
31
32           // Print some spacing.
33           echo '<p><br /></p>';
34
35       } else { // Invalid submitted values.
36           echo '<h1 id="mainhead">Error!</h1>
37           <p class="error">Please enter a valid quantity and price.</p><p><br /></p>';
38       }
39
40   } // End of main isset() IF.
41
```

(script continues on next page)

3. Initialize the $total variable outside of the function.

```
$total = NULL;
```

As a matter of good programming form, the $total variable is defined with a NULL value before the function call will make it global.

4. Change the function call lines to

```
if (is_numeric($_POST['tax'])) {
    calculate_total ($_POST['tax']);
} else {
    calculate_total ();
}
```

Since the function will automatically access the $_POST variables, the function call lines now only need to send the function a tax value if one has been submitted.

5. Change the echo() statement to read

```
echo '<p>The total cost of
→ purchasing ' . $_POST['quantity']
→ . ' widget(s) at $' . number_format
→ ($_POST['price'], 2) . ' each is $'
→ . $total . '.</p>';
```

Instead of referring to $total_cost (which was previously returned from the function), the global $total variable is printed here.

6. Save the file, upload to your server, and test in your Web browser (**Figure 3.18**).

Script 3.11 *continued*

```
script
42   // Leave the PHP section and create the
     HTML form.
43   ?>
44   <h2>Widget Cost Calculator</h2>
45   <form action="calculator.php"
     method="post">
46       <p>Quantity: <input type="text"
         name="quantity" size="5" maxlength="10"
         value="<?php if (isset($_POST
         ['quantity'])) echo $_POST['quantity'];
         ?>" /></p>
47       <p>Price: <input type="text"
         name="price" size="5" maxlength="10"
         value="<?php if (isset($_POST['price']))
         echo $_POST['price']; ?>" /></p>
48       <p>Tax (%): <input type="text"
         name="tax" size="5" maxlength="10"
         value="<?php if (isset($_POST['tax']))
         echo $_POST['tax']; ?>" /> (optional)</p>
49       <p><input type="submit" name="submit"
         value="Calculate!" /></p>
50       <input type="hidden" name="submitted"
         value="TRUE" />
51   </form>
52   <?php
53   include ('./includes/footer.html');
54   ?>
```

Figure 3.18 Again, the same end result (what the user sees) can be created using variations on your function definition.

✔ Tips

- Another confusing aspect of variable scope and functions comes from where in a script you define a function. A function's code is executed when that function is called, not when it is defined. Thus, you only need to define a global variable prior to calling a function that references it.

- A *static* variable is one that belongs to a function but whose value is initialized the first time that function is called and remembered by the function for each subsequent call. The following function will print the number *1* the first time called by the script, the number *2* the second time, and so forth.

```
function counter () {
    static $var = 1;
    echo $var++;
}
```

- Another method for circumventing scope is to pass a variable by reference rather than by value, allowing any changes made to that variable within the function to be applied to the variable outside of it. See the PHP manual for more information on passing values by reference.

- To adjust for scope, you can also use the $GLOBALS array, which contains all of the script's global variables.

- The $_SESSION and $_COOKIE variables can have values that are accessible by multiple pages. You'll learn more about both in Chapter 9, "Cookies and Sessions."

- Even though you can use the global statement and superglobals to rewrite your functions as I've done here, it won't always make the most sense to do so. The preceding version of the function was actually better because it received three values and returned one, without caring what the form input names (corresponding to the $_POST variables) were.

Date and Time Functions

Changing the direction of the chapter just a bit, I'll introduce a couple of PHP's date- and time-related functions. The most important of these is the aptly named `date()` function, which returns a string of text for a certain date and time according to a format you specify.

```
date ('format', [timestamp]);
```

The timestamp is an optional argument representing the number of seconds since the Unix Epoch (midnight on January 1, 1970) for the date in question. It allows you to get information, like the day of the week, for a particular date. If a timestamp is not specified, PHP will just use the current time on the server.

There are myriad formatting parameters available (**Table 3.1**), and these can be used in conjunction with literal text. For example,

```
echo date('F j, Y'); // January 26, 2005
```

```
echo date('H:i'); // 23:14
```

```
echo date('Today is D'); // Today is Mon
```

You can find the timestamp for a particular date using the `mktime()` function.

```
$stamp = mktime (hour, minute, second,
→ month, day, year);
```

Finally, the `getdate()` function can be used to return an array of values (**Table 3.2**) for a date and time. For example,

```
$dates = getdate();
```

```
echo $dates['month']; // January
```

This function also takes an optional timestamp argument. If that argument is not used, `getdate()` returns information for the current date and time.

To practice working with these functions, the simple `dateform.php` script will be rewritten to preselect the current date.

Date Function Formatting

CHARACTER	MEANING	EXAMPLE
Y	year as 4 digits	2005
y	year as 2 digits	05
n	month as 1 or 2 digits	2
m	month as 2 digits	02
F	month	February
M	month as 3 letters	Feb
j	day of the month as 1 or 2 digits	8
d	day of the month as 2 digits	08
l (lowercase L)	day of the week	Monday
D	day of the week as 3 letters	Mon
g	hour, 12-hour format as 1 or 2 digits	6
G	hour, 24-hour format as 1 or 2 digits	18
h	hour, 12-hour format as 2 digits	06
H	hour, 24-hour format as 2 digits	18
i	minutes	45
s	seconds	18
a	am or pm	am
A	AM or PM	PM

Table 3.1 The `date()` function can take any combination of these parameters to determine its returned results.

The getdate() Array

KEY	VALUE	EXAMPLE
year	year	2005
mon	month	12
month	month name	December
mday	day of the month	25
weekday	day of the week	Tuesday
hours	hours	11
minutes	minutes	56
seconds	seconds	47

Table 3.2 The `getdate()` function returns this associative array.

Script 3.12 This script makes use of the date() and getdate() functions.

```
1    <?php # Script 3.12 - dateform.php (2nd
     version after Script 3.7)
2    $page_title = 'Calendar Form';
3    include ('./includes/header.html');
4
5    // This function makes three pull-down
     menus for the months, days, and years.
6    function make_calendar_pulldowns($m =
     NULL, $d = NULL, $y = NULL) {
7
8        // Make the months array.
9        $months = array (1 => 'January',
         'February', 'March', 'April', 'May',
         'June', 'July', 'August', 'September',
         'October', 'November', 'December');
10
11       // Make the months pull-down menu.
12       echo '<select name="month">';
13       foreach ($months as $key => $value) {
14           echo "<option value=\"$key\"";
15           if ($key == $m) { // Preselect.
16               echo ' selected="selected"';
17           }
18           echo ">$value</option>\n";
19       }
20       echo '</select>';
21
22       // Make the days pull-down menu.
23       echo '<select name="day">';
24       for ($day = 1; $day <= 31; $day++) {
25           echo "<option value=\"$day\"";
26           if ($day == $d) { // Preselect.
27               echo ' selected="selected"';
28           }
29           echo ">$day</option>\n";
30       }
31       echo '</select>';
32
33       // Make the years pull-down menu.
34       echo '<select name="year">';
35       for ($year = 2005; $year <= 2015;
         $year++) {
```

(script continues on next page)

To use the date functions:

1. Open `dateform.php` (Script 3.7) in your text editor.

2. Change the function definition to begin (**Script 3.12**).

   ```
   function make_calendar_pulldowns
   → ($m = NULL, $d = NULL, $y = NULL) {
   ```

   Now this function will be able to take three arguments: a day, a month, and a year. The purpose of these will be to pre-set the pull-down menu values, as if this were part of a sticky form.

3. Change the months `foreach` loop so that it pre-selects a particular month.

   ```
   foreach ($months as $key => $value) {
       echo "<option value=\"$key\"";
       if ($key == $m) {
           echo ' selected="selected"';
       }
       echo ">$value</option>\n";
   }
   ```

   The code is as it was before except for the inclusion of the conditional. If the function is called with an `$m` value (for a particular month), the corresponding month should be selected in the form. To test for this, see if `$m` is equal to `$key`, where `$key` is the array's key, a value from 1 to 12. In such a case, the `selected="selected"` code will be added to the appropriate `option` tag.

4. Modify the day `for` loop so that it is also sticky.

   ```
   for ($day = 1; $day <= 31; $day++) {
       echo "<option value=\"$day\"";
       if ($day == $d) {
           echo ' selected="selected"';
       }
       echo ">$day</option>\n";
   }
   ```

continues on next page

DATE AND TIME FUNCTIONS

115

This is exactly like the months foreach loop except that it's a simple for loop. If the $day value is equal to the $d value, assigned when calling the function, the selected="selected" is added to the option tag.

5. Modify the year for loop so that it is also sticky.

```
for ($year = 2005; $year <= 2015;
→ $year++) {
    echo "<option value=\"$year\"";
    if ($year == $y) {
        echo ' selected="selected"';
    }
    echo ">$year</option>\n";
}
```

6. Alter the function call line so that it is called with today's date.

```
$dates = getdate();
make_calendar_pulldowns
→ ($dates['mon'], $dates['mday'],
→ $dates['year']);
```

To send the month, day, and year parameters to the function, I'll first use the getdate() function to retrieve an array of values for today. Then I call the function, supplying the appropriate array elements.

7. Print the current day and time.

```
echo '<p>Today is ' . date ('l') . '.
→ The current time is ' . date
→ ('g:i a') . '.</p>';
```

This final string will print something along the lines of *<p>Today is Tuesday. The current time is 11:14 pm.</p>* using the appropriate formatting parameters for the date() function.

8. Save the file as dateform.php, upload to your Web server, and test in your Web browser (**Figure 3.19**).

Script 3.12 *continued*

```
36          echo "<option value=\"$year\"";
37          if ($year == $y) { // Preselect.
38              echo ' selected="selected"';
39          }
40          echo ">$year</option>\n";
41      }
42      echo '</select>';
43
44  } // End of the function definition.
45
46  // Create the form tags.
47  echo '<h1 id="mainhead">Select a Date:</h1>
48  <p><br /></p><form action="dateform.php"
    method="post">';
49
50  // Get today's information and call the
    function.
51  $dates = getdate();
52  make_calendar_pulldowns ($dates['mon'],
    $dates['mday'], $dates['year']);
53
54  echo '</form><p><br /></p>'; // End of form.
55
56  // Print the current day and time.
57  echo '<p>Today is ' . date ('l') . '. The
    current time is ' . date ('g:i a') .
    '.</p>';
58
59  include ('./includes/footer.html');
60  ?>
```

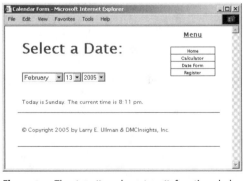

Figure 3.19 The date() and getdate() functions help add some dynamic behavior to this page.

9. If you want, view the source code of the page to see how the select menus were made sticky (**Figure 3.20**).

✔ Tips

■ As you'll see in Chapter 4, "Introduction to SQL and MySQL," MySQL has its own date functions.

■ PHP's date functions reflect the time on the server (because PHP runs on the server); you'll need to use JavaScript if you want to determine the date and time on the client computer.

■ The checkdate() function takes three parameters—month, day, and year—and checks if it is a valid date (one that actually exists or existed).

```
Source of http://localhost/ch03/dateform.php
<h1 id="mainhead">Select a date.</h1>
<p><br /></p><form action="dateform.php" method="post"><select name="month"><option
value="1">January</option>
<option value="2" selected="selected">February</option>
<option value="3">March</option>
<option value="4">April</option>
<option value="5">May</option>
<option value="6">June</option>
<option value="7">July</option>
<option value="8">August</option>
<option value="9">September</option>
<option value="10">October</option>
<option value="11">November</option>
<option value="12">December</option>
</select><select name="day"><option value="1">1</option>
<option value="2">2</option>
<option value="3">3</option>
<option value="4">4</option>
<option value="5">5</option>
<option value="6">6</option>
<option value="7">7</option>
<option value="8">8</option>
<option value="9">9</option>
<option value="10">10</option>
<option value="11">11</option>
<option value="12">12</option>
<option value="13" selected="selected">13</option>
<option value="14">14</option>
<option value="15">15</option>
<option value="16">16</option>
<option value="17">17</option>
<option value="18">18</option>
<option value="19">19</option>
<option value="20">20</option>
```

Figure 3.20 The source code reveals how the selected="selected" attribute makes the pull-down menus sticky.

DATE AND TIME FUNCTIONS

Sending Email

One of my absolute favorite things about PHP is how easy it is to send an email. On a properly configured server, the process is as simple as using the `mail()` function.

```
mail ($to, $subject, $body);
```

The `$to` value should be an email address or a series of addresses, separated by commas. The `$subject` value will create the email's subject line, and `$body` is where you put the contents of the email. Use the newline character (\n) within double quotation marks when creating your body to make the text go over multiple lines.

The `mail()` function takes a fourth, optional parameter for additional headers. This is where you could set the From, Reply-To, Cc, Bcc, and similar settings. For example,

```
mail ('phpmysql2@dmcinsights.com',
→ 'Question regarding Script 3.13',
→ $body, 'From: person@address.com');
```

To use multiple headers of different types in your email, separate each with \r\n:

```
$headers = "From: John@Doe.com\r\n";
```

```
$headers .= "Cc: Jane@Doe.com, Joe@Doe.
→ com\r\n";
```

```
mail ('phpmysql2@dmcinsights.com',
→ 'Question regarding Script 3.13',
→ $body, $headers);
```

As the last example in this chapter, a simple registration form will be created that will also send an email upon successful registration. While I'm at it, this example will also demonstrate an easy way to handle and report multiple form-submission errors.

To send email:

1. Begin a new PHP script in your text editor (**Script 3.13**).

   ```
   <?php # Script 3.13 - register.php
   $page_title = 'Register';
   include ('./includes/header.html');
   ```

2. Create the conditional for checking if the form has been submitted and then create a variable to track registration errors.

   ```
   if (isset($_POST['submitted'])) {
       $errors = array();
   ```

   The `$errors` variable will store all of the accumulated errors from validating the form data. It's initialized here as an array, which is not technically required but is good programming style.

3. Validate the name and email address.

   ```
   if (empty($_POST['name'])) {
       $errors[] = 'You forgot to enter
   → your name.';
   }
   if (empty($_POST['email'])) {
       $errors[] = 'You forgot to enter
   → your email address.';
   }
   ```

   These two text inputs are validated using the most minimal technique: making sure they aren't empty. If either is empty, a specific message is added as an element to the `$errors` array.

   In Chapter 10, "Web Application Security," you'll see how to use regular expressions to help validate a submitted email address.

   continues on page 120

Script 3.13 PHP's mail() function is surprisingly easy to use.

```
                               script
1    <?php # Script 3.13 - register.php
2    $page_title = 'Register';
3    include ('./includes/header.html');
4
5    // Check if the form has been submitted.
6    if (isset($_POST['submitted'])) {
7
8        $errors = array(); // Initialize error array.
9
10       // Check for a name.
11       if (empty($_POST['name'])) {
12           $errors[] = 'You forgot to enter your name.';
13       }
14
15       // Check for an email address.
16       if (empty($_POST['email'])) {
17           $errors[] = 'You forgot to enter your email address.';
18       }
19
20       // Check for a password and match against the confirmed password.
21       if (!empty($_POST['password1'])) {
22           if ($_POST['password1'] != $_POST['password2']) {
23               $errors[] = 'Your password did not match the confirmed password.';
24           }
25       } else {
26           $errors[] = 'You forgot to enter your password.';
27       }
28
29       if (empty($errors)) { // If everything's okay.
30
31           // Register the user.
32
33           // Send an email.
34           $body = "Thank you for registering with our site!\nYour password is '{$_POST['password1']}
             '.\n\nSincerely,\nUs";
35           mail ($_POST['email'], 'Thank you for registering!', $body, 'From: admin@site.com');
36
37           echo '<h1 id="mainhead">Thank you!</h1>
38           <p>You are now registered. An email has been sent to your email address confirming the
             information.</p><p><br /></p>';
39
```

(script continues on next page)

4. Validate the password.

```
if (!empty($_POST['password1'])) {
  if ($_POST['password1'] != $_POST
  → ['password2']) {
    $errors[] = 'Your password did
    → not match the confirmed
    → password.';
  }
} else {
  $errors[] = 'You forgot to enter
  → your password.';
}
```

There are two different validations for the password. First you must check that it's not empty. Second, the password must match the confirmed password. If either condition is false, another error message is added to the array.

5. Create a conditional that checks if errors occurred.

```
if (empty($errors)) {
```

If no errors occurred, then the $errors array is still empty, and the email can be sent.

6. Send the email.

```
$body = "Thank you for registering
→ with our site!\nYour password is
→ '{$_POST['password1']}'.
→ \n\nSincerely,\nUs";
mail ($_POST['email'], 'Thank you
→ for registering!', $body, 'From:
→ admin@site.com');
```

To send the email, I first build up my email body and assign that to the *$body* variable, and then I use the mail() function.

Script 3.13 *continued*

```
40     } else { // Report the errors.
41
42         echo '<h1 id="mainhead">Error!</h1>
43         <p class="error">The following
           error(s) occurred:<br />';
44         foreach ($errors as $msg) { // Print
           each error.
45             echo " - $msg<br />\n";
46         }
47         echo '</p><p>Please go back and try
           again.</p><p><br /></p>';
48
49     } // End of if (empty($errors)) IF.
50
51 } else { // Display the form.
52 ?>
53 <h2>Register</h2>
54 <form action="register.php" method="post">
55     <p>Name: <input type="text" name="name"
       size="20" maxlength="40" /></p>
56     <p>Email Address: <input type="text"
       name="email" size="20" maxlength="40"
       /> </p>
57     <p>Password: <input type="password"
       name="password1" size="10"
       maxlength="20" /></p>
58     <p>Confirm Password: <input
       type="password" name="password2"
       size="10" maxlength="20" /></p>
59     <p><input type="submit" name="submit"
       value="Register" /></p>
60     <input type="hidden" name="submitted"
       value="TRUE" />
61 </form>
62 <?php
63 } // Close the main IF-ELSE.
64 include ('./includes/footer.html');
65 ?>
```

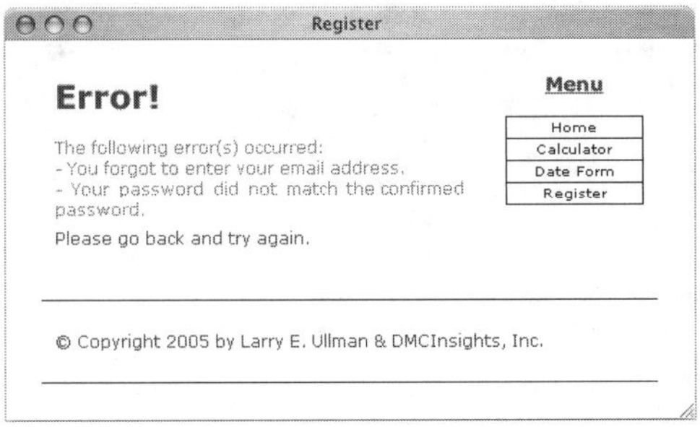

Figure 3.21 If the form isn't filled out completely, error messages are generated.

7. Print a message to the user.

```
echo '<h1 id="mainhead">Thank you!
→ </h1>
<p>You are now registered. An email
→ has been sent to your email address
→ confirming the information.
→ </p><p><br /></p>';
```

Obviously the script doesn't yet register the user, but that functionality will be added in due time.

8. Complete the inner conditional, reporting on the errors.

```
} else {
    echo '<h1 id="mainhead">Error!</h1>
    <p class="error">The following
    → error(s) occurred:<br />';
    foreach ($errors as $msg) {
        echo " - $msg<br />\n";
    }
    echo '</p><p>Please go back and
    → try again.</p><p><br /></p>';
}
```

Since **$errors** is an array, all of the error messages can easily be printed out using a **foreach** loop. The result will be a simply formatted list of problems (**Figure 3.21**).

9. Complete the main **if** and close the PHP tags.

```
} else {
?>
```

This closes the **if** block that checks if the form has been submitted. Now the form itself will be created, outside of the PHP tags.

continues on next page

10. Create the HTML form.

```
<h2>Register</h2>
<form action="register.php"
→ method="post">
  <p>Name: <input type="text"
→ name="name" size="20"
→ maxlength="40" /></p>
  <p>Email Address: <input
→ type="text" name="email"
→ size="20" maxlength="40" /> </p>
  <p>Password: <input
→ type="password"
→ name="password1" size="10"
→ maxlength="20" /></p>
  <p>Confirm Password: <input
→ type="password"
→ name="password2" size="10"
→ maxlength="20" /></p>
  <p><input type="submit"
→ name="submit" value="Register"
→ /></p>
  <input type="hidden"
→ name="submitted" value="TRUE" />
</form>
```

There's nothing particularly new here, except that the password is requested twice. This is a smart step to take, since the password is an unreadable input (**Figure 3.22**). If you only take the password once and the user mistypes their entry, they may not know what their password actually is.

11. Complete the PHP page.

```
<?php
}
include ('./includes/footer.html');
?>
```

The closing curly brace completes the main conditional (that checks if the form has been submitted and displays it otherwise).

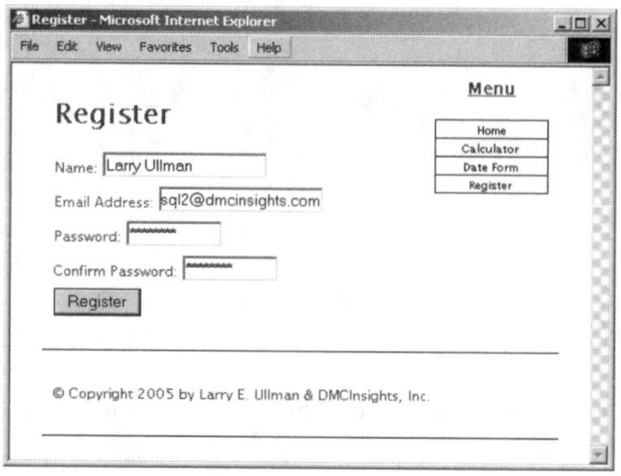

Figure 3.22 The registration form...

SENDING EMAIL

Figure 3.23 ...and its successful completion.

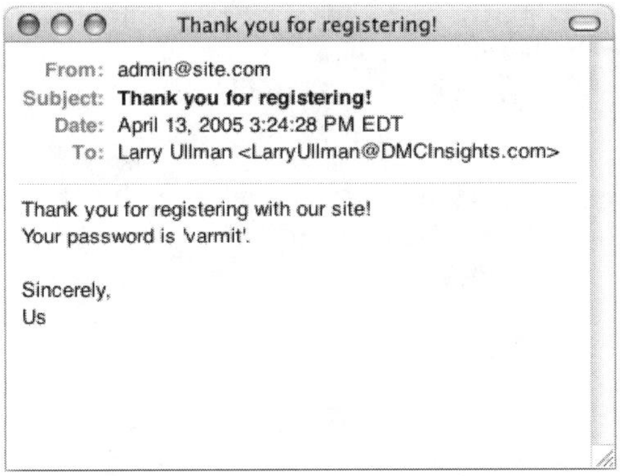

Figure 3.24 The email I received from the registration page.

12. Save the file as `register.php`, upload to your Web server, and test in your Web browser (**Figure 3.23**).

See the sidebar "PHP mail() Dependencies" if you see an odd error message (about From headers missing or no SMTP server) or if you never receive the email.

13. Check your email to confirm that you received the message (**Figure 3.24**).

✔ Tips

■ On some—primarily Unix—systems, the \r\n characters aren't handled properly. If you have problems with them, use just \n instead.

■ The `mail()` function returns a 1 or a 0 indicating the success of the function call. This is not the same thing as the email successfully being sent or received. You cannot easily test for either using PHP.

■ While it's easy to send a simple message with the `mail()` function, sending HTML emails or emails with attachments involves more work. In Chapter 11, "Extended Topics," I discuss the PEAR library of code. One of the classes in PEAR—*Mime_Mail*—can send HTML emails.

PHP mail() Dependencies

PHP's `mail()` function doesn't actually send the email itself. Instead, it tells the mail server running on the computer to do so. What this means is that your computer must have a working mail server in order for this function to work.

If you have a computer running a Unix variant or if you are running your Web site through a professional host, this should not be a problem. But if you are running PHP on your own computer, you'll probably need to make adjustments.

If you are running Windows and have an Internet service provider (ISP) that provides you with an SMTP server (like *smtp.comcast.net*), this information can be set in the `php.ini` file. Unfortunately, this will only work if your ISP does not require authentication—a username and password combination—to use the SMTP server. Otherwise, you'll need to install an SMTP server on your computer. There are plenty available, and they're not that hard to install and use: just search the Internet for *free windows smtp server* and you'll see some options.

If you are running Mac OS X, you'll need to enable the built-in SMTP server (either sendmail or postfix, depending upon the specific version of Mac OS X you are running). You can find instructions online for doing so (search with *enable sendmail "Mac OS X"*).

INTRODUCTION TO SQL AND MySQL

This chapter is a departure from its predecessors in that I'll be temporarily leaving PHP behind to delve into SQL and MySQL. Because this book discusses how to integrate two different technologies (PHP and MySQL), a solid understanding of each individually is important before you begin writing PHP scripts that use SQL and interact with MySQL.

SQL, short for Structured Query Language, is a group of special words used exclusively for interacting with databases. Every major database uses SQL, and MySQL is no exception. SQL was created shortly after Dr. E.F. Codd came up with the theory of relational databases in the early 1970s. In 1989, the American National Standards Institute—the organization responsible for maintaining the language—released the first SQL standard, referred to now as *SQL89*. *SQL2* was released in 1992 and is still the current, working version (also called *SQL92* or just plain *SQL*).

MySQL is the world's most popular open source database application (according to MySQL's Web site, `www.mysql.com`) and is commonly used with PHP. The MySQL software comes with the database server, different client applications, and several utilities. This chapter and the next will demonstrate how to use SQL and MySQL to store and retrieve data. Chapter 7, "Using PHP with MySQL," will then apply this same information to PHP scripts.

This chapter assumes you have access to a running MySQL server. If you are working on your own computer, see Appendix A, "Installation," for installation, user-creation, and starting MySQL instructions. If you are using a hosted server, your Web host should provide you with the database access.

Choosing Your Column Types

Before you start working with SQL and MySQL, you have to identify your application's needs. This then dictates the database design. For the examples in this chapter, I'll create a database (generically called *site-name*) that stores some user registration information (which will then be incorporated into Chapter 7). The database will consist of a single table, *users*, that contains columns to store user ID, first name, last name, email address, password, and registration date. **Table 4.1** shows the current layout, using MySQL's naming rules for column titles (alphanumeric names, plus the underscore, with no spaces).

Once you have identified all of the tables and columns that the database will need, you should determine each field's MySQL data type. When creating the database, MySQL requires that you define what sort of information each field will contain. There are three primary categories, which is true for almost every database application:

◆ Text

◆ Numbers

◆ Dates and times

Within each of these, there are a number of variants—some of which are MySQL-specific—you can use. Choosing your column types correctly not only dictates what information can be stored and how but also affects the database's overall performance. **Table 4.2** lists most of the available types for MySQL, how much space they take up, and brief descriptions of each type.

users Table	
COLUMN NAME	EXAMPLE
user_id	834
first_name	Hannah
last_name	Mauck
email	phpmysql2@dmcinsights.com
password	bethany
registration_date	2004-12-15 17:00:00

Table 4.1 The *users* table will have these six columns, to store records like the sample data here.

Many of the types can take an optional *Length* attribute, limiting their size. (The square brackets, [], indicate an optional parameter to be put in parentheses.) You should keep in mind that if you insert a string five characters long into a CHAR(2) field, the final three characters will be truncated. This is true for any field in which the length is set (CHAR, VARCHAR, INT, etc.). So your length should always correspond to the maximum possible value (as a number) or longest possible string (as text) that might be stored.

The various date types have all sorts of unique behaviors, which are documented in the MySQL manual. You'll use the DATE and TIME fields primarily without modification, so you need not worry too much about their intricacies.

There are also two special types—ENUM and SET—that allow you to define a series of acceptable values for that field. An ENUM column can have only one value of a possible several thousand values, while SET allows for several of up to 64 possible values. These are available in MySQL but aren't present in every database application.

MySQL Data Types

TYPE	SIZE	DESCRIPTION
CHAR[Length]	*Length* bytes	A fixed-length field from 0 to 255 characters long
VARCHAR[Length]	String length + 1 bytes	A variable-length field from 0 to 255 characters long
TINYTEXT	String length + 1 bytes	A string with a maximum length of 255 characters
TEXT	String length + 2 bytes	A string with a maximum length of 65,535 characters
MEDIUMTEXT	String length + 3 bytes	A string with a maximum length of 16,777,215 characters
LONGTEXT	String length + 4 bytes	A string with a maximum length of 4,294,967,295 characters
TINYINT[Length]	1 byte	Range of –128 to 127 or 0 to 255 unsigned
SMALLINT[Length]	2 bytes	Range of –32,768 to 32,767 or 0 to 65,535 unsigned
MEDIUMINT[Length]	3 bytes	Range of –8,388,608 to 8,388,607 or 0 to 16,777,215 unsigned
INT[Length]	4 bytes	Range of –2,147,483,648 to 2,147,483,647 or 0 to 4,294,967,295 unsigned
BIGINT[Length]	8 bytes	Range of –9,223,372,036,854,775,808 to 9,223,372,036,854,775,807 or 0 to 18,446,744,073,709,551,615 unsigned
FLOAT	4 bytes	A small number with a floating decimal point
DOUBLE[Length, Decimals]	8 bytes	A large number with a floating decimal point
DECIMAL[Length, Decimals]	Length + 1 or Length + 2 bytes	A DOUBLE stored as a string, allowing for a fixed decimal point
DATE	3 bytes	In the format of YYYY-MM-DD
DATETIME	8 bytes	In the format of YYYY-MM-DD HH:MM:SS
TIMESTAMP	4 bytes	In the format of YYYYMMDDHHMMSS; acceptable range ends in the year 2037
TIME	3 bytes	In the format of HH:MM:SS
ENUM	1 or 2 bytes	Short for *enumeration*, which means that each column can have one of several possible values
SET	1, 2, 3, 4, or 8 bytes	Like ENUM except that each column can have more than one of several possible values

Table 4.2 The common MySQL data types you can use for defining columns.

To select the column types:

1. Identify whether a column should be a text, number, or date type (**Table 4.3**).

   This is normally an easy and obvious step. You will find that numbers such as ZIP codes and dollar amounts will be text fields if you include their corresponding punctuation (dollar signs, commas, and hyphens), but you'll get better results if you store them as numbers and address the formatting elsewhere.

2. Choose the most appropriate subtype for each column (**Table 4.4**).

   In my example, I'll set the *user_id* as a MEDIUMINT, allowing for up to nearly 17 million values (as an *unsigned*, or non-negative, number). The *registration_date* will be a DATETIME, storing both the day and the specific moment a user registered. When deciding among the date types, consider whether or not you'll want to access just the date, the time, or possibly both.

   The other fields will be mostly VARCHAR, since their lengths will differ from record to record. The only exception is the password, which will be a fixed-length CHAR (you'll see why when inserting records later in this chapter). See the sidebar "CHAR vs. VARCHAR" for more information on these two types.

3. Set the maximum lengths for text and number columns (**Table 4.5**).

   The size of any field should be restricted to the smallest possible value, based upon the largest possible input. For example, if the largest a number such as *user_id* can be is in the hundreds, set the column as a three-digit SMALLINT (allowing for up to 999 values).

users Table

COLUMN NAME	TYPE
user_id	number
first_name	text
last_name	text
email	text
password	text
registration_date	date/time

Table 4.3 The *users* table with generic data types.

users Table

COLUMN NAME	TYPE
user_id	MEDIUMINT
first_name	VARCHAR
last_name	VARCHAR
email	VARCHAR
password	CHAR
registration_date	DATETIME

Table 4.4 The *users* table with more specific data types.

users Table

COLUMN NAME	TYPE
user_id	MEDIUMINT
first_name	VARCHAR(15)
last_name	VARCHAR(30)
email	VARCHAR(40)
password	CHAR(40)
registration_date	DATETIME

Table 4.5 The *users* table with set length attributes.

CHAR vs. VARCHAR

Both of these types store strings and can be set with a fixed maximum length. One primary difference between the two is that anything stored as a CHAR will always be stored as a string the length of the column (using spaces to pad it). Conversely, VARCHAR strings will be only as long as the stored string itself.

The implications of this are

◆ VARCHAR columns tend to take up less disk space.

◆ Unless you are using the InnoDB table type, CHAR columns are faster to access than VARCHAR.

Granted, the speed and disk space differences between the two types may be imperceptible in most cases, and as the InnoDB table type becomes the norm, any speed difference will disappear.

There is also a third, minor difference between these two: MySQL trims off extra spaces from CHAR columns when data is retrieved and from VARCHAR when it's inserted.

If a string field will always be of a set length (e.g., a state abbreviation), use CHAR; otherwise, use VARCHAR. You may notice, though, that in some cases MySQL defines a column as the one type (like CHAR) even though you created it as the other (VARCHAR). This is perfectly normal and is MySQL's way of improving performance.

✔ Tips

■ In Chapter 5, "Advanced SQL and MySQL," I'll develop a more complex database and discuss database design in more detail.

■ Many of the data types have synonymous names: INT and INTEGER, DEC and DECIMAL, etc.

■ The TIMESTAMP field type is automatically set as the current date and time when an INSERT or UPDATE occurs, even if no value is specified for that particular field. If a table has multiple TIMESTAMP columns, only the first one will be updated when an INSERT or UPDATE is performed.

■ There is also a BLOB type, which is a variant on TEXT that allows for storing binary files (like images) in a table. This type is also used for some encrypted data.

CHOOSING YOUR COLUMN TYPES

Choosing Other Column Properties

Besides deciding what data types and sizes you should use for your columns, you should consider a handful of other properties.

First, every type can also be set as NOT NULL. The NULL value, in databases and programming, is equivalent to saying that the field has no value. Ideally, every field of every record in a database should have a value, but that is rarely the case in reality. To force a field to have a value, you add the NOT NULL description to its column type. For example, a required dollar amount can be described as

cost DECIMAL(5,2) NOT NULL

When creating a table, you can also specify a default value for any type. In cases where a majority of the records will have the same value for a column, presetting a default will save you from having to specify a value when inserting new rows (unless that row's value for that column is different from the norm).

gender ENUM('M', 'F') default 'F'

If no value is specified for a column when adding a record, the default will be used if set or an error will occur if the column is defined as NOT NULL.

The number types can be marked as UNSIGNED, which limits the stored data to positive numbers and zero. This also effectively doubles the range of positive numbers that can be stored (because no negative numbers will be kept). You can also flag the number types as ZEROFILL, which means that any extra room will be padded with zeros (ZEROFILLs are also automatically UNSIGNED).

Finally, when designing a database, you'll need to consider creating indexes, adding keys, and using the AUTO_INCREMENT property. Chapter 5 discusses these concepts in greater detail, but in the meantime, check out the sidebar "Indexes, Keys, and AUTO_INCREMENT" to learn how they affect the *users* table.

To finish defining your columns:

1. Identify your primary key.

   The primary key is quixotically both arbitrary and critically important. Almost always a number value, the primary key is a unique way to refer to a particular record. For example, your phone number has no inherent value but is uniquely a way to reach you.

   In the *users* table, the *user_id* will be the primary key: an arbitrary number used to refer to a row of data.

2. Identify which columns cannot have a NULL value.

   In this example, every field is required (cannot be NULL). If you stored peoples' addresses, by contrast, you might have *address_line1* and *address_line2*, with the latter one being optional.

3. Make any numeric type UNSIGNED if it won't ever store negative numbers.

   The *user_id*, which will be a number, is UNSIGNED so that it's always positive.

users Table

COLUMN NAME	TYPE
user_id	MEDIUMINT UNSIGNED NOT NULL
first_name	VARCHAR(15) NOT NULL
last_name	VARCHAR(30) NOT NULL
email	VARCHAR(40) NOT NULL
password	CHAR(40) NOT NULL
registration_date	DATETIME NOT NULL

Table 4.6 The final description of the *users* table. Also remember that the *user_id* will be marked as an auto-incremented primary key.

4. Establish the default value for any column.

   None of the columns here logically implies a default value.

5. Confirm the final column definitions (**Table 4.6**).

   Before creating your tables, you should revisit the type and range of data you'll store to make sure that your database effectively accounts for everything.

Indexes, Keys, and AUTO_INCREMENT

Two concepts closely related to database design are indexes and keys. An *index* in a database is a way of requesting that the database keep an eye on the values of a specific column or combination of columns (loosely stated). The end result of this is improved performance when retrieving records but slightly hindered performance when inserting or updating them.

A *key* in a database table is integral to the normalization process used for designing more complicated databases. There are two types of keys: *primary* and *foreign*. Each table should have one primary key, and as you'll discover in the next chapter, the primary key in a table is often linked as a foreign key in another.

A table's primary key is an artificial way to refer to a record and should abide by three rules:

1. It must always have a value.

2. That value must never change.

3. That value must be unique for each record in the table.

In the *users* table, the *user_id* will be designated as a PRIMARY KEY, which is both a description of the column and an indication to MySQL to index it. Since the *user_id* is a number (which primary keys almost always will be), I'll also add the AUTO_INCREMENT description to the column, which tells MySQL to use the next-highest number as the *user_id* value for each added record. You'll see what this means in practice when you begin inserting records.

Using the mysql Client

In order to create tables, add records, and request information from a database, some sort of *client* application is necessary to communicate with the database server. Although there are oodles of client applications available (see the sidebar "Alternatives to the mysql Client"), I'll focus on using the *mysql client* (or *mysql monitor,* as it is also called). Although this application does not have a pretty graphical interface, it's a reliable, standard tool that's easy to use and behaves consistently on many different operating systems.

The mysql client is accessed from a command-line interface, be it the Terminal application in Linux or Mac OS X, or a DOS prompt in Windows. It can take several arguments up front, including the username, password, and hostname (computer name or URL). You establish these arguments like so:

```
mysql -u username -p -h hostname
```

The -p option will cause the client to prompt you for the password. You can also specify the password on this line if you prefer— by typing it directly after the -p prompt— but it will be visible, which is insecure. The -h hostname argument is optional, and I tend to leave it off unless I cannot connect to the MySQL server otherwise.

Within the mysql client, every statement (SQL command) needs to be terminated by a semicolon. These semicolons are an indication to MySQL that the query is complete; the semicolons are not part of the SQL itself. What this does mean is that you can continue the same SQL statement over several lines within the mysql client, to make it easier to read.

As a quick demonstration of accessing and using the mysql client, I will show you how to start the mysql client, select a database to use, and quit the client. Before following these steps,

◆ The MySQL server must be running.

◆ You must have a username and password with proper access.

Both of these steps are explained in Appendix A. If you are using MySQL hosted on another computer (such as a Web host), that system's administrator should provide you with access and you may need to use another interface tool, such as phpMyAdmin (again, see the sidebar). If you are using another client application, where and how you run your SQL commands will vary, but the SQL commands themselves and most of the results will be exactly the same.

As a side note, in the following steps and throughout the rest of the chapter, I will continue to provide images using the mysql client on both Windows and Mac OS X. While the appearance differs, the steps and results will be identical. So in short, don't be concerned about why one image shows the DOS prompt and the next a Terminal.

To use the mysql client:

1. Access your system from a command-line interface.

   On Unix systems and Mac OS X, this is just a matter of bringing up the Terminal or a similar application.

   If you are using Windows and followed the instructions in Appendix A, you can choose Start > Programs > MySQL > MySQL Server *X.X* > MySQL Command Line Client (**Figure 4.1**). Then you can skip to Step 3. If you don't have a MySQL Command Line Client option available, you'll need to choose Run from the Start menu, type cmd in the window, and press Enter to bring up a DOS prompt (then follow the instructions in the next step).

continues on next page

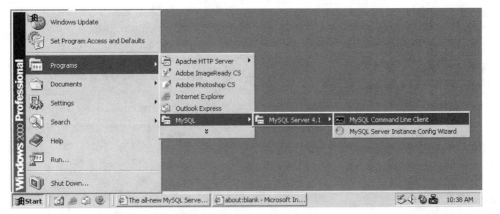

Figure 4.1 The MySQL Windows installer creates a link in your Start menu so that you can easily get into the mysql client.

2. Invoke the mysql client, using the appropriate command (**Figure 4.2**).

```
/path/to/mysql/bin/mysql -u
→ username -p
```

The */path/to/mysql* part of this step will be largely dictated by the operating system you are running and where MySQL was installed. This might therefore be

▲ `/usr/local/mysql/bin/mysql - u`
`→ username -p` (on Mac OS X and Unix)

or

▲ `C:\mysql\bin\mysql -u username -p` (on Windows)

The basic premise is that you are running the mysql client, connecting as *username*, and requesting to be prompted for the password. For this and the next chapter, you can use the *root* user, if you have that access information, but any user that has permission to create tables and databases is fine.

3. Enter the password at the prompt and press Return/Enter.

The password you use here should be for the user you specified in the preceding step. If you used the MySQL Command Line Client link on Windows (Figure 4.1), the user is *root*, so you should use that password (probably established during installation and configuration, see Appendix A).

If you used the proper username/password combination (i.e., someone with valid access), you should be greeted as shown in **Figure 4.3**.

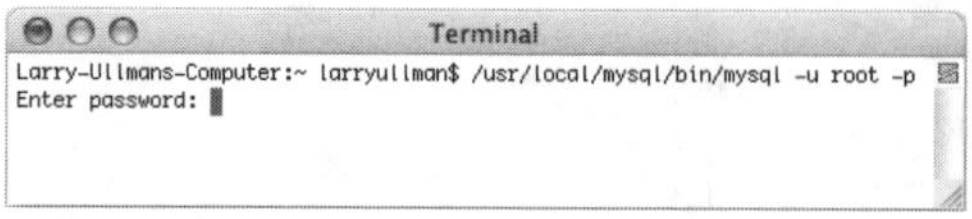

Figure 4.2 Access the mysql client by entering the full path to the utility, along with the proper arguments.

Alternatives to the mysql Client

Since the mysql client is a command-line tool, you may not be able to use it if you are working with an ISP's or Web host's server. Here are two things you can try:

◆ Telnet or SSH into the remote server and then use mysql.

◆ Install the MySQL software on your computer and use the mysql client to connect to the remote server by specifying it as the hostname (`mysql -u username -p -h www.site.com`).

If neither of these options work, you have other choices, beginning with phpMyAdmin. A popular open source tool written in PHP, phpMyAdmin, provides a Web-based interface for MySQL. Available from `www.phpmyadmin.net`, this software is so common that many Web hosting companies offer it as the default way for their users to interface with a MySQL database.

If you cannot access MySQL through the mysql client, you can still do practically everything with phpMyAdmin. The SQL tab in the latest version allows you to directly type in SQL commands, although many common commands have their own shortcuts in the program.

The good people at MySQL have other tools available for download, including the MySQL Query Browser, which will let you interact with the server through a graphical interface. If this isn't to your liking, there are dozens of others available (from third parties) if you search the Web.

USING THE MYSQL CLIENT

Figure 4.3 If you are successfully able to log in, you'll see a welcome message like this.

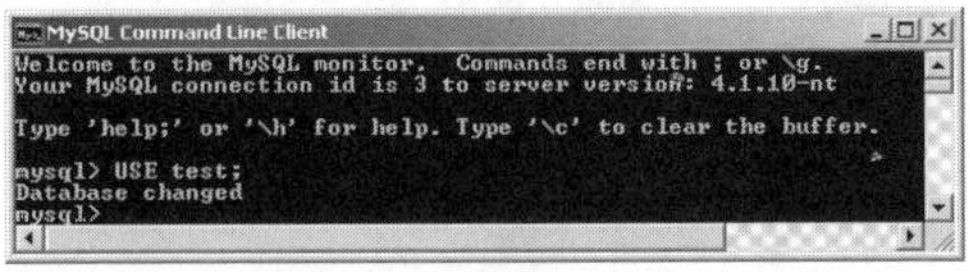

Figure 4.4 The USE command selects a database to use.

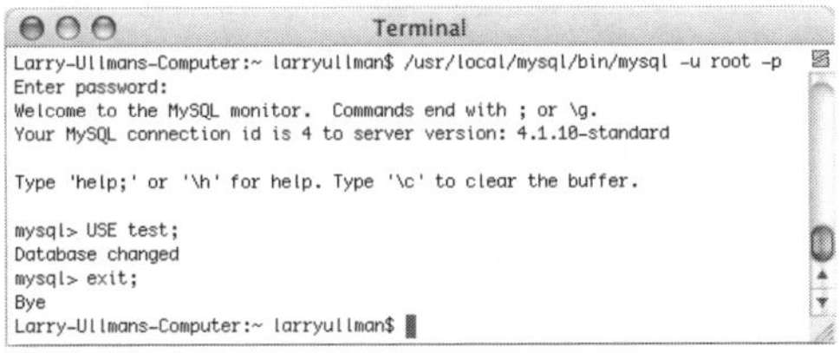

```
Terminal
Larry-Ullmans-Computer:~ larryullman$ /usr/local/mysql/bin/mysql -u root -p
Enter password:
Welcome to the MySQL monitor.  Commands end with ; or \g.
Your MySQL connection id is 4 to server version: 4.1.10-standard

Type 'help;' or '\h' for help. Type '\c' to clear the buffer.

mysql> USE test;
Database changed
mysql> exit;
Bye
Larry-Ullmans-Computer:~ larryullman$
```

Figure 4.5 Type either exit or quit to terminate your session and leave the mysql client.

4. Select the database you want to use (**Figure 4.4**).

   `USE test;`

   The USE command tells MySQL which database you want to deal with from here on out (saving typing the database name over and over again later). The *test* database is one of two that MySQL installs by default. Assuming it exists on your server, all users should be able to access it.

5. Quit out of mysql (**Figure 4.5**).

   `exit`

   You can also use the command `quit` to leave the client. This step—unlike most other commands you enter in the mysql client—does not require a semicolon at the end.

   If you used the MySQL Command Line Client, this will also close the DOS prompt window.

✔ Tips

- If you know in advance which database you will want to use, you can simplify matters by starting mysql with

   */path/to/mysql/bin/*mysql -u *username*
   → -p *databasename*

- To see what else you can do with the mysql utility, type

   */path/to/mysql/bin/*mysql --help

- The mysql client on most systems allows you to use the up and down arrows to scroll through previously entered commands. This can save you oodles of time when working with a database.

- If you are in a long statement and make a mistake, cancel the current operation by typing c and pressing Return or Enter. If mysql thinks a closing single or double quotation mark is missing (as indicated by the '> and "> prompts), you'll need to enter the appropriate quotation mark first.

- To be particularly safe when using mysql, start the application using the --i-am-a-dummy argument. And no, I am not making this up (the argument limits what you can and cannot do).

Creating Databases and Tables

The first logical use of SQL and MySQL will be to create a database. The syntax for creating a new database is

CREATE DATABASE *databasename*

The CREATE term is also used for making tables.

CREATE TABLE *tablename* (

column1name description,

column2name description

...)

As you can see from this syntax, after naming the table, you define each column—in order—within parentheses. Each column-description pair should be separated from the next by a comma. Should you choose to create indexes at this time, you can add those at the end of the creation statement, but you can add indexes at a later time as well.

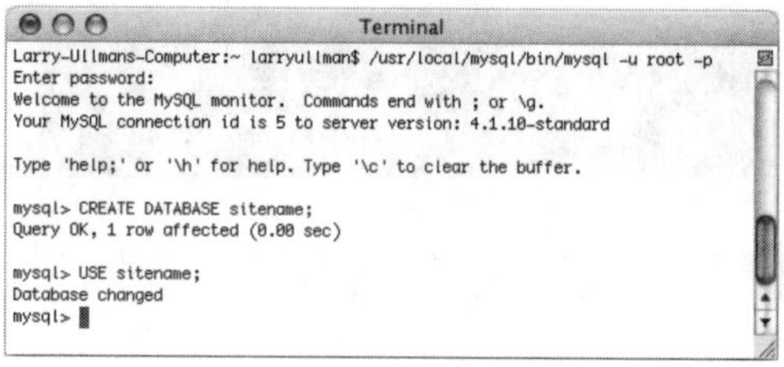

To create databases and tables:

1. Access the mysql client using the steps outlined previously.

   Throughout the rest of this chapter, all of the SQL will be entered using the mysql client. Using the steps in the preceding section of this chapter, open the mysql client, entering the proper syntax (username, password, etc.) for your system and configuration. You can also use phpMyAdmin or any other interface tool.

2. Create and select the new database (**Figure 4.6**).

   CREATE DATABASE sitename;
   USE sitename;

Figure 4.6 I'll be using the *sitename* database throughout the remainder of this chapter.

Figure 4.7 This CREATE SQL command will make the *users* table.

This first line creates the database (assuming that you are logged into mysql as a user with permission to create new databases). The second line tells MySQL that you want to work within this database from here on out. Remember that within the mysql client, you must terminate every SQL command with a semicolon, although these semi-colons aren't technically part of SQL itself.

If you are using a hosting company's MySQL, they will probably create the database for you.

3. Create the *users* table (**Figure 4.7**).

CREATE TABLE users (

user_id MEDIUMINT UNSIGNED NOT NULL
→ AUTO_INCREMENT,

first_name VARCHAR(15) NOT NULL,

last_name VARCHAR(30) NOT NULL,

email VARCHAR(40) NOT NULL,

password CHAR(40) NOT NULL,

registration_date DATETIME NOT NULL,

PRIMARY KEY (user_id)

);

This step takes the design for the *users* table and integrates that within the CREATE table syntax. The order in which you enter the columns here will dictate the order in which the columns appear in the table.

Because the mysql client will not run a query until it encounters a semicolon, you can enter statements over multiple lines as I did in Figure 4.7 (by pressing Return or Enter at the end of each line). This often makes a query easier to read and debug.

continues on next page

CREATING DATABASES AND TABLES

4. Confirm the existence of the table (**Figure 4.8**).

SHOW TABLES;

SHOW COLUMNS FROM users;

The SHOW command reveals the tables in a database or the column names and types in a table, if named.

Also, you might notice in Figure 4.8 that the default value for *user_id* is NULL, even though this column was defined as NOT NULL. This is actually correct and has to do with *user_id* being an automatically incremented primary key.

✔ Tips

■ Throughout the rest of this chapter, I will assume that you are using the mysql client or comparable tool and have already selected the *sitename* database with USE.

■ Although SQL is case-insensitive, I make it a habit to capitalize the SQL words, helping to separate them from the database, table, and column names. If you would rather not capitalize these terms, you have that option.

■ When creating a table, you have the option of specifying a type, with MyISAM, BDB, InnoDB, temporary, and HEAP being the most common. If you do not specify a table type, MySQL will automatically create the table using the default, most likely MyISAM. Chapter 5 discusses the various table types in more detail.

■ DESCRIBE *tablename*, which you might see in other resources, is the same statement as SHOW COLUMNS FROM *tablename*.

```
● ● ●                          Terminal
mysql> SHOW TABLES;
+--------------------+
| Tables_in_sitename |
+--------------------+
| users              |
+--------------------+
1 row in set (0.00 sec)

mysql> SHOW COLUMNS FROM users;
+-------------------+----------------------+------+-----+---------------------+----------------+
| Field             | Type                 | Null | Key | Default             | Extra          |
+-------------------+----------------------+------+-----+---------------------+----------------+
| user_id           | mediumint(8) unsigned |      | PRI | NULL                | auto_increment |
| first_name        | varchar(15)          |      |     |                     |                |
| last_name         | varchar(30)          |      |     |                     |                |
| email             | varchar(40)          |      |     |                     |                |
| password          | varchar(40)          |      |     |                     |                |
| registration_date | datetime             |      |     | 0000-00-00 00:00:00 |                |
+-------------------+----------------------+------+-----+---------------------+----------------+
6 rows in set (0.00 sec)

mysql> █
```

Figure 4.8 I can confirm the existence and layout of a table using the SHOW command.

Inserting Records

After your database and its table(s) have been created, you can start populating them using the INSERT command. Before demonstrating the syntax, I want to be explicit as to how you should treat the different data types in your SQL commands. Always abide by these rules:

◆ Numeric values shouldn't be quoted.

◆ String values (for CHAR, VARCHAR, and TEXT column types) must always be quoted.

◆ Date and time values must always be quoted.

◆ Functions cannot be quoted.

◆ The word NULL must not be quoted.

With that in mind, there are two formats for inserting data. With the first, you specify the columns to be used:

```
INSERT INTO tablename (column1,
→ column2 …) VALUES ('value1',
→ 'value2' …)
```

```
INSERT INTO tablename (column4,
→ column8) VALUES ('valueX', 'valueY')
```

Using this structure, you can add rows of records, populating only the columns that matter. The result will be that any columns not given a value will be treated as NULL (or given a default value, if that was defined). Note that if a column cannot have a NULL value (it was set as NOT NULL), not specifying a value will cause an error.

The second format for inserting records is not to specify any columns at all but to include values for every one.

```
INSERT INTO tablename VALUES ('value1',
→ NULL, 'value3', 30, …)
```

If you use this second method, you must specify a value, even if it's NULL, for every column. If there are six columns in the table, you must list six values. Failure to match the number of values to the number of columns will cause an error. For this and other reasons, the first format of inserting records is generally preferable.

MySQL also allows you to insert multiple rows at one time, separating each record by a comma.

```
INSERT INTO tablename (column1,
→ column4) VALUES ('valueA', 'valueB'),
→ ('valueC', 'valueD'), ('valueE',
→ 'valueF')
```

While you can do this with MySQL, it is not acceptable within the ANSI SQL2 standard and is therefore not supported by all database applications.

To insert data into a table:

1. Insert a new row of data into the *users* table (**Figure 4.9**).

   Your syntax would be one of the following:

   ▲ INSERT INTO users (first_name,
      → last_name, email, password,
      → registration_date) VALUES
      → ('Larry', 'Ullman',
      → 'phpmysql2@DMCInsights.com',
      → SHA('password'), NOW());

   or

   ▲ INSERT INTO users VALUES (NULL,
      → 'Larry', 'Ullman',
      → 'phpmysql2@DMCInsights.com',
      → SHA('password'), NOW());

   Again, the first syntax (where the specific columns are named) is more foolproof but not always the most convenient. Two functions are used in both cases (see the sidebar "Two MySQL Functions" for more on these). I use the NOW() function to set the *registration_date* as this moment (notice the function is not enclosed by quotation marks). Another function, SHA(), is used to store an encrypted form of the password. It's available in versions 4.0.2 and later of MySQL (if you have an earlier version, use MD5() instead of SHA()).

   In the second example (where I must insert a value for the *user_id*), I set the *user_id* field as NULL, which will cause MySQL to use the next logical number, per its AUTO_INCREMENT description. This wasn't necessary in the first example, as no value was specified at all.

Two MySQL Functions

Although I'll be discussing functions in more detail later in this chapter, I want to introduce two MySQL functions here: SHA() and NOW().

The SHA() function is one way to encrypt data. This function creates an encrypted string that is always exactly 40 characters long (which is why I set the *users* table's *password* column as CHAR(40)). SHA() is a one-way encryption technique, meaning that it cannot be reversed. It's useful for storing sensitive data that need not be viewed in an unencrypted form again, but it's obviously not a good choice for sensitive data that should be protected but later viewed (like credit card numbers). If you are not using a version of MySQL later than 4.0.1, you can use the MD5() function instead, and set the password column as CHAR(32). This function does the same task, using a different algorithm, and returns a 32-character long string.

The NOW() function is handy for date, time, and timestamp columns, since it will insert the current date and time (on the server) for that field.

When using any function in a SQL statement, do not place it within quotation marks. You also must not have any spaces between the function's name and the following parenthesis (so NOW() not NOW ()).

```
mysql> INSERT INTO users (first_name, last_name, email, password, registration_date)
VALUES ('Larry', 'Ullman', 'phpmysql2@DMCInsights.com', SHA('password'), NOW());
Query OK, 1 row affected (0.12 sec)

mysql>
```

Figure 4.9 This query inserts a single record into the *users* table.

2. Insert several values into the *users* table (**Figure 4.10**).

```
INSERT INTO users (first_name,
→ last_name, email, password,
→ registration_date) VALUES
('John', 'Lennon', 'john@beatles.
→ com', SHA('Happin3ss'), NOW()),
('Paul', 'McCartney', 'paul@beatles.
→ com', SHA('letITbe'), NOW()),
('George', 'Harrison',
→ 'george@beatles.com',
→ SHA('something'), NOW()),
('Ringo', 'Starr', 'ringo@beatles.
→ com', SHA('thisboy'), NOW());
```

Since MySQL allows you to insert multiple values at once, you can take advantage of this and fill up the table with records.

3. Continue Steps 1 and 2 until you've thoroughly populated the *users* table.

Throughout the rest of this chapter I will be performing queries based upon the records I entered into my database. Should your database not have the same specific records as mine, change the particulars accordingly. The fundamental thinking behind the following queries should still apply regardless of the data, since the *sitename* database has a set column and table structure.

✔ Tips

- On the scripts page of the book's supporting Web site (www.DMCInsights.com/php-mysql2), you can download all of the SQL commands for the book. Using some of these commands, you can populate your *users* table exactly as I have.

- If you need to insert a value containing a single quotation mark, escape it with a backslash:

```
INSERT INTO tablename (last_name,
→ first_name) VALUES ('O\'Toole',
→ 'Peter');
```

- The term INTO in INSERT statements is optional in current versions of MySQL.

```
mysql> INSERT INTO users (first_name, last_name, email, password, registration_date) VALUES
    -> ('John', 'Lennon', 'john@beatles.com', SHA('Happin3ss'), NOW()),
    -> ('Paul', 'McCartney', 'paul@beatles.com', SHA('letITbe'), NOW()),
    -> ('George', 'Harrison', 'george@beatles.com ', SHA('something'), NOW()),
    -> ('Ringo', 'Starr', 'ringo@beatles.com', SHA('thisboy'), NOW());
Query OK, 4 rows affected (0.00 sec)
Records: 4  Duplicates: 0  Warnings: 0

mysql>
```

Figure 4.10 This one query—which MySQL allows but other databases will not—inserts several records into the table at once.

INSERTING RECORDS

Selecting Data

Now that the database has some records in it, you can begin to retrieve the information with the most used of all SQL terms, SELECT. This type of query returns rows of records that match certain criteria, using the syntax

SELECT *which_columns* FROM *which_table*

The simplest SELECT query is

SELECT * FROM *tablename*

The asterisk means that you want to view every column. Your other choice would be to specify the columns to be returned, with each separated from the next by a comma.

SELECT user_id, first_name, last_name
→ FROM users

There are a few benefits to being explicit about which columns are selected. The first is performance: There's no reason to fetch columns you will not be using. The second is order: You can return columns in an order other than their layout in the table. Third— and you'll see this later in the chapter—it allows you to manipulate the values in those columns using functions.

To select data from a table:

1. Retrieve all the data from the *users* table (**Figure 4.11**).

   SELECT * FROM users;

   This very basic SQL command will retrieve every column of every row stored within that table.

```
mysql> SELECT * FROM users;
+---------+------------+-----------+----------------------------+----------------------------------+---------------------+
| user_id | first_name | last_name | email                      | password                         | registration_date   |
+---------+------------+-----------+----------------------------+----------------------------------+---------------------+
|       1 | Larry      | Ullman    | phpmysql2@DMCInsights.com  | 5baa61e4c9b93f3f0682250b6cf8331b7ee68fd8 | 2005-02-20 13:42:49 |
|       2 | John       | Lennon    | john@beatles.com           | 2a50435b0f512f60988db719106a258fb7e338ff | 2005-02-20 13:43:34 |
|       3 | Paul       | McCartney | paul@beatles.com           | 6ae16792c502a5b47da180ce8456e5ae7d65e262 | 2005-02-20 13:43:34 |
|       4 | George     | Harrison  | george@beatles.com         | 1af17e73721dbe0c40011b82ed4bb1a7dbe3ce29 | 2005-02-20 13:43:34 |
|       5 | Ringo      | Starr     | ringo@beatles.com          | 520f73691bcf89d508d923a2dbc8e6fa58efb522 | 2005-02-20 13:43:34 |
|       6 | David      | Jones     | davey@monkees.com          | ec23244e40137ef72763267f17ed6c7ebb2b019f | 2005-02-20 13:56:39 |
|       7 | Peter      | Tork      | peter@monkees.com          | b8f6bc0c646f68ec6f27653f8473ae4ae81fd302 | 2005-02-20 13:56:39 |
|       8 | Micky      | Dolenz    | micky@monkees.com          | 0599b6e3c9206ef135c83a921294ba6417dbc673 | 2005-02-20 13:56:39 |
|       9 | Mike       | Nesmith   | mike@monkees.com           | 804a1773e9985abeb1f2605e0cc22211cc58cb1b | 2005-02-20 13:56:39 |
|      10 | David      | Sedaris   | david@authors.com          | f54e748ae9624210402eeb2c15a9f506a110ef72 | 2005-02-20 13:56:39 |
|      11 | Nick       | Hornby    | nick@authors.com           | 815f12d7b9d7cd690d4781015c2a0a5b3ae207c0 | 2005-02-20 13:56:39 |
|      12 | Melissa    | Bank      | melissa@authors.com        | 15ac6793642add347cbf24b8884b97947f637091 | 2005-02-20 13:56:39 |
|      13 | Toni       | Morrison  | toni@authors.com           | ce3a79105879624f762c01ecb8abee7b31e67df5 | 2005-02-20 13:56:39 |
|      14 | Jonathan   | Franzen   | jonathan@authors.com       | c969581a0a7d6f790f4b520225f34fd90a09c86f | 2005-02-20 13:56:39 |
|      15 | Don        | DeLillo   | don@authors.com            | 01a3ff9a11b328afd3e5affcba4cc9e539c4c455 | 2005-02-20 13:56:39 |
|      16 | Graham     | Greene    | graham@authors.com         | 7c16ec1fcbc8c3ec99790f25c310ef63febb1bb3 | 2005-02-20 13:56:39 |
|      17 | Michael    | Chabon    | michael@authors.com        | bd58cc413f97c33930778416a6dbd2d67720dc41 | 2005-02-20 13:56:39 |
|      18 | Richard    | Brautigan | richard@authors.com        | b1f8414005c218fb53b661f17b4f671bccecea3d | 2005-02-20 13:56:39 |
|      19 | Russell    | Banks     | russell@authors.com        | 6bc4056557e33f1e209870ab578ed362f8b3c1b8 | 2005-02-20 13:56:39 |
|      20 | Homer      | Simpson   | homer@simpson.com          | 54a0b2dcbc5a944907d29304405f0552344b3847 | 2005-02-20 13:56:39 |
|      21 | Marge      | Simpson   | marge@simpson.com          | cea9be7b57e183dea0e4cf000489fe073908c0ca | 2005-02-20 13:56:39 |
|      22 | Bart       | Simpson   | bart@simpson.com           | 73265774abd1028ed8ef06afc5fa0f9a7ccbb6aa | 2005-02-20 13:56:39 |
|      23 | Lisa       | Simpson   | lisa@simpson.com           | a09bb16971ec0759dffff75c088f004e205c9e27b | 2005-02-20 13:56:39 |
|      24 | Maggie     | Simpson   | maggie@simpson.com         | 0e87350b393ceced1d4751b828d18102be123edb | 2005-02-20 13:56:39 |
|      25 | Abe        | Simpson   | abe@simpson.com            | 6591827c8e3d4624e8fc1ee324f31fa389fdafb4 | 2005-02-20 13:56:39 |
+---------+------------+-----------+----------------------------+----------------------------------+---------------------+
25 rows in set (0.08 sec)

mysql>
```

Figure 4.11 The SELECT * FROM *tablename* query returns every column for every record.

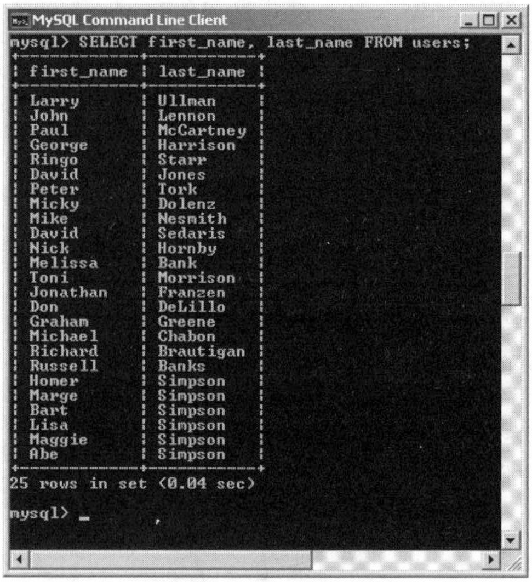

```
MySQL Command Line Client
mysql> SELECT first_name, last_name FROM users;
+------------+-----------+
| first_name | last_name |
+------------+-----------+
| Larry      | Ullman    |
| John       | Lennon    |
| Paul       | McCartney |
| George     | Harrison  |
| Ringo      | Starr     |
| David      | Jones     |
| Peter      | Tork      |
| Micky      | Dolenz    |
| Mike       | Nesmith   |
| David      | Sedaris   |
| Nick       | Hornby    |
| Melissa    | Bank      |
| Toni       | Morrison  |
| Jonathan   | Franzen   |
| Don        | DeLillo   |
| Graham     | Greene    |
| Michael    | Chabon    |
| Richard    | Brautigan |
| Russell    | Banks     |
| Homer      | Simpson   |
| Marge      | Simpson   |
| Bart       | Simpson   |
| Lisa       | Simpson   |
| Maggie     | Simpson   |
| Abe        | Simpson   |
+------------+-----------+
25 rows in set (0.04 sec)

mysql> _
```

Figure 4.12 All of the records but only two of the columns are returned by this query.

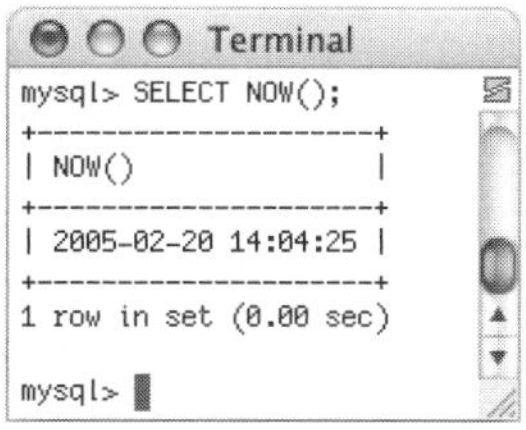

```
Terminal
mysql> SELECT NOW();
+---------------------+
| NOW()               |
+---------------------+
| 2005-02-20 14:04:25 |
+---------------------+
1 row in set (0.00 sec)

mysql>
```

Figure 4.13 Many queries can be run without specifying a database or table. This query returns the current date and time, according to MySQL.

2. Retrieve just the first and last names from *users* (**Figure 4.12**).

   ```
   SELECT first_name, last_name FROM
   → users;
   ```

   Instead of showing the data from every field in the *users* table, you can use the SELECT statement to limit yourself to only the pertinent information.

✔ Tips

- Strange as it may sound, you can actually use SELECT without naming tables or columns. For example, SELECT NOW(); (**Figure 4.13**).
- The order in which you list columns in your SELECT statement (assuming you are not retrieving everything) dictates the order in which the values are presented (compare Figure 4.12 with **Figure 4.14**).
- With SELECT, you can even retrieve the same column multiple times, a feature that enables you to manipulate the column's data in many different ways.

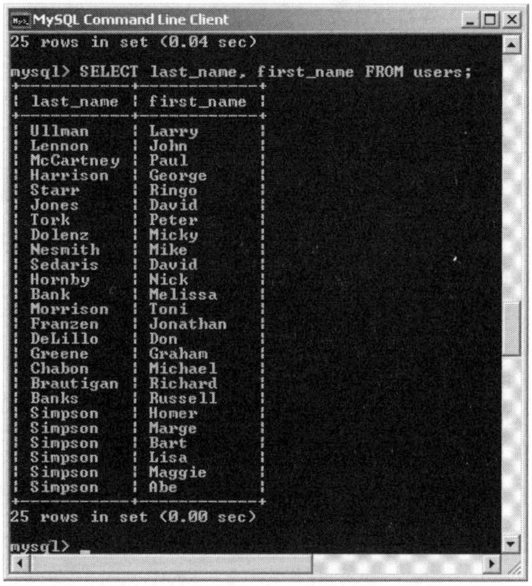

```
MySQL Command Line Client
25 rows in set (0.04 sec)

mysql> SELECT last_name, first_name FROM users;
+-----------+------------+
| last_name | first_name |
+-----------+------------+
| Ullman    | Larry      |
| Lennon    | John       |
| McCartney | Paul       |
| Harrison  | George     |
| Starr     | Ringo      |
| Jones     | David      |
| Tork      | Peter      |
| Dolenz    | Micky      |
| Nesmith   | Mike       |
| Sedaris   | David      |
| Hornby    | Nick       |
| Bank      | Melissa    |
| Morrison  | Toni       |
| Franzen   | Jonathan   |
| DeLillo   | Don        |
| Greene    | Graham     |
| Chabon    | Michael    |
| Brautigan | Richard    |
| Banks     | Russell    |
| Simpson   | Homer      |
| Simpson   | Marge      |
| Simpson   | Bart       |
| Simpson   | Lisa       |
| Simpson   | Maggie     |
| Simpson   | Abe        |
+-----------+------------+
25 rows in set (0.00 sec)

mysql> _
```

Figure 4.14 Columns will be displayed by MySQL in the order dictated by your query when you specify them.

Using Conditionals

The problem with the SELECT statement as I have used it thus far is that it will automatically retrieve every record. While this isn't a big issue when dealing with a few rows of information, it will greatly hinder the performance of your database as the number of records grows. To improve the efficiency of your SELECT statements, you can use different conditionals in an almost limitless number of combinations. These conditionals use the SQL term WHERE and are written much as you'd write a conditional in PHP.

```
SELECT * FROM tablename WHERE columnname
→ = 'value'
```

```
SELECT email FROM users WHERE last_name
→ = 'Lennon'
```

```
SELECT name FROM people WHERE birth_date
→ = '2005-01-26'
```

Table 4.7 lists the most common operators you would use within a WHERE conditional. These operators can be used together, along with parentheses, to create more complex expressions.

```
SELECT * FROM users WHERE (user_id >= 10)
→ AND (user_id <= 20)
```

```
SELECT * FROM users WHERE (last_name =
→ 'Bank') OR (last_name = 'Banks')
```

To demonstrate using conditionals, I'll retrieve more specific data from the *sitename* database. The examples that follow will be just a few of the possibilities. Over the course of this chapter and the entire book you will see any number of variants on SELECT conditionals.

MySQL Operators

Operator	Meaning
=	equals
<	less than
>	greater than
<=	less than or equal to
>=	greater than or equal to
!=	not equal to
IS NOT NULL	has a value
IS NULL	does not have a value
BETWEEN	within a range
NOT BETWEEN	outside of a range
OR (also ||)	where one of two conditionals is true
AND (also &&)	where both conditionals are true
NOT (also !)	where the condition is not true

Table 4.7 These MySQL operators are frequently (but not exclusively) used with WHERE expressions.

To use conditionals:

1. Select the records for every user registered on a specific date (**Figure 4.15**).

   ```
   SELECT * FROM users WHERE
   → (registration_date > '2005-02-23
   → 00:00:00') AND (registration_date
   → < '2005-02-24 00:00:00');
   ```

   To get the users who registered on February 23, 2005, I select those whose registration date is greater than midnight on that day and less than midnight on the following day (I could have also used the BETWEEN operator). If the *registration_date* was of type DATE (meaning of the form *YYYY-MM-DD*), I could use an equals here (registration_date = '2005-02-23').

2. Select all the first names of users whose last name is *Simpson* (**Figure 4.16**).

   ```
   SELECT first_name FROM users WHERE
   → last_name = 'Simpson';
   ```

   Here I'm just returning one field (*first_name*) for each row. The returned records themselves are determined by the value of another field (*last_name*).

   continues on next page

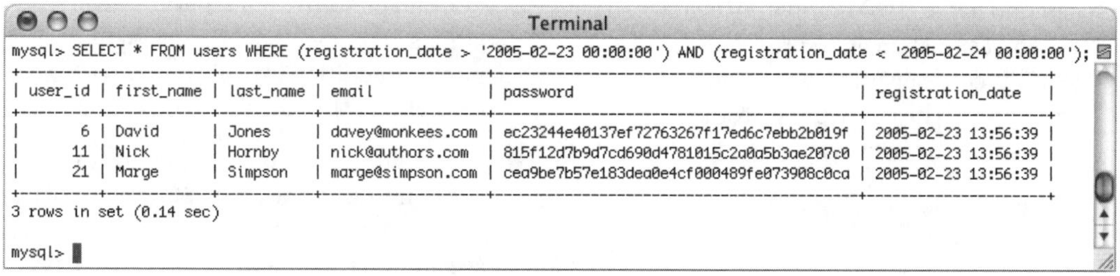

Figure 4.15 Using WHERE with two statements and the AND allows me to pinpoint which records are returned.

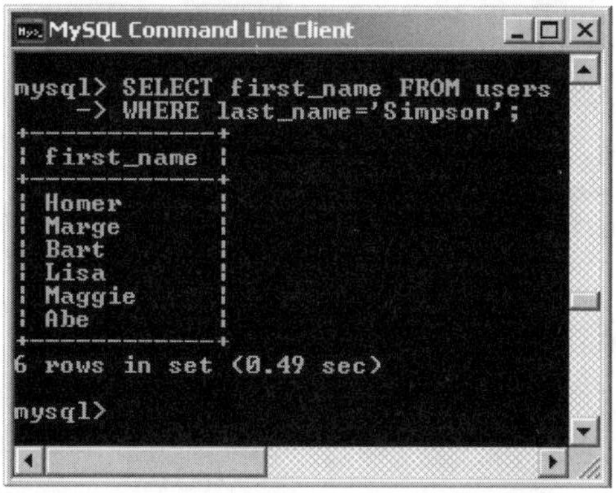

Figure 4.16 All of the Simpsons who have registered.

3. Select everything from every record in the *users* table that does not have an email address (**Figure 4.17**).

```
SELECT * FROM users WHERE email IS
→ NULL;
```

The IS NULL conditional is the same as saying *does not have a value*. Keep in mind that an empty string is the same thing as a value, in NULL terms, and therefore would not match this condition. Such a case would, however, match

```
SELECT * FROM users WHERE email='';
```

4. Select the record in which the password is *password* (**Figure 4.18**).

```
SELECT * FROM users WHERE password=
→ SHA('password');
```

Since the stored passwords were encrypted with the SHA() function, you can find a match by comparing the stored version against an encrypted version. SHA() is case-sensitive, so this query will work only if the passwords (stored vs. queried) match exactly.

✔ Tips

■ Strange as it may seem, you do not have to select a column on which you are performing a WHERE.

```
SELECT user_id FROM users WHERE
→ first_name = 'Brent'
```

The reason for this is that the columns listed after SELECT indicate only what fields to return and the columns listed in a WHERE indicate which records to use as a basis for retrieval.

■ You can also use the IN and NOT IN operators to determine if a column's value is or is not one of a listed set of values.

```
SELECT * FROM people WHERE
→ birth_date IN ('2005-01-24',
→ '2004-04-26', '2004-04-28')
```

■ You can perform mathematical calculations within your queries using the numeric addition (+), subtraction (-), multiplication (*), and division (/) characters.

■ Although the previous demonstrations use conditionals with SELECT, they will be used with many types of queries, as you'll see later in this chapter.

Figure 4.17 No records are returned by this query because email cannot have a NULL value. So this query did work; it just had no matching records.

```
mysql> SELECT * FROM users WHERE password= SHA('password');
+---------+------------+-----------+-------------------------+------------------------------------------+---------------------+
| user_id | first_name | last_name | email                   | password                                 | registration_date   |
+---------+------------+-----------+-------------------------+------------------------------------------+---------------------+
|       1 | Larry      | Ullman    | phpmysql2@DMCInsights.com | 5baa61e4c9b93f3f0682250b6cf8331b7ee68fd8 | 2005-02-20 13:42:49 |
+---------+------------+-----------+-------------------------+------------------------------------------+---------------------+
1 row in set (0.02 sec)

mysql>
```

Figure 4.18 Use the same encryption function again (SHA()) to check against encrypted, stored values.

Using LIKE and NOT LIKE

Using numbers, dates, and NULLs in conditionals is a straightforward process, but strings can be trickier. You can check for string equality with a query such as

```
SELECT * FROM users WHERE last_name = 'Bluth'
```

However, comparing strings in a more liberal manner requires extra operators and characters. If, for example, you wanted to match a person's last name that could be *Smith* or *Smiths* or *Smithson*, you would need a more flexible conditional. This is where the LIKE and NOT LIKE terms come in. These are used—primarily with strings—in conjunction with two wildcard characters: the underscore (_), which matches a single character, and the percentage sign (%), which matches zero or more characters. In the last-name example, the query I would write would be

```
SELECT * FROM users WHERE last_name LIKE
→ 'Smith%'
```

This query will return all rows whose *last_name* value begins with *Smith*. Because it's a case-insensitive search by default, it would also apply to names that begin with *smith*.

To use LIKE:

1. Select all of the records in which the last name starts with *Bank* (**Figure 4.19**).

   ```
   SELECT * FROM users WHERE last_name
   → LIKE 'Bank%';
   ```

continues on next page

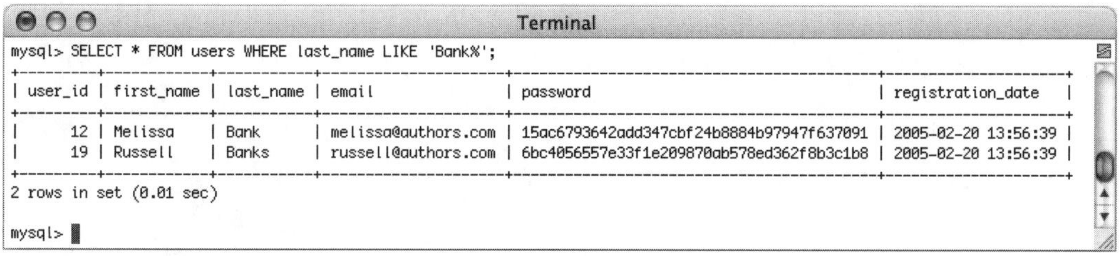

Figure 4.19 The LIKE SQL term adds flexibility to your conditionals.

2. Select the name for every record whose email address is not of the form *something@authors.com* (**Figure 4.20**).

```
SELECT first_name, last_name
→ FROM users WHERE email NOT LIKE
→ '%@authors.com';
```

If I want to rule out certain possibilities, I can use NOT LIKE with the wildcard.

✔ Tips

- Queries with a LIKE conditional are generally slower because they can't take advantage of indexes, so use this format sparingly.

- The wildcard characters can be used at the front and/or back of a string in your queries.

```
SELECT * FROM users WHERE user_name
→ = '_smith%'
```

- Although LIKE and NOT LIKE are normally used with strings, they can also be applied to numeric columns.

- To use either the literal underscore or the percentage sign in a LIKE or NOT LIKE query, you will need to escape it (by preceding the character with a backslash) so that it is not confused with a wildcard.

- The underscore can be used in combination with itself; as an example, LIKE '__' would find any two-letter combination.

- In the next chapter you'll learn about FULLTEXT searches, which are often better than LIKE searches.

Figure 4.20 A NOT LIKE conditional returns records based upon what a value *isn't*.

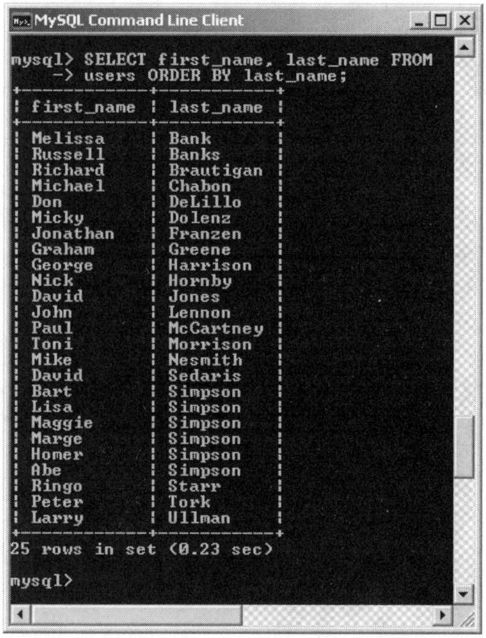

Figure 4.21 The records in alphabetical order by last name.

Sorting Query Results

Whereas the WHERE conditional places restrictions on what records are returned, the ORDER BY clause will affect how those records are presented. Much as listing the columns of a table arranges the returned order (compare Figures 4.12 and 4.14), ORDER BY structures the entire list. When you do not dictate the order of the returned data, it will be presented to you in somewhat unpredictable ways (although probably on the primary key in ascending order).

SELECT * FROM *tablename* ORDER BY *column*

SELECT email FROM users ORDER BY
→ registration_date

The default order when using ORDER BY is ascending (abbreviated ASC), meaning that numbers increase from small to large and dates go from older to most recent. You can reverse this order by specifying DESC.

SELECT email FROM users ORDER BY
→ registration_date DESC

You can even order the returned values by multiple columns, as I'll show in the following example.

To sort data:

1. Select all of the users in alphabetical order by last name (**Figure 4.21**).

   SELECT first_name, last_name FROM
   → users ORDER BY last_name;

   If you compare these results with those in Figure 4.12, you'll see the benefits of using ORDER BY.

   continues on next page

2. Display all of the users in alphabetical order by last name and then first name (**Figure 4.22**).

```
SELECT first_name, last_name FROM
→ users ORDER BY last_name ASC,
→ first_name ASC;
```

In this query, the effect would be that every row is returned, first ordered by the *last_name*, and then by *first_name* within the *last_name*s. The effect is most evident among the Simpsons.

3. Show all of the users by date registered (**Figure 4.23**).

```
SELECT * FROM users ORDER BY
→ registration_date DESC;
```

You can use an ORDER BY on any column type, including numbers and dates.

Figure 4.22 The records in alphabetical order, first by last name, and then by first name within that.

Figure 4.23 All of the users displayed by date registered, with the most recent listed first.

✔ Tips

- As part of the nature of databases, the order records are stored in a table is inconsequential. To give significance to the order records are returned in, use an ORDER BY on a column.

- Because MySQL works naturally with any number of languages, the ORDER BY will be based upon the language being used by the database (English as a default).

- If the column that you choose to sort on contains NULL values, those will appear first, both in ascending and descending order.

- You can, and frequently will, use ORDER BY with WHERE or other clauses. When doing so, place the ORDER BY after the other conditions:

```
SELECT * FROM users WHERE
→ registration_date >= '2005-03-01'
→ ORDER BY last_name ASC
```

Limiting Query Results

Another SQL term you can add to your query statement is LIMIT. Unlike WHERE, which affects which records to return, or ORDER BY, which decides how those records are sorted, LIMIT states how many records to return. It is used like so:

```
SELECT * FROM tablename LIMIT 10
```

```
SELECT * FROM tablename LIMIT 10, 20
```

In the first example, only the initial 10 records from the query will be returned. In the second, 20 records will be returned, starting with the 11th. Like arrays in PHP, the indexes in databases begin at 0 when it comes to LIMITs, so 10 is the 11th record.

You can use LIMIT with WHERE and/or ORDER BY, appending it to the end of your query.

```
SELECT * FROM users WHERE last_name =
→ 'Simpson' ORDER BY registration_date
→ DESC LIMIT 5
```

Even though LIMIT does not reduce the strain of a query on the database (since it has to assemble every record and then truncate the list), it will minimize the amount of data to handle when it comes to the mysql client or your PHP scripts. As a rule, when writing queries, there is never any reason to return columns or rows you will not use.

To limit the amount of data returned:

1. Select the last five registered users (**Figure 4.24**).

SELECT * FROM users ORDER BY
→ registration_date DESC LIMIT 5;

To return the latest of anything, I must sort the data by date, in descending order. Then, to see just the most recent five, I apply a LIMIT 5 to the query.

2. Select the second person to register (**Figure 4.25**).

SELECT * FROM users ORDER BY
→ registration_date ASC LIMIT 1, 1;

This may look strange, but it's just a good application of the information learned so far. First I order all of the records by *registration_date* ascending, so the first people to register would be returned first. Then I limit this group to start at 1 (which is the second row) and to return just one record.

✔ Tips

■ The LIMIT x, y clause is most frequently used when displaying multiple pages of query results where you would want to show the first 20 results, then the second 20, and so forth.

■ In the next chapter, you'll learn one last clause to use with your SELECT statements, GROUP BY.

■ The LIMIT term is not part of the SQL standard and is therefore (sadly) not available on all databases.

■ The LIMIT clause can be used with most types of queries, not just SELECTs.

```
mysql> SELECT * FROM users ORDER BY registration_date DESC LIMIT 5;
+---------+------------+-----------+-------------------+----------------------------------+---------------------+
| user_id | first_name | last_name | email             | password                         | registration_date   |
+---------+------------+-----------+-------------------+----------------------------------+---------------------+
|      21 | Marge      | Simpson   | marge@simpson.com | cea9be7b57e183dea0e4cf000489fe073908c0ca | 2005-02-24 13:56:39 |
|      11 | Nick       | Hornby    | nick@authors.com  | 815f12d7b9d7cd690d4781015c2a0a5b3ae207c0 | 2005-02-23 13:56:39 |
|       6 | David      | Jones     | davey@monkees.com | ec23244e40137ef72763267f17ed6c7ebb2b019f | 2005-02-23 13:56:39 |
|      25 | Abe        | Simpson   | abe@simpson.com   | 6591827c8e3d4624e8fc1ee324f31fa389fdafb4 | 2005-02-21 13:56:39 |
|      16 | Graham     | Greene    | graham@authors.com | 7c16ec1fcbc8c3ec99790f25c310ef63febb1bb3 | 2005-02-21 13:56:39 |
+---------+------------+-----------+-------------------+----------------------------------+---------------------+
5 rows in set (0.00 sec)

mysql>
```

Figure 4.24 Using the LIMIT clause, I can return a more specific number of records.

```
mysql> SELECT * FROM users ORDER BY registration_date ASC LIMIT 1, 1;
+---------+------------+-----------+------------------+----------------------------------+---------------------+
| user_id | first_name | last_name | email            | password                         | registration_date   |
+---------+------------+-----------+------------------+----------------------------------+---------------------+
|       2 | John       | Lennon    | john@beatles.com | 2a50435b0f512f60988db719106a258fb7e338ff | 2005-02-20 13:43:34 |
+---------+------------+-----------+------------------+----------------------------------+---------------------+
1 row in set (0.01 sec)

mysql>
```

Figure 4.25 With SQL, you can even return records from the middle of a group, using the LIMIT x, y format.

Figure 4.26 Before updating a record, determine which primary key to use in your WHERE clause.

Updating Data

Once your tables contain some data, you have the option of changing existing records. The most frequent reason for doing this would be if information were entered incorrectly—or in the case of user information, if data gets changed (such as a last name or email address) and that needs to be reflected in the database.

The syntax for updating records is

UPDATE *tablename* SET *column*='value'

You can alter multiple columns of one record at a single time, separating each from the next by a comma.

UPDATE *tablename* SET *column1*='value',
→ *column2*='value2'…

Normally you will want to use a WHERE clause to specify what rows to affect; otherwise, the change would be applied to every row.

UPDATE *tablename* SET *column1*='value'
→ WHERE *column2*='value2'

Updates, along with deletions, are one of the most important reasons to use a primary key. This number—which should never change—can be a reference point in WHERE clauses, even if every other field needs to be altered.

To update records:

1. Determine which record will be updated (**Figure 4.26**).

   SELECT user_id FROM users WHERE
   → first_name = 'Michael'
   → AND last_name='Chabon';

   In my example, I'll change the email for this author's record. To do so, I must first find that record's primary key, which this query accomplishes.

continues on next page

UPDATING DATA

2. Update the record (**Figure 4.27**).

```
UPDATE users SET email=
→ 'mike@authors.com' WHERE
→ user_id = 17;
```

To change the email address, I use an UPDATE query, being certain to specify to which record this should apply, using the primary key (*user_id*). MySQL will report upon the success of the query and how many rows were affected.

3. Confirm that the change was made (**Figure 4.28**).

```
SELECT * FROM users WHERE
→ user_id=17;
```

Although MySQL already indicated the update was successful (see Figure 4.27), it can't hurt to select the record again to confirm that the proper changes occurred.

✔ Tips

- Be extra certain to use a WHERE conditional whenever you use UPDATE unless you want the changes to affect every row.

- If you run an update query that doesn't actually change any values (like UPDATE users SET first_name='mike' WHERE first_name='mike'), you won't see any errors but no rows will be affected.

- To protect yourself against accidentally updating too many rows, apply a LIMIT clause to your UPDATEs.

  ```
  UPDATE users SET email=
  → 'mike@authors.com' WHERE
  → user_id = 17 LIMIT 1
  ```

- You should never have to perform an UPDATE on the primary-key column, because this value should never change. Altering a primary key in one table could destroy the integrity of a relationship with another table.

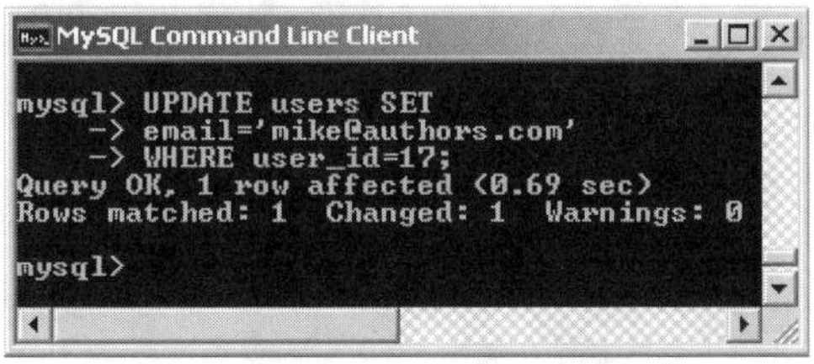

Figure 4.27 This query altered the value of one column in just one row.

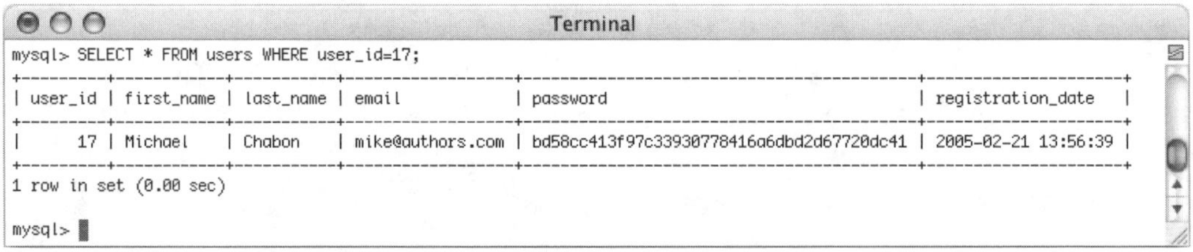

Figure 4.28 As a final step, I confirm the update by selecting the record again.

Deleting Data

Another step you can easily take on existing data is to entirely remove it from the database. To do this, you use the DELETE command.

```
DELETE FROM tablename WHERE
→ column='value'
```

Note that once you have deleted a record, there is no way of retrieving it, so you may want to back up your database before performing any deletes. Also, you should get in the habit of using WHERE when deleting data, or else you will delete all of the data in a table. The query DELETE FROM *tablename* will empty out a table, while still retaining its structure. Similarly, the command TRUNCATE TABLE *tablename* will delete an entire table (both the records and the structure) and then re-create the structure. The end result is the same, but this method is faster and safer.

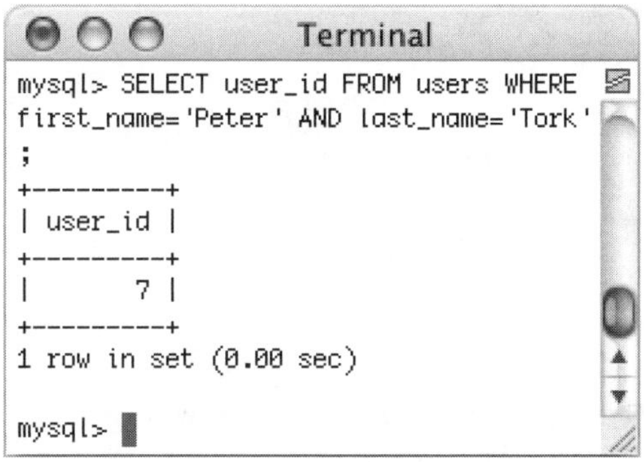

```
mysql> SELECT user_id FROM users WHERE
first_name='Peter' AND last_name='Tork'
;
+---------+
| user_id |
+---------+
|       7 |
+---------+
1 row in set (0.00 sec)

mysql>
```

Figure 4.29 The *user_id* will be used to refer to this record in my DELETE query.

To delete data:

1. Determine which record will be deleted (**Figure 4.29**).

   ```
   SELECT user_id FROM users WHERE
   → first_name='Peter' AND
   → last_name='Tork';
   ```

   Just as in the UPDATE example, I first need to determine which primary key to use for the delete.

2. Preview what will happen when the delete is made (**Figure 4.30**).

   ```
   SELECT * FROM users WHERE
   → user_id = 7;
   ```

   A really good trick for safeguarding against errant deletions is to first run the query using SELECT * instead of DELETE. The results of this query will represent which row(s) will be affected by the deletion.

continues on next page

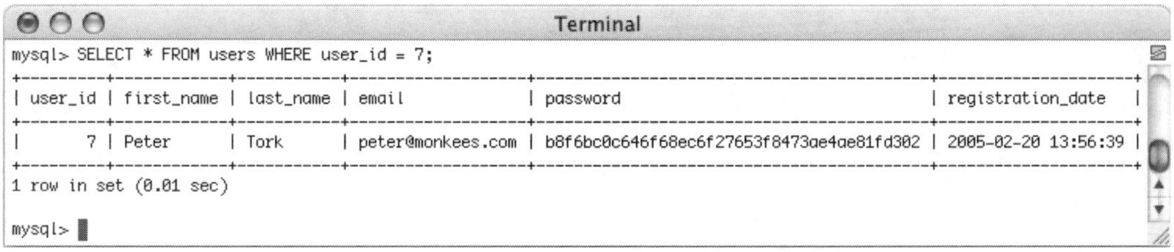

```
mysql> SELECT * FROM users WHERE user_id = 7;
+---------+------------+-----------+-------------------+------------------------------------------+---------------------+
| user_id | first_name | last_name | email             | password                                 | registration_date   |
+---------+------------+-----------+-------------------+------------------------------------------+---------------------+
|       7 | Peter      | Tork      | peter@monkees.com | b8f6bc0c646f68ec6f27653f8473ae4ae81fd302 | 2005-02-20 13:56:39 |
+---------+------------+-----------+-------------------+------------------------------------------+---------------------+
1 row in set (0.01 sec)

mysql>
```

Figure 4.30 To preview the effect of my DELETE query, I run a syntactically similar SELECT query.

3. Delete the record (**Figure 4.31**).

`DELETE FROM users WHERE user_id = 7;`

As with the update, MySQL will report on the successful execution of the query and how many rows were affected. At this point, there is no way of reinstating the deleted records unless you backed up the database beforehand (or are using transactions, see Chapter 11, "Extended Topics").

4. Confirm that the change was made (**Figure 4.32**).

`SELECT user_id, first_name,`
`→ last_name FROM users ORDER BY`
`→ user_id ASC;`

✔ Tips

■ To delete all of the data in a table, as well as the table itself, use `DROP TABLE`:

`DROP TABLE tablename`

■ To delete an entire database, including every table therein and all of its data, use

`DROP DATABASE databasename`

■ Beginning with MySQL version 4.0, you can run a `DELETE` query across multiple tables at the same time.

■ For extra security when deleting records, you can add a `LIMIT` clause (assuming you want to delete only a set number of records):

`DELETE FROM tablename WHERE id=4`
`LIMIT 1`

```
● ● ●          Terminal
mysql> DELETE FROM users WHERE user_id = 7;
Query OK, 1 row affected (0.07 sec)

mysql>
```

Figure 4.31 Deleting one record from the table.

```
● ● ●                    Terminal
mysql> SELECT user_id, first_name, last_name FROM
    users ORDER BY user_id ASC;
+---------+------------+------------+
| user_id | first_name | last_name  |
+---------+------------+------------+
|       1 | Larry      | Ullman     |
|       2 | John       | Lennon     |
|       3 | Paul       | McCartney  |
|       4 | George     | Harrison   |
|       5 | Ringo      | Starr      |
|       6 | David      | Jones      |
|       8 | Micky      | Dolenz     |
|       9 | Mike       | Nesmith    |
|      10 | David      | Sedaris    |
|      11 | Nick       | Hornby     |
|      12 | Melissa    | Bank       |
|      13 | Toni       | Morrison   |
|      14 | Jonathan   | Franzen    |
|      15 | Don        | DeLillo    |
|      16 | Graham     | Greene     |
|      17 | Michael    | Chabon     |
|      18 | Richard    | Brautigan  |
|      19 | Russell    | Banks      |
|      20 | Homer      | Simpson    |
|      21 | Marge      | Simpson    |
|      22 | Bart       | Simpson    |
|      23 | Lisa       | Simpson    |
|      24 | Maggie     | Simpson    |
|      25 | Abe        | Simpson    |
+---------+------------+------------+
24 rows in set (0.00 sec)

mysql>
```

Figure 4.32 The record whose *user_id* was 7 is no longer part of this table.

Using Functions

To wrap up this chapter, you'll learn about a number of functions that you can use in your MySQL queries. You have already seen two—NOW() and SHA()—but those are just the tip of the iceberg. Most of the functions you'll see here are used with SELECT queries to format and alter the returned data, but you may use MySQL functions in any number of different queries.

To use any function, you need to modify your query so that you specify to which column or columns the function should be applied.

```
SELECT FUNCTION(column) FROM tablename
```

To specify multiple columns, you can write a query like either of these:

◆ `SELECT *, FUNCTION(column) FROM`
    `→ tablename`

◆ `SELECT column1, FUNCTION(column2),`
    `→ column3 FROM tablename`

While the function names themselves are case-insensitive, I will continue to write them in an all-capitalized format, to help distinguish them from table and column names (as I also capitalize SQL terms). One important rule with functions is that you cannot have spaces between the function name and the opening parenthesis in MySQL, although spaces within the parentheses are acceptable.

When using functions to format returned data, you'll normally want to make uses of *aliases*, a concept discussed in the sidebar.

Aliases

An *alias* is merely a symbolic renaming of a table or column, giving you a new way to refer to something. Aliases are created using the term AS:

```
SELECT registration_date AS reg FROM
→ users WHERE user_id=2
```

Aliases are case-sensitive strings composed of numbers, letters, and the underscore but are normally kept to a very short length, allowing you to write queries more succinctly. As you'll see in the following examples, the aliases will be reflected in the headings of the returned results.

If you've defined an alias on a table or a column, the entire query must consistently use that same alias rather than the original name. For example,

```
SELECT registration_date AS reg FROM
→ users ORDER BY reg
```

Text functions

The first group of functions I will demonstrate are those meant for manipulating the various text and character columns. Most of the functions in this category are listed in **Table 4.8**.

CONCAT(), perhaps the most useful of the text functions, deserves special attention. The CONCAT() function accomplishes concatenation, for which PHP uses the period (see Chapter 1, "Introduction to PHP"). The syntax for concatenation requires you to place, within parentheses, the various values you want assembled, in order and separated by commas:

```
SELECT CONCAT(column1, column2) FROM
→ tablename
```

While you can—and normally will—apply CONCAT() to columns, you can also incorporate strings, entered within single quotation marks. To format a person's name as *Surname, First* from two columns, you would use

```
SELECT CONCAT(last_name, ', ',
→ first_name) FROM users
```

Because concatenation normally returns a new form of a column, it's an excellent time to use an alias.

```
SELECT CONCAT(last_name, ', ',
→ first_name) AS Name FROM users
```

Text Functions		
FUNCTION	**USAGE**	**PURPOSE**
CONCAT()	CONCAT(x, y, ...)	Creates a new string of the form *xy*.
LENGTH()	LENGTH(column)	Returns the length of the value stored in the column.
LEFT()	LEFT(column, x)	Returns the leftmost *x* characters from a column's value.
RIGHT()	RIGHT(column, x)	Returns the rightmost *x* characters from a column's value.
TRIM()	TRIM(column)	Trims excess spaces from the beginning and end of the stored value.
UPPER()	UPPER(column)	Capitalizes the entire stored string.
LOWER()	LOWER(column)	Turns the stored string into an all-lowercase format.
SUBSTRING()	SUBSTRING(column, start, length)	Returns *length* characters from *column* beginning with *start* (indexed from 0).

Table 4.8 MySQL's text-based functions.

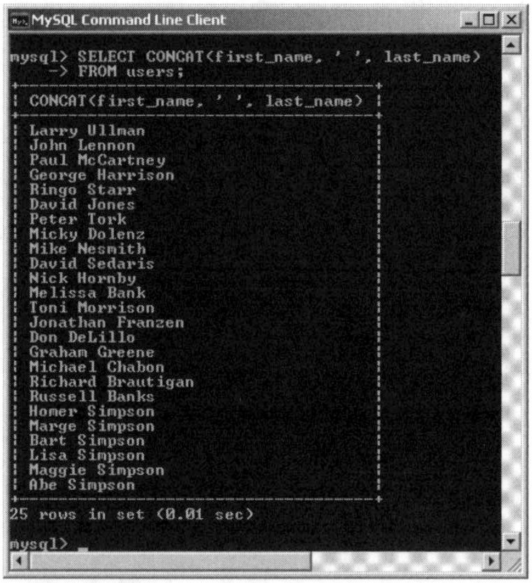

Figure 4.33 This simple concatenation pulls out the users' full names. Make a note of the column's heading.

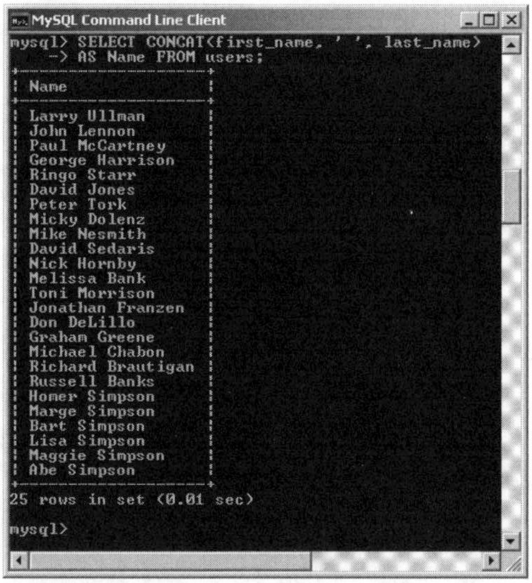

Figure 4.34 By using an alias, the returned data is under the column heading of *Name*.

To format text:

1. Concatenate the names *without* using an alias (**Figure 4.33**).

   ```
   SELECT CONCAT(last_name, ', ',
   → first_name) FROM users
   ```

   Two points are demonstrated here. First, the users' first names, last names, and a space are concatenated together to make one string. Second, as the figure shows, if you don't use an alias, the returned data's column heading is very literal and often unwieldy.

2. Concatenate the names while using an alias (**Figure 4.34**).

   ```
   SELECT CONCAT(last_name, ', ',
   → first_name) AS Name FROM users
   ```

   To use an alias, just add AS *aliasname* after the item to be renamed. The alias will be the new title for the returned data.

continues on next page

3. Find the longest last name (**Figure 4.35**).

```
SELECT LENGTH(last_name) AS L,
→ last_name FROM users ORDER BY L
→ DESC LIMIT 1;
```

This query first determines the length of each last name and calls that *L*. Then the whole list is sorted by that value from highest to lowest, and the string length and first name of the first row is returned.

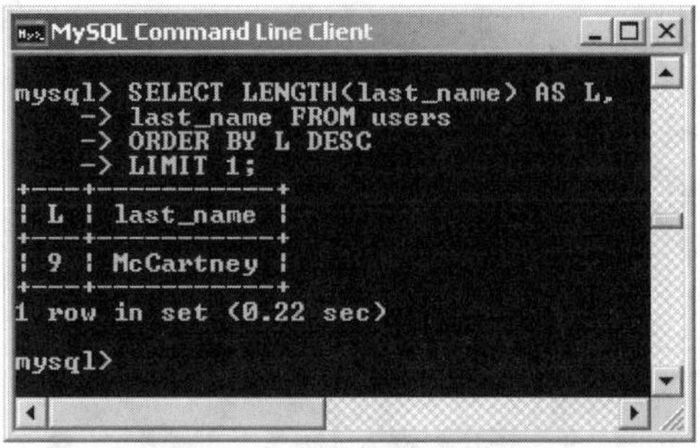

✔ Tips

- A query like that in Step 3 (also Figure 4.35) may be useful for helping to fine-tune your column lengths once your database has some records in it.

- You can use most of the MySQL functions while running queries other than SELECT. Most frequently, you might use a function to format or trim data during an INSERT.

- Functions can be equally applied to both columns and manually entered strings. For example, the following is perfectly acceptable:

```
SELECT UPPER('makemebig')
```

- CONCAT() has a corollary function called CONCAT_WS(), which stands for *with separator*. The syntax is CONCAT_ WS(*separator*, *column1*, *column2*, …). The separator will be inserted between each of the columns listed.

Figure 4.35 The LENGTH() function returns the length of a column's value.

Numeric functions

Besides the standard math operators that MySQL uses (for addition, subtraction, multiplication, and division), there are about two dozen functions dedicated to formatting and performing calculations on numeric values. **Table 4.9** lists the most common of these, some of which I will demonstrate shortly.

I want to specifically mention three of these functions: FORMAT(), ROUND(), and RAND(). The first—which is not technically number-specific—turns any number into a more conventionally formatted layout. For example, if you stored the cost of a car as *20198.20*, FORMAT(car_cost, 2) would turn that number into the more common *20,198.20*.

ROUND() will take one value, presumably from a column, and round that to a specified number of decimal places. If no decimal places are indicated, it will round the number to the nearest integer. If more decimal places are indicated than exist in the original number, the remaining spaces are padded with zeros (to the right of the decimal point).

The RAND() function, as you might infer, is used for returning random numbers.

SELECT RAND()

A further benefit to the RAND() function is that it can be used with your queries to return the results in a random order.

SELECT * FROM *tablename* ORDER BY RAND()

Numeric Functions

Function	Usage	Purpose
ABS()	ABS(x)	Returns the absolute value of *x*.
CEILING()	CEILING(x)	Returns the next-highest integer based upon the value of *x*.
FLOOR()	FLOOR(x)	Returns the integer value of *x*.
FORMAT()	FORMAT(x, y)	Returns *x* formatted as a number with *y* decimal places and commas inserted every three spaces.
MOD()	MOD(x, y)	Returns the remainder of dividing *x* by *y* (either or both can be a column).
RAND()	RAND()	Returns a random number between 0 and 1.0.
ROUND()	ROUND(x, y)	Returns the number *x* rounded to *y* decimal places.
SIGN()	SIGN(x)	Returns a value indicating whether a number is negative (–1), zero (0), or positive (+1).
SQRT()	SQRT(x)	Calculates the square root of *x*.

Table 4.9 Some of MySQL's numeric functions.

To use numeric functions:

1. Display a number, formatting the amount as dollars (**Figure 4.36**).

   ```
   SELECT CONCAT('$', FORMAT(5639.6,
   → 2)) AS cost;
   ```

   Using the FORMAT() function, as just described, with CONCAT(), you can turn any number into a currency format as you might display it in a Web page.

2. Retrieve a random email address from the table (**Figures 4.37** and **4.38**).

   ```
   SELECT email FROM users ORDER BY
   → RAND() LIMIT 1;
   ```

   In MySQL, what happens with this query is this: All of the email addresses are selected; the order they are in is shuffled (ORDER BY RAND()); and then the first one is returned. Running this same query multiple times will produce different random results. Notice that you do not specify to which column the RAND() is applied.

✔ Tips

- Along with the mathematical functions listed here, there are several trigonometric, exponential, and other types of numeric functions available.

- The MOD() function is the same as using the percent sign:

  ```
  SELECT MOD(9,2)
  ```
  ```
  SELECT 9%2
  ```

  It returns the remainder of a division (*1* in the above examples).

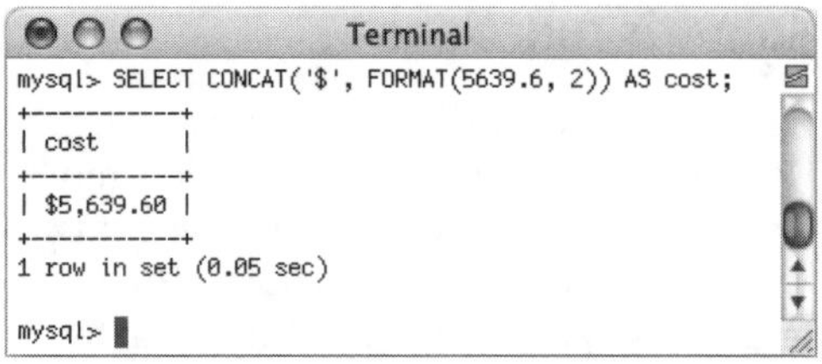

Figure 4.36 Using an arbitrary example, this query shows how the FORMAT() function works.

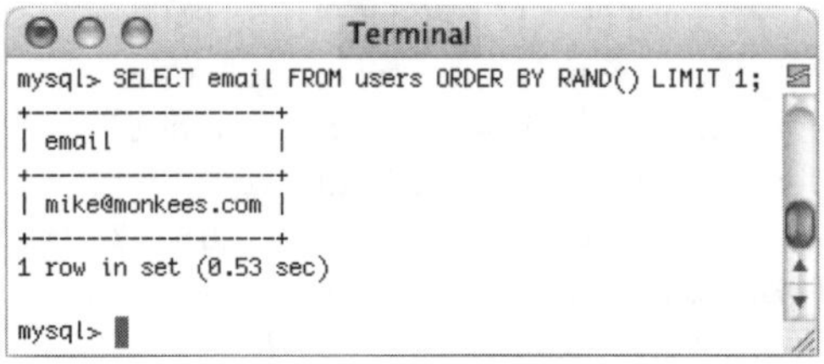

Figure 4.37 The RAND() function can be used to return a random record from the database.

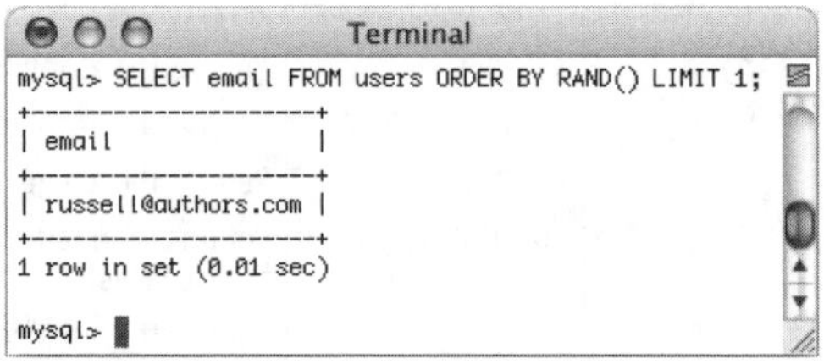

Figure 4.38 Subsequent executions of the same query (compare with Figure 4.37) return different random results.

Date and time functions

The date and time column types in MySQL are particularly flexible and utilitarian. But because many database users are not familiar with all of the available date and time functions, these options are frequently underused.

Whether you want to make calculations based upon a date or return only the month name from a stored value, MySQL has a function for that purpose. **Table 4.10** lists most of these.

As you can tell, the many date and time functions range from those returning portions of a date column to those that return the current date or time. These are all best taught by example.

Date and Time Functions

Function	Usage	Purpose
HOUR()	HOUR(column)	Returns just the hour value of a stored date.
MINUTE()	MINUTE(column)	Returns just the minute value of a stored date.
SECOND()	SECOND(column)	Returns just the second value of a stored date.
DAYNAME()	DAYNAME(column)	Returns the name of the day for a date value.
DAYOFMONTH()	DAYOFMONTH(column)	Returns just the numerical day value of a stored date.
MONTHNAME()	MONTHNAME(column)	Returns the name of the month in a date value.
MONTH()	MONTH(column)	Returns just the numerical month value of a stored date.
YEAR()	YEAR(column)	Returns just the year value of a stored date.
ADDDATE()	ADDDATE(column, INTERVAL x type)	Returns the value of x units added to *column* (see the sidebar on page 165).
SUBDATE()	SUBDATE(column, INTERVAL x type)	Returns the value of x units subtracted from *column* (see the sidebar on page 165).
CURDATE()	CURDATE()	Returns the current date.
CURTIME()	CURTIME()	Returns the current time.
NOW()	NOW()	Returns the current date and time.
UNIX_TIMESTAMP()	UNIX_TIMESTAMP(date)	Returns the number of seconds since the epoch until the current moment or until the date specified.

Table 4.10 Most of MySQL's date- and time-related functions.

To use date and time functions:

1. Display the first and last name for every user registered on the 21st of the month (**Figure 4.39**).

   ```
   SELECT first_name, last_name FROM
   → users WHERE DAY(registration_date)
   → =21;
   ```

   The `DAY()` function returns the day of the month part of a date column. So seeing if the returned result is equal to some value is an easy way to restrict what records are selected.

2. Show the current date and time, according to MySQL (**Figure 4.40**).

   ```
   SELECT CURDATE(), CURTIME();
   ```

   To show what date and time MySQL currently thinks it is, you can select the `CURDATE()` and `CURTIME()` functions, which return these values. This is another example of a query that can be run without referring to a particular table name.

✔ Tips

- The date and time returned by MySQL's date and time functions correspond to those on the server, not on the client accessing the database.
- Be careful when using the `ADDDATE()` function to include all three *D*s. It's all too easy to write `ADDATE()`, causing an error. If you continue to make this mistake, use `DATE_ADD()` instead.

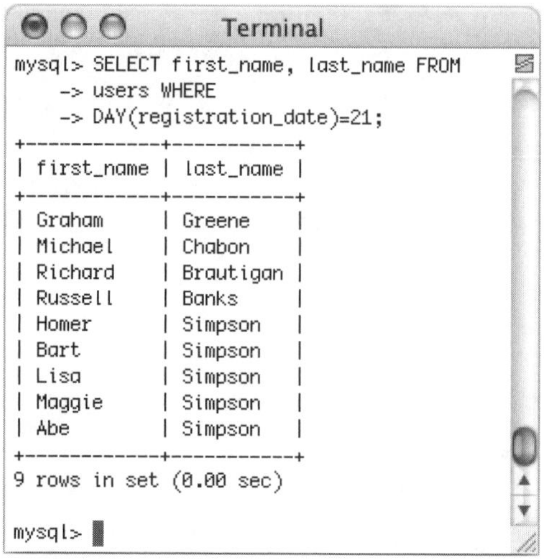

```
Terminal
mysql> SELECT first_name, last_name FROM
    -> users WHERE
    -> DAY(registration_date)=21;
+------------+-----------+
| first_name | last_name |
+------------+-----------+
| Graham     | Greene    |
| Michael    | Chabon    |
| Richard    | Brautigan |
| Russell    | Banks     |
| Homer      | Simpson   |
| Bart       | Simpson   |
| Lisa       | Simpson   |
| Maggie     | Simpson   |
| Abe        | Simpson   |
+------------+-----------+
9 rows in set (0.00 sec)

mysql>
```

Figure 4.39 The date functions can be used to format columns or limit which records are returned (as in this example).

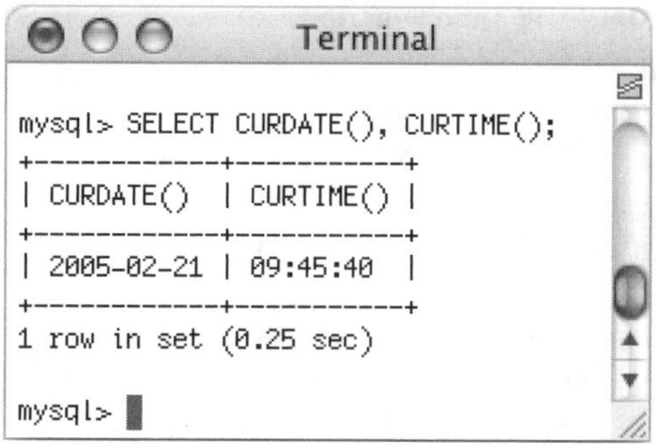

```
Terminal
mysql> SELECT CURDATE(), CURTIME();
+------------+-----------+
| CURDATE()  | CURTIME() |
+------------+-----------+
| 2005-02-21 | 09:45:40  |
+------------+-----------+
1 row in set (0.25 sec)

mysql>
```

Figure 4.40 This query, not run on any particular table, returns the current date and time.

ADDDATE() and SUBDATE()

The `ADDDATE()` and `SUBDATE()` functions, which are synonyms for `DATE_ADD()` and `DATE_SUB()`, perform calculations upon date values. The syntax for using them is

```
ADDDATE(date, INTERVAL x type)
```

In the example, *date* can be either an entered date or a value retrieved from a column. The *x* value differs, depending upon which *type* you specify. The available types are `SECOND, MINUTE, HOUR, DAY, MONTH`, and `YEAR`. There are even combinations of these: `MINUTE_SECOND, HOUR_MINUTE, DAY_HOUR`, and `YEAR_MONTH`.

To add two hours to a date, you would write

```
ADDDATE(date, INTERVAL 2 HOUR)
```

To add two weeks from December 31, 2005:

```
ADDDATE('2005-12-31', INTERVAL 14 DAY)
```

To subtract 15 months from a date:

```
SUBDATE(date, INTERVAL '1-3' YEAR_MONTH)
```

This last query tells MySQL that you want to subtract one year and three months from the value stored in the *date* column.

Formatting the date and time

There are two additional date and time functions that you might find yourself using more than all of the others combined: DATE_FORMAT() and TIME_FORMAT(). There is some overlap between the two and when you would use one or the other.

DATE_FORMAT() can be used to format both the date and time if a value contains both (e.g., *YYYY-MM-DD HH:MM:SS*). Comparatively, TIME_FORMAT() can format only the time value and must be used if only the time value is being stored (e.g. *HH:MM:SS*). The syntax is

```
SELECT DATE_FORMAT(date_column,
→ 'formatting') FROM tablename
```

The *formatting* relies upon combinations of key codes and the percent sign to indicate what values you want returned. **Table 4.11** lists the available date- and time-formatting parameters. You can use these in any combination, along with textual additions, such as punctuation, to return a date and time in a more presentable form.

Assuming that a column called *the_date* has the date and time of *2005-04-30 23:07:45* stored in it, common formatting tasks and results would be

◆ Time (11:07:45 PM)

  TIME_FORMAT(the_date, '%r')

◆ Time without seconds (11:07 PM)

  TIME_FORMAT(the_date, '%l:%i %p')

◆ Date (April 30th, 2005)

  DATE_FORMAT(the_date, '%M %D, %Y')

DATE_FORMAT() and TIME_FORMAT() Parameters

TERM	USAGE	EXAMPLE
%e	Day of the month	1-31
%d	Day of the month, two digit	01-31
%D	Day with suffix	1st-31st
%W	Weekday name	Sunday-Saturday
%a	Abbreviated weekday name	Sun-Sat
%c	Month number	1-12
%m	Month number, two digit	01-12
%M	Month name	January-December
%b	Month name, abbreviated	Jan-Dec
%Y	Year	2002
%y	Year	02
%l	Hour	1-12 (lowercase L)
%h	Hour, two digit	01-12
%k	Hour, 24-hour clock	0-23
%H	Hour, 24-hour clock, two digit	00-23
%i	Minutes	00-59
%S	Seconds	00-59
%r	Time	8:17:02 PM
%T	Time, 24-hour clock	20:17:02
%p	AM or PM	AM or PM

Table 4.11 Use these parameters with the DATE_FORMAT() and TIME_FORMAT() functions.

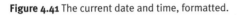

Figure 4.41 The current date and time, formatted.

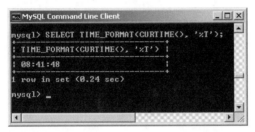

Figure 4.42 The current time, in a 24-hour format.

```
● ● ●                    Terminal
mysql> SELECT email, DATE_FORMAT(registration_date, '%a %b %e %Y')
    AS Date FROM users ORDER BY registration_date DESC;
+--------------------------+--------------+
| email                    | Date         |
+--------------------------+--------------+
| marge@simpson.com        | Thu Feb 24 2005 |
| nick@authors.com         | Wed Feb 23 2005 |
| davey@monkees.com        | Wed Feb 23 2005 |
| abe@simpson.com          | Mon Feb 21 2005 |
| graham@authors.com       | Mon Feb 21 2005 |
| mike@authors.com         | Mon Feb 21 2005 |
| richard@authors.com      | Mon Feb 21 2005 |
| russell@authors.com      | Mon Feb 21 2005 |
| homer@simpson.com        | Mon Feb 21 2005 |
| bart@simpson.com         | Mon Feb 21 2005 |
| lisa@simpson.com         | Mon Feb 21 2005 |
| maggie@simpson.com       | Mon Feb 21 2005 |
| don@authors.com          | Sun Feb 20 2005 |
| jonathan@authors.com     | Sun Feb 20 2005 |
| micky@monkees.com        | Sun Feb 20 2005 |
| mike@monkees.com         | Sun Feb 20 2005 |
| david@authors.com        | Sun Feb 20 2005 |
| melissa@authors.com      | Sun Feb 20 2005 |
| toni@authors.com         | Sun Feb 20 2005 |
| ringo@beatles.com        | Sun Feb 20 2005 |
| george@beatles.com       | Sun Feb 20 2005 |
| paul@beatles.com         | Sun Feb 20 2005 |
| john@beatles.com         | Sun Feb 20 2005 |
| phpmysql2@DMCInsights.com | Sun Feb 20 2005 |
+--------------------------+--------------+
24 rows in set (0.00 sec)

mysql>
```

Figure 4.43 The DATE_FORMAT() function is used to pre-format the registration date when selecting records from the *users* table.

To format the date and time:

1. Return the current date and time as *Month DD, YYYY - HH:MM* (**Figure 4.41**).

   SELECT DATE_FORMAT(NOW(),'%M %e,
   → %Y - %l:%i');

   Using the NOW() function, which returns the current date and time, I can practice my formatting to see what results are returned.

2. Display the current time, using 24-hour notation (**Figure 4.42**).

   SELECT TIME_FORMAT(CURTIME(),'%T');

3. Select every email address and date registered, ordered by date registered, formatting the date as *Weekday (abbreviated) Month (abbreviated) Day Year* (**Figure 4.43**).

   SELECT email, DATE_FORMAT
   → (registration_date, '%a %b %e %Y')
   → AS Date FROM users ORDER BY
   → registration_date DESC;

   This is just one more example of how you can use these formatting functions to alter the output of a SQL query.

✔ Tips

- In your Web applications, use SQL and functions to format any dates arising from the database.

- The only way to access the date or time on the client (the user's machine) is to use JavaScript. It cannot be done with PHP or MySQL.

USING FUNCTIONS

ADVANCED SQL AND MySQL

This chapter picks up where its predecessor left off, discussing more advanced SQL and MySQL topics. While the basics of both technologies will certainly get you by, it's these more complex features that will take your database-driven applications to the next level.

I'll begin by discussing database design in greater detail, using part of a content management system as an example. This naturally leads into the SQL topic of joins, an integral part of any relational database. From there I'll describe a new category of functions that are specifically used when grouping your query results.

After that discussion, the subject matter becomes more advanced, starting with indexes, how to change the structure of existing tables, and what the available MySQL table types are. Then, a newer MySQL feature is covered: performing full text searches. The final topic in the chapter teaches how to optimize your tables and SQL queries. (In Chapter 11, "Extended Topics," two other new and advanced MySQL concepts will be discussed.)

Database Design

Whenever you are working with a relational database management system such as MySQL, the first step in creating and using a database is to establish the database's structure (also called the database *schema*). Database design, aka *data modeling*, is crucial for successful long-term management of your information. Using a process called *normalization*, you carefully eliminate redundancies and other problems that will undermine the integrity of your database.

The techniques you will learn in this chapter will help to ensure the viability, performance, and reliability of your databases. The specific example I will start with—a content management system for storing Web links—will be more explicitly used in Chapter 12, "Example—Content Management," but the principles of normalization apply to any database application you might create.

Normalization

Normalization was developed by an IBM researcher named E.F. Codd in the early 1970s (he also invented the relational database). A relational database is merely a collection of data, organized in a particular manner, and Dr. Codd created a series of rules called *normal forms* that help define that organization. In this chapter I will discuss the first three of the normal forms, which are sufficient for most database designs.

Before you begin normalizing your database, you must define the role of the application being developed. Whether it means that you thoroughly discuss the subject with a client or figure it out for yourself, understanding how the information will be accessed dictates the modeling. Thus, this process will require paper and pen rather than the MySQL software itself (although database design is applicable to any relational database, not just MySQL).

In my example I want to store Web links (URLs). I have listed a sample row of data in **Table 5.1**.

✔ Tips

- One of the best ways to determine what information should be stored in a database is to think about what questions will be asked of the database and what data would be included in the answers.

- The example in Chapter 4, "Introduction to SQL and MySQL," used only a single table and did not require more advanced normalization.

Sample Content Data	
ITEM	**EXAMPLE**
URL	www.php.net
Title	PHP: Hypertext Preprocessor
Description	The home page of ...
Categories	General PHP, Programming, Web Development
Date Submitted	5/15/2005
Approved	Yes

Table 5.1 A record for the kind of information I want to store in my database.

DATABASE DESIGN

Keys

As briefly mentioned in the previous chapter, keys are pieces of data that help to identify a row of information in a table. There are two types of keys you will deal with: *primary* and *foreign*. A primary key is a unique identifier that has to abide by certain rules. They must

◆ Always have a value (they cannot be NULL)

◆ Have a value that remains the same (never changes)

◆ Have a unique value for each record in the table

The best real-world example of a primary key is the U.S. Social Security number: each individual has a unique Social Security number, and that number never changes. Just as the Social Security number is an artificial construct used to identify people, you'll frequently find creating an arbitrary primary key for each table to be the best design practice.

The second type of key is a foreign key. Foreign keys are the representation of the primary key from Table A in Table B. If you have a *cinema* database with a *movies* table and a *directors* table, the primary key from *directors* would be linked as a foreign key in *movies*. You'll see better how this works as the normalization process continues.

The *content* database is just a simple table as it stands (Table 5.1), but before I begin the normalization process, I'll want to ensure at least one primary key (the foreign keys will come in later steps).

To assign a primary key:

1. Look for any fields that meet the three tests for a primary key.

In this example, the only column that may fit all of the criteria is the URL itself, but strings make for lousy keys, and there is always the possibility that the same URL is submitted multiple times. Furthermore, a URL could change, violating one of the rules of primary keys.

2. If no logical primary key exists, invent one (**Table 5.2**).

Frequently, you will need to create a primary key because no good solution presents itself. In this example, I'll manufacture a *URL ID*.

Sample Content Data, Extended	
ITEM	EXAMPLE
URL ID	1
URL	www.php.net
Title	PHP: Hypertext Preprocessor
Description	The home page of ...
Categories	General PHP, Programming, Web Development
Date Submitted	5/15/2005
Approved	Yes

Table 5.2 I've added a primary key to the table as an easy way to reference the records.

✔ Tips

- As a rule of thumb, I name my primary keys using at least part of the table's name (e.g., *URL*) and the word *id*. Some database developers like to add the abbreviation *pk* to the name as well.

- MySQL allows for only one primary key per table, although you can base a primary key on multiple columns (this means the combination of those columns must be unique and never change).

- Ideally, your primary key should always be an integer, which results in better MySQL performance.

- In many database applications, the integrity of the primary key–foreign key relationship is monitored and ensured. Currently, MySQL formally implements foreign keys only when using the InnoDB table type but generally ignores their existence otherwise. Hence, foreign keys in MySQL are more of a theoretical presence than a binding one, although this should change in later versions of the software.

Relationships

When I speak of database relationships, I specifically mean how the data in one table relates to the data in another. A relationship between two tables can be *one-to-one*, *one-to-many*, or *many-to-many*.

The relationship is one-to-one if one and only one item in Table A applies to one and only one item in Table B (e.g., each U.S. citizen has only one Social Security number, and each Social Security number applies to only one U.S. citizen; no citizen can have two Social Security numbers, and no Social Security number can refer to two citizens).

A relationship is one-to-many if one item in Table A can apply to multiple items in Table B. The terms *female* and *male* will apply to many people, but each person can be only one or the other (in theory). A one-to-many relationship is the most common one between tables in normalized databases.

Finally, a relationship is many-to-many if multiple items in Table A can apply to multiple items in Table B. For example, a record album can contain songs by multiple artists, and artists can make multiple albums. You should try to avoid many-to-many relationships in your design because they lead to data redundancy and integrity problems. Instead you'll end up creating an intermediary table so that a many-to-many relationship can be broken down into two one-to-many relationships (you'll see this soon enough).

Relationships and keys work together in that a key in one table will normally relate to a field in another, as I mentioned earlier.

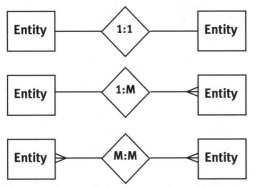

Figure 5.1 These symbols are commonly used to represent relationships in database modeling schemes.

✔ Tips

■ Database modeling uses certain conventions to represent the structure of the database, which I'll follow through a series of images in this chapter. The symbols for the three types of relationships are shown in **Figure 5.1**.

■ The process of database design results in an *ERD* (entity-relationship diagram). This graphical representation of a database uses boxes for tables, ovals for columns, and the symbols from Figure 5.1 to represent the relationships.

■ The term "relational" in RDBMS actually stems from the tables, which are technically called *relations*.

First Normal Form

As I said before, normalizing a database is the process of adjusting the database's structure according to several rules, called *forms*. Your database should adhere to each rule exactly, and the forms must be followed in order.

Every table in a database must have the following two qualities in order to be in First Normal Form (1NF):

◆ Each column must contain only one value (this is sometimes described as being *atomic* or *indivisible*).

◆ No table can have repeating columns for related data.

DATABASE DESIGN

A table containing one field for a person's entire address (street, city, state, ZIP code, country) would *not* be 1NF compliant, because it has multiple values in one column, violating the first property listed. As for the second, a *movies* table that had columns such as *actor1*, *actor2*, *actor3*, and so on would fail to be 1NF compliant because of the repeating columns all listing the exact same kind of information.

I'll begin the normalization process by checking the existing structure for 1NF compliance. Any columns that are not atomic will be broken into multiple columns. If a table has repeating similar columns, then those will be turned into their own, separate table.

To make a database 1NF compliant:

1. Identify any field that contains multiple pieces of information.

   Looking back at Table 5.2, one field is not 1NF compliant: *Categories*. The example record had three different applicable categories, although other records could have more or less.

   The *Date Submitted* field contains a day, a month, and a year, but subdividing past that level of specificity is really not warranted.

   If your table used just one column for a person's name (instead of separate first and last) or stored multiple phone numbers (mobile, home, work) in a single column, you would also want to subdivide those, too.

2. Break up any fields found in Step 1 into distinct fields (**Table 5.3**).

   To fix this problem, I'll create separate *Category1*, *Category2*... fields, each of which contains only one value.

Content Database, Atomic	
ITEM	EXAMPLE
URL ID	1
URL	www.php.net
Title	PHP: Hypertext Preprocessor
Description	The home page of ...
Category1	General PHP
Category2	Programming
Category3	Web Development
Date Submitted	5/15/2005
Approved	Yes

Table 5.3 The table with atomic columns.

Content Database: URLs

ITEM	EXAMPLE
URL ID	1
URL	www.php.net
Title	PHP: Hypertext Preprocessor
Description	The home page of ...
Date Submitted	5/15/2005
Approved	Yes

Table 5.4 The 1NF-compliant *URLs* table stores all of the pertinent URL information, aside from what categories they are associated with.

Content Database: Associated URLs

ID	URL	CATEGORY
1	www.php.net	General PHP
2	www.php.net	Programming
3	www.php.net	Web Development
4	www.mysql.com	General MySQL

Table 5.5 This table is required in order to allow each URL to be associated with multiple categories.

3. Turn any repeating column groups into their own table (**Tables 5.4** and **5.5**).

There are two problems with the table structure as it stands (having multiple category fields). First of all, there's no getting around the fact that each record will be limited to a certain number of categories. Even if you add columns *Category1* through *Category100*, there will still be that limit (of a hundred). Second, any record that doesn't have the maximum number of categories will have NULL values in those extra columns. You should generally avoid columns with NULL values in your database schema. To fix this, a new table has been created.

Notice that I've also added a primary key column to the newly created table. The idea that each table has a primary key is implicit in the First Normal Form.

4. Double-check that all new fields created in Steps 2 and 3 pass the 1NF test.

✔ Tips

■ The simplest way to think about 1NF is that this rule analyzes a table horizontally. You inspect all of the columns within a single row to guarantee specificity and avoid repetition of similar data.

■ Various resources will describe the normal forms in somewhat different ways, often with much more technical jargon. What is most important is the spirit—and end result—of the normalization process, not the technical wording of the rules.

■ If you limited each URL so that it could be associated with only a single category, then this example would be much easier. For starters, the separate *Associated URLs* table wouldn't be necessary.

Second Normal Form

For a database to be in Second Normal Form (2NF), the database must first already be in 1NF (you must normalize in order). Then you must identify any columns whose values are the same in multiple rows. Such columns must be turned into their own table and related back to the original table.

As an example, the fictional *movies* table would have the director Martin Scorsese listed twenty times. This violates the 2NF rule, so a separate *directors* table would be created and the two tables would be linked through a primary key–foreign key one-to-many relationship.

Looking at the *content* database (see Tables 5.4 and 5.5), there are two obvious problems: the *URL* value will be the same for many rows in the *Associated URLs* table (Table 5.5), and similarly, the *Category* will most likely have repetitions for different URLs. To put this database into 2NF, I'll need to separate out these columns into their own tables, where each value will be represented only once. In fact, normalization could be summarized as the process of creating more and more tables until potential redundancies have been eliminated.

To make a database 2NF compliant:

1. Identify any fields that could have repeating values.

   As I just stated, the *URL* and *Category* fields will likely have repeating values over multiple rows. The *URLs* table, as it stands, has no significant issues (although the *Approved* value will repeat as either *Yes* or *No*).

2. Create new tables accordingly (**Figure 5.2**).

   The most logical modification for the existing structure is to make a separate *Categories* table. The *URLs* table is fine as is. I do need to yank the *URL* column out of the *Associated URLs* table, as that value repeats and is already represented within *URLs* (the tables will be linked shortly).

   In my visual representation of the database, I create a box for each table, with the table name as a header and all of its columns (also called its *attributes*) underneath.

3. Assign or create new primary keys (**Figure 5.3**).

   Using the techniques described earlier in the chapter, ensure that each new table has a primary key. Here I've added a *Category ID* field to the *Categories* table to act as its primary key.

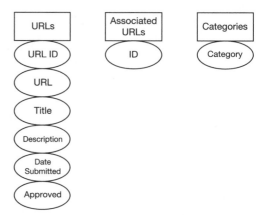

Figure 5.2 To make the database 2NF compliant, I create a third table (*Categories*).

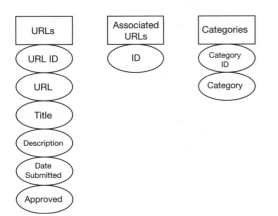

Figure 5.3 Each table should have its own primary key.

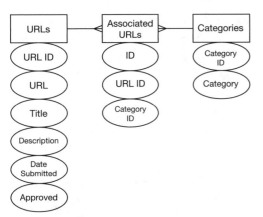

Figure 5.4 To relate the three tables, I add two foreign keys to the *Associated URLs* table, relating it to the other two tables.

- A primary key can actually be derived from multiple columns. Regardless, the rules for primary keys still count, so the combination of the column values must be unique, must not be null, and must never change. I repeat this fact because the *Associated URLs* table doesn't need its own *ID* column; *URL ID* and *Category ID* together could form the primary key. I'm leaving *ID* in as the primary key to minimize confusion.

4. Create the requisite foreign keys and indicate the relationships (**Figure 5.4**).

The final step in achieving 2NF compliance is to incorporate foreign keys to identify how all of the data and tables are associated. Remember that a primary key in one table will most likely be a foreign key in another.

With this example, the *URL ID* from the *URLs* table links to the *URL ID* column in the *Associated URLs* table. Therefore, *URLs* has a one-to-many relationship with *Associated URLs* (because each URL can be associated with many different categories).

Also, the two *Category ID* columns are linked, creating a one-to-many relationship between *Categories* and *Associated URLs* (because each category can be associated with many different URLs).

✔ Tips

- Another way to test for 2NF is to look at the relationships between tables. The ideal is to create one-to-many situations. Tables that have a many-to-many relationship may need to be restructured.

- A properly normalized database should never have duplicate rows (two or more rows in which the values in every column match) in the same table.

- As you may have surmised, the *Associated URLs* table is actually just an intermediary. It solves the problem arising from the fact that there's a many-to-many relationship between the URLs and the categories.

- To simplify how you conceive of the normalization process, remember that 1NF is a matter of inspecting a table horizontally, and 2NF is a vertical analysis (hunting for repeating values over multiple rows).

Third Normal Form

A database is in Third Normal Form (3NF) if it is in 2NF and every nonkey column is dependent upon the primary key. If you followed the normalization process properly to this point, you may not have 3NF issues. In my example (see Figure 5.4), there aren't any 3NF problems, but I'll explain a hypothetical situation where this rule would come into play.

Take, as a common example, a single table that stores the information for registered clients: first name, last name, email address, phone number, mailing address, and so on. Such a table would not be 3NF compliant because many of the columns would not be dependent upon the primary key: street would actually be dependent upon the city; city would be dependent upon the state; and the ZIP code would be an issue, too. These values are subservient to each other, not to the person whose record it is. To normalize this database, you would have to create one table for the states, another for the cities (with a foreign key linking to the states table), and another for the ZIP codes. All of these would then be linked back to the clients table.

If you feel that all that may be overkill, you are correct. To be frank, this higher level of normalization is often unnecessary. The point is that you should strive to normalize your databases but that sometimes you'll make concessions to keep things simple (see the sidebar "Overruling Normalization"). The needs of your application and the particulars of your database will help dictate just how far into the normalization process you should go.

As I said, the *content* example is fine as is, so I'll outline the 3NF steps just the same using an abbreviated version of the just-mentioned *Clients* example.

To make a database 3NF compliant:

1. Identify any fields in any tables that do not relate directly to the primary key.

   As I just stated, what you look for are columns that depend more upon each other (like city and state) than they do on the record as a whole.

   In the *content* database, this isn't an issue. Just looking at the *URL* table, each *URL* will be specific to a *URL ID*, each title will be specific to that *URL ID* (to the *URL* actually, but the *URL* and *URL ID*s are essentially the same thing, as the one is a numeric representation of the other), and so forth.

2. Create new tables accordingly (**Figure 5.5**).

   If you found any problematic columns in Step 1, like city and state, you would create a separate *Cities* and *States* tables.

3. Assign or create new primary keys (**Figure 5.6**).

   Every table must have a primary key, so I add *City ID* and *State ID* to the new tables.

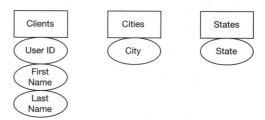

Figure 5.5 Going with an minimal version of the hypothetical *clients* database, two new tables are created for storing the city and state values.

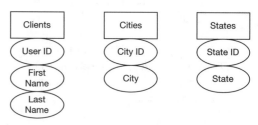

Figure 5.6 Primary keys are added to the two new tables.

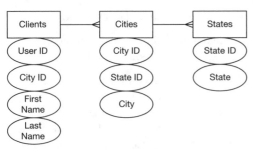

Figure 5.7 Finally, the foreign keys are added and the relationships are formally defined.

4. Create the requisite foreign keys that link any of the relationships (**Figure 5.7**).

Finally, I've added a *State ID* to the *Cities* table and a *City ID* to the *Clients* table. This effectively links each client's record to the city and state in which they live. I also indicate that there are one-to-many relationships between the three tables.

✔ Tips

■ As a general rule, I would probably not normalize this particular example— *Clients*—to this extent. If I left the city and state fields in the *Clients* table, the worst thing that would happen is that a city would change its name and this fact would need to be updated for all of the users living in that city. But this—cities changing their names—is not a common occurrence.

■ If you wanted to expand the *Clients* example, there are two ways of handling the street (e.g., *1234 Main Street*). You could store the entire value in the *Clients* table while still linking to the *Cities* table. Alternatively, you could store just the street number (*1234*) in the *Clients* table but create a separate *Streets* table, storing the street names (*Main Street*), linked to the *Cities* table. This method would be much more tedious but truer to the normalization rules.

Overruling Normalization

As much as ensuring that a database is in 3NF will help guarantee stability and endurance, you won't fully normalize every database with which you work. Before undermining the proper methods though, understand that doing so may have devastating long-term consequences.

The two primary reasons to overrule normalization are convenience and performance. Fewer tables are easier to manipulate and comprehend than more. Further, because of their more intricate nature, normalized databases will most likely be slower for updating, retrieving data from, and modifying. Normalization, in short, is a trade-off between data integrity/scalability and simplicity/speed. On the other hand, there are ways to improve your database's performance but few to remedy corrupted data that can result from poor design.

Practice and experience will teach you how best to model your database, but do try to err on the side of normalization, particularly as you are still mastering the concept.

CREATING THE DATABASE

The final step in designing your database is to identify the column types and set the column, table, and database names. While MySQL is very flexible on how you name your databases, tables, and columns, here are some good rules to go by (some of which are required):

◆ Use alphanumeric characters and the underscore to separate words (MySQL cannot use spaces or punctuation in names).

◆ Do not use an existing keyword (you shouldn't name a table or column *table* or *database* or *varchar*, and so on).

◆ Limit yourself to fewer than 64 characters.

◆ Use entirely lowercase words (this is definitely a personal preference rather than a rule).

◆ Use plural table names (to indicate multiple values stored) and singular column names.

◆ End primary and foreign key columns with *id* (or *ID*), or *pk* and *fk*.

◆ List the primary key first in a table, followed by foreign keys.

◆ Field names should be descriptive.

◆ Field names should be unique across every table, except for the keys.

These are largely recommendations and are therefore not absolute, except for limiting yourself to alphanumeric names without spaces that are fewer than 64 characters long. Some developers prefer to use capital letters to break up words (instead of underscores). Others like to indicate the column type or its table in its name. The most important consideration is that you remain consistent.

Table 5.6 shows the final database design. One alteration from the previous scheme is that I have decided to move the *Approved* and *Date Submitted* fields into the *Associated URLs* table (**Figure 5.8**). This is just a matter of personal preference, though; the database design would work either way.

As for the table names, each will begin with *url* (*urls*, *url_associations*, *url_categories*). This convention makes it clear that the tables are related, and it also means they will be listed together when viewing all of a database's tables (because they are alphabetically close to one another).

THE CONTENT DATABASE WITH TYPES

COLUMN NAME	TABLE	COLUMN TYPE
url_id	urls	SMALLINT(4) UNSIGNED NOT NULL AUTO_INCREMENT
url	urls	VARCHAR(60) NOT NULL
title	urls	VARCHAR(60) NOT NULL
description	urls	TINYTEXT NOT NULL
ua_id	url_associations	SMALLINT(4) UNSIGNED NOT NULL AUTO_INCREMENT
url_id	url_associations	SMALLINT (4) UNSIGNED NOT NULL
url_category_id	url_associations	TINYINT(3) UNSIGNED NOT NULL
date_submitted	url_associations	TIMESTAMP
approved	url_associations	CHAR(1) NOT NULL
url_category_id	url_categories	TINYINT(3) UNSIGNED NOT NULL AUTO_INCREMENT
category	url_categories	VARCHAR(20) NOT NULL

Table 5.6 THE FINAL PLAN FOR THE *content* DATABASE.

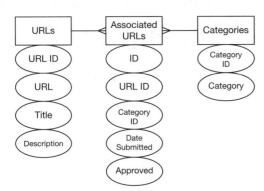

Figure 5.8 The last change in my database design is to have the *Date Submitted* and *Approved* columns be attributes of the *Associated URLs* table.

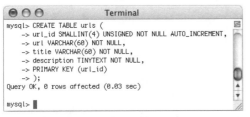

Figure 5.9 The first steps are to create and select the database.

Figure 5.10 Creating the first table.

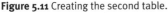

Figure 5.11 Creating the second table.

To create the database:

1. Log in to the mysql client.

As with the previous chapter, this one will also use the mysql client (or *monitor* or *command line client*) for all of its examples. You are welcome to use phpMyAdmin or other tools as the interface to MySQL.

2. Create the *content* database (**Figure 5.9**).

CREATE DATABASE content;

USE content;

Depending upon your setup, you may not be allowed to create your own databases. If not, just use your given database and add the following tables to it.

3. Create the *urls* table (**Figure 5.10**).

CREATE TABLE urls (

url_id SMALLINT(4) UNSIGNED NOT NULL
→ AUTO_INCREMENT,

url VARCHAR(60) NOT NULL,

title VARCHAR(60) NOT NULL,

description TINYTEXT NOT NULL,

PRIMARY KEY (url_id)

);

It does not matter in what order you create your tables, but I'll make the *urls* table first. Remember that you can enter your SQL queries over multiple lines for convenience.

4. Create the *url_categories* table (**Figure 5.11**).

CREATE TABLE url_categories (

url_category_id TINYINT(3) UNSIGNED
→ NOT NULL AUTO_INCREMENT,

category VARCHAR(20) NOT NULL,

PRIMARY KEY (url_category_id)

);

The primary key for this table is a bit smaller—a TINYINT(3) instead of a SMALLINT(4)—as I expect it to contain fewer records.

continues on next page

DATABASE DESIGN

5. Create the *url_associations* table (**Figure 5.12**).

```
CREATE TABLE url_associations (
ua_id SMALLINT(4) UNSIGNED NOT NULL
→ AUTO_INCREMENT,
url_id SMALLINT(4) UNSIGNED
→ NOT NULL,
url_category_id TINYINT(3) UNSIGNED
→ NOT NULL,
date_submitted TIMESTAMP,
approved CHAR(1) DEFAULT 'N'
→ NOT NULL,
PRIMARY KEY (ua_id)
);
```

For brevity sake, I'm calling the primary key just `ua_id` instead of the full `url_association_id`. Also, I'll set a default value for the `approved` column. Since it is defined as `NOT NULL`, if no `approved` value is inserted when adding a record, it will be given a value of *N*.

The `date_submitted` column will automatically be `NOT NULL` because of the unique nature of `TIMESTAMP` columns. Such columns are automatically updated to the current date and time whenever a record is inserted or updated.

6. If desired, confirm the database's structure (**Figure 5.13**).

```
SHOW TABLES;
SHOW COLUMNS FROM urls;
SHOW COLUMNS FROM url_categories;
SHOW COLUMNS FROM url_associations;
```

This step is optional because MySQL reports on the success of each query as it is entered. But it's always nice to remind yourself of a database's structure.

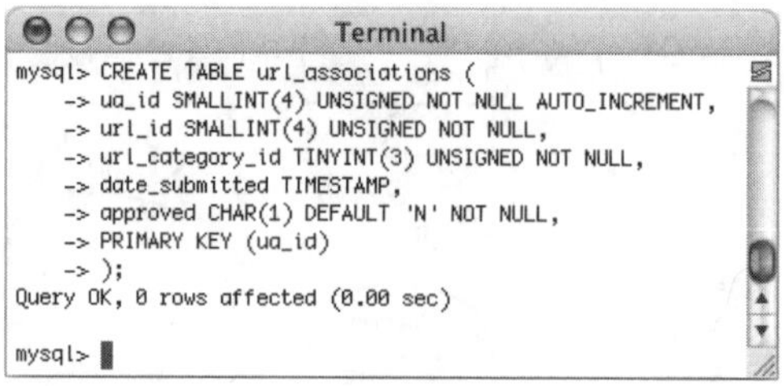

Figure 5.12 The database's third and final table.

✔ Tips

- In my tables, I set the *approved* column as a CHAR(1) so that it can be either *Y* or *N* (you could also make it a TINYINT(1), storing *1* or *0* instead). I decided to use a TIMESTAMP for the date, which can be used like DATETIME but takes up half the space.

- When you have a primary key–foreign key link (like urls_id in urls to urls_id in url_associations), both columns should be of the same type (in this case, SMALLINT(4) UNSIGNED NOT NULL).

- Once you've sketched out a database on paper, you could create a series of spreadsheets that reflect the design (or use an application specifically tailored to this end). This file can act both as a good reference to the Web developers working on the database as well as a nice thing to give over to the client when the project is completed.

- Database and table names are case-sensitive on Unix systems but insensitive under Windows. Column names are always case-insensitive.

- By strictly adhering to any set of database design principles, you minimize errors that could occur when programming a database interface, as you will in Chapter 7, "Using PHP with MySQL."

```
mysql> SHOW TABLES;
+--------------------+
| Tables_in_content  |
+--------------------+
| url_associations   |
| url_categories     |
| urls               |
+--------------------+
3 rows in set (0.00 sec)

mysql> SHOW COLUMNS FROM urls;
+-------------+--------------------+------+-----+---------+----------------+
| Field       | Type               | Null | Key | Default | Extra          |
+-------------+--------------------+------+-----+---------+----------------+
| url_id      | smallint(4) unsigned |    | PRI | NULL    | auto_increment |
| url         | varchar(60)        |      |     |         |                |
| title       | varchar(60)        |      |     |         |                |
| description | tinytext           |      |     |         |                |
+-------------+--------------------+------+-----+---------+----------------+
4 rows in set (0.01 sec)

mysql> SHOW COLUMNS FROM url_categories;
+-----------------+-------------------+------+-----+---------+----------------+
| Field           | Type              | Null | Key | Default | Extra          |
+-----------------+-------------------+------+-----+---------+----------------+
| url_category_id | tinyint(3) unsigned |    | PRI | NULL    | auto_increment |
| category        | varchar(20)       |      |     |         |                |
+-----------------+-------------------+------+-----+---------+----------------+
2 rows in set (0.01 sec)

mysql> SHOW COLUMNS FROM url_associations;
+-----------------+-------------------+------+-----+-------------------+----------------+
| Field           | Type              | Null | Key | Default           | Extra          |
+-----------------+-------------------+------+-----+-------------------+----------------+
| ua_id           | smallint(4) unsigned |    | PRI | NULL           | auto_increment |
| url_id          | smallint(4) unsigned |    |     | 0              |                |
| url_category_id | tinyint(3) unsigned |    |     | 0               |                |
| date_submitted  | timestamp         | YES  |     | CURRENT_TIMESTAMP |                |
| approved        | char(1)           |      |     | N                 |                |
+-----------------+-------------------+------+-----+-------------------+----------------+
5 rows in set (0.00 sec)

mysql>
```

Figure 5.13 You can check the structure of any database or table using SHOW.

To populate the database:

1. Add some new records to the *url_categories* table (**Figure 5.14**).

```
INSERT INTO url_categories
→ (category) VALUES ('General
→ PHP'), ('Web Development'), ('Code
→ Libraries'), ('Programming'),
→ ('General MySQL'), ('General
→ Database');
```

Since the *url_associations* table relies on values retrieved from both the *categories* and *urls* tables, I'll need to populate these first.

2. Add new records to the *urls* table (**Figure 5.15**).

```
INSERT INTO urls (url, title,
→ description) VALUES

('www.php.net', 'PHP: Hypertext
→ Preprocessor', 'The home page of
→ PHP...'),

('www.mysql.com', 'MySQL: The
→ World\'s Most Popular Open Source
→ Database', 'The home page of
→ MySQL...'),

('www.w3.org', 'World Wide Web
→ Consortium', 'The home page of the
→ W3C...'),

('www.Zend.com', 'Zend', 'The home
→ page of Zend...');
```

You can either use the examples I'm entering here or come up with your own (the SQL statements are also available for download from the book's supporting Web site). Be careful with problematic characters (like the apostrophe in the MySQL record), escaping them as needed.

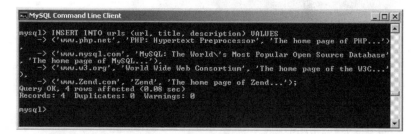

Figure 5.14 Adding records to the *url_categories* table.

Figure 5.15 Adding records to the *urls* table.

3. Add new records to the *url_associations* table (**Figure 5.16**).

```
SELECT * FROM url_categories;
SELECT url_id, title FROM urls;
INSERT INTO url_associations
(url_id, url_category_id, approved)
VALUES
(1,1,'Y'),
(1,4,'Y'),
(1,2,'Y'),
(2,5,'Y'),
(2,2,'Y'),
(3,2,'Y'),
(4,1,'Y'),
(4,3,'Y');
```

Because two of the fields in the *url_associations* table (*url_id* and *url_category_id*) relate to values in other tables, I'll select those values before inserting my records. For example, to create a new URL record for *www.PHP.net* (*url_id* of 1) under the *General PHP* category (*url_category_id* of 1), I would use

```
INSERT INTO url_associations
→ (url_id, url_category_id,
→ approved) VALUES
(1,1,'Y');
```

With your PHP scripts—once you've created an interface for this database, this process will be much easier, but it's important to comprehend the theory in SQL terms first.

You should also notice here that I'm not entering a value for the `date_submitted` field. MySQL will automatically insert the current date and time for this `TIMESTAMP` column.

4. Repeat Steps 1 through 3 to populate the database.

The rest of the examples in this chapter will use the populated database. You can use the example `INSERT`s I've defined here, create your own, or use the SQL for this chapter from the book's Web site.

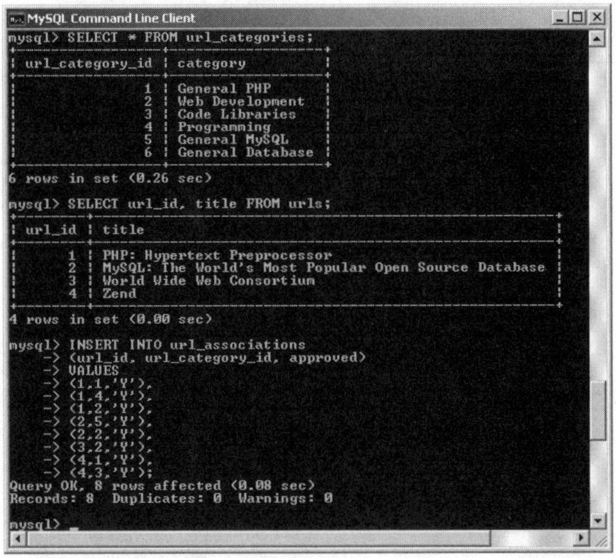

Figure 5.16 NORMALIZED DATABASES WILL OFTEN REQUIRE YOU TO KNOW VALUES FROM ONE TABLE IN ORDER TO ENTER RECORDS INTO ANOTHER.

DATABASE DESIGN

Performing Joins

Because relational databases are more complexly structured, they sometimes require special query statements to retrieve the information you need most. For example, if you wanted to know what categories the *www.php.net* URL is filed under, you would need to find its *url_id* from the *urls* table, use that to retrieve all the *url_category_id*s from the *url_associations* table, and then retrieve the actual *category* values from the *url_categories* table for those *url_category_id*s. As you can see, this requires several steps and queries. By using a *join*—an SQL query performed by cross-referencing tables—you can accomplish all of that in one fell swoop.

Several types of joins are conceivable according to SQL. Beginning to intermediate users will find that the two most basic joins, which I'll teach in this chapter, will suffice for almost every application. The most used join is called an *inner* join.

```
SELECT * FROM url_associations,
→ url_categories WHERE url_associations.
→ url_category_id = url_categories.
→ url_category_id
```

The benefit of this join is that it will retrieve all of the information from both the *url_associations* and *url_categories* tables wherever a *url_associations.url_category_id* is the same as the *url_categories.url_category_id* (**Figure 5.17**). In other words, the query will replace the *url_category_id* foreign key in the *url_associations* table with all of the information for that type from the *url_categories* table. An inner join like this will return records only where a match is made (so if a URL category were not being used by an existing URL, it would not be displayed).

```
mysql> SELECT * FROM url_associations, url_categories WHERE url_associations.url_category_id = url_categories.url_
category_id;
+-------+--------+----------------+---------------------+----------+----------------+------------------+
| ua_id | url_id | url_category_id | date_submitted      | approved | url_category_id | category         |
+-------+--------+----------------+---------------------+----------+----------------+------------------+
|     1 |      1 |              1 | 2005-03-19 16:58:55 | Y        |              1 | General PHP      |
|     2 |      1 |              4 | 2005-03-19 16:58:55 | Y        |              4 | Programming      |
|     3 |      1 |              2 | 2005-03-19 16:58:55 | Y        |              2 | Web Development  |
|     4 |      2 |              5 | 2005-03-19 16:58:55 | Y        |              5 | General MySQL    |
|     5 |      2 |              2 | 2005-03-19 16:58:55 | Y        |              2 | Web Development  |
|     6 |      3 |              2 | 2005-03-19 16:58:55 | Y        |              2 | Web Development  |
|     7 |      4 |              1 | 2005-03-19 16:58:55 | Y        |              1 | General PHP      |
|     8 |      4 |              3 | 2005-03-19 16:58:55 | Y        |              3 | Code Libraries   |
+-------+--------+----------------+---------------------+----------+----------------+------------------+
8 rows in set (0.65 sec)

mysql>
```

Figure 5.17 This join returns every column from both tables where the *url_category_id* values are equal.

When selecting from multiple tables and columns, you must use the dot syntax (*table.column*) if they have columns with the same name. This is normally the case when dealing with relational databases because a primary key from one table will have the same name as a foreign key in another. If you are not explicit when referencing your columns, you'll get an error (**Figure 5.18**).

The second type of join I'll discuss—an *outer* or *left* join—differs from an inner join in that it could return records not matched by a conditional. An example of a left join is

```
SELECT * FROM url_categories LEFT JOIN
→ url_associations ON url_associations.
→ url_category_id = url_categories.
→ url_category_id
```

Note that the comma from the inner join is replaced by the words LEFT JOIN and the word WHERE is replaced with ON. The most important consideration with left joins is which table gets named first. In this example, all of the *url_categories* records will be returned along with all of the *url_associations* information, if a match is made. If no *url_associations* match exists for a *url_categories* row, then NULL values will be returned instead (**Figure 5.19**).

If both tables in a left join have the same column name, you can simplify your query with

```
SELECT * FROM url_categories LEFT JOIN
→ url_associations USING
→ (url_category_id)
```

Because of the complicated syntax with joins, the SQL concept of an alias—introduced in the Chapter 4—will come in handy when writing them.

```
● ● ●                          Terminal
mysql> SELECT * FROM url_associations, url_categories
    -> WHERE
    -> url_category_id = url_categories.url_category_id;
ERROR 1052 (23000): Column 'url_category_id' in where clause is ambiguous
mysql> ▮
```

Figure 5.18 Generically referring to a column present in multiple tables will cause an ambiguity error.

```
● ● ●                                    Terminal
mysql> SELECT * FROM url_categories LEFT JOIN url_associations ON url_associations.url_category_id = url_categories
.url_category_id;
+-----------------+------------------+-------+--------+-----------------+---------------------+----------+
| url_category_id | category         | ua_id | url_id | url_category_id | date_submitted      | approved |
+-----------------+------------------+-------+--------+-----------------+---------------------+----------+
|               1 | General PHP      |     1 |      1 |               1 | 2005-03-19 16:58:55 | Y        |
|               1 | General PHP      |     7 |      4 |               1 | 2005-03-19 16:58:55 | Y        |
|               2 | Web Development  |     3 |      1 |               2 | 2005-03-19 16:58:55 | Y        |
|               2 | Web Development  |     5 |      2 |               2 | 2005-03-19 16:58:55 | Y        |
|               2 | Web Development  |     6 |      3 |               2 | 2005-03-19 16:58:55 | Y        |
|               3 | Code Libraries   |     8 |      4 |               3 | 2005-03-19 16:58:55 | Y        |
|               4 | Programming      |     2 |      1 |               4 | 2005-03-19 16:58:55 | Y        |
|               5 | General MySQL    |     4 |      2 |               5 | 2005-03-19 16:58:55 | Y        |
|               6 | General Database |  NULL |   NULL |            NULL |                NULL | NULL     |
+-----------------+------------------+-------+--------+-----------------+---------------------+----------+
9 rows in set (0.08 sec)

mysql> ▮
```

Figure 5.19 This left join returns more records than the comparative inner join (see Figure 5.17).

To use joins:

1. Retrieve the URL category for every record in the *url_associations* table (**Figure 5.20**).

   SELECT category FROM url_
   → associations AS ua, url_categories
   → AS uc WHERE ua.url_category_id=uc.
   → url_category_id;

   This query, which includes an inner join, will effectively replace the *url_category_id* value from the *url_associations* table with the corresponding *category* value from the *url_categories* table for each of the records in the *url_associations* table. The end result is that it displays the textual version of the category for each stored URL.

2. Retrieve the URL and the URL category for every record in the *url_associations* table, sorted by category (**Figure 5.21**).

   SELECT category, url FROM urls AS u,
   → url_categories AS uc,
   → url_associations AS ua

   WHERE ua.url_category_id=uc.
   → url_category_id

   AND u.url_id=ua.url_id

   ORDER BY uc.category ASC;

   This join has two differences from its predecessor. First, I also want to return the actual URL as well, which means that I need to join in the *urls* table. Second, I've added an ORDER BY to sort the results.

   Take note of how a three-table inner join is written (with an AND conditional) and how the aliases are used for shorthand when referring to the three tables and their columns. In simplest terms, what is returned by this query is every record from the *urls* table, with the textual version of the category replacing the *url_category_id* value and the textual version of the URL replacing the *url_id* value.

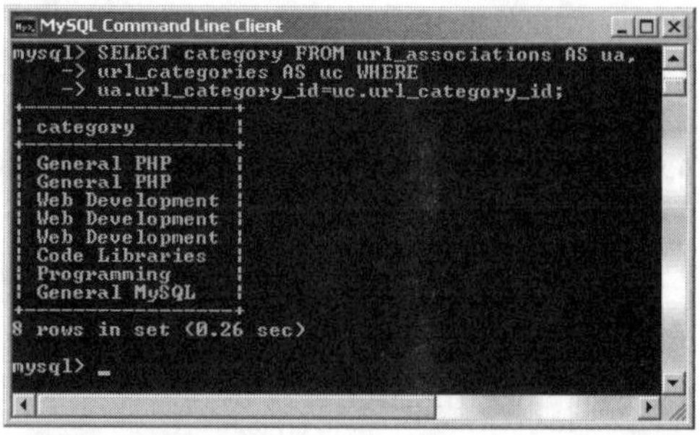

Figure 5.20 A basic inner join that returns only one column of values.

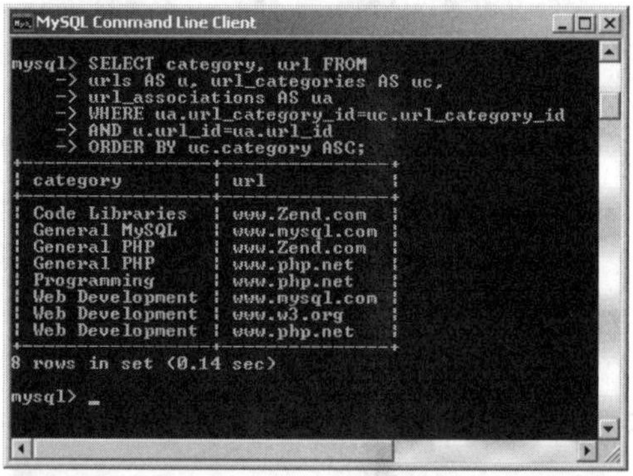

Figure 5.21 A slightly more complicated version of an inner join, using all three tables in the *content* database.

3. Retrieve the URL and the URL type for every URL type (**Figure 5.22**).

```
SELECT category, url FROM
→ url_categories LEFT JOIN
→ url_associations USING
→ (url_category_id) LEFT JOIN urls
→ USING (url_id) ORDER BY
→ url_categories.category;
```

This is a left join variant on the inner join from Step 2. Whereas that join returned only the URL and category for records in the *urls* table, this one returns all of the URLs and categories based upon the *url_categories* table. The end result is that one more record is returned here (*General Database*), and the URL, which is not matched through an inner join (no URL has been assigned this type), is given a NULL value.

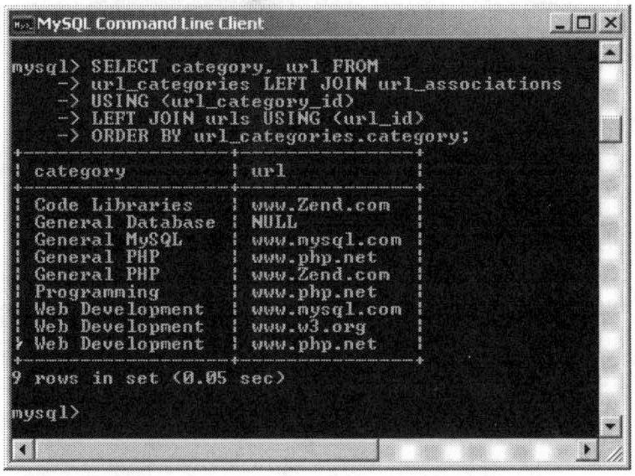

Figure 5.22 This left join returns more records than the comparative inner join (see Figure 5.21).

✔ Tips

- You can even join a table with itself (a *self-join*)!

- Joins can be created using conditionals involving any columns, not just the primary and foreign keys, as I have here.

- You can perform joins across multiple databases using the *database.table.column* syntax, as long as every database is on the same server (you cannot do this across a network).

- Joins that do not include a WHERE clause (e.g., SELECT * FROM urls, url_associations) are called *full* joins and will return every record from both tables. This construct can have unwieldy results with larger tables.

- A NULL value in a column referenced in a join will never be returned, because a NULL matches no other value, including NULL.

- Because the syntax of joins is more complicated than standard SELECT queries, successfully writing them takes some practice and experimentation. If your PHP script will be using a join, make sure it works in the mysql client (or phpMyAdmin) first.

Grouping Selected Results

In the preceding chapter, two different clauses—ORDER BY and LIMIT—were introduced as ways of affecting the returned results. The former dictates the order in which the selected rows are returned; the latter dictates which of the selected rows are actually returned. This next clause, GROUP BY, is different in that it works by grouping the returned data into similar blocks of information. For example, to group all of the URLs by category, you would use

```
SELECT * FROM url_associations, urls
→ WHERE url_associations.url_id=urls.
→ url_id GROUP BY url_category_id
```

The returned data is altered in that you've now aggregated the information instead of returned just the specific itemized records. So where you might have seven URLs of one type, the GROUP BY would return all seven of those records as one row. You will often use one of several grouping (or aggregate) functions with GROUP BY. **Table 5.7** lists these.

You can apply combinations of WHERE, ORDER BY, and LIMIT conditions to a GROUP BY, normally structuring your query like this:

```
SELECT what_columns FROM table WHERE
condition GROUP BY column ORDER BY
column LIMIT x, y
```

To group data:

1. Select all of the titles that have been submitted (**Figure 5.23**).

   ```
   SELECT url FROM urls AS u,
   url_associations AS ua WHERE
   u.url_id=ua.url_id GROUP BY u.url_id;
   ```

   This is one of many ways to achieve the desired result of returning the URLs currently in the *urls* table. Whereas these URLs have been submitted (using the earlier INSERT statements) as eight distinct records (with different categories), only four distinct URLs were used.

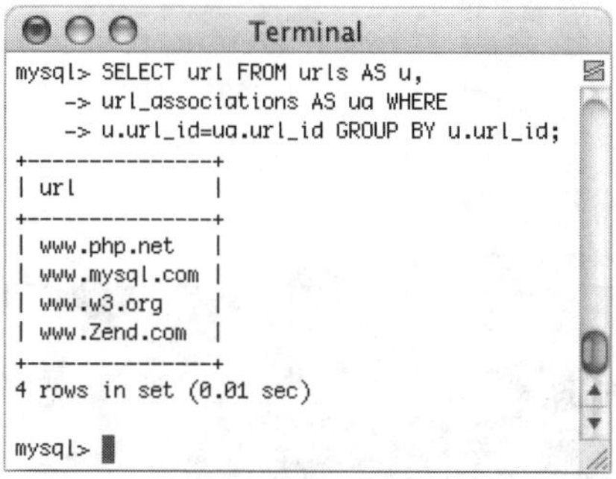

Figure 5.23 This GROUP BY query returns records grouped by URL, without using an aggregate function.

Grouping Functions

FUNCTION	USAGE	PURPOSE
AVG()	AVG(column)	Returns the average value of the column.
COUNT()	COUNT(column)	Counts the number of rows.
MAX()	MAX(column)	Returns the largest value from the column.
MIN()	MIN(column)	Returns the smallest value from the column.
SUM()	SUM(column)	Returns the sum of all the values in the column.

Table 5.7 MySQL's grouping functions.

2. Count the number of times each URL is listed (**Figure 5.24**).

```
SELECT url, COUNT(*) AS Number FROM
urls AS u, url_associations AS ua
WHERE u.url_id=ua.url_id
GROUP BY u.url_id;
```

This query is an extension of that in Step 1, adding the COUNT() function to return a number for how many times each URL has been submitted (each submission is a different type). COUNT() is normally but not necessarily applied to every column (*).

```
mysql> SELECT url, COUNT(*) AS Number FROM
    -> urls AS u, url_associations AS ua
    -> WHERE u.url_id=ua.url_id
    -> GROUP BY u.url_id;
+---------------+--------+
| url           | Number |
+---------------+--------+
| www.php.net   |      3 |
| www.mysql.com |      2 |
| www.w3.org    |      1 |
| www.Zend.com  |      2 |
+---------------+--------+
4 rows in set (0.00 sec)

mysql>
```

Figure 5.24 This GROUP BY query counts the number of times each URL is listed (in other words, how many categories each URL is associated with).

```
mysql> SELECT url, COUNT(*) AS Number FROM
    -> urls AS u, url_associations AS ua
    -> WHERE u.url_id=ua.url_id
    -> GROUP BY u.url_id
    -> ORDER BY Number DESC;
+---------------+--------+
| url           | Number |
+---------------+--------+
| www.php.net   |      3 |
| www.mysql.com |      2 |
| www.Zend.com  |      2 |
| www.w3.org    |      1 |
+---------------+--------+
4 rows in set (0.00 sec)

mysql>
```

Figure 5.25 Finally, a sort is added to organize the URLs by their number of listings.

3. Sort the URLs by the number of times they are listed (**Figure 5.25**).

```
SELECT url, COUNT(*) AS Number FROM
urls AS u, url_associations AS ua
WHERE u.url_id=ua.url_id
GROUP BY u.url_id
ORDER BY Number DESC;
```

With grouping, you can order the results as you would with any other query. Assigning the value of COUNT(*) as the alias *Number* facilitates this process.

✔ Tips

- NULL is a peculiar value and it's interesting to know that GROUP BY will group NULL values together, since they have the same nonvalue.

- The COUNT() function will count only nonnull values. Be certain to use it on either every column (*) or on columns that will not contain NULL values (like the primary key).

- The GROUP BY clause, and the functions listed here, take some time to figure out, and MySQL will report an error whenever your syntax is inapplicable. Experiment within the mysql client to determine the exact wording of any query you might want to run in an application.

- Another related clause is HAVING, which is like a WHERE condition applied to a group.

Creating Indexes

Indexes are a special system that databases use to improve the overall performance. By setting indexes on your tables, you are telling MySQL to pay particular attention to that column (loosely said). In fact, MySQL creates extra files to store and track indexes efficiently.

MySQL allows for at least 16 indexes for each table, and each index can incorporate up to 15 columns. While a multicolumn index may not seem obvious, it will come in handy for searches frequently performed on the same combinations of columns (e.g., first and last name, city and state, etc.).

On the other hand, you should not go overboard with indexing. While it does improve the speed of reading from databases, it slows down the process of altering data in a database (because the changes need to be recorded in the index). Indexes are best used on columns

◆ That are frequently used in the WHERE part of a query

◆ That are frequently used in an ORDER BY part of a query

Altering Tables

The ALTER SQL term is primarily used to modify the structure of a table in your database. Commonly this means adding, deleting, or changing the columns therein, but it also includes the addition of indexes. An ALTER statement can even be used for renaming the table as a whole. While proper database design should give you the structure you need, in the real world, making alterations is commonplace. The basic syntax of ALTER is

```
ALTER TABLE tablename CLAUSE
```

Because there are so many possible clauses, I've listed the common ones in **Table 5.8**. If you need to rename a table, you can alternatively use the RENAME TABLE syntax:

```
RENAME TABLE old_name TO new_name
```

ALTER TABLE Clauses

CLAUSE	USAGE	MEANING
ADD COLUMN	ALTER TABLE *tablename* ADD COLUMN *column_name* VARCHAR(40)	Adds a new column to the end of the table.
CHANGE COLUMN	ALTER TABLE *tablename* CHANGE COLUMN *column_name column_name* VARCHAR(60)	Allows you to change the data type and properties of a column.
DROP COLUMN	ALTER TABLE *tablename* DROP COLUMN *column_name*	Removes a column from a table, including all of its data.
ADD INDEX	ALTER TABLE *tablename* ADD INDEX indexname (*column_name*)	Adds a new index on *column_name*.
DROP INDEX	ALTER TABLE *tablename* DROP INDEX *indexname*	Removes an existing index.
RENAME AS	ALTER TABLE *tablename* RENAME AS *new_tablename*	Changes the name of a table.

Table 5.8 Common variants on the ALTER command. See the MySQL manual for the full specifications.

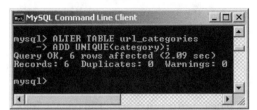

Figure 5.26 A unique index is placed on the category column. This will improve the efficiency of certain queries and protect against redundant entries.

Figure 5.27 An index has been added to the *urls* table. MySQL will report on the success of a query and how many rows were affected when using ALTER statements.

◆ That are frequently used as the focal point of a join

◆ That have many different values (columns with numerous repeating values ought not to be indexed)

MySQL has four types of indexes: INDEX (the standard), UNIQUE (which requires each row to have a unique value for that column), FULLTEXT (for performing FULLTEXT searches), and PRIMARY KEY (which is just a particular UNIQUE index and one you've already been using).

With this in mind, I'll modify my tables by adding indexes to them. To do so, I'll use the ALTER command, as described in the sidebar.

To add an index to an existing table:

1. Add an index on the *category* column in the *url_categories* table (**Figure 5.26**).

   ALTER TABLE url_categories ADD
   → UNIQUE(category);

   The *url_categories* table already has a primary key index on the *url_category_id*. Since the *category* may also be a frequently referenced field and since its value should be unique across every row, I add a UNIQUE index to the table.

2. Add an UNIQUE index on the *url* column in the *urls* table (**Figure 5.27**).

   ALTER TABLE urls ADD UNIQUE(url);

   Similar to the *url_categories* table, the *urls* table already has a primary key index on the *url_id*. The *url* may also be a frequently referenced field—as you've seen—and since its value should be unique across every row, I add a UNIQUE index to the table. Neither the *title* nor *description* fields are used in such a way that they would benefit from indexes.

continues on next page

CREATING INDEXES

3. Add indexes to the *url_associations* table (**Figure 5.28**).

```
ALTER TABLE url_associations ADD
→ INDEX (url_id), ADD INDEX
→ (url_category_id), ADD INDEX
→ (date_submitted);
```

Finally, I'll add three indexes to the *url_associations* table. First I'll want to add nonunique indexes to the foreign keys, *url_id* and *url_category_id*, since these are used in WHERE conditionals and joins. Then I'll also index the submission date, which will come up in my conditionals. The table's *ua_id* field is automatically indexed as a primary key, and the *approved* column shouldn't be indexed, since its value will never be anything but *Y* or *N*.

4. View the current structure of each table (**Figure 5.29**).

```
DESCRIBE url_categories;
DESCRIBE urls;
DESCRIBE url_associations;
```

The DESCRIBE SQL term will tell you information about a table's column names and order, column types, and index types (under *Key*). It also indicates whether or not a field can be NULL, what default value has been set (if any), and more.

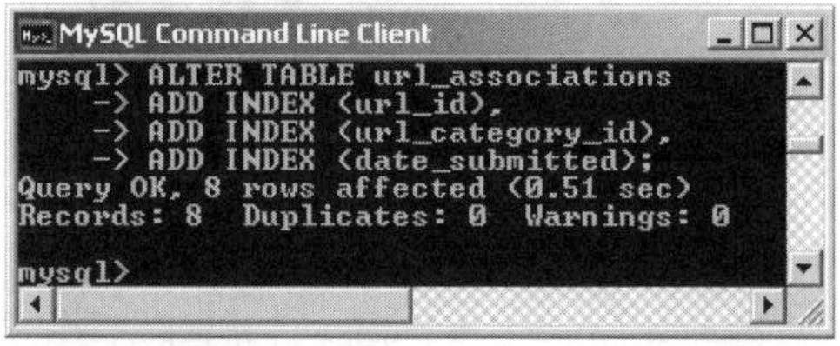

Figure 5.28 With SQL, I am allowed to add multiple indexes at once.

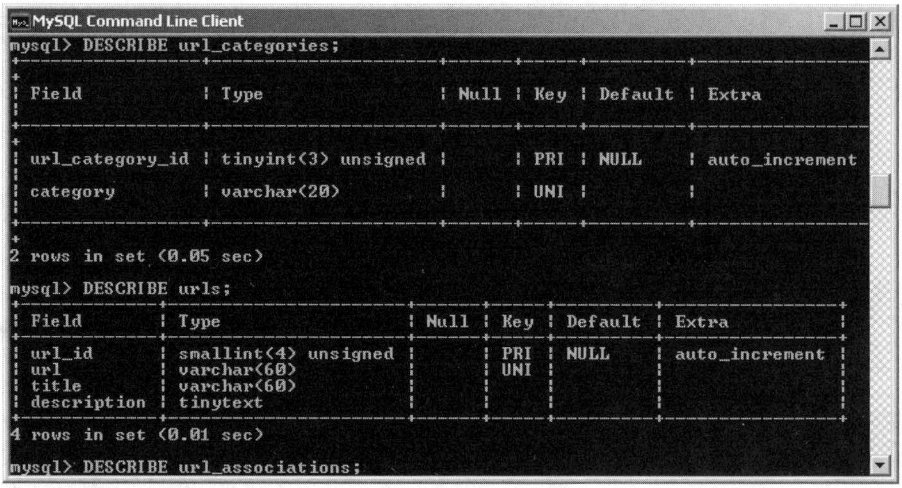

Figure 5.29 To view the details of a table's structure, use DESCRIBE.

✔ Tips

- Indexes are less efficient on variable-length columns, just as MySQL is generally slower dealing with fields that are not of a fixed length.

- Indexes can be named when they are created:
  ```
  ALTER TABLE tablename ADD INDEX
  → indexname (columnname)
  ```
  If they are not, they will take the name of the column to which they are applied.

- You can also add indexes to a table using the `CREATE INDEX` command. I prefer `ALTER`, though, as it's used for other table modifications (in other words, you'll probably need to know `ALTER` regardless).

- Because an `ALTER` command could have serious repercussions on a table, you should always back up the table before execution.

- The word `COLUMN` in most `ALTER` statements is optional.

- When adding a new column to a table, you can use the `AFTER columnname` description to indicate where in the table the new column should be placed.
  ```
  ALTER TABLE clients ADD COLUMN
  → last_name VARCHAR(25)
  → AFTER first_name
  ```

- Indexes can have set lengths, so that only a certain number of characters in a column are indexed. The following index will track only the first five characters in the `last_name` column:
  ```
  ALTER TABLE clients ADD INDEX
  → start_name (last_name(5))
  ```

- At the end of the chapter, the `EXPLAIN` command will be used to indicate when and what indexes are involved in a query.

Using Different Table Types

The MySQL database application supports several different types of tables (a table's type is also called its *storage engine*). Although each type supports a different feature set, how you interact with them—in terms of running queries—is generally consistent.

The most important table type is *MyISAM*. MyISAM tables are great for most applications, handling `SELECT`s and `INSERT`s very quickly. But the MyISAM storage engine cannot manage transactions, a feature I talk about in Chapter 11.

After MyISAM, the two most popular storage engines are *InnoDB* and *MEMORY* (which used to be called *HEAP*). InnoDB tables have been part of the default MySQL installation since version 4.0 (if you are using an earlier version, you must enable InnoDB support; see the MySQL manual). InnoDB tables can be used for transactions and perform `UPDATE`s nicely. But the InnoDB storage engine is generally slower than MyISAM and requires more disk space on the server.

The MEMORY table type is the best performer of the bunch, as such tables store all data in memory, not in files. This comes at a price, as MEMORY tables can only deal with fixed-length column types, have no support for `AUTO_INCREMENT`, and lose all data in a crash.

To specify the storage engine when you define a table, add a clause to the end of the creation statement:

```
CREATE TABLE tablename (

column1name COLUMNTYPE,

column1name COLUMNTYPE…

) ENGINE = INNODB
```

continues on next page

(Prior to MySQL 4.0.18, you have to use the word TYPE instead of ENGINE). If you don't specify a storage engine when creating tables, MySQL will use the default type. This is normally MyISAM, but it is InnoDB if you installed MySQL on Windows using the MySQL Configuration Wizard.

To change the type of an existing table—which is perfectly acceptable—use an ALTER command:

```
ALTER TABLE tablename ENGINE = MYISAM
```

Because the next example in this chapter will require a MyISAM table, I'll run through the steps necessary for setting the storage engine on the *urls* table. The first couple of steps will show you how to see the current storage engine being used (as you may not need to change the *urls* table's type).

To change a table's type:

1. Log into the mysql client and select the *contents* database.

2. View the current table information (**Figure 5.30**).

   ```
   SHOW TABLE STATUS;
   ```

   The SHOW TABLE STATUS command returns all sorts of useful information about your database's tables. The returned result will be hard to read, though, as it is a wide table displayed over multiple lines. What you're looking for is this: The first item on each row is the table's name, and the second item is the table's engine, or table type. The engine will most likely be either *MyISAM* or *InnoDB*.

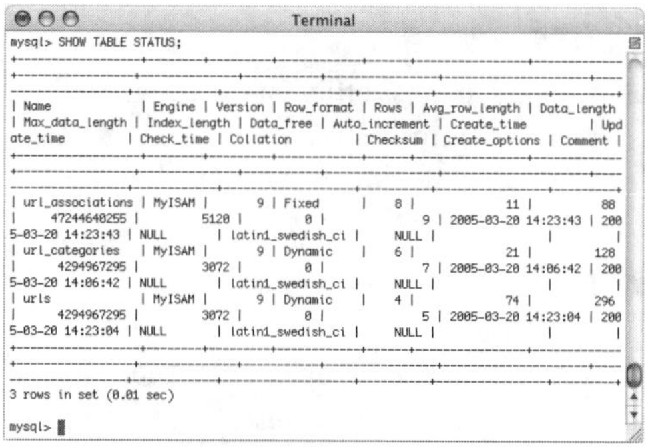

Figure 5.30 Before altering a table's type, I view its current type with the SHOW TABLES STATUS command.

MySQL Command Line Client
mysql> ALTER TABLE urls ENGINE=MYISAM;
Query OK, 4 rows affected (0.69 sec)
Records: 4 Duplicates: 0 Warnings: 0
mysql>

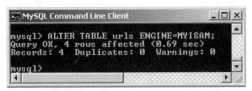

Figure 5.31 I've changed the table's type (or storage engine) using an `ALTER` command.

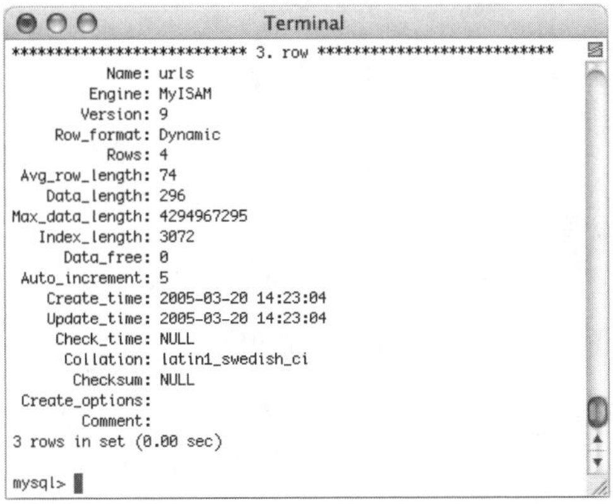

Terminal
*************************** 3. row ***************************
Name: urls
Engine: MyISAM
Version: 9
Row_format: Dynamic
Rows: 4
Avg_row_length: 74
Data_length: 296
Max_data_length: 4294967295
Index_length: 3072
Data_free: 0
Auto_increment: 5
Create_time: 2005-03-20 14:23:04
Update_time: 2005-03-20 14:23:04
Check_time: NULL
Collation: latin1_swedish_ci
Checksum: NULL
Create_options:
Comment:
3 rows in set (0.00 sec)
mysql>

Figure 5.32 For a more legible version of the query results, I've added the `\G` option in the mysql client.

3. Change the *urls* table to MyISAM, if necessary (**Figure 5.31**).

```
ALTER TABLE urls ENGINE=MYISAM;
```

If the results in Step 2 (Figure 5.30) indicate that the engine is anything other than MyISAM, you'll need to change it over to MyISAM using this command (capitalization doesn't matter). With the default MySQL installation and configuration, changing the table's type wasn't necessary on Mac OS X but was on Windows.

4. If desired, confirm the engine change by rerunning the `SHOW TABLE STATUS` command.

✔ Tips

- To make any query's results easier to view in the mysql client, you can add the `\G` parameter (**Figure 5.32**):

  ```
  SHOW TABLE STATUS \G
  ```

  This flag states that the table of results should be displayed vertically instead of horizontally. Notice that you don't need to use a terminating semicolon now, because the `\G` ends the command.

- The same database can have tables of different types. This may be true for your *contents* database now (depending upon your default table type). You may also see this with an e-commerce database that uses MyISAM for customers and products but InnoDB for orders (to allow for transactions).

- The MyISAM table type uses upward of three files for each table. There will be a ***tablename*.frm** file that has the table's definition, a ***tablename*.myd** that stores the actual data, and a ***tablename*.myi** that stores the indexes.

- There are a number of configuration options for the InnoDB storage engine. See the MySQL manual for specifics.

Performing FULLTEXT Searches

In Chapter 4, the LIKE keyword was introduced as a way to perform somewhat simple string matches like

```
SELECT * FROM users WHERE last_name
→ LIKE 'Smith%'
```

This type of conditional is effective enough but is still very limiting. For example, it would not allow you to do Google-like searches using multiple words. For those kinds of situations, you need FULLTEXT searches.

FULLTEXT searches require a FULLTEXT index, which you'll create next. Then you'll learn the special SQL syntax for performing these searches. Finally, you'll read about some capabilities added in MySQL 4.0.1 to make your FULLTEXT searches more exacting.

Creating a FULLTEXT Index

The FULLTEXT index is just a special type of index necessary to run FULLTEXT searches. You can create one on any CHAR, VARCHAR, or TEXT column in a MyISAM table.

```
CREATE TABLE comments (

comment_id INT UNSIGNED NOT NULL
→ AUTO_INCREMENT,

subject VARCHAR(100),

comment TEXT,

PRIMARY KEY (comment_id),

FULLTEXT (comment)

)
```

In this chapter's example, I'll add a FULLTEXT index to the *urls* table, on the *description* column. Since that table already exists, I'll use an ALTER command.

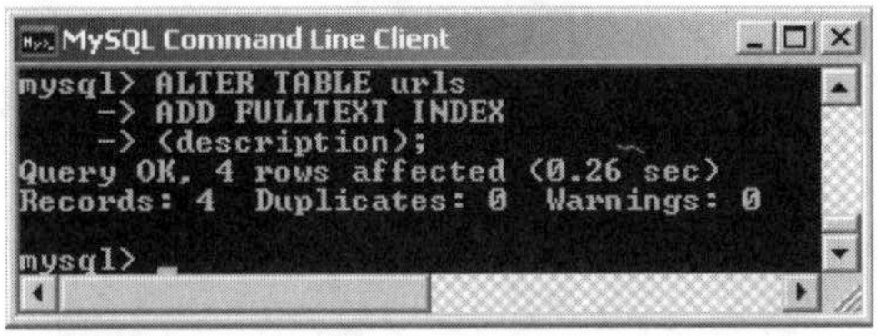

Figure 5.33 The FULLTEXT index is added to the *urls* table.

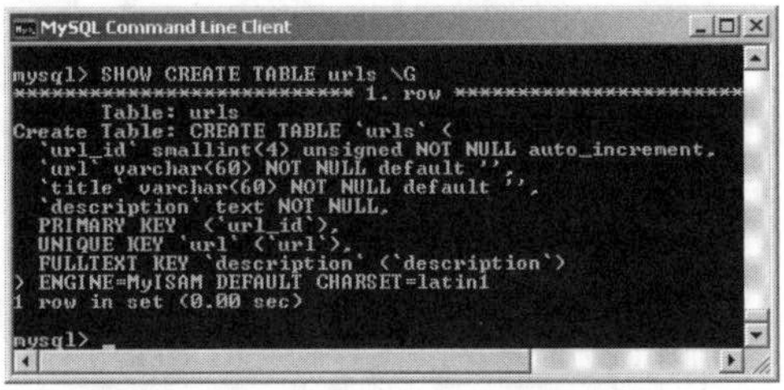

Figure 5.34 Viewing the table's creation statement reveals the FULLTEXT index, among other things.

To create a FULLTEXT index:

1. Open the mysql client and select the *contents* database.

2. Add the FULLTEXT index (**Figure 5.33**).

   ```
   ALTER TABLE urls ADD FULLTEXT INDEX
   → (description);
   ```

   This syntax is familiar to those used earlier to create standard and unique indexes.

3. Confirm the table's structure by viewing its CREATE syntax (**Figure 5.34**).

   ```
   SHOW CREATE TABLE urls \G
   ```

   You've already seen a couple of SHOW commands by now, so hopefully this one isn't too surprising. The SHOW CREATE TABLE *tablename* command asks MySQL to print out the SQL command used to create (or recreate) the named table. Using the \G trick (mentioned in a tip in the previous section) makes the results are easier to view.

✔ Tips

- Inserting records into tables with FULLTEXT indexes can be much slower because of the complex index that's required.

- You can add FULLTEXT indexes on multiple columns, if those columns will all be used in searches.

Performing Basic FULLTEXT Searches

Once you've established a FULLTEXT index on a column, you can start querying against it, using the MATCH and AGAINST functions.

```
SELECT * FROM tablename WHERE MATCH
→ (somecolumn) AGAINST ('keywords')
```

```
SELECT * FROM tablename WHERE MATCH
→ (somecolumn) AGAINST ('keyword1
→ keyword2')
```

MySQL will return matching rows in order of a mathematically-calculated relevance, just like a search engine. When doing so, certain rules apply:

◆ Strings are broken down into their individual keywords.

◆ Keywords less than four characters long are ignored.

◆ Very popular words, called *stopwords*, are ignored.

◆ If more than fifty percent of the records match the keywords, no records are returned.

This last fact is problematic to many users as they begin with FULLTEXT searches and wonder why no results are retrieved. When you have a sparsely populated table, there just won't be sufficient records for MySQL to return *relevant* results.

To perform FULLTEXT searches:

1. Thoroughly populate the *urls* table, focusing on adding lengthy, descriptive definitions.

   Once again, SQL INSERT commands can be downloaded from this book's corresponding Web site.

2. Run a simple FULLTEXT search on the word *security* (**Figure 5.35**).

   ```
   SELECT url FROM urls WHERE MATCH
   → (description) AGAINST('security');
   ```

   This is a very simple example that will return some results as long as at least one and less than fifty percent of the records in the *urls* table have the word *security* in their description.

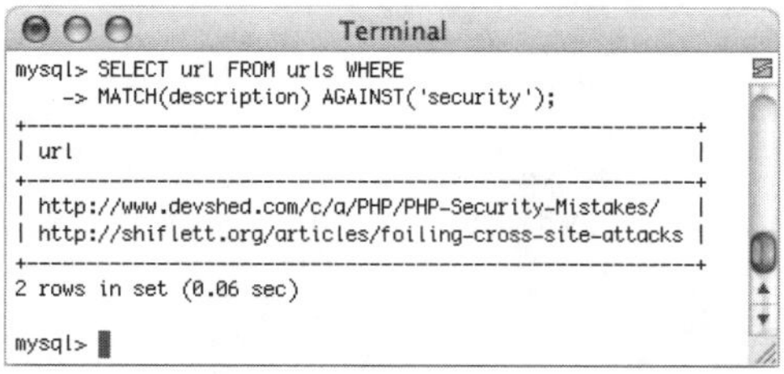

Figure 5.35 A basic FULLTEXT search.

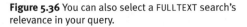

```
mysql> SELECT url, MATCH(description)
    -> AGAINST('security') AS R
    -> FROM urls WHERE
    -> MATCH(description) AGAINST('security')
    -> ;
+-----------------------------------------------------+--------------------+
| url                                                 | R                  |
+-----------------------------------------------------+--------------------+
| http://www.devshed.com/c/a/PHP/PHP-Security-Mistakes/ | 0.84802478551865   |
| http://shiflett.org/articles/foiling-cross-site-attacks | 0.81339609622955 |
+-----------------------------------------------------+--------------------+
2 rows in set (0.01 sec)

mysql>
```

Figure 5.36 You can also select a FULLTEXT search's relevance in your query.

```
mysql> SELECT url FROM urls WHERE
    -> MATCH(description) AGAINST('MYSQL database');
+---------------+
| url           |
+---------------+
| www.mysql.com |
+---------------+
1 row in set (0.02 sec)

mysql>
```

Figure 5.37 Using the FULLTEXT search, you can easily find descriptions that contain multiple keywords.

3. Run the same FULLTEXT search while also showing the relevance (**Figure 5.36**).

SELECT url, MATCH(description)
→ AGAINST('security') AS R FROM
→ urls WHERE MATCH(description)
→ AGAINST('security');

If you use the same MATCH...AGAINST expression as a selected value, the actual relevance will be returned.

4. Run a FULLTEXT search using multiple keywords (**Figure 5.37**).

SELECT url FROM urls WHERE MATCH
→ (description) AGAINST('mysql
→ database');

With this query, a match will be made only if a description contains both *mysql* and *database*.

✔ Tips

■ Remember that if a FULLTEXT search returns no records, this means that either no matches were made or that over half of the records match.

■ For sake of simplicity, I wrote all of the queries in this section as simple SELECT statements. You can certainly use FULLTEXT searches within joins or more complex queries.

■ MySQL comes with several hundred stop-words already defined. These are part of the application's source code.

■ The minimum keyword length—four characters by default—is a configuration setting you can change in MySQL.

■ FULLTEXT searches are case-insensitive by default.

Performing Boolean FULLTEXT Searches

The basic FULLTEXT search is nice, but a more sophisticated FULLTEXT search can be accomplished using its Boolean mode. This feature has been present in MySQL since version 4.0.1.

Boolean mode uses a number of operators (**Table 5.9**) to dictate how each keyword is treated. With the operators you also use the phrase IN BOOLEAN MODE in your query:

```
SELECT * FROM tablename WHERE

MATCH(column) AGAINST('+database
→ -mysql' IN BOOLEAN MODE)
```

In that example, a match will be made if the word *database* is found and *mysql* is not present. Alternatively, the tilde (~) is used as a milder form of the minus sign, meaning that the keyword can be present in a match, but such matches should be considered less relevant.

The wildcard character (*) matches variations on a word, so cata* matches *catalog*, *catalina*, and so on. Two operators explicitly state what keywords are more (>) or less (<) important. Finally, you can use double quotation marks to hunt for exact phrases and parentheses to make subexpressions.

The following query would look for records with the phrase *Web develop* with the word *html* being required and the word *JavaScript* detracting from a match's relevance:

```
SELECT * FROM tablename WHERE

MATCH(column) AGAINST('>"Web develop"
→ +html ~JavaScript' IN BOOLEAN MODE)
```

When using Boolean mode, there are several differences as to how FULLTEXT searches work:

◆ If a keyword is not preceded by an operator, the word is optional but a match will be ranked higher if it is present.

◆ Results will be returned even if more than fifty percent of the records match the search.

◆ The results are not automatically sorted by relevance.

Because of this last fact, you'll also want to sort the returned records by their relevance, as I'll demonstrate in the next sequence of steps. One important rule that's the same with Boolean searches is that the minimum word length (four characters by default) still applies. So trying to require a shorter word using a plus sign (+php) still won't work.

Boolean Mode Operators	
OPERATOR	MEANING
+	Must be present in every match
-	Must not be present in any match
~	Lowers a ranking if present
*	Wildcard
<	Decrease a word's importance
>	Increase a word's importance
" "	Must match the exact phrase
( )	Create subexpressions

Table 5.9 Use these operators to fine-tune your FULLTEXT searches.

To perform FULLTEXT Boolean searches:

1. Run a simple FULLTEXT search on variations of the word *develop* (**Figure 5.38**).

   SELECT url, description FROM
   → urls WHERE MATCH(description)
   → AGAINST('develop*' IN BOOLEAN
   → MODE) \G

   This query will find records that contain *develop*, *developer*, *development*, etc. To confirm this, I'm also selecting the actual description column, and I'm using the \G trick to make the result easier to view.

   continues on next page

```
mysql> SELECT url, description FROM urls WHERE MATCH(description) AGAINST('develop*' IN BOOLEAN MODE) \G
*************************** 1. row ***************************
        url: www.Zend.com
description: The home page of Zend, the company behind the heart of PHP (since version 3). This is a good resour
ce for anyone wanting to develop dynamic Web applications using PHP.
*************************** 2. row ***************************
        url: www.w3.org
description: The home page of the W3C, the caretakers of the World Wide Web. Every Web developer should be famil
iar with this site. Even though the content is sometimes technical, it's a valuable resource.
*************************** 3. row ***************************
        url: http://shiflett.org/articles/foiling-cross-site-attacks
description: A great article focusing on one type of security risks Web developers need to worry about. Written
with the PHP programmer in mind.
*************************** 4. row ***************************
        url: http://www.secureprogramming.com
description: A site dedicate to the subject of secure programming. The topics include Web development and PHP.
4 rows in set (0.00 sec)

mysql>
```

Figure 5.38 A simple Boolean mode FULLTEXT search.

2. Find matches involving secure programming, with the emphasis on security (**Figure 5.39**).

```
SELECT url FROM urls WHERE MATCH
→ (description) AGAINST('>secur*
→ +program*' IN BOOLEAN MODE);
```

This query first finds all records that have both secur* (*secure, security, …*) and program* (*program, programmer, programming, …*) in them. Then the results are ranked, with secur* outweighing program*.

3. Run the same query but in order of relevance (**Figure 5.40**).

```
SELECT url, MATCH(description)
→ AGAINST('>secur* +program*' IN
→ BOOLEAN MODE) AS R FROM urls WHERE
→ MATCH(description) AGAINST
→ ('>secur* +program*' IN BOOLEAN
→ MODE) ORDER BY R DESC;
```

As I mentioned earlier, Boolean mode searches do not return the results in order. To make that happen, you'll need to also select the relevance and add an ORDER BY that sorts using those values.

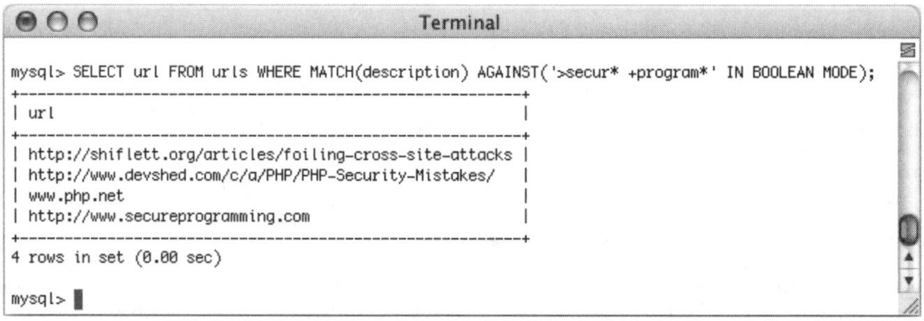

Figure 5.39 This search looks for variations on two different keywords, ranking the one higher than the other.

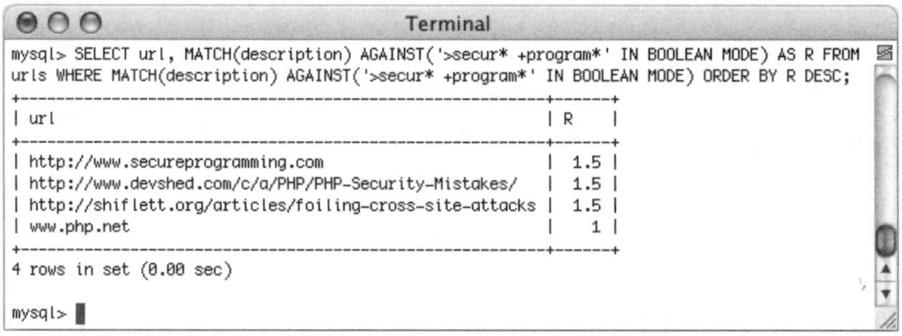

Figure 5.40 When doing Boolean mode searches, you must sort the returned results yourself (compare with Figure 5.39).

Database Optimization

As a conclusion to this chapter, I want to mention several performance-related techniques with respect to databases. The busier a site is, the more important each little tweak will become.

The performance of your database is primarily dependent upon its structure and indexes. When creating databases, try to

◆ Choose the best storage engine

◆ Use the smallest data type possible for each column

◆ Define columns as NOT NULL whenever possible

◆ Use integers as primary keys

◆ Judiciously define indexes, selecting the correct type and applying them to the right column or columns

◆ Limit indexes to a certain number of characters, if applicable

Along with these tips, there are two simple techniques for optimizing databases. I'll discuss each next.

✔ Tips

■ Another way to improve the speed of your databases is to tune how MySQL runs. You can do this by specifying different options, such as the key_buffer (memory allotted for indexes), max_connections (how many connections can be handled at one time), and table_cache (table buffer). More information on these parameters can be found in the MySQL manual.

■ Suppose you define an index on multiple columns, like this:

```
ALTER TABLE tablename ADD INDEX
→ (col1, col2, col3)
```

This effectively creates an index for searches on *col1*, on *col1* and *col2* together, or on all three columns together. It does not provide an index for searching just *col2* or *col3* or those two together.

Optimizing tables

MySQL manages its tables rather nicely, and you normally do not need to worry about them. But deleting records, as just one example, creates gaps in the tables, resulting in extra overhead.

One way to improve MySQL's performance is to run an OPTIMIZE command on such tables. This query will rid a table of any unnecessary overhead, thereby speeding any interactions with it.

To optimize a table:

1. Check the table's status (**Figure 5.41**).

   SHOW TABLE STATUS \G

   Using the query explained earlier in the chapter, I'll inspect each table for gaps (the \G option makes it easier to read). The *Data_free* value shows the number of bytes that have been allocated but are not being used.

2. Optimize the *url_associations* table (**Figure 5.42**).

   OPTIMIZE TABLE url_associations;

   After running this query, MySQL will indicate the status of the table.

3. Recheck the table's status.

   SHOW TABLE STATUS \G

   You should now see *0* for the *Data_free* value.

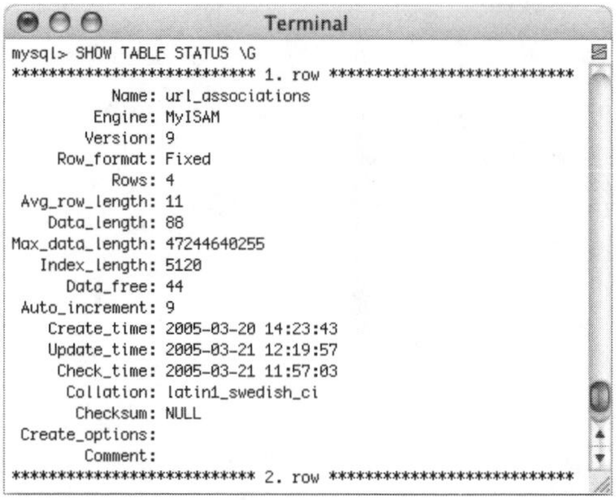

✔ Tips

■ Optimizing a table to clear out 44 bytes is definitely overkill, used to demonstrate a process. You should not need to take this step very often, except after significant changes like deleting lots of rows or changing variable-length column definitions.

Figure 5.41 The *url_associations* table has 44 unused bytes.

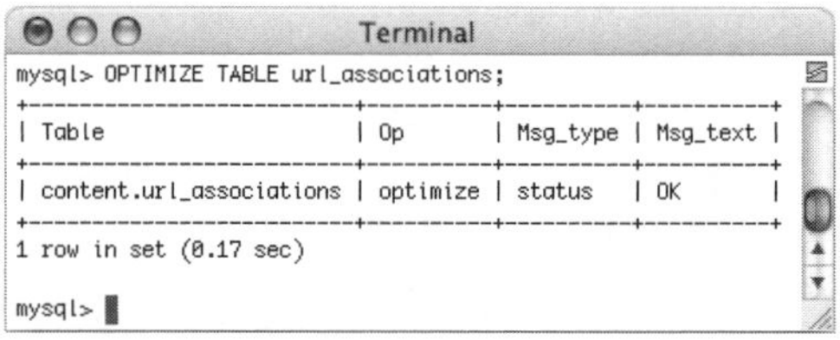

Figure 5.42 Running an OPTIMIZE query on a table.

■ A common misconception for people new to the concept of an automatically incrementing primary key (like *url_id*) is that there shouldn't be gaps in the sequence (which occur after deleting a record). Such gaps are perfectly fine, and you should *in no way* consider renumbering the sequence (because primary keys shouldn't change).

■ MySQL tables of the MyISAM table type (the default in current versions of the software) can also be optimized using the separate myisamchk utility.

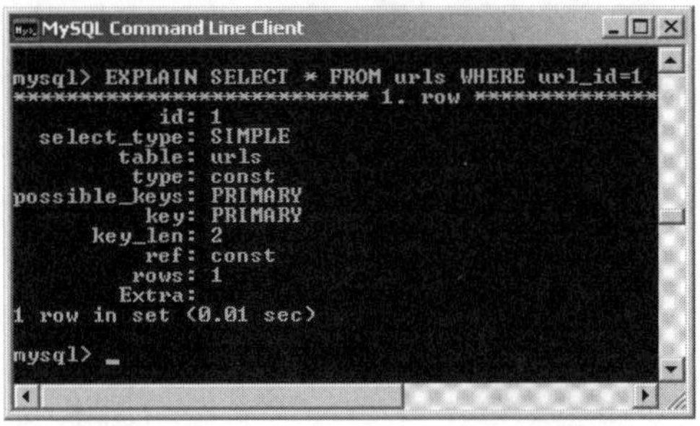

Figure 5.43 USE EXPLAIN TO SHOW HOW MYSQL HANDLES QUERIES.

EXPLAIN TYPE VALUES

VALUE	NOTES
system	A SPECIAL KIND OF *const*
const	GREAT: ONLY ONE POSSIBLE MATCHING ROW (E.G., url_id=2)
eq_ref	VERY GOOD SIGN; INDICATES THAT PRIMARY OR UNIQUE INDEXES ARE BEING USED
ref	NOT AS GOOD AS *eq_ref* BECAUSE IT CAN'T USE THE PROPER INDEXES
ref_or_null	LIKE *ref*, BUT MAY INVOLVE NULL VALUES
index	LIKE *all* BUT AN INDEX IS USED
all	WORST POSSIBLE VALUE; ADD INDEXES!

Table 5.10 THESE ARE THE MOST COMMON *type* VALUES YOU'LL SEE IN EXPLAIN RESULTS (*system* AND *const* ARE THE BEST; *all* IS THE WORST).

EXPLAINING QUERIES

The heart of a MySQL-driven application is the queries being run on the database, so making these as efficient as possible is of the utmost importance. To improve a query's efficiency, it helps to understand how exactly MySQL will run that query. This can be accomplished using the EXPLAIN SQL keyword. For example (**Figure 5.43**):

EXPLAIN SELECT * FROM urls WHERE url_id=1

The explanation given by MySQL for the query will help you understand where to add indexes to your tables and how to better tailor your SQL. The explanation will list tables involved, the type of join used, what possible indexes (or keys) MySQL might use for this query, which index is actually used, and the number of rows that MySQL must look at to run this query. I'll briefly describe what each value means and how it relates to you.

To start, *select_type* is the type of query being run. Normally this will be SIMPLE, unless you are using subqueries. The *table* column shows the table being used by the query. Queries involving multiple tables will list each in the order that the query will access them. The *type* is very important, reflecting the type of join being used. **Table 5.10** lists these options, from most efficient to least. If your type value says *const*, *eq_ref*, or *ref*, you're in good shape. If it says *all*, you may have a much slower query than you should.

The *rows* information is a major factor for how long a query takes to run. It indicates approximately how many rows will need to be scanned in order to execute the query. By multiplying the row *values* from all of the tables involved in a query, you get a sense of how big the scanning process is.

continues on next page

Finally, the *possible_keys* value indicates what indexes are available for use. The *key* value is what index will actually be used. If either or both of these are `NULL`, there may be a problem.

This is a lot of information and somewhat sophisticated at that, so I'll run through a quick sample as to how you might use this information.

To use explain:

1. Run an `EXPLAIN` query (**Figure 5.44**).

   ```
   EXPLAIN SELECT category, url FROM
   → url_associations AS ua, urls
   → AS u, url_categories AS uc WHERE
   → u.url_id=ua.url_id AND ua.url_
   → category_id=uc.url_category_id
   → ORDER BY uc.category \G
   ```

   This is an advanced join that uses all three tables and is therefore a good candidate for explanation. As you can see in the resulting image,

   - The final two tables both have a type of *eq_ref* and *PRIMARY* key values, which is great.
   - Only one row in each of the final two tables needs to be referenced for each row in the first, which is perfect. (The product of 4 * 1 * 1 is very small, and even if there are hundreds of records, the sum will still only be *X* * 1 * 1.)
   - The first table has a type of *index*, which isn't great but is better than *all* and is not uncommon with the first table involved in a join.
   - The first table does use an index.

   All in all, this query is as efficient as it can be. The *Using filesort* value for the *ua* table reflects the fact that I'm sorting the query results. If I remove the `ORDER BY` clause, the query will run somewhat faster.

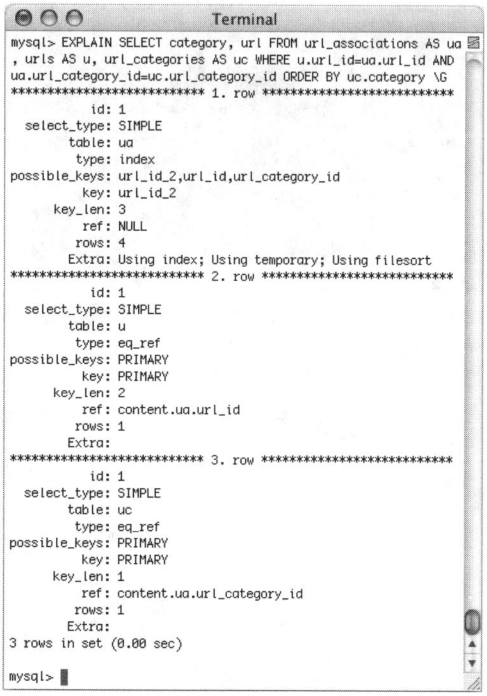

```
Terminal
mysql> EXPLAIN SELECT category, url FROM url_associations AS ua
, urls AS u, url_categories AS uc WHERE u.url_id=ua.url_id AND
ua.url_category_id=uc.url_category_id ORDER BY uc.category \G
*************************** 1. row ***************************
           id: 1
  select_type: SIMPLE
        table: ua
         type: index
possible_keys: url_id_2,url_id,url_category_id
          key: url_id_2
      key_len: 3
          ref: NULL
         rows: 4
        Extra: Using index; Using temporary; Using filesort
*************************** 2. row ***************************
           id: 1
  select_type: SIMPLE
        table: u
         type: eq_ref
possible_keys: PRIMARY
          key: PRIMARY
      key_len: 2
          ref: content.ua.url_id
         rows: 1
        Extra:
*************************** 3. row ***************************
           id: 1
  select_type: SIMPLE
        table: uc
         type: eq_ref
possible_keys: PRIMARY
          key: PRIMARY
      key_len: 1
          ref: content.ua.url_category_id
         rows: 1
        Extra:
3 rows in set (0.00 sec)

mysql>
```

Figure 5.44 Here an `EXPLAIN` shows how MySQL will handle a join across three tables.

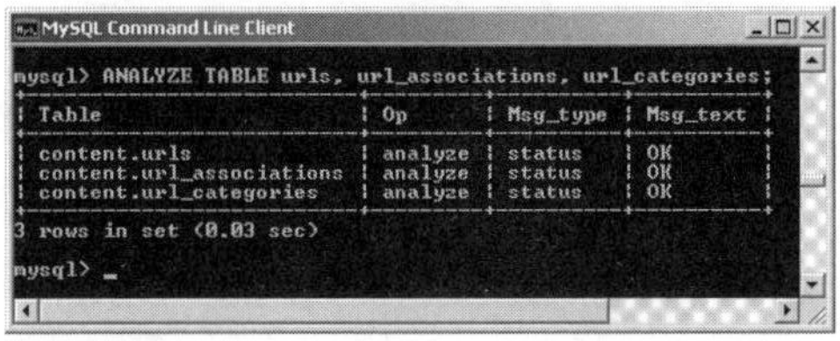

Figure 5.45 Have MySQL ANALYZE your tables to make sure it makes the most of your indexes.

Looking Ahead to MySQL 5

As MySQL ages, the developers have been adding more and more features (features long present in other database applications, to be frank). Some of the new topics discussed in this chapter were added in versions 4 and 4.1 of MySQL, and there is a lot planned for version 5.

The two big new expected features are *views* and *stored procedures*. Views are like saved query results. They're great if you have complex queries, like joins, that you frequently run or that require further querying.

Stored procedures are saved SQL commands. They offer better performance and greater security over standard SQL commands hard-coded into your applications.

2. If necessary, change your query or add indexes as needed.

This particular query is fine as is, because I already added the proper indexes to the tables. If indexes aren't available, you would want to add some. Alternatively, you can try redefining your query so that it's as efficient as possible.

3. Run an ANALYZE TABLE query to update MySQL's index information (**Figure 5.45**).

ANALYZE TABLE urls, url_associations,
→ url_categories;

The ANALYZE TABLE query forces MySQL to update its statistics for a table. It may improve the effectiveness of queries and EXPLAINs.

4. Run the EXPLAIN query a second time to see if improvements have been made.

Not all queries can be improved, but what you should keep an eye on are:

▲ The *type* values

▲ If keys are being used

▲ The product of all the *rows* values

✔ Tips

■ For more information on EXPLAIN and ANALYZE, see the MySQL manual.

■ If your query relies on equating two columns (…WHERE col1=col2), MySQL cannot take advantage of any indexes if the two columns are of different sizes.

DATABASE OPTIMIZATION

ERROR HANDLING AND DEBUGGING

Before getting into the heart of developing PHP- and MySQL-driven Web sites, I'm going to spend a few pages discussing the bane of the programmer: errors. As you gain experience, you'll make fewer errors and pick up your own debugging methodologies, but there are plenty of tools and techniques you can use to help ease the learning process.

This chapter has three main threads. One focus is on learning about the various kinds of errors that can occur when developing dynamic Web sites and what their likely causes are. Second, a multitude of debugging techniques are taught, in a step-by-step format. Finally, you'll see different techniques for handling the errors that occur in the most graceful manner possible.

Before I begin, a word on errors: they happen to the best of us. Even the author of this here book sees plenty of errors in his Web development duties (but rest assured that the code in this book should be bug-free). Thinking that you'll get to a skill level where errors never occur is a fool's dream, but knowing how to quickly catch, handle, and fix errors is a major skill in its own right. So try not to become frustrated as you make errors; instead, bask in the knowledge that you're becoming a better debugger!

General Error Types and Debugging

When developing Web applications with PHP and MySQL, you end up with potential bugs in one of four or more technologies. You could have HTML issues, PHP problems, SQL errors, or MySQL mistakes. To be able to fix the bug, you must first determine in what realm the bug resides.

HTML problems are often the least disruptive and the easiest to catch. You normally know there's a problem when your layout is all messed up. Some steps for catching and fixing these, as well as general debugging processes, are discussed in the next section.

PHP errors are the ones you'll see most often, as this language will be at the heart of your applications. PHP errors fall into three general areas:

- Syntactical
- Run time
- Logical

Syntactical errors are the most common and the easiest to fix. You'll see them if you merely omit a semicolon. Such errors stop the script from executing, and if *display_errors* is on in your PHP configuration, PHP will show an error, including the line PHP thinks it's on (**Figure 6.1**). If *display_errors* is off, you'll see a blank page.

The second category includes those things that don't stop a PHP script from beginning to run (like parse errors do) but do stop the script from doing everything it was supposed to do, such as calling a function using the wrong number or types of parameters. With these errors, PHP will normally display a message (**Figure 6.2**) indicating the exact problem (again, assuming that *display_errors* is on).

http://192.168.0.100/handle.inc.php - Microsoft Internet Explorer
File Edit View Favorites Tools Help
Parse error: parse error, unexpected T_VARIABLE, expecting ',' or ';' in /Users/larryullman/Sites/handle.inc.php on line 36
Done
Internet

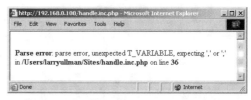

Figure 6.1 Parse errors—which you've probably seen many times over by now—are the most common sort of PHP error, particularly for beginning programmers.

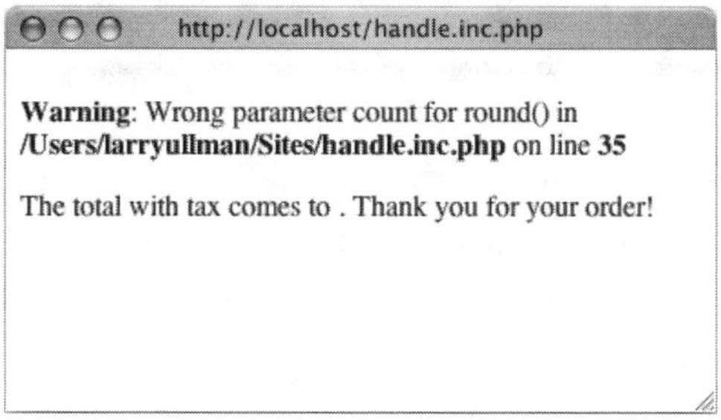

http://localhost/handle.inc.php
Warning: Wrong parameter count for round() in /Users/larryullman/Sites/handle.inc.php on line 35
The total with tax comes to . Thank you for your order!

Figure 6.2 Misusing a function (calling it with improper parameters) will create errors during the execution of the script.

The final category of error is actually the worst, because PHP won't necessarily report it to you. These are out-and-out bugs: problems that aren't obvious and don't stop the execution of a script. Tricks for solving all of these PHP errors will be demonstrated in just a few pages.

SQL errors are normally a matter of syntax, and they'll be reported when you try to run the query on MySQL. For example, I've done this many times:

```
DELETE * FROM tablename
```

The syntax is just wrong, confused with the SELECT syntax (`SELECT * FROM tablename`). The right syntax is

```
DELETE FROM tablename
```

Again, MySQL will raise a red flag when you have SQL errors, so these aren't that difficult to find and fix. With dynamic Web sites, the trick is that PHP will often generate the SQL query, so PHP ends up being the real culprit.

Besides reporting on SQL errors, MySQL has its own to consider. An inability to access the database is a common one and a show-stopper at that (**Figure 6.3**). You'll also see errors when you misuse a MySQL function or ambiguously refer to a column in a join. Again, MySQL will report any such error in specific detail. Keep in mind that when a query doesn't have the result you expect, that's not a MySQL or SQL error, but rather a logical one. Toward the end of this chapter you'll see how to solve SQL and MySQL errors.

But as you have to walk before you can run, I'll begin by covering the fundamentals of debugging dynamic Web sites, starting with the basic checks you should make and how to fix HTML problems.

Basic Debugging Steps

This first sequence of steps may seem obvious, but when it comes to debugging, missing one of these steps leads to an unproductive and extremely frustrating debugging experience. And while I'm at it, I should mention that the best piece of general debugging advice is this: *When you get frustrated, step away from the computer!* I have solved almost all of the most perplexing issues I've come across by taking a break, clearing my head, and coming back to the code with fresh eyes.

```
Terminal — 84x5
Larry-Ullmans-Computer:~ larryullman$ /usr/local/mysql/bin/mysql -u root -p
Enter password:
ERROR 1045 (28000): Access denied for user 'root'@'localhost' (using password: YES)
Larry-Ullmans-Computer:~ larryullman$ ▮
```

Figure 6.3 An inability to connect to a MySQL server or a specific database is a common MySQL error.

To begin debugging any problem:

◆ Make sure that you are running the right page.

It's altogether too common that you try to fix a problem and no matter what you do, it never goes away. The reason: you've actually been editing a different page than you thought.

◆ Make sure that you have saved your latest changes.

◆ Make sure that you run all PHP pages through the URL.

Because PHP requires the use of a Web server, running any PHP code requires that you access the page through a URL (http://www.sitename.com/page.php or http://localhost/page.php). If you double-click a PHP page to open it in a browser (or use the browser's File > Open option), you'll see the PHP code, not the executed result.

◆ Know what versions of PHP and MySQL you are running.

Some problems are specific to a certain version of PHP or MySQL. For example, some functions are added in later versions of PHP, and MySQL has added significant new features in versions 4, 4.1, and 5. Run a phpinfo() script (**Figure 6.4**, see Appendix A, "Installation," for a script example) and open a mysql client session (**Figure 6.5**) to determine this information.

◆ Know what Web server you are running.

Similarly, some problems and features are unique to your Web serving application—Apache, IIS, and PWS. You should know which one you are using, and which version, from when you installed the application.

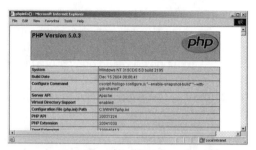

Figure 6.4 A phpinfo() script is one of your best tools for debugging, informing you of the PHP version and how it's configured.

Figure 6.5 When you connect to a MySQL server, it should let you know the version number.

◆ Try executing pages in a different Web browser.

Every Web developer should have and use at least two Web browsers. If you test your pages in different ones, you'll see if the problem has to do with your script or a particular browser.

◆ If possible, try executing the page using a different Web server.

PHP and MySQL errors sometimes stem from particular configurations and versions on one server. If something works on one server but not another, then you'll know that the script isn't inherently at fault. From there it's a matter of using `phpinfo()` scripts to see what server settings may be different.

✔ Tips

■ If taking a break is one thing you should do when you become frustrated, here's what you *shouldn't* do: send off one or multiple panicky and persnickety emails to the author, to a newsgroup or mailing list, or to anyone else. When it comes to asking for free help from strangers, patience and pleasantries garner much better and faster results.

■ There's another different realm of errors that you could classify as *usage* errors: what goes wrong when the site's user doesn't do what you thought they would. These are very difficult to find on your own because it's hard for the programmer to use an application in a way other than she intended. As a golden rule, try to make sure that a PHP script has all of the data—and in the right format—that it needs before proceeding. Don't assume that the pages will always be used exactly as you had intended them to be!

Book Errors

If you've followed an example in this book and something's not working right, what should you do?

1. Double-check your code or steps against those in the book.

2. Use the index at the back of the book to see if I reference a script or function in an earlier page (you may have missed an important usage rule or tip).

3. View the PHP manual for a specific function to see if it's available in only a certain version and to verify how the function is used.

4. Check out the book's errata page (through the supporting Web site) to see if an error in the code does exist and has been reported. Don't post your particular problem there yet, though!

5. Triple-check your code and use all the debugging techniques outlined in this chapter.

6. Search the book's supporting forum to see if others have had this problem and if a solution has already been determined.

7. If all else fails, use the book's supporting forum to ask for assistance.

Debugging HTML

Debugging HTML is relatively easy. The source code is very accessible, most problems are overt, and attempts at fixing the HTML don't normally make things worse (as can happen with PHP). Still, there are some basic steps you should follow to find and fix an HTML problem.

To debug an HTML error:

◆ Check the source code.

If you have an HTML problem, you'll almost always need to check the source code of the page to find it. How you view the source code depends upon the browser being used, but different steps—variations on View > Page Source—were introduced back in Chapter 1, "Introduction to PHP."

◆ Use a validation tool (**Figure 6.6**).

Validation tools, like the one at `http://validator.w3.org`, are great for finding mismatched tags, broken tables, and other problems. On the other hand, validation tools will also report on nonstandard but perfectly functional HTML, which may not be the problem you were hoping to solve.

◆ Add borders to your tables.

Frequently layouts are messed up because tables are incomplete. To confirm this, add a prominent border to your table to make it obvious where the different columns and rows are.

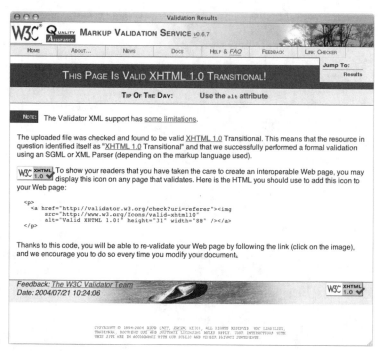

Figure 6.6 Validation tools like the one provided by the W3C (World Wide Web Consortium) are good for finding problems and making sure your HTML conforms to standards.

◆ Use Firefox's Web Developer widget (**Figure 6.7**).

Besides being just a great Web browser, the very popular Firefox browser (available for free from www.mozilla.org) has a ton of features that the Web developer will appreciate. Furthermore, you can expand Firefox's functionality by installing any of the free widgets that are available. The Web Developer widget in particular provides quick access to great tools, such as showing a table's borders, revealing the CSS, validating a page, and more.

◆ Test the page in another browser.

PHP code is generally browser-independent, meaning you'll get consistent results regardless of the client. Not so with HTML. Sometimes a particular browser has a quirk that affects the rendered page. Running the same page in another browser is the easiest way to know if it's an HTML problem or a browser quirk.

✔ Tips

■ Although Internet Explorer is still the most popular Web browser, particularly on Windows, Web developers are better served by using Firefox, Safari (on Mac OS X), and others. As just one motivating example, how Firefox lets you see and handle cookies can make debugging cookie problems infinitely easier. Obviously, you'll need to test your applications using IE, as most Web users run it, but develop your scripts with better tools, like Firefox.

■ The first step toward fixing any kind of problem is understanding what's causing it. Remember the role each technology—HTML, PHP, SQL, and MySQL—plays as you debug. If your page doesn't look right, that's an HTML problem. If your HTML is dynamically generated by PHP, it's still an HTML problem but you'll need to work with the PHP code to make it right.

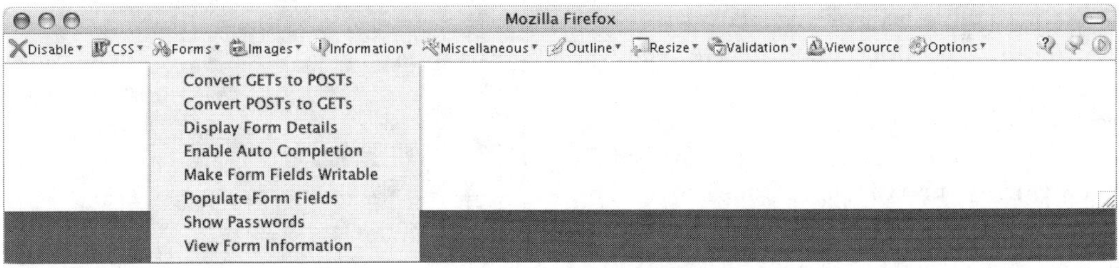

Figure 6.7 Firefox's Web Developer widget provides quick access to several useful developer tools.

Displaying PHP Errors

PHP provides remarkably useful and descriptive error messages when things go awry. Unfortunately, PHP doesn't show these errors when running using its default configuration. This policy makes sense for live servers, where you don't want the end users seeing PHP-specific error messages, but it also makes everything that much more confusing for the beginning PHP developer. To see PHP's errors, you must turn on the *display_errors* directive, either in an individual script or for the PHP configuration as a whole.

To turn on *display_errors* in a script, use the `ini_set()` function. As its arguments, this function takes a directive name and what setting it should have:

```
ini_set('display_errors', 1);
```

Including this line in a script will turn on *display_errors* for that script. The only downside is that if your script has a syntax error that prevents it from running at all, then you'll still see a blank page. To have PHP display errors for the entire server, edit your `php.ini` file, assuming you can (unless you host your site on your own computer, it probably won't be an option). If you don't yet know where to find the `php.ini` file, see the "Configuring PHP" section of Appendix A.

To turn on display_errors:

1. Open the active `php.ini` file in any text editor.

2. Find the line that reads

   ```
   display_errors = Off
   ```

   Note that the `php.ini` file will include this line twice. The first time, it's just a reference and is preceded by a semicolon, meaning that the line is not active. Find the line that does not begin with a semicolon.

3. Change the line to read

   ```
   display_errors = On
   ```

4. Save the `php.ini` file.

5. Restart your Web server application.

   You do not have to restart the entire computer, just the Web serving application (Apache, IIS, etc.). How you do this depends upon the Web server being used, the operating system, and the installation method. See Appendix A for instructions.

6. If you want, rerun a `phpinfo.php` script to confirm that the change was made (**Figure 6.8**).

   Again, the first appendix discusses the `phpinfo.php` script if you don't already have one.

phpinfo()		
disable_functions	*no value*	*no value*
display_errors	On	On
display_startup_errors	Off	Off
doc_root	*no value*	*no value*
docref_ext	*no value*	*no value*
docref_root	*no value*	*no value*
enable_dl	On	On
error_append_string	*no value*	*no value*
error_log	*no value*	*no value*
error_prepend_string	*no value*	*no value*
error_reporting	2047	2047
expose_php	On	On
extension_dir	./	./
file_uploads	On	On

Figure 6.8 My `phpinfo.php` page now reflects that *display_errors* is On.

✔ Tips

- While in the `php.ini` file, you can adjust other directives. For example, the *log_errors* and *error_log* settings control whether and to where errors are logged. If *log_errors* is *On*, a text file will store all of the problems that occur. You probably don't want this during development—when lots of problems exist—but do for a live server.

- If your `php.ini` file has *track_errors* set to *1* (or *on*), every error will automatically be stored in an array called `$php_errormsg`.

- The `ini_set()` function cannot be used to adjust every possible PHP setting. See the PHP manual for specifics as to what can and cannot be controlled.

- The `php.ini` file includes pretty good instructions as to what the most relevant settings are, how you would change them, and why you might not want to. Pay attention to these instructions and perhaps make a backup copy of the file before editing it (just in case).

Adjusting Error Reporting in PHP

Once you have PHP set to reveal what errors occur, you might want to adjust the level of error reporting. Your PHP installation as a whole or individual scripts can be set to report or ignore different levels of errors. **Table 6.1** lists most of the levels, but they can generally be one of these three kinds:

- *Notices*, which do not stop the execution of a script and may not necessarily be a problem.

- *Warnings*, which indicate a problem but don't stop a script's execution.

- *Errors*, which stop a script from continuing (including the ever-common parse error, which prevent scripts from running at all).

As a rule of thumb, you'll want PHP to report on any kind of error while you're developing a site but report no specific errors once the site goes live. For security and aesthetic purposes, it's generally unwise for a public user to see PHP's detailed error messages.

ADJUSTING ERROR REPORTING IN PHP

Error-Reporting Levels

NUMBER	CONSTANT	REPORT ON
1	E_ERROR	Fatal run-time errors (that stop execution of the script).
2	E_WARNING	Run-time warnings (nonfatal errors).
4	E_PARSE	Parse errors.
8	E_NOTICE	Notices (things that could or could not be a problem).
256	E_USER_ERROR	User-generated error messages, generated by the `trigger_error()` function.
512	E_USER_WARNING	User-generated warnings, generated by the `trigger_error()` function.
1024	E_USER_NOTICE	User-generated notices, generated by the `trigger_error()` function.
2047	E_ALL	All errors and warnings.
2048	E_STRICT	E_ALL plus recommendations.

Table 6.1 PHP's error-reporting settings, to be used with the `error_reporting()` function or in the `php.ini` file.

Frequently, error messages—particularly those dealing with the database—will reveal certain behind-the-scenes aspects of your Web application that are best not shown. While you hope all of these will be worked out during the development stages, that's rarely the case.

You can follow the instructions in the previous section for altering the `php.ini` file specifically for error reporting or set this on a script-by-script basis using the `error_reporting()` function. This function is used to establish what type of errors PHP should report on within a specific page. The function takes either a number or a constant, using the values in Table 6.1 (the PHP manual lists a few others, related to the core of PHP itself).

```
error_reporting(0); // Show no errors.
```

A setting of *0* turns error reporting off entirely (errors will still occur; you just won't see them anymore). Conversely, `error_reporting (E_ALL)` will tell PHP to report on every error that occurs. The numbers can be added up to customize the level of error reporting, or you could use the bitwise operators—| (or), ~ (not), & (and)—with the constants. With this following setting any non-notice error will be shown:

```
error_reporting (E_ALL & ~E_NOTICE);
```

Because you'll probably want to adjust error reporting on a site-wide basis and change the level of reporting depending upon whether or not the site is live, you'll want to call the `error_reporting()` function in one file common to the entire Web site. To do this, a configuration file will be created for handling a dynamic application's errors.

To adjust error reporting for an application:

1. Create a new PHP script in your text editor (**Script 6.1**).

   ```
   <?php # Script 6.1 - config.inc.php
   ```

   This is a plain PHP page; there will be no HTML in it at all.

2. Set the error reporting on the highest level.

   ```
   error_reporting (E_ALL);
   ```

   For development purposes, I'd like PHP to notify me of all errors and warnings. This line will accomplish that. Because E_ALL is a constant, it is not enclosed in quotation marks.

3. Close the PHP script and save the file as `config.inc.php`.

   ```
   ?>
   ```

   You can give your file just about any extension, but `.inc.php` indicates that it's both an included file and a PHP file.

Script 6.1 This configuration file sets error reporting on nearly the highest level.

```
1   <?php # Script 6.1 - config.inc.php
2   // Set the level of error reporting.
3   error_reporting (E_ALL);
4   ?>
```

4. To use the file in a Web application, include the following line at the top of every script:

```
include ('config.inc.php');
```

This configuration file will set the behavior for an entire application. Including it first in every PHP script will apply the error reporting to that script. You'll see this concept in action in Chapter 13, "Example—User Registration."

✔ TIPS

■ E_STRICT has been added in version 5 of PHP. Using it means that PHP will make recommendations for optimal coding and let you know when you're using outdated functions or variables.

■ In current versions of PHP, error reporting is set to E_ALL & ~E_NOTICE (report on all errors except for notices) by default.

■ The scripts written in this book were all programmed with PHP's error reporting on the highest level (in the hopes of catching every possible problem).

SUPPRESSING ERRORS WITH @

Individual errors can be suppressed in PHP using the @ operator. For example, if you don't want PHP to report if it couldn't open a file, you would code

```
@include ('config.inc.php');
```

Or if you don't want to see a "division by zero" error:

```
$x = 8;

$y = 0;

$num = @($x/$y);
```

The @ symbol will work only on expressions, like function calls or mathematical operations. You cannot use @ before conditionals, loops, function definitions, and so forth.

As a rule of thumb, I recommend that @ be used on functions whose execution, should they fail, will not affect the functionality of the script as a whole. Or you can suppress PHP's errors when you will handle them more gracefully yourself.

Creating Custom Error Handlers

Another option for error management with your sites (aside from adjusting the error reporting) is to alter how PHP handles errors. You can create your own functions that will overrule PHP's default behavior (printing them out in HTML tags). For example,

```
function report_errors ($num, $msg) {

    // Do whatever here.

}

set_error_handler ('report_errors');
```

The `set_error_handler()` determines what function handles errors. Feeding this function the name of another function will result in that second function (e.g., *report_errors*) being called whenever an error is encountered. This function (*report_errors*) will, at that time, receive two arguments—an error number and a textual error message—which can be used in any possible manner.

This function can also be written to take up to five arguments, the extra three being the name of the file where the error was found, the specific line number, and the variables that existed at the time of the error.

```
function report_errors ($num, $msg,
→ $file, $line, $vars) {…
```

This next file will define an error handler, which will then be included in a second file that purposefully causes a couple of errors (in order to test the system).

To create your own error handler:

1. Begin a new PHP script in your text editor or IDE (**Script 6.2**).

   ```
   <?php # Script 6.2 - handle.inc.php
   ```

Script 6.2 A special function is created to handle any errors that occur in a more customized manner.

```
1    <?php # Script 6.2 - handle.inc.php
2
3    // Flag variable for site status:
4    $live = FALSE;
5
6    // Create the error handler.
7    function my_error_handler ($e_number,
     $e_message, $e_file, $e_line, $e_vars) {
8
9        global $live;
10
11       // Build the error message.
12       $message = "An error occurred in script
         '$e_file' on line $e_line: $e_message\n";
13
14       // Append $e_vars to the $message.
15       $message .= print_r ($e_vars, 1);
16
17       if ($live) { // Don't show the error.
18           echo '<div class="error">A
             system error occurred. We apologize
             for the inconvenience.</div><br />';
19       } else { // Development (print the
         error).
20           echo '<div class="error">' .
             $message . '</div><br />';
21       }
22
23   } // End of my_error_handler() definition.
24
25   // Use my error handler.
26   set_error_handler ('my_error_handler');
27   ?>
```

2. Create a flag variable.

```
$live = FALSE;
```

This variable will be a flag used to indicate whether or not the site is currently live. It's an important distinction, as how you handle errors and what you reveal in the browser should differ greatly when you're developing a site and when a site is live.

3. Begin defining the error handling function.

```
function my_error_handler
→ ($e_number, $e_message, $e_file,
→ $e_line, $e_vars) {
```

The my_error_handler() function is set to receive the full five arguments that a custom error handler can.

4. Make the $live variable global.

```
global $live;
```

This variable, defined in Step 2, is the flag indicating what stage the site is in (development or live). To access the variable, the global keyword must be used here. See the section on variable scope in Chapter 3, "Creating Dynamic Web Sites," for more.

5. Create the error message using the received values.

```
$message = "An error occurred in
→ script '$e_file' on line $e_line:
→ $e_message\n";
```

The error message will begin by referencing the filename and number where the error occurred. Added to this is the actual error message.

6. Add any existing variables to the error message.

```
$message .= print_r ($e_vars, 1);
```

The $e_vars variable will receive all of the variables that exist, and their values, when the error happens. Because this might contain useful debugging information, I add it to the message.

The print_r() function is normally used to print out a variable's structure and value; it is particularly useful with arrays. If you call the function using the second argument (*1*), the result is returned instead of printed. So this line adds all of the variable information to $message.

7. Print a message that will vary, depending upon whether or not the site is live.

```
if ($live) {
    echo '<div class="error">A system
    → error occurred. We apologize
    → for the inconvenience.</div>
    → <br />';
} else {
    echo '<div class="error">' .
    → $message . '</div><br />';
}
```

If the site is live, a simple mea culpa will be printed, letting the user know that an error occurred but not what the specific problem is. If $live is false (when the site is being developed), the full message is printed instead.

8. Complete the function and tell PHP to use it.

```
}
set_error_handler ('my_error_
→ handler');
```

This second line is the important one, telling PHP to use the custom error handler instead of PHP's default handler.

9. Finish the PHP page.

```
?>
```

10. Save the file as handle.inc.php and upload it to your Web server.

To test the error handler, I'll create a dummy file that uses it to handle two silly mistakes.

To create errors:

1. Begin a new PHP document in your text editor, starting with the HTML head (**Script 6.3**).

   ```
   <!DOCTYPE html PUBLIC "-//W3C//DTD
   → XHTML 1.0 Transitional//EN"
   "http://www.w3.org/TR/xhtml1/DTD/
   → xhtml1-transitional.dtd">
   <html xmlns="http://www.w3.org/1999/
   → xhtml" xml:lang="en" lang="en">
   <head>
      <meta http-equiv="content-type"
   → content="text/html;
   → charset=iso-8859-1" />
      <title>OOPS!</title>
   </head>
   <body>
   ```

2. Open a section of PHP and include the error handling file.

   ```
   <?php # Script 6.3 - error.php
   include ('handle.inc.php');
   ```

   For this, or any, script to use the custom error handler, the handle.inc.php page just needs to be included.

3. Create a couple of purposeful errors to test the script.

   ```
   echo $variable;
   $result = 200/0;
   ```

   In order to see how the error reporting works, two simple errors are created. The problem with the first line is that the $variable variable is referenced before it has been assigned a value (this normally causes a *notice* in PHP).

   The second line is a classic division by zero, which is not allowed in programming languages or in math.

Script 6.3 This page includes the custom error handler and then makes two mistakes.

```
1   <!DOCTYPE html PUBLIC "-//W3C//DTD XHTML
    1.0 Transitional//EN"
2        "http://www.w3.org/TR/xhtml1/DTD/
         xhtml1-transitional.dtd">
3   <html xmlns="http://www.w3.org/1999/xhtml"
    xml:lang="en" lang="en">
4   <head>
5      <meta http-equiv="content-type" content=
       "text/html; charset=iso-8859-1" />
6      <title>OOPS!</title>
7   </head>
8   <body>
9   <?php # Script 6.3 - error.php
10  // Include the error handling file.
11  include ('handle.inc.php');
12
13  // Create some problems.
14  echo $variable;
15  $result = 200/0;
16  ?>
17  </body>
18  </html>
```

Figure 6.9 During the development phase, detailed error messages are printed in the Web browser.

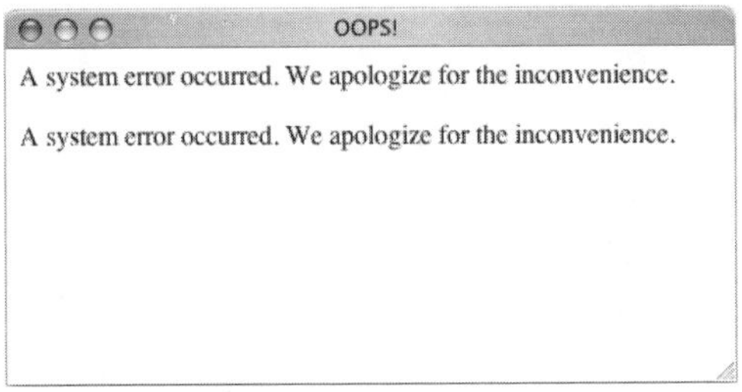

Figure 6.10 Once a site has gone live, more user-friendly (and less revealing) errors are printed.

4. Close the PHP code and the HTML page.

```
?>
</body>
</html>
```

5. Save the file as error.php, upload it to your Web server (in the same directory as handle.inc.php), and run in your Web browser (**Figure 6.9**).

6. Open handle.inc.php and change the value of $live to *TRUE*.

To see how the error handler behaves with a live site, just change this one value.

7. Save the file, upload it to your Web server, and test again by rerunning error.php (**Figure 6.10**).

✔ Tips

■ If your PHP page uses special HTML formatting—like CSS tags to affect the layout and font treatment—add this information to your error reporting function.

■ Obviously in a live site you'll probably need to do more than apologize for the inconvenience (particularly if a significantly affecting error occurs). Still, this example demonstrates how you can easily adjust error handling to suit the situation.

■ You can also invoke your error handling function using trigger_error().

■ New to PHP 4.3 is the debug_backtrace() function, which provides a *backtrace*, a list of information similar to that sent to an error handler. PHP 5 takes this one step further with debug_print_backtrace(), which prints out the backtrace data.

Logging PHP Errors

In the previous example, errors were handled by simply printing them out in detail or not. Another option is to log the errors: make a permanent note of them somehow. For this purpose, the error_log() function instructs PHP how to file an error.

```
error_log (message, type, destination,
→ extra headers);
```

The *message* value should be the text of the logged error. The *type* dictates how the error is logged. **Table 6.2** lists the types of error logging you can use. The *destination* parameter can be either the name of a file (for log type 3) or an email address (for log type 1). The *extra headers* argument is used only when sending emails (log type 1). Both the destination and extra headers are optional.

With this in mind, the error handling function will be modified so that it can email the errors that occur to you, the site's administrator.

Error Log Types	
NUMBER	MEANING
0	The message is logged using the operating system's default method.
1	The message is sent by email to the *destination* address.
2	The message is sent to a remote debugger (for example, another server).
3	The message is recorded in a text file.

Table 6.2 PHP can log errors using these four techniques.

Using die() and exit()

In Chapter 3, "Creating Dynamic Web Sites," the continue and break statements were used to control the execution of a script, specifically within control structures. For example, continue will halt the current execution of a loop and move on to the next iteration. Or the break statement can be used to exit loops and switch conditionals. Similar to these are die() and exit(), two synonymous functions (or language constructs, technically).

When a die() or exit() is called in your script, the entire script is terminated. These are useful for stopping a script from continuing should something important—like establishing a database connection—fail to happen. You can also pass die() and exit() a string that will be printed out in the browser.

You'll commonly see die() or exit() used in an OR conditional. For example:

```
include('config.inc.php') OR die ('Could not open the file.');
```

With a line like that, if PHP could not include the configuration file, the die() statement will be executed and the *Could not open the file.* message will be printed. You'll see variations on this throughout this book and in the PHP manual, as it's a quick (but potentially excessive) way to handle errors without using a custom error handler.

Script 6.4 This modified version of the error handling file sends emails when errors occur.

```
        script
1    <?php # Script 6.4 - handle.inc.php
2
3    // Flag variable for site status:
4    $live = FALSE;
5
6    // Error log email address:
7    $email = 'me@address.com';
8
9    // Create the error handler.
10   function my_error_handler ($e_number,
     $e_message, $e_file, $e_line, $e_vars) {
11
12       global $live, $email;
13
14       // Build the error message.
15       $message = "An error occurred in script
         '$e_file' on line $e_line: $e_message\n";
16
17       // Append $e_vars to the $message.
18       $message .= print_r ($e_vars, 1);
19
20       if ($live) { // Don't show the error.
21
22           error_log ($message, 1, $email); //
             Send email.
23           echo '<div class="error">A
             system error occurred. We apologize
             for the inconvenience.</div><br />';
24
25       } else { // Development (print the
         error).
26           echo '<div class="error">' .
             $message . '</div><br />';
27       }
28
29   } // End of my_error_handler() definition.
30
31   // Use my error handler.
32   set_error_handler ('my_error_handler');
33   ?>
```

To use error logging:

1. Open `handle.inc.php` (refer to Script 6.2) in your text editor.

2. After declaring the `$live` variable, define an email address (**Script 6.4**).

   `$email = 'me@address.com';`

   The email address should be yours, where the errors that occur should be sent.

3. Change the `global` line inside of the function so that the email address is available.

   `global $live, $email;`

   In order to use the email address, it must also be global.

4. If the site is live, also send the error message to an email address.

   `error_log ($message, 1, $email);`

   This function will send the error message to that email address.

5. Save the file and upload it to the same directory as `error.php`.

6. Rerun `error.php` with the `$live` variable equal to *TRUE*.

7. Check your email to see the error messages (**Figures 6.11** and **6.12** on next page).

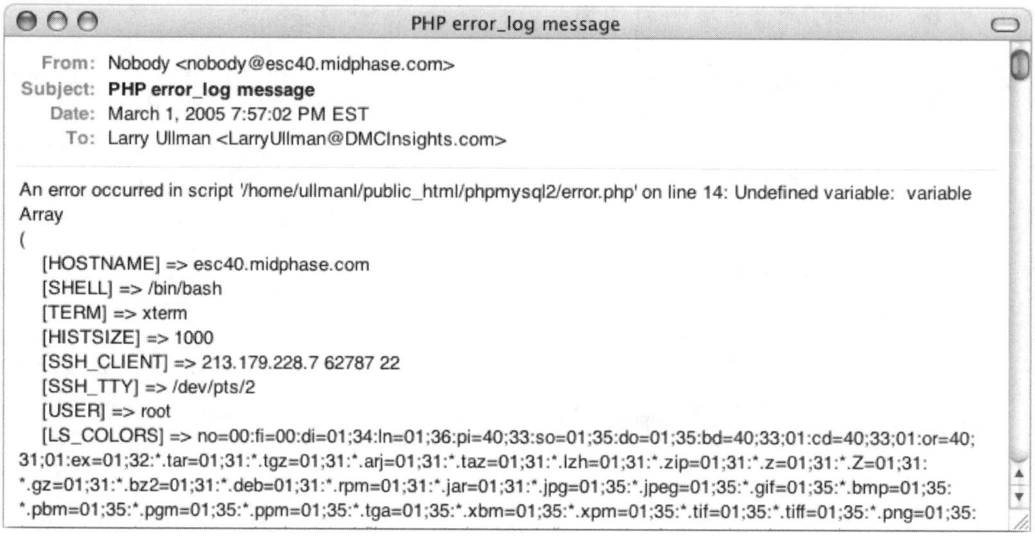

Figure 6.11 While the user stills sees a simple message in the browser, a detailed error message is emailed to the system administrator.

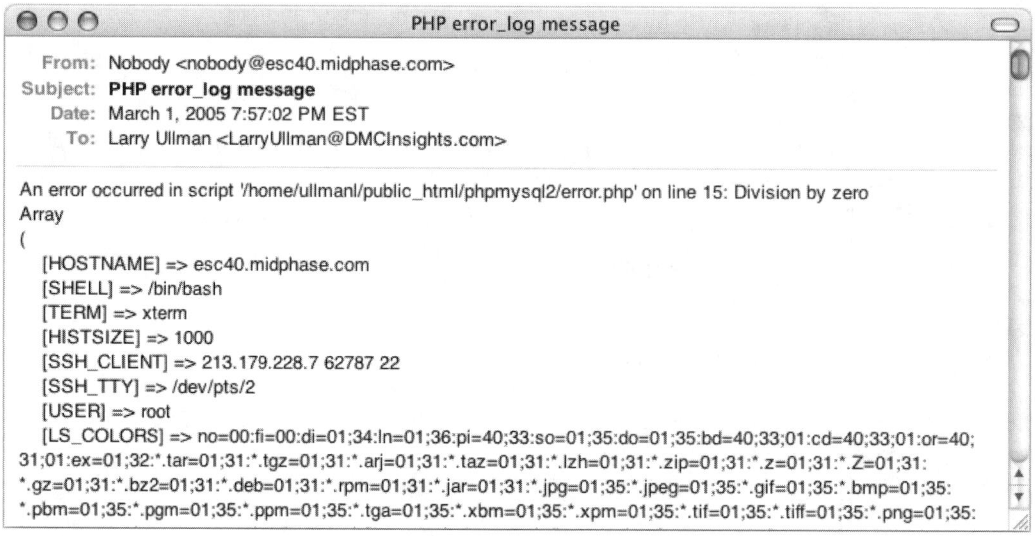

Figure 6.12 This is the second email, for the second error that occurred. Notice that the list of variables will differ from server to server (compare with those in Figure 6.9).

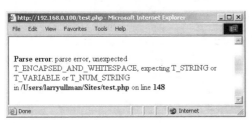

Figure 6.13 The parse error prevents a script from running because of invalid PHP syntax. This one was caused by failing to enclose `$array['key']` within curly braces when printing its value.

PHP Debugging Techniques

When it comes to debugging, what experience teaches you most is the causes of certain types of errors. Knowing this makes fixing the error much, much faster. To shorten the chase, **Table 6.3** lists the likely reasons for the most common PHP errors.

The first, and most common, type of error that you'll run across is syntactical and will prevent your scripts from executing. An error like this will result in messages like the one in **Figure 6.13**, which every PHP developer has seen too many times. To avoid making this sort of mistake when you program, be sure to:

◆ End every statement (but not language constructs like loops and conditionals) with a semicolon.

◆ Balance all quotation marks, parentheses, curly braces, and square brackets (each opening character must be closed).

continues on next page

Common PHP Errors

Error	Likely Cause
Blank Page	HTML problem, or PHP error and *display_errors* is off.
Parse error	Missing semicolon; unbalanced curly braces, parentheses, or quotation marks; or use of an unescaped quotation mark in a string.
Empty variable value	Forgot the initial **$**, misspelled or miscapitalized the variable name, inappropriate variable scope (with functions), or the `register_globals` setting is turned off.
Undefined variable	Reference made to a variable before it is given a value or an empty variable value (see those potential causes).
Call to undefined function	Misspelled function name, PHP is not configured to use that function (like a MySQL function), or document that contains the function definition is not properly included.
Cannot redeclare function	Two definitions of your own function exist, check within included files.
Headers already sent	White space exists in the script before the PHP tags, data has already been printed, or a file has been included.

Table 6.3 These are some of the most common errors you'll see in PHP, along with their most probable causes.

PHP DEBUGGING TECHNIQUES

- Be consistent with your quotation marks (single quotes can be closed only with single quotes and double quotes with double quotes).

- Escape, using the backslash, all single- and double-quotation marks within a `print()` statement, as appropriate.

One thing you should also understand about syntactical errors is that just because the PHP error message says the error is occurring on line 12, that doesn't mean that the mistake is actually on that line. At the very least, it is not uncommon for there to be a difference between what PHP thinks is line 12 and what your text editor indicates is line 12. So while PHP's direction is useful in tracking down a problem, treat the line number referenced as more of a starting point than an absolute.

If PHP reports an error on the last line of your document, this is almost always because a mismatched parenthesis, curly brace, or quotation mark was not caught until that moment.

The second type of error you'll encounter results from misusing a function. This error occurs, for example, when a function is called without the proper arguments. This error is discovered by PHP when attempting to execute the code. In later chapters you'll probably see such errors when using the `header()` function, cookies, or sessions.

To fix errors, you'll need to do a little detective work to see what mistakes were made and where. For starters, though, always thoroughly read and trust the error message PHP offers. Although the referenced line number may not always be correct, a PHP error is very descriptive.

To debug your scripts:

- Turn on *display_errors*.

  Use the earlier steps to enable *display_errors* for your entire server as you develop your applications.

- Use comments.

  Just as you can use comments to document your scripts, you can also use them to rule out problematic lines. If PHP is giving you an error on line 12, then commenting out that line should get rid of the error. If not, then you know the error is elsewhere. Just be careful that you don't introduce more errors by improperly commenting out only a portion of a code block: the syntax of your scripts must be maintained.

- Call the `print()` and `echo()` functions.

  In more complicated scripts, I frequently use `print()` statements to leave me notes as to what is happening as the script is executed (**Figure 6.14**). When a script has several steps, it may not be easy to know if the problem is occurring in step 2 or step 5. By using the `print()` statement, you can narrow the problem down to the specific juncture.

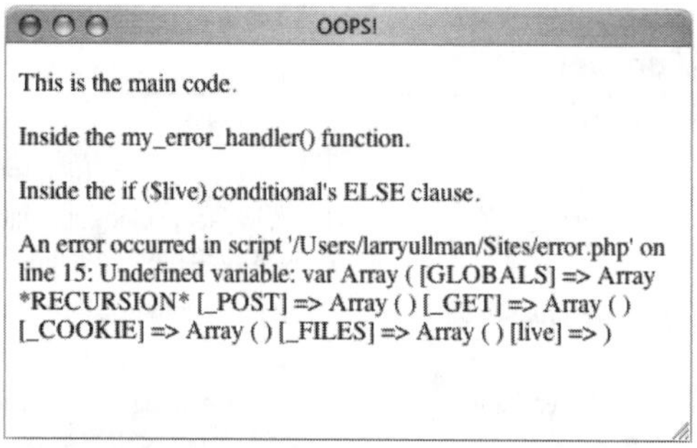

Figure 6.14 More complex debugging can be accomplished by leaving yourself notes as to what the script is doing.

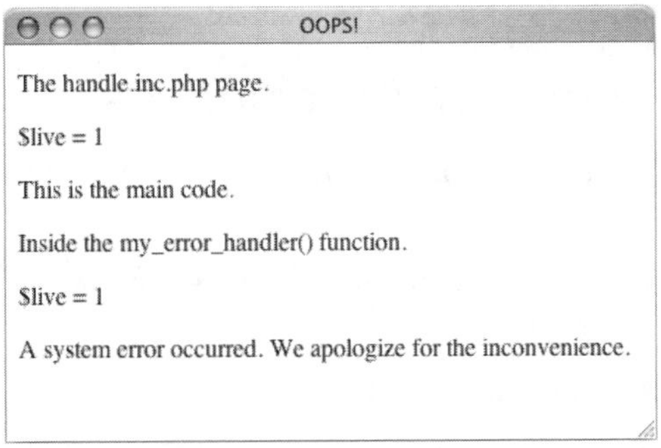

Figure 6.15 Using the `print()` and `echo()` functions is the easiest way to track the values of variables over the course of a script.

◆ Check what quotation marks are being used for printing variables.

It's not uncommon for programmers to mistakenly use single quotation marks and then wonder why their variables are not printed properly. Remember that single quotation marks treat text literally and that you must use double quotation marks to print out the values of variables.

◆ Track variables (**Figure 6.15**).

It is pretty easy for a script not to work because you referred to the wrong variable or the right variable by the wrong name or because the variable does not have the value you would expect. To check for these possibilities, use the `print()` or `echo()` statements to print out the values of variables at important points in your scripts. This is simply a matter of

```
echo "\$var = $var <br />\n";
```

The first dollar sign is escaped so that the variable's name is printed. The second reference of the variable will print its value.

◆ Print array values.

For more complicated variable types (arrays and objects), the `print_r()` and `var_dump()` functions will print out their values without the need for loops. Both functions accomplish the same task, although `var_dump()` is more detailed in its reporting than `print_r()`.

PHP DEBUGGING TECHNIQUES

✔ Tips

- Many text editors include utilities to check for balanced parentheses, brackets, and quotation marks.

- If you cannot find the parse error in a complex script, begin by using the /* */ comments to render the entire PHP code inert. Then continue to uncomment sections at a time (by moving the opening or closing comment characters) and rerun the script until you deduce what lines are causing the error. Watch how you comment out control structures, though, as the curly braces must continue to be matched in order to avoid parse errors. For example:

```
if (condition) {
/* Start comment.
Inert code.
End comment. */
}
```

- Some programmers advocate reverse testing to minimize the occurrence of logical errors. Reverse testing is the policy of switching your conditionals. For example,

```
if ($variable = 5) { …
```

may not seem incorrect among 500 lines of code but still causes problems because that condition will always be TRUE. Changing it to

```
if (5 = $variable) { …
```

will immediately send up a red flag because the number 5 cannot be assigned a value.

- To make the results of either print_r() or var_dump() more readable in the Web browser, I will frequently wrap them within HTML <pre> (preformatted) tags:

```
echo '<pre>';
print_r ($var);
echo '</pre>';
```

SQL and MySQL Debugging Techniques

The most common SQL errors are caused by the following issues:

- Unbalanced use of quotation marks or parentheses

- Unescaped apostrophes in column values

- Misspelling a column name, table name, or function

- Ambiguously referring to a column in a join

- Placing a query's clauses (WHERE, GROUP BY, ORDER BY, LIMIT) in the wrong order

Furthermore, when using MySQL you can also run across the following:

- Unpredictable or inappropriate query results

- Inability to access the database

- Difficulty starting MySQL

Since you'll be running the queries for your dynamic Web sites from PHP, you need a methodology for debugging SQL and MySQL errors within that context (PHP will not report a problem with your SQL).

Debugging SQL problems

To decide if you are experiencing a MySQL (or SQL) problem rather than a PHP one, you need a methodology for finding and fixing the issue. Fortunately, the steps you should take to debug MySQL and SQL problems are easy to define and should be followed without thinking. If you ever have any MySQL or SQL errors to debug, just abide by this sequence of steps.

Figure 6.16 Knowing exactly what query a PHP script is attempting to execute is the most useful first step for solving SQL and MySQL problems.

Figure 6.17 To understand what result a PHP script is receiving, run the same query through a separate interface. In this case the problem is the lack of quotes around *mypass*, so MySQL tries to treat it as a column (and such a column doesn't exist).

✔ Tips

- Another common MySQL problem is trying to run queries or connect using the mysql client when the MySQL server isn't even running. Be sure that MySQL is available for querying!

- As an alternative to printing out the query to the browser, you could print it out as an HTML comment (viewable only in the HTML source), using

  ```
  echo "<!-- $query -->";
  ```

To debug your SQL queries:

1. Print out any applicable queries in your PHP script (**Figure 6.16**).

   As you'll see in the next chapter, SQL queries will often be assigned to a `$query` variable, particularly as you use PHP to dynamically write them. Using the code `echo $query` (or variations on this) in your PHP scripts, you can send to the browser the exact query being run. Sometimes this step alone will help you see what the real problem is.

2. Run the query in the mysql client or other tool (**Figure 6.17**).

   The most foolproof method of debugging a SQL or MySQL problem is to run the query used in your PHP scripts through an independent application: the mysql client, phpMyAdmin, or the like. Doing so will give you the same result as the original PHP script receives but without the overhead and hassle.

   If the independent application returns the expected result but you are still not getting the proper behavior in your PHP script, then you will know that the problem lies within the script itself, not your SQL or MySQL database.

3. Rewrite the query in its most basic form, then keep adding dimensions back in until you discover which clause is causing the problem.

   Sometimes it's difficult to debug a query because there's too much going on. Like commenting out most of a PHP script, taking a query down to its bare minimum structure and slowly building it back up can be the easiest way to debug complex SQL commands.

Debugging access problems

Access denied error messages are the most common problem beginning developers encounter when using PHP to interact with MySQL. These are among the common solutions:

◆ Reload MySQL after altering the privileges so that the changes take effect. Either use the mysqladmin tool or run FLUSH PRIVILEGES in the mysql client. You must be logged in as a user with the appropriate permissions to do this (see Appendix A for more).

◆ Double-check the password used. The error message *Access denied for user: 'user@localhost' (Using password: YES)* frequently indicates that the password is wrong or mistyped. (This is not always the cause but is the first thing to check.)

◆ Do not forget to use the PASSWORD() function when setting privileges or updating a password.

◆ The error message *Can't connect to...* (error number 2002) indicates that MySQL either is not running or is not running on the socket or TCP/IP port tried by the client.

✔ Tips

■ MySQL keeps its own error logs, which are very useful in solving MySQL problems (like why MySQL won't even start). MySQL's error log will be located in the data directory and titled *hostname*.err.

■ The MySQL manual is very detailed, containing SQL examples, function references, and the meanings of error codes. Make the manual your friend and turn to it when confusing errors pop up.

PHP's mysql_error() Function

Error handling, which is important in any script, is even more of an issue when dealing with databases, since the probability for errors will increase dramatically. Printing out your queries and then running them through the mysql client is a key debugging technique but is certainly not the only tool.

To have your scripts give informative reports about errors that occur, make use of the mysql_error() function. It will return the error that MySQL had with the previous database interaction. Whether an error occurs in trying to connect to MySQL, in selecting the database to use, or in running a query (like that in Figure 6.17), the mysql_error() function will report on any problems, just as if the command was run in the mysql client. In the next and subsequent chapters you'll use this function extensively.

SQL AND MYSQL DEBUGGING TECHNIQUES

Using PHP with MySQL

Now that you have a sufficient amount of PHP, SQL, and MySQL experience under your belt, it's time to put all of the technologies together. PHP's strong integration with MySQL is just one reason so many programmers have embraced it, and you'll be amazed at how easily you can use the two together.

In this chapter I will use the existing *sitename* database—created in Chapter 4, "Introduction to SQL and MySQL"—to build a PHP interface for interacting with the *users* table. The knowledge taught and the examples used here will be the basis for all of your PHP-MySQL Web applications, as the principles involved are the same for any PHP-MySQL interaction.

Before heading into this chapter, you should be comfortable with everything covered in the first four chapters. Also, understanding the error debugging and handling techniques covered in Chapter 6 will make the learning process easier. Finally, remember that you need a PHP-enabled Web server and access to a running MySQL server in order to test the following examples.

Modifying the Template

Since all of the pages in this and the following chapter will be part of the same Web application, it'll be worthwhile to use a common template system. Instead of creating a new template from scratch, the layout from Chapter 3, "Creating Dynamic Web Sites," will be used again, with only a minor modification to the header file's navigation links.

To make the header file:

1. Open header.html (Script 3.2) in your text editor.

2. Change the list of links to read (**Script 7.1**)

   ```
   <li class="navtop"><a href="index.
   → php" title="Go to the Home
   → Page">Home</a></li>
   ```

   ```
   <li><a href="register.php" title=
   → "Register">Register</a></li>
   ```

   ```
   <li><a href="view_users.php"
   → title="View the Existing
   → Users">View Users</a></li>
   ```

   ```
   <li><a href="password.php" title=
   → "Change Your Password">Change
   → Password</a></li>
   ```

   All of the examples in this chapter will involve the registration, view users, and change password pages. The dateform and calculator links from Chapter 3 can be deleted.

3. Save the file as header.html.

4. Upload the new header file to your Web server, placing it into the includes directory along with footer.html (Script 3.3) and layout.css (available for download from the book's supporting Web site).

Script 7.1 The site's header file has been modified with new navigation links.

```
1   <!DOCTYPE html PUBLIC "-//W3C//DTD XHTML
    1.0 Transitional//EN"
2        "http://www.w3.org/TR/xhtml1/DTD/
         xhtml1-transitional.dtd">
3   <html xmlns="http://www.w3.org/1999/xhtml"
    xml:lang="en" lang="en">
4   <head>
5       <meta http-equiv="content-type" content=
        "text/html; charset=iso-8859-1" />
6       <title><?php echo $page_title;
        ?></title>
7       <style type="text/css" media="all">
        @import "./includes/layout.css"
        ;</style>
8   </head>
9   <body>
10  <div id="wrapper"><!-- Goes with the CSS
    layout. -->
11
12      <div id="content"><!-- Goes with the CSS
        layout. -->
13
14          <div id="nav"><!-- Links section -->
15              <h3>Menu</h3>
16              <ul>
17                  <li class="navtop"><a href=
                    "index.php" title="Go to the
                    Home Page">Home</a></li>
18                  <li><a href="register.php"
                    title="Register">Register
                    </a></li>
19                  <li><a href="view_users.php"
                    title="View the Existing
                    Users">View Users</a></li>
20                  <li><a href="password.php"
                    title="Change Your Password">
                    Change Password</a></li>
21              </ul>
22          </div>
23          <!-- Script 7.1 - header.html -->
24          <!-- Start of page-specific content.
            -->
```

5. Test the new header file by running `index.php` in your Web browser (**Figure 7.1**).

✔ Tips

- For a preview of this site's structure, see the "Organizing Your Documents" sidebar in the next section.

- Remember that you can use any file extension for your template files, including `.inc` or `.php`.

- To refresh your memory on the template-creation process or the specifics of this layout, see the first few pages of Chapter 3.

Figure 7.1 The dynamically generated home page.

Connecting to MySQL and Selecting the Database

The first step when dealing with MySQL—connecting to the server—requires the appropriately named `mysql_connect()` function:

```
$dbc = mysql_connect ($host, $user,
→ $password);
```

The arguments sent to the function (host, username, and password) are based upon the users and privileges set up within the *mysql* database (see Appendix A, "Installation," for more information). Commonly (but not always), the host to specify will be *localhost* (naming a different host will allow you to connect to MySQL running on a different server).

If the connection was made, the `$dbc` variable will become a reference point for all of your subsequent database interactions. Most of the PHP functions for working with MySQL can take this as an optional argument, but if it is omitted, the functions will automatically use the open connection.

Once you have connected to MySQL, you will need to select the database with which you want to work. This is the equivalent of saying USE *databasename* within the mysql client and is accomplished with the `mysql_select_db()` function:

```
mysql_select_db($database_name);
```

I'll start the demonstration of connecting to MySQL by creating a special file just for that purpose. Other PHP scripts that require a MySQL connection can include this file. I'll also make use of the `mysql_error()` function, which was briefly introduced at the end of the preceding chapter.

To connect to and select a database:

1. Create a new PHP document in your text editor (**Script 7.2**).

   ```php
   <?php # Script 7.2 - mysql_connect.php
   ```

2. Set the database host, username, password, and database name as constants.

   ```php
   DEFINE ('DB_USER', 'username');
   DEFINE ('DB_PASSWORD', 'password');
   DEFINE ('DB_HOST', 'localhost');
   DEFINE ('DB_NAME', 'sitename');
   ```

   I prefer to establish these variables as constants for security reasons (they cannot be changed this way), but that isn't required. In general, setting these values as some sort of variable makes sense so that you can separate the configuration parameters from the functions that use them, but again, this is not obligatory.

   When writing your script, change these values to ones that will work with your database. Or do what I did and grant the proper permissions to a user called *username* with a password of *password*.

3. Connect to MySQL.

   ```php
   $dbc = @mysql_connect (DB_HOST,
   → DB_USER, DB_PASSWORD) OR die
   → ('Could not connect to MySQL: '
   →  . mysql_error() );
   ```

   The mysql_connect() function, if it successfully connects to MySQL, will return a resource link that corresponds to the open connection. This link will be assigned to the $dbc variable (for *database connection*), which gives me the option of referring to the connection explicitly when using the other MySQL-specific functions.

   The function call is preceded by the error suppression operator (@). This prevents the PHP error from being displayed in the Web browser (which is preferred, as the error will be handled by the OR die() clause).

Script 7.2 The mysql_connect.php script will be used by every other script in this application. It establishes a connection to MySQL and selects the database.

```php
1    <?php # Script 7.2 - mysql_connect.php
2
3    // This file contains the database access
     information.
4    // This file also establishes a connection
     to MySQL and selects the database.
5
6    // Set the database access information as
     constants.
7    DEFINE ('DB_USER', 'username');
8    DEFINE ('DB_PASSWORD', 'password');
9    DEFINE ('DB_HOST', 'localhost');
10   DEFINE ('DB_NAME', 'sitename');
11
12   // Make the connection.
13   $dbc = @mysql_connect (DB_HOST, DB_USER,
     DB_PASSWORD) OR die ('Could not connect to
     MySQL: ' . mysql_error() );
14
15   // Select the database.
16   @mysql_select_db (DB_NAME) OR die ('Could
     not select the database: ' .
     mysql_error() );
17   ?>
```

Figure 7.2 A visual representation of a server's Web documents, where `mysql_connect.php` is not stored within the main directory (*html*).

If the `mysql_connect()` function cannot return a valid resource link, then the `OR die()` part of the statement is executed (because the first part of the `OR` will be false, so the second part must be true). As discussed in the preceding chapter, the `die()` function terminates the execution of the script. The function can also take as an argument a string that will be printed to the Web browser. In this case, the string is a combination of *Could not connect to MySQL:* and the specific MySQL error. Using this blunt error management system makes debugging much easier as you develop your sites.

4. Select the database to be used and close the PHP page.

```
@mysql_select_db (DB_NAME) OR die
→ ('Could not select the database:
→ ' . mysql_error() );
?>
```

This final step tells MySQL on what database every query should be run. Failure to select the database will create problems in later scripts, although if an application uses multiple databases, you might not want to select one here.

Again, the `OR die()` construct is used to handle any MySQL problems, and the `@` suppresses the original PHP error.

5. Save the file as `mysql_connect.php`.

Since this file contains information that must be kept private (the database access data), I'll use a `.php` extension. With a `.php` extension, even if malicious users ran this script in their Web browser, they would not see the page's actual content.

6. Upload the file to your server, outside of the Web document root (**Figure 7.2**).

continues on next page

Because the file contains sensitive MySQL access information, it ought to be stored securely. If you can, place it in the directory immediately above or otherwise outside of the Web directory. This way the file will not be accessible from a Web browser.

7. Temporarily place a copy of the script within the Web document root and run the script in your Web browser (**Figures 7.3** and **7.4**).

In order to test the script, you'll want to place a copy on the server so that it's accessible from the Web browser (which means it must be in the Web directory). If the script works properly, the result should be a blank page (see Figure 7.3). If you see an *Access denied...* or similar message (see Figure 7.4), it means that the combination of username, password, and host does not have permission to access the particular database.

8. Remove the temporary copy from the Web directory.

✔ Tips

■ The same values used in Chapter 4, "Introduction to SQL and MySQL," and Chapter 5, "Advanced SQL and MySQL," to log into the mysql client should work from your PHP scripts.

■ If you receive an error that claims `mysql_connect()` is an undefined function, it means that PHP has not been compiled with MySQL support. See the first appendix for installation information.

■ If you see an *Access denied...* error message when running the script (see Figure 7.4), use the mysql client to test your connection information. Also confirm that MySQL is running.

Figure 7.3 If the MySQL connection script works properly, the end result will be a blank page (no HTML is generated by the script).

Figure 7.4 If there were problems connecting to MySQL, an informative message is displayed and the script is halted.

```
●●●          http://localhost/mysql_connect.php

Warning: mysql_connect() [function.mysql-connect]: Access denied for
user 'username'@'localhost' (using password: YES) in
/Users/larryullman/Sites/mysql_connect.php on line 13
Could not connect to MySQL: Access denied for user
'username'@'localhost' (using password: YES)
```

Figure 7.5 If you don't use the error suppression operator (@), you'll see both the PHP error and the custom OR die() error.

■ Once you've written one `mysql_connect.php` file, you can easily make changes to the `define()` lines to use the script for other projects.

■ In case you are curious, **Figure 7.5** shows what would happen if you didn't use @ before `mysql_connect()` and an error occurred.

■ If you need to connect to multiple database servers in the same script, you can use multiple `mysql_connect()` calls, assigning the returned results to different PHP variables.

Executing Simple Queries

Once you have successfully connected to and selected a database, you can start performing queries. These queries can be as basic as inserts, updates, and deletions or as involved as complex joins returning numerous rows. In any case, the PHP function for executing a query is `mysql_query()`:

```
$result = mysql_query($query);
```

For simple queries like INSERT, UPDATE, DELETE, etc. (which do not return records), the `$result` variable will be either TRUE or FALSE depending upon whether the query executed successfully. For complex queries that do return records (SELECT, SHOW, DESCRIBE, and EXPLAIN), the `$result` variable will be a resource link to the results of the query if it worked or be FALSE if it did not.

One final, albeit optional, step in your script would be to close the existing MySQL connection once you're finished with it:

```
mysql_close();
```

This function is not required, because PHP will automatically close the connection at the end of a script, but it does make for good programming form to incorporate it.

To demonstrate this process, I'll write another registration script like the one from Chapter 3 (refer to Script 3.13). In this version, the user's information will actually be entered into the *users* table of the *sitename* database.

Organizing Your Documents

I introduced the concept of site structure back in Chapter 3 when developing the first Web application. Now that I'll begin using a database connection script, the topic is more important.

Should the database connectivity information (username, password, host, and database) fall into malicious hands, it could be used to steal your information or wreak havoc upon the database as a whole. Therefore, you cannot keep a script like `mysql_connect.php` too secure.

The most important recommendation for securing such a file is to store it outside of the Web documents directory. If, for example, the *html* folder in Figure 7.2 is the root of the Web directory (in other words, the URL `www.DMCInsights.com` leads there), then not storing `mysql_connect.php` anywhere within the *html* directory means it will never be accessible via the Web browser. Granted, the source code of PHP scripts is not viewable from the Web browser (only the data sent to the browser by the script is), but you can never be too careful.

Secondarily, I would recommend using a `.php` extension for your connection scripts. A properly configured and working server will execute rather than display code in such a file. Conversely, if you use just `.inc` as your extension, that page's contents would be displayed in the Web browser if accessed directly.

To execute simple queries:

1. Create a new PHP script in your text editor (**Script 7.3**).

   ```php
   <?php # Script 7.3 - register.php
   $page_title = 'Register';
   include ('./includes/header.html');
   ```

   Although most of the script will be similar to register.php from Chapter 3, I'll write it from scratch as a refresher.

2. Create the submission conditional and initialize the $errors array.

   ```php
   if (isset($_POST['submitted'])) {
       $errors = array();
   ```

   This script will both display and handle the HTML form. This conditional will check whether or not to process the form. The $errors variable is initialized so that no warnings are created when I build upon it later. It will be used as it was in Chapter 3.

3. Validate the first name.

   ```php
   if (empty($_POST['first_name'])) {
       $errors[] = 'You forgot to enter
       → your first name.';
   } else {
       $fn = trim($_POST['first_name']);
   }
   ```

   As in the previous examples, the empty() function is used as a minimal way of ensuring that a text field was filled out. If the first name field was not filled out, an error message is added to the $errors array. Otherwise, $fn is set to the submitted value, after trimming off any extraneous spaces. By using this new variable—which is obviously short for *first_name*—I make it syntactically easier to write my query later.

4. Validate the last name and email address.

   ```php
   if (empty($_POST['last_name'])) {
       $errors[] = 'You forgot to enter
       → your last name.';
   } else {
       $ln = trim($_POST['last_name']);
   }
   if (empty($_POST['email'])) {
       $errors[] = 'You forgot to enter
       → your email address.';
   } else {
       $e = trim($_POST['email']);
   }
   ```

   These lines are syntactically the same as those validating the first name field. In both cases a new variable will be created, assuming that the minimal validation was passed.

5. Validate the password.

   ```php
   if (!empty($_POST['password1'])) {
       if ($_POST['password1'] != $_POST
       → ['password2']) {
           $errors[] = 'Your password did
           → not match the confirmed
           → password.';
       } else {
           $p = trim($_POST['password1']);
       }
   } else {
       $errors[] = 'You forgot to enter
       → your password.';
   }
   ```

   To validate the password I need to check the *password1* input for a value and then confirm that the *password1* value matches the *password2* value (so the password and confirmed password are the same).

continues on page 244

Script 7.3 The registration script adds a record to the database.

```
1    <?php # Script 7.3 - register.php
2
3    $page_title = 'Register';
4    include ('./includes/header.html');
5
6    // Check if the form has been submitted.
7    if (isset($_POST['submitted'])) {
8
9        $errors = array(); // Initialize error array.
10
11       // Check for a first name.
12       if (empty($_POST['first_name'])) {
13           $errors[] = 'You forgot to enter your first name.';
14       } else {
15           $fn = trim($_POST['first_name']);
16       }
17
18       // Check for a last name.
19       if (empty($_POST['last_name'])) {
20           $errors[] = 'You forgot to enter your last name.';
21       } else {
22           $ln = trim($_POST['last_name']);
23       }
24
25       // Check for an email address.
26       if (empty($_POST['email'])) {
27           $errors[] = 'You forgot to enter your email address.';
28       } else {
29           $e = trim($_POST['email']);
30       }
31
32       // Check for a password and match against the confirmed password.
33       if (!empty($_POST['password1'])) {
34           if ($_POST['password1'] != $_POST['password2']) {
35               $errors[] = 'Your password did not match the confirmed password.';
36           } else {
37               $p = trim($_POST['password1']);
38           }
39       } else {
40           $errors[] = 'You forgot to enter your password.';
41       }
42
```

(script continues on page 245)

EXECUTING SIMPLE QUERIES

6. Check if it's OK to register the user.

```
if (empty($errors)) {
```

If the submitted data passed all of the conditions, this condition will be TRUE and it's safe to proceed. If not, then the appropriate error messages should be printed and the user given another opportunity to register.

7. Add the user to the database.

```
require_once ('../mysql_connect.
→ php');
$query = "INSERT INTO users
→ (first_name, last_name, email,
→ password, registration_date)
→ VALUES ('$fn', '$ln', '$e',
→ SHA('$p'), NOW() )";
$result = @mysql_query ($query);
```

The first line of code will insert the contents of the mysql_connect.php file into this script, thereby creating a connection to MySQL and selecting the database. You may need to change the reference to the location of the file as it is on your server.

The query itself is similar to those demonstrated in Chapter 4. The SHA() function is used to encrypt the password, and NOW() is used to set the registration date as this moment.

After assigning the query to a variable, it is run through the mysql_query() function, which sends the SQL command to the MySQL database. As in the mysql_connect.php script, the mysql_query() call is preceded by @ in order to suppress any ugly errors. If a problem occurs, the error will be handled more directly in the next step.

8. Report on the success of the registration.

```
if ($result) {
    echo '<h1 id="mainhead">Thank you!
    → </h1>
```

```
<p>You are now registered.
→ In Chapter 9 you will actually
→ be able to log in!</p><p>
→ <br /></p>';
include ('./includes/footer.html');
exit();

} else {
    echo '<h1 id="mainhead">System
    → Error</h1>
<p class="error">You could not be
→ registered due to a system
→ error. We apologize for any
→ inconvenience.</p>';
    echo '<p>' . mysql_error()
    → . '<br /><br />Query: ' . $query
    → . '</p>';
    include ('./includes/footer.html');
    exit();
}
```

The $result variable, which is assigned the value returned by mysql_query(), can be used in a conditional to indicate the successful operation of the query. In this example, you could also save yourself a line of code by writing the conditional as

```
if (@mysql_query ($query)) {
```

If $result is TRUE, then a message is displayed, the footer is included, and the script is halted (using exit()). If I didn't include the footer here and exit the script, then the registration form would be displayed again. You could also send an email upon successful registration, as I had in Chapter 3.

If $result is FALSE, error messages are printed. For debugging purposes, the error messages will include both the error spit out by MySQL (thanks to the mysql_error() function) and the query that was run. Again, the footer is included and the page's execution is halted so that the form is not redisplayed.

continues on page 246

Script 7.3 *continued*

```
43      if (empty($errors)) { // If everything's okay.
44
45          // Register the user in the database.
46          require_once ('../mysql_connect.php'); // Connect to the db.
47
48          // Make the query.
49          $query = "INSERT INTO users (first_name, last_name, email, password, registration_date)
            VALUES ('$fn', '$ln', '$e', SHA('$p'), NOW() )";
50          $result = @mysql_query ($query); // Run the query.
51          if ($result) { // If it ran OK.
52
53              // Send an email, if desired.
54
55              // Print a message.
56              echo '<h1 id="mainhead">Thank you!</h1>
57          <p>You are now registered. In Chapter 9 you will actually be able to log in!</p><p><br />
            </p>';
58
59              // Include the footer and quit the script (to not show the form).
60              include ('./includes/footer.html');
61              exit();
62
63          } else { // If it did not run OK.
64              echo '<h1 id="mainhead">System Error</h1>
65          <p class="error">You could not be registered due to a system error. We apologize for any
            inconvenience.</p>'; // Public message.
66              echo '<p>' . mysql_error() . '<br /><br />Query: ' . $query . '</p>'; // Debugging message.
67              include ('./includes/footer.html');
68              exit();
69          }
70
```

(script continues on page 247)

9. Close the database connection.

```
mysql_close();
```

This isn't required but is a good policy.

10. Print out any error messages and close the submit conditional.

```
    } else {
        echo '<h1 id="mainhead">Error!
→ </h1>
        <p class="error">The following
→ error(s) occurred:<br />';
        foreach ($errors as $msg) {
                echo " - $msg<br />\n";
        }
        echo '</p><p>Please try again.
→ </p><p><br /></p>';
    }
}
```

The `else` clause is invoked if there were any errors. In that case, all of the errors are displayed using a `foreach` loop, exactly as in Chapter 3.

The final closing curly brace closes the main submit conditional. In Chapter 3, the main conditional was an `if-else`, so that either the form was displayed or it was handled. In order for the form to be sticky (again, see Chapter 3), a different structure is used here.

11. Close the PHP code and begin the HTML form.

```
?>
<h2>Register</h2>
<form action="register.php"
→ method="post">
  <p>First Name: <input type="text"
→ name="first_name" size="15"
→ maxlength="15" value="<?php if
→ (isset($_POST['first_name']))
→ echo $_POST['first_name'];
→ ?>" /></p>
  <p>Last Name: <input type="text"
→ name="last_name" size="15"
→ maxlength="30" value="<?php if
→ (isset($_POST['last_name']))
→ echo $_POST['last_name'];
→ ?>" /></p>
```

The form itself is nearly identical to its brethren in Chapter 3, although I have broken the name into separate first and last inputs and made the text fields sticky.

Also, I would strongly recommend that you use the same name for your form inputs as the corresponding column in the database where that value will be stored. Further, you should set the maximum input length in the form equal to the maximum column length in the database. Both of these habits help to minimize errors.

continues on page 248

EXECUTING SIMPLE QUERIES

Script 7.3 *continued*

```
                                              script
71        mysql_close(); // Close the database connection.
72
73    } else { // Report the errors.
74
75        echo '<h1 id="mainhead">Error!</h1>';
76        <p class="error">The following error(s) occurred:<br />';
77        foreach ($errors as $msg) { // Print each error.
78            echo " - $msg<br />\n";
79        }
80        echo '</p><p>Please try again.</p><p><br /></p>';
81
82    } // End of if (empty($errors)) IF.
83
84  } // End of the main Submit conditional.
85  ?>
86  <h2>Register</h2>
87  <form action="register.php" method="post">
88      <p>First Name: <input type="text" name="first_name" size="15" maxlength="15" value="<?php if
        (isset($_POST['first_name'])) echo $_POST['first_name']; ?>" /></p>
89      <p>Last Name: <input type="text" name="last_name" size="15" maxlength="30" value="<?php if
        (isset($_POST['last_name'])) echo $_POST['last_name']; ?>" /></p>
90      <p>Email Address: <input type="text" name="email" size="20" maxlength="40" value="<?php if
        (isset($_POST['email'])) echo $_POST['email']; ?>"  /> </p>
91      <p>Password: <input type="password" name="password1" size="10" maxlength="20" /></p>
92      <p>Confirm Password: <input type="password" name="password2" size="10" maxlength="20" /></p>
93      <p><input type="submit" name="submit" value="Register" /></p>
94      <input type="hidden" name="submitted" value="TRUE" />
95  </form>
96  <?php
97  include ('./includes/footer.html');
98  ?>
```

EXECUTING SIMPLE QUERIES

12. Complete the HTML form.

```
<p>Email Address: <input
→ type="text" name="email"
→ size="20" maxlength="40"
→ value="<?php if (isset($_POST
→ ['email'])) echo $_POST
→ ['email']; ?>" /> </p>

<p>Password: <input
→ type="password" name=
→ "password1" size="10"
→ maxlength="20" /></p>

<p>Confirm Password: <input
→ type="password" name=
→ "password2" size="10"
→ maxlength="20" /></p>

<p><input type="submit" name=
→ "submit" value="Register"
→ /></p>

<input type="hidden" name=
→ "submitted" value="TRUE" />

</form>
```

Again, most of this form is exactly as it was in Chapter 3. As a side note, I don't need to follow my `maxlength` recommendation (from Step 11) with the password inputs, because they will be encrypted with `SHA()`, which always creates a string 40 characters long.

13. Complete the page using the HTML footer.

```
<?php
include ('./includes/footer.html');
?>
```

14. Save the file as `register.php`, upload to your Web server in the same directory as `index.php`, and test the file by running the script in your Web browser (**Figures 7.6**, **7.7**, and **7.8**).

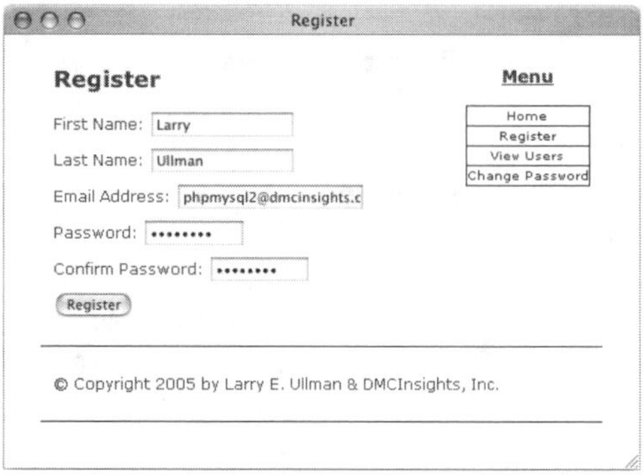

Figure 7.6 The registration form.

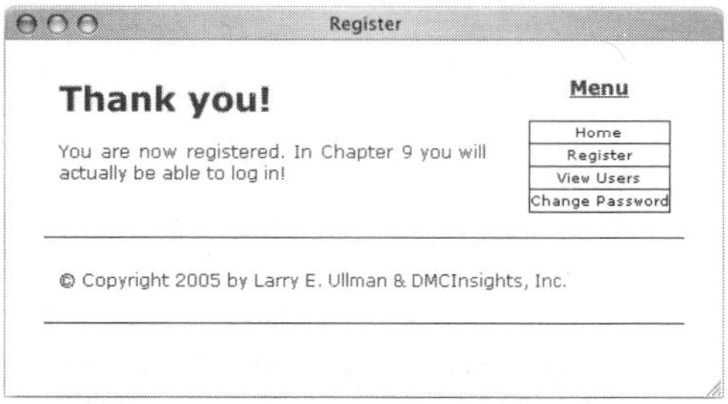

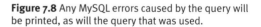

Figure 7.7 If the user could be registered in the database, this message is displayed.

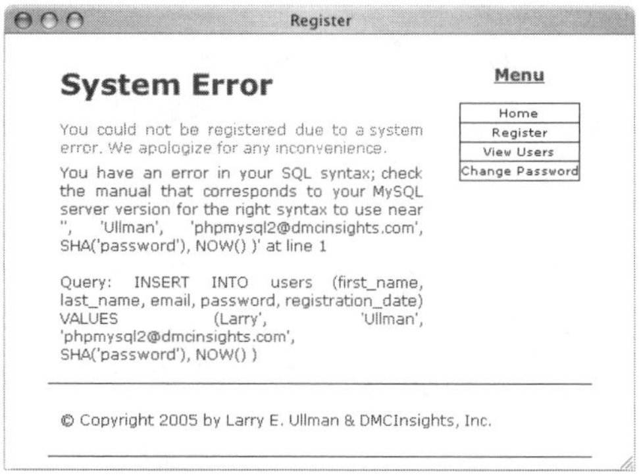

Figure 7.8 Any MySQL errors caused by the query will be printed, as will the query that was used.

✔ Tips

- After running the script, you can always ensure that it worked by using the mysql client to view the values in the table.

- As you saw in Chapter 6, there are many ways of handling errors. In these scripts, the `mysql_error()` function will be called and the query will be printed, should the query not successfully run. These steps are only for easier debugging and shouldn't be used in a live site.

- You should not end your queries with a semicolon in PHP, as you did when using the mysql client. When working with MySQL, this is a common, albeit harmless, mistake to make. When working with other database applications (Oracle, for one), doing so will make your queries unusable.

- The `mysql_query()` function returns TRUE if the query could be executed on the database. This does not necessarily mean that the result of the query is what you were expecting. Later scripts will demonstrate how to more accurately gauge the success of a query.

- Remember that the best method of debugging PHP scripts that interact with MySQL is to use the `mysql_error()` function, have PHP print out your query, and, if still confused, run the query through the mysql client or a similar tool.

- You are not necessarily obligated to create a `$query` variable as I tend to do (you could directly insert your query text into `mysql_query()`). However, as the construction of your queries becomes more complex, using a variable will be the only option.

- Practically any query you would run in the mysql client can also be executed using `mysql_query()`.

Retrieving Query Results

In the preceding section of this chapter I discussed and demonstrated how to execute simple queries on a MySQL database. A simple query, as I'm calling it, could be defined as one that begins with INSERT, UPDATE, DELETE, or ALTER. What all four of these have in common is that they return no data, just an indication of their success. Conversely, a SELECT query generates information (i.e., it will return rows of records) that has to be handled by other PHP functions.

The primary tool for handling SELECT query results is mysql_fetch_array(), which takes the query result variable (that I've been calling $result) and returns one row of data at a time, in an array format. You'll want to use this function within a loop that will continue to access every returned row as long as there are more to be read. The basic construction for reading every record from a query is

```
while ($row = mysql_fetch_array
→ ($result)) {

    // Do something with $row.

}
```

The mysql_fetch_array() function takes an optional parameter specifying what type of array is returned: associative, indexed, or both. An associative array allows you to refer to column values by name, whereas an indexed array requires you to use only numbers (starting at 0 for the first column returned). Each parameter is defined by a constant listed in **Table 7.1**. The MYSQL_NUM setting is marginally faster (and uses less memory) than the other options. Conversely, MYSQL_ASSOC is more specific ($row['column'] rather than $row[3]) and will continue to work even if the table structure or query changes.

An optional step you can take when using mysql_fetch_array() would be to free up the query result resources once you are done using them:

```
mysql_free_result ($result);
```

This line removes the overhead (memory) taken by $result. It's an optional step, since PHP will automatically free up the resources at the end of a script, but—like using mysql_close()—it does make for good programming form.

To demonstrate how to handle results returned by a query, I will create a script for viewing all of the currently registered users.

mysql_fetch_array() Constants

CONSTANT	EXAMPLE
MYSQL_ASSOC	$row['column']
MYSQL_NUM	$row[0]
MYSQL_BOTH	$row[0] or $row['column']

Table 7.1 Adding one of these constants as an optional parameter to the mysql_fetch_array() function dictates how you can access the values returned. The default setting of the function is MYSQL_BOTH.

Script 7.4 The `view_users.php` script runs a static query on the database and prints all of the returned rows.

```
1   <?php # Script 7.4 - view_users.php
2   // This script retrieves all the records
    from the users table.
3
4   $page_title = 'View the Current Users';
5   include ('./includes/header.html');
6
7   // Page header.
8   echo '<h1 id="mainhead">Registered Users
    </h1>';
9
10  require_once ('../mysql_connect.php');
    // Connect to the db.
11
12  // Make the query.
13  $query = "SELECT CONCAT(last_name, ', ',
    first_name) AS name, DATE_FORMAT
    (registration_date, '%M %d, %Y') AS dr
    FROM users ORDER BY registration_date
    ASC";
14  $result = @mysql_query ($query); //
    Run the query.
15
16  if ($result) { // If it ran OK, display the
    records.
17
18    // Table header.
19    echo '<table align="center"
      cellspacing="0" cellpadding="5">
20    <tr><td align="left"><b>Name</b></td>
      <td align="left"><b>Date Registered</b>
      </td></tr>
21  ';
22
23    // Fetch and print all the records.
24    while ($row = mysql_fetch_array
      ($result, MYSQL_ASSOC)) {
25      echo '<tr><td align="left">' .
        $row['name'] . '</td><td align=
        "left">' . $row['dr'] . '</td></tr>
26      ';
27    }
28
```

(script continues on next page)

To retrieve query results:

1. Create a new PHP document in your text editor (**Script 7.4**).

```
<?php # Script 7.4 - view_users.php
$page_title = 'View the Current
→Users';
include ('./includes/header.html');
echo '<h1 id="mainhead">Registered
→Users</h1>';
```

2. Connect to and query the database.

```
require_once ('../mysql_connect.
→php');
$query = "SELECT CONCAT(last_name,
→', ', first_name) AS name,
→DATE_FORMAT(registration_date,
→'%M %d, %Y') AS dr FROM users ORDER
→BY registration_date ASC";
$result = @mysql_query ($query);
```

The query here will return two columns: the users' names (formatted as *Last Name, First Name*) and the date they registered (formatted as *Month DD, YYYY*). Because both columns are formatted using MySQL functions, aliases are given to the returned results (*name* and *dr*, accordingly). See Chapter 4 if you are confused by any of this syntax.

continues on next page

3. Display the query results.

```
if ($result) {
    echo '<table align="center"
    → cellspacing="0" cellpadding="5">
    <tr><td align="left"><b>Name
    → </b></td><td align="left">
    → <b>Date Registered</b></td></tr>
';
    while ($row = mysql_fetch_array
    → ($result, MYSQL_ASSOC)) {
        echo '<tr><td align="left">'
        → . $row['name'] . '</td>
        → <td align="left">' .
        → $row['dr'] . '</td></tr>
        ';
    }
    echo '</table>';
```

To display the results, I first make a table and header row in HTML. Then I loop through the results using `mysql_fetch_array()` and print each subsequent row. Finally, I close the table.

Notice that within the `while` loop, I refer to each returned value using the proper alias: $row['name'] and $row['dr']. I could not refer to $row['first_name'] or $row['date_registered'] because no such field name was returned (you can confirm this by running the same query in the mysql client).

4. Free up the query resources.

```
mysql_free_result ($result);
```

Again, this is an optional step but a good one to take.

Script 7.4 *continued*

```
29      echo '</table>';
30
31      mysql_free_result ($result); // Free up
        the resources.
32
33  } else { // If it did not run OK.
34      echo '<p class="error">The current users
        could not be retrieved. We apologize for
        any inconvenience.</p>'; // Public
        message.
35      echo '<p>' . mysql_error() . '<br />
        <br />Query: ' . $query . '</p>'; //
        Debugging message.
36  }
37
38  mysql_close(); // Close the database
    connection.
39
40  include ('./includes/footer.html'); //
    Include the HTML footer.
41  ?>
```

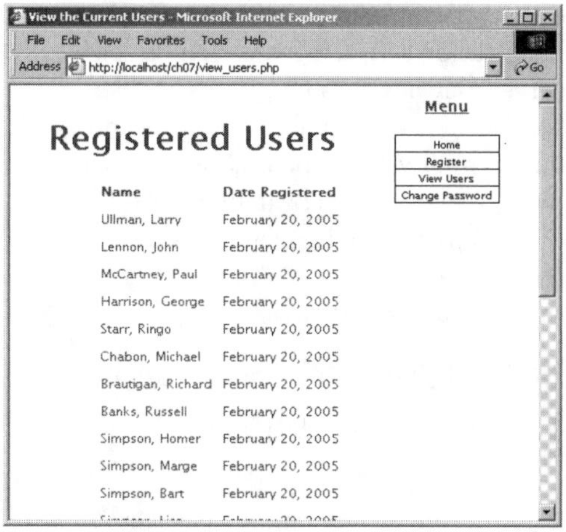

Figure 7.9 All of the user records are retrieved from the database and displayed in the Web browser.

5. Complete the conditional.

```
} else {
    echo '<p class="error">The current
    → users could not be retrieved.
    → We apologize for any
    → inconvenience.</p>';
    echo '<p>' . mysql_error() .
    → '<br /><br />Query: ' . $query .
    → '</p>';
}
```

As in the previous example, there are two error messages here. The first is a generic message, the kind you'd show in a live site. The second is much more detailed, printing both the MySQL error and the query, and is critical for debugging purposes.

6. Close the database connection and finish the page.

```
mysql_close();
include ('./includes/footer.html');
?>
```

7. Save the file as view_users.php, upload to your Web server, and test in your browser (**Figure 7.9**).

✔ Tips

■ If you are in a situation where you need to run a second query inside of your while loop, be certain to use different variable names for it ($result2 and $row2 instead of $result and $row), or else you'll encounter logical errors.

■ I frequently see beginning PHP developers muddle the process of fetching query results. Remember that you must execute the query using mysql_query(), then use mysql_fetch_array() to retrieve a single row of information. If you have multiple rows to retrieve, use a while loop (not for or foreach).

■ The function mysql_fetch_row() (which you might run across) is the equivalent of mysql_fetch_array ($result, MYSQL_NUM);

■ The function mysql_fetch_assoc() is the equivalent of mysql_fetch_array ($result, MYSQL_ASSOC);

■ As with any array, when you retrieve records from the database, you must refer to the columns exactly as they are defined in the database if using the array associatively (that is to say, the keys are case-sensitive).

Ensuring Secure SQL

Database security with respect to PHP comes down to two broad issues:

1. Protecting the database access information

2. Being cautious when running queries, particular those involving user-submitted data

You can accomplish the first objective by securing the MySQL connection script outside of the Web directory so that it is never viewable through a Web browser. I discussed this is some detail earlier in the chapter.

For the second objective, there are numerous steps you can and should take. First, as I've been doing in this chapter, be sure to use the $_POST array (or $_GET) instead of global variables. Second, validate that some data has been submitted, or that it is of the proper type (number, string, etc.). Third, use regular expressions to make sure that submitted data matches what you would expect it to be. Regular expressions will also be covered in Chapter 10. A fourth recommendation is to use the specific mysql_real_escape_string() function. This function cleans data by escaping what could be problematic characters:

$data = mysql_real_escape_string
→ ($data, $dbc);

This function acts like addslashes()—and should be used with any text fields from your forms—but is more database-specific. It was added in version 4.3 of PHP. If you are using an older version of PHP, use this function and syntax instead (notice that no database connection is required):

$data = mysql_escape_string ($data);

I'll incorporate this new function into the registration script. However, since your server may have Magic Quotes enabled, the script will need to make sure that submitted data is not over-escaped. Thus, the escape_data() function will be defined, making use of a new function, ini_get(), as described in the sidebar on page 257 "Magic Quotes and mysql_real_escape_string()."

To use mysql_real_escape_string():

1. Open register.php (Script 7.3) in your text editor.

2. After the submit conditional (line 7), add the following (**Script 7.5**).

```
require_once ('../mysql_connect.
→ php');
function escape_data ($data) {
   global $dbc;
   if (ini_get('magic_quotes_gpc')) {
      $data = stripslashes($data);
   }
   return mysql_real_escape_string
   → (trim($data), $dbc);
}
```

The escape_data() function will take a string, trim any extra spaces from it, apply the mysql_real_escape_string() function to it, and then return the results. If the data has already been run through Magic Quotes (if ini_get('magic_quotes_gpc') is TRUE), the data is first stripped of its slashes so that the data is not over-escaped (where every appropriate character would be escaped twice).

Because this function requires a database connection, the mysql_connect.php script must be required before this function is called and the database connection itself—$dbc—must be made available as a global variable.

continues on page 258

Script 7.5 The register.php script now uses the mysql_real_escape_string() function to clean the submitted data.

```
1    <?php # Script 7.5 - register.php (2nd version after Script 7.3)
2
3    $page_title = 'Register';
4    include ('./includes/header.html');
5
6    // Check if the form has been submitted.
7    if (isset($_POST['submitted'])) {
8
9        require_once ('../mysql_connect.php'); // Connect to the db.
10
11       // Create a function for escaping the data.
12       function escape_data ($data) {
13          global $dbc; // Need the connection.
14          if (ini_get('magic_quotes_gpc')) {
15             $data = stripslashes($data);
16          }
17          return mysql_real_escape_string(trim($data), $dbc);
18       } // End of function.
19
20       $errors = array(); // Initialize error array.
21
22       // Check for a first name.
23       if (empty($_POST['first_name'])) {
24          $errors[] = 'You forgot to enter your first name.';
25       } else {
26          $fn = escape_data($_POST['first_name']);
27       }
28
29       // Check for a last name.
30       if (empty($_POST['last_name'])) {
31          $errors[] = 'You forgot to enter your last name.';
32       } else {
33          $ln = escape_data($_POST['last_name']);
34       }
35
36       // Check for an email address.
37       if (empty($_POST['email'])) {
38          $errors[] = 'You forgot to enter your email address.';
39       } else {
40          $e = escape_data($_POST['email']);
41       }
42
43       // Check for a password and match against the confirmed password.
```

(script continues on next page)

Script 7.5 *continued.*

```
                                          script
44        if (!empty($_POST['password1'])) {
45            if ($_POST['password1'] != $_POST['password2']) {
46                $errors[] = 'Your password did not match the confirmed password.';
47            } else {
48                $p = escape_data($_POST['password1']);
49            }
50        } else {
51            $errors[] = 'You forgot to enter your password.';
52        }
53
54        if (empty($errors)) { // If everything's okay.
55
56            // Register the user in the database.
57
58            // Make the query.
59            $query = "INSERT INTO users (first_name, last_name, email, password, registration_date)
                  VALUES ('$fn', '$ln', '$e', SHA('$p'), NOW() )";
60            $result = @mysql_query ($query); // Run the query.
61            if ($result) { // If it ran OK.
62
63                // Send an email, if desired.
64
65                // Print a message.
66                echo '<h1 id="mainhead">Thank you!</h1>
67        <p>You are now registered. In Chapter 9 you will actually be able to log in!</p><p><br /></p>';
68
69                // Include the footer and quit the script (to not show the form).
70                include ('./includes/footer.html');
71                exit();
72
73            } else { // If it did not run OK.
74                echo '<h1 id="mainhead">System Error</h1>
75                <p class="error">You could not be registered due to a system error. We apologize for any
                  inconvenience.</p>'; // Public message.
76                echo '<p>' . mysql_error() . '<br /><br />Query: ' . $query . '</p>'; // Debugging message.
77                include ('./includes/footer.html');
78                exit();
79            }
80
81        } else { // Report the errors.
82
83            echo '<h1 id="mainhead">Error!</h1>
```

(script continues on next page)

Script 7.5 *continued.*

```
84              <p class="error">The following error(s) occurred:<br />';
85              foreach ($errors as $msg) { // Print each error.
86                  echo " - $msg<br />\n";
87              }
88              echo '</p><p>Please try again.</p><p><br /></p>';
89
90          } // End of if (empty($errors)) IF.
91
92          mysql_close(); // Close the database connection.
93
94      } // End of the main Submit conditional.
95      ?>
96      <h2>Register</h2>
97      <form action="register.php" method="post">
98          <p>First Name: <input type="text" name="first_name" size="15" maxlength="15" value="<?php if
                (isset($_POST['first_name'])) echo $_POST['first_name']; ?>" /></p>
99          <p>Last Name: <input type="text" name="last_name" size="15" maxlength="30" value="<?php if
                (isset($_POST['last_name'])) echo $_POST['last_name']; ?>" /></p>
100         <p>Email Address: <input type="text" name="email" size="20" maxlength="40" value="<?php if
                (isset($_POST['email'])) echo $_POST['email']; ?>"  /> </p>
101         <p>Password: <input type="password" name="password1" size="10" maxlength="20" /></p>
102         <p>Confirm Password: <input type="password" name="password2" size="10" maxlength="20" /></p>
103         <p><input type="submit" name="submit" value="Register" /></p>
104         <input type="hidden" name="submitted" value="TRUE" />
105     </form>
106     <?php
107     include ('./includes/footer.html');
108     ?>
```

Magic Quotes and mysql_real_escape_string()

Magic Quotes, which I discussed in Chapter 2, "Programming with PHP," will automatically escape problematic characters in text entered in forms. When querying databases this is particularly useful because those quotation marks will create errors in your SQL commands. However, the mysql_real_escape_string() function is a slightly better way to achieve the same result, since it's database- and language-specific. With this in mind, I want to create a way to use mysql_real_escape_string() and not Magic Quotes (using both will over-escape the values).

My solution in this script is to test the Magic Quotes status using the ini_get() function. This function will return the setting in PHP's configuration file (php.ini) for a particular option. If ini_get() returns TRUE—meaning Magic Quotes is on—I'll strip the existing slashes before applying mysql_real_escape_string().

In current versions of PHP, Magic Quotes is turned off by default, so ini_get() will return FALSE and there's no need to strip any existing slashes.

3. Change the validation routines to use this function, replacing each occurrence of $var = trim($_POST['var']) with $var = escape_data($_POST['var']).

```
$fn = escape_data($_POST
→ ['first_name']);

$ln = escape_data($_POST
→ ['last_name']);

$e = escape_data($_POST['email']);

$p = escape_data($_POST
→ ['password1']);
```

Instead of just assigning the submitted value to each variable ($fn, $ln, etc.), I'll run the value through the escape_data() function first.

4. Delete the original require_once ('../mysql_connect.php') line (refer to Script 7.3, line 46).

Since I've moved this line near the top of the script, I should remove it here.

5. Move the mysql_close() line so that it's called before the end of the main submit conditional.

To be consistent, since the database connection is opened as the first step of the main conditional, it should be closed as the last step of this same conditional.

6. Save the file as register.php, upload it to your Web server, and test in your Web browser (**Figures 7.10** and **7.11**).

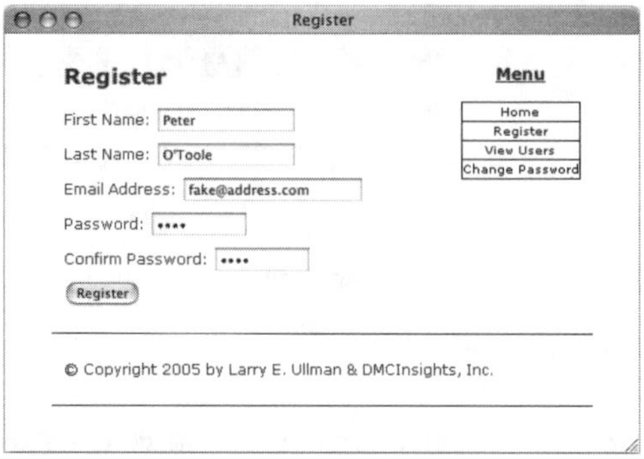

Figure 7.10 Values with apostrophes in them will be handled properly whether or not Magic Quotes is enabled (see Figure 7.11).

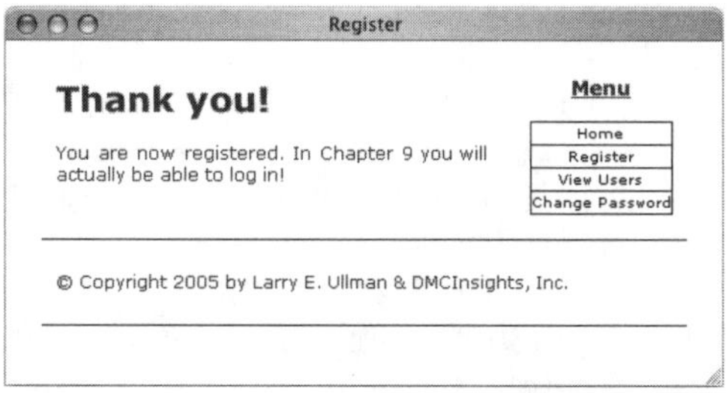

Figure 7.11 Now the script works—and is more database secure—with or without Magic Quotes.

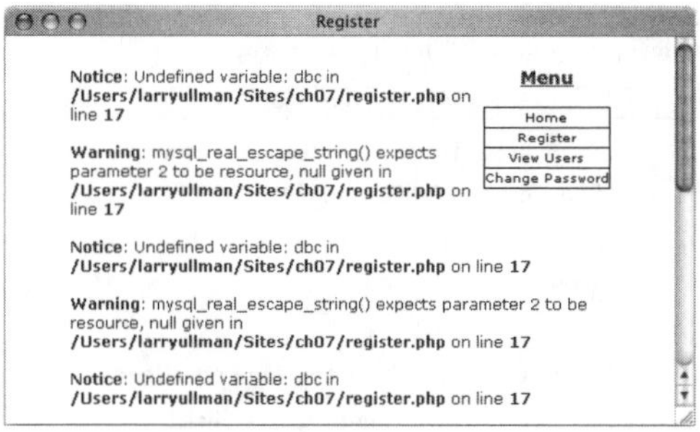

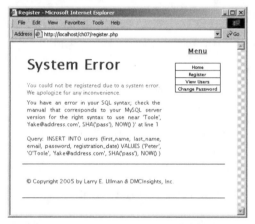

Figure 7.12 Since the `mysql_real_escape_string()` requires a database connection, improperly using it can lead to other errors.

Figure 7.13 Apostrophes in form values can be problematic in queries, if not accounted for.

Figure 7.14 With Magic Quotes enabled, escaped values reprinted in a form will be inaccurate unless the `stripslashes()` function is used.

✔ Tips

- The `mysql_real_escape_string()` function escapes a string in accordance with the language being used, which is an added advantage over `addslashes()` or the `mysql_escape_string()` function.

- If you see results like those in **Figure 7.12** it means that the `mysql_real_escape_string()` function cannot access the database (because it has no connection, like `$dbc`).

- Without the use of this function and without Magic Quotes turned on, a common name like O'Toole will generate a MySQL error (**Figure 7.13**) because the apostrophe in the name will conflict with the apostrophes used in the query.

- With Magic Quotes turned on, you may want to use the `stripslashes()` function before printing a submitted value back to the sticky form (see the Last Name input in **Figure 7.14**).

- The `get_magic_quotes_gpc()` function can also be used to return the current Magic Quotes setting. I prefer to use `ini_get()`, as this function can be used to get the setting of many different `php.ini` settings, not just Magic Quotes.

Counting Returned Records

The next logical function to discuss is `mysql_num_rows()`. This function returns the number of rows retrieved by a SELECT query, taking the query result as a parameter.

```
$num = mysql_num_rows($result);
```

I'll use this function in two different ways. First, I'll modify `view_users.php` to list the total number of registered users. Second, I'll modify `register.php` to test if an email address has already been taken before letting a user register with it.

To modify view_users.php:

1. Open `view_users.php` (refer to Script 7.4) in your text editor.

2. Before the `if ($result)` conditional, add this line (**Script 7.6**)

   ```
   $num = mysql_num_rows ($result);
   ```

   This line will assign the number of returned rows to the $num variable.

3. Change the original $result conditional to

   ```
   if ($num > 0) {
   ```

   The conditional as it was written before was based upon whether the query did or did not work, not whether or not any records were returned. Now it will be more accurate.

4. Print out the number of registered users.

   ```
   echo "<p>There are currently $num
   → registered users.</p>\n";
   ```

Script 7.6 Now the `view_users.php` script will display the total number of registered users.

```
1   <?php # Script 7.6 - view_users.php
    (2nd version after Script 7.4)
2   // This script retrieves all the records
    from the users table.
3
4   $page_title = 'View the Current Users';
5   include ('./includes/header.html');
6
7   // Page header.
8   echo '<h1 id="mainhead">Registered Users
    </h1>';
9
10  require_once ('../mysql_connect.php');
    // Connect to the db.
11
12  // Make the query.
13  $query = "SELECT CONCAT(last_name, ', ',
    first_name) AS name, DATE_FORMAT
    (registration_date, '%M %d, %Y') AS dr FROM
    users ORDER BY registration_date ASC";
14  $result = @mysql_query ($query); //
    Run the query.
15  $num = mysql_num_rows($result);
16
17  if ($num > 0) { // If it ran OK, display
    the records.
18
19      echo "<p>There are currently $num
        registered users.</p>\n";
20
21      // Table header.
22      echo '<table align="center" cellspacing=
        "0" cellpadding="5">
23      <tr><td align="left"><b>Name</b></td>
        <td align="left"><b>Date Registered</b>
        </td></tr>
24      ';
25
26      // Fetch and print all the records.
27      while ($row = mysql_fetch_array($result,
        MYSQL_ASSOC)) {
```

(script continues on next page)

Script 7.6 *continued*

```
          script
28        echo '<tr><td align="left">' . $row
          ['name'] . '</td><td align="left">'
          . $row['dr'] . '</td></tr>
29        ';
30    }
31
32    echo '</table>';
33
34    mysql_free_result ($result); // Free up
      the resources.
35
36    } else { // If it did not run OK.
37        echo '<p class="error">There are
          currently no registered users.</p>';
38    }
39
40    mysql_close(); // Close the database
      connection.
41
42    include ('./includes/footer.html');
      // Include the HTML footer.
43    ?>
```

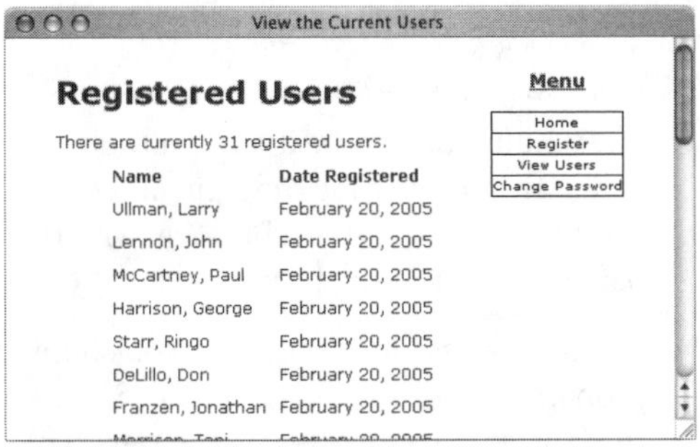

Figure 7.15 The number of registered users is now displayed at the top of the page.

5. Change the else part of the conditional to read

echo '<p class="error">There are
→ currently no registered users.
→ </p>';

The original conditional was based upon whether or not the query worked. Hopefully you've successfully debugged the query so that it is working and the original error messages are no longer needed. Now the error message just indicates if no records were returned.

6. Save the file as view_users.php, upload to your Web server, and test in your Web browser (**Figure 7.15**).

To modify register.php:

1. Open `register.php` (refer to Script 7.5) in your text editor.

2. Before the INSERT query (line 59), add (**Script 7.7**)

   ```
   $query = "SELECT user_id FROM users
   → WHERE email='$e'";
   $result = mysql_query($query);
   if (mysql_num_rows($result) == 0) {
   ```

   This query will check if the submitted email address (`$e`) is currently in the database by attempting to select that record. If the number of rows returned by the result is equal to 0, it's safe to register the new user.

   I don't have any debugging code in place here, as I assume the query will run without problems. (Even if the user enters a bad email address and no records are returned, that's not a MySQL error, just a usage problem.) If you have difficulties with this, remember to use the `mysql_error()` function and print out the query being run.

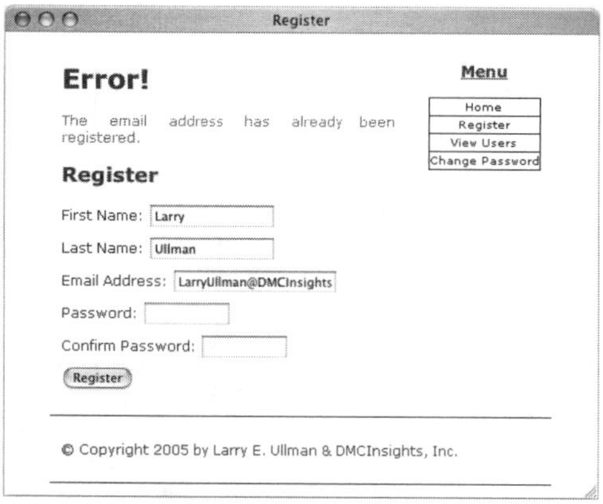

3. After the `if ($result)` conditional ends (line 79 of the original script), add

   ```
   } else {
       echo '<h1 id="mainhead">Error!
   → </h1>
       <p class="error">The email address
   → has already been registered.
   → </p>';
   }
   ```

   This `else` is the conclusion of the `if (mysql_num_rows($result) == 0)` conditional. It reports that an email address is already taken.

4. Save the file as `register.php`, upload to your Web server, and test in your Web browser (**Figure 7.16**).

✔ Tips

- You can, and probably should, also guarantee unique email addresses by placing a UNIQUE index on the column in MySQL. Once you've done that, trying to insert a duplicate value will cause a MySQL error (which is why you'll still want a PHP check like the one added to `register.php`).

- Every registration/login system requires one unique column, be it an email address or a username. During the login process, this unique value, in combination with the password, will verify the user.

- If you haven't done so already, you should probably use the mysql client to ensure that the email addresses in the users table are unique. If you don't, you might run into problems when using the data in later chapters.

Figure 7.16 The registration process will no longer allow a user to register an existing email address (each address must be unique in the database).

Script 7.7 The register.php script will now check if a username is taken.

```
1    <?php # Script 7.7 - register.php (3rd version after Scripts 7.3 & 7.5)
2
3    $page_title = 'Register';
4    include ('./includes/header.html');
5
6    // Check if the form has been submitted.
7    if (isset($_POST['submitted'])) {
8
9        require_once ('../mysql_connect.php'); // Connect to the db.
10
11       // Create a function for escaping the data.
12       function escape_data ($data) {
13           global $dbc; // Need the connection.
14           if (ini_get('magic_quotes_gpc')) {
15               $data = stripslashes($data);
16           }
17           return mysql_real_escape_string(trim($data), $dbc);
18       } // End of function.
19
20       $errors = array(); // Initialize error array.
21
22       // Check for a first name.
23       if (empty($_POST['first_name'])) {
24           $errors[] = 'You forgot to enter your first name.';
25       } else {
26           $fn = escape_data($_POST['first_name']);
27       }
28
29       // Check for a last name.
30       if (empty($_POST['last_name'])) {
31           $errors[] = 'You forgot to enter your last name.';
32       } else {
33           $ln = escape_data($_POST['last_name']);
34       }
35
36       // Check for an email address.
37       if (empty($_POST['email'])) {
38           $errors[] = 'You forgot to enter your email address.';
39       } else {
40           $e = escape_data($_POST['email']);
```

(script continues on next page)

COUNTING RETURNED RECORDS

Script 7.7 *continued*

```
41      }
42
43      // Check for a password and match against the confirmed password.
44      if (!empty($_POST['password1'])) {
45          if ($_POST['password1'] != $_POST['password2']) {
46              $errors[] = 'Your password did not match the confirmed password.';
47          } else {
48              $p = escape_data($_POST['password1']);
49          }
50      } else {
51          $errors[] = 'You forgot to enter your password.';
52      }
53
54      if (empty($errors)) { // If everything's okay.
55
56          // Register the user in the database.
57
58          // Check for previous registration.
59          $query = "SELECT user_id FROM users WHERE email='$e'";
60          $result = mysql_query($query);
61          if (mysql_num_rows($result) == 0) {
62
63              // Make the query.
64              $query = "INSERT INTO users (first_name, last_name, email, password, registration_date)
                    VALUES ('$fn', '$ln', '$e', SHA('$p'), NOW() )";
65              $result = @mysql_query ($query); // Run the query.
66              if ($result) { // If it ran OK.
67
68                  // Send an email, if desired.
69
70                  // Print a message.
71                  echo '<h1 id="mainhead">Thank you!</h1>
72              <p>You are now registered. In Chapter 9 you will actually be able to log in!</p><p>
                <br /></p>';
73
74                  // Include the footer and quit the script (to not show the form).
75                  include ('./includes/footer.html');
76                  exit();
77
78              } else { // If it did not run OK.
79                  echo '<h1 id="mainhead">System Error</h1>
```

(script continues on next page)

Script 7.7 *continued*

```
                          script

80              <p class="error">You could not be registered due to a system error. We apologize for
                any inconvenience.</p>'; // Public message.
81              echo '<p>' . mysql_error() . '<br /><br />Query: ' . $query . '</p>'; //
                Debugging message.
82              include ('./includes/footer.html');
83              exit();
84          }
85
86      } else { // Already registered.
87          echo '<h1 id="mainhead">Error!</h1>
88          <p class="error">The email address has already been registered.</p>';
89      }
90
91  } else { // Report the errors.
92
93      echo '<h1 id="mainhead">Error!</h1>
94      <p class="error">The following error(s) occurred:<br />';
95      foreach ($errors as $msg) { // Print each error.
96          echo " - $msg<br />\n";
97      }
98      echo '</p><p>Please try again.</p><p><br /></p>';
99
100 } // End of if (empty($errors)) IF.
101
102 mysql_close(); // Close the database connection.
103
104 } // End of the main Submit conditional.
105 ?>
106 <h2>Register</h2>
107 <form action="register.php" method="post">
108     <p>First Name: <input type="text" name="first_name" size="15" maxlength="15" value="<?php if
        (isset($_POST['first_name'])) echo $_POST['first_name']; ?>" /></p>
109     <p>Last Name: <input type="text" name="last_name" size="15" maxlength="30" value="<?php if
        (isset($_POST['last_name'])) echo $_POST['last_name']; ?>" /></p>
110     <p>Email Address: <input type="text" name="email" size="20" maxlength="40" value="<?php if
        (isset($_POST['email'])) echo $_POST['email']; ?>" /> </p>
111     <p>Password: <input type="password" name="password1" size="10" maxlength="20" /></p>
112     <p>Confirm Password: <input type="password" name="password2" size="10" maxlength="20" /></p>
113     <p><input type="submit" name="submit" value="Register" /></p>
114     <input type="hidden" name="submitted" value="TRUE" />
115 </form>
116 <?php
117 include ('./includes/footer.html');
118 ?>
```

Updating Records with PHP

The last technique I'll introduce in this chapter is how to update database records with a PHP script. Doing so requires use of the UPDATE query, and its successful execution can be verified with PHP's mysql_affected_rows() function.

While the mysql_num_rows() function will return the number of rows generated by a SELECT query, mysql_affected_rows() returns the number of rows affected by an INSERT, UPDATE, or DELETE query. It's used like so:

$num = mysql_affected_rows($dbc);

The one argument the function takes is the database connection ($dbc), not the results of the previous query ($result). This argument is optional, though, so I'll often omit it in order to avoid problems (like inadvertently using $result).

The following example will be a script that allows registered users to change their password. It'll demonstrate two important ideas:

◆ Checking a submitted username and password against registered values (the key to a login system as well)

◆ Updating database records using the primary key as a reference point

To update records with PHP:

1. Create a new PHP script in your text editor (**Script 7.8**).

   ```
   <?php # Script 7.8 - password.php
   $page_title = 'Change Your Password';
   include ('./includes/header.html');
   ```

Script 7.8 The change_password.php script runs an UPDATE query on the database and uses the mysql_affected_rows() function to confirm the change.

```
1    <?php # Script 7.8 - password.php
2    // This page lets a user change their
     password.
3
4    // Set the page title and include the HTML
     header.
5    $page_title = 'Change Your Password';
6    include ('./includes/header.html');
7
8    // Check if the form has been submitted.
9    if (isset($_POST['submitted'])) {
10
11       require_once ('../mysql_connect.php');
         // Connect to the db.
12
13       // Create a function for escaping the
         data.
14       function escape_data ($data) {
15          global $dbc; // Need the connection.
16          if (ini_get('magic_quotes_gpc')) {
17             $data = stripslashes($data);
18          }
19          return mysql_real_escape_string
            (trim($data), $dbc);
20       } // End of function.
21
22       $errors = array(); // Initialize error
         array.
23
24       // Check for an email address.
25       if (empty($_POST['email'])) {
26          $errors[] = 'You forgot to enter your
            email address.';
27       } else {
28          $e = escape_data($_POST['email']);
29       }
30
31       // Check for an existing password.
32       if (empty($_POST['password'])) {
```

(script continues on next page)

Script 7.8 *continued*

```
                       script

33        $errors[] = 'You forgot to enter your
          existing password.';
34    } else {
35        $p = escape_data($_POST
          ['password']);
36    }
37
38    // Check for a password and match
      against the confirmed password.
39    if (!empty($_POST['password1'])) {
40        if ($_POST['password1'] != $_POST
          ['password2']) {
41            $errors[] = 'Your new password
              did not match the confirmed new
              password.';
42        } else {
43            $np = escape_data($_POST
              ['password1']);
44        }
45    } else {
46        $errors[] = 'You forgot to enter your
          new password.';
47    }
48
49    if (empty($errors)) { // If everything's
      OK.
50
51        // Check that they've entered the
          right email address/password
          combination.
52        $query = "SELECT user_id FROM users
          WHERE (email='$e' AND
          password=SHA('$p') )";
53        $result = mysql_query($query);
54        $num = mysql_num_rows($result);
55        if (mysql_num_rows($result) == 1)
          { // Match was made.
56
57            // Get the user_id.
58            $row = mysql_fetch_array
              ($result, MYSQL_NUM);
59
60            // Make the UPDATE query.
```

(script continues on page 269)

2. Create the main conditional.

```
if (isset($_POST['submitted'])) {
```

Since this page both displays and handles the form, I'll use my standard submit conditional.

3. Include the database connection and write the escape_data() function.

```
require_once ('../mysql_connect.
→ php');
function escape_data ($data) {
    global $dbc;
    if (ini_get('magic_quotes_gpc')) {
        $data = stripslashes($data);
    }
    return mysql_real_escape_string
    → (trim($data), $dbc);
}
```

The initial part of this script will mimic the registration form, including the safeguarding of submitted data with the escape_data() function. In order for any registration-login process to work, the data must be managed in the same way for both steps.

continues on next page

4. Check the submitted data.

```
$errors = array();
if (empty($_POST['email'])) {
    $errors[] = 'You forgot to enter
    → your email address.';
} else {
    $e = escape_data($_POST['email']);
}
if (empty($_POST['password'])) {
    $errors[] = 'You forgot to enter
    → your existing password.';
} else {
    $p = escape_data($_POST
    → ['password']);
}
if (!empty($_POST['password1'])) {
    if ($_POST['password1'] != $_POST
    → ['password2']) {
        $errors[] = 'Your new password
        → did not match the confirmed
        → new password.';
    } else {
        $np = escape_data($_POST
        → ['password1']);
    }
} else {
    $errors[] = 'You forgot to enter
    → your new password.';
}
```

The processes themselves are exactly like those in `register.php`. The form will have four inputs: the email address, the existing password, the new password, and a confirmation of the new password.

5. If all the tests are passed, retrieve the user's ID.

```
if (empty($errors)) {
    $query = "SELECT user_id FROM
    → users WHERE (email='$e' AND
    → password=SHA('$p') )";
    $result = mysql_query($query);
    $num = mysql_num_rows($result);
    if (mysql_num_rows($result) == 1) {
        $row = mysql_fetch_array
        → ($result, MYSQL_NUM);
```

This first query will return just the user_id field for the record that matches the submitted email address and password. To compare the submitted password against the stored one, encrypt it again with the SHA() function. If the user is registered and has correctly entered both the email address and password, exactly one row will be selected (since the email value must be unique across all rows). Finally, this one record is assigned as an array (of one element) to the $row variable.

6. Update the database.

```
$query = "UPDATE users SET password=
→ SHA('$np') WHERE user_id=$row[0]";
$result = @mysql_query ($query);
```

This query will change the password—using the new submitted value—where the user_id column is equal to the number retrieved from the previous query.

continues on page 270

UPDATING RECORDS WITH PHP

Script 7.8 *continued*

```
████                         script                          ██
61          $query = "UPDATE users SET password=SHA('$np') WHERE user_id=$row[0]";
62          $result = @mysql_query ($query);
63          if (mysql_affected_rows() == 1) { // If it ran OK.
64
65              // Send an email, if desired.
66
67              // Print a message.
68              echo '<h1 id="mainhead">Thank you!</h1>
69              <p>Your password has been updated. In Chapter 9 you will actually be able to log in!
                </p><p><br /></p>';
70
71              // Include the footer and quit the script (to not show the form).
72              include ('./includes/footer.html');
73              exit();
74
75          } else { // If it did not run OK.
76              echo '<h1 id="mainhead">System Error</h1>
77              <p class="error">Your password could not be changed due to a system error. We apologize
                for any inconvenience.</p>'; // Public message.
78              echo '<p>' . mysql_error() . '<br /><br />Query: ' . $query . '</p>'; //
                Debugging message.
79              include ('./includes/footer.html');
80              exit();
81          }
82
83      } else { // Invalid email address/password combination.
84          echo '<h1 id="mainhead">Error!</h1>
85          <p class="error">The email address and password do not match those on file.</p>';
86      }
87
88  } else { // Report the errors.
89
90      echo '<h1 id="mainhead">Error!</h1>
91      <p class="error">The following error(s) occurred:<br />';
92      foreach ($errors as $msg) { // Print each error.
93          echo " - $msg<br />\n";
94      }
95      echo '</p><p>Please try again.</p><p><br /></p>';
96
97  } // End of if (empty($errors)) IF.
98
```

(script continues on page 271)

7. Check the results of the query.

```
if (mysql_affected_rows() == 1) {
    echo '<h1 id="mainhead">Thank
    → you!</h1>
    <p>Your password has been updated.
    → In Chapter 9 you will actually
    → be able to log in!</p><p><br
    → /></p>';
    include ('./includes/footer.
    → html');
    exit();
} else {
    echo '<h1 id="mainhead">System
    → Error</h1>
    <p class="error">Your password
    → could not be changed due to a
    → system error. We apologize for
    → any inconvenience.</p>';
    echo '<p>' . mysql_error() .
    → '<br /><br />Query: ' . $query .
    → '</p>';
    include ('./includes/footer.
    → html');
    exit();
}
```

This part of the script again works similar to register.php. In this case, if mysql_affected_rows() returns the number 1, the record has been updated, a message will be printed, the footer included, and the script concluded. If not, the database error is printed.

8. Complete the conditionals.

```
} else {
    echo '<h1 id="mainhead">Error!
    → </h1>
    <p class="error">The email address
    → and password do not match those
    → on file.</p>';
}
```

If mysql_num_rows() does not equal *1*, then the submitted email address and password do not match those on file and this error is printed.

9. Print any error messages and complete the PHP.

```
} else {
    echo '<h1 id="mainhead">
    → Error!</h1>
    <p class="error">The following
    → error(s) occurred:<br />';
    foreach ($errors as $msg) {
        echo " - $msg<br />\n";
    }
    echo '</p><p>Please try again.
    → </p><p><br /></p>';
}
mysql_close();
}
?>
```

Script 7.8 *continued*

```
                    script
99      mysql_close(); // Close the database
        connection.
100
101     } // End of the main Submit conditional.
102     ?>
103     <h2>Change Your Password</h2>
104     <form action="password.php" method="post">
105         <p>Email Address: <input type="text"
            name="email" size="20" maxlength="40"
            value="<?php if
            (isset($_POST['email'])) echo $_POST
            ['email']; ?>"  /> </p>
106         <p>Current Password: <input type=
            "password" name="password" size="10"
            maxlength="20" /></p>
107         <p>New Password: <input type="password"
            name="password1" size="10"
            maxlength="20" /></p>
108         <p>Confirm New Password: <input type=
            "password" name="password2" size="10"
            maxlength="20" /></p>
109         <p><input type="submit" name="submit"
            value="Change My Password" /></p>
110         <input type="hidden" name="submitted"
            value="TRUE" />
111     </form>
112     <?php
113     include ('./includes/footer.html');
114     ?>
```

10. Display the form.

```
<h2>Change Your Password</h2>
<form action="password.php"
→ method="post">
    <p>Email Address: <input type=
    → "text" name="email" size="20"
    → maxlength="40" value="<?php
    → if (isset($_POST['email'])) echo
    → $_POST['email']; ?>"  /> </p>
    <p>Current Password: <input type=
    → "password" name="password"
    → size="10" maxlength="20" /></p>
    <p>New Password: <input type=
    → "password" name="password1"
    → size="10" maxlength="20" /></p>
    <p>Confirm New Password: <input
    → type="password"
    → name="password2" size="10"
    → maxlength="20" /></p>
    <p><input type="submit" name=
    → "submit" value="Change My Password"
    → /></p>
    <input type="hidden" name=
    → "submitted" value="TRUE" />
</form>
```

Again, the form takes three different password inputs—the current password, the new one, and a confirmation of the new password—and the email address. The email address input is sticky (password inputs cannot be).

continues on next page

11. Include the footer file.

```php
<?php
include ('./includes/footer.html');
?>
```

12. Save the file as password.php, upload to your Web server, and test in your Web browser (**Figures 7.17**, **7.18**, and **7.19**).

✔ Tips

■ If you delete every record from a table, mysql_affected_rows() will return 0, even if the query was successful and every row was removed. This is just a quirk.

■ If an UPDATE query runs but does not actually change the value of any column (for example, a password is replaced with the same password), mysql_affected_rows() will return 0.

■ The mysql_affected_rows() conditional used here could (and maybe should) also be applied to the register.php script to see if one record was added. That would be a more exacting condition to check than if ($result).

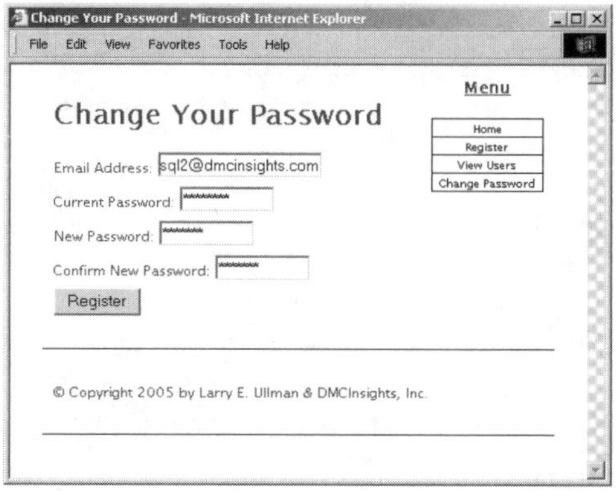

Figure 7.17 The form for changing a user's password.

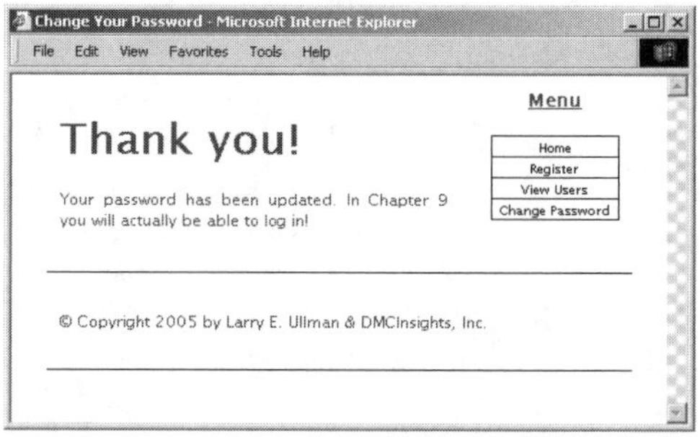

Figure 7.18 The password was changed in the database.

Figure 7.19 If the entered email address and password don't match those on file, the password will not be updated.

Looking Ahead

This chapter is a basic introduction to using PHP and MySQL together. Although all of the techniques covered here are fundamental and all of the scripts were practical, real-world examples, there's still much to be learned.

In the next chapter you'll see three important concepts:

◆ How to delete data from a database using PHP.

◆ How to update the data in the database by first retrieving the current values.

◆ How to paginate a query's results over multiple pages.

In Chapter 11, "Extended Topics," you'll be introduced to the new Improved MySQL Extension interface. These functions provide a system for taking advantage of the new features in MySQL 4.1 and later. Furthermore, there are speed and security benefits to using the `mysqli_*` functions instead of the `mysql_*` ones. (Improved MySQL support must be built into PHP, and you must be using version 4.1.3 or later of MySQL to use these functions, which is why the older, standard functions are discussed here first.)

Finally, Chapter 12, "Example—Content Management," introduces one last important MySQL function, `mysql_insert_id()`. This function returns the automatically-incremented primary key of freshly added records.

Of course, the PHP manual includes documentation on *every* MySQL-related function, so don't forget about using that critical reference.

WEB
APPLICATION
DEVELOPMENT

Now that you have a little PHP and MySQL interaction under your belt, it's time to take things up a notch. This chapter is similar to Chapter 3, "Creating Dynamic Web Sites," in that it covers a myriad of somewhat independent topics. Naturally, most of the examples in this chapter will involve MySQL, as you continue to develop those skills.

Some of the scripts broaden the application started in the preceding chapter by adding new, popular features. First of all, you'll learn methods of making your applications more flexible by adjusting their behavior to correspond to certain server settings. Also, you'll see several tricks for managing database information, in particular editing and deleting records. At that same time a couple new ways of passing data to your PHP pages will be introduced. Next, three new features will be added to the view_users. php script from the preceding chapter. This chapter concludes with a tangential topic: You'll discover what HTTP headers are, why they're important, and how to control them with PHP.

As you can see, this chapter presents a long list of valuable information. The common denominator here is that these features are all present in more sophisticated Web applications and their proper usage distinguishes the more seasoned programmer from the beginner.

Adjusting Behavior for Server Settings

In the last chapter, the escape_data() function was defined as a way to sanctify user input before storing it in a database. At that time I briefly discussed the ini_get() function, which returns the php.ini setting for a submitted configuration option. In that example, I checked if Magic Quotes (*magic_quotes_gpc*, specifically) was on, as I don't want to over-escape submitted data. Using the ini_get() function is just one way you can improve the portability of your PHP applications by making scripts behave differently according to server-specific information.

Complementing the ini_get() function is ini_set(), which changes a PHP configuration for the duration of that script. This tool was mentioned in Chapter 3 as a way of turning on PHP's *display_errors* setting:

```
ini_set('display_errors', 1);
```

While useful for many things, this function's powers are limited. Some features cannot be altered using ini_set(), like Magic Quotes and *register_globals* (in both cases because the form data will be received by the page before any ini_set() alterations can occur).

Another useful tool for checking out a server's configuration is function_exists(). As you might expect from the name, this function returns either TRUE or FALSE to indicate whether a function exists in your PHP installation. You can use it to check if:

◆ A user-defined function exists (has been defined).

◆ A function added in a recent version of PHP is available.

◆ A function that requires external libraries is available for use, like mysql_connect().

Using the function is simple:

```
if (function_exists('mysql_connect')) {…
```

A final category of useful information can be found within the $_SERVER array. You already used this variable once: back in Chapter 1, "Introduction to PHP," to print out the server's PHP version and operating system. In this chapter, you'll see many references to the $_SERVER array.

But first, a slightly new version of the mysql_connect.php script will be written utilizing function_exists().

Script 8.1 The escape_data() function is now defined within this, the latest version of the mysql_connect.php script. The escape_data() function now checks for the availability of the mysql_real_escape_string() function before calling it.

```
1    <?php # Script 8.1 - mysql_connect.php
2
3    // This file contains the database access
     information.
4    // This file also establishes a connection
     to MySQL and selects the database.
5    // This file also defines the escape_data()
     function.
6
7    // Set the database access information as
     constants.
8    DEFINE ('DB_USER', 'username');
9    DEFINE ('DB_PASSWORD', 'password');
10   DEFINE ('DB_HOST', 'localhost');
11   DEFINE ('DB_NAME', 'sitename');
12
13   // Make the connection.
14   $dbc = @mysql_connect (DB_HOST, DB_USER,
     DB_PASSWORD) OR die ('Could not connect to
     MySQL: ' . mysql_error() );
15
16   // Select the database.
17   @mysql_select_db (DB_NAME) OR die ('Could
     not select the database: ' . mysql_error() );
18
19   // Create a function for escaping the data.
20   function escape_data ($data) {
21
22       // Address Magic Quotes.
23       if (ini_get('magic_quotes_gpc')) {
24           $data = stripslashes($data);
25       }
26
27       // Check for mysql_real_escape_string()
         support.
28       if (function_exists('mysql_real_
         escape_string')) {
29           global $dbc; // Need the connection.
```

(script continues on next page)

To use function_exists():

1. Open `mysql_connect.php` (Script 7.2) in your text editor or IDE.

2. After you have connected to and selected the database, begin defining the escape_data() function (**Script 8.1**).

   `function escape_data($data) {`

   As multiple scripts within this application will need this function, you'll define it within the `mysql_connect.php` page instead of within each individual page.

3. Check for, and respond to, the Magic Quotes setting.

   ```
   if (ini_get('magic_quotes_gpc')) {
       $data = stripslashes($data);
   }
   ```

   This is a repetition of what you've seen before. The `ini_get()` function will return TRUE or FALSE indicating whether Magic Quotes GPC is on. If it is, the data will have already been escaped and I'll want to remove those slashes before using the database-specific escaping function.

continues on next page

4. Check for, and respond to, the existence of the `mysql_real_escape_string()` function.

```
if (function_exists('mysql_real_
→ escape_string')) {
  global $dbc;
  $data = mysql_real_escape_string
  → (trim($data), $dbc);
} else {
  $data = mysql_escape_string
  → (trim($data));
}
```

The conditional checks if the `mysql_real_escape_string()` function is available for use (it was added in version 4.3 of PHP, which your server may not be running). If it is, the database connection—`$dbc`—is made available via the `global` statement. Next, the `mysql_real_escape_string()` function is applied to the trimmed data.

If that particular function is not available, the older `mysql_escape_string()` function is used instead. This function works in much the same way but does not require a database connection.

5. Complete the function definition.

```
  return $data;
}
```

The last step is to return the escaped data back to the script that called this function.

6. Save the file and upload it to your server.

Remember to place this file outside of your Web root directory, if at all possible. See the preceding chapter for details.

Script 8.1 *continued*

```
30        $data = mysql_real_escape_string
          (trim($data), $dbc);
31    } else {
32        $data = mysql_escape_string
          (trim($data));
33    }
34
35    // Return the escaped value.
36    return $data;
37
38 } // End of function.
39 ?>
```

✔ Tips

- Similar to the `function_exists()` function is `extension_loaded()`. This function returns `TRUE` or `FALSE` to indicate whether the extension name given as an argument is loaded in your PHP configuration. You can use it to check, for example, if PHP has MySQL support enabled.

- To see the list of configurable options, see `www.php.net/manual/en/ini.php`. Any option marked as either `PHP_INI_ALL` or `PHP_INI_USER` can be adjusted with `ini_set()`.

- This version of the `mysql_connect.php` script will be used several times over the course of this book, so make sure that you are comfortable with its syntax and functionality.

Sending Values to a Script Manually

In the examples so far, all of the data received in the PHP script came from what the user entered in a form. There are, however, two different ways you can pass variables and values to a PHP script, both worth knowing.

The first method is to make use of HTML's hidden input type:

```
<input type="hidden" name="name"
→ value="Brian" />
```

Script 8.2 The view_users.php script has been modified so that it presents *Edit* and *Delete* links, passing the user's ID number along in each URL.

```
1    <?php # Script 8.2 - view_users.php
2    # (3rd version after Scripts 7.4 & 7.6)
3
4    // This script retrieves all the records
     from the users table.
5    // This new version links to edit and
     delete pages.
6
7    $page_title = 'View the Current Users';
8    include ('./includes/header.html');
9
10   // Page header.
11   echo '<h1 id="mainhead">Registered Users
     </h1>';
12
13   require_once ('../mysql_connect.php'); //
     Connect to the db.
14
15   // Make the query.
16   $query = "SELECT last_name, first_name,
     DATE_FORMAT(registration_date, '%M
     %d, %Y') AS dr, user_id FROM users ORDER
     BY registration_date ASC";
17   $result = mysql_query ($query); // Run the
     query.
```

(script continues on page 285)

As long as this code is anywhere between the `form` tags, the variable `$_POST['name']` will have a value of *Brian* in the handling PHP script (assuming that the form uses the `POST` method). This technique will be demonstrated shortly.

The second method is to append a value to the PHP script's URL:

`www.dmcinsights.com/page.php?name=Brian`

This technique emulates the `GET` method of an HTML form. With this specific example, `page.php` receives a variable called `$_GET['name']` with a value of *Brian*.

To demonstrate this `GET` method trick, a new version of the `view_users.php` script will be written. This one will provide links to edit or delete an existing user. The links will pass the user's ID to the handling pages, both of which will be written subsequently.

To manually send values to a PHP script:

1. Open `view_users.php` (Script 7.6) in your text editor or IDE.

2. Change the SQL query to read (**Script 8.2**).
   ```
   $query = "SELECT last_name,
   → first_name, DATE_FORMAT
   → (registration_date, '%M %d, %Y')
   → AS dr, user_id FROM users ORDER BY
   → registration_date ASC";
   ```
   I have changed this query in a couple of ways. First, I select the first and last names as separate values, instead of as one concatenated value. Second, I now also select the `user_id` value, which will be necessary in creating the links.

continues on next page

3. Add three more columns to the main table.

```
echo '<table align="center"
→ cellspacing="0" cellpadding="5">
<tr>
    <td align="left"><b>Edit</b></td>
    <td align="left"><b>Delete</b>
    → </td>
    <td align="left"><b>Last Name</b>
    → </td>
    <td align="left"><b>First Name</b>
    → </td>
    <td align="left"><b>Date
    → Registered</b></td>
</tr>
';
```

In the previous version of the script, there were only two columns: one for the name and another for the date the user registered. I've separated out the name column into its two parts and created one column for the *Edit* link and another for the *Delete* link.

4. Change the echo statement within the while loop to match the table's new structure.

```
echo '<tr>
    <td align="left"><a href="edit_
    → user.php?id=' . $row['user_id']
    → . '">Edit</a></td>
    <td align="left"><a href="delete_
    → user.php?id=' . $row['user_id']
    → . '">Delete</a></td>
    <td align="left">' . $row['last_
    → name'] . '</td>
    <td align="left">' . $row['first_
    → name'] . '</td>
    <td align="left">' . $row['dr']
    → . '</td>
</tr>
';
```

For each record returned from the database, this line will print out a row with five columns. The last three columns are obvious and easy to create: just refer to the returned column name.

For the first two columns, which provide links to edit or delete the user, the syntax is slightly more complicated. The desired end result is HTML code like `<a href="edit_user.php?id=X">Edit</a>`, where *X* is the user's ID. Having established this, all I have to do is print $row['user_id'] for *X*, being mindful of the quotation marks to avoid parse errors.

continues on page 282

Script 8.2 *continued*

```
          script
18   $num = mysql_num_rows($result);
19
20   if ($num > 0) { // If it ran OK, display the records.
21
22       echo "<p>There are currently $num registered users.</p>\n";
23
24       // Table header.
25       echo '<table align="center" cellspacing="0" cellpadding="5">
26       <tr>
27           <td align="left"><b>Edit</b></td>
28           <td align="left"><b>Delete</b></td>
29           <td align="left"><b>Last Name</b></td>
30           <td align="left"><b>First Name</b></td>
31           <td align="left"><b>Date Registered</b></td>
32       </tr>
33   ';
34
35       // Fetch and print all the records.
36       while ($row = mysql_fetch_array($result, MYSQL_ASSOC)) {
37           echo '<tr>
38               <td align="left"><a href="edit_user.php?id=' . $row['user_id'] . '">Edit</a></td>
39               <td align="left"><a href="delete_user.php?id=' . $row['user_id'] . '">Delete</a></td>
40               <td align="left">' . $row['last_name'] . '</td>
41               <td align="left">' . $row['first_name'] . '</td>
42               <td align="left">' . $row['dr'] . '</td>
43           </tr>
44           ';
45       }
46
47       echo '</table>';
48
49       mysql_free_result ($result); // Free up the resources.
50
51   } else { // If it did not run OK.
52       echo '<p class="error">There are currently no registered users.</p>';
53   }
54
55   mysql_close(); // Close the database connection.
56
57   include ('./includes/footer.html'); // Include the HTML footer.
58   ?>
```

5. Save the file as `view_users.php`, upload it to your server, and run in your Web browser (**Figure 8.1**).

6. If you want, view the HTML source of the page to see each dynamically generated link (**Figure 8.2**).

✔ Tips

■ To append multiple variables to a URL, use this syntax: `page.php?name1=value1 &name2=value2&name3=value3`. It's simply a matter of using the ampersand, plus another *name=value* pair.

■ One trick to adding variables to URLs is that strings should be encoded to ensure that the value is handled properly. For example, the space in the string *Elliott Smith* would be problematic. The solution then is to use the `urlencode()` function:

```
$url = 'page.php?name=' .
→ urlencode('Elliott Smith');
```

You only need to do this when *manually* adding values to a URL. When a form uses a `GET` method, it automatically encodes the data properly.

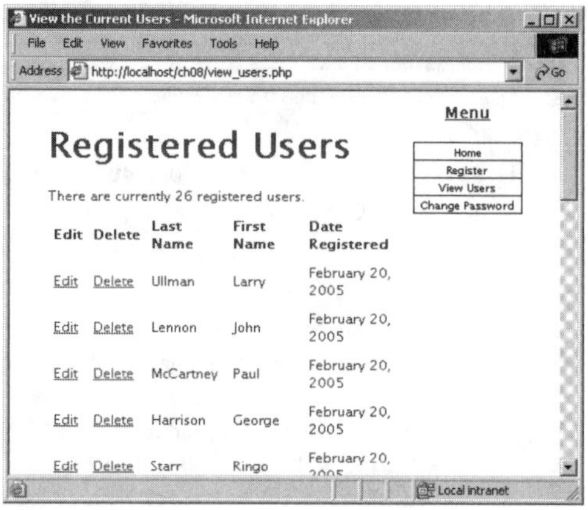

Figure 8.1 The latest version of the `view_users.php` page, with new columns and links.

Figure 8.2 The source of the page (see Figure 8.1) shows how the user's ID is added to each link's URL.

Using Hidden Form Inputs

In the preceding example, a new version of the view_users.php script was written. This one now includes links to the edit_user.php and delete_user.php pages, passing each a user's ID through the URL. This next example, delete_user.php, will take the passed user ID and allow the administrator to delete that user. Although you could have this page simply execute a DELETE query on the database, for security purposes (and to prevent an inadvertent deletion), there will be multiple steps:

Script 8.3 This script expects a user ID to be passed to it through the URL. It then presents a confirmation form and deletes the user upon submission.

```
        ▤▤▤▤▤▤▤  script  ▤▤▤▤▤▤
1    <?php # Script 8.3 - delete_user.php
2
3    // This page deletes a user.
4    // This page is accessed through view_
     users.php.
5
6    $page_title = 'Delete a User';
7    include ('./includes/header.html');
8
9    // Check for a valid user ID, through GET
     or POST.
10   if ( (isset($_GET['id'])) && (is_numeric
     ($_GET['id'])) ) { // Accessed through
     view_users.php
11       $id = $_GET['id'];
12   } elseif ( (isset($_POST['id'])) &&
     (is_numeric($_POST['id'])) ) { // Form
     has been submitted.
13       $id = $_POST['id'];
14   } else { // No valid ID, kill the script.
15       echo '<h1 id="mainhead">Page Error
         </h1>
16       <p class="error">This page has been
         accessed in error.</p><p><br /><br />
         </p>';
17       include ('./includes/footer.html');
18       exit();
19   }
```

(script continues on next page)

1. The page must check that it received a numeric user ID.

2. A message will confirm that this user should be deleted.

3. The user ID will be stored in a hidden form input.

4. Upon submission of this form, the user will actually be deleted.

To use hidden form inputs:

1. Create a new PHP document in your text editor or IDE (**Script 8.3**).

   ```
   <?php # Script 8.3 - delete_user.php
   ```

2. Include the page header.

   ```
   $page_title = 'Delete a User';
   include ('./includes/header.html');
   ```

   This document will use the same template system as the other pages in the application.

3. Check for a valid user ID value.

   ```
   if ( (isset($_GET['id'])) &&
   → (is_numeric($_GET['id'])) ) {
       $id = $_GET['id'];
   } elseif ( (isset($_POST['id'])) &&
   → (is_numeric($_POST['id'])) ) {
       $id = $_POST['id'];
   } else {
       echo '<h1 id="mainhead">
       → Page Error</h1>
       <p class="error">This page has
       → been accessed in error.</p><p>
       → <br /><br /></p>';
       include ('./includes/footer.
       → html');
       exit();
   }
   ```

continues on next page

This script relies upon having a valid user ID, which will be used in a DELETE query's WHERE clause. The first time this page is accessed, the user ID should be passed in the URL (the page's URL will end with delete_user.php?id=X), after clicking the *Delete* link in the view_users.php page. The first if condition checks for such a value and that the value is numeric.

As you will see, the script will then store the user ID value in a hidden form input. When the form is submitted (back to this same page), the page will receive the ID through $_POST. The second condition checks this and, again, that the ID value is numeric.

If neither of these conditions are TRUE, then the page cannot proceed, so an error message is displayed and the script's execution is terminated.

4. Include the MySQL connection script.

    require_once ('../mysql_connect.
    → php');

    Both of this script's processes—showing the form and handling the form—require a database connection, so this line is outside of the main submit conditional (Step 5).

5. Begin the main submit conditional.

    if (isset($_POST['submitted'])) {

6. Delete the user, if appropriate.

    if ($_POST['sure'] == 'Yes') {
      $query = "DELETE FROM users WHERE
    → user_id=$id";
      $result = @mysql_query ($query);

    The form (**Figure 8.3**) will make the user click a radio button to confirm the deletion. This little step prevents any accidents. Thus, the handling process first checks that the right radio button was selected. If so, a basic DELETE query is defined, using the user's ID in the WHERE clause.

Script 8.3 *continued*

```
20
21    require_once ('../mysql_connect.php'); //
      Connect to the db.
22
23    // Check if the form has been submitted.
24    if (isset($_POST['submitted'])) {
25
26        if ($_POST['sure'] == 'Yes') { // Delete
          them.
27
28            // Make the query.
29            $query = "DELETE FROM users WHERE
              user_id=$id";
30            $result = @mysql_query ($query); //
              Run the query.
```

(script continues on next page)

Figure 8.3 The page confirms the user deletion using this simple form.

Script 8.3 *continued*

```
                  script
31        if (mysql_affected_rows() == 1) { //
          If it ran OK.
32
33            // Print a message.
34            echo '<h1 id="mainhead">Delete a
              User</h1>
35        <p>The user has been deleted.</p><p>
          <br /><br /></p>';
36
37        } else { // If the query did not
          run OK.
38            echo '<h1 id="mainhead">System
              Error</h1>
39            <p class="error">The user could
              not be deleted due to a system
              error.</p>'; // Public message.
40            echo '<p>' . mysql_error() .
              '<br /><br />Query: ' . $query .
              '</p>'; // Debugging message.
41        }
42
43    } else { // Wasn't sure about deleting
      the user.
44        echo '<h1 id="mainhead">Delete a
          User</h1>
45        <p>The user has NOT been deleted.
          </p><p><br /><br /></p>';
46    }
47
```

(script continues on page 287)

7. Check if the deletion worked and respond accordingly.

```
if (mysql_affected_rows() == 1) {
    echo '<h1 id="mainhead">Delete a
    → User</h1>
<p>The user has been deleted.
→ </p><p><br /><br /></p>';
} else {
    echo '<h1 id="mainhead">System
    → Error</h1>
    <p class="error">The user could
    → not be deleted due to a system
    → error.</p>';
    echo '<p>' . mysql_error() .
    → '<br /><br />Query: ' . $query .
    → '</p>';
}
```

The `mysql_affected_rows()` function checks that exactly one row was affected by the `DELETE` query. If so, a happy message is displayed. If not, an error message is sent out.

Keep in mind that it's possible that no rows were affected without a MySQL error occurring. For example, if the query tries to delete the record where the user ID is equal to *42000* (which presumably doesn't exist), no rows will be deleted but no MySQL error will occur.

8. Complete the `$_POST['sure']` conditional.

```
} else {
    echo '<h1 id="mainhead">Delete a
    → User</h1>
    <p>The user has NOT been deleted.
    → </p><p><br /><br /></p>';
}
```

If the page user did not explicitly check the *Yes* box, the user will not be deleted and this message is displayed.

continues on next page

9. Begin the else clause of the main submit conditional.

```
} else {
```

The page will either handle the form or display it. Most of the code prior to this takes effect if the form has been submitted (if `$_POST['submitted']` is set). The code from here on takes effect if the form has not yet been submitted, in which case the form should be displayed.

10. Retrieve the information for the user being deleted.

```
$query = "SELECT CONCAT(last_name,
→', ', first_name) FROM users WHERE
→user_id=$id";

$result = @mysql_query ($query);

if (mysql_num_rows($result) == 1) {
```

To confirm that the script received a valid user ID and to state exactly who is being deleted (refer back to Figure 8.3), the to-be-deleted user's name is retrieved from the database.

The conditional—checking that a single row was returned—ensures that a valid user ID was provided.

11. Display the form.

```
$row = mysql_fetch_array ($result,
→MYSQL_NUM);

echo '<h2>Delete a User</h2>

<form action="delete_user.php"
→method="post">

<h3>Name: ' . $row[0] . '</h3>

<p>Are you sure you want to delete
→this user?<br />

<input type="radio" name="sure"
→value="Yes" /> Yes

<input type="radio" name="sure"
→value="No" checked="checked" />
No</p>

<p><input type="submit" name=
→"submit" value="Submit" /></p>
```

```
<input type="hidden" name=
→"submitted" value="TRUE" />

<input type="hidden" name="id"
→value="' . $id . '" />

</form>';
```

First, the database information is retrieved using the `mysql_fetch_array()` function. Then the form is printed, showing the name value retrieved from the database at the top. An important step here is that the user ID (`$id`) is stored as a hidden form input so that the handling process can also access this value.

12. Complete the `mysql_num_rows()` conditional.

```
} else {

    echo '<h1 id="mainhead">Page
→Error</h1>

    <p class="error">This page has
→been accessed in error.</p>
→<p><br /><br /></p>';

}
```

If no record was returned from the database (because an invalid user ID was submitted), this message is displayed.

If you are unsure of your MySQL query, you could call the `mysql_error()` function here and print out the query to check for errors. Again though, an invalid user ID can cause no records to be returned without a MySQL error having occurred.

13. Complete the PHP page.

```
}

mysql_close();

include ('./includes/footer.html');

?>
```

The closing brace finishes the main submit conditional. Then the MySQL connection is closed and the footer is included.

continues on page 288

Script 8.3 *continued*

```
████████████████████████████████    script    ████████████████████████████████
48   } else { // Show the form.
49
50      // Retrieve the user's information.
51      $query = "SELECT CONCAT(last_name, ', ', first_name) FROM users WHERE user_id=$id";
52      $result = @mysql_query ($query); // Run the query.
53
54      if (mysql_num_rows($result) == 1) { // Valid user ID, show the form.
55
56         // Get the user's information.
57         $row = mysql_fetch_array ($result, MYSQL_NUM);
58
59         // Create the form.
60         echo '<h2>Delete a User</h2>
61      <form action="delete_user.php" method="post">
62      <h3>Name: ' . $row[0] . '</h3>
63      <p>Are you sure you want to delete this user?<br />
64      <input type="radio" name="sure" value="Yes" /> Yes
65      <input type="radio" name="sure" value="No" checked="checked" /> No</p>
66      <p><input type="submit" name="submit" value="Submit" /></p>
67      <input type="hidden" name="submitted" value="TRUE" />
68      <input type="hidden" name="id" value="' . $id . '" />
69      </form>';
70
71      } else { // Not a valid user ID.
72         echo '<h1 id="mainhead">Page Error</h1>
73         <p class="error">This page has been accessed in error.</p><p><br /><br /></p>';
74      }
75
76   } // End of the main Submit conditional.
77
78   mysql_close(); // Close the database connection.
79
80   include ('./includes/footer.html');
81   ?>
```

USING HIDDEN FORM INPUTS

14. Save the file as `delete_user.php` and upload it to your Web server (it should be placed in the same directory as `view_users.php`).

15. Run the page by first clicking a *Delete* link in the `view_users.php` page (**Figures 8.4** and **8.5**).

✔ Tips

■ Another way of writing this script would be to have the form use the `GET` method. Then the validation conditional (lines 10–19) would only have to validate `$_GET['id']`, as the ID would be passed in the URL whether the page was first being accessed or the form had been submitted.

■ Hidden form elements don't display in the Web browser but are still present in the HTML source code (**Figure 8.6**). For this reason, never store anything there that must be kept truly secure.

■ Using hidden form inputs and appending values to a URL are just two ways to make data available to other PHP pages. Two more methods—cookies and sessions—are thoroughly covered in the next chapter.

■ PHP's `parse_url()` function can be used to break a URL down into its subparts. See the PHP manual for more information.

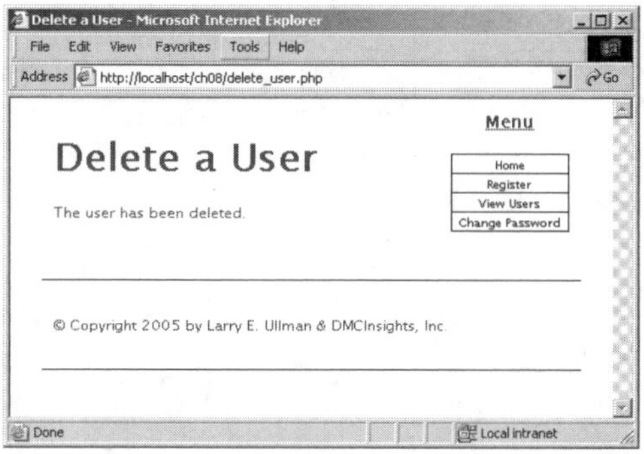

Figure 8.4 If you select *Yes* in the form (see Figure 8.3) and click Submit, this should be the result.

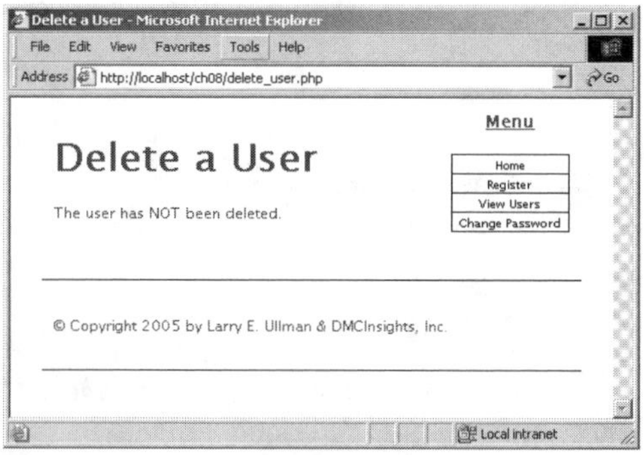

Figure 8.5 If you do not select *Yes* in the form, no database changes are made.

Figure 8.6 The user ID is stored as a hidden input so that it's available when the form is handled.

Editing Existing Records

A common practice with database-driven Web sites is having a system in place so that you can easily edit existing records. This concept seems daunting to many beginning programmers, but it's surprisingly straight-forward. For the following example, editing registered user records, the process combines three skills you should already have:

◆ Making sticky forms

◆ Using hidden inputs

◆ Registering new users

Script 8.4 The edit_user.php page first displays the user's current information in a form. Upon submission of the form, the record will be updated in the database.

```
script

1   <?php # Script 8.4 - edit_user.php
2
3   // This page edits a user.
4   // This page is accessed through
    view_users.php.
5
6   $page_title = 'Edit a User';
7   include ('./includes/header.html');
8
9   // Check for a valid user ID, through GET
    or POST.
10  if ( (isset($_GET['id'])) && (is_numeric
    ($_GET['id'])) ) { // Accessed through
    view_users.php
11     $id = $_GET['id'];
12  } elseif ( (isset($_POST['id'])) &&
    (is_numeric($_POST['id'])) ) { // Form
    has been submitted.
13     $id = $_POST['id'];
14  } else { // No valid ID, kill the script.
15     echo '<h1 id="mainhead">Page Error</h1>
16     <p class="error">This page has been
       accessed in error.</p><p><br /><br />
       </p>';
17     include ('./includes/footer.html');
18     exit();
19  }
```

(script continues on page 291)

This next example is generally very similar to delete_user.php and will also be linked from the view_users.php script (when a person clicks *Edit*). A form will be displayed with the user's current information, allowing for those values to be changed. Upon submitting the form, an UPDATE query will be run to update the database.

To edit an existing database record:

1. Create a new PHP document in your text editor or IDE (**Script 8.4**).

   ```
   <?php # Script 8.4 - edit_user.php
   $page_title = 'Edit a User';
   include ('./includes/header.html');
   ```

2. Check for a valid user ID value.

   ```
   if ( (isset($_GET['id'])) &&
   → (is_numeric($_GET['id'])) ) {
      $id = $_GET['id'];
   } elseif ( (isset($_POST['id'])) &&
   → (is_numeric($_POST['id'])) ) {
      $id = $_POST['id'];
   } else {
      echo '<h1 id="mainhead">Page
   → Error</h1>
      <p class="error">This page has
   → been accessed in error.</p>
   → <p><br /><br /></p>';
      include ('./includes/footer.
   → html');
      exit();
   }
   ```

   This validation routine is exactly the same as that in delete_user.php, confirming that a numeric user ID has been received.

   continues on next page

3. Include the MySQL connection script and begin the main submit conditional.

```
require_once ('../mysql_connect.
→ php');
if (isset($_POST['submitted'])) {
  $errors = array();
```

Like the registration examples you have already done, this script makes use of an array to track errors.

4. Validate the form data.

```
if (empty($_POST['first_name'])) {
  $errors[] = 'You forgot to enter
  → your first name.';
} else {
  $fn = escape_data($_POST
  → ['first_name']);
}
if (empty($_POST['last_name'])) {
  $errors[] = 'You forgot to enter
  → your last name.';
} else {
  $ln = escape_data($_POST
  → ['last_name']);
}
if (empty($_POST['email'])) {
  $errors[] = 'You forgot to enter
  → your email address.';
} else {
  $e = escape_data($_POST['email']);
}
```

The form (**Figure 8.7**) is like a registration form but without the password fields. The form data can therefore be validated using the same methods used in the registration scripts.

5. If there were no errors, check that the submitted email address is not already in use.

```
if (empty($errors)) {
  $query = "SELECT user_id FROM
  → users WHERE email='$e' AND
  → user_id != $id";
  $result = mysql_query($query);
  if (mysql_num_rows($result) == 0) {
```

The integrity of the database and of the application as a whole partially depends upon having unique email address values in the *users* table. This guarantees that the login system (developed in the next chapter) works. Because the form allows for altering the user's email address (see Figure 8.7), special steps have to be taken to ensure uniqueness. Consider two possibilities...

In the first, the user's email address is being changed. In this case you just need to run a query making sure that that particular email address isn't already registered (i.e., SELECT user_id FROM users WHERE email='$e').

In the second possibility, the user's email address will remain the same. In this case, it's okay if the email address is already in use, because it's already in use for this user.

To write one query that will work for both possibilities, don't check to see if the email address is being used, but rather see if it's being used by *anyone else*: SELECT user_id FROM users WHERE email='$e' AND user_id != $id.

continues on page 292

Figure 8.7 The form for editing a user's record.

Script 8.4 *continued*

```
20
21    require_once ('../mysql_connect.php'); // Connect to the db.
22
23    // Check if the form has been submitted.
24    if (isset($_POST['submitted'])) {
25
26        $errors = array(); // Initialize error array.
27
28        // Check for a first name.
29        if (empty($_POST['first_name'])) {
30            $errors[] = 'You forgot to enter your first name.';
31        } else {
32            $fn = escape_data($_POST['first_name']);
33        }
34
35        // Check for a last name.
36        if (empty($_POST['last_name'])) {
37            $errors[] = 'You forgot to enter your last name.';
38        } else {
39            $ln = escape_data($_POST['last_name']);
40        }
41
42        // Check for an email address.
43        if (empty($_POST['email'])) {
44            $errors[] = 'You forgot to enter your email address.';
45        } else {
46            $e = escape_data($_POST['email']);
47        }
48
49        if (empty($errors)) { // If everything's OK.
50
51            //  Test for unique email address.
52            $query = "SELECT user_id FROM users WHERE email='$e' AND user_id != $id";
53            $result = mysql_query($query);
54            if (mysql_num_rows($result) == 0) {
55
56                // Make the query.
```

(script continues on page 293)

6. Update the database.

```
$query = "UPDATE users SET
→ first_name='$fn', last_name='$ln',
→ email='$e' WHERE user_id=$id";
$result = @mysql_query ($query);
if (mysql_affected_rows() == 1) {
    echo '<h1 id="mainhead">Edit a
    → User</h1>
    <p>The user has been edited.</p>
    → <p><br /><br /></p>';
} else {
    echo '<h1 id="mainhead">System
    → Error</h1>
    <p class="error">The user could
    → not be edited due to a system
    → error. We apologize for any
    → inconvenience.</p>';
    echo '<p>' . mysql_error() .
    → '<br /><br />Query: ' . $query .
    → '</p>';
    include ('./includes/footer.
    → html');
    exit();
}
```

The UPDATE query is similar to examples you may have seen in Chapter 4, "Introduction to SQL and MySQL." The query updates all three fields—first name, last name, and email address—using the values submitted by the form. This system works because the form is preset with the existing values. So, if you edit the first name in the form but nothing else, the first name value in the database is updated using this new value, but the last name and email address values are "updated" using their current values. This system is much easier than trying to determine which form values have changed and updating just those in the database.

The mysql_affected_rows() function is used to report upon the success of the operation.

7. Complete the email, $errors, and submit conditionals.

```
    } else {
        echo '<h1 id="mainhead">
        → Error!</h1>
        <p class="error">The email
        → address has already been
        → registered.</p>';
    }
} else {
    echo '<h1 id="mainhead">
    → Error!</h1>
    <p class="error">The following
    → error(s) occurred:<br />';
    foreach ($errors as $msg) {
        echo " - $msg<br />\n";
    }
    echo '</p><p>Please try again.
    → </p><p><br /></p>';
}
}
```

This first else completes the conditional that checked if an email address was already being used by another user. The second else is used to report any errors in the form (namely, a lack of a first name, last name, or email address). The final closing brace completes the main submit conditional.

In this example, the form will be displayed whenever the page is accessed. So after submitting the form, the database will be updated, and the form will be shown again, now displaying the latest information.

continues on page 294

Script 8.4 *continued*

```
57          $query = "UPDATE users SET first_name='$fn', last_name='$ln', email='$e' WHERE
            user_id=$id";
58          $result = @mysql_query ($query); // Run the query.
59          if (mysql_affected_rows() == 1) { // If it ran OK.
60
61              // Print a message.
62              echo '<h1 id="mainhead">Edit a User</h1>
63              <p>The user has been edited.</p><p><br /><br /></p>';
64
65          } else { // If it did not run OK.
66              echo '<h1 id="mainhead">System Error</h1>
67              <p class="error">The user could not be edited due to a system error. We apologize for
                any inconvenience.</p>'; // Public message.
68              echo '<p>' . mysql_error() . '<br /><br />Query: ' . $query . '</p>'; // Debugging
                message.
69              include ('./includes/footer.html');
70              exit();
71          }
72
73          } else { // Already registered.
74              echo '<h1 id="mainhead">Error!</h1>
75              <p class="error">The email address has already been registered.</p>';
76          }
77
78      } else { // Report the errors.
79
80          echo '<h1 id="mainhead">Error!</h1>
81          <p class="error">The following error(s) occurred:<br />';
82          foreach ($errors as $msg) { // Print each error.
83              echo " - $msg<br />\n";
84          }
85          echo '</p><p>Please try again.</p><p><br /></p>';
86
87      } // End of if (empty($errors)) IF.
88
89  } // End of submit conditional.
90
91  // Always show the form.
92
93  // Retrieve the user's information.
```

(script continues on page 295)

8. Retrieve the information for the user being edited.

```
$query = "SELECT first_name,
→ last_name, email FROM users WHERE
→ user_id=$id";

$result = @mysql_query ($query);

if (mysql_num_rows($result) == 1) {
```

This query is similar to the one in `delete_user.php`, although three individual values are retrieved from the database. Again, the conditional—checking that a single row was returned—ensures that a valid user ID was provided.

9. Display the form.

```
$row = mysql_fetch_array ($result,
→ MYSQL_NUM);

echo '<h2>Edit a User</h2>

<form action="edit_user.php"
→ method="post">

<p>First Name: <input type="text"
→ name="first_name" size="15"
→ maxlength="15" value="' . $row[0]
→ . '" /></p>

<p>Last Name: <input type="text"
→ name="last_name" size="15"
→ maxlength="30" value="' . $row[1]
→ . '" /></p>

<p>Email Address: <input
→ type="text" name="email" size="20"
→ maxlength="40" value="' . $row[2]
→ . '"  /> </p>

<p><input type="submit"
→ name="submit" value="Submit"
→ /></p>

<input type="hidden"
→ name="submitted" value="TRUE" />

<input type="hidden" name="id"
→ value="' . $id . '" />

</form>';
```

The form has but three text inputs, each of which is made sticky using the data retrieved from the database. Again, the user ID (`$id`) is stored as a hidden form input so that the handling process can also access this value.

10. Complete the `mysql_num_rows()` conditional.

```
} else {
    echo '<h1 id="mainhead">Page
→ Error</h1>
    <p class="error">This page has
→ been accessed in error.</p><p>
→ <br /><br /></p>';
}
```

If no record was returned from the database, because an invalid user ID was submitted, this message is displayed.

11. Complete the PHP page.

```
mysql_close();
include ('./includes/footer.html');
?>
```

continues on page 296

Script 8.4 *continued*

```
94   $query = "SELECT first_name, last_name, email FROM users WHERE user_id=$id";
95   $result = @mysql_query ($query); // Run the query.
96
97   if (mysql_num_rows($result) == 1) { // Valid user ID, show the form.
98
99       // Get the user's information.
100      $row = mysql_fetch_array ($result, MYSQL_NUM);
101
102      // Create the form.
103      echo '<h2>Edit a User</h2>
104  <form action="edit_user.php" method="post">
105  <p>First Name: <input type="text" name="first_name" size="15" maxlength="15" value="' . $row[0]
     . '" /></p>
106  <p>Last Name: <input type="text" name="last_name" size="15" maxlength="30" value="' . $row[1]
     . '" /></p>
107  <p>Email Address: <input type="text" name="email" size="20" maxlength="40" value="' . $row[2]
     . '"  /> </p>
108  <p><input type="submit" name="submit" value="Submit" /></p>
109  <input type="hidden" name="submitted" value="TRUE" />
110  <input type="hidden" name="id" value="' . $id . '" />
111  </form>';
112
113  } else { // Not a valid user ID.
114      echo '<h1 id="mainhead">Page Error</h1>
115      <p class="error">This page has been accessed in error.</p><p><br /><br /></p>';
116  }
117
118  mysql_close(); // Close the database connection.
119
120  include ('./includes/footer.html');
121  ?>
```

EDITING EXISTING RECORDS

12. Save the file as `edit_user.php` and upload it to your Web server.

13. Run the page by first clicking an *Edit* link in the `view_users.php` page (**Figures 8.8** and **8.9**).

✔ Tips

■ This edit page does not include the functionality to change the password. That concept was already demonstrated in `password.php` (Script 7.8). If you would like to incorporate that functionality here, keep in mind that you cannot display the current password, as it is encrypted. Instead, just present two boxes for changing the password (the new password input and a confirmation). If these values are submitted, update the password in the database as well. If these inputs are left blank, do not update the password in the database.

■ The `mysql_affected_rows()` function will return a value of *0* if an UPDATE command successfully ran but didn't actually affect any records. So if you submit this form without changing any of the form values, a system error is displayed, which may not technically be correct. Once you have this script effectively working, you could change the error message to indicate that no alterations were made in such a case.

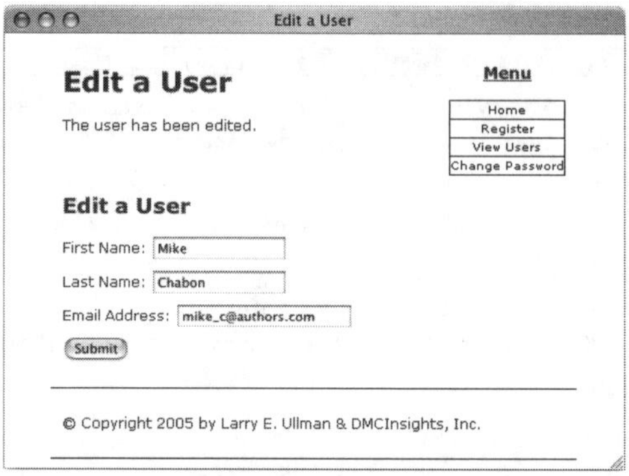

Figure 8.8 The new values are displayed in the form after successfully updating the database (compare with the form values in Figure 8.7).

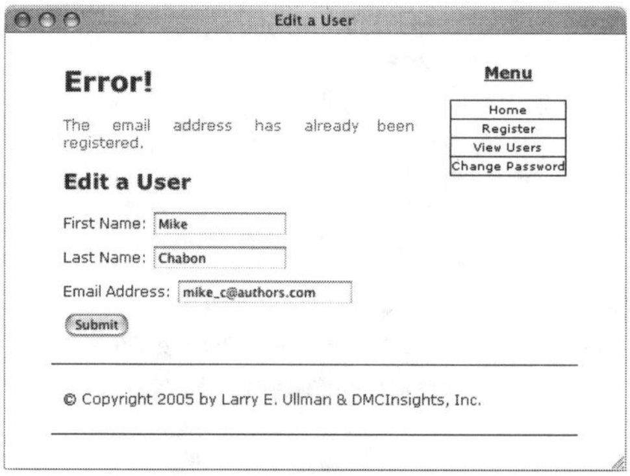

Figure 8.9 If you try to change a record to an existing email address or if you omit an input, errors are reported.

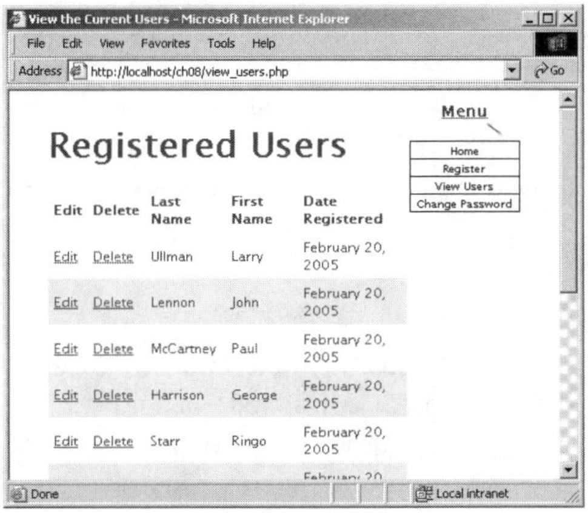

Figure 8.10 Alternating the table row colors makes this list of users more legible (every other row has a light gray background).

Paginating Query Results

Pagination is a concept you're familiar with even if you don't know the term. When you use a search engine like Google, it displays the results as a series of pages and not as one long list. The `view_users.php` script could benefit from this same feature.

Paginating query results makes extensive use of the `LIMIT` SQL clause introduced in Chapter 4. `LIMIT` restricts which subset of the matched records are actually returned. To paginate the returned results of a query, each page will run the same query using different `LIMIT` parameters. These parameters will also be passed from page to page in the URL, like the user IDs passed from the `view_users.php` page.

Another, more cosmetic technique will be demonstrated here: displaying each row of the table—each returned record—using an alternating background color (**Figure 8.10**). This effect will be achieved with ease, using the ternary operator (see the sidebar "The Ternary Operator" on page 304).

There's a lot of good, new information here, so be careful as you follow along and make sure that your script matches this one exactly. If altering the existing script seems like too much of a hassle, make your life easier by just writing this one from scratch (you'll obviously have to fill in a few steps on your own using what you already know from the previous version).

TO PAGINATE VIEW _ USERS.PHP:

1. Open `view_users.php` (Script 8.2) in your text editor or IDE.

2. After including the database connection, set the number of records to display per page (**Script 8.5**).

   ```
   $display = 10;
   ```

   By establishing this value as a variable here, you'll make it easy to change the number of records displayed on each page at a later date.

3. Check if the number of required pages has been determined.

   ```
   if (isset($_GET['np'])) {
      $num_pages = $_GET['np'];
   } else {
   ```

   For this script to display the users over several pages, it will need to determine how many total pages of results will be required. The first time the script is run, this number will be calculated. From then on, the number of pages will be passed to the script as part of the URL, as the `$_GET['np']` variable. If this variable is set, its value will be assigned to the `$num_pages` variable. If not, then the number of pages will need to be calculated.

4. Count the number of records in the database.

   ```
   $query = "SELECT COUNT(*) FROM users
   → ORDER BY registration_date ASC";
   $result = mysql_query ($query);
   $row = mysql_fetch_array ($result,
   → MYSQL_NUM);
   $num_records = $row[0];
   ```

   Using the `COUNT()` function, introduced in Chapter 5, "Advanced SQL and MySQL," you can easily see the number of records in the *users* table. This query will return a single row with a single column: the number of records.

5. Mathematically calculate how many pages are required.

   ```
       if ($num_records > $display) {
          $num_pages = ceil ($num_
          → records/$display);
       } else {
          $num_pages = 1;
       }
   }
   ```

   The number of pages used to display the records is based upon the total number of records to be shown and the number to display per page (as set by the `$display` variable). If there are more rows than there are records to be displayed per page, multiple pages will be required. To calculate exactly how many pages, take the next highest integer from the division of the two (the `ceil()` function returns the next highest integer). If `$num_records` is not greater than `$display`, only one page is necessary.

continues on page 300

PAGINATING QUERY RESULTS

Script 8.5 This new version of `view_users.php` incorporates pagination so that the users are listed over multiple Web browser pages.

```
1    <?php # Script 8.5 - view_users.php
2    # (4th version after Scripts 7.4, 7.6, & 8.2)
3
4    // This script retrieves all the records from the users table.
5    // This new version paginates the query results.
6
7    $page_title = 'View the Current Users';
8    include ('./includes/header.html');
9
10   // Page header.
11   echo '<h1 id="mainhead">Registered Users</h1>';
12
13   require_once ('../mysql_connect.php'); // Connect to the db.
14
15   // Number of records to show per page:
16   $display = 10;
17
18   // Determine how many pages there are.
19   if (isset($_GET['np'])) { // Already been determined.
20
21       $num_pages = $_GET['np'];
22
23   } else { // Need to determine.
24
25       // Count the number of records
26       $query = "SELECT COUNT(*) FROM users ORDER BY registration_date ASC";
27       $result = mysql_query ($query);
28       $row = mysql_fetch_array ($result, MYSQL_NUM);
29       $num_records = $row[0];
30
31       // Calculate the number of pages.
32       if ($num_records > $display) { // More than 1 page.
33           $num_pages = ceil ($num_records/$display);
34       } else {
35           $num_pages = 1;
36       }
37
38   } // End of np IF.
39
```

(script continues on page 301)

PAGINATING QUERY RESULTS

6. Determine the starting point in the database.

```
if (isset($_GET['s'])) {
    $start = $_GET['s'];
} else {
    $start = 0;
}
```

The second parameter the script will receive—on subsequent viewings of the page—will be the starting record. Upon initially calling the script, the first 10 records should be retrieved. The second page would show records 10 through 20; the third, 20 through 30; and so forth. The first page will not have an $_GET['s'] variable set, and so $start will be 0 (the first record in a LIMIT clause is indexed at 0). Subsequent pages will receive the $_GET['s'] variable from the URL, and it will be assigned to $start.

7. Change the query so that it uses the LIMIT clause.

```
$query = "SELECT last_name, first_
→ name, DATE_FORMAT(registration_
→ date, '%M %d, %Y') AS dr, user_id
→ FROM users ORDER BY registration_
→ date ASC LIMIT $start, $display";
```

The LIMIT clause dictates which record to begin retrieving ($start) and how many to return ($display) from that point. The first time the page is run, the query will be SELECT last_name, first_name … LIMIT 0, 10. Clicking to the next page will result in SELECT last_name, first_name … LIMIT 10, 10.

8. Delete the references to the $num variable. In order to simplify this script a little bit, I'm deleting both the assignment of the $num variable and the if ($num > 0) conditional. I'm assuming that there are records to be displayed.

9. Before the while loop, initialize the background color variable.

```
$bg = '#eeeeee';
```

I initialize a $bg variable (to *#eeeeee*, a light gray), which will be used as the background color for every other row.

10. Within the while loop, add.

```
$bg = ($bg=='#eeeeee' ? '#ffffff' :
→ '#eeeeee');
```

The background color used by each row in the table is assigned to the $bg variable. Because I want this color to alternate, I use this line of code to assign the opposite color to $bg. If it's equal to *#eeeeee*, then it will be assigned the value of *#ffffff* and vice versa (again, see the sidebar for the syntax and explanation of the ternary operator). For the first row, $bg is equal to *#eeeeee* and will therefore be assigned *#ffffff*, making a white background. For the second row, $bg is not equal to *#eeeeee*, so it will be assigned that value, making a gray background.

11. Modify the while loop's echo statement so that it prints the table row's background color.

```
echo '<tr bgcolor="' . $bg . '">
```

continues on page 302

Script 8.5 *continued*

```
40    // Determine where in the database to start returning results.
41    if (isset($_GET['s'])) {
42        $start = $_GET['s'];
43    } else {
44        $start = 0;
45    }
46
47    // Make the query.
48    $query = "SELECT last_name, first_name, DATE_FORMAT(registration_date, '%M %d, %Y') AS dr, user_id
      FROM users ORDER BY registration_date ASC LIMIT $start, $display";
49    $result = mysql_query ($query); // Run the query.
50
51    // Table header.
52    echo '<table align="center" cellspacing="0" cellpadding="5">
53    <tr>
54        <td align="left"><b>Edit</b></td>
55        <td align="left"><b>Delete</b></td>
56        <td align="left"><b>Last Name</b></td>
57        <td align="left"><b>First Name</b></td>
58        <td align="left"><b>Date Registered</b></td>
59    </tr>
60    ';
61
62    // Fetch and print all the records.
63    $bg = '#eeeeee'; // Set the background color.
64    while ($row = mysql_fetch_array($result, MYSQL_ASSOC)) {
65        $bg = ($bg=='#eeeeee' ? '#ffffff' : '#eeeeee'); // Switch the background color.
66        echo '<tr bgcolor="' . $bg . '">
67            <td align="left"><a href="edit_user.php?id=' . $row['user_id'] . '">Edit</a></td>
68            <td align="left"><a href="delete_user.php?id=' . $row['user_id'] . '">Delete</a></td>
69            <td align="left">' . $row['last_name'] . '</td>
70            <td align="left">' . $row['first_name'] . '</td>
71            <td align="left">' . $row['dr'] . '</td>
72        </tr>
73        ';
74    }
75
76    echo '</table>';
77
78    mysql_free_result ($result); // Free up the resources.
79
80    mysql_close(); // Close the database connection.
81
```

(script continues on next page)

PAGINATING QUERY RESULTS

12. After completing the HTML table, begin a section for displaying links to other pages, if necessary.

```
if ($num_pages > 1) {
   echo '<br /><p>';
   $current_page = ($start/$display)
→ + 1;
   if ($current_page != 1) {
      echo '<a href="view_users.
→ php?s=' . ($start -
→ $display) . '&np=' . $num_
→ pages . '">Previous</a> ';
   }
```

If the script requires multiple pages to display all of the records, I'll want to make the appropriate links at the bottom of the page (see **Figure 8.11**). For these links I'll first determine the current page, which can be calculated as the start number divided by the display number, plus 1. For example, on the second instance of this script, $start will be 10 (because on the first instance, $start is 0), so 10/10 + 1 = 2.

If the current page is not the first page, I'll display a *Previous* link to the earlier result set (**Figure 8.12**).

Each link will be made up of the script name, plus the starting point and the number of pages. The starting point for the previous page will be the current starting point minus the number being displayed.

Script 8.5 *continued*

```
┌────────────────── script ──────────────────┐
82   // Make the links to other pages, if
     necessary.
83   if ($num_pages > 1) {
84
85      echo '<br /><p>';
86      // Determine what page the script is on.
87      $current_page = ($start/$display) + 1;
88
89      // If it's not the first page, make a
        Previous button.
90      if ($current_page != 1) {
91         echo '<a href="view_users.php?s='
           . ($start - $display) . '&np=' .
           $num_pages . '">Previous</a> ';
92      }
93
94      // Make all the numbered pages.
95      for ($i = 1; $i <= $num_pages; $i++) {
96         if ($i != $current_page) {
97            echo '<a href="view_users.php
              ?s=' . (($display * ($i - 1))) .
              '&np=' . $num_pages . '">' . $i
              . '</a> ';
98         } else {
99            echo $i . ' ';
100        }
101     }
102
103     // If it's not the last page, make a
        Next button.
104     if ($current_page != $num_pages) {
105        echo '<a href="view_users.php?s='
           . ($start + $display) . '&np=' .
           $num_pages . '">Next</a>';
106     }
107
108     echo '</p>';
109
110  } // End of links section.
111
112  include ('./includes/footer.html'); //
     Include the HTML footer.
113  ?>
```

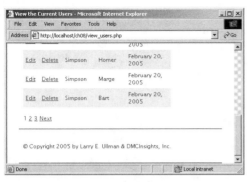

Figure 8.11 After all of the returned records, links are generated to the other result pages.

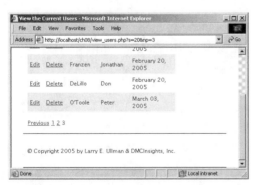

Figure 8.12 The *Previous* link will appear only if the current page is not the first one.

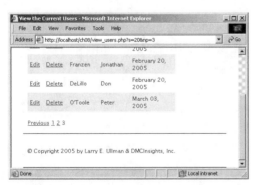

Figure 8.13 The final results page will not display a *Next* link.

13. Finish making the links.

```
for ($i = 1; $i <= $num_pages;
→ $i++) {
    if ($i != $current_page) {
        echo '<a href="view_
        → users.php?s=' . (($display
        → * ($i - 1))) . '&np=' .
        → $num_pages . '">' . $i .
        → '</a> ';
    } else {
        echo $i . ' ';
    }
}
if ($current_page != $num_pages) {
    echo '<a href="view_users.
    → php?s=' . ($start + $display)
    → . '&np=' . $num_pages .
    → '">Next</a>';
}
echo '</p>';
}
```

The bulk of the links will be created by looping from 1 to the total number of pages. Each page will be linked except for the current one.

Finally, a *Next* page link will be displayed, assuming that this is not the final page (**Figure 8.13**).

14. Save the file as view_users.php, upload it to your Web server, and test in your Web browser.

✔ Tips

- From a security standpoint, it would be better if this script validated $_GET['np'] and $_GET['s'] to ensure they are numeric. Such steps have been omitted for brevity, but note that you should not assume that data received by a PHP page will necessarily be of a certain type or value.

- Also, no error handling has been included in this script, as I know the queries function as written. If you have problems, remember your MySQL/SQL debugging steps: print the query, run it using the mysql client or phpMyAdmin to confirm the results, and invoke the mysql_error() function as needed.

- The ternary operator derives its name from the fact that there are three parts to its structure (the conditional and the two returned values). It is also sometimes referred to as the *trinary* operator.

The Ternary Operator

In this example, I'll be using an operator I have not introduced before, called the *ternary* operator. Its structure is

```
(condition) ? valueT : valueF
```

The condition in parentheses will be evaluated; if it is TRUE, the first value will be returned (*valueT*). If the condition is FALSE, the second value (*valueF*) will be returned.

Because the ternary operator returns a value, the entire structure is often the argument of a function. For example, the line

```
echo (isset($var)) ? 'SET' : 'NOT SET';
```

will print out *SET* or *NOT SET*, depending upon the status of the variable $var.

In this version of the view_users.php script, the ternary operator assigns a value to a variable. The variable itself will then be used to dictate the background color of each record in the table. There are certainly other ways to set this value, but the ternary operator is the most concise.

Script 8.6 This latest version of the `view_users.php` script creates clickable links out of the table's column headings. Clicking one of these links redisplays the results in a different order.

```
script
1    <?php # Script 8.6 - view_users.php
2    # (5th version after Scripts 7.4, 7.6, 8.2
     & 8.5)
3
4    // This script retrieves all the records
     from the users table.
5    // This new version allows the results to
     be sorted in different ways.
6
7    $page_title = 'View the Current Users';
8    include ('./includes/header.html');
9
10   // Page header.
11   echo '<h1 id="mainhead">Registered Users
     </h1>';
12
13   require_once ('../mysql_connect.php'); //
     Connect to the db.
14
15   // Number of records to show per page:
16   $display = 10;
17
18   // Determine how many pages there are.
19   if (isset($_GET['np'])) { // Already been
     determined.
20       $num_pages = $_GET['np'];
21   } else { // Need to determine.
22
23       // Count the number of records
24       $query = "SELECT COUNT(*) FROM users
         ORDER BY registration_date ASC";
25       $result = @mysql_query ($query);
26       $row = mysql_fetch_array ($result,
         MYSQL_NUM);
27       $num_records = $row[0];
28
29       // Calculate the number of pages.
30       if ($num_records > $display) { // More
         than 1 page.
```

(script continues on page 307)

Making Sortable Displays

There's one final feature that I want to add to `view_users.php` while I'm at it. In its current state the list of users is displayed in order by the date they registered. It would be nice to be able to view them by name as well.

From a MySQL perspective, accomplishing this task is easy: just change the ORDER BY clause. Therefore, all I need to do is add some functionality in PHP that will change the ORDER BY clause. The logical way to do this is to link the column headings so that clicking them changes the display order. As you hopefully can guess, this involves using the GET method to pass a parameter back to this page indicating the preferred sort order.

To take this concept just a little bit further, I want the sorting links to be contextual. For example, clicking the *Last Name* column the first time will sort the results in ascending order by last name. Clicking that same column again should sort the results in *descending* order by last name. This is easily accomplished by toggling the link's parameters.

To make sortable links:

1. Open `view_users.php` (Script 8.5) in your text editor or IDE.

2. Before the main query, define the default links (**Script 8.6**).
   ```
   $link1 = "{$_SERVER['PHP_SELF']}
   → ?sort=lna";

   $link2 = "{$_SERVER['PHP_SELF']}
   → ?sort=fna";

   $link3 = "{$_SERVER['PHP_SELF']}
   → ?sort=dra";
   ```

continues on next page

These variables define the default link values for the *Last Name* ($link1), *First Name* ($link2), and *Date Registered* ($link3) columns. Each link should be something like `view_users.php?sort=XXX`, where *XXX* represents the new sorting order.

I've decided not to hard-code `view_users.php` as the link because if I later want to apply this same technique to another script, I'll need to find and change the link name multiple times. Instead I use `$_SERVER['PHP_SELF']`, which is a way for a script to refer to itself (the curly braces are used to avoid parse errors, in case you've forgotten).

The abbreviations for the three links stand for *last name ascending, first name ascending*, and *date registered ascending*.

3. Check if a sorting order has already been determined.

```
if (isset($_GET['sort'])) {
```

As with `$_GET['np']` and `$_GET['s']`, the sorting order will be passed in the URL, so it should be available in `$_GET['sort']`. This only applies when the user accesses multiple results pages, though.

4. Begin defining a `switch` conditional that determines how the results should be sorted.

```
switch ($_GET['sort']) {
   case 'lna':
      $order_by = 'last_name ASC';
      $link1 = "{$_SERVER['PHP_SELF']
      ⇀ }?sort=lnd";
      break;
   case 'lnd':
      $order_by = 'last_name DESC';
      $link1 = "{$_SERVER['PHP_SELF']
      ⇀ }?sort=lna";
      break;
```

The switch checks `$_GET['sort']` against several expected values. If, for example, it is equal to *lna*, then the results should be ordered by the last name in ascending order. The assigned `$order_by` variable will be used in the SQL query.

Because I want the links to be contextual, I also change the appropriate link value based upon `$_GET['sort']`. If the results are going to be displayed in ascending order by last name (*lna*), then the *Last Name* column link should be to display the result in *descending* order by last name (*lnd*). So for each case in the `switch`, the appropriate link is given a new value.

continues on page 308

Script 8.6 *continued*

```
31         $num_pages = ceil ($num_records/$display);
32    } else {
33         $num_pages = 1;
34    }
35
36 } // End of np IF.
37
38 // Determine where in the database to start returning results.
39 if (isset($_GET['s'])) {
40    $start = $_GET['s'];
41 } else {
42    $start = 0;
43 }
44
45 // Default column links.
46 $link1 = "{$_SERVER['PHP_SELF']}?sort=lna";
47 $link2 = "{$_SERVER['PHP_SELF']}?sort=fna";
48 $link3 = "{$_SERVER['PHP_SELF']}?sort=dra";
49
50 // Determine the sorting order.
51 if (isset($_GET['sort'])) {
52
53    // Use existing sorting order.
54    switch ($_GET['sort']) {
55       case 'lna':
56          $order_by = 'last_name ASC';
57          $link1 = "{$_SERVER['PHP_SELF']}?sort=lnd";
58          break;
59       case 'lnd':
60          $order_by = 'last_name DESC';
61          $link1 = "{$_SERVER['PHP_SELF']}?sort=lna";
62          break;
63       case 'fna':
64          $order_by = 'first_name ASC';
65          $link2 = "{$_SERVER['PHP_SELF']}?sort=fnd";
66          break;
67       case 'fnd':
68          $order_by = 'first_name DESC';
69          $link2 = "{$_SERVER['PHP_SELF']}?sort=fna";
70          break;
71       case 'dra':
72          $order_by = 'registration_date ASC';
73          $link3 = "{$_SERVER['PHP_SELF']}?sort=drd";
74          break;
```

(script continues on next page)

MAKING SORTABLE DISPLAYS

5. Complete the `switch` conditional.

```
    case 'fna':
        $order_by = 'first_name ASC';
        $link2 = "{$_SERVER['PHP_SELF']}
→ ?sort=fnd";
        break;
    case 'fnd':
        $order_by = 'first_name DESC';
        $link2 = "{$_SERVER['PHP_SELF']}
→ ?sort=fna";
        break;
    case 'dra':
        $order_by = 'registration_date
→ ASC';
        $link3 = "{$_SERVER['PHP_SELF']}
→ ?sort=drd";
        break;
    case 'drd':
        $order_by = 'registration_date
→ DESC';
        $link3 = "{$_SERVER['PHP_SELF']}
→ ?sort=dra";
        break;
    default:
        $order_by = 'registration_date
→ DESC;
        break;
}
```

There are six total conditions to check against, plus the default (just in case). For each the `$order_by` variable is defined as it will be used in the query and the appropriate link is redefined. Since each link has already been given a default value (Step 2), I only need to change a single link's value for each case.

Script 8.6 *continued*

```
script
75         case 'drd':
76             $order_by = 'registration_date
               DESC';
77             $link3 = "{$_SERVER['PHP_SELF']}
               ?sort=dra";
78             break;
79         default:
80             $order_by = 'registration_date
               DESC';
81             break;
82     }
83
84     // $sort will be appended to the
       pagination links.
85     $sort = $_GET['sort'];
86
87 } else { // Use the default sorting order.
88     $order_by = 'registration_date ASC';
89     $sort = 'drd';
90 }
91
92 // Make the query.
93 $query = "SELECT last_name, first_name,
   DATE_FORMAT(registration_date, '%M %d, %Y')
   AS dr, user_id FROM users ORDER BY $order_
   by LIMIT $start, $display";
94 $result = @mysql_query ($query); // Run the
   query.
95
96 // Table header.
97 echo '<table align="center" cellspacing="0"
   cellpadding="5">
98 <tr>
99     <td align="left"><b>Edit</b></td>
100    <td align="left"><b>Delete</b></td>
101    <td align="left"><b><a href="' .
       $link1 . '">Last Name</a></b></td>
102    <td align="left"><b><a href="' .
       $link2 . '">First Name</a></b></td>
103    <td align="left"><b><a href="' .
       $link3 . '">Date Registered</a></b>
       </td>
104 </tr>
105 ';
106
```

(script continues on page 311)

Figure 8.14 THE FIRST TIME VIEWING THE PAGE, THE RESULTS ARE SHOWN IN DESCENDING ORDER OF REGISTRATION DATE.

6. Complete the `isset()` conditional.

   ```
   $sort = $_GET['sort'];
   } else {
       $order_by = 'registration_date ASC;
       $sort = 'drd';
   }
   ```

   The `$sort` variable will need to be appended to the pagination links, like `$s` and `$np`. If `$_GET['sort']` is set, then `$sort` should have that value. Otherwise, the page's default `$order_by` and `$sort` values are used (**Figure 8.14**).

7. Modify the query to use the new `$order_by` variable.

   ```
   $query = "SELECT last_name, first_
   → name, DATE_FORMAT(registration_
   → date, '%M %d, %Y') AS dr, user_id
   → FROM users ORDER BY $order_by LIMIT
   → $start, $display";
   ```

   By this point, the `$order_by` variable has a value indicating how the returned results should be ordered (for example, *registration_date DESC*), so it can be easily added to the query. Remember that the ORDER BY clause comes before the LIMIT clause. If the resulting query doesn't run properly for you, print it out and inspect the dynamically-generated syntax.

continues on next page

MAKING SORTABLE DISPLAYS

8. Modify the table header echo statement to create links out of the column headings.

```
echo '<table align="center"
→ cellspacing="0" cellpadding="5">
<tr>
    <td align="left"><b>Edit</b></td>
    <td align="left"><b>Delete</b>
    → </td>
    <td align="left"><b><a href="' .
    → $link1 . '">Last Name</a></b>
    → </td>
    <td align="left"><b><a href="' .
    → $link2 . '">First Name</a></b>
    → </td>
    <td align="left"><b><a href="' .
    → $link3 . '">Date Registered</a>
    → </b></td>
</tr>
';
```

To make the column headings clickable links, just surround them with the <a> tags. The value of the href attribute for each link has already been determined and assigned to $link1, $link2, and $link3.

Script 8.6 *continued*

```
107   // Fetch and print all the records.
108   $bg = '#eeeeee'; // Set the background
      color.
109   while ($row = mysql_fetch_array($result,
      MYSQL_ASSOC)) {
110       $bg = ($bg=='#eeeeee' ? '#ffffff' :
          '#eeeeee'); // Switch the background
          color.
111       echo '<tr bgcolor="' . $bg . '">
112           <td align="left"><a href="edit_user.
              php?id=' . $row['user_id'] .
              '">Edit</a></td>
113           <td align="left"><a href="delete_
              user.php?id=' . $row['user_id'] .
              '">Delete</a></td>
114           <td align="left">' . $row['last_
              name'] . '</td>
115           <td align="left">' . $row['first_
              name'] . '</td>
116           <td align="left">' . $row['dr'] .
              '</td>
117       </tr>
118       ';
119   }
120
121   echo '</table>';
122
123   mysql_free_result ($result); // Free up the
      resources.
124
125   mysql_close(); // Close the database
      connection.
126
127   // Make the links to other pages, if
      necessary.
128   if ($num_pages > 1) {
129
130       echo '<br /><p>';
131       // Determine what page the script is on.
132       $current_page = ($start/$display) + 1;
133
```

(script continues on next page)

Script 8.6 *continued*

```
┌─────────────── script ───────────────┐
134    // If it's not the first page, make a
       Previous button.
135    if ($current_page != 1) {
136        echo '<a href="view_users.php?s=' .
           ($start - $display) . '&np=' .
           $num_pages . '&sort=' . $sort .
           '">Previous</a> ';
137    }
138
139    // Make all the numbered pages.
140    for ($i = 1; $i <= $num_pages; $i++) {
141        if ($i != $current_page) {
142            echo '<a href="view_users.php?s='
               . (($display * ($i - 1))) .
               '&np=' . $num_pages . '&sort=' .
               $sort . '">' . $i . '</a> ';
143        } else {
144            echo $i . ' ';
145        }
146    }
147
148    // If it's not the last page, make a
       Next button.
149    if ($current_page != $num_pages) {
150        echo '<a href="view_users.php?s='
           . ($start + $display) . '&np=' .
           $num_pages . '&sort=' . $sort .
           '">Next</a>';
151    }
152
153    echo '</p>';
154
155  } // End of links section.
156
157  include ('./includes/footer.html'); //
     Include the HTML footer.
158  ?>
```

9. Modify the echo statement that creates the *Previous* link so that the sort value is also passed.

```
echo '<a href="view_users.php?s='
→ . ($start - $display) . '&np='
→ . $num_pages . '&sort=' . $sort
→ .'">Previous</a> ';
```

I've added another *name=value* pair to the *Previous* link so that the sort order is also sent to each page of results.

10. Repeat Step 9 for the numbered pages and the *Next* link.

```
echo '<a href="view_users.php?s='
→ . (($display * ($i - 1))) . '&np='
→ . $num_pages . '&sort=' . $sort
→ .'">' . $i . '</a> ';
echo '<a href="view_users.php?s='
→ . ($start + $display) . '&np='
→ . $num_pages . '&sort=' . $sort
→ .'">Next</a>';
```

continues on next page

MAKING SORTABLE DISPLAYS

11. Save the file as view_users.php, upload it to your Web server, and run in your Web browser (**Figures 8.15** and **8.16**).

✔ Tip

■ A very important security concept was also demonstrated in this example. Instead of using the value of $_GET['sort'] directly in the query, I check it against assumed values in a switch. If, for some reason, $_GET['sort'] has a value other than I would expect, the query uses a default sorting order. The point is this: don't make assumptions about received data and don't use unvalidated data in a SQL query.

Figure 8.15 Clicking the *Last Name* column displays the results in order by last name ascending.

Figure 8.16 Clicking the *Last Name* column again (from Figure 8.15) displays the results in order by last name descending.

Understanding HTTP Headers

Switching gears, I want to conclude this chapter by discussing how you can use HTTP headers in your application. HTTP (Hypertext Transfer Protocol) is the technology at the heart of the World Wide Web because it defines the way clients and servers communicate (in layman's terms). When a browser requests a Web page, it receives a series of HTTP headers in return.

PHP's built-in header() function can be used to take advantage of this protocol. The most common example of this will be demonstrated here, when the header() function will be used to redirect the Web browser from the current page to another. However, in Chapter 12, "Example—Content Management," you'll use it to send files to the Web user.

To use header() to redirect the Web browser, type

```
header ('Location: http://www.url.com/
→ page.php');
```

Because this should be the last thing to occur on the current page (since the browser will soon be leaving it), this line would normally be followed by a call to the exit() function, which stops execution of the current script.

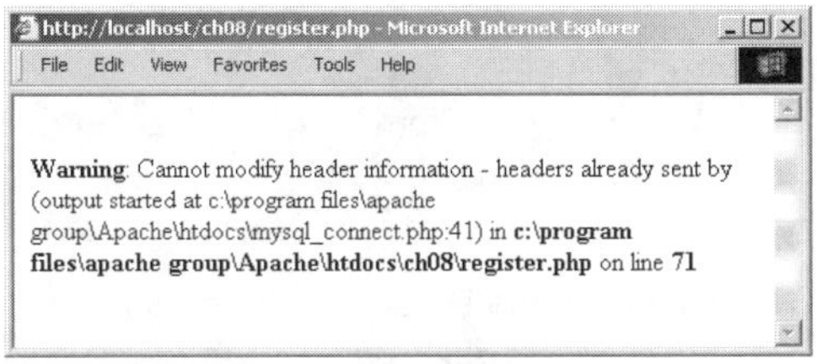

Figure 8.17 The *headers already sent* error is a common occurrence when learning how to use the header() function.

The absolutely critical thing to remember about the header() function is that it must be called before *anything* is sent to the Web browser. This includes HTML or even blank spaces. If your code has any echo() or print() statements, has blank lines outside of PHP tags, or includes files that do any of these things before calling header(), you'll see an error message like that in **Figure 8.17**.

You can avoid this problem using the headers_sent() function, which checks whether or not data has been sent to the Web browser.

```
if (!headers_sent()) {

    header ('Location: http://www.url.
    → com/page.php');

    exit();

} else {

    echo 'Wanted to redirect you but I
    → could not do it!';

}
```

I'll rewrite the registration script (from previous chapters) so that the user is redirected to a thank-you page upon successful registration. To do so will require that I restructure the page to ensure that no text is sent to the browser before I call header(). Also, since header() calls should use an absolute URL (http://www.somesite.com/page.php) instead of a relative one (page.php), the $_SERVER variable will be used to dynamically determine the full redirection URL (see the sidebar on page 321 "Using Absolute URLs with header()").

To use the header() function:

1. Create a new PHP page in your text editor or IDE (**Script 8.7**).

   ```php
   <?php # Script 8.7 - register.php
   ```

2. Check if the form has been submitted.

   ```php
   if (isset($_POST['submitted'])) {
   ```

   Notice that I am not including the HTML header before this line as I have in previous examples. I need the script to be able to redirect the user once they've registered, so I cannot include the header file (sending its HTML to the Web browser) beforehand.

3. Include the MySQL connection script and initialize the $errors array.

   ```php
   require_once ('../mysql_connect.
   → php');

   $errors = array();
   ```

   I no longer need to define the escape_data() function in this script, as it is now defined within mysql_connect.php.

4. Validate the form inputs.

   ```php
   if (empty($_POST['first_name'])) {
       $errors[] = 'You forgot to enter
       → your first name.';
   } else {
       $fn = escape_data($_POST['first_
       → name']);
   }
   if (empty($_POST['last_name'])) {
       $errors[] = 'You forgot to enter
       → your last name.';
   } else {
       $ln = escape_data($_POST['last_
       → name']);
   }
   if (empty($_POST['email'])) {
       $errors[] = 'You forgot to enter
       → your email address.';
   } else {
       $e = escape_data($_POST['email']);
   }
   if (!empty($_POST['password1'])) {
       if ($_POST['password1'] != $_POST
       → ['password2']) {
           $errors[] = 'Your password did
           → not match the confirmed
           → password.';
       } else {
           $p = escape_data($_POST
           → ['password1']);
       }
   } else {
       $errors[] = 'You forgot to enter
       → your password.';
   }
   ```

   This entire process is exactly the same as it has been in other registration examples.

continues on page 316

Script 8.7 The registration script will now redirect the user to a Thank You page once they've successfully registered. Doing so requires that nothing be sent to the Web browser prior to invoking the header() function.

```php
1    <?php # Script 8.7 - register.php
2    // Send NOTHING to the Web browser prior to the header() line!
3
4    // Check if the form has been submitted.
5    if (isset($_POST['submitted'])) {
6
7        require_once ('../mysql_connect.php'); // Connect to the db.
8
9        $errors = array(); // Initialize error array.
10
11       // Check for a first name.
12       if (empty($_POST['first_name'])) {
13           $errors[] = 'You forgot to enter your first name.';
14       } else {
15           $fn = escape_data($_POST['first_name']);
16       }
17
18       // Check for a last name.
19       if (empty($_POST['last_name'])) {
20           $errors[] = 'You forgot to enter your last name.';
21       } else {
22           $ln = escape_data($_POST['last_name']);
23       }
24
25       // Check for an email address.
26       if (empty($_POST['email'])) {
27           $errors[] = 'You forgot to enter your email address.';
28       } else {
29           $e = escape_data($_POST['email']);
30       }
31
32       // Check for a password and match against the confirmed password.
33       if (!empty($_POST['password1'])) {
34           if ($_POST['password1'] != $_POST['password2']) {
35               $errors[] = 'Your password did not match the confirmed password.';
36           } else {
37               $p = escape_data($_POST['password1']);
38           }
39       } else {
40           $errors[] = 'You forgot to enter your password.';
41       }
```

(script continues on page 317)

UNDERSTANDING HTTP HEADERS

5. If there were no registration errors, check if the email address has already been registered, and then run the INSERT query.

```php
if (empty($errors)) {
    $query = "SELECT user_id FROM
    → users WHERE email='$e'";
    $result = mysql_query($query);
    if (mysql_num_rows($result) == 0) {
        $query = "INSERT INTO users
        → (first_name, last_name,
        → email, password, registration_
        → date) VALUES ('$fn', '$ln',
        → '$e', SHA('$p'), NOW() )";
        $result = @mysql_query ($query);
        if ($result) {
```

Again, there's nothing new here. Refer to previous register.php scripts in Chapter 7 if you're confused by any of this code.

6. Dynamically determine the redirection URL and then call the header() function.

```php
$url = 'http://' . $_SERVER['HTTP_
→ HOST'] . dirname($_SERVER['PHP_
→ SELF']);
if ((substr($url, -1) == '/') OR
→ (substr($url, -1) == '\\') ) {
    $url = substr ($url, 0, -1);
}
$url .= '/thanks.php';
header("Location: $url");
exit();
```

Before calling the header() function, I need to determine the absolute URL (you can just make $url equal to *thanks.php*, but it's better to be absolute). To start, I assign $url the value of *http://* plus the host name (which could be either *localhost* or *www.dmcinsights.com*). To this I add the name of the current directory using the dirname() function, in case the redirection is taking place within a subfolder.

Because the existence of a subfolder might add an extra slash (/) or backslash (\, for

Windows), I have to check for and remove this. To do so, I use the substr() function to see if the last character in $url is either / or \. But since the backslash is the escape character in PHP, I need to use \\ to refer to a single backslash. If $url concludes with either of these characters, the substr() function is then called again to assign $url the value of $url minus this last character. Finally, the specific page name is appended to the $url. This may all seem to be quite complicated, but it's a very effective way to ensure that the redirection works no matter on what server, or from what directory, the script is being run.

The header() function will then send the user to a thank-you page if everything went OK. Then the script is exited, which means that everything else in the script will not be executed.

7. Complete the INSERT, email, and $errors conditionals.

```php
    } else {
        $errors[] = 'You could not be
        → registered due to a system
        → error. We apologize for any
        → inconvenience.';
        $errors[] = mysql_error() .
        → '<br /><br />Query: ' .
        → $query;
    }
} else {
    $errors[] = 'The email address
    → has already been registered.';
}
}
```

In previous versions of this script, these errors would immediately be printed. But since the HTML header has not yet been included, that's not an option. So instead, the existing $errors array is used to handle all errors, even system ones.

continues on page 318

Script 8.7 *continued*

```
42
43    if (empty($errors)) { // If everything's OK.
44
45        // Register the user in the database.
46
47        // Check for previous registration.
48        $query = "SELECT user_id FROM users WHERE email='$e'";
49        $result = mysql_query($query);
50        if (mysql_num_rows($result) == 0) {
51
52            // Make the query.
53            $query = "INSERT INTO users (first_name, last_name, email, password, registration_date)
                  VALUES ('$fn', '$ln', '$e', SHA('$p'), NOW() )";
54            $result = @mysql_query ($query); // Run the query.
55            if ($result) { // If it ran OK.
56
57                // Send an email, if desired.
58
59                // Redirect the user to the thanks.php page.
60                // Start defining the URL.
61                $url = 'http://' . $_SERVER['HTTP_HOST'] . dirname($_SERVER['PHP_SELF']);
62
63                // Check for a trailing slash.
64                if ((substr($url, -1) == '/') OR (substr($url, -1) == '\\') ) {
65                    $url = substr ($url, 0, -1); // Chop off the slash.
66                }
67
68                // Add the page.
69                $url .= '/thanks.php';
70
71                header("Location: $url");
72                exit();
73
74            } else { // If it did not run OK.
75                $errors[] = 'You could not be registered due to a system error. We apologize for any
                  inconvenience.'; // Public message.
76                $errors[] = mysql_error() . '<br /><br />Query: ' . $query; // Debugging message.
77            }
78
79        } else { // Email address is already taken.
80            $errors[] = 'The email address has already been registered.';
81        }
```

(script continues on page 319)

8. Close the database connection and complete the submission conditional.

```
   mysql_close();
} else {
   $errors = NULL;
}
```

The else clause takes effect if the page has not yet been submitted. In that case, I need to indicate that there are no errors, which I do by initializing that variable with a NULL value.

9. Include the HTML header.

```
$page_title = 'Register';
include ('./includes/header.html');
```

After the main conditional and once the header() function would have been called, it's now safe to use the included file.

10. Print out any error messages.

```
if (!empty($errors)) {
   echo '<h1 id="mainhead">Error!
→ </h1>
   <p class="error">The following
→ error(s) occurred:<br />';
   foreach ($errors as $msg) {
      echo " - $msg<br />\n";
   }
   echo '</p><p>Please try again.
→ </p>';
}
```

Web users will be seeing this page under two circumstances: once when they first arrive and again if they fail to fill out the form completely. Under this second situation, the $errors variable will have a value (of what went wrong) and its values will be printed here, above the form.

11. Create the HTML form and complete the PHP page.

```
?>
<h2>Register</h2>
<form action="register.php"
→ method="post">
   <p>First Name: <input type="text"
→ name="first_name" size="15"
→ maxlength="15" value="<?php if
→ (isset($_POST['first_name']))
→ echo $_POST['first_name']; ?>"
→ /></p>
   <p>Last Name: <input type="text"
→ name="last_name" size="15"
→ maxlength="30" value="<?php if
→ (isset($_POST['last_name']))
→ echo $_POST['last_name']; ?>"
→ /></p>
   <p>Email Address: <input
→ type="text" name="email"
→ size="20" maxlength="40"
→ value="<?php if (isset($_POST
→ ['email'])) echo $_POST
→ ['email']; ?>" /> </p>
   <p>Password: <input
→ type="password"
→ name="password1" size="10"
→ maxlength="20" /></p>
   <p>Confirm Password: <input
→ type="password"
→ name="password2" size="10"
→ maxlength="20" /></p>
   <p><input type="submit"
→ name="submit" value="Register"
→ /></p>
   <input type="hidden"
→ name="submitted" value="TRUE" />
</form>
<?php
include ('./includes/footer.html');
?>
```

12. Save the file as register.php and upload it to your Web server.

Now I'll put together a quick thank-you page.

Script 8.7 *continued*

```
                                    script

82
83        } // End of if (empty($errors)) IF.
84
85        mysql_close(); // Close the database connection.
86
87    } else { // Form has not been submitted.
88
89        $errors = NULL;
90
91    } // End of the main Submit conditional.
92
93    // Begin the page now.
94    $page_title = 'Register';
95    include ('./includes/header.html');
96
97    if (!empty($errors)) { // Print any error messages.
98        echo '<h1 id="mainhead">Error!</h1>
99        <p class="error">The following error(s) occurred:<br />';
100       foreach ($errors as $msg) { // Print each error.
101           echo " - $msg<br />\n";
102       }
103       echo '</p><p>Please try again.</p>';
104   }
105
106   // Create the form.
107   ?>
108   <h2>Register</h2>
109   <form action="register.php" method="post">
110       <p>First Name: <input type="text" name="first_name" size="15" maxlength="15" value="<?php if
          (isset($_POST['first_name'])) echo $_POST['first_name']; ?>" /></p>
111       <p>Last Name: <input type="text" name="last_name" size="15" maxlength="30" value="<?php if
          (isset($_POST['last_name'])) echo $_POST['last_name']; ?>" /></p>
112       <p>Email Address: <input type="text" name="email" size="20" maxlength="40" value="<?php if
          (isset($_POST['email'])) echo $_POST['email']; ?>"  /> </p>
113       <p>Password: <input type="password" name="password1" size="10" maxlength="20" /></p>
114       <p>Confirm Password: <input type="password" name="password2" size="10" maxlength="20" /></p>
115       <p><input type="submit" name="submit" value="Register" /></p>
116       <input type="hidden" name="submitted" value="TRUE" />
117   </form>
118   <?php
119   include ('./includes/footer.html');
120   ?>
```

To create a thank-you page:

1. Create a new PHP document in your text editor (**Script 8.8**).

```
<?php # Script 8.8 - thanks.php
$page_title = 'Thank You!';
include ('./includes/header.html');
?>
<h1 id="mainhead">Thank you!</h1>
<p>You are now registered. In
→ Chapter 9--just around the
→ corner--you will actually be able
→ to log in!</p><p><br /></p>
<?php
include ('./includes/footer.html');
?>
```

2. Save the script as thanks.php, upload to your Web server along with the modified register.php, and test in your Web browser (**Figures 8.18** and **8.19**).

Script 8.8 The user will be redirected to this simple page upon successfully registering.

```
1   <?php # Script 8.8 - thanks.php
2   $page_title = 'Thank You!';
3   include ('./includes/header.html');
4   ?>
5   <h1 id="mainhead">Thank you!</h1>
6   <p>You are now registered. In Chapter 9--
    just around the corner--you will actually
    be able to log in!</p><p><br /></p>
7   <?php
8   include ('./includes/footer.html');
9   ?>
```

Figure 8.18 Once the user has been registered in the database, they are redirected to thanks.php.

Figure 8.19 If any registration errors occurred, those errors are displayed above the registration form, as they had been in the past.

Using Absolute URLs with header()

You should ideally use an absolute URL with the header() function when using the *Location* directive (e.g., http://www. dmcinsights.com/admin/page.php rather than just page.php). To do so in your scripts, you have two choices. First, you could hard-code the absolute URL using

```
header ('Location: http://www.
→ dmcinsights.com/admin/page.php');
```

This method will work unless the server configuration changes, the URL changes, or you move the script.

A more flexible method is to make use of the $_SERVER superglobal and the dirname() function (which returns the directory path of the current script). The PHP manual recommends the following code to redirect to a page located in the same directory as the current script:

```
header ('Location: http://' .
→ $_SERVER['HTTP_HOST'] . dirname($_
→ SERVER['PHP_SELF']) . '/newpage.
→ php');
```

This will effectively redirect the user to the current domain (*www.dmcinsights.com*), the current directory (*admin*), and the new page. This is the format I use in this chapter with just a minor modification.

✔ Tips

- I cannot stress strongly enough that *nothing* can be sent to the Web browser before using the header() function. Even if your mysql_connect.php file has a blank line after the closing PHP tag, this will make the header() function unusable.

- On the bright side, PHP's error messages when it comes to headers having already been sent are quite informative. The error in Figure 8.17 indicates that line 41 of mysql_connect.php sent some output to the browser that meant that line 71 of register.php couldn't do its thing. So open up mysql_connect.php to find and fix the problem.

- The substr() function is a very useful one that has not been given much attention in the book so far. For more information about its syntax and how you can use it, check out the PHP manual.

- The header() function is also frequently used when you have a PHP script that generates PDFs, images, and other non-HTML media.

- For everything you might want to know about HTTP and more, see www.w3.org/Protocols/.

- HTTP is a stateless protocol, which means it has no memory from one Web page to another. Chapter 9, "Cookies and Sessions," will show PHP's work-around for this.

- You can add *name=value* pairs to the URL in a header() call to pass values to the target page. In this example, if you added this line to the script, prior to redirection:

```
$url .= '?name=' . urlencode
→ ("$fn $ln");
```

then the thanks.php page could greet the user by $_GET['name'].

UNDERSTANDING HTTP HEADERS

COOKIES AND SESSIONS

The Hypertext Transfer Protocol (HTTP) is a stateless technology, meaning that each individual HTML page is an unrelated entity. HTTP has no method for tracking users or retaining variables as a person traverses a site. Using a Web scripting language like PHP, you can overcome the statelessness of the Web. You have a few options to choose from, the most popular two being cookies and sessions.

Prior to the existence of cookies, surfing a Web site was a trip without a history. Although your browser tracked the pages you visited, allowing you to use the back button to return to previously visited pages, the server kept no record of who had seen what. Without the server being able to track a user, there can be no shopping carts or custom Web site personalization.

Sessions improve upon cookies, allowing the Web application to store and retrieve far more information than cookies alone can. Both technologies are easy to use with PHP and are worth knowing. In this chapter I'll explain each, using a login system, based upon the existing *users* database, as my example.

Using Cookies

Cookies are a way for a server to store information on the user's machine. This is one way that a site can remember or track a user over the course of a visit. Think of a cookie like a name tag: you tell the server your name and it gives you a sticker to wear. Then it can know who you are by referring back to that name tag.

Some people are suspicious of cookies because they believe that cookies allow a server to know too much about them. However, a cookie can only be used to store information that the server is given, so it's no less secure than most anything else online. Unfortunately, many people still have misconceptions about the technology, which is a problem as those misconceptions can undermine the functionality of your Web application.

In this section you will learn how to set a cookie, retrieve information from a stored cookie, alter a cookie's settings, and then delete a cookie.

Testing for Cookies

To effectively program using cookies, you need to be able to accurately test for their presence. The best way to do so is to have your Web browser ask what to do when receiving a cookie. In such a case, the browser will prompt you with the cookie information each time PHP attempts to send a cookie.

Different versions of different browsers on different platforms all define their cookie handling policies in different places. I'll quickly run through a couple of options for popular Web browsers.

To set this up using Internet Explorer on Windows XP, choose Tools > Internet Options. Then click the Privacy tab, followed by the Advanced button under Settings. Click "Override automatic cookie handling" and then choose "Prompt" for both First- and Third-party Cookies.

Using Firefox on Windows, choose Tools > Options. Then click Privacy and expand the Cookies section. Finally, select "ask me every time" in the Keep Cookies drop-down menu. If you are using Firefox on Mac OS X, the steps are the same, but you must start by choosing Firefox > Preferences.

Unfortunately, Safari on Mac OS X does not have a cookie prompting option, but it will allow you to view existing cookies, which is still a useful debugging tool. This option can be found under the Security Preferences panel.

Figure 9.1 The *headers already sent...* error message is all too common when creating cookies. Pay attention to what the error message says in order to find and fix the problem.

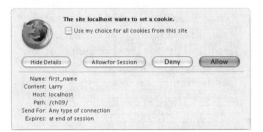

Figure 9.2 If I have my browser set to ask for permission when receiving cookies, I'll see a message like this when a site attempts to send one.

Setting cookies

The most important thing to understand about cookies is that they must be sent from the server to the client prior to *any other information*. Should the server attempt to send a cookie after the Web browser has already received HTML—even an extraneous white space—an error message will result and the cookie will not be sent (**Figure 9.1**). This is by far the most common cookie-related error.

Cookies are sent via the setcookie() function:

setcookie (*name*, *value*);

setcookie ('first_name', 'Larry');

The second line of code will send a cookie to the browser with a name of *first_name* and a value of *Larry* (**Figure 9.2**).

You can continue to send more cookies to the browser with subsequent uses of the setcookie() function:

setcookie ('ID', 263);

setcookie ('email', 'phpmysql2@
→ dmcinsights.com');

As when using any variable in PHP, when naming your cookies, do not use white spaces or punctuation, but do pay attention to the exact case used.

To send a cookie:

1. Create a new PHP document in your text editor (**Script 9.1**).

   ```php
   <?php # Script 9.1 - login.php
   ```

   For this example, I'll make a new login. php script (which works in conjunction with the scripts from Chapter 7, "Using PHP with MySQL").

2. Validate the form.

   ```php
   if (isset($_POST['submitted'])) {
       require_once ('../mysql_connect.
       → php');
       $errors = array();
       if (empty($_POST['email'])) {
           $errors[] = 'You forgot to enter
           → your email address.';
       } else {
           $e = escape_data($_POST
           → ['email']);
       }
       if (empty($_POST['password'])) {
           $errors[] = 'You forgot to enter
           → your password.';
       } else {
           $p = escape_data($_POST
           → ['password']);
       }
   ```

   These steps are very similar to those in Chapter 7. The main conditional checks if the form has been submitted. Then the database connection is made by including the connection script (which also defines the escape_data() function as of Chapter 8, "Web Application Development"). Finally, the email address and password inputs are checked for values.

3. Retrieve the user_id and first_name for this user from the database.

   ```php
   if (empty($errors)) {
       $query = "SELECT user_id,
       → first_name FROM users WHERE
       → email='$e' AND password=
       → SHA('$p')";
       $result = @mysql_query ($query);
       $row = mysql_fetch_array
       → ($result, MYSQL_NUM);
   ```

   If both validation tests were passed, the database will be queried, retrieving the user_id and first_name values for the record where the email column matches the submitted email address and the password matches an encrypted version of the submitted password.

4. If the user entered the correct information, log the user in.

   ```php
   if ($row) {
       setcookie ('user_id', $row[0]);
       setcookie ('first_name', $row[1]);
   ```

   The $row variable will have a value only if the preceding query returned at least one record (indicating the submitted email address and password match those on file). In this case, two cookies will be created.

continues on page 328

Script 9.1 The login.php script creates cookies upon a successful login.

```
1    <?php # Script 9.1 - login.php
2    // Send NOTHING to the Web browser prior to the setcookie() lines!
3
4    // Check if the form has been submitted.
5    if (isset($_POST['submitted'])) {
6
7        require_once ('../mysql_connect.php'); // Connect to the db.
8
9        $errors = array(); // Initialize error array.
10
11       // Check for an email address.
12       if (empty($_POST['email'])) {
13           $errors[] = 'You forgot to enter your email address.';
14       } else {
15           $e = escape_data($_POST['email']);
16       }
17
18       // Check for a password.
19       if (empty($_POST['password'])) {
20           $errors[] = 'You forgot to enter your password.';
21       } else {
22           $p = escape_data($_POST['password']);
23       }
24
25       if (empty($errors)) { // If everything's OK.
26
27           /* Retrieve the user_id and first_name for
28           that email/password combination. */
29           $query = "SELECT user_id, first_name FROM users WHERE email='$e' AND password=SHA('$p')";
30           $result = @mysql_query ($query); // Run the query.
31           $row = mysql_fetch_array ($result, MYSQL_NUM); // Return a record, if applicable.
32
33           if ($row) { // A record was pulled from the database.
34
35               // Set the cookies & redirect.
36               setcookie ('user_id', $row[0]);
37               setcookie ('first_name', $row[1]);
38
```

(script continues on page 333)

5. Redirect the user to another page.

```php
$url = 'http://' . $_SERVER
→ ['HTTP_HOST'] . dirname($_SERVER
→ ['PHP_SELF']);
if ((substr($url, -1) == '/') OR
→ (substr($url, -1) == '\\') ) {
   $url = substr ($url, 0, -1);
}
$url .= '/loggedin.php';
header("Location: $url");
exit();
```

Using the steps outlined in Chapter 8, the redirection URL is first dynamically generated. To do so, various $_SERVER values are referenced, along with the dirname() function. Any trailing slashes are also chopped off should this script be within a subdirectory (this is all covered in Chapter 8).

Finally the header() function is called to redirect the user and the script's execution is terminated with exit().

6. Complete the $row conditional (started in Step 4) and the $errors conditional, and then close the database connection.

```php
   } else {
      $errors[] = 'The email address
→ and password entered do not
→ match those on file.';
      $errors[] = mysql_error() .
→ '<br /><br />Query: ' .
$query;
   }
}
mysql_close();
```

The error management in this script is much like that in the register.php script in Chapter 8. Because nothing can be sent to the Web browser before calling the setcookie() and header() lines, the errors have to be saved and printed later.

The second error message here is for debugging purposes only and shouldn't be used on a live site.

7. Complete the main submit conditional, include the HTML header, and print any error messages.

```php
} else {
   $errors = NULL;
}
$page_title = 'Login';
include ('./includes/header.html');
if (!empty($errors)) {
   echo '<h1 id="mainhead">Error!
→ </h1>
   <p class="error">The following
→ error(s) occurred:<br />';
   foreach ($errors as $msg) {
→ echo " - $msg<br />\n";
   }
   echo '</p><p>Please try again.
→ </p>';
}
?>
```

Again, this and the previous steps are like those in Chapter 8's register.php script. The first else conditional sets the $errors variable to NULL, indicating that no errors need to be printed out when this page is first run. Then the page's title is set and the template's header file is included (this application uses the same template as those in Chapters 7 and 8). Finally, any existing errors—from the form's submission—are printed.

continues on page 330

Script 9.1 *continued*

```
39          // Redirect the user to the loggedin.php page.
40          // Start defining the URL.
41          $url = 'http://' . $_SERVER['HTTP_HOST'] . dirname($_SERVER['PHP_SELF']);
42          // Check for a trailing slash.
43          if ((substr($url, -1) == '/') OR (substr($url, -1) == '\\') ) {
44              $url = substr ($url, 0, -1); // Chop off the slash.
45          }
46          // Add the page.
47          $url .= '/loggedin.php';
48
49          header("Location: $url");
50          exit(); // Quit the script.
51
52      } else { // No record matched the query.
53          $errors[] = 'The email address and password entered do not match those on file.';
            // Public message.
54          $errors[] = mysql_error() . '<br /><br />Query: ' . $query; // Debugging message.
55      }
56
57  } // End of if (empty($errors)) IF.
58
59  mysql_close(); // Close the database connection.
60
61  } else { // Form has not been submitted.
62
63      $errors = NULL;
64
65  } // End of the main Submit conditional.
66
67  // Begin the page now.
68  $page_title = 'Login';
69  include ('./includes/header.html');
70
71  if (!empty($errors)) { // Print any error messages.
72      echo '<h1 id="mainhead">Error!</h1>
73      <p class="error">The following error(s) occurred:<br />';
74      foreach ($errors as $msg) { // Print each error.
75          echo " - $msg<br />\n";
76      }
77      echo '</p><p>Please try again.</p>';
78  }
79
```

(script continues on next page)

8. Display the HTML form.

```
<h2>Login</h2>
<form action="login.php"
→ method="post">
    <p>Email Address: <input type=
    → "text" name="email" size="20"
    → maxlength="40" /> </p>
    <p>Password: <input type=
    → "password" name="password"
    → size="20" maxlength="20" /></p>
    <p><input type="submit" name=
    → "submit" value="Login" /></p>
    <input type="hidden" name=
    → "submitted" value="TRUE" />
</form>
```

The HTML form takes two inputs—an email address and a password—and submits the data back to this same page. You can make the email address input sticky by presetting a value attribute, if you'd like.

9. Include the PHP footer.

```
<?php
include ('./includes/footer.html');
?>
```

10. Save the file as login.php, upload it to your Web server in the same directory as the files from Chapter 7, and load the form in your Web browser (**Figure 9.3**).

✔ Tips

- Cookies are limited to about 4 KB of total data, and each Web browser can remember only 20 cookies from any one server.

- Because cookies rely upon the HTTP header, you can set them in PHP using the header() function. It's very important to remember that the setcookie() and header() functions must be called before any data is sent to the Web browser.

Script 9.1 *continued*

```
80   // Create the form.
81   ?>
82   <h2>Login</h2>
83   <form action="login.php" method="post">
84       <p>Email Address: <input type="text"
         name="email" size="20" maxlength="40"
         /> </p>
85       <p>Password: <input type="password"
         name="password" size="20" maxlength="20"
         /></p>
86       <p><input type="submit" name="submit"
         value="Login" /></p>
87       <input type="hidden" name="submitted"
         value="TRUE" />
88   </form>
89   <?php
90   include ('./includes/footer.html');
91   ?>
```

Figure 9.3 The login form.

- The setcookie() function is one of the few functions in PHP that could generate different results in different browsers, since browsers will treat cookies differently. Be sure to test your Web sites in multiple browsers on different platforms to ensure consistency.

- In Chapter 11, "Extended Topics," I'll show how to control browser output so that cookies can be sent at nearly any point in a script.

Script 9.2 The `loggedin.php` script prints a greeting to a user based upon a stored cookie.

```
                      script
1   <?php # Script 9.2 - loggedin.php
2   # User is redirected here from login.php.
3
4   // If no cookie is present, redirect the
    user.
5   if (!isset($_COOKIE['user_id'])) {
6
7       // Start defining the URL.
8       $url = 'http://' . $_SERVER['HTTP_HOST']
        . dirname($_SERVER['PHP_SELF']);
9       // Check for a trailing slash.
10      if ((substr($url, -1) == '/') OR
        (substr($url, -1) == '\\') ) {
11          $url = substr ($url, 0, -1); // Chop
            off the slash.
12      }
13      $url .= '/index.php'; // Add the page.
14      header("Location: $url");
15      exit(); // Quit the script.
16  }
17
18  // Set the page title and include the HTML
    header.
19  $page_title = 'Logged In!';
20  include ('./includes/header.html');
21
22  // Print a customized message.
23  echo "<h1>Logged In!</h1>
24  <p>You are now logged in, {$_COOKIE
    ['first_name']}!</p>
25  <p><br /><br /></p>";
26
27  include ('./includes/footer.html');
28  ?>
```

Accessing cookies

To retrieve a value from a cookie, you only need to refer to the `$_COOKIE` superglobal, using the appropriate cookie name as the key (as you would with any array). For example, to retrieve the value of the cookie established with the line

```
setcookie ('username', 'Trout');
```

you would use `$_COOKIE['username']`.

In the following example, the cookies set by the `login.php` script will be accessed in two ways. First a check will be made that the user is logged in (otherwise, they shouldn't be accessing this page). Next, the user will be greeted by their first name, which was stored in a cookie.

To access a cookie:

1. Create a new PHP document in your text editor (**Script 9.2**).

   ```
   <?php # Script 9.2 - loggedin.php
   ```

   The user will be redirected to this page after successfully logging in. It will print a user-specific greeting.

2. Check for the presence of a cookie.

   ```
   if (!isset($_COOKIE['user_id'])) {
   ```

   Since I don't want a user to access this page unless that user is logged in, I first check for the cookie that should have been set (in `login.php`).

   continues on next page

USING COOKIES

3. Complete the `if` conditional.

```
$url = 'http://' . $_SERVER
→['HTTP_HOST'] . dirname($_SERVER
→['PHP_SELF']);
if ((substr($url, -1) == '/') OR
→(substr($url, -1) == '\\') ) {
   $url = substr ($url, 0, -1);
}
$url .= '/index.php';
header("Location: $url");
exit();
}
```

If the user is not logged in, they will be automatically redirected to the main page. This is a simple way to limit access to logged-in users.

4. Include the page header.

```
$page_title = 'Logged In!';
include ('./includes/header.html');
```

5. Welcome the user, using the cookie.

```
echo "<h1>Logged In!</h1>
<p>You are now logged in, {$_COOKIE
→['first_name']}!</p>
<p><br /><br /></p>";
```

To greet the user by name, I refer to the `$_COOKIE['first_name']` variable (enclosed within curly braces to avoid parse errors).

6. Complete the HTML page.

```
include ('./includes/footer.html');
?>
```

7. Save the file as `loggedin.php`, upload to your Web server (in the same directory as `login.php`), and test in your Web browser by logging in through `login.php` (**Figure 9.4**).

Since these examples use the same database as those in Chapter 7, you should be able to log in using the registered username and password submitted at that time.

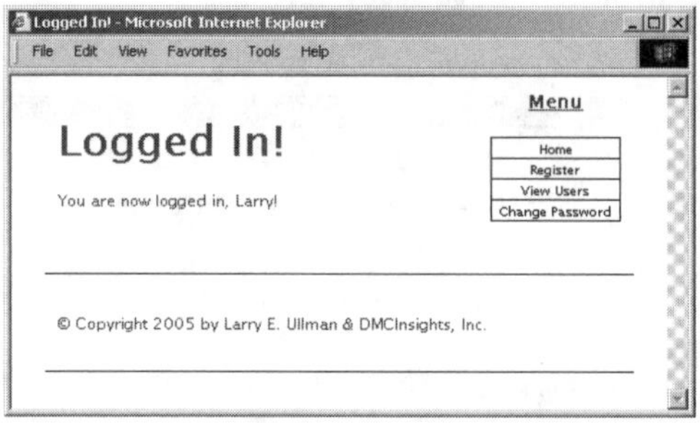

Figure 9.4 If you used the correct username and password, you'll be redirected here after logging in.

USING COOKIES

Figure 9.5 To see the effect of the setcookie() function, set your Web browser to ask before storing a cookie.

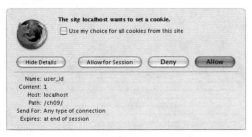

Figure 9.6 The user_id cookie with a value of 1.

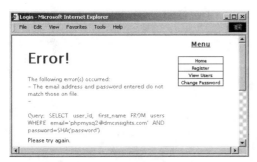

Figure 9.7 If no record was returned from the database, this will be the result. The blank space after the second dash is for the mysql_error(), which doesn't exist (since the query ran fine).

8. If you like, change the cookie settings for your browser (**Figure 9.5**) and test again (**Figure 9.6**).

✔ Tips

■ If the submitted email address and username do not match those on file, a public message is displayed, followed by the query (**Figure 9.7**). Remember to delete the debugging message (the MySQL error plus the query) before using this code on a live site.

■ If your mysql_connect.php file sends anything to the Web browser or even has blank lines or spaces after the closing PHP tag, you'll see a *headers already sent* error.

■ With *register_globals* enabled, PHP will load variables in a specific order (depending upon the setting in the php.ini file), normally: get, post, cookie, session. If you do not use the superglobal arrays to refer to variables, then the value of a $username variable in a form could be overridden by the value of a $username variable stored in a cookie. This is one reason why you should program without relying upon *register_globals*.

■ A cookie is not accessible until the setting page (e.g., login.php) has been reloaded or another page has been accessed (in other words, you cannot set and access a cookie in the same page).

■ If users decline a cookie or have their Web browser set not to accept them, they will automatically be redirected to the home page in this example, even if they successfully logged in. For this reason you may want to let the user know when cookies are required.

USING COOKIES

Setting cookie parameters

Although passing just the name and value arguments to the setcookie() function will suffice, you ought to be aware of the other arguments available. The function can take up to four more parameters, each of which will alter the definition of the cookie.

```
setcookie ('name', 'value', expiration,
→ 'path', 'domain', secure);
```

The expiration argument is used to set a definitive length of time for a cookie to exist, specified in seconds since the *epoch* (the epoch is midnight on January 1, 1970). If it is not set, the cookie will continue to be functional until the user closes his or her browser. Normally, the expiration time is determined by adding a particular number of minutes or hours to the current moment, retrieved using the time() function. The following line will set the expiration time of the cookie to be 1 hour (60 seconds times 60 minutes) from the current moment:

```
setcookie ('name', 'value', time()+
→ 3600);
```

The path and domain arguments are used to limit a cookie to a specific folder within a Web site (the path) or to a specific host. For example, you could restrict a cookie to exist only while a user is within the *admin* folder of a domain (and the *admin* folder's subfolders):

```
setcookie ('name', 'value', time()+
→ 3600, '/admin/');
```

Finally, the secure value dictates that a cookie should only be sent over a secure HTTPS connection. A *1* indicates that a secure connection must be used, and a *0* says that a standard connection is fine.

```
setcookie ('name', 'value', time()+
→ 3600, '/admin/', '', 1);
```

As with all functions that take arguments, you must pass the setcookie() values in order. To skip any parameter, use NULL or an empty string. The expiration and secure values are both integers and are therefore not quoted.

To demonstrate this information, I'll add an expiration setting to the login cookies so that they last for only one hour.

Script 9.3 The login.php script now uses every argument the setcookie() function can take.

```
1   <?php # Script 9.3 - login.php (2nd version
    after Script 9.1)
2   // Send NOTHING to the Web browser prior to
    the setcookie() lines!
3
4   // Check if the form has been submitted.
5   if (isset($_POST['submitted'])) {
6
7       require_once ('../mysql_connect.php');
        // Connect to the db.
8
9       $errors = array(); // Initialize error
        array.
10
11      // Check for an email address.
12      if (empty($_POST['email'])) {
13          $errors[] = 'You forgot to enter your
            email address.';
14      } else {
15          $e = escape_data($_POST['email']);
16      }
17
18      // Check for a password.
19      if (empty($_POST['password'])) {
20          $errors[] = 'You forgot to enter your
            password.';
21      } else {
```

(script continues on next page)

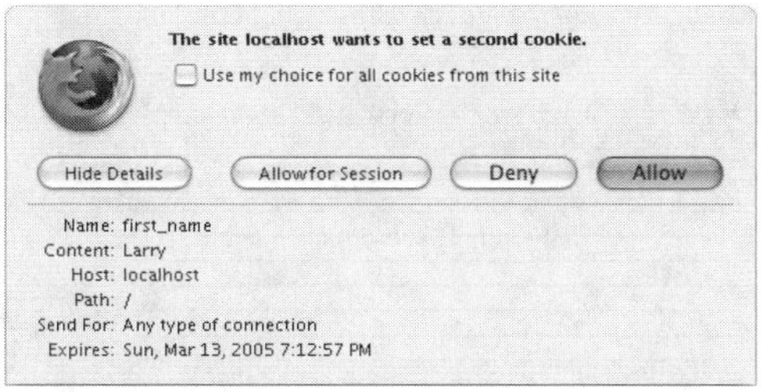

Figure 9.8 Once an expiration date or time has been set, it will be reflected in the cookie sent to the Web browser.

To set a cookie's expiration date:

1. Open login.php in your text editor (refer to Script 9.1).

2. Change the two setcookie() lines to include an expiration date that's 60 minutes away (**Script 9.3**):

   ```
   setcookie ('user_id', $row[0],
   → time()+3600, '/', '', 0);
   ```

   ```
   setcookie ('first_name', $row[1],
   → time()+3600, '/', '', 0);
   ```

   With the expiration date set to time() + 3600 (60 minutes times 60 seconds), the cookie will continue to exist for an hour after it is set. While I'm at it, I explicitly state the other cookie parameters.

3. Save the script, upload to your Web server, and test in your Web browser (**Figure 9.8**).

Script 9.3 *continued*

```
22          $p = escape_data($_POST['password']);
23      }
24
25      if (empty($errors)) { // If everything's OK.
26
27          /* Retrieve the user_id and first_name for
28          that email/password combination. */
29          $query = "SELECT user_id, first_name FROM users WHERE email='$e' AND password=SHA('$p')";
30          $result = @mysql_query ($query); // Run the query.
31          $row = mysql_fetch_array ($result, MYSQL_NUM); // Return a record, if applicable.
32
33          if ($row) { // A record was pulled from the database.
34
35              // Set the cookies & redirect.
36              setcookie ('user_id', $row[0], time()+3600, '/', '', 0);
37              setcookie ('first_name', $row[1], time()+3600, '/', '', 0);
38
39              // Redirect the user to the loggedin.php page.
40              // Start defining the URL.
41              $url = 'http://' . $_SERVER['HTTP_HOST'] . dirname($_SERVER['PHP_SELF']);
42              // Check for a trailing slash.
43              if ((substr($url, -1) == '/') OR (substr($url, -1) == '\\') ) {
44                  $url = substr ($url, 0, -1); // Chop off the slash.
45              }
46              // Add the page.
47              $url .= '/loggedin.php';
48
49              header("Location: $url");
50              exit(); // Quit the script.
51
52          } else { // No record matched the query.
53              $errors[] = 'The email address and password entered do not match those on file.';
                // Public message.
54              $errors[] = mysql_error() . '<br /><br />Query: ' . $query; // Debugging message.
55          }
56
57      } // End of if (empty($errors)) IF.
58
59      mysql_close(); // Close the database connection.
60
```

(script continues on next page)

Script 9.3 *continued*

```
script
61  } else { // Form has not been submitted.
62
63      $errors = NULL;
64
65  } // End of the main Submit conditional.
66
67  // Begin the page now.
68  $page_title = 'Login';
69  include ('./includes/header.html');
70
71  if (!empty($errors)) { // Print any error
    messages.
72      echo '<h1 id="mainhead">Error!</h1>
73      <p class="error">The following error(s)
        occurred:<br />';
74      foreach ($errors as $msg) { // Print
        each error.
75          echo " - $msg<br />\n";
76      }
77      echo '</p><p>Please try again.</p>';
78  }
79
80  // Create the form.
81  ?>
82  <h2>Login</h2>
83  <form action="login.php" method="post">
84      <p>Email Address: <input type="text"
        name="email" size="20" maxlength="40"
        /> </p>
85      <p>Password: <input type="password"
        name="password" size="20" maxlength="20"
        /></p>
86      <p><input type="submit" name="submit"
        value="Login" /></p>
87      <input type="hidden" name="submitted"
        value="TRUE" />
88  </form>
89  <?php
90  include ('./includes/footer.html');
91  ?>
```

✔ Tips

- Some browsers have difficulties with cookies that do not list every argument. Explicitly stating every parameter—even as an empty string, as I did here—will achieve more reliable results across all browsers.

- Here are some general guidelines for cookie expirations: If the cookie should last as long as the session, do not set an expiration time; if the cookie should continue to exist after the user has closed and reopened his or her browser, set an expiration time months ahead; and if the cookie can constitute a security risk, set an expiration time of an hour or fraction thereof so that the cookie does not continue to exist too long after a user has left his or her browser.

- For security purposes, you could set a five- or ten-minute expiration time on a cookie and have the cookie resent with every new page the user visits (assuming that the cookie exists). This way, the cookie will continue to persist as long as the user is active but will automatically die five or ten minutes after the user's last action.

- Setting the path to '/' will make the cookie visible within an entire domain (Web site).

- Setting the domain to '.site.com' will make the cookie visible within an entire domain and every subdomain (www.site.com, admin.site.com, pages.site.com, etc.).

- E-commerce and other privacy-related Web applications should use an SSL (Secure Sockets Layer) connection for all transactions, including the cookie.

USING COOKIES

Deleting cookies

The final thing to understand about using cookies is how to delete one. While a cookie will automatically expire when the user's browser is closed or when the expiration date/ time is met, sometimes you'll want to manually delete the cookie instead. For example, in Web sites that have registered users and login capabilities, you will probably want to delete any cookies when the user logs out.

Although the `setcookie()` function can take up to six arguments, only one is actually required—the cookie name. If you send a cookie that consists of a name without a value, it will have the same effect as deleting the existing cookie of the same name. For example, to create the cookie *first_name*, you use this line:

```
setcookie('first_name', 'Larry');
```

To delete the *first_name* cookie, you would code:

```
setcookie('first_name');
```

As an added precaution, you can also set an expiration date that's in the past.

```
setcookie('first_name', '', time()-300);
```

To demonstrate all of this, I'll add logout capability to the site, which will appear only to logged-in users. As an added bonus, the header file will be altered so that a *Logout* link appears when the user is logged-in and a *Login* link appears when the user is logged-out.

To delete a cookie:

1. Create a new PHP document in your text editor (**Script 9.4**).

   ```
   <?php # Script 9.4 - logout.php
   ```

Script 9.4 The `logout.php` script deletes the previously established cookies.

```
1   <?php # Script 9.4 - logout.php
2   // This page lets the user logout.
3
4   // If no cookie is present, redirect the
    user.
5   if (!isset($_COOKIE['user_id'])) {
6
7       // Start defining the URL.
8       $url = 'http://' . $_SERVER['HTTP_HOST']
        . dirname($_SERVER['PHP_SELF']);
9       // Check for a trailing slash.
10      if ((substr($url, -1) == '/') OR
        (substr($url, -1) == '\\') ) {
11          $url = substr ($url, 0, -1); // Chop
            off the slash.
12      }
13      $url .= '/index.php'; // Add the page.
14      header("Location: $url");
15      exit(); // Quit the script.
16
17  } else { // Delete the cookies.
18      setcookie ('first_name', '',
        time()-300, '/', '', 0);
19      setcookie ('user_id', '',
        time()-300, '/', '', 0);
20  }
21
22  // Set the page title and include the HTML
    header.
23  $page_title = 'Logged Out!';
24  include ('./includes/header.html');
25
26  // Print a customized message.
27  echo "<h1>Logged Out!</h1>
28  <p>You are now logged out, {$_COOKIE
    ['first_name']}!</p>
29  <p><br /><br /></p>";
30
31  include ('./includes/footer.html');
32  ?>
```

2. Check for the existence of a *user_id* cookie; if it is present, delete both cookies.

```php
if (!isset($_COOKIE['user_id'])) {
    $url = 'http://' . $_SERVER
    → ['HTTP_HOST'] . dirname($_SERVER
    → ['PHP_SELF']);
    if ((substr($url, -1) == '/') OR
    → (substr($url, -1) == '\\') ) {
        $url = substr ($url, 0, -1);
    }
    $url .= '/index.php';
    header("Location: $url");
    exit();
} else {
    setcookie ('first_name', '',
    → time()-300, '/', '', 0);
    setcookie ('user_id', '',
    → time()-300, '/', '', 0);
}
```

As with my loggedin.php page, if the user is not already logged in, I want this page to redirect the user to the home page. If the user is logged in, these two cookies will effectively delete the existing ones.

3. Make the remainder of the PHP page.

```php
$page_title = 'Logged Out!';
include ('./includes/header.html');
echo "<h1>Logged Out!</h1>
<p>You are now logged out, {$_COOKIE
→ ['first_name']}!</p>
<p><br /><br /></p>";
include ('./includes/footer.html');
?>
```

The page itself is also much like the loggedin.php page. Although it may seem odd that you can still refer to the *first_name* cookie (that you just deleted in this script), it makes perfect sense considering the process:

A) This page is requested by the client.

B) The server reads the appropriate cookies from the client's browser.

C) The page is run and does its thing (including sending new cookies).

So, in short, the original *first_name* cookie data is available to this script when it first runs. The set of cookies sent by this page (the delete cookies) aren't available to this page, so the original values are still usable.

4. Save the file as logout.php.

To create the logout link:

1. Open `header.html` (refer to Script 7.1) in your text editor.

2. Change the links to (**Script 9.5**)

```
<li class="navtop"><a href=
→ "index.php" title="Go to the Home
→ Page">Home</a></li>
<li><a href="register.php" title=
→ "Register">Register</a></li>
<li><?php
if ( (isset($_COOKIE['user_id'])) &&
→ (!strpos($_SERVER['PHP_SELF'],
→ 'logout.php')) ) {
   echo '<a href="logout.php" title=
→ "Logout">Logout</a>';
} else {
   echo '<a href="login.php" title=
→ "Login">Login</a>';
}
?></li>
```

Instead of having a permanent login link in my template, I'll have it display a *Logout* link if the user is logged in or a *Login* link if the user is not. The preceding conditional will accomplish just that based upon the presence of a cookie.

Because the `logout.php` script would ordinarily display a logout link (because the cookie exists when the page is first being viewed), I have to add a statement to my conditional, checking that the current page is not the `logout.php` script. The `strpos()` function, which checks if one string is found within another string, is an easy way to accomplish this.

Script 9.5 The `header.html` file now displays either a login or a logout link depending upon the user's current status.

```
1   <!DOCTYPE html PUBLIC "-//W3C//DTD XHTML
    1.0 Transitional//EN"
2        "http://www.w3.org/TR/xhtml1/DTD/
         xhtml1-transitional.dtd">
3   <html xmlns="http://www.w3.org/1999/xhtml"
    xml:lang="en" lang="en">
4   <head>
5       <meta http-equiv="content-type" content=
        "text/html; charset=iso-8859-1" />
6       <title><?php echo $page_title; ?></title>
7       <style type="text/css" media="all">
        @import "./includes/layout.css";</style>
8   </head>
9   <body>
10  <div id="wrapper"><!-- Goes with the CSS
    layout. -->
11
12      <div id="content"><!-- Goes with the CSS
        layout. -->
13
14          <div id="nav"><!-- Links section -->
15              <h3>Menu</h3>
16              <ul>
17                  <li class="navtop"><a href=
                    "index.php" title="Go to the Home
                    Page">Home</a></li>
18                  <li><a href="register.php" title=
                    "Register">Register</a></li>
19                  <li><?php
20  // Create a login/logout link.
21  if ( (isset($_COOKIE['user_id'])) &&
    (!strpos($_SERVER['PHP_SELF'], 'logout.
    php')) ) {
22      echo '<a href="logout.php" title=
        "Logout">Logout</a>';
23  } else {
24      echo '<a href="login.php" title=
        "Login">Login</a>';
25  }
26  ?></li>
27              </ul>
28          </div>
29          <!-- Script 9.5 - header.html -->
30          <!-- Start of page-specific content. -->
```

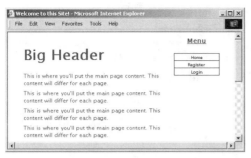

Figure 9.9 The home page with a *Login* link.

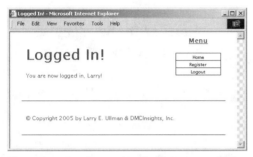

Figure 9.10 After the user logs in, the page now has a *Logout* link.

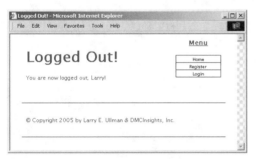

Figure 9.11 The result after logging out.

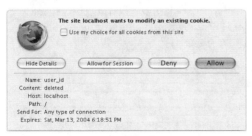

Figure 9.12 This is how the deletion cookie appears in a Firefox prompt.

3. Save the file, upload to the Web server (placed within the *includes* directory), and test the login/logout process in your Web browser (**Figures 9.9**, **9.10**, and **9.11**).

✔ Tips

- To see the result of the setcookie() calls in the logout.php script, turn on cookie prompting in your browser (**Figure 9.12**).

- Due to a bug in how Internet Explorer on Windows handles cookies, you may need to set the *domain* parameter to false (without quotes) in order to get the logout process to work when developing on your own computer (i.e., through *localhost*).

- When deleting a cookie, you should always use the same parameters that were used to set the cookie. If you set the domain and path in the creation cookie, use them again in the deletion cookie.

- To hammer the point home, remember that the deletion of a cookie does not take effect until the page has been reloaded or another page has been accessed (in other words, the cookie will still be available to a page after that page has deleted it). This is why I needed to add the && (!strpos($_SERVER['PHP_SELF'], 'logout.php') clause to the header.html conditional (because the cookie itself would still be available on the logout.php page).

Using Sessions

Another method of making data available to multiple pages of a Web site is to use sessions. The premise of a session is that data is stored on the server, not in the Web browser, and a session identifier is used to locate a particular user's record (session data). This session identifier is normally stored in the user's Web browser via a cookie, but the sensitive data itself—like the user's ID, name, and so on—always remains on the server.

The question may arise: why use sessions at all when cookies work just fine? First of all, sessions are more secure in that all of the recorded information is stored on the server and not continually sent back and forth between the server and the client. Second, some users reject cookies or turn them off completely. Sessions, while designed to work with a cookie, can function without them, as you'll see in the next section of this chapter.

To demonstrate sessions—and to compare them with cookies—I will rewrite the previous scripts.

Setting session variables

The most important rule with respect to sessions is that each page that will use them must begin by calling the `session_start()` function. This function tells PHP to either begin a new session or access an existing one.

The first time this function is used, `session_start()` will attempt to send a cookie with a name of *PHPSESSID* (the session name) and a value of something like *a61f867 0baa8e90a30c878df89a2074b* (32 hexadecimal letters, the session ID). Because of this attempt to send a cookie, `session_start()` must be called before any data is sent to the Web browser, as is the case when using the `setcookie()` and `header()` functions.

Once the session has been started, values can be registered to the session using

```
$_SESSION['key'] = 'value';

$_SESSION['name'] = 'Jessica';

$_SESSION['id'] = 48;
```

I'll rewrite the `login.php` script with this in mind.

Allowing for Sessions on Windows

Sessions in PHP requires a temporary directory on the server where PHP can store the session data. For Unix and Mac OS X users, this isn't a problem, as the `/tmp` directory is available explicitly for purposes such as this. For Windows users, you also do not need to do anything special as of version 4.3.6 of PHP. But if you are running Windows and an earlier version of PHP, you must configure the server. Here's how:

1. Create a new folder on your server, such as `C:\temp`.

2. Make sure that *Everyone* (or just the Web server user, if you know that value) can read and write to this folder.

3. Edit your `php.ini` file (see Appendix A, "Installation"), setting the value of *session.save_path* to this folder (`C:\temp`).

4. Restart the Web server.

If you see errors about the *session. save_path* when you first use sessions, pay attention to what the error messages say. Also double-check your path name and that you edited the correct `php.ini` file.

Script 9.6 The login.php script now uses sessions instead of cookies.

```
1    <?php # Script 9.6 - login.php (3rd version
     after Scripts 9.1 & 9.3)
2    // Send NOTHING to the Web browser prior to
     the session_start() line!
3
4    // Check if the form has been submitted.
5    if (isset($_POST['submitted'])) {
6
7        require_once ('../mysql_connect.php');
         // Connect to the db.
8
9        $errors = array(); // Initialize error
         array.
10
11       // Check for an email address.
12       if (empty($_POST['email'])) {
13           $errors[] = 'You forgot to enter your
             email address.';
14       } else {
15           $e = escape_data($_POST['email']);
16       }
17
18       // Check for a password.
19       if (empty($_POST['password'])) {
20           $errors[] = 'You forgot to enter your
             password.';
21       } else {
22           $p = escape_data($_POST
             ['password']);
23       }
24
25       if (empty($errors)) { // If everything's
         OK.
26
27           /* Retrieve the user_id and
             first_name for
28           that email/password combination. */
29           $query = "SELECT user_id,
             first_name FROM users WHERE
             email='$e' AND password=SHA('$p')";
```

(script continues on next page)

To begin a session:

1. Open login.php (refer to Script 9.3) in your text editor.

2. Replace the setcookie() lines (36–37) with these lines (**Script 9.6**):

```
session_start();
$_SESSION['user_id'] = $row[0];
$_SESSION['first_name'] = $row[1];
```

The first step is to begin the session. Since there are no echo() statements, include calls, or HTML prior to this point in the script, it will be safe to use session_start() now, although I could have placed it at the top of the script as well. Then, I add two *key-value* pairs to the $_SESSION superglobal array to register the user's first name and user ID to the session.

continues on page 346

USING SESSIONS

Script 9.6 *continued*

```
                                        script

30          $result = @mysql_query ($query); // Run the query.
31          $row = mysql_fetch_array ($result, MYSQL_NUM); // Return a record, if applicable.
32
33          if ($row) { // A record was pulled from the database.
34
35              // Set the session data & redirect.
36              session_start();
37              $_SESSION['user_id'] = $row[0];
38              $_SESSION['first_name'] = $row[1];
39
40              // Redirect the user to the loggedin.php page.
41              // Start defining the URL.
42              $url = 'http://' . $_SERVER['HTTP_HOST'] . dirname($_SERVER['PHP_SELF']);
43              // Check for a trailing slash.
44              if ((substr($url, -1) == '/') OR (substr($url, -1) == '\\') ) {
45                  $url = substr ($url, 0, -1); // Chop off the slash.
46              }
47              // Add the page.
48              $url .= '/loggedin.php';
49
50              header("Location: $url");
51              exit(); // Quit the script.
52
53          } else { // No record matched the query.
54              $errors[] = 'The email address and password entered do not match those on file.';
                // Public message.
55              $errors[] = mysql_error() . '<br /><br />Query: ' . $query; // Debugging message.
56          }
57
58      } // End of if (empty($errors)) IF.
59
60      mysql_close(); // Close the database connection.
61
62  } else { // Form has not been submitted.
63
64      $errors = NULL;
65
66  } // End of the main Submit conditional.
67
68  // Begin the page now.
69  $page_title = 'Login';
```

(script continues on next page)

Script 9.6 *continued*

```
70   include ('./includes/header.html');
71
72   if (!empty($errors)) { // Print any error messages.
73       echo '<h1 id="mainhead">Error!</h1>
74       <p class="error">The following error(s) occurred:<br />';
75       foreach ($errors as $msg) { // Print each error.
76           echo " - $msg<br />\n";
77       }
78       echo '</p><p>Please try again.</p>';
79   }
80
81   // Create the form.
82   ?>
83   <h2>Login</h2>
84   <form action="login.php" method="post">
85       <p>Email Address: <input type="text" name="email" size="20" maxlength="40" /> </p>
86       <p>Password: <input type="password" name="password" size="20" maxlength="20" /></p>
87       <p><input type="submit" name="submit" value="Login" /></p>
88       <input type="hidden" name="submitted" value="TRUE" />
89   </form>
90   <?php
91   include ('./includes/footer.html');
92   ?>
```

Sessions in Older Versions of PHP

Prior to version 4.1 of PHP (when the $_SESSION superglobal became available), session variables were set using the special `session_register()` function. The syntax was

```
session_start();

$name = 'Jessica';

session_register('name');
```

It's very important to notice that the `session_register()` function takes the name of a variable to register without the initial dollar sign (so *name* rather than *$name*).

Once a session variable is registered, you can refer to is using `$HTTP_SESSION_VARS['var']`.

To delete a session variable, you use the `session_unregister()` function.

To repeat, you only need to use these functions if you are using an *old* version of PHP (between 4.0 and 4.1). As always, see the PHP manual for more information on these functions.

3. Save the page as `login.php`, upload to your server, and test in your Web browser (**Figure 9.13**).

Although `loggedin.php` and the header and script will need to be rewritten, you can still test the login script and see the resulting cookie (**Figure 9.14**). The `loggedin.php` page should redirect you back to the home page, though, as it's still checking for the presence of a `$_COOKIE` variable.

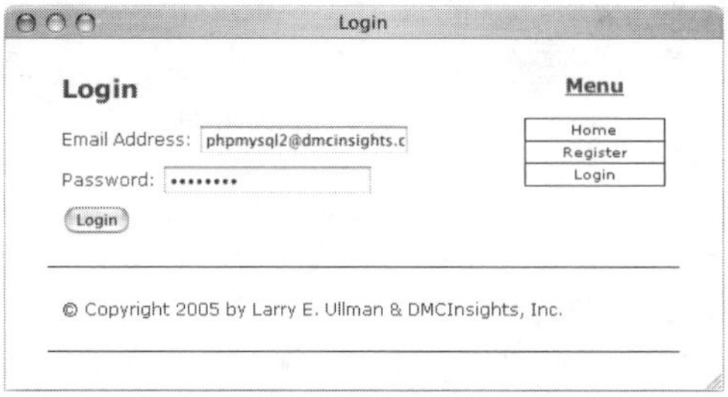

✔ Tips

■ Because sessions will normally send and read cookies, you should always try to begin them as early in the script as possible. Doing so will help you avoid the problem of attempting to send a cookie after the headers (HTML or white space) have already been sent (see Figure 9.1).

■ If you want, you can set *session.auto_start* in the `php.ini` file to 1, making it unnecessary to use `session_start()` on each page. This does put a greater toll on the server and, for that reason, shouldn't be used without some consideration of the circumstances.

■ You can store arrays in sessions (making `$_SESSION` a multidimensional array), just as you can strings or numbers.

Figure 9.13 The login form remains unchanged to the end user, but the underlying functionality now uses sessions.

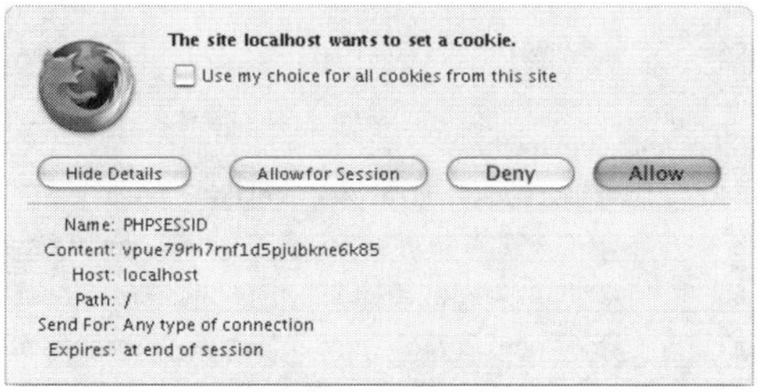

Figure 9.14 This cookie, created by PHP's `session_start()` function, stores the session ID.

Script 9.7 I've updated `loggedin.php` so that it refers to `$_SESSION` and not `$_COOKIE`.

```
script
1   <?php # Script 9.7 - loggedin.php (2nd
    version after Script 9.2)
2   # User is redirected here from login.php.
3
4   session_start(); // Start the session.
5
6   // If no session value is present, redirect
    the user.
7   if (!isset($_SESSION['user_id'])) {
8
9       // Start defining the URL.
10      $url = 'http://' . $_SERVER['HTTP_HOST']
        . dirname($_SERVER['PHP_SELF']);
11      // Check for a trailing slash.
12      if ((substr($url, -1) == '/') OR
        (substr($url, -1) == '\\') ) {
13          $url = substr ($url, 0, -1); // Chop
            off the slash.
14      }
15      $url .= '/index.php'; // Add the page.
16      header("Location: $url");
17      exit(); // Quit the script.
18  }
19
20  // Set the page title and include the HTML
    header.
21  $page_title = 'Logged In!';
22  include ('./includes/header.html');
23
24  // Print a customized message.
25  echo "<h1>Logged In!</h1>
26  <p>You are now logged in, {$_SESSION
    ['first_name']}!</p>
27  <p><br /><br /></p>";
28
29  include ('./includes/footer.html');
30  ?>
```

Accessing session variables

Once a session has been started and variables have been registered to it, you can create other scripts that will access those variables. To do so, each script must first enable sessions, again using `session_start()`.

This function will give the current script access to the previously started session (if it can read the *PHPSESSID* value stored in the cookie) or create a new session if it cannot (in which case, it won't be able to access stored values because a new session will have been created).

To then refer to a session variable, use `$_SESSION['var']`, as you would refer to any other array.

To access session variables:

1. Open `loggedin.php` (refer to Script 9.2) in your text editor.

2. Add a call to the `session_start()` function (**Script 9.7**).

   `session_start();`

   Every PHP script that either sets or accesses session variables must use the `session_start()` function. This line must be called before the `header.html` file is included and before anything is sent to the Web browser.

   continues on next page

USING SESSIONS

3. Replace the references to $_COOKIE with $_SESSION (lines 5 and 24 of the original file).

```
if (!isset($_SESSION['user_id'])) {
```

and

```
echo "<h1>Logged In!</h1>
<p>You are now logged in, {$_SESSION
→ ['first_name']}!</p>
<p><br /><br /></p>";
```

Switching a script from cookies to sessions requires only that you change uses of $_COOKIE to $_SESSION.

4. Save the file as loggedin.php, upload to your Web server, and test in your browser (**Figure 9.15**).

5. Replace the reference to $_COOKIE with $_SESSION in header.html (from Script 9.5 to **Script 9.8**).

```
if ( (isset($_SESSION['user_id']))
→ && (!strpos($_SERVER['PHP_SELF'],
→ 'logout.php')) ) {
```

For the *Login/Logout* links to function properly (notice the incorrect link in Figure 9.15), the reference to the cookie variable within the header file must be switched over to sessions. The header file does not need to call the session_start() function, as it'll be included by pages that do.

6. Save the header file, upload to the Web server, and test in your browser (**Figure 9.16**).

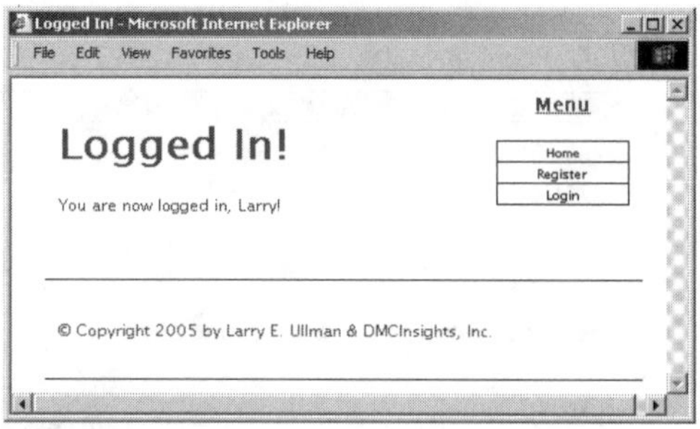

Figure 9.15 After logging in, the user is redirected to loggedin.php, which will welcome the user by name using the stored session value.

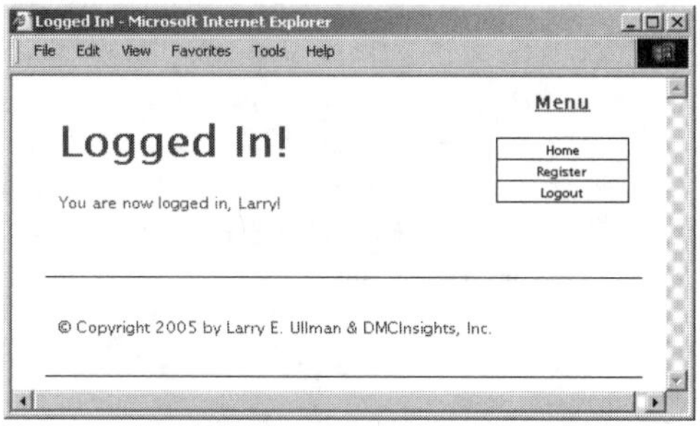

Figure 9.16 With the header file altered for sessions, the proper *Login/Logout* links will be displayed (compare with Figure 9.15).

USING SESSIONS

Script 9.8 The header.html file now also references $_SESSION.

```
1    <!DOCTYPE html PUBLIC "-//W3C//DTD XHTML
     1.0 Transitional//EN"
2         "http://www.w3.org/TR/xhtml1/DTD/
          xhtml1-transitional.dtd">
3    <html xmlns="http://www.w3.org/1999/xhtml"
     xml:lang="en" lang="en">
4    <head>
5        <meta http-equiv="content-type" content=
         "text/html; charset=iso-8859-1" />
6        <title><?php echo $page_title; ?></title>
7        <style type="text/css" media="all">
         @import "./includes/layout.css";</style>
8    </head>
9    <body>
10   <div id="wrapper"><!-- Goes with the CSS
     layout. -->
11
12       <div id="content"><!-- Goes with the CSS
         layout. -->
13
14           <div id="nav"><!-- Links section -->
15               <h3>Menu</h3>
16               <ul>
17               <li class="navtop"><a href=
                 "index.php" title="Go to the Home
                 Page">Home</a></li>
18               <li><a href="register.php" title=
                 "Register">Register</a></li>
19               <li><?php
20   // Create a login/logout link.
21   if ( (isset($_SESSION['user_id'])) &&
     (!strpos($_SERVER['PHP_SELF'], 'logout.
     php')) ) {
22       echo '<a href="logout.php" title=
         "Logout">Logout</a>';
23   } else {
24       echo '<a href="login.php" title=
         "Login">Login</a>';
25   }
26   ?></li>
27           </ul>
28           </div>
29           <!-- Script 9.8 - header.html -->
30           <!-- Start of page-specific content. -->
```

✔ Tips

■ For the *Login/Logout* links to work on the other pages (register.php, index. php, etc.), you'll need to add the session_ start() command to each of those.

■ If you have an application where the session data does not seem to be accessible from one page to the next, it could be because a new session is being created on each page. To check for this, compare the session ID (the last few characters of the value will suffice) to see if it is the same. You can see the session's ID by viewing the session cookie as it is sent or by using the session_id() function:

```
echo session_id();
```

■ Session variables are available as soon as you've established them. So, unlike when using cookies, you can assign a value to $_SESSION['var'] and then refer to $_SESSION['var'] later in that same script.

Deleting session variables

When using sessions—particularly with a login/logout system as I've established here—you need to create a method to delete the session variables. In the current example, this would be necessary when the user logs out.

Whereas a cookie system only requires that another cookie be sent to destroy the existing cookie, sessions are more demanding, since there are both the cookie on the client and the data on the server to consider.

To delete an individual session variable, you can use the unset() function (which works with any variable in PHP):

```php
unset($_SESSION['var']);
```

To delete every session variable, reset the entire $_SESSION array:

```php
$_SESSION = array();
```

Finally, to remove all of the session data from the server, use session_destroy():

```php
session_destroy();
```

Note that prior to using any of these methods, the page must begin with session_start() so that the existing session is accessed.

To delete a session:

1. Create a new PHP script in your text editor (**Script 9.9**).

   ```php
   <?php # Script 9.9 - logout.php
   ```

   The logout script will log out the user and delete all the session information.

2. Invoke the session.

   ```php
   session_start();
   ```

   Anytime you are using sessions, you must use the session_start() function, preferably at the very beginning of a page. This is true even if you are deleting a session.

Script 9.9 Destroying a session requires special syntax.

```
1    <?php # Script 9.9 - logout.php (2nd
     version after Script 9.4)
2    // This page lets the user logout.
3
4    session_start(); // Access the existing
     session.
5
6    // If no session variable exists, redirect
     the user.
7    if (!($_SESSION['user_id'])) {
8
9        // Start defining the URL.
10       $url = 'http://' . $_SERVER['HTTP_HOST']
         . dirname($_SERVER['PHP_SELF']);
11       // Check for a trailing slash.
12       if ((substr($url, -1) == '/') OR (substr
         ($url, -1) == '\\') ) {
13           $url = substr ($url, 0, -1); // Chop
             off the slash.
14       }
15       $url .= '/index.php'; // Add the page.
16       header("Location: $url");
17       exit(); // Quit the script.
18
19   } else { // Cancel the session.
20       $_SESSION = array(); // Destroy the
         variables.
21       session_destroy(); // Destroy the
         session itself.
22       setcookie ('PHPSESSID', '', time()-300,
         '/', '', 0); // Destroy the cookie.
23   }
24
25   // Set the page title and include the HTML
     header.
26   $page_title = 'Logged Out!';
27   include ('./includes/header.html');
28
29   // Print a customized message.
30   echo "<h1>Logged Out!</h1>
31   <p>You are now logged out!</p>
32   <p><br /><br /></p>";
33
34   include ('./includes/footer.html');
35   ?>
```

USING SESSIONS

3. Check for the presence of the
$_SESSION['user_id'] variable.

```
if (!($_SESSION['user_id'])) {
  $url = 'http://' . $_SERVER
→['HTTP_HOST'] . dirname($_SERVER
→['PHP_SELF']);
  if ((substr($url, -1) == '/') OR
→(substr($url, -1) == '\\') ) {
    $url = substr ($url, 0, -1);
  }
  $url .= '/index.php';
  header("Location: $url");
  exit();
```

As with the logout.php script in the cookie examples, if the user is not currently logged in, he or she will be redirected.

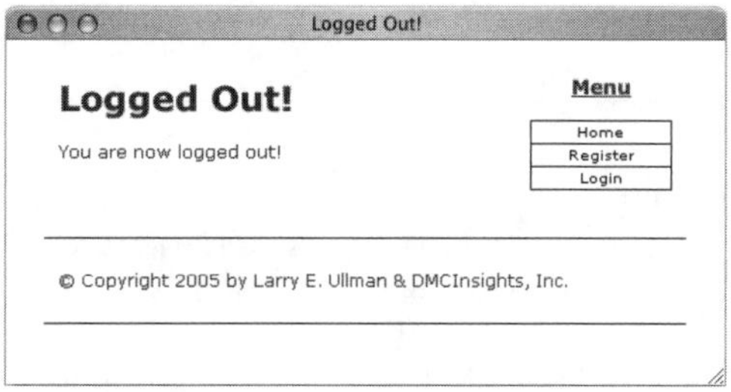

Figure 9.17 The logout page.

4. Destroy all of the session material.

```
} else {
  $_SESSION = array();
  session_destroy();
  setcookie ('PHPSESSID', '',
→time()-300, '/', '', 0);
}
```

The second line here will reset the entire $_SESSION variable as a new array, erasing its existing values. The third line removes the data from the server, and the fourth sends a cookie to replace the existing session cookie in the browser.

5. Create the HTML and print a message.

```
$page_title = 'Logged Out!';
include ('./includes/header.html');
echo "<h1>Logged Out!</h1>
<p>You are now logged out!</p>
<p><br /><br /></p>";
include ('./includes/footer.html');
?>
```

Unlike when using the cookie logout. php script, you cannot refer to the user by their first name anymore, as all of that data has been deleted.

6. Save the file as logout.php, upload to your Web server, and test in your browser (**Figure 9.17**).

✔ Tips

■ If you are using an older version of PHP (prior to version 4.1) and the $_SESSION array is not available, use session_unset() in lieu of $_SESSION = array().

■ Never set $_SESSION equal to NULL, because that could cause problems on some servers.

■ To delete just one session variable, use unset($_SESSION['var']).

Changing the session behavior

As part of PHP's support for sessions, there are about 20 different configuration options you can set for how PHP handles sessions. **Table 9.1** lists the most important of these.

Each of these settings, except for *session. use_trans_sid*, can be set within your PHP script using the ini_set() function (covered in the preceding chapter):

```
ini_set (parameter, new_setting);
```

For example, to change where PHP stores the session data, use

```
ini_set ('session.save_path',
→ '/path/to/folder');
```

To set the name of the session (perhaps to make a more user-friendly one), you can use either ini_set() or the simpler session_name() function.

```
session_name('YourSession');
```

The benefits of creating your own session name are twofold: it's marginally more secure and it may be better received by the end user (since the session name is the cookie name the end user will see). That being said, for session_name() to work, it must be called before every use of session_start() in your entire Web application. I'll rewrite the example with this in mind.

Session Configuration Settings		
SETTING	EXAMPLE	MEANING
session.auto_start	0	If sessions should be automatically used (0 means no).
session.cookie_domain	www.dmcinsights.com	The URL wherein the session cookie should be accessible.
session.cookie_lifetime	0	How long, in seconds, the session cookie should exist (0 means for the life of the browser).
session.cookie_path	/	The domain path wherein the cookie should be accessible.
session.cookie_secure	0	Whether or not the cookie must be sent over a secure connection (0 means no).
session.gc_probability	1	The odds of performing garbage collection from 1 to 100.
session.gc_maxlifetime	1440	The time period in seconds a session should last.
session.name	PHPSESSID	The name given to all sessions.
session.save_handler	files	How the session data will be stored.
session.save_path	/tmp	Where session data will be stored.
session.serialize_handler	php	What method should be used to serialize the session variables.
session.use_cookies	1	Whether or not the session ID should be stored in a cookie (0 means no).
session.use_only_cookies	0	Whether or not the session ID must be stored in a cookie (0 means no).
session.use_trans_sid	0	Whether or not PHP should add the session ID to every link in an application (0 means no).

Table 9.1 PHP's session configuration options, with the default setting listed as most of the examples.

Script 9.10 The login.php script now uses an original session name.

```
1   <?php # Script 9.10 - login.php (4th
    version after Scripts 9.1, 9.3 & 9.6)
2   // Send NOTHING to the Web browser prior to
    the session_start() line!
3
4   // Check if the form has been submitted.
5   if (isset($_POST['submitted'])) {
6
7       require_once ('../mysql_connect.php');
        // Connect to the db.
8
9       $errors = array(); // Initialize error
        array.
10
11      // Check for an email address.
12      if (empty($_POST['email'])) {
13          $errors[] = 'You forgot to enter your
            email address.';
14      } else {
15          $e = escape_data($_POST['email']);
16      }
17
18      // Check for a password.
19      if (empty($_POST['password'])) {
20          $errors[] = 'You forgot to enter your
            password.';
21      } else {
22          $p = escape_data($_POST
            ['password']);
23      }
24
25      if (empty($errors)) { // If everything's
        OK.
26
27          /* Retrieve the user_id and
            first_name for
28          that email/password combination. */
29          $query = "SELECT user_id, first_name
            FROM users WHERE email='$e' AND
            password=SHA('$p')";
```

(script continues on next page)

To use your own session names:

1. Open login.php (refer to Script 9.6) in your text editor.

2. Before the session_start() call (line 36), add the following (**Script 9.10**):

   session_name ('YourVisitID');

   Instead of having the session be named *PHPSESSID*, which may be imposing as a cookie name, I'll use the friendlier *YourVisitID*.

continues on page 356

Script 9.10 *continued*

```
         script
30       $result = @mysql_query ($query); // Run the query.
31       $row = mysql_fetch_array ($result, MYSQL_NUM); // Return a record, if applicable.
32
33       if ($row) { // A record was pulled from the database.
34
35           // Set the session data & redirect.
36           session_name ('YourVisitID');
37           session_start();
38           $_SESSION['user_id'] = $row[0];
39           $_SESSION['first_name'] = $row[1];
40
41           // Redirect the user to the loggedin.php page.
42           // Start defining the URL.
43           $url = 'http://' . $_SERVER['HTTP_HOST'] . dirname($_SERVER['PHP_SELF']);
44           // Check for a trailing slash.
45           if ((substr($url, -1) == '/') OR (substr($url, -1) == '\\') ) {
46               $url = substr ($url, 0, -1); // Chop off the slash.
47           }
48           // Add the page.
49           $url .= '/loggedin.php';
50
51           header("Location: $url");
52           exit(); // Quit the script.
53
54       } else { // No record matched the query.
55           $errors[] = 'The email address and password entered do not match those on file.';
             // Public message.
56           $errors[] = mysql_error() . '<br /><br />Query: ' . $query; // Debugging message.
57       }
58
59   } // End of if (empty($errors)) IF.
60
61   mysql_close(); // Close the database connection.
62
63 } else { // Form has not been submitted.
64
65   $errors = NULL;
66
67 } // End of the main Submit conditional.
68
```

(script continues on next page)

Script 9.10 *continued*

```
script
69    // Begin the page now.
70    $page_title = 'Login';
71    include ('./includes/header.html');
72
73    if (!empty($errors)) { // Print any error messages.
74        echo '<h1 id="mainhead">Error!</h1>
75        <p class="error">The following error(s) occurred:<br />';
76        foreach ($errors as $msg) { // Print each error.
77            echo " - $msg<br />\n";
78        }
79        echo '</p><p>Please try again.</p>';
80    }
81
82    // Create the form.
83    ?>
84    <h2>Login</h2>
85    <form action="login.php" method="post">
86        <p>Email Address: <input type="text" name="email" size="20" maxlength="40" /> </p>
87        <p>Password: <input type="password" name="password" size="20" maxlength="20" /></p>
88        <p><input type="submit" name="submit" value="Login" /></p>
89        <input type="hidden" name="submitted" value="TRUE" />
90    </form>
91    <?php
92    include ('./includes/footer.html');
93    ?>
```

3. Repeat the process for loggedin.php (compare Script 9.7 with **Script 9.11**).

Because every page must use the same session name, this line of code has to be added to the loggedin.php and logout.php scripts for them to work properly.

Script 9.11 The same session name (*YourVisitID*) must be used across every script.

```
1    <?php # Script 9.11 - loggedin.php (3rd
     version after Scripts 9.2 & 9.7)
2    # User is redirected here from login.php.
3
4    session_name ('YourVisitID');
5    session_start(); // Start the session.
6
7    // If no session value is present, redirect
     the user.
8    if (!isset($_SESSION['user_id'])) {
9
10       // Start defining the URL.
11       $url = 'http://' . $_SERVER['HTTP_HOST']
         . dirname($_SERVER['PHP_SELF']);
12       // Check for a trailing slash.
13       if ((substr($url, -1) == '/') OR (substr
         ($url, -1) == '\\') ) {
14          $url = substr ($url, 0, -1); // Chop
            off the slash.
15       }
16       $url .= '/index.php'; // Add the page.
17       header("Location: $url");
18       exit(); // Quit the script.
19   }
20
21   // Set the page title and include the HTML
     header.
22   $page_title = 'Logged In!';
23   include ('./includes/header.html');
24
25   // Print a customized message.
26   echo "<h1>Logged In!</h1>
27   <p>You are now logged in, {$_SESSION
     ['first_name']}!</p>
28   <p><br /><br /></p>";
29
30   include ('./includes/footer.html');
31   ?>
```

Script 9.12 The logout.php page uses the session_name() function to also determine the name of the cookie to be sent.

```
1    <?php # Script 9.12 - logout.php (3rd
     version after Scripts 9.4 & 9.9)
2    // This page lets the user logout.
3
4    session_name ('YourVisitID');
5    session_start(); // Access the existing
     session.
6
7    // If no session variable exists, redirect
     the user.
8    if (!($_SESSION['user_id'])) {
9
10       // Start defining the URL.
11       $url = 'http://' . $_SERVER['HTTP_HOST']
          . dirname($_SERVER['PHP_SELF']);
12       // Check for a trailing slash.
13       if ((substr($url, -1) == '/') OR (substr
          ($url, -1) == '\\') ) {
14          $url = substr ($url, 0, -1); // Chop
             off the slash.
15       }
16       $url .= '/index.php'; // Add the page.
17       header("Location: $url");
18       exit(); // Quit the script.
19
20    } else { // Cancel the session.
21       $_SESSION = array(); // Destroy the
          variables.
22       session_destroy(); // Destroy the
          session itself.
23       setcookie (session_name(), '',
          time()-300, '/', '', 0); // Destroy
          the cookie.
24    }
25
26    // Set the page title and include the HTML
     header.
27    $page_title = 'Logged Out!';
28    include ('./includes/header.html');
29
30    // Print a customized message.
```

(script continues on next page)

4. Add the following line to logout.php (compare Script 9.9 with **Script 9.12**):

```
session_name ('YourVisitID');
```

5. Change the setcookie() line of logout.php so that it uses the session_name() function:

```
setcookie (session_name(), '',
→ time()-300, '/', '', 0);
```

The session_name() function will set the session name or return the current session name (if no argument is given). Since I want to send a cookie using the same cookie name as was used to create the cookie, the session_name() function will set that value appropriately.

continues on next page

USING SESSIONS

6. Save all the files, upload to your Web server, and test in your Web browser.

7. If desired, view the cookie that was set during the login process (**Figure 9.18**).

Script 9.12 *continued*

```
31    echo "<h1>Logged Out!</h1>
32    <p>You are now logged out!</p>
33    <p><br /><br /></p>";
34
35    include ('./includes/footer.html');
36    ?>
```

Figure 9.18 The cookie's name will correspond to the session name.

Sessions and Cookies

In the previous examples I've accomplished the same tasks (logging in and logging out) using cookies and sessions. Obviously, both are easy to use in PHP, but the true question is when to use one or the other.

Sessions have the following advantages over cookies:

◆ They are generally more secure (because the data is being retained on the server).

◆ They allow for more data to be stored.

◆ They can be used without cookies.

Whereas cookies have the following advantages over sessions:

◆ They are easier to program.

◆ They require less of the server.

In general, to store and retrieve just a couple of small pieces of information, use cookies. For most of your Web applications, though, you'll use sessions. But since sessions do rely upon cookies by default, I'll discuss how to better manage this relationship.

Changing the session cookie settings

As it stands, the cookie sent by the `session_start()` function uses certain default parameters: an expiration of `0` (meaning the cookie will last as long as the browser remains open), a path of `'/'` (the cookie is available in the current folder and all of its subfolders), and no domain name. To change any of these settings, you can use the `session_set_cookie_params()` function:

```
session_set_cookie_params(expiration,
→ 'path', 'domain', secure);
```

The expiration setting is the only required value and is set in seconds with `0` as the default. This is not the number of seconds from the epoch (as is the case with the `setcookie()` function), and therefore you would use just *300* (for five minutes) rather than *time() + 300* (for five minutes from now).

To change the session cookie settings:

1. Open login.php (refer to Script 9.10) in your text editor.

2. Prior to the session_start() call (line 37), add the following (**Script 9.13**):

   session_set_cookie_params (900,
   → '/ch09/', 'www.domain.com');

   The session_set_cookie_params() function must be used before session_start() to be effective. Change the path and domain setting to those values that make sense for your application, or omit the values to use the defaults. In this example, I'll give the cookie an expiration time that's 15 minutes from now.

3. Save the file as login.php, upload to your Web server, and test in your browser.

   After 15 minutes, the cookie will expire and the PHP scripts should no longer be able to access the session values (*first_ name* and *user_id*).

continues on page 362

Script 9.13 This version of the login.php script sets explicit cookie parameters.

```
                            script
1    <?php # Script 9.13 - login.php (5th
     version after Scripts 9.1, 9.3, 9.6 & 9.10)
2    // Send NOTHING to the Web browser prior to
     the session_start() line!
3
4    // Check if the form has been submitted.
5    if (isset($_POST['submitted'])) {
6
7        require_once ('../mysql_connect.php');
         // Connect to the db.
8
9        $errors = array(); // Initialize error
         array.
10
11       // Check for an email address.
12       if (empty($_POST['email'])) {
13           $errors[] = 'You forgot to enter your
             email address.';
14       } else {
15           $e = escape_data($_POST['email']);
16       }
17
18       // Check for a password.
19       if (empty($_POST['password'])) {
20           $errors[] = 'You forgot to enter your
             password.';
21       } else {
22           $p = escape_data($_POST
             ['password']);
23       }
24
25       if (empty($errors)) { // If everything's
OK.
26
27           /* Retrieve the user_id and
             first_name for
28           that email/password combination. */
29           $query = "SELECT user_id,
             first_name FROM users WHERE email=
             '$e' AND password=SHA('$p')";
30           $result = @mysql_query ($query); //
             Run the query.
```

(script continues on next page)

Script 9.13 *continued*

```
31         $row = mysql_fetch_array ($result, MYSQL_NUM); // Return a record, if applicable.
32
33         if ($row) { // A record was pulled from the database.
34
35             // Set the session data & redirect.
36             session_name ('YourVisitID');
37             session_set_cookie_params (900, '/ch09/', 'www.domain.com');
38             session_start();
39             $_SESSION['user_id'] = $row[0];
40             $_SESSION['first_name'] = $row[1];
41
42             // Redirect the user to the loggedin.php page.
43             // Start defining the URL.
44             $url = 'http://' . $_SERVER['HTTP_HOST'] . dirname($_SERVER['PHP_SELF']);
45             // Check for a trailing slash.
46             if ((substr($url, -1) == '/') OR (substr($url, -1) == '\\') ) {
47                 $url = substr ($url, 0, -1); // Chop off the slash.
48             }
49             // Add the page.
50             $url .= '/loggedin.php';
51
52             header("Location: $url");
53             exit(); // Quit the script.
54
55         } else { // No record matched the query.
56             $errors[] = 'The email address and password entered do not match those on file.';
                // Public message.
57             $errors[] = mysql_error() . '<br /><br />Query: ' . $query; // Debugging message.
58         }
59
60     } // End of if (empty($errors)) IF.
61
62     mysql_close(); // Close the database connection.
63
64 } else { // Form has not been submitted.
65
66     $errors = NULL;
67
68 } // End of the main Submit conditional.
69
70 // Begin the page now.
71 $page_title = 'Login';
```

(script continues on next page)

4. View the cookie being sent (**Figure 9.19**).

5. Alter `loggedin.php` and `logout.php` so that the `setcookie()` function uses the same parameters as `login.php` (except for the expiration time on the logout page, of course).

✔ Tips

■ The `session_get_cookie_params()` function returns an array of the current session cookie settings.

■ The session cookie parameters can also be altered using the `ini_set()` function.

■ The expiration time of the cookie refers only to the longevity of the cookie in the Web browser, not to how long the session data will be stored on the server.

Script 9.13 *continue*

```
72    include ('./includes/header.html');
73
74    if (!empty($errors)) { // Print any error
      messages.
75        echo '<h1 id="mainhead">Error!</h1>';
76        <p class="error">The following error(s)
        occurred:<br />';
77        foreach ($errors as $msg) { // Print
        each error.
78            echo " - $msg<br />\n";
79        }
80        echo '</p><p>Please try again.</p>';
81    }
82
83    // Create the form.
84    ?>
85    <h2>Login</h2>
86    <form action="login.php" method="post">
87        <p>Email Address: <input type="text"
        name="email" size="20" maxlength="40"
        /> </p>
88        <p>Password: <input type="password"
        name="password" size="20" maxlength="20"
        /></p>
89        <p><input type="submit" name="submit"
        value="Login" /></p>
90        <input type="hidden" name="submitted"
        value="TRUE" />
91    </form>
92    <?php
93    include ('./includes/footer.html');
94    ?>
```

Figure 9.19 The session cookie now has an expiration time set.

Using sessions without cookies

One of the problems with sessions is that, by default, they rely on the use of a cookie to work properly. When a session is started, it sends a cookie that resides in the user's Web browser. Every subsequent page that calls `session_start()` makes use of the cookie, which contains the session name and ID, to know to use an existing session and to not create a new one. The problem is that users may have cookies turned off in their Web browser or may not accept the cookie because they do not understand its purpose. If this is the case, PHP will create a new session for each page and none of the registered variables will be accessible.

You can use sessions without cookies by passing along the session name and ID from page to page. This is simple enough to do, but if you forget to pass the session in only one instance, the entire process is shot.

To pass the session name from page to page, you can use the `SID` constant, which stands for *session ID* and has a value like *session_name=session_ID*. If this value is appended to every URL within the site, the sessions will still work even if the user did not accept the cookie. Note, though, that PHP only assigns a value to `SID` if no session cookie is present.

Garbage Collection

Garbage collection with respect to sessions is the process of deleting the session files (where the actual data is stored). Creating a logout system that destroys a session is ideal, but there's no guarantee all users will formally log out as they should. For this reason, PHP includes a cleanup process.

Whenever the `session_start()` function is called, PHP's garbage collection kicks in, checking the last modification date of each session (a session is modified whenever variables are set or retrieved). The server overhead of all this can become costly for busy sites, so you can tweak PHP's behavior in this regard.

Two settings dictate garbage collection: `session_gc_maxlifetime` and `session.gc_probability`. The first states after how many seconds of inactivity a session is considered idle and will therefore be deleted. The second setting determines the probability that garbage collection is performed, on a scale of 1 to 100. So, with the default settings, each call to `session_start()` has a 1 percent chance of invoking garbage collection. If PHP does start the cleanup, any sessions that have not been used in more than 1,440 seconds will be deleted.

With this in mind, you can alter PHP's garbage collection habits to better suit your application. Twenty-four minutes is a reasonable amount of idle time, but you'll want to increase the probability to somewhere closer to 30 percent so that there is a good balance between performance and clutter.

To use sessions without cookies:

1. Open login.php (refer to Script 9.13) in your text editor.

2. Replace the session_set_cookie_params() line with this one (**Script 9.14**):

   ini_set('session.use_cookies', 0);

   This code will tell PHP to specifically not use any cookies.

3. Alter the final $url creation line to be

   $url .= '/loggedin.php?' . SID;

   The addition of ? and SID to the redirect will add *?session_name=session_ID* to the URL, effectively passing the session ID to the loggedin.php script.

continues on page 366

Script 9.14 This version of the login.php script does not use cookies at all, instead maintaining the state by passing the session ID in the URL.

```
                           script

1    <?php # Script 9.14 - login.php (6th version
     after Scripts 9.1, 9.3, 9.6, 9.10 & 9.13)
2    // Send NOTHING to the Web browser prior to
     the session_start() line!
3
4    // Check if the form has been submitted.
5    if (isset($_POST['submitted'])) {
6
7        require_once ('../mysql_connect.php');
         // Connect to the db.
8
9        $errors = array(); // Initialize error
     array.
10
11       // Check for an email address.
12       if (empty($_POST['email'])) {
13           $errors[] = 'You forgot to enter your
             email address.';
14       } else {
15           $e = escape_data($_POST['email']);
16       }
17
18       // Check for a password.
19       if (empty($_POST['password'])) {
20           $errors[] = 'You forgot to enter your
             password.';
21       } else {
22           $p = escape_data($_POST['password']);
23       }
24
25       if (empty($errors)) { // If everything's
     OK.
26
27           /* Retrieve the user_id and
             first_name for
28           that email/password combination. */
29           $query = "SELECT user_id, first_name
             FROM users WHERE email='$e' AND
             password=SHA('$p')";
30           $result = @mysql_query ($query); //
             Run the query.
```

(script continues on next page)

Script 9.14 *continued*

```
31        $row = mysql_fetch_array ($result, MYSQL_NUM); // Return a record, if applicable.
32
33        if ($row) { // A record was pulled from the database.
34
35            // Set the session data & redirect.
36            session_name ('YourVisitID');
37            ini_set('session.use_cookies', 0); // Don't use cookies.
38            session_start();
39            $_SESSION['user_id'] = $row[0];
40            $_SESSION['first_name'] = $row[1];
41
42            // Redirect the user to the loggedin.php page.
43            // Start defining the URL.
44            $url = 'http://' . $_SERVER['HTTP_HOST'] . dirname($_SERVER['PHP_SELF']);
45            // Check for a trailing slash.
46            if ((substr($url, -1) == '/') OR (substr($url, -1) == '\\') ) {
47                $url = substr ($url, 0, -1); // Chop off the slash.
48            }
49            // Add the page.
50            $url .= '/loggedin.php?' . SID; // Add the session name & ID.
51
52            header("Location: $url");
53            exit(); // Quit the script.
54
55        } else { // No record matched the query.
56            $errors[] = 'The email address and password entered do not match those on file.';
                // Public message.
57            $errors[] = mysql_error() . '<br /><br />Query: ' . $query; // Debugging message.
58        }
59
60    } // End of if (empty($errors)) IF.
61
62    mysql_close(); // Close the database connection.
63
64 } else { // Form has not been submitted.
65
66    $errors = NULL;
67
68 } // End of the main Submit conditional.
69
70 // Begin the page now.
71 $page_title = 'Login';
```

(script continues on next page)

4. Save the file, upload to your Web server, and test in your Web browser (**Figure 9.20**).

5. Copy the URL from the browser and paste it into another browser (**Figure 9.21**).

Called *session hijacking*, this is one of the reasons to rely upon cookies whenever possible. The next section of this chapter will introduce preventive measures.

To spare you from having to review minor modifications to the same scripts yet again (and to save precious book space), I am not including new versions of header.html, loggedin.php, and logout.php. But since you should know how to edit these files in order to use sessions without cookies, I'll quickly outline the necessary changes.

Script 9.14 *continue*

```
72    include ('./includes/header.html');
73
74    if (!empty($errors)) { // Print any error
      messages.
75        echo '<h1 id="mainhead">Error!</h1>';
76        <p class="error">The following error(s)
          occurred:<br />';
77        foreach ($errors as $msg) { // Print
          each error.
78            echo " - $msg<br />\n";
79        }
80        echo '</p><p>Please try again.</p>';
81    }
82
83    // Create the form.
84    ?>
85    <h2>Login</h2>
86    <form action="login.php" method="post">
87        <p>Email Address: <input type="text"
          name="email" size="20" maxlength="40"
          /> </p>
88        <p>Password: <input type="password"
          name="password" size="20" maxlength="20"
          /></p>
89        <p><input type="submit" name="submit"
          value="Login" /></p>
90        <input type="hidden" name="submitted"
          value="TRUE" />
91    </form>
92    <?php
93    include ('./includes/footer.html');
94    ?>
```

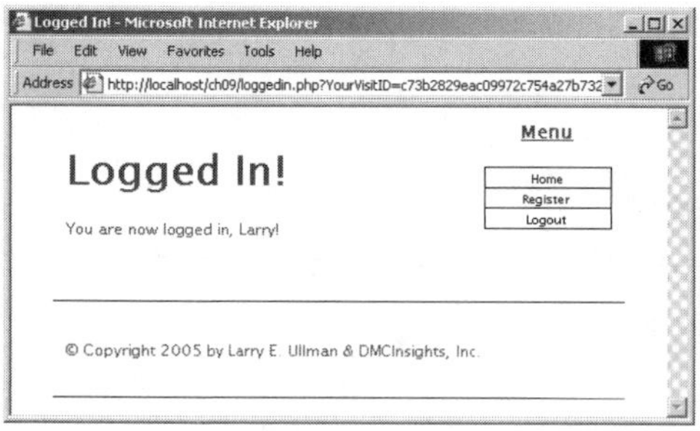

Figure 9.20 When the browser is redirected to the loggedin.php page, the session name and ID will be appended to the URL.

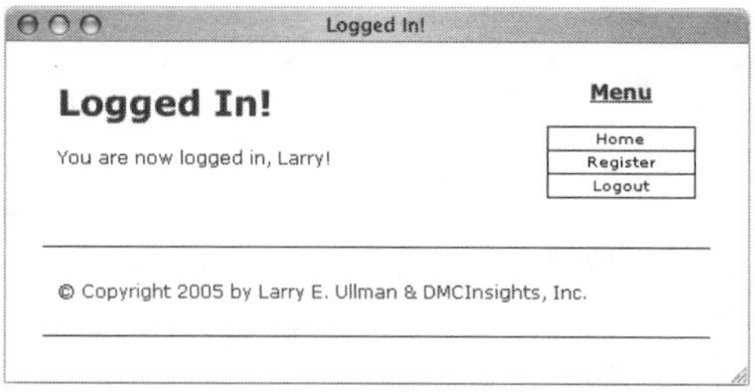

Figure 9.21 By using an existing session ID in a new browser, I can hijack another user's session and have access to all of that user's registered session data.

To edit the other files:

1. Edit `header.html` so that every link includes *?session_name=session_ID* (script not shown).

   The other problem with using sessions without cookies (besides the security issue) is that you must account for every link in your entire application. To modify the header file, you'll need to define the links like so:

   ```
   <a href="index.php?<?php echo
   → SID; ?>" title="Go to the Home
   → Page">Home</a>
   ```

2. Edit `loggedin.php` so that it also includes the `ini_set()` line.

   This script would then begin like so:

   ```
   session_name ('YourVisitID');
   ini_set('session.use_cookies', 0);
   session_start();
   ```

   You would also need to do this step for any other page that uses sessions.

3. Make the same changes to `logout.php`.

4. Remove the `setcookie()` line from `logout.php`.

   Since a session cookie is no longer being used, there is no reason to set another cookie deleting it.

✔ Tips

- If you have access to your `php.ini` file, you can set *session.use_trans_sid* to *1* or *On*. Doing so will have PHP automatically append `SID` to every URL as you have done manually here. It will slow down execution of the scripts, though, because PHP will need to check every page for URLs.

- The `session_id()` function returns the current session value (or allows you to specify which session to use).

- You can also pass `SID` from one page to another by storing it as a hidden input type in a form.

- Depending on the Web browser being used by the client, a session may be either browser-specific or window-specific. If the latter is the case, a pop-up window in your site will not be part of the same session unless it has received the session ID.

- Remember that using this method of storing and passing the session ID is less secure than using cookies for that purpose. If security isn't really a concern for your Web site (for example, if you're not dealing with personal information or e-commerce), then this is less of an issue.

Improving Session Security

Because important information is normally stored in a session (as opposed to a cookie), security becomes more of an issue. Remember that with sessions there are two considerations: the session ID, which is a reference point to the session data, and the session data itself, stored on the server. A malicious person is far more likely to hack into a session through the session ID than the data on the server, so I'll focus on that side of things here.

Storing the session ID in a cookie is considered the more secure method of using sessions, as opposed to passing the session ID along in URLs or storing it in hidden form inputs. Those alternatives are less secure because the session could easily be *hijacked* by another user, as you already witnessed. If I can learn another user's session ID, I can easily trick a server into thinking that it is *my* session ID. At that point I have effectively taken over the original user's entire session and may have access to their data. So storing the session ID in a cookie makes it somewhat harder to steal.

One method of preventing hijacking is to store some sort of user identifier in the session, and then to repeatedly double-check this value. The *HTTP_USER_AGENT*—a combination of the browser and operating system being used—is a likely candidate for this purpose. This adds a layer of security in that I could only hijack another user's session if I am running the exact same browser and operating system. For example, a login page would have

```
$_SESSION['agent'] = $_SERVER
→['HTTP_USER_AGENT'];
```

Then subsequent pages would check the stored *HTTP_USER_AGENT* against the user's *HTTP_USER_AGENT* (which should be the same).

```
if ($_SERVER['HTTP_USER_AGENT'] !=
→ $_SESSION['agent']) {

    /* The session has probably

    been hijacked! */

}
```

As a demonstration of this, I'll modify the examples one last time. While I'm focusing on security, I'll encrypt the $_SERVER['HTTP_USER_AGENT'] information using the md5() function to make it harder to fake.

Preventing Session Fixation

Another specific kind of session attack is known as *session fixation*. This is where one user specifies the session ID that another user should use. This session ID could be randomly generated or legitimately created. In either case, the real user will go into the site using the fixed session ID and do whatever. Then the malicious user can access that session because they know what the session ID is. You can help protect against these types of attack by changing the session ID. The session_regenerate_id() does just that, providing a new session ID to refer to the current session data. You can use this function should anything of consequence change during a user's session.

Script 9.15 This final version of the login.php script also stores an encrypted form of the user's *HTTP_USER_AGENT* (the browser and operating system of the client) in a session.

```
1   <?php # Script 9.15 - login.php (7th
    version after Scripts 9.1, 9.3, 9.6, 9.10.
    9.13 & 9.14)
2   // Send NOTHING to the Web browser prior to
    the session_start() line!
3
4   // Check if the form has been submitted.
5   if (isset($_POST['submitted'])) {
6
7       require_once ('../mysql_connect.php');
        // Connect to the db.
8
9       $errors = array(); // Initialize error
        array.
10
11      // Check for an email address.
12      if (empty($_POST['email'])) {
13          $errors[] = 'You forgot to enter your
            email address.';
14      } else {
15          $e = escape_data($_POST['email']);
16      }
17
18      // Check for a password.
19      if (empty($_POST['password'])) {
20          $errors[] = 'You forgot to enter your
            password.';
21      } else {
22          $p = escape_data($_POST
            ['password']);
23      }
24
25      if (empty($errors)) { // If everything's
        OK.
26
27          /* Retrieve the user_id and
            first_name for
28          that email/password combination. */
```

(script continues on next page)

To use sessions more securely:

1. Open login.php (refer to Script 9.14) in your text editor.

2. Delete the ini_set() line and remove the reference to SID (**Script 9.15**).

   For security purposes, I'll revert to using cookies to store the session ID. I also no longer need to append SID to the header() redirection URL.

3. After assigning the other session variables, store the *HTTP_USER_AGENT*.

   $_SESSION['agent'] = md5($_SERVER
   → ['HTTP_USER_AGENT']);

   The *HTTP_USER_AGENT* is part of the $_SERVER array (you may recall using it way back in Chapter 1, "Introduction to PHP"). It will have a value like *Mozilla/4.0 (compatible; MSIE 6.0; Windows NT 5.0; .NET CLR 1.1.4322)*. This variable is run through the md5() function, which will turn it into a 32-character hexadecimal *hash* (although it's just easier to say that the data is encrypted).

4. Save the file and upload to your Web server.

continues on page 372

IMPROVING SESSION SECURITY

Script 9.15 *continued*

```
29        $query = "SELECT user_id, first_name FROM users WHERE email='$e' AND password=SHA('$p')";
30        $result = @mysql_query ($query); // Run the query.
31        $row = mysql_fetch_array ($result, MYSQL_NUM); // Return a record, if applicable.
32
33        if ($row) { // A record was pulled from the database.
34
35            // Set the session data & redirect.
36            session_name ('YourVisitID');
37            session_start();
38            $_SESSION['user_id'] = $row[0];
39            $_SESSION['first_name'] = $row[1];
40            $_SESSION['agent'] = md5($_SERVER['HTTP_USER_AGENT']);
41
42            // Redirect the user to the loggedin.php page.
43            // Start defining the URL.
44            $url = 'http://' . $_SERVER['HTTP_HOST'] . dirname($_SERVER['PHP_SELF']);
45            // Check for a trailing slash.
46            if ((substr($url, -1) == '/') OR (substr($url, -1) == '\\') ) {
47                $url = substr ($url, 0, -1); // Chop off the slash.
48            }
49            // Add the page.
50            $url .= '/loggedin.php';
51
52            header("Location: $url");
53            exit(); // Quit the script.
54
55        } else { // No record matched the query.
56            $errors[] = 'The email address and password entered do not match those on file.';
                        // Public message.
57            $errors[] = mysql_error() . '<br /><br />Query: ' . $query; // Debugging message.
58        }
59
60    } // End of if (empty($errors)) IF.
61
62    mysql_close(); // Close the database connection.
63
64 } else { // Form has not been submitted.
65
66    $errors = NULL;
67
```

(script continues on next page)

Script 9.15 *continued*

```
68    } // End of the main Submit conditional.
69
70    // Begin the page now.
71    $page_title = 'Login';
72    include ('./includes/header.html');
73
74    if (!empty($errors)) { // Print any error messages.
75        echo '<h1 id="mainhead">Error!</h1>
76        <p class="error">The following error(s) occurred:<br />';
77        foreach ($errors as $msg) { // Print each error.
78            echo " - $msg<br />\n";
79        }
80        echo '</p><p>Please try again.</p>';
81    }
82
83    // Create the form.
84    ?>
85    <h2>Login</h2>
86    <form action="login.php" method="post">
87        <p>Email Address: <input type="text" name="email" size="20" maxlength="40" /> </p>
88        <p>Password: <input type="password" name="password" size="20" maxlength="20" /></p>
89        <p><input type="submit" name="submit" value="Login" /></p>
90        <input type="hidden" name="submitted" value="TRUE" />
91    </form>
92    <?php
93    include ('./includes/footer.html');
94    ?>
```

5. Open `loggedin.php` (Script 9.11) in your text editor.

6. Change the `!isset($_SESSION['user_id'])` conditional to (**Script 9.16**)

```
if (!isset($_SESSION['agent'])
→ OR ($_SESSION ['agent'] != md5
→ ($_SERVER['HTTP_USER_AGENT'])) ) {
```

This conditional checks for two things. First, it sees if the `$_SESSION['agent']` variable is not set (this part is just as it was before, although *agent* is being used instead of *user_id*). The second part of the conditional checks if the `md5()` version of `$_SERVER['HTTP_USER_AGENT']` does not equal the value stored in `$_SESSION['agent']`. If either of these conditions are true, the user will be redirected.

Script 9.16 This `loggedin.php` script now confirms that the user accessing this page has the same *HTTP_USER_AGENT* as they did when they logged in.

```
1    <?php # Script 9.16 - loggedin.php
     (4th version after Scripts 9.2, 9.7 & 9.11)
2    # User is redirected here from login.php.
3
4    session_name ('YourVisitID');
5    session_start(); // Start the session.
6
7    // If no session value is present, redirect
     the user.
8    if (!isset($_SESSION['agent']) OR
     ($_SESSION ['agent'] != md5($_SERVER
     ['HTTP_USER_AGENT'])) ) {
9
10       // Start defining the URL.
11       $url = 'http://' . $_SERVER['HTTP_HOST']
         . dirname($_SERVER['PHP_SELF']);
12       // Check for a trailing slash.
13       if ((substr($url, -1) == '/') OR (substr
         ($url, -1) == '\\') ) {
14           $url = substr ($url, 0, -1); // Chop
             off the slash.
15       }
16       $url .= '/index.php'; // Add the page.
17       header("Location: $url");
18       exit(); // Quit the script.
19   }
20
21   // Set the page title and include the HTML
     header.
22   $page_title = 'Logged In!';
23   include ('./includes/header.html');
24
25   // Print a customized message.
26   echo "<h1>Logged In!</h1>
27   <p>You are now logged in, {$_SESSION
     ['first_name']}!</p>
28   <p><br /><br /></p>";
29
30   include ('./includes/footer.html');
31   ?>
```

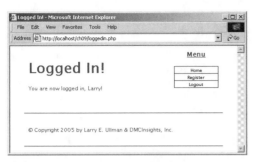

Figure 9.22 You cannot tell any difference by running the application, but this final version of the login system is more secure. Specifically, it helps to prevent session hijacking.

7. Save this file, upload to your Web server, and test in your Web browser by logging in (**Figure 9.22**).

✔ Tips

■ For critical uses of sessions, require the use of cookies and transmit them over a secure connection, if at all possible. You can even set PHP to only use cookies by setting *session.use_only_cookies* to *1* (as of PHP 4.3).

■ If you are using a server shared with other domains, changing the *session.save_path* from its default setting—which is accessible by all users—to something more local will be more secure.

■ On the server side of security, the session data itself can be stored in a database rather than a text file. This is a more secure, but more programming-intensive, option.

■ The user's IP address (the network address from which the user is connecting) is *not* a good unique identifier, for two reasons. First, a user's IP address can, and normally does, change frequently (ISP's dynamically assign them for short periods of time). Second, many users accessing a site from the same network (like a home network or an office) could all have the same IP address.

IMPROVING SESSION SECURITY

WEB APPLICATION SECURITY

The security of your Web applications is such an important topic that I always include a specific chapter on the subject in my books. Although I've been mentioning security-related issues throughout this book, this chapter will help to fill in certain gaps and finalize other points.

The most important concept to understand about security is that your Web site will not be either *secure* or *not secure*. What it will be is *more* secure or *less* secure. Security isn't a switch that you turn on and off; it's a scale that you can move up and down. Also, keep in mind that improved security normally comes at a cost of convenience (to both you, the programmer, and to the end user) and performance. Increased security normally means more code, more checks, and more required of the server. So when developing your Web applications, think about these considerations and make the right decisions—for the particular situation—from the outset.

The topics discussed here include extended form validation with PHP, accounting for HTML in submitted form data, using type casting, form validation with JavaScript, using regular expressions, and database security. Unlike the past couple chapters—which used a cohesive series of examples—this chapter will use several discrete scripts.

More Secure Form Validation

In this book, form validation has been discussed several times, using different methods. The golden rule of validating *any* data received by a PHP page is to assume that it's invalid until it passes the right tests indicating otherwise. At a bare minimum, you should

- Use the superglobals (e.g., `$_POST['name']`) rather than the registered globals (`$name`).

- Check text, password, and textarea form inputs for values using `empty()`.

- Check other form inputs for values using `isset()`.

- Check any form input by verifying that it has a positive length.

A better way to validate data is to see if it conforms to a certain type (like an integer), as will be covered shortly. An even more exacting method of form validation requires the use of regular expressions, discussed later in this chapter. You can also use JavaScript to perform basic validation on the client (within the Web browser) before the data is sent to the server. This will also be discussed in this chapter. But first, there's an entirely different kind of validation you can use: validating that a form has only been submitted once and that the right form has been submitted to a page. These first two topics are the focus over the next few pages.

Preventing multiple submissions

A common question I see is how to prevent someone from submitting the same form multiple times. Whether a user repeatedly submits a form on accident or on purpose, such occurrences can be a minor nuisance or a major problem for your Web site. There are many different ways to prevent multiple submissions, and I'll discuss two options here.

First, if you are already using sessions, an easy solution is to create a session variable indicating whether a specific form has been submitted or not.

```
if (isset($_SESSION['form_name'])) {

    // Do not handle the form.

} else {

    // Handle the form.

    // Indicate that the form

    // has been handled.

    $_SESSION['form_name'] = TRUE;

}
```

This technique is both effective and simple but does require the use of sessions.

In the following steps, I'll demonstrate another option, which is viable for applications that use a database to store the submitted information. The premise is this: A generated identifier will be stored in the HTML form (as a hidden input). This value will be inserted into the database (see the sidebar on page 384) along with the other submitted information. To prevent repeated submissions, this identifier can be stored in the database only once. A user wishing to submit the form again will have to reload the HTML form so that another unique identifier is created.

Script 10.1 PHP is used in this basic HTML form to store a random key in a hidden form input.

```
1   <!DOCTYPE html PUBLIC "-//W3C//DTD XHTML
    1.0 Transitional//EN"
2       "http://www.w3.org/TR/xhtml1/DTD/
        xhtml1-transitional.dtd">
3   <html xmlns="http://www.w3.org/1999/xhtml"
    xml:lang="en" lang="en">
4   <head>
5       <meta http-equiv="content-type" content=
        "text/html; charset=iso-8859-1" />
6       <title>Enter Your Comments</title>
7   </head>
8   <body>
9   <!-- Script 10.1 - comments.php -->
10
11  <form action="handle_comments.php"
    method="post">
12
13      <fieldset><legend>Enter your comments in
        the form below:</legend>
14      <p><b>Name:</b> <input type="text"
        name="name" size="20" maxlength="40" />
        </p>
15      <p><b>Comments:</b> <textarea
        name="comments" rows="3" cols="40">
        </textarea></p>
16      </fieldset>
17      <div align="center"><input type="submit"
        name="submit" value="Submit" /></div>
18
19      <input type="hidden" name="stamp"
        value="<?php echo md5(uniqid(rand(),
        true)); ?>" />
20
21  </form>
22  </body>
23  </html>
```

To prevent multiple form submissions:

1. Begin a new PHP document in your text editor or IDE (**Script 10.1**).

```
<!DOCTYPE html PUBLIC "-//W3C//DTD
XHTML 1.0 Transitional//EN"
"http://www.w3.org/TR/xhtml1/DTD/
xhtml1-transitional.dtd">
<html xmlns="http://www.w3.org/1999/
xhtml" xml:lang="en" lang="en">
<head>
    <meta http-equiv="content-type"
→ content="text/html; charset=
→ iso-8859-1" />
    <title>Enter Your Comments</title>
</head>
<body>
<!-- Script 10.1 - comments.php -->
```

2. Begin defining the form.

```
<form action="handle_comments.php"
→ method="post">
    <fieldset><legend>Enter your
→ comments in the form below:
→ </legend>
    <p><b>Name:</b> <input type="text"
→ name="name" size="20"
→ maxlength="40" /></p>
    <p><b>Comments:</b> <textarea
→ name="comments" rows="3"
→ cols="40"></textarea></p>
    </fieldset>
    <div align="center"><input
→ type="submit" name="submit"
→ value="Submit" /></div>
```

I'm keeping this form simple, taking only the user's name and comments.

continues on next page

3. Store a unique identifier in a hidden form input.

```
<input type="hidden" name="stamp"
→ value="<?php echo md5(uniqid
→ (rand(), true)); ?>" />
```

To achieve the specific goal—avoiding duplicate form submissions—this is the most important line. Each time this page is loaded, a unique 32-character stamp is generated. Doing so requires use of the `rand()`, `uniqid()`, and `md5()` functions. Of these, `uniqid()` is the most important; it creates a unique identifier. It's fed the `rand()` function to help generate a more random value. Finally, the returned result is *hashed* using `md5()`, which creates a string exactly 32 characters long (a hash is a mathematically calculated representation of a piece of data). You do not need to fully comprehend these three functions, just note that the result will be a unique 32-character string.

4. Complete the form and the page.

```
</form>
</body>
</html>
```

5. Save the file as `comments.php`, upload to your Web server, and run in your Web browser (**Figure 10.1**).

Note that this has to be a PHP page, not an HTML one, as it has a line of PHP code.

6. View the HTML source to see the value of the hidden stamp (**Figure 10.2**).

7. Reload the page, and then review the HTML source to confirm that the stamp value has changed (**Figure 10.3**).

Now that the form itself has been written, a quick PHP page will be made that will handle the form data.

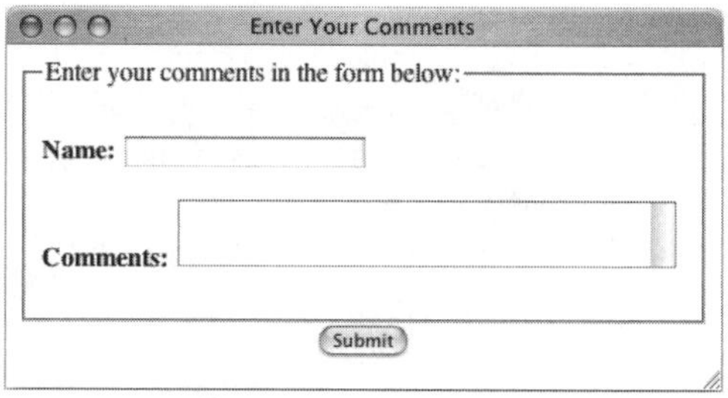

Figure 10.1 The HTML form looks much like any other.

Figure 10.2 The source of the HTML form reveals the PHP-generated stamp.

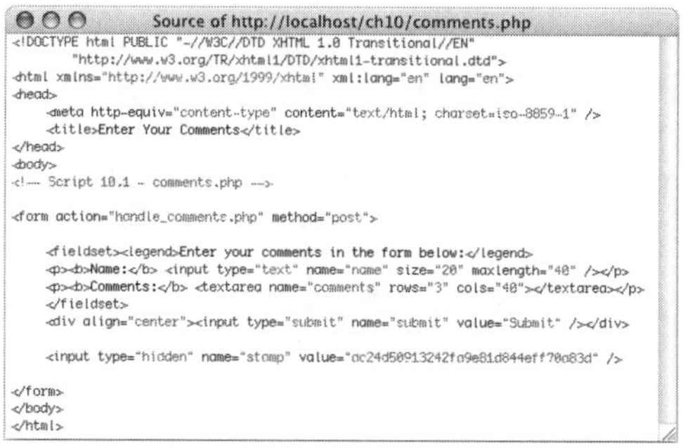

Figure 10.3 Each running of the same form should create a different stamp value.

Script 10.2 Because the stamp value in the database has to be unique, this script will not allow the same form data to be recorded twice.

```
1   <!DOCTYPE html PUBLIC "-//W3C//DTD XHTML
    1.0 Transitional//EN"
2        "http://www.w3.org/TR/xhtml1/DTD/
         xhtml1-transitional.dtd">
3   <html xmlns="http://www.w3.org/1999/xhtml"
    xml:lang="en" lang="en">
4   <head>
5      <meta http-equiv="content-type" content=
       "text/html; charset=iso-8859-1" />
6      <title>Handle Comments</title>
7   </head>
8   <body>
9   <?php # Script 10.2 - handle_comments.php
10
11  require_once ('../mysql_connect.php');
    // Connect to the db.
12  // The escape_data() function is defined in
    mysql_connect.php!
13  // Make sure that mysql_connect.php selects
    the 'test' database!
14
```

(script continues on page 381)

To write handle_comments.php:

1. Begin a new PHP document in your text editor or IDE (**Script 10.2**).

   ```
   <!DOCTYPE html PUBLIC "-//W3C//DTD
   → XHTML 1.0 Transitional//EN"
   "http://www.w3.org/TR/xhtml1/DTD/
   → xhtml1-transitional.dtd">
   <html xmlns="http://www.w3.org/1999/
   → xhtml" xml:lang="en" lang="en">
   <head>
      <meta http-equiv="content-type"
   →   content="text/html; charset=
   →   iso-8859-1" />
      <title>Handle Comments</title>
   </head>
   <body>
   <?php # Script 10.2 - handle_
   → comments.php
   ```

2. Include the database connection script.

   ```
   require_once ('../mysql_connect.
   → php');
   ```

   I haven't included this script in this chapter, but it will be very similar to the one created in Chapter 8, "Web Application Development." Besides connecting to the MySQL server, it should select the *test* database and define the escape_data() function.

   continues on next page

3. Validate the name and comments fields.

```
if (!empty($_POST['name'])) {
    $n = escape_data($_POST['name']);
} else {
    echo '<p><font color="red">You
    → forgot to enter your name.
    → </font></p>';
    $n = FALSE;
}
if (!empty($_POST['comments'])) {
    $c = escape_data($_POST
    → ['comments']);
} else {
    echo '<p><font color="red">You
    → forgot to enter your comments.
    → </font></p>';
    $c = FALSE;
}
```

To validate the person's name, I check that the *name* value isn't empty. If it isn't, then the value is escaped using the escape_data() function and assigned to the $n variable. Otherwise, an error message is printed and $n is set to FALSE. This process is repeated for the comments.

4. Validate the stamp.

```
if (strlen($_POST['stamp']) == 32 ) {
    $s = escape_data($_POST['stamp']);
} else {
    echo '<p><font color="red">This
    → page has been accessed in error.
    → </font></p>';
    $s = FALSE;
}
```

Just because the stamp value is a hidden input generated by PHP doesn't mean it shouldn't be validated. The stamp value should always be 32 characters long—as the md5() function always returns a string of that length—so I can be precise in my validation routine. Although the submitted stamp shouldn't contain any problematic characters, you can never be too careful, so the value is also run through escape_data().

5. If all tests passed, attempt to insert the new record into the database.

```
if ($n && $c && $s) {
    $query = "INSERT INTO comments
    → (name, comment, stamp) VALUES
    → ('$n', '$c', '$s')";
    $result = @mysql_query ($query);
```

If all three tests were passed, then $n, $c, and $s will all be true, making this conditional true. Inside the conditional, a simple INSERT query is defined and executed. The error suppression operator is used here, and any errors that occur will be handled later in the script.

continues on page 382

Script 10.2 *continued*

```
┌─────────────────────────── script ───────────────────────────┐
│ 15   // Check for a name.                                      │
│ 16   if (!empty($_POST['name'])) {                            │
│ 17       $n = escape_data($_POST['name']);                    │
│ 18   } else {                                                  │
│ 19       echo '<p><font color="red">You forgot to enter your name.</font></p>'; │
│ 20       $n = FALSE;                                           │
│ 21   }                                                         │
│ 22                                                             │
│ 23   // Check for comments (assume at least 5 characters).     │
│ 24   if (!empty($_POST['comments'])) {                        │
│ 25       $c = escape_data($_POST['comments']);                │
│ 26   } else {                                                  │
│ 27       echo '<p><font color="red">You forgot to enter your comments.</font></p>'; │
│ 28       $c = FALSE;                                           │
│ 29   }                                                         │
│ 30                                                             │
│ 31   // Check for the stamp.                                   │
│ 32   if (strlen($_POST['stamp']) == 32 ) {                    │
│ 33       $s = escape_data($_POST['stamp']);                   │
│ 34   } else {                                                  │
│ 35       echo '<p><font color="red">This page has              │
│          been accessed in error.</font></p>';                 │
│ 36       $s = FALSE;                                           │
│ 37   }                                                         │
│ 38                                                             │
│ 39   if ($n && $c && $s) { // If everything's OK.              │
│ 40                                                             │
│ 41       // Enter the record into the database.                │
│ 42       $query = "INSERT INTO comments (name, comment, stamp) VALUES ('$n', '$c', '$s')"; │
│ 43       $result = @mysql_query ($query); // Run the query.    │
│ 44                                                             │
└───────────────────────────────────────────────────────────────┘
```

(script continues on next page)

MORE SECURE FORM VALIDATION

6. Report on the results of the query.

```
if (mysql_affected_rows() == 1) {
    echo '<p>Thank you for your
    → comments.</p>';
} else {
    echo '<p><font color="red">Your
    → comments could not be added.
    → </font></p>';
    echo mysql_error() . '<br /><br />
    → Query: ' . $query;
}
```

If one row was successfully inserted, then `mysql_affected_rows()` will return *1*, and a thank-you message is printed. If one row was not inserted (or affected), an error occurred. For debugging purposes only, I'll print out the MySQL error and the query itself.

While developing the script, you may have errors because of improper query syntax, referring to a table or column that doesn't exist, and so forth. Once you've worked out these quirks, the only error that should occur is if the same form is submitted multiple times. In such cases, MySQL will cough up a duplicate key error (**Figure 10.4**), which is actually what you want. Naturally in a live site you would not reveal this information to the end user.

For a live site, you could also change the public error message to something like *Your comments have already been processed.*

7. Complete the main conditional.

```
} else {
    echo '<p><font color="red">Please
    → go back and try again.</font>
    → </p>';
}
```

If $n or $c or $s is not true, then this message is printed.

Script 10.2 *continued*

```
45      if (mysql_affected_rows() == 1) { // A
        record was added.
46          echo '<p>Thank you for your comments.
            </p>';
47      } else { // Insert failed.
48          echo '<p><font color="red">Your
            comments could not be added.</font>
            </p>'; // Public message.
49          echo mysql_error() . '<br /><br />
            Query: ' . $query; // Debugging
            message.
50      }
51
52  } else { // Error occurred.
53      echo '<p><font color="red">Please go
        back and try again.</font></p>';
54  }
55
56  mysql_close(); // Close the database
        connection.
57
58  ?>
59  </body>
60  </html>
```

```
● ● ●          Handle Comments
Your comments could not be added.

Duplicate entry 'ac24d50913242fa9e81d844eff70a83d' for key 2

Query: INSERT INTO comments (name, comment, stamp)
VALUES ('Larry Ullman', 'These are my \"comments\"! I\'m
pleased.', 'ac24d50913242fa9e81d844eff70a83d')
```

Figure 10.4 Resubmitting the same form with the same stamp value will cause a MySQL error.

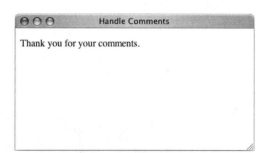

Figure 10.5 If the form is submitted for the first time, meaning that a unique stamp value was used, the data will be inserted into the database and the user will be thanked.

8. Close the database connection and complete the page.

```
mysql_close();
?>
</body>
</html>
```

9. Save the file as handle_comments.php, upload it to your Web server (in the same directory as comments.php), and test by submitting the HTML form (**Figure 10.5**).

✔ Tips

■ There's no way using PHP that you can determine a form's name. The only option is to store that value in a hidden form input.

■ If you're comfortable with JavaScript, you can add JavaScript code to your form to ensure that it is submitted only once. Search the Web for examples.

■ As a reminder, it's more secure to use the POST method with forms than the GET. If your form includes passwords or other sensitive information, you really must use POST.

■ Remember that hidden inputs in forms are still viewable in the HTML source and therefore aren't a secure way of temporarily storing information. You should never store a password or other secret information there.

MORE SECURE FORM VALIDATION

Validating the right form

PHP programmers often spend a lot of time fixating on form data—and rightly so—but do not think about the forms themselves. Say you have, as part of your site, a `contact.html` page with a form that is handled by `contact.php`. The assumption is that `contact.php` will be receiving data from `contact.html`, but that's not necessarily the case.

The fact of the matter is that a malicious user could create their own HTML page with a form whose action attribute is `http://www.yoursite.com/contact.php`. Using this form, they could send any data of any type to your page. If your handling page isn't looking for specific form fields and data, this could be a major security concern.

In this example I'll show a nifty little trick for validating that the received form data matches what is expected. The premise is that you make a list of what form inputs the page should receive and then check for a match. I'll rewrite the `handle_comments.php` using this technique.

> ### Using the Test Database
>
> MySQL creates two databases as part of its normal installation process. The first, called *mysql*, is the most important. MySQL access permissions are controlled by this database.
>
> The second database is called *test*. This database, appropriately enough, is intended for testing purposes. It is somewhat unique in that anyone has permission to access this database (you do not need to establish a username/password combination for it). Since this first example is unrelated to any other project, I'll create a new table within *test*. Here is the CREATE statement required to make the table:
>
> ```
> CREATE TABLE comments (
>
>     comment_id INT UNSIGNED NOT NULL
>     → AUTO_INCREMENT,
>
>     name VARCHAR(60) NOT NULL,
>
>     comment TEXT NOT NULL,
>
>     stamp CHAR(32) NOT NULL,
>
>     date_entered TIMESTAMP,
>
>     PRIMARY KEY (comment_id),
>
>     UNIQUE (stamp)
>
> )
> ```
>
> To make things easier, I'm storing the person's name in one field, but I generally recommend that you use separate first and last name columns. Also, a UNIQUE index is placed on the stamp column, which will help prevent duplicate submissions.

Script 10.3 By referring to the keys of the $_POST array, you can confirm if all the correct inputs were submitted to this page.

```
1   <!DOCTYPE html PUBLIC "-//W3C//DTD XHTML
    1.0 Transitional//EN"
2       "http://www.w3.org/TR/xhtml1/DTD/
        xhtml1-transitional.dtd">
3   <html xmlns="http://www.w3.org/1999/xhtml"
    xml:lang="en" lang="en">
4   <head>
5       <meta http-equiv="content-type" content=
        "text/html; charset=iso-8859-1" />
6       <title>Handle Comments</title>
7   </head>
8   <body>
9   <?php # Script 10.3 - handle_comments.php
10  # (2nd version after Script 10.2)
11
12  // Set the expected form inputs.
13  $allowed = array('name', 'comments',
    'submit', 'stamp');
14
15  // Get the received inputs.
16  $received = array_keys($_POST);
17
18  // Check that the two arrays match.
19  if ($allowed == $received) {
20
21      require_once ('../mysql_connect.php');
        // Connect to the db.
22      // The escape_data() function is defined
        in mysql_connect.php!
23      // Make sure that mysql_connect.php
        selects the 'test' database!
24
25      // Check for a name.
26      if (!empty($_POST['name'])) {
27          $n = escape_data($_POST['name']);
28      } else {
29          echo '<p><font color="red">You
            forgot to enter your name.</font>
            </p>';
30          $n = FALSE;
31      }
```

(script continues on next page)

To validate a form:

1. Open `handle_comments.php` (Script 10.2) in your text editor or IDE.

2. After the initial PHP tag, define what form inputs are expected (**Script 10.3**).

   ```
   $allowed = array('name', 'comments',
   → 'submit', 'stamp');
   ```

   Using the `array()` function, I create an array of allowed inputs. Remember that you must include the *submit* input here, as that will also be passed to this page. Also, the inputs should be listed in the same order as they appear in the form and have the exact same name (so *submit*, not *Submit*).

3. Assign the received variable names to a new array.

   ```
   $received = array_keys($_POST);
   ```

   This function—`array_keys()`—returns the names of the keys for a given array. In this case, it should return *name*, *comments*, *submit*, and *stamp* (in that order), assuming that the proper form has been submitted to this page.

4. Create a conditional that checks if the two arrays are the same.

   ```
   if ($allowed == $received) {
   ```

   You can easily compare one array to another using the equality operator. This conditional merely checks that the received keys (the form input names) exactly match the expected keys. If that's the case, the form can be handled as it was before.

continues on page 387

Script 10.3 *continued*

```
32
33      // Check for comments (assume at least 5 characters).
34      if (!empty($_POST['comments'])) {
35          $c = escape_data($_POST['comments']);
36      } else {
37          echo '<p><font color="red">You forgot to enter your comments.</font></p>';
38          $c = FALSE;
39      }
40
41      // Check for the stamp.
42      if (strlen($_POST['stamp']) == 32 ) {
43          $s = escape_data($_POST['stamp']);
44      } else {
45          echo '<p><font color="red">This page has been accessed in error.</font></p>';
46          $s = FALSE;
47      }
48
49      if ($n && $c && $s) { // If everything's OK.
50
51          // Enter the record into the database.
52          $query = "INSERT INTO comments (name, comment, stamp) VALUES ('$n', '$c', '$s')";
53          $result = @mysql_query ($query); // Run the query.
54
55          if (mysql_affected_rows() == 1) { // A record was added.
56              echo '<p>Thank you for your comments.</p>';
57          } else { // Insert failed.
58              echo '<p><font color="red">Your comments could not be added.</font></p>';
                // Public message.
59              echo mysql_error() . '<br /><br />Query: ' . $query; // Debugging message.
60          }
61
62      } else { // Error occurred.
63          echo '<p><font color="red">Please go back and try again.</font></p>';
64      }
65
66      mysql_close(); // Close the database connection.
67
68  } else { // Form mismatch.
69      echo '<p><font color="red">This page has been accessed in error.</font></p>';
70  }
71
72  ?>
73  </body>
74  </html>
```

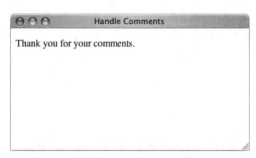

Figure 10.6 If the right form with the right inputs was submitted to this page, it will be handled as normal.

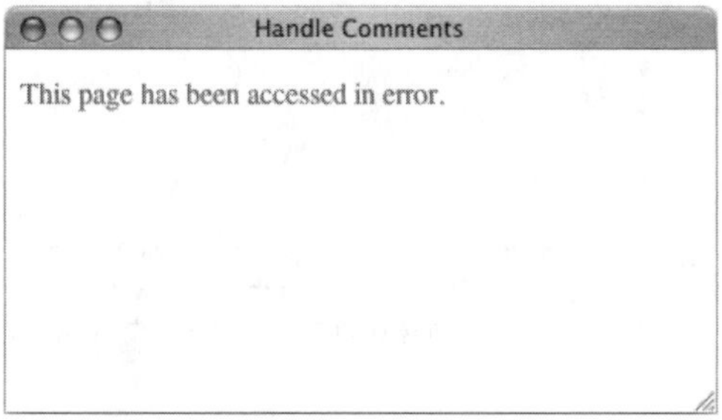

Figure 10.7 If the wrong form inputs are submitted to this page (presumably through malicious intent), the data will be ignored.

5. After the `mysql_close()` line, complete the `$allowed == $received` conditional.

```
} else {
    echo '<p><font color="red">This
    → page has been accessed in error.
    → </font></p>';
}
```

If the submitted inputs do not exactly match the expected inputs, the form is not handled and this error message is printed.

6. Save the page as `handle_comments.php`, upload to your Web server, and test in your Web browser (**Figure 10.6**).

7. If you'd like to play the role of a hacker, make a fake form that submits different values to the `handle_comments.php` page to see the results (**Figure 10.7**).

✔ Tips

- This trick was devised by Chris Shiflett, a PHP security consultant. For similar security-related tips and tricks, check out the PHP Security Consortium at `www.phpsec.org`.

- The `$_SERVER['HTTP_REFERER']` variable reflects the previous page the user accessed before the current one. Using this variable would seem to be a good way to validate that a form was properly submitted from the correct source. Unfortunately, `$_SERVER['HTTP_REFERER']` is not reliable, as some browsers will not support it.

Handling HTML

HTML is simply plain text, like <b>, which is given special meaning by Web browsers (as by making text bold). Because of this fact, your Web site's user could easily add HTML or JavaScript to their form data, like the comments field in the previous example (**Figure 10.8**). What's wrong with that, you might ask?

Many dynamically driven Web applications take the information submitted by a user, store it in a database, and then redisplay that information on another page. Think of a forum, as just one example. At the very least, if a user enters HTML code in their data, such code could throw off the layout and aesthetic of your site. Worse yet, bad code could create pop-up windows (**Figure 10.9**) or redirections to other sites. In the worst-case scenario, HTML and JavaScript could be used for what's called cross-site scripting (XSS), a common type of hack.

PHP includes a handful of functions for handling HTML and other code found within strings. These include:

◆ htmlspecialchars(), which turns &, ', ", <, and > into an HTML entity format (*&*, *"*, etc.)

◆ htmlentities(), which turns all applicable characters into their HTML entity format

◆ strip_tags(), which removes all HTML and PHP tags

These three functions are roughly listed in order from least disruptive to most. Which you'll want to use depends upon the application at hand. To demonstrate this concept, I'll apply the htmlspecialchars() function to the submitted name and comments data.

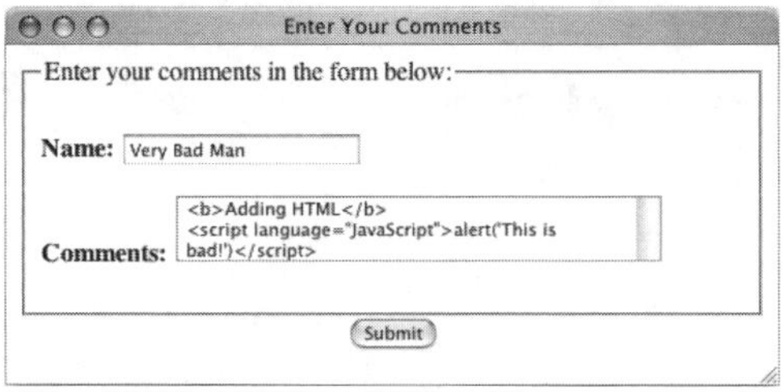

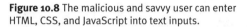

Figure 10.8 The malicious and savvy user can enter HTML, CSS, and JavaScript into text inputs.

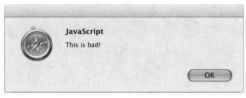

Figure 10.9 The JavaScript entered into the comments field (see Figure 10.8) would create this alert window when the comments were displayed in the Web browser.

Script 10.4 Calls to the htmlspecialchars() function help to sanctify the submitted name and comments values.

```
                    script
1   <!DOCTYPE html PUBLIC "-//W3C//DTD XHTML
    1.0 Transitional//EN"
2           "http://www.w3.org/TR/xhtml1/DTD/
            xhtml1-transitional.dtd">
3   <html xmlns="http://www.w3.org/1999/xhtml"
    xml:lang="en" lang="en">
4   <head>
5       <meta http-equiv="content-type" content=
        "text/html; charset=iso-8859-1" />
6       <title>Handle Comments</title>
7   </head>
8   <body>
9   <?php # Script 10.4 - handle_comments.php
10  # (3rd version after Scripts 10.2 and 10.3)
11
12  // Set the expected form inputs.
13  $allowed = array('name', 'comments',
    'submit', 'stamp');
14
15  // Get the received inputs.
16  $received = array_keys($_POST);
17
18  // Check that the two arrays match.
19  if ($allowed == $received) {
20
21      require_once ('../mysql_connect.php');
        // Connect to the db.
22      // The escape_data() function is defined
        in mysql_connect.php!
23      // Make sure that mysql_connect.php
        selects the 'test' database!
24
25      // Check for a name.
26      if (!empty($_POST['name'])) {
27          $n = escape_data
            (htmlspecialchars($_POST['name']));
28      } else {
29          echo '<p><font color="red">You
            forgot to enter your name.</font>
            </p>';
30          $n = FALSE;
31      }
```

(script continues on next page)

To handle HTML in form submissions:

1. Open handle_comments.php (Script 10.3) in your text editor or IDE.

2. Change the assignment of the $n variable (**Script 10.4**).

   ```
   $n = escape_data(htmlspecialchars
   → ($_POST['name']));
   ```

   Presumably the name data would be something that might be displayed in a Web application (as on a view_comments. php page). To keep submitted information from messing up such a page, it's run through the htmlspecialchars() function prior to escape_data(). So, any double quotation mark in $_POST['name'] will be turned into ", and < and > will become < and > respectively. Then the escape_data() function will do its thing, escaping problematic characters like the single quotation mark.

3. Repeat the change for the comments field.

   ```
   $c = escape_data(htmlspecialchars
   → ($_POST['comments']));
   ```

   As you've already seen (Figures 10.8 and 10.9), the comments field could be used maliciously, so its value should be run through htmlspecialchars() as well.

4. Alter the thank-you message so that it also prints out the safe version of the user's comments.

   ```
   echo '<p>Thank you for your
   → comments: <br />' .
   → stripslashes($c) . '</p>';
   ```

   To demonstrate how the htmlspecial- chars() function affects a string, I'll print out the value of $c. But since $c is also derived by calling the escape_data() function, I want to strip any slashes from it first.

continues on page 391

HANDLING HTML

Script 10.4 *continued*

```
32
33      // Check for comments (assume at least 5 characters).
34      if (!empty($_POST['comments'])) {
35          $c = escape_data(htmlspecialchars($_POST['comments']));
36      } else {
37          echo '<p><font color="red">You forgot to enter your comments.</font></p>';
38          $c = FALSE;
39      }
40
41      // Check for the stamp.
42      if (strlen($_POST['stamp']) == 32 ) {
43          $s = escape_data($_POST['stamp']);
44      } else {
45          echo '<p><font color="red">This page has been accessed in error.</font></p>';
46          $s = FALSE;
47      }
48
49      if ($n && $c && $s) { // If everything's OK.
50
51          // Enter the record into the database.
52          $query = "INSERT INTO comments (name, comment, stamp) VALUES ('$n', '$c', '$s')";
53          $result = @mysql_query ($query); // Run the query.
54
55          if (mysql_affected_rows() == 1) { // A record was added.
56              echo '<p>Thank you for your comments: <br />' . stripslashes($c) . '</p>';
57          } else { // Insert failed.
58              echo '<p><font color="red">Your comments could not be added.</font></p>';
                // Public message.
59              echo mysql_error() . '<br /><br />Query: ' . $query; // Debugging message.
60          }
61
62      } else { // Error occurred.
63          echo '<p><font color="red">Please go back and try again.</font></p>';
64      }
65
66      mysql_close(); // Close the database connection.
67
68  } else { // Form mismatch.
69      echo '<p><font color="red">This page has been accessed in error.</font></p>';
70  }
71
72  ?>
73  </body>
74  </html>
```

HANDLING HTML

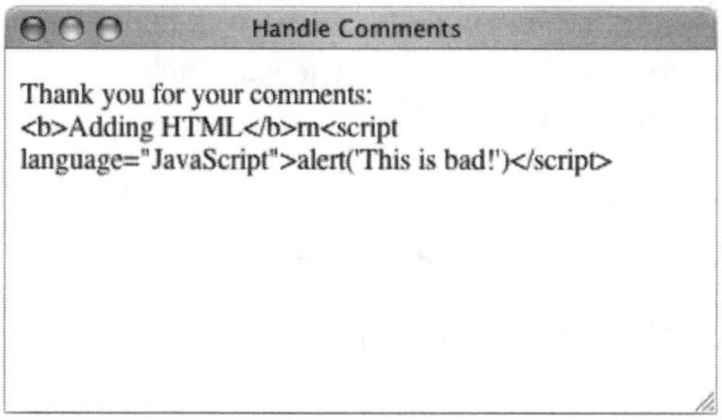

Figure 10.10 Thanks to the `htmlspecialchars()` function, malicious code entered into the comments field (see Figure 10.8) is rendered inert.

5. Save the page as `handle_comments.php`, upload to your Web server, and test in your Web browser (**Figure 10.10**).

✔ Tips

■ Both `htmlspecialchars()` and `htmlentities()` take an optional parameter indicating how quotation marks should be handled. See the PHP manual for specifics.

■ The `strip_tags()` function takes an optional parameter indicating what tags should not be stripped.

```
$var = strip_tags ($var, '<p><br />');
```

■ The `strip_tags()` function will remove even invalid HTML tags, which may cause problems. For example, `strip_tags()` will yank out all of the code it thinks is an HTML tag, even if it's improperly formed, like *<b I forgot to close the tag*.

■ Unrelated to security but quite useful is the `nl2br()` function. It turns every return (such as those entered into a text area) into an HTML `<br />` tag. If applied in this example, you wouldn't see the *rn* after `</b>` in Figure 10.10 (the *rn* is the stripped version of \r\n, which was created by the Return after `</b>` in Figure 10.8).

Validating Data by Type

For the most part, the form validation I've demonstrated has been rather minimal, often just checking if a variable has any value at all. In many situations, this really is the best you can do. For example, there's no clear pattern for what a valid street address is or what a user might enter into a comments field. Still, much of the data you'll work with can be validated in stricter ways. Later in the chapter, the sophisticated concept of regular expressions will demonstrate just that. But here I'll cover the more approachable ways you can validate some data by type.

PHP supports many types of data: strings, numbers (integers and floats), arrays, and so on. For each of these, there's a specific function that checks if a variable is of that type (**Table 10.1**). You've probably already seen the is_numeric() function in action in earlier chapters, and is_array() is a great for confirming a variable's type before attempting to use it in a foreach loop.

In PHP, you can even change a variable's type, after it's been assigned a value. Doing so is called *type casting* and is accomplished by preceding a variable's name by the type in parentheses:

```
$var = 20.2;

echo (int) $var; // 20
```

Depending upon the original and destination types, PHP will convert the variable's value accordingly:

```
$var = 20;

echo (float) $var; // 20.0
```

With numeric values, the conversion is straightforward, but with other variable types, more complex rules apply:

```
$var = 'trout';

echo (int) $var; // 0
```

In most circumstances you don't need to cast a variable from one type to another, as PHP will often automatically do so as needed. But forcibly casting a variable's type can be a good security measure in your Web applications. To show how you might use this notion, I'll create a calculator script for determining the total purchase price of an item, similar to that defined in earlier chapters.

Type Validation Functions

FUNCTION	CHECKS FOR
is_array()	Arrays
is_bool()	Booleans (TRUE, FALSE)
is_float()	Floating-point numbers
is_int()	Integers
is_null()	NULLs
is_numeric()	Numeric values, even as a string (e.g., "20")
is_resource()	Resources, like a database connection
is_scalar()	Scalar (single-valued) variables
is_string()	Strings

Table 10.1 These functions return TRUE if the submitted variable is of a certain type and FALSE otherwise.

Script 10.5 By type-casting variables, this script more definitively validates that data is of the correct format.

```
script
1    <!DOCTYPE html PUBLIC "-//W3C//DTD XHTML
     1.0 Transitional//EN"
2           "http://www.w3.org/TR/xhtml1/DTD/
            xhtml1-transitional.dtd">
3    <html xmlns="http://www.w3.org/1999/xhtml"
     xml:lang="en" lang="en">
4    <head>
5      <meta http-equiv="content-type" content=
       "text/html; charset=iso-8859-1" />
6      <title>Widget Cost Calculator</title>
7    </head>
8    <body>
9    <?php # Script 10.5 - calculator.php
10
11   // Check if the form has been submitted.
12   if (isset($_POST['submitted'])) {
13
14     // Cast all the variables to a specific
       type.
15     $quantity = (int) $_POST['quantity'];
16     $price = (float) $_POST['price'];
17     $tax = (float) $_POST['tax'];
18
```

(script continues on page 395)

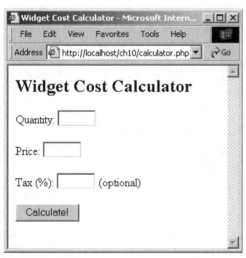

Figure 10.11 The HTML form takes three inputs: a quantity, a price, and a tax rate.

To use type casting:

1. Begin a new PHP document in your text editor or IDE (**Script 10.5**).

   ```
   <!DOCTYPE html PUBLIC "-//W3C//DTD
   → XHTML 1.0 Transitional//EN"
   "http://www.w3.org/TR/xhtml1/DTD/
   → xhtml1-transitional.dtd">
   <html xmlns="http://www.w3.org/1999/
   → xhtml" xml:lang="en" lang="en">
   <head>
     <meta http-equiv="content-type"
   → content="text/html; charset=
   → iso-8859-1" />
     <title>Widget Cost Calculator
   → </title>
   </head>
   <body>
   <?php # Script 10.5 - calculator.php
   ```

2. Check if the form has been submitted.

   ```
   if (isset($_POST['submitted'])) {
   ```

   Like many previous examples, this one script will both display the HTML form and handle its submission. By checking for the presence of a specific $_POST element, I'll know if the form has been submitted.

3. Cast all the variables to a specific type.

   ```
   $quantity = (int) $_POST
   → ['quantity'];
   $price = (float) $_POST['price'];
   $tax = (float) $_POST['tax'];
   ```

   The form itself has three text boxes (**Figure 10.11**), into which practically anything could be typed (there's no number type of input for HTML forms). But I know that the quantity must be an integer and that both price and tax should be floats (contain decimal points). To force the issue, I'll cast each one to a specific type.

   continues on next page

393

4. Check if the variables have proper values, and then calculate and print the results.

```
if ( ($quantity > 0) && ($price > 0)
→ && ($tax > 0)) {
   $total = ($quantity * $price) *
   → (($tax/100) + 1);
   echo '<p>The total cost of
   → purchasing ' . $quantity . '
   → widget(s) at $' . number_format
   → ($price, 2) . ' each is $' .
   → number_format ($total, 2) .
   → '.</p>';
```

Besides knowing what type each variable should be, I also know that they must all be positive numbers. This conditional checks for that prior to performing the calculations.

The calculation itself and the printing of the results proceed much as in previous examples of the calculator. Essentially the quantity is multiplied by the price. This is then multiplied by the tax divided by 100 (so 8% becomes *.08*) plus 1 (*1.08*). The number_format() function is used to print both the price and total values in the proper format.

5. Complete the conditionals.

```
   } else {
      echo '<p><font color="red">
      → Please enter a valid quantity,
      → price, and tax rate.</font>
      → </p>';
   }
}
```

6. Create the HTML form.

```
?>
<h2>Widget Cost Calculator</h2>
<form action="calculator.php"
→ method="post">
   <p>Quantity: <input type="text"
   → name="quantity" size="5"
   → maxlength="10" value="<?php if
   → (isset($quantity)) echo
   → $quantity; ?>" /></p>
   <p>Price: <input type="text"
   → name="price" size="5"
   → maxlength="10" value="<?php if
   → (isset($price)) echo $price;
   → ?>" /></p>
   <p>Tax (%): <input type="text"
   → name="tax" size="5"
   → maxlength="10" value="<?php
   → if (isset($tax)) echo $tax;
   → ?>" /> (optional)</p>
   <p><input type="submit"
   → name="submit" value="Calculate!"
   → /></p>
   <input type="hidden"
   → name="submitted" value="TRUE" />
</form>
```

The HTML form is fairly simple. I did give the inputs a sticky quality, so the user can see what was previously entered. By referring to $quantity etc. instead of $_POST['quantity'] etc., the form will reflect the value for each input *as it was type-casted.*

7. Complete the HTML code.

```
</body>
</html>
```

continues on page 396

Script 10.5 *continued*

```
 19    // All variables should be positive!
 20    if ( ($quantity > 0) && ($price > 0) && ($tax > 0)) {
 21
 22       // Calculate the total.
 23       $total = ($quantity * $price) * (($tax/100) + 1);
 24
 25       // Print the result.
 26       echo '<p>The total cost of purchasing ' . $quantity . ' widget(s) at $' . number_format
          ($price, 2) . ' each is $' . number_format ($total, 2) . '.</p>';
 27
 28    } else { // Invalid submitted values.
 29       echo '<p><font color="red">Please enter a valid quantity, price, and tax rate.</font></p>';
 30    }
 31
 32 } // End of main isset() IF.
 33
 34 // Leave the PHP section and create the HTML form.
 35 ?>
 36 <h2>Widget Cost Calculator</h2>
 37 <form action="calculator.php" method="post">
 38    <p>Quantity: <input type="text" name="quantity" size="5" maxlength="10" value="<?php if
       (isset($quantity)) echo $quantity; ?>" /></p>
 39    <p>Price: <input type="text" name="price" size="5" maxlength="10" value="<?php if
       (isset($price)) echo $price; ?>" /></p>
 40    <p>Tax (%): <input type="text" name="tax" size="5" maxlength="10" value="<?php if (isset($tax))
       echo $tax; ?>" /> (optional)</p>
 41    <p><input type="submit" name="submit" value="Calculate!" /></p>
 42    <input type="hidden" name="submitted" value="TRUE" />
 43 </form>
 44 </body>
 45 </html>
```

VALIDATING DATA BY TYPE

8. Save the file as calculator.php, upload it to your Web server, and test in your Web browser (**Figures 10.12** and **10.13**).

✔ Tips

■ You should definitely use type casting when working with numbers within SQL queries. Numbers aren't quoted in queries, so if a string is somehow used in a number's place, there will be a SQL syntax error. If you type-cast such variables to an integer or float first, the query may not work (in terms of returning a record) but will still be syntactically valid. You'll frequently see this in the book's last three chapters.

■ As I implied, regular expressions are a more advanced method of data validation and are sometimes your best bet. But using type-based validation, when feasible, will certainly be faster (in terms of processor speed) and less prone to programmer error (did I mention that regular expressions are complex?).

■ To repeat myself, the rules of how values are converted from one data type to another are somewhat complex. If you want to get into the details, see the PHP manual.

■ The gettype() function returns the type of a submitted variable.

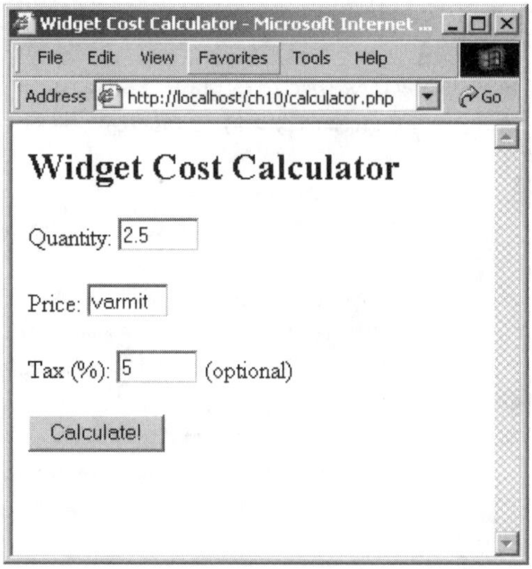

Figure 10.12 If invalid values are entered, such as floats for the quantity or strings for the price...

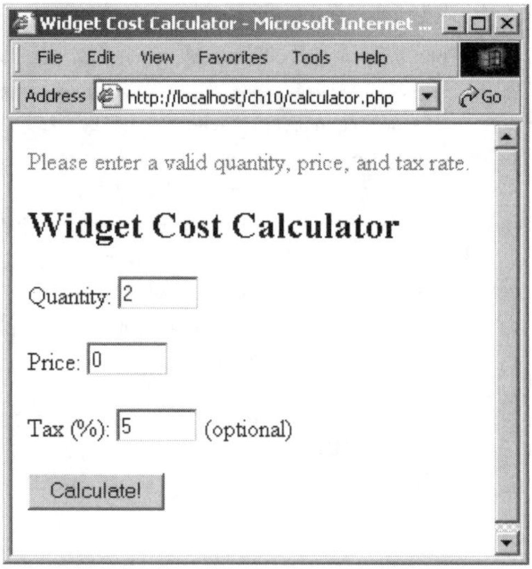

Figure 10.13 ...they'll be cast into more appropriate formats.

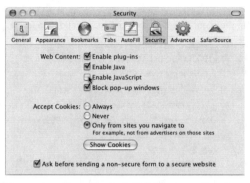

Figure 10.14 Most of today's Web browsers allow for disabling all JavaScript.

Form Validation with JavaScript

JavaScript is not a true security measure in itself, but rather an added level of security and a convenience to your users. Because JavaScript is a client-side technology (whereas PHP is server-side), incorporating it into your pages can save users the hassle of having to send the form data back to the server before seeing there are problems. Instead, you can use JavaScript to immediately run through some tests and then, if the data passes, send the form information along to PHP.

I say that JavaScript in itself is not a security measure because it can be easily turned off in a user's browser (**Figure 10.14**), rendering it completely useless. It is critical that you view JavaScript in this light and continue to use PHP as your primary security measure.

As a demonstration of this, I'll create a form for submitting URLs. Some basic, easy-to-follow JavaScript will be incorporated to validate the data in the Web browser. In the next section of this chapter, PHP scripts will further check the submitted data using regular expressions.

To validate forms with JavaScript:

1. Create a new HTML document in your text editor (**Script 10.6**).

   ```
   <!DOCTYPE html PUBLIC "-//W3C//DTD
   → XHTML 1.0 Transitional//EN"
   "http://www.w3.org/TR/xhtml1/DTD/
   → xhtml1-transitional.dtd">
   <html xmlns="http://www.w3.org/1999/
   → xhtml" xml:lang="en" lang="en">
   <head>
      <meta http-equiv="content-type"
      → content="text/html; charset=
      → iso-8859-1" />
      <title>Submit a URL</title>
   ```

   For this example, I'll be making one HTML page that displays the form and a separate PHP script that handles it.

2. Create a JavaScript section and begin a function.

   ```
   <script type="text/javascript"
   → language="Javascript">
   <!-- // Hide script contents from old
   → browsers.
   function check_data(my_form) {
      var problem = false;
   ```

   JavaScript can go anywhere within an HTML document using the script tags, but preferably it'll be placed within the HTML head.

   The check_data() function will be called when the form is submitted. Its only purpose will be to validate all the form inputs. This function receives one argument: the form being validated. The problem variable (variables in JavaScript do not use an initial dollar sign) will be used as a flag indicating if there are any problems.

Script 10.6 The submit_url.html page uses JavaScript in the client (the Web browser) to prevalidate a form.

```
script
1    <!DOCTYPE html PUBLIC "-//W3C//DTD XHTML
     1.0 Transitional//EN"
2            "http://www.w3.org/TR/xhtml1/DTD/
             xhtml1-transitional.dtd">
3    <html xmlns="http://www.w3.org/1999/xhtml"
     xml:lang="en" lang="en">
4    <head>
5        <meta http-equiv="content-type" content=
         "text/html; charset=iso-8859-1" />
6        <title>Submit a URL</title>
7
8        <script type="text/javascript"
         language="Javascript">
9        <!-- // Hide script contents from old
         browsers.
10
11       function check_data(my_form) {
12
13          var problem = false; // Flag
             variable.
14
15          // Validate the name.
16          if (my_form.name.value == "") {
17             alert ("Enter your name.");
18             my_form.name.value = "*** Name";
19             my_form.name.focus();
20             problem = true;
21          }
22
23          // Validate the email.
24          if (my_form.email.value == "") {
25             alert ("Enter your email
                address.");
26             my_form.email.value = "*** Email
                Address";
27             my_form.email.focus();
28             problem = true;
29          }
30
```

(script continues on next page)

Script 10.6 *continued*

```
                   script
31        // Validate the URL.
32        if (my_form.url.value == "") {
33            alert ("Enter the URL.");
34            my_form.url.value = "*** URL";
35            my_form.url.focus();
36            problem = true;
37        }
38
```

(script continues on page 401)

Figure 10.15 JavaScript's alert() function will make a pop-up box like this one.

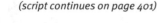

Figure 10.16 JavaScript's focus() function will highlight an element like the text box here (the actual results will vary by browser).

3. Validate that the user entered a name.

```
if (my_form.name.value == "") {
    alert ("Enter your name.");
    my_form.name.value = "*** Name";
    my_form.name.focus();
    problem = true;
}
```

A barebones validation checks that the field isn't empty. To do so, I refer to the field's value, using the *formname.fieldname. value* syntax. If the user did not enter a value, then an alert pop-up window will be created (**Figure 10.15**) by the alert() line. Next, the *name* field will be given the value of **** Name* to highlight it, and the user's attention will be directed to the name field in the Web browser (**Figure 10.16**) via JavaScript's focus() method. Finally, if there was a problem, the problem variable is set to *true*.

4. Repeat the process for the email address and the URL.

```
if (my_form.email.value == "") {
    alert ("Enter your email
→ address.");
    my_form.email.value = "*** Email
→ Address";
    my_form.email.focus();
    problem = true;
}
if (my_form.url.value == "") {
    alert ("Enter the URL.");
    my_form.url.value = "*** URL";
    my_form.url.focus();
    problem = true;
}
```

The two validation routines are variants on the steps taken to check the name input, replacing instances of *name* with *email* and *url* accordingly.

continues on next page

FORM VALIDATION WITH JAVASCRIPT

5. Validate that a URL category was selected.

```
if ((my_form.url_category.
→ selectedIndex == 0) || (my_form.
→ url_category.value == 0) ) {
    alert ("Please select a category
    → for this URL.");
    problem = true;
}
```

Using JavaScript on pull-down menus is one of the many ways in which Web browsers differ. The `my_form.url_cate-gory.value == 0` code will work for some browsers, but you have to use `my_form.url_category.selectedIndex == 0` for others to function properly. I've included both as my conditional with an OR (the double pipe) linking them.

6. Check if there was a problem and then complete the JavaScript.

```
    if (problem) {
        return false;
    } else {
        return true;
    }
}
//-->
</script>
```

The logic here may seem a little backward, so I'll explain in detail. The value returned by this function—*true* or *false*—determines whether or not the form will be submitted to the handling page (*true* means go ahead and submit the data). If a problem was found, then *false* should be returned, indicating that the form data should not be submitted.

Turning to the `problem` variable, it was initially assigned the value of *false* (i.e., no problem exists). If the form passed all four tests, `problem` will still be equal to *false* and the function can return *true*, indicating that the data is valid. If the form failed one or more tests, `problem` will be equal to *true*, so the function should return *false*, leaving the user on this form page.

7. Complete the HTML head, begin the body, and start the form.

```
</head>
<body>
<!-- Script 10.6 - submit_url.html -->
<form name="url_form"
→ action="handle_submit_url.php"
→ method="post" onsubmit="return
→ check_data(this)">
```

When validating forms with JavaScript, the most important line of code is this last one here, which begins the form. In it, I have named the form (*url_form*) and requested that when the submit button is pressed (`onsubmit`), the `check_data()` function be called. The function call passes the current object—in JavaScript `this` always refers to the current object—to the `check_data()` function.

continues on page 402

Script 10.6 *continued*

```
                                 script

39          // Validate the URL category.
40          if ((my_form.url_category.selectedIndex == 0) || (my_form.url_category.value == 0) ) {
41              alert ("Please select a category for this URL.");
42              problem = true;
43          }
44
45          // Return true/false based upon problem.
46          if (problem) {
47              return false;
48          } else {
49              return true;
50          }
51
52      } // End of function definition.
53
54      //-->
55      </script>
56
57   </head>
58   <body>
59   <!-- Script 10.6 - submit_url.html -->
60
61   <form name="url_form" action="handle_submit_url.php" method="post" onsubmit="return
     check_data(this)">
62
```

(script continues on next page)

FORM VALIDATION WITH JAVASCRIPT

8. Complete the form.

```
<fieldset><legend>Enter your
→ information in the form below:
→ </legend>
<p><b>Your Name:</b> <input
→ type="text" name="name" size="40"
→ maxlength="60" /></p>
<p><b>Email Address:</b> <input
→ type="text" name="email" size="40"
→ maxlength="60" /> </p>
<p><b>URL:</b> <input type="text"
→ name="url" size="40"
→ maxlength="80" /></p>
<p><b>URL Category:</b> <select
→ name="url_category">
  <option>Choose One</option>
  <option value="3">Code Libraries
  → </option>
  <option value="6">General Database
  → </option>
  <option value="5">General MySQL
  → </option>
  <option value="1">General PHP
  → </option>
  <option value="4">Programming
  → </option>
  <option value="2">Web Development
  → </option>
</select></p>
</fieldset>
<div align="center"><input
→ type="submit" name="submit"
→ value="Submit" /></div>
</form>
```

In the formal application of this script in Chapter 12, "Example—Content Management," I'll generate the pull-down menu using the *content* database. For now I've hard-coded the *url_category* values (although they do correlate to those established in Chapter 5, "Advanced SQL and MySQL").

Script 10.6 *continued*

```
                      script
63    <fieldset><legend>Enter your
      information in the form below:</legend>
64
65    <p><b>Your Name:</b> <input type="text"
      name="name" size="40" maxlength="60"
      /></p>
66
67    <p><b>Email Address:</b> <input
      type="text" name="email" size="40"
      maxlength="60" /> </p>
68
69    <p><b>URL:</b> <input type="text"
      name="url" size="40" maxlength="80"
      /></p>
70
71    <p><b>URL Category:</b> <select
      name="url_category">
72      <option>Choose One</option>
73      <option value="3">Code Libraries
        </option>
74      <option value="6">General Database
        </option>
75      <option value="5">General MySQL
        </option>
76      <option value="1">General PHP
        </option>
77      <option value="4">Programming
        </option>
78      <option value="2">Web Development
        </option>
79    </select></p>
80
81    </fieldset>
82    <div align="center"><input type="submit"
      name="submit" value="Submit" /></div>
83
84  </form>
85  </body>
86  </html>
```

FORM VALIDATION WITH JAVASCRIPT

Figure 10.17 A pop-up alert will be created if any field is omitted.

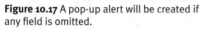

Figure 10.18 Each text field that is not filled out is highlighted using asterisks.

■ JavaScript does support regular expressions, although only in more recent versions of the language. For the code to be more backward-compatible, I avoided using JavaScript regular expressions here.

■ Online surveys claim that anywhere between 10 and 20 percent of Web users do not have JavaScript enabled in their Web browsers.

9. Finish the HTML page.

   ```
   </body>
   </html>
   ```

10. Save the file as `submit_url.html` and test in your Web browser (**Figures 10.17** and **10.18**).

    You do not need to upload this to your Web server if you would prefer not to, since it's a simple HTML page. In any case, once the form passes validation, you'll see a *Page Not Found* error because the handling script has yet to be written.

✔ Tips

■ Another way to refer to a form's element is to use the formal *document.form-name.inputname* syntax. By passing the `check_data()` function the form (`this`), I was able to refer just to `my_form.input-name`, which I find to be easier.

■ Many people find alert prompts to be annoying (because, well, they are). When using JavaScript to validate forms, you may want to reserve alert boxes for only the most critical fields.

■ Alternatively, you can check for empty fields by seeing if their length—the number of characters entered—is less than or equal to 0. The code would be

   ```
   if (my_form.inputname.value.
   → length <= 0)
   ```

■ Using JavaScript for security is kind of like having a *This house is protected by...* sticker on your site's window: it implies that security measures are in force, but it does no actual protection on its own (because people can disable JavaScript).

Regular Expressions

Regular expressions are an amazingly powerful (but tedious) tool available in most of today's programming languages. Think of regular expressions as an elaborate system of matching patterns. You first write the pattern and then use one of PHP's built-in functions to apply the pattern to a text string (regular expressions are normally used with strings).

PHP supports two types of regular expressions: POSIX Extended and Perl-compatible (PCRE). The POSIX version is somewhat less powerful and potentially slower than PCRE but is far easier to learn. For this reason, I'll cover POSIX regular expressions here.

With both types of regular expressions, PHP has two functions for simple pattern matches (one case-sensitive and one not) and two for matching patterns and replacing matched text with other text (again, one case-sensitive and one not). Although I'll be using the POSIX functions here, if you are already comfortable with the Perl-compatible syntax, you need only replace the names of the POSIX functions with the PCRE equivalents in the following examples (and change the patterns accordingly).

✔ Tips

- Some text editors, such as BBEdit and emacs, allow you to use regular expressions to match and replace patterns within and throughout several documents.

- Another difference between POSIX and PCRE regular expressions is that the latter can be used on binary data while the former cannot.

Defining a pattern

Before you can use one of PHP's built-in regular expression functions, you have to be able to define a pattern that the function will use for matching purposes. PHP has a number of rules for creating a pattern. You can use these rules separately or in combination, making your pattern either quite simple or very complex.

Before I get into the rules, though, a word on the effectiveness of regular expressions. *For most cases, it is nearly impossible to write a pattern that is 100 percent accurate!* The goal, then, is to create a pattern that catches *most invalid* submissions but allows for *all valid* submissions. In other words, err on the side of being too permissive. Like most security systems, regular expressions are a deterrent, not an absolutely perfect fix. That being said, on with the show....

To explain how patterns are created, I'll start by introducing the symbols used in regular expressions, then discuss how to group characters together, and finish with character classes. Once all of this has been covered, you can begin to use this knowledge within PHP functions. As a formatting rule, I'll define my patterns within straight quotes (`'pattern'`) and will indicate what the corresponding pattern matches in *italics*.

The first type of character you will use for defining patterns is a *literal*. A literal is a value that is written exactly as it is interpreted. For example, the pattern `'a'` will match the letter *a*, `'ab'` will match *ab*, and so forth. Therefore, assuming a case-insensitive search is performed, `'rom'` will match any of the following strings since they all contain *rom*:

- ◆ CD-ROM

- ◆ Rommel crossed the desert.

- ◆ I'm writing a roman à clef.

Along with literals, your patterns will use *metacharacters*. These are special symbols that have a meaning beyond their literal value (**Table 10.2**). While `'a'` simply means *a*, the period (`.`) will match any single character (`'.'` matches *a*, *b*, *c*, the underscore, a space, etc.). To match any metacharacter, you will need to escape it, much as you escape a quotation mark to print it. Hence `'\.'` will match the period itself.

Two metacharacters specify where certain characters must be found. There is the caret (^), which will match a string that begins with the letter following the caret. There is also the dollar sign ($), for anything that ends with the preceding letter. Accordingly, `'^a'` will match any string beginning with an *a*, while `'a$'` will correspond to any string ending with an *a*. Therefore, `'^a$'` will only match *a* (a string that both begins and ends with *a*).

Regular expressions also make use of the pipe (|) as the equivalent of *or*. Therefore, `'a|b'` will match strings containing either *a* or *b*. (Using the pipe within patterns is called *alternation* or *branching*).

Next, there are three metacharacters that allow for multiple occurrences: `'a*'` will match zero or more *a*'s (no *a*'s, *a*, *aa*, *aaa*, etc.); `'a+'` matches one or more *a*'s (*a*, *aa*, *aaa*, etc., but there must be at least one); and `'a?'` will match up to one *a* (*a* or no *a*'s match). These metacharacters all act as quantifiers in your patterns, as do the curly braces.

To match a certain quantity of a letter, put the quantity between curly braces ({}), stating a specific number, just a minimum, or both a minimum and a maximum. Thus, `'a{3}'` will match *aaa*; `'a{3,}'` will match *aaa*, *aaaa*, etc. (three or more *a*'s); and `'a{3,5}'` will match just *aaa*, *aaaa*, and *aaaaa* (between three and five). **Table 10.3** lists all of the quantifiers.

Once you comprehend the basic symbols, then you can begin to use parentheses to group characters into more involved patterns. Grouping works as you might expect: `'(abc)'` will match *abc*, `'(trout)'` will match *trout*. Think of parentheses as being used to establish a new literal of a larger size. So `'(yes)|(no)'` accepts either of those two words in their entirety.

Regardless of how you combine your literals into various groups, they will only ever be useful for matching specific strings. But what if you wanted to match any four-letter lowercase word or any number sequence? For this, you define and utilize *character classes*.

continues on next page

Metacharacters

Character	Name	Meaning
^	caret	Indicates the beginning of a string
$	dollar sign	Indicates the end of a string
.	period	Any single character
|	pipe	Alternatives (or)

Table 10.2 The metacharacters have unique meanings inside of regular expressions.

Quantifiers

Character	Meaning
?	0 or 1
*	0 or more
+	1 or more
{x}	exactly *x* occurrences
{x, y}	between *x* and *y* (inclusive)
{x,}	at least *x* occurrences

Table 10.3 The quantifiers allow you to dictate how many times something can or must appear.

REGULAR EXPRESSIONS

Classes are created by placing characters within square brackets ([]). For example, you can match any one vowel with '[aeiou]' (by comparison, '(aeiou)' would match that entire five-character string). Or you can use the hyphen to indicate a range of characters: '[a-z]' is any single lowercase letter and '[A-Z]' is any uppercase, '[A-Za-z]' is any letter in general, and '[0-9]' matches any digit. As an example, '[a-z]{3}' would match *abc*, *def*, *oiw*, etc.

PHP has already defined some classes that will be most useful to you in your programming. These use a syntax like [[:*name*:]]. The [[:alpha:]] class matches letters and is the equivalent of '[A-Za-z]'.

By defining your own classes and using those already defined in PHP (**Table 10.4**), you can make better patterns for regular expressions.

Character Classes

CLASS	MEANING
[a-z]	Any lowercase letter
[a-zA-Z]	Any letter
[0-9]	Any number
[\f\r\t\n\v]	Any white space
[aeiou]	Any vowel
[[:alnum:]]	Any letter or number
[[:alpha:]]	Any letter (same as [a-zA-Z])
[[:blank:]]	Any tabs or spaces
[[:digit:]]	Any number (same as [0-9])
[[:lower:]]	Any lowercase letter
[[:upper:]]	Any uppercase letter
[[:punct:]]	Punctuation characters (. , ; : -)
[[:space:]]	Any white space

Table 10.4 Character classes are a more flexible tool for defining patterns.

✔ Tips

- Because many escaped characters within double quotation marks have special meaning, I advocate using single quotation marks to define your patterns. For example, to match a backslash using single quotes, you would code \\ (the one slash indicates that the next slash should be treated literally). To match a backslash in double quotes, you would have to code \\\\.

- When using curly braces to specify a number of characters, you must always include the minimum number. The maximum is optional: 'a{3}' and 'a{3,}' are acceptable, but 'a{,3}' is not.

- To include special characters (^.[]$()|*?{}\) in a pattern, they need to be escaped (a backslash put before them).

- Within the square brackets (i.e., in a class definition), the caret symbol, which is normally used to indicate an accepted beginning of a string, is used to exclude a character.

- The dollar sign and period have no special meaning inside of a class.

- To match any word that does not use punctuation, use '^[[:alpha:]]+$' (which states that the string must begin and end with only letters).

- You should never use regular expressions if you're trying to just match a literal string. In such cases, use one of PHP's string functions, which will be faster.

Matching patterns

Two functions are built in to PHP expressly for the purpose of matching a pattern within a string: ereg() and eregi() (Perl-compatible regular expressions use preg_match() instead). The only difference between the two is that ereg() treats patterns as case-sensitive, whereas eregi() is case-insensitive, making it less particular. The latter is generally recommended for common use, unless you need to be more explicit (perhaps for security purposes). Both functions will be evaluated to TRUE if the pattern is matched, FALSE if it is not. Here are two ways to use these functions (you can also hybridize the methods):

```
ereg('pattern', 'string');
```

or

```
$pattern = 'pattern';

$string = 'string';

eregi($pattern, $string);
```

The second method is easier to digest, but the first saves a step or two. If you find the examples that follow to be cumbersome, start by separating out the pattern itself as a variable.

To match a pattern:

1. Create a new PHP document in your text editor (**Script 10.7**).

   ```
   <!DOCTYPE html PUBLIC "-//W3C//DTD
   → XHTML 1.0 Transitional//EN"
   "http://www.w3.org/TR/xhtml1/DTD/
   → xhtml1-transitional.dtd">
   <html xmlns="http://www.w3.org/1999/
   → xhtml" xml:lang="en" lang="en">
   <head>
      <meta http-equiv="content-type"
      → content="text/html; charset=
      → iso-8859-1" />
      <title>Submit a URL</title>
   </head>
   <body>
   <?php # Script 10.7 - handle_submit_
   → url.php
   ```

   This script will receive the data from the form on submit_url.html (refer to Script 10.6).

   continues on next page

Script 10.7 This script handles the submit_url.html form using primarily regular expressions to validate the submitted data.

```
script
1   <!DOCTYPE html PUBLIC "-//W3C//DTD XHTML 1.0 Transitional//EN"
2        "http://www.w3.org/TR/xhtml1/DTD/xhtml1-transitional.dtd">
3   <html xmlns="http://www.w3.org/1999/xhtml" xml:lang="en" lang="en">
4   <head>
5      <meta http-equiv="content-type" content="text/html; charset=iso-8859-1" />
6      <title>Submit a URL</title>
7   </head>
8   <body>
9   <?php # Script 10.7 - handle_submit_url.php
10
```

(script continues on next page)

2. Create the error-checking variables.

```
$message = '<font color="red">The
→ following errors occurred:<br />';
$problem = FALSE;
```

The $message variable will be used to store the accumulated errors. The $problem variable (like its JavaScript counterpart) will be used to test for problems, naturally.

3. Validate the submitted name.

```
if (!eregi ('^[[:alpha:]\.\' \-]
→ {4,}$', stripslashes(trim($_POST
→ ['name'])))) {
  $problem = TRUE;
  $message .= '<p>Please enter a
  → valid name.</p>';
}
```

This conditional will check the submitted name against a particular pattern. If the submitted value does not meet the criteria of the regular expression, the $problem variable will be set to TRUE.

The pattern in question is a class consisting of [:alpha:] (all letters), the period, the apostrophe, a blank space, and the dash. The pattern says that the name must begin and end with these characters (meaning only those are allowed) and must be at least four characters long.

Each of the inputs will be stripped of any slashes (presuming that Magic Quotes is on) and trimmed of extraneous white spaces (both of which could invalidate a regular expression).

Script 10.7 *continued*

```
      ┌─────────────── script ───────────────┐
11    // Initialize the variables.
12    $message = '<font color="red">The following
      errors occurred:<br />';
13    $problem = FALSE;
14
15    // Check the name.
16    if (!eregi ('^[[:alpha:]\.\' \-]{4,}$',
      stripslashes(trim($_POST['name'])))) {
17        $problem = TRUE;
18        $message .= '<p>Please enter a valid
          name.</p>';
19    }
20
```

(script continues on next page)

Script 10.7 *continued*

```
              script

21   // Check the email address.
22   if (!eregi ('^[[:alnum:]][a-z0-9_\.\-]
     *@[a-z0-9\.\-]+\.[a-z]{2,4}$',
     stripslashes(trim($_POST['email'])))) {
23       $problem = TRUE;
24       $message .= '<p>Please enter a valid
         email address.</p>';
25   }
26
27   // Check the URL.
28   if (!eregi ('^((http|https|ftp)://)?
     ([[:alnum:]\-\.])+(\.)([[:alnum:]])
     {2,4}([[:alnum:]/+=%&_\.~?\-]*)$',
     stripslashes(trim($_POST['url'])))) {
29       $problem = TRUE;
30       $message .= '<p>Please enter a valid
         URL.</p>';
31   }
32
```

(script continues on next page)

4. Validate the email address.

```
if (!eregi ('^[[:alnum:]][a-z0-9_\.
→ \-]*@[a-z0-9\.\-]+\.[a-z]{2,4}$',
→ stripslashes(trim($_POST
→ ['email'])))) {
    $problem = TRUE;
    $message .= '<p>Please enter a
→ valid email address.</p>';
}
```

Email addresses and URLs are notoriously difficult to validate with absolute accuracy. The pattern I am using here mandates that the email address begin with a letter or number and then continue with some combination of letters, numbers, the underscore, the period, and the hyphen. An email address must have an @, which will be followed by some combination of letters, numbers, the period, and the hyphen. Finally, there will be a period, followed by a two- to four-letter string (e.g., *com*, *edu*, *uk*, *info*).

5. Validate the URL.

```
if (!eregi ('^((http|https|ftp)
→ ://)?([[:alnum:]\-\.])+(\.)([[:
→ alnum:]]){2,4}([[:alnum:]/+=%&_
→ \.~?\-]*)$', stripslashes(trim
→ ($_POST['url'])))) {
    $problem = TRUE;
    $message .= '<p>Please enter a
→ valid URL.</p>';
}
```

To validate the URL, I first check for the optional *http://*, *https://*, or *ftp://*. Then I want to see letters, numbers, or the dash, followed by a period (*sitename.*), followed by a two- to four-letter string (*com*, *edu*, etc.). Finally, I allow for the possibility of many other characters, which would constitute a specific filename, parameters being passed to it, and so forth.

continues on next page

6. Validate the URL category.

```
if (!isset($_POST['url_category'])
→ OR !is_numeric($_POST['url_
→ category'])) {
    $message .= '<p>Please select a
    → valid URL category.</p>';
    $problem = TRUE;
}
```

Since the url_category comes from a pull-down menu and should be a number, I can verify it without regular expressions.

7. Create the conditional checking on the status of the tests.

```
if (!$problem) {
    echo '<p>Thank you for the URL
    → submission.</p>';
} else {
    echo $message;
    echo '</font><p>Please go back and
    → try again.</p>';
}
```

If no problem occurred, a simple thank you is displayed (in Chapter 12 the information will be stored in the database). If any problem was found, the error message is displayed.

8. Complete the PHP code and the HTML page.

```
?>
</body>
</html>
```

Script 10.7 *continued*

```
33    // Check the URL category.
34    if (!isset($_POST['url_category']) OR
      !is_numeric($_POST['url_category'])) {
35        $message .= '<p>Please select a valid
          URL category.</p>';
36        $problem = TRUE;
37    }
38
39    if (!$problem) { // Nothing went wrong.
40        // Do whatever with the submitted
          information.
41        echo '<p>Thank you for the URL
          submission.</p>';
42    } else { // At least one test failed.
43        echo $message;
44        echo '</font><p>Please go back and try
          again.</p>';
45    }
46    ?>
47    </body>
48    </html>
```

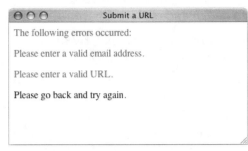

Figure 10.19 If any data fails to match the regular expressions, error messages are displayed.

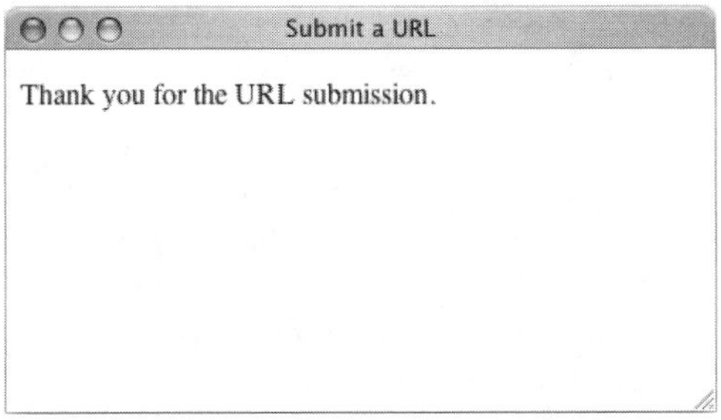

Figure 10.20 If the submitted data matches the appropriate patterns, a thank-you message is printed.

9. Save the file as handle_submit_url.php, upload to your Web server (in the same directory as submit_url.html), and test in your Web browser (**Figures 10.19** and **10.20**).

✔ Tips

- Although it demonstrates good dedication to programming to learn how to write and execute your own regular expressions, numerous working examples are available already by searching the Internet.

- Remember that regular expressions in PHP are case-sensitive by default. The eregi() function overrules this standard behavior.

- If you are looking to match an exact string within another string, use the strstr() function, which is faster than regular expressions. In fact, as a rule of thumb, you should use regular expressions only if the task at hand cannot be accomplished using any other function or technique.

Matching and replacing patterns

While the ereg() and eregi() functions are great for validating a string, you can take your programming one step further by matching a pattern and then replacing it with a slightly different pattern or with specific text. The syntax for doing so is

```
ereg_replace('pattern', 'replace',
→ 'string');
```

or

```
$pattern = 'pattern';

$replace = 'replace';

$string = 'string';

eregi_replace($pattern, $replace,
→ $string);
```

The ereg_replace() function is case-sensitive, whereas eregi_replace() is not. One reason you might want to use either function would be to turn a user-entered Web site address (a URL) into a clickable HTML link, by encapsulating it in the <a href="url"></a> tags.

There is a related concept to discuss that is involved with these two functions: *back referencing*.

In a ZIP code matching pattern—'^([0-9]{5})(\-[0-9]{4})?$'—there are two groupings within parentheses (the first representing the obligatory initial five digits and the second representing the optional dash plus four-digit extension). Within a regular expression pattern, PHP will automatically number parenthetical groupings beginning at 1. Back referencing allows you to refer to each individual section by using a double backslash in front of the corresponding number. For example, if you match the ZIP code *94710-0001* with this pattern, referring back to \\1 will give you *94710*. The code \\0 refers to the whole initial string.

To match and replace a pattern:

1. Open handle_submit_url.php (refer to Script 10.7) in your text editor.

2. Add the following to the email validation (**Script 10.8**).

```
} else {
    $email = eregi_replace ('^[[:
    → alnum:]][a-z0-9_\.\-]*@[a-z0-9\.
    → \-]+\.[a-z]{2,4}$', '<a href=
    → "mailto:\\0">Email</a>',
    → stripslashes(trim($_POST
    → ['email'])));
}
```

If the email address passed the original regular expression, I'll run it through eregi_replace() using that same pattern. This function will turn an email address (say phpmysql2@dmcinsights.com) into the HTML code

```
<a href="mailto:phpmysql2@
→ dmcinsights.com">Email</a>.
```

continues on page 414

Script 10.8 The modified version of the `handle_submit_url.php` script uses `eregi_replace()` to create new strings based upon matched patterns in existing ones.

```
1    <!DOCTYPE html PUBLIC "-//W3C//DTD XHTML 1.0 Transitional//EN"
2         "http://www.w3.org/TR/xhtml1/DTD/xhtml1-transitional.dtd">
3    <html xmlns="http://www.w3.org/1999/xhtml" xml:lang="en" lang="en">
4    <head>
5      <meta http-equiv="content-type" content="text/html; charset=iso-8859-1" />
6      <title>Submit a URL</title>
7    </head>
8    <body>
9    <?php # Script 10.8 - handle_submit_url.php
10   # 2nd version after Script 10.7
11
12   // Initialize the variables.
13   $message = '<font color="red">The following errors occurred:<br />';
14   $problem = FALSE;
15
16   // Check the name.
17   if (!eregi ('^[[:alpha:]\.\' \-]{4,}$', stripslashes(trim($_POST['name'])))) {
18      $problem = TRUE;
19      $message .= '<p>Please enter a valid name.</p>';
20   }
21
22   // Check the email address.
23   if (!eregi ('^[[:alnum:]][a-z0-9_\.\-]*@[a-z0-9\.\-]+\.[a-z]{2,4}$', stripslashes(trim($_POST
     ['email'])))) {
24      $problem = TRUE;
25      $message .= '<p>Please enter a valid email address.</p>';
26   } else {
27      $email = eregi_replace ('^[[:alnum:]][a-z0-9_\.\-]*@[a-z0-9\.\-]+\.[a-z]{2,4}$',
        '<a href="mailto:\\0">Email</a>', stripslashes(trim($_POST['email'])));
28   }
```

(script continues on next page)

REGULAR EXPRESSIONS

3. Replace the URL validation with these lines:

```
if (eregi ('^((http|https|ftp)
→ ://)([[:alnum:]\-\.])+(\.)([[:
→ alnum:]]){2,4}([[:alnum:]/+=%&_\.
→ ~?\-]*)$', stripslashes(trim
→ ($_POST['url'])))) {
    $url = eregi_replace ('^((http|
    → https|ftp)://)([[:alnum:]\-\.])+
    → (\.)([[:alnum:]]){2,4}([[:
    → alnum:]/+=%&_\.~?\-]*)$', '<a
    → href="\\0">\\0</a>', stripslashes
    → (trim($_POST['url'])));
} elseif (eregi ('^([[:alnum:]]
→ \-\.])+(\.)([[:alnum:]]){2,4}
→ ([[:alnum:]/+=%&_\.~?\-]*)$',
→ stripslashes(trim($_POST['url']
→ )))) {
    $url = eregi_replace ('^([[:
    → alnum:]\-\.])+(\.)([[:alnum:]])
    → {2,4}([[:alnum:]/+=%&_\.~?\-
    → ]*)$', '<a href="http://\\0">
    → \\0</a>', stripslashes(trim
    → ($_POST['url'])));
} else {
    $problem = TRUE;
    $message .= '<p>Please enter a
    → valid URL.</p>';
}
```

This is a more complicated extension of the previous example. Here I'll first test for whether or not the initial *http://*, *https://*, or *ftp://* string is present. If it is (and the URL matches the overall pattern), the entire URL will be used in creating an HTML link.

If that initial string is not present, the HTML link will manually include it, followed by the submitted value.

Script 10.8 *continued*

```
script
29
30  // Check the URL.
31  if (eregi ('^((http|https|ftp)://)
    ([[:alnum:]\-\.])+(\.)([[:alnum:]])
    {2,4}([[:alnum:]/+=%&_\.~?\-]*)$',
    stripslashes(trim($_POST['url'])))) {
32      $url = eregi_replace
        ('^((http|https|ftp)://)([[:alnum:]
        \-\.])+(\.)([[:alnum:]]){2,4}
        ([[:alnum:]/+=%&_\.~?\-]*)$',
        '<a href="\\0">\\0</a>', stripslashes
        (trim($_POST['url'])));
33  } elseif (eregi ('^([[:alnum:]\-\.])+
        (\.)([[:alnum:]]){2,4}([[:alnum:]/+=%&_
        \.~?\-]*)$', stripslashes(trim($_POST
        ['url'])))) {
34      $url = eregi_replace ('^([[:alnum:]]
        \-\.])+(\.)([[:alnum:]]){2,4}([[:alnum:]
        /+=%&_\.~?\-]*)$', '<a href="http:
        //\\0">\\0</a>', stripslashes(trim
        ($_POST['url'])));
35  } else {
36      $problem = TRUE;
37      $message .= '<p>Please enter a valid
            URL.</p>';
38  }
39
40  // Check the URL category.
41  if (!isset($_POST['url_category']) OR
        !is_numeric($_POST['url_category'])) {
42      $message .= '<p>Please select a valid
            URL category.</p>';
43      $problem = TRUE;
44  }
45
46  if (!$problem) { // Nothing went wrong.
47      // Do whatever with the submitted
            information.
```

(script continues on next page)

Script 10.8 *continued*

```
48    echo "<p>Thank you for the URL
      submission. We have received the
      following information:</p>\n{$_POST
      ['name']}<br />\n$email<br />\n$url";
49    } else { // At least one test failed.
50      echo $message;
51      echo '</font><p>Please go back and try
      again.</p>';
52    }
53    ?>
54    </body>
55    </html>
```

Figure 10.21 The form now prints out the values submitted and creates links using the email address and URL.

4. Change the problem conditional so that the first part reads

```
echo "<p>Thank you for the URL
→ submission. We have received
→ the following information:</p>
→ \n{$_POST['name']}<br />\
→ n$email<br />\n$url";
```

The thank-you message will now also print out the submitted values, including the reformatted email address and URL.

5. Save the file, upload to your Web server, and test in your Web browser (**Figure 10.21**).

6. View the page source to see the results of the eregi_replace() function (**Figure 10.22**).

✔ Tips

■ The ereg() and eregi() functions will also return matched patterns in an optional third argument, meaning that the code in this example could be replicated using those two functions.

■ PHP's split() function works like explode() in that it turns a string into an array, but it allows you to use regular expressions to define your separator.

■ The Perl-compatible version of the ereg_replace() function is preg_replace().

Figure 10.22 The HTML source of the page shows the generated links.

Database Security and Encryption

As a brief conclusion to this chapter, I should mention a few of the security issues to consider when using and administering your databases. Then I will demonstrate a few more MySQL functions that can be used to encrypt and decrypt data.

Security practices

If you have administrative-level control over your database, you should keep in mind the following:

◆ Do not allow anonymous users to connect to MySQL.

◆ Always require a password to connect to MySQL.

◆ Require users to also specify a hostname. This limits from what computers users can and cannot access MySQL (although this requirement can be tedious).

◆ Assign each user the absolute minimum required privileges.

◆ Limit the root user to *localhost* access only.

◆ Delete the *test* database, which, by default, any user can access.

◆ Delete unused user accounts.

◆ When storing sensitive information in a table, particularly passwords, protect the data first using an encryption function.

◆ Validate user-submitted data before inserting it into a database as discussed earlier in the chapter and throughout the book.

◆ Use the .php extension for the file containing your database connectivity information.

◆ If at all possible, store the database connection script outside of the Web root directory.

Most of these issues relate to permissions, which is discussed in Appendix A, "Installation."

Encryption

MySQL has several encryption and decryption functions built into the software. You've already seen one of these, SHA(), since I've been using it to encrypt passwords stored in the database.

Another function, ENCRYPT(), is like SHA() in that it encrypts a string but differs in that you can add a *salt* parameter to help randomize the encryption process.

```
INSERT INTO users (username, password)
→ VALUES ('trout', ENCRYPT('password',
→ 'salt'));
```

ENCRYPT() uses the Unix crypt() software, so it may not be available on your particular system (in particular, on Windows). MySQL has another encryption function called DES_ENCRYPT(), usable only over an SSL connection.

Both the SHA() and ENCRYPT() functions create an encrypted string that cannot be decrypted. This is a great safety feature because it means that stored information cannot be retrieved in readable form.

If you require data to be stored in an encrypted form that can be decrypted, you'll need to use either ENCODE() and DECODE() or AES_ENCRYPT() and AES_DECRYPT(). These functions also take a *salt* argument, which helps to randomize the encryption.

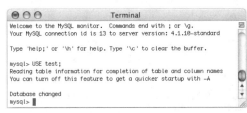

Figure 10.23 The following examples will all be run in the mysql client, on the *test* database.

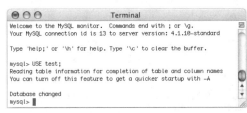

Figure 10.24 The *encode* table, consisting of only two columns, is added to the database.

```
INSERT INTO users (username, password)
→ VALUES ('trout', ENCODE('password',
→ 'salt'));

SELECT DECODE(password, 'salt') AS
→ passwd FROM users WHERE username=
→ 'trout';
```

The AES_ENCRYPT() function is considered to be the most secure encryption option, but it is only available as of MySQL version 4.0.2. Because of this restriction, I'll begin by demonstrating ENCODE() and DECODE(). To do so, I'll run some queries on the *test* database using the mysql client.

To encrypt and decrypt data:

1. Log into the mysql client and select the *test* database (**Figure 10.23**).

   ```
   USE test;
   ```

   Follow the steps outlined in Chapter 4, "Introduction to SQL and MySQL," to connect to the mysql client. Alternatively, you can use phpMyAdmin or another interface to run the queries in the following steps.

2. Create a new *encode* table (**Figure 10.24**).

   ```
   CREATE TABLE encode (
   id INT UNSIGNED NOT NULL AUTO_
   → INCREMENT,
   card_number TINYBLOB,
   PRIMARY KEY (id)
   );
   ```

   This table, *encode*, will contain fields for just an id and a (credit) card_number. The card_number will be encrypted using ENCODE() so that it can be decoded. ENCODE() returns a binary value that ought to be stored in a BLOB (or TINYBLOB here) column type.

   continues on next page

DATABASE SECURITY AND ENCRYPTION

3. Insert a new record (**Figure 10.25**).

```
INSERT INTO encode (id, card_number)
→ VALUES (NULL, ENCODE
→ (1234567890123456, 'eLL10tT'));
```

Here I am adding a new record to the table, using the ENCODE() function with a salt of *eLL10tT* to encrypt the card number. Always try to use a unique salt with your encryption functions.

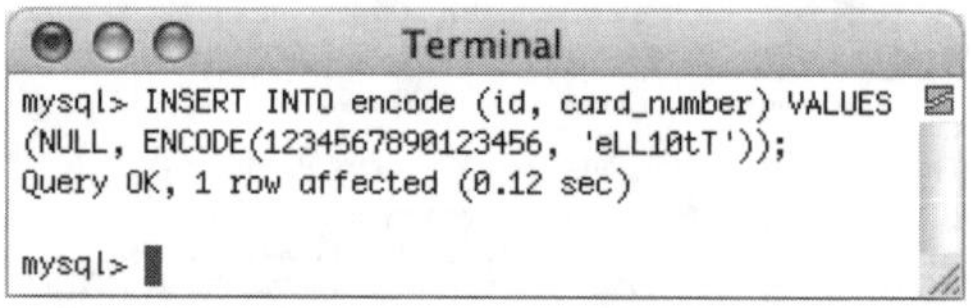

4. Retrieve the record in an unencrypted form (**Figure 10.26**).

```
SELECT id, DECODE(card_number,
→ 'eLL10tT') AS cc FROM encode;
```

This query returns all of the records, decrypting the credit card number in the process. Any value stored using ENCODE() can be retrieved (and matched) using DECODE(), as long as the same salt is used (here, *eLL10tT*).

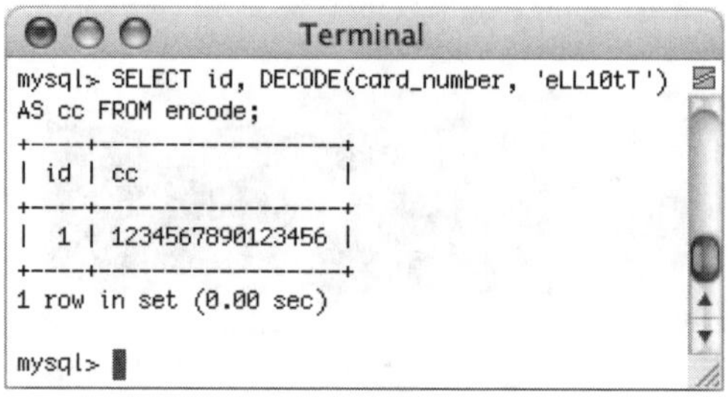

5. Check out the table's contents without using decryption (**Figure 10.27**).

```
SELECT * FROM encode;
```

As you can see in the figure, the encrypted version of the credit card number is unreadable. This is exactly the kind of security measure required by e-commerce applications.

✔ Tips

■ When using ENCRYPT(), ENCODE(), or DECODE() from a PHP script, be sure to store the salt in a secure place. Alternatively, you can use the technique demonstrated in the next section to store the salt in the database.

Figure 10.25 A record is inserted, using an encryption function to protect the credit card number.

Figure 10.26 The record has been retrieved, decrypting the credit card number in the process.

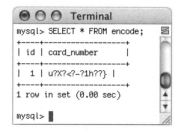

Figure 10.27 Encrypted data is stored in an unreadable format (here, as a binary string of data).

■ As a rule of thumb, use SHA() for information that will never need to be viewable, such as passwords and perhaps usernames. Use AES_ENCRYPT() (or ENCODE() on older versions of MySQL) for information that needs to be protected but may need to be viewable at a later date, such as credit card information, Social Security numbers, addresses (perhaps), and so forth.

■ The ENCRYPT() function will return a NULL value if it is not available on an operating system.

Secure salt storage

While the preceding sequence of steps demonstrates how you can add a level of security to your Web applications by encrypting and decrypting sensitive data, there's still room for improvement. For starters, the AES_ENCRYPT() function is a more secure option and is recommend if you are using MySQL 4.0.2 or later. Its syntax is the same as that of the ENCODE() function:

```
INSERT INTO users (username, userpass)
→ VALUES ('trout', AES_ENCRYPT
→ ('password', 'salt'))
```

```
SELECT AES_DECRYPT(userpass, 'salt') AS
→ passwd FROM users WHERE username=
→ 'trout'
```

Another issue is the encryption salt, which is key to the encryption process. In order for a Web application to use a salt in its queries, PHP must store this value somewhere, most likely in the database connection script (as a constant). But storing this value in a plain text format on the server makes it more vulnerable. Instead, I'll store the salt in a database table. To use it in a query without going through PHP, I then select it and assign the value to a MySQL user-set variable. To just establish a user-defined variable, use this SQL command:

```
SELECT @var:='value'
```

To define a variable based upon a value stored in a table, the syntax is

```
SELECT @var:=some_column FROM tablename
```

Once you've established @var, it can be used in other queries:

```
INSERT INTO encode (card_number) VALUES
→ (AES_ENCRYPT(1234567890123456, @var))
```

This last sequence of steps will demonstrate this approach in action.

To use a database-stored salt:

1. Log into the mysql client and select the *test* database, if you haven't already.

2. Empty the *encode* table (**Figure 10.28**).
   ```
   TRUNCATE TABLE encode;
   ```
   Because I'm going to be using a different encryption function, I'll want to clear out all the existing data before repopulating it. The TRUNCATE command is the best way to do so.

3. Create and populate an *aes_salt* table (**Figure 10.29**).
   ```
   CREATE TABLE aes_salt (
     salt VARCHAR(12) NOT NULL
   );
   INSERT INTO aes_salt (salt) VALUES
   → ('0bfuscate');
   ```

   continues on next page

Figure 10.28 Run a TRUNCATE query to empty a table.

Figure 10.29 The *aes_salt* table has one column and should only ever have one row of data. The INSERT query stores the salt value in this table.

This table, *aes_salt*, will store the encryption salt value in its one column. The INSERT query stores the salt, which will be retrieved and assigned to a user-defined variable as needed.

4. Retrieve the stored salt value and use it to insert a new record into the *encode* table (**Figure 10.30**).

```
SELECT @salt:=salt FROM aes_salt;
INSERT INTO encode (card_number)
→ VALUES (AES_ENCRYPT
→ (1234567890123456, @salt));
```

The first line retrieves the stored salt value from the *aes_salt* table and assigns this to @salt (the figure shows the results of the SELECT statement). Then a standard INSERT query is run to add a record to the *encode* table. In this case, @salt is used in the query instead of a hard-coded salt value.

5. Decrypt the stored credit card number (**Figure 10.31**).

```
SELECT @salt:=salt FROM aes_salt;
SELECT id, AES_DECRYPT(card_number,
→ @salt) AS cc FROM encode;
```

The first step retrieves the salt value so that it can be used for decryption purposes. (If you followed these steps without closing the MySQL session, this step wouldn't actually be necessary, as @salt would already be established.) The @salt variable is then used with the AES_DECRYPT() function.

Figure 10.30 These two queries show how you can use an established salt that was previously stored in a database table.

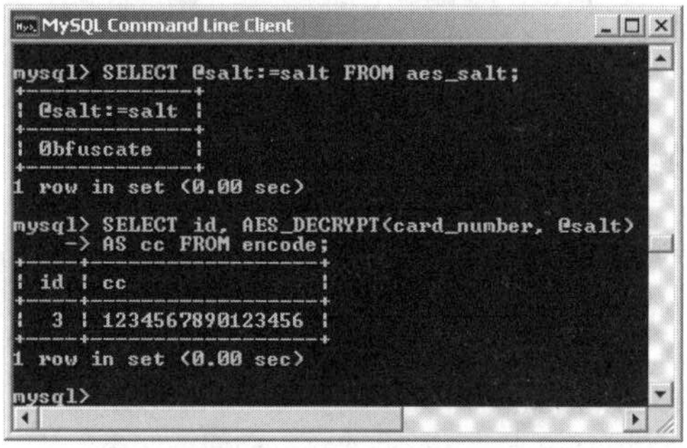

Figure 10.31 A similar process (see Figure 10.30) is used to decrypt stored information using a database-stored salt.

✔ Tips

- User variables are particular to each connection. When one script or one mysql client session connects to MySQL and establishes a variable, only that one script or sessions has access to that variable.

- Prior to version 5.0 of MySQL, user variable names are case-sensitive.

- You cannot use a user-defined variable as a parameter in a LIMIT clause.

- Never establish and use a user-defined variable within the same SQL statement.

EXPEDIA.COM
SAN JOSE INTERNATIONAL AIRPORT
WELCOME!!

956 Carlos   PAGE 2

115/1   3924   851
AUG30 05 8.08PM

TAX   2.38
AMOUNT   31.35 $

COMMENTS OR SUGGESTIONS,
PLEASE CALL (408)294-5108.

THANK YOU FOR CHOOSING
EXPEDIA.com AT THE
SAN JOSE AIRPORT

HAVE A NICE DAY

EXPEDIA.COM
SAN   INTERNATIONAL AIRPORT
WELCOME !!

9562 Carlos   PAGE 2

115/1   3924   GST 1
     AUG30'05 6:06PM

  TAX   2.39
  AMOUNT   31.35 $

  COMMENTS OR SUGGESTIONS,
PLEASE CALL (408)294-5108

   THANK YOU FOR CHOOSING
    EXPEDIA.com AT THE
    SAN JOSE AIRPORT

   HAVE A NICE DAY

EXTENDED TOPICS

This chapter represents the last of the book's "content," in which the primary focus will be on discussing new information (the remaining three chapters will deal with specific applications). The extended topics covered here are not applicable to every Web application but are certainly worth your consideration.

First up is the relatively easy task of handling file uploads with PHP. After that, I'll demonstrate how you can use PHP and JavaScript together. Third on the list is output buffering, which controls when data is sent to the Web browser.

From there I head back into the world of MySQL, starting with the set of new Improved MySQL Extension functions. These have been added to PHP in version 5 and were specifically made for working with MySQL version 4.1 and above. Then, a couple of recent additions to the MySQL software are covered, specifically transactions and prepared statements.

This chapter concludes with an introduction and demonstration of PEAR. PEAR is a special framework of PHP code that can save you lots of development and debugging time.

Not every application you write will require all of these features. In fact, the special server requirements of some of them constitute a limitation. But being aware of their existence and having an understanding of the syntax will be a great asset when the time does come to incorporate any of these concepts.

Handling File Uploads

I'm going to begin this chapter by demonstrating how to accept file uploads in your forms. Like handling any HTML form using PHP, the process of uploading a file has two dimensions. First the HTML form must be displayed, with the proper code to allow for file uploads. Then upon submission of the form, the PHP script must copy the uploaded file to the proper location.

However, for this process to work, several things must be in place:

◆ PHP must run with the proper settings.

◆ A temporary storage directory must exist with the proper permissions.

◆ The final storage directory must exist with the proper permissions.

With this in mind, I'll first adjust the server to ensure that file uploads are allowed. Then I'll create the upload script itself.

Allowing for file uploads

As I said, certain settings must be established in order for PHP to be able to handle file uploads. I'll first discuss why or when you'd need to make these adjustments before walking you through the steps.

The first issue is PHP itself. There are several settings in the `php.ini` file that dictate how PHP handles uploads, specifically dictating how large of a file can be uploaded and where the upload should temporarily be stored. Generally speaking, you'll need to edit this file if either of these two conditions apply:

◆ You installed PHP on your own Windows computer.

◆ You will be uploading very large files (larger than 2 MB).

If you don't have access to your `php.ini` file, meaning that you're using a hosted site, presumably the host has already made the necessary alterations. If you installed PHP on Mac OS X or Unix, you should also be good to go (assuming reasonable-sized files).

The second issue is the location of, and permissions on, the temporary directory. This is where PHP will store the uploaded file until your PHP script moves it to its final destination. If you installed PHP on your own Windows computer, you'll need to take steps here. Mac OS X and Unix users need not worry about this.

Finally, the final destination folder must be created and have the proper permissions established on it. This is a step that *everyone* must take for *every* application that handles file uploads. Because there are important security issues involved in this step, please also make sure that you read and understand the sidebar , "Secure Folder Permissions," on page 426.

With all of that in mind, I'll now walk you through the steps.

To prepare the server:

1. Open `php.ini` in your text editor.

If you do not know where your `php.ini` file is, see Appendix A, "Installation," which covers how to identify and edit this file. If you are not allowed to edit your `php.ini` file (if, for instance, you're using a hosted server), then presumably any necessary edits would have already been made to allow for file uploads. You can confirm this by checking the settings listed in Step 2 in a `phpinfo()` script (again, see the first appendix).

2. Under the File Uploads section (approximately line 475), adjust the following lines as needed (**Figure 11.1**):

`file_uploads = On`

`;upload_tmp_dir =`

`upload_max_filesize = 2M`

The first line dictates whether or not uploads are allowed. The second states where the uploaded files should be temporarily stored. On most operating systems, including Mac OS X and Unix, this setting can be left commented out (preceeded by a semicolon) without any problem. If you are running Windows, set this value to `C:\tmp`, making sure that the line is *not* preceded by a semicolon.

Finally, a maximum upload file size is set, in megabytes.

3. Save the `php.ini` file and restart your Web server.

How you restart your Web server depends upon the operating system and Web serving application being used. Using Apache on Mac OS X, it's just a matter of going through the System Preferences > Sharing panel.

Windows users running Apache can type

`NET STOP APACHE`

`NET START APACHE`

within a DOS prompt.

Unix and Linux users will normally use the command

`apachectl graceful`

continues on next page

```
546  ;;;;;;;;;;;;;;;;;
547  ; File Uploads ;
548  ;;;;;;;;;;;;;;;;;
549
550  ; Whether to allow HTTP file uploads.
551  file_uploads = On
552
553  ; Temporary directory for HTTP uploaded files (will use system default if not
554  ; specified).
555  ;upload_tmp_dir =
556
557  ; Maximum allowed size for uploaded files.
558  upload_max_filesize = 2M
```

Figure 11.1 Various `php.ini` settings affect your ability to manage file uploads in PHP.

4. If you are running Windows, create a `tmp` folder within `C:\` and make sure that everyone can write to that directory (**Figure 11.2**).

PHP, through your Web server, will temporarily store the uploaded file in the *upload_tmp_dir*. For this to work, the Web user (if your Web server runs as a particular user) must have permission to write to the folder.

You may not actually have to change the permissions, but to do so, depending upon what version of Windows you are running, you can normally adjust the permissions by right-clicking the folder and selecting Properties. With the Properties window, there should be a Security tab where permissions are set. It may also be under Sharing.

Mac OS X and Unix users can skip this step as the temporary directory—/tmp—has open permissions already.

5. Create a new directory, called *uploads*, in the same directory where you'll be placing the file upload script.

All of the uploaded files will be permanently stored in the *uploads* directory. If you'll be placing your script in the `C:\inetpub\wwwroot\ch11` directory, then create a `C:\inetpub\wwwroot\ch11\uploads` directory. Or if the files are going in `/Users/<username>/Sites/ch11`, make a `/Users/<username>/Sites/ch11/uploads` folder.

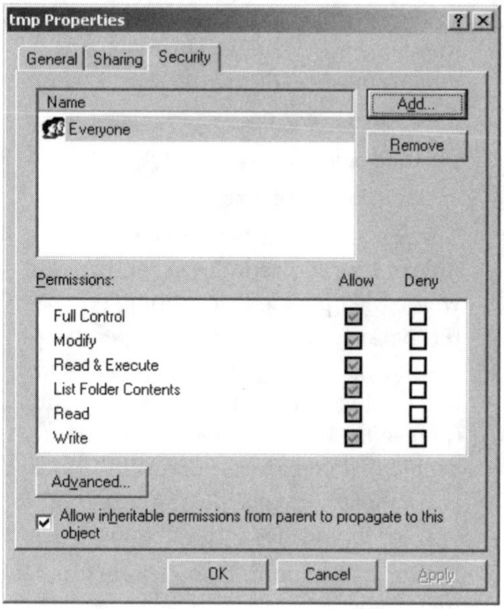

Figure 11.2 Windows users need to make sure that the `C:\tmp` directory is writable.

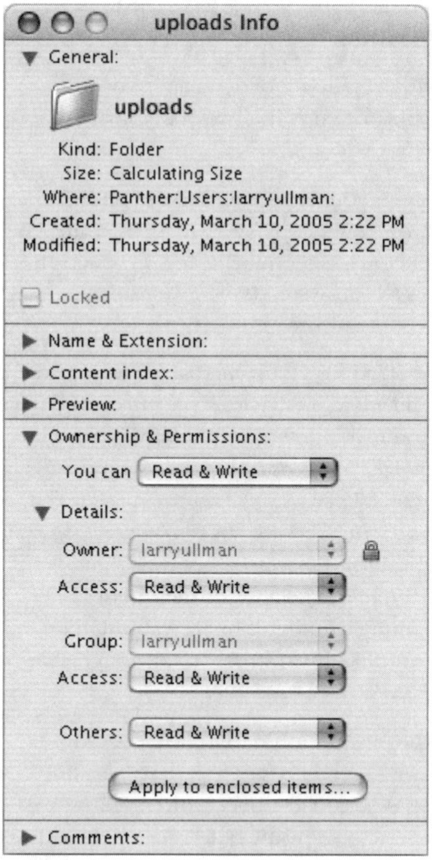

Figure 11.3 Adjusting the properties on the *uploads* folder in Mac OS X.

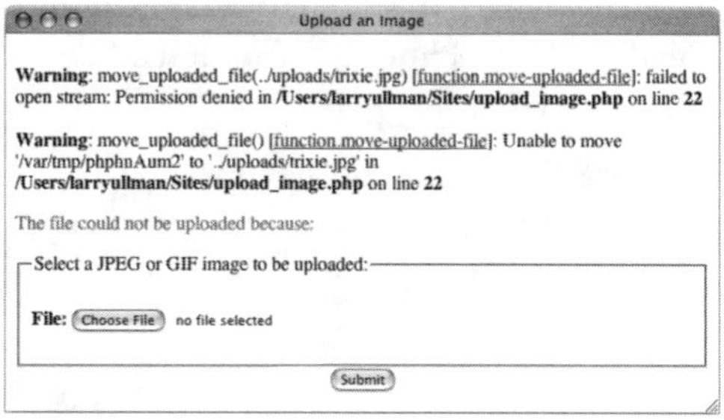

Figure 11.4 If PHP could not move the upload image over to the *uploads* folder because of a permissions issue, you'll see an error message like this one. Fix the permissions on *uploads* to correct this.

6. Set the permissions on the *uploads* directory so that the Web server can write to it.

Again, Windows users should use the Properties window to make these changes. Mac OS X users can...

A) Select the folder in the Finder.

B) Press Command+I.

C) Allow everyone to Read & Write, under the Ownership & Permissions panel (**Figure 11.3**).

Depending upon your operating system, you may be able to upload files without first taking this step. You should try the following script before altering the permissions, just to check. If you see messages like those in **Figure 11.4**, then you will need to make some adjustments.

Check out the sidebar for information related to the security issues involved with this step.

✔ Tips

■ Unix people can use the chmod command to adjust a folder's permissions.

■ The post_max_size setting in the php. ini file dictates the total amount of data (in megabytes) that can be uploaded by a single script. It's set at 8 MB by default. If you want to accept a large file upload, you must also increase this value accordingly.

■ Because of the time it may take to upload a large file, you may also need to change the max_execution_time value in the php. ini file or temporarily bypass it using the set_time_limit() function in your script.

Secure Folder Permissions

As I've said before, increased security normally comes with a trade-off of decreased convenience. With this example, I have practically no security but the convenience of being able to easily demonstrate the file upload process. I'll explain in more detail....

The permissions I've set on the *uploads* folder—allowing everyone read and write access—is heavy-handed and quite insecure. Literally anyone can now move, copy, or write files to the *uploads* folder (assuming that they know it exists). A malicious user could write a PHP script to your *uploads* directory and then run that script in the Web browser, doing all kinds of damage. There are several possible fixes to make this process more secure.

Storing uploaded files outside of the Web directory is preferred for security reasons. Doing so will deny users access to the files directly and avoid placing a folder with loose permissions in a publicly accessible place. For example, if you are running Windows and the root of your Web directory (where `http://localhost` points) is `C:\inetpub\wwwroot`, then you would create a `C:\inetpub\uploads` directory. On Mac OS X, where `/Users/<username>/Sites` is the Web root (`http://localhost/~username` points there), you would create `/Users/<username>/uploads`. Unfortunately placing the *uploads* folder outside of the Web directory would render the set of scripts that display the uploaded images—written in the JavaScript section of the chapter—completely useless. The uploaded images simply would not be viewable. One work-around for this is demonstrated in Chapter 14, "Example—E-Commerce," although that involves a bit more programming.

If you must keep the *uploads* folder publicly accessible, the permissions could be tweaked. For security purposes, you ideally want to allow only the Web server user to read, write, and browse this directory. This means knowing what user the Web server runs as and making that user—and no one else—ruler of the uploads. This isn't a perfect solution, but it does help a bit. This change also limits *your* access to that folder, though, as its contents would belong to only the Web server.

Finally, if you're using Apache, you could limit access to the *uploads* folder using an `.htaccess` file. Basically, you would state that only image files in the folder be publicly viewable, meaning that even if a PHP script were to be placed there, it could not be executed. Information on how to use `.htaccess` files can be found online (search on *.htaccess tutorial*).

Sometimes even the most conservative programmer will make security concessions. The important point is that you're aware of the potential concerns and that you do the most you can to minimize the danger.

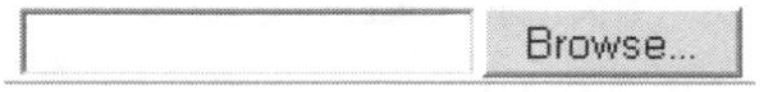

Figure 11.5 The file input as it appears in IE 6 on Windows.

Choose File   no file selected

Figure 11.6 The file input as it appears in Safari on Mac OS X.

The $_FILES Array

INDEX	MEANING
name	The original name of the file (as it was on the user's computer).
type	The MIME type of the file, as provided by the browser.
size	The size of the uploaded file in bytes.
tmp_name	The temporary filename of the uploaded file as it was stored on the server.
error	The error code associated with any problem in uploading.

Table 11.1 The data for an uploaded file will be available through these array elements.

Uploading files with PHP

Now that the server has (hopefully) been set up to properly allow for file uploads, you can create the PHP script that does the actual file handling. There are two parts to such a script: the HTML form and the PHP code.

The required syntax for a form to handle a file upload has three parts:

```
<form enctype="multipart/form-data"
→ action="script.php" method="post">
```

```
<input type="hidden" name="MAX_FILE_SIZE"
→ value="30000" />
```

```
File <input type="file" name="upload" />
```

The `enctype` part of the initial form tag indicates that the form should be able to handle multiple types of data, including files. Also note that the form *must use* the `POST` method. The `MAX_FILE_SIZE` hidden input is a form restriction on how large the chosen file can be, in bytes, and must come before the file input. Finally, the `file` input type will create the proper button in the form (**Figures 11.5** and **11.6**).

As of PHP 4.1, the uploaded file can be accessed using the `$_FILES` superglobal. The variable will be an array of values, listed in **Table 11.1**.

Once the file has been received by the PHP script, the `move_uploaded_file()` function can transfer it from the temporary directory to its permanent location.

```
move_uploaded_file ('temporary_
filename',
→ '/path/to/destination/filename');
```

If the move was successful, then the temporary version of the file will have been moved over to its new destination.

continues on next page

HANDLING FILE UPLOADS

This next script will let the user select a file on their computer and will then store it in the *uploads* directory. The script will check that the file is of an image type. In the next section of this chapter, another script will list, and create links to, the uploaded images.

To handle file uploads in PHP:

1. Create a new PHP document in your text editor (**Script 11.1**).

```
<!DOCTYPE html PUBLIC "-//W3C//DTD
→ XHTML 1.0 Transitional//EN"
"http://www.w3.org/TR/xhtml1/DTD/
→ xhtml1-transitional.dtd">
<html xmlns="http://www.w3.org/1999/
→ xhtml" xml:lang="en" lang="en">
<head>
   <meta http-equiv="content-type"
   → content="text/html; charset=
   → iso-8859-1" />
   <title>Upload an Image</title>
</head>
<body>
<?php # Script 11.1 - upload_image.
→ php
```

2. Check if the form has been submitted and that a file was selected.

```
if (isset($_POST['submitted'])) {
    if (isset($_FILES['upload'])) {
```

Since this form will have no other fields to be validated, this is the only conditional required. You could also validate the size of the uploaded file to determine if it fits within the acceptable range (refer to the $_FILES['upload']['size'] value).

3. Check that the uploaded file is of the proper type.

```
$allowed = array ('image/gif',
→ 'image/jpeg', 'image/jpg',
→ 'image/pjpeg');
if (in_array($_FILES['upload']
→ ['type'], $allowed)) {
```

The file's type is its *MIME* type, indicating what kind of file it is. The browser will determine and provide this information, depending upon the properties of the selected file. An image should have a type of *image/gif*, *image/jpeg*, or *image/jpg* (you could also allow for *image/png*). Microsoft Internet Explorer also uses the *image/pjpeg* for type, so I allow for that.

To validate the file's type, I first create an array of allowed options. If the uploaded file's type is in this array, the file is valid and should be handled.

4. Copy the file to its new location on the server.

```
if (move_uploaded_file($_FILES
→ ['upload']['tmp_name'], "uploads/
→ {$_FILES['upload']['name']}")) {
    echo '<p>The file has been
    → uploaded!</p>';
```

I'll use the move_uploaded_file() function to move the temporary file to its permanent location (in the *uploads* folder). The file will retain its original name. In the next chapter, you'll see how to give the file a new name, which is generally a good idea.

As a rule, you should always use a conditional to confirm that a file was successfully moved, instead of just assuming that the move worked.

continues on page 430

Script 11.1 This script allows the user to upload an image file from their computer to the server.

```
1    <!DOCTYPE html PUBLIC "-//W3C//DTD XHTML 1.0 Transitional//EN"
2          "http://www.w3.org/TR/xhtml1/DTD/xhtml1-transitional.dtd">
3    <html xmlns="http://www.w3.org/1999/xhtml" xml:lang="en" lang="en">
4    <head>
5       <meta http-equiv="content-type" content="text/html; charset=iso-8859-1" />
6       <title>Upload an Image</title>
7    </head>
8    <body>
9    <?php # Script 11.1 - upload_image.php
10
11   // Check if the form has been submitted.
12   if (isset($_POST['submitted'])) {
13
14      // Check for an uploaded file.
15      if (isset($_FILES['upload'])) {
16
17         // Validate the type. Should be jpeg, jpg, or gif.
18         $allowed = array ('image/gif', 'image/jpeg', 'image/jpg', 'image/pjpeg');
19         if (in_array($_FILES['upload']['type'], $allowed)) {
20
21            // Move the file over.
22            if (move_uploaded_file($_FILES['upload']['tmp_name'], "uploads/{$_FILES['upload']
               ['name']}")) {
23
24               echo '<p>The file has been uploaded!</p>';
25
26            } else { // Couldn't move the file over.
27
```

(script continues on page 431)

5. Report on any errors if the file could not be moved.

```
} else {
  echo '<p><font color="red">The
→ file could not be uploaded
→ because: <b>';
  switch ($_FILES['upload']
→ ['error']) {
    case 1:
      print 'The file exceeds the
→ upload_max_filesize setting
→ in php.ini';
      break;
    case 2:
      print 'The file exceeds the
→ MAX_FILE_SIZE setting in
→ the HTML form';
      break;
    case 3:
      print 'The file was only
→ partially uploaded';
      break;
    case 4:
      print 'No file was uploaded';
      break;
    case 6:
      print 'No temporary folder
→ was available';
      break;
    default:
      print 'A system error
→ occurred.';
      break;
  }
  print '</b></font>.</p>';
}
```

There are several possible reasons a file could not be moved. The first and most obvious one is if the permissions are not set properly on the destination directory.

In such a case, you'll see an appropriate error message (refer back to Figure 11.4). PHP will often also store an error number in the $_FILES['upload']['error'] variable. The numbers correspond to specific problems, from 0 to 4, plus 6 (oddly enough, there is no 5). The switch conditional here prints out the problem according to the error number. The default case is added because $_FILES['upload']['error'] may not always have a value.

6. Complete the conditionals and the PHP section.

```
    } else {
      echo '<p><font color="red">
→ Please upload a JPEG or GIF
→ image.</font></p>';
      unlink ($_FILES['upload']
→ ['tmp_name']);
    }
  } else {
    echo '<p><font color="red">
→ Please upload a JPEG or GIF
→ image smaller than 512KB.
→ </font></p>';
  }
}
?>
```

The first else clause concludes the type in_array() conditional. If the file was not of the right type, an error message is printed. Also, the uploaded file is deleted from the server using the unlink() function.

The second else clause concludes the isset($_FILES['upload']) conditional. That variable may not be set either because the user failed to select a file for uploading or because the file was larger than the MAX_FILE_SIZE value.

continues on pge 438

Script 11.1 *continued*

```
script
28            echo '<p><font color="red">The file could not be uploaded because: <b>';
29
30            // Print a message based upon the error.
31            switch ($_FILES['upload']['error']) {
32                case 1:
33                    print 'The file exceeds the upload_max_filesize setting in php.ini.';
34                    break;
35                case 2:
36                    print 'The file exceeds the MAX_FILE_SIZE setting in the HTML form.';
37                    break;
38                case 3:
39                    print 'The file was only partially uploaded.';
40                    break;
41                case 4:
42                    print 'No file was uploaded.';
43                    break;
44                case 6:
45                    print 'No temporary folder was available.';
46                    break;
47                default:
48                    print 'A system error occurred.';
49                    break;
50            } // End of switch.
51
52            print '</b></font>.</p>';
53
54        } // End of move... IF.
55
56    } else { // Invalid type.
57        echo '<p><font color="red">Please upload a JPEG or GIF image.</font></p>';
58        unlink ($_FILES['upload']['tmp_name']); // Delete the file.
59    }
60
61    } else { // No file uploaded.
62        echo '<p><font color="red">Please upload a JPEG or GIF image smaller than 512KB.</font></p>';
63    }
64
65 } // End of the submitted conditional.
66 ?>
67
```

(script continues on next page)

7. Create the HTML form.

```
<form enctype="multipart/form-data"
→ action="upload_image.php"
→ method="post">
  <input type="hidden" name=
  → "MAX_FILE_SIZE" value="524288" />
  <fieldset><legend>Select a JPEG or
  → GIF image to be uploaded:
  → </legend>
  <p><b>File:</b> <input type="file"
  → name="upload" /></p>
  </fieldset>
  <div align="center"><input type=
  → "submit" name="submit" value=
  → "Submit" /></div>
  <input type="hidden" name=
  → "submitted" value="TRUE" />
</form>
```

This form is very simple (**Figure 11.7**), but it contains the three necessary parts for file uploads: the form's enctype attribute, the MAX_FILE_SIZE hidden input, and the file input.

8. Complete the HTML page.

```
</body>
</html>
```

HANDLING FILE UPLOADS

Script 11.1 *continued*

```
      ┌─────────────────── script ───────────────────┐
68    <form enctype="multipart/form-data"
      action="upload_image.php" method="post">
69
70        <input type="hidden" name=
          "MAX_FILE_SIZE" value="524288" />
71
72        <fieldset><legend>Select a JPEG or GIF
          image to be uploaded:</legend>
73
74        <p><b>File:</b> <input type="file"
          name="upload" /></p>
75
76        </fieldset>
77        <div align="center"><input type="submit"
          name="submit" value="Submit" /></div>
78        <input type="hidden" name="submitted"
          value="TRUE" />
79    </form>
80    </body>
81    </html>
```

Figure 11.7 The HTML form, indicating that a file has been selected (in Safari on Mac OS X).

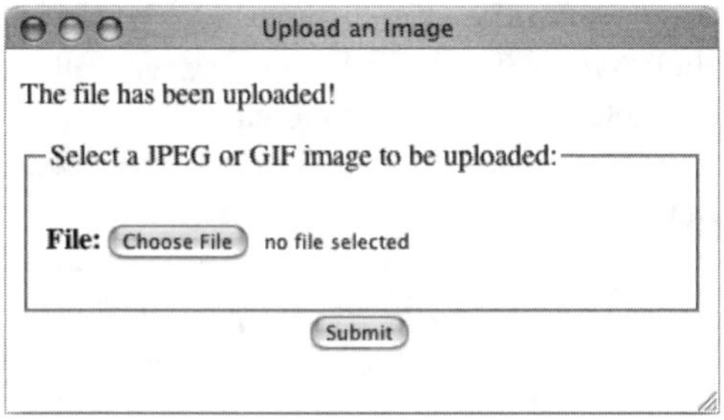

Figure 11.8 If the file was successfully uploaded and moved to its final destination, a simple message is printed.

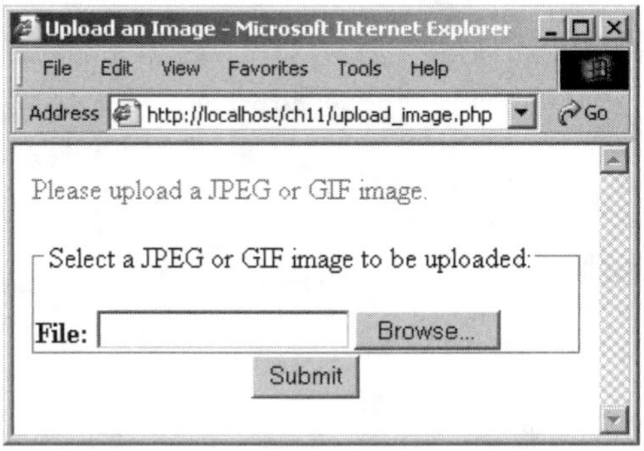

Figure 11.9 If an invalid file type is uploaded, this error message is displayed and the file is deleted (behind the scenes).

9. Save the file as upload_image.php, upload to your Web server, and test in your Web browser (**Figures 11.8** and **11.9**).

✔ Tips

- Omitting the enctype form attribute is a common reason for file uploads to mysteriously fail.

- The existence of an uploaded file can also be validated with the is_uploaded_file() function.

- Windows users must use forward slashes or double backslashes to refer to directories (so C:\\ or C/: rather than C:\). This is because the backslash is the escape character in PHP.

- The move_uploaded_file() function will overwrite an existing file without warning if the new and existing files both have the same name.

- In Chapter 12, you'll learn how to upload multiple files at once. At that time you'll also store the names of the uploaded files in a database and give the uploaded files new names on the server.

- The MAX_FILE_SIZE is a restriction in the browser as to how large a file can be, although not all browsers abide by this restriction. The PHP configuration file has its own restrictions. You can also validate the uploaded file size within the receiving PHP script.

- A file's MIME type can also be detected in PHP 4.3 and later using the mime_content_type() function.

PHP and JavaScript

Despite its limitations and cross-browser compliance issues, JavaScript is still a very popular and useful technology in today's Web pages. Unfortunately, many new PHP programmers have difficulty grasping how PHP and JavaScript interact and differ.

The most significant difference between the two languages is that JavaScript is client-side (meaning it runs in the Web browser) and PHP is server-side. Therefore, JavaScript can detect the size of the browser in pixels, create pop-up windows, and make image mouseovers, whereas PHP cannot.

But while PHP cannot do certain things that JavaScript can, PHP can be used to create or work with JavaScript (just as PHP can create HTML). In this example, PHP will list all the images uploaded by the upload_image.

php script and make clickable links using their names. The links themselves will call a JavaScript function that creates a pop-up window. Three new PHP functions are used in this example. The first, getimagesize(), returns an array of information for a given image (**Table 11.2**). The second, scandir(), returns an array listing the files in a given directory (it was added in PHP 5). The third, filesize(), returns the size of a file in bytes.

The getimagesize() Array

ELEMENT	VALUE	EXAMPLE
0	image's width in pixels	423
1	image's height in pixels	368
2	image's type	2 (representing JPG)
3	appropriate HTML img data	*height="xx" width="yy"*

Table 11.2 The getimagesize() function returns this array of data.

Sending JavaScript Data to PHP

As the example in this section shows, sending data from PHP to JavaScript is rather easy— as simple as creating any HTML. Transferring data from JavaScript to PHP, however, is a bit more complicated. There are three obvious methods for doing so:

◆ Use JavaScript to set a cookie and then retrieve this cookie on another page using PHP.

◆ Append the variable and value to a URL (e.g., *script.php?name=Jude*) with JavaScript, and then use JavaScript to redirect the Web browser to that URL.

◆ Have JavaScript set the value of a hidden input type in an HTML form, and then have the user submit the form to the PHP script.

For example, if I wanted to determine the size of a browser window, I would need to first detect this in JavaScript (it cannot be done with PHP). If I wanted this information passed to a PHP script (to store in a database, maybe), I would need to use one of the preceding methods to accomplish this task.

Notice that in every JavaScript-to-PHP transfer, one HTML page must use JavaScript to perform the detection and a separate PHP script must be used to receive the information. You cannot pass JavaScript data to PHP without requesting a PHP page from the server after JavaScript has done its thing.

Script 11.2 The images.php script uses JavaScript and PHP to create links to images stored on the server.

```
script
1    <!DOCTYPE html PUBLIC "-//W3C//DTD XHTML
     1.0 Transitional//EN"
2          "http://www.w3.org/TR/xhtml1/DTD/
     xhtml1-transitional.dtd">
3    <html xmlns="http://www.w3.org/1999/xhtml"
     xml:lang="en" lang="en">
4    <head>
5        <meta http-equiv="content-type" content=
     "text/html; charset=iso-8859-1" />
6        <title>Images</title>
7        <script language="JavaScript">
8        <!-- // Hide from old browsers.
9
10       // Make a pop-up window function.
11       function create_window (image, width,
     height) {
12
13           // Add some pixels to the width and
     height.
14           width = width + 25;
15           height = height + 50;
16
17           // If the window is already open,
     resize it to the new dimensions.
```

(script continues on page 437)

To create JavaScript with PHP:

1. Begin a new PHP document in your text editor (**Script 11.2**).

   ```
   <!DOCTYPE html PUBLIC "-//W3C//DTD
   → XHTML 1.0 Transitional//EN"
   "http://www.w3.org/TR/xhtml1/DTD/
   → xhtml1-transitional.dtd">
   <html xmlns="http://www.w3.org/1999/
   → xhtml" xml:lang="en" lang="en">
   <head>
       <meta http-equiv="content-type"
   → content="text/html; charset=
   → iso-8859-1" />
       <title>Images</title>
   ```

   This first script will display a list of images, along with their file sizes, and create a link to view the actual image itself in a pop-up window. The pop-up window will be created by JavaScript, although PHP will be used to set certain parameters.

2. Begin the JavaScript function.

   ```
   <script language="JavaScript">
   <!-- // Hide from old browsers.
   function create_window (image,
   → width, height) {
   width = width + 25;
   height = height + 50;
   ```

   The JavaScript create_window() function will accept three parameters: the image name, its width, and its height. Each of these will be passed to this function when the user clicks a link, the exact values of the image name, width, and height being determined by PHP.

   Some pixels will be added to the width and height values to create a window slightly larger than the image itself.

continues on next page

3. Resize the pop-up window if it is already open.

```
if (window.popup_window && !window.
→ popup_window.closed) {
    window.popup_window.resizeTo
    → (width, height);
}
```

This code first checks if the pop-up window exists and if it is not closed. If it passes both tests (which is to say it's already open), the window will be resized according to the new image dimensions. The purpose of this code is to resize the existing window from one image to another if it was left open.

4. Determine the properties of the pop-up window and the URL, and then create the window.

```
var window_specs = "location=no,
→ scrollbars=no, menubars=no,
→ toolbars=no, resizable=yes,
→ left=0, top=0, width=" + width + ",
→ height=" + height;
var url = "image_window.php?image="
→ + image;
popup_window = window.open(url,
→ "PictureWindow", window_specs);
popup_window.focus();
```

The first line sets the properties of the pop-up window (the window will have no location bar, scroll bars, menus, or toolbars; it should be resizable; it will be located in the upper-left corner of the screen; and it will have a width of *width* and a height of *height*). The plus sign is used to perform concatenation in JavaScript, allowing me to add a variable's value to a string.

The second line sets the URL of the pop-up window, which is *image_window. php?image=* plus the name of the image.

Finally, the pop-up window is created using the defined properties and URL, and focus is given to it, meaning it should appear above the current window.

5. Conclude the JavaScript function and the HTML head.

```
    }
    //--></script>
</head>
```

6. Create the introductory text and begin the table.

```
<body>
<div align="center">Click on an
→ image to view it in a separate
→ window.</div><br />
<table align="center" cellspacing=
→ "5" cellpadding="5" border="1">
    <tr>
        <td align="center"><b>
        → Image Name</b></td>
        <td align="center"><b>
        → Image Size</b></td>
    </tr>
```

I'm not putting a lot of effort into the appearance of the page. It will be just one table with a caption.

7. Start the PHP code and create an array of images by referring to the *uploads* directory.

```
<?php # Script 11.2 - images.php
$dir = 'uploads';
$files = scandir($dir);
```

This script will automatically list and link all of the images stored in the *uploads* folder (presumably put there by upload_ image.php, Script 11.1). I begin by defining the directory as a variable, so that it's easier to refer to. Then I use the scan- dir() function, which returns an array of files and directories found within a folder. This array is assigned to $files.

If you are not running PHP version 5 or later, see the manual's page for the scan- dir() function, which lists an alternative syntax you can use.

continues on page 438

Script 11.2 *continued*

```
                                    script
18          if (window.popup_window && !window.popup_window.closed) {
19              window.popup_window.resizeTo(width, height);
20          }
21
22          // Set the window properties.
23          var window_specs = "location=no, scrollbars=no, menubars=no, toolbars=no, resizable=yes,
            left=0, top=0, width=" + width + ", height=" + height;
24
25          // Set the URL.
26          var url = "image_window.php?image=" + image;
27
28          // Create the pop-up window.
29          popup_window = window.open(url, "PictureWindow", window_specs);
30          popup_window.focus();
31
32      } // End of function.
33      //--></script>
34  </head>
35  <body>
36  <div align="center">Click on an image to view it in a separate window.</div><br />
37  <table align="center" cellspacing="5" cellpadding="5" border="1">
38      <tr>
39          <td align="center"><b>Image Name</b></td>
40          <td align="center"><b>Image Size</b></td>
41      </tr>
42  <?php # Script 11.2 - images.php
43  // This script lists the images in the uploads directory.
44
45  $dir = 'uploads'; // Define the directory to view.
46
47  $files = scandir($dir); // Read all the images into an array.
48
49  // Display each image caption as a link to the JavaScript function.
```

(script continues on next page)

8. Loop through the $files array, linking each image to the JavaScript function.

```
foreach ($files as $image) {
    if (substr($image, 0, 1) != '.') {
        $image_size = getimagesize
→ ("$dir/$image");
        $file_size = round ( (filesize
→ ("$dir/$image")) / 1024) .
→ "kb";
        echo "  <tr>
            <td><a href=\"javascript:
            → create_window('$image',
            → $image_size[0],$image_
            → size[1])\">$image</a></td>
    <td>$file_size</td>
        </tr>";
    }
}
```

This loop will go through every image in the array and create a row in the table for it. There are two PHP functions I'm using here that I have not used before (for more information on either, check the PHP manual): getimagesize() and file-size(). The former returns an array of information about an image. The values returned by this function will be used to set the width and height sent to the create_window() JavaScript function.

The filesize() function returns the size of a file in bytes. To calculate the kilobytes of a file, I divide this number by 1,024 (there are that many bytes in a kilobyte) and round it off.

Finally, the loop creates the HTML table row, consisting of the linked image name and the image size. The caption is linked as a call to the JavaScript create_window() function so that when the link is clicked, that function is executed.

Script 11.2 *continued*

```
script
50   foreach ($files as $image) {
51
52       if (substr($image, 0, 1) != '.') { //
         Ignore anything starting with a period.
53
54           // Get the image's size in pixels.
55           $image_size = getimagesize
             ("$dir/$image");
56
57           // Calculate the image's size in
             kilobytes.
58           $file_size = round ( (filesize
             ("$dir/$image")) / 1024) . "kb";
59
60           // Print the information.
61           echo "  <tr>
62               <td><a href=\"javascript:
                 create_window('$image',$image_
                 size[0],$image_size[1])
                 \">$image</a></td>
63               <td>$file_size</td>
64           </tr>";
65
66       } // End of the IF.
67
68   } // End of the foreach loop.
69   ?>
70   </table>
71   </body>
72   </html>
```

Figure 11.10 The `images.php` file (Script 11.2) lists all of the files stored in the *uploads* directory, creating JavaScript links to each (see Figure 11.11).

9. Complete the PHP code and the HTML page.

   ?>

   </table>

   </body>

   </html>

10. Save the file as `images.php`, upload to your Web server (in the same directory as `upload_image.php` and the *uploads* folder), and test in your Web browser (**Figure 11.10**).

11. View the source code to see the dynamically generated links (**Figure 11.11**).

    Notice how the parameters to each function call are appropriate to the specific image. The `getimagesize()` function is used to determine the image's width and height.

    The last step here is to make the `image_window.php` script, which is used by the pop-up window. This script simply shows the image.

Figure 11.11 Each image is linked as a call to a JavaScript function. The function call's parameters were created by PHP.

To make the image viewing script:

1. Begin a new PHP document in your text editor (**Script 11.3**).

```
<!DOCTYPE html PUBLIC "-//W3C//DTD
→ XHTML 1.0 Transitional//EN"
"http://www.w3.org/TR/xhtml1/DTD/
→ xhtml1-transitional.dtd">
<html xmlns="http://www.w3.org/1999/
→ xhtml" xml:lang="en" lang="en">
<head>
    <meta http-equiv="content-type"
    → content="text/html; charset=
    → iso-8859-1" />
    <title>View Image</title>
</head>
<body>
```

2. Begin the PHP section and create a new variable.

```
<?php # Script 11.3 - image_window.
→ php
$okay = FALSE;
```

The $okay variable will be used to confirm that the image was displayed. If it could not be—because no valid image name was received by the script or because the image could not be accessed—$okay will still be FALSE and an error message will be displayed.

Script 11.3 This script displays an image, using the `getimagesize()` function to determine its dimensions.

```
                          script
1    <!DOCTYPE html PUBLIC "-//W3C//DTD XHTML
     1.0 Transitional//EN"
2           "http://www.w3.org/TR/xhtml1/DTD/
            xhtml1-transitional.dtd">
3    <html xmlns="http://www.w3.org/1999/xhtml"
     xml:lang="en" lang="en">
4    <head>
5        <meta http-equiv="content-type" content=
         "text/html; charset=iso-8859-1" />
6        <title>View Image</title>
7    </head>
8    <body>
9    <?php # Script 11.3 - image_window.php
10
11   // Set a variable for problem reporting.
12   $okay = FALSE;
13
14   // Make sure an image name was passed to
     the script.
```

(script continues on next page)

Script 11.3 *continued*

```
                    script
15   if (isset($_GET['image'])) {
16
17       // Get the extension of the image name.
18       $ext = substr ($_GET['image'], -4);
19
20       // Test if it's a valid image extension.
21       if ((strtolower($ext) == '.jpg')
         OR (strtolower($ext) == 'jpeg') OR
         (strtolower($ext) == '.gif')) {
22
23           // Get the image information and
             display the image.
```

(script continues on next page)

3. Validate the received image name.

```
if (isset($_GET['image'])) {
$ext = substr ($_GET['image'], -4);
if ((strtolower($ext) == '.jpg')
→ OR (strtolower($ext) == 'jpeg') OR
→ (strtolower($ext) == '.gif')) {
```

Before attempting to access the image on the server, I validate it twice. The first conditional just checks that an image value was sent to the page through the URL. The second conditional makes sure that the image name (i.e., the filename) has a valid extension (.jpg, jpeg, or .gif) by checking the last four characters of the received filename (notice that the four-character extensions include *jpeg* without the initial period). To also allow for files with an extension of .JPG, .GIF, and .JPEG, I call the strtolower() function.

There are two assumptions being made here regarding the received image name. First, it shouldn't contain spaces or other problematic characters, as that will cause problems when passed in the URL. Second, I assume that the image name has an extension. Alternatively, you could use the mime_content_type() function to check the file's type, regardless of the presence of an extension.

continues on next page

PHP AND JAVASCRIPT

4. Display the image.

```
if ($image = @getimagesize
→ ('uploads/' . $_GET['image'])) {
   echo "<img src=\"uploads/{$_GET
→ ['image']}\" $image[3] border=
→ \"2\" />";
   $okay = TRUE;
}
```

If the script can retrieve the image information, the image will be displayed (by creating the appropriate HTML code) and the $okay variable set to TRUE. The fourth array element returned by the getimagesize() function makes it easy to generate the proper HTML for the image.

5. Complete the conditionals and print an error message if necessary.

```
      }
   }
   if (!$okay) {
      echo '<div align="center">
→ <font color="red" size="+1">
→ This script must receive a valid
→ image name!</font></div>';
   }
```

If $okay is not TRUE, then some problem occurred and a generic error message is printed to the Web browser.

6. Complete the PHP code and the HTML page.

```
?>
<br />
<div align="center"><a href=
→ "javascript:self.close();">Close
→ This Window</a></div>
</body>
</html>
```

This final bit of JavaScript will create a link that, when clicked, will close the pop-up window.

Script 11.3 *continued*

```
24        if ($image = @getimagesize
          ('uploads/' . $_GET['image'])) {
25           echo "<img src=\"uploads/{$_GET
             ['image']}\" $image[3] border=
             \"2\" />";
26           $okay = TRUE; // No problems.
27        }
28
29     } // End of extension IF.
30
31  } // End of isset() IF.
32
33  // If something went wrong...
34  if (!$okay) {
35     echo '<div align="center"><font
        color="red" size="+1">This script must
        receive a valid image name!</font>
        </div>';
36  }
37  ?>
38  <br />
39  <div align="center"><a href="javascript:
    self.close();">Close This Window</a></div>
40  </body>
41  </html>
```

Figure 11.12 The image is displayed by having PHP create the appropriate HTML.

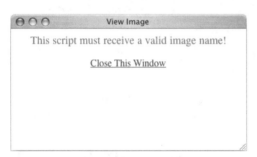

Figure 11.13 If no image name or an invalid image name is supplied to this page, this error message is displayed.

7. Save the file as `image_window.php`, upload to your Web server (in the same directory as `images.php`), and test in your Web browser (**Figure 11.12**).

If any problems are encountered, the `image_window.php` script will look like **Figure 11.13**.

✔ Tips

- Not to belabor the point, but most everything Web developers do with JavaScript (for example, resize or move the browser window) cannot be done using the server-side PHP.

- There is *a little* overlap between the PHP and JavaScript. Both can set and read cookies, create HTML, and do some browser detection.

- The PHP function `file_exists()`—it tests for the existence of a file on the server—could also be used in both of these scripts to validate the presence of an image before linking to or displaying it.

PHP AND JAVASCRIPT

Using Output Buffering

An interesting feature added in version 4 of PHP is output control. *Output control* (or output buffering) allows you to write and execute your scripts as normal but send data to the Web browser only at select points. The main benefit of this system is that you can call the header(), setcookie(), and session_start() functions at nearly any spot in your script without concern for the *headers already sent* error messages.

To begin output buffering, use the ob_start() function. Once you call it, every echo(), print(), and similar function will send data to a memory buffer rather than the Web browser. Conversely, HTTP calls (like header() and setcookie()) will not be buffered and will operate as usual.

At the conclusion of the script, call the ob_end_flush() function to send the accumulated buffer to the Web browser. Or, use the ob_end_clean() function to delete the buffered data without sending it. Both functions have the secondary effect of turning off output buffering.

From a programmer's perspective, output buffering allows you to structure a script in a more linear form, without concern for HTTP headers. To demonstrate how you might use output buffering, I'll create a straightforward version of a login.php script, similar to those written in Chapter 9, "Cookies and Sessions."

To use output buffering:

1. Create a new PHP document in your text editor (**Script 11.4**).

   ```
   <?php # Script 11.4 - login.php
   ```

2. Begin output buffering and close the PHP section.

   ```
   ob_start();

   ?>
   ```

   The key to using output buffering is to call the ob_start() function as early as possible in a script. It should be the very first line (not counting the opening PHP tag).

3. Add the HTML header.

   ```
   <!DOCTYPE html PUBLIC "-//W3C//DTD
   → XHTML 1.0 Transitional//EN"
   "http://www.w3.org/TR/xhtml1/DTD/
   → xhtml1-transitional.dtd">
   <html xmlns="http://www.w3.org/1999/
   → xhtml" xml:lang="en" lang="en">
   <head>
       <meta http-equiv="content-type"
       → content="text/html; charset=
       → iso-8859-1" />
       <title>Login</title>
   </head>
   <body>
   ```

   Since this code comes after output buffering has started, the HTML will be stored in memory, rather than sent to the Web browser.

   If you are using a template system in your page, you could include the header file here instead.

Script 11.4 The login.php script can be written in a more logical structure without regard to HTTP headers, thanks to the use of output buffering.

```
script
1    <?php # Script 11.4 - login.php
2    ob_start(); // Start output buffering.
3    ?>
4    <!DOCTYPE html PUBLIC "-//W3C//DTD XHTML
     1.0 Transitional//EN"
5            "http://www.w3.org/TR/xhtml1/DTD/
            xhtml1-transitional.dtd">
6    <html xmlns="http://www.w3.org/1999/xhtml"
     xml:lang="en" lang="en">
7    <head>
8        <meta http-equiv="content-type" content=
         "text/html; charset=iso-8859-1" />
9        <title>Login</title>
10   </head>
11   <body>
12   <?php
13
14   // Check if the form has been submitted.
15   if (isset($_POST['submitted'])) {
16
17       require_once ('../mysql_connect.php');
         // Connect to the db.
18       // The escape_data() function is defined
         in mysql_connect.php!
19       // Make sure that mysql_connect.php
         selects the 'sitename' database!
20
21       // Check for an email address.
22       if (!empty($_POST['email'])) {
23           $e = escape_data($_POST['email']);
24       } else {
25           echo '<p><font color="red">You
             forgot to enter your email address!
             </font></p>';
26           $e = FALSE;
27       }
28
29       // Check for a password.
30       if (!empty($_POST['password'])) {
31           $p = escape_data($_POST
             ['password']);
```

(script continues on page 447)

4. Check if the form has been submitted and include the database connection script.

```
if (isset($_POST['submitted'])) {
    require_once ('../mysql_connect.
    → php');
```

In this script I assume that a mysql_connect.php script exists that establishes the database connection. That page should also define the escape_data() function. See the example in Chapter 9 if you don't have such a script sitting around already.

5. Validate the email address and password.

```
if (!empty($_POST['email'])) {
    $e = escape_data($_POST['email']);
} else {
    echo '<p><font color="red">
    → You forgot to enter your email
    → address!</font></p>';
    $e = FALSE;
}
if (!empty($_POST['password'])) {
    $p = escape_data($_POST
    → ['password']);
} else {
    echo '<p><font color="red">
    → You forgot to enter your password!
    → </font></p>';
    $p = FALSE;
}
```

Instead of using an $errors array to handle errors (as I have in previous incarnations), I can now directly print the messages. Each string will be added to the current buffer, rather than sent to the Web browser.

continues on next page

6. Query the database.

```
if ($e && $p) {
    $query = "SELECT user_id,
    → first_name FROM users WHERE
    → email='$e' AND password=
    → SHA('$p')";
    $result = @mysql_query ($query);
    $row = mysql_fetch_array
    → ($result, MYSQL_NUM);
```

Hopefully this part of the code is second nature to you by now. A query is run retrieving the user's ID and first name from the database, using the submitted email address and password in the WHERE conditional.

7. If a match was made, store the data in the session, delete the buffer, and redirect the user.

```
if ($row) {
    session_start();
    $_SESSION['user_id'] = $row[0];
    $_SESSION['first_name'] = $row[1];
    ob_end_clean();
    $url = 'http://' . $_SERVER
    → ['HTTP_HOST'] . dirname($_SERVER
    → ['PHP_SELF']);
    if ((substr($url, -1) == '/') OR
    → (substr($url, -1) == '\\') ) {
        $url = substr ($url, 0, -1);
    }
    $url .= '/loggedin.php';
    header("Location: $url");
    exit();
```

If the submitted email address and password match those in the database, then $row will have a value and I can register the first name and user_id values to the session. Thanks to output buffering, I can call the session_start() function here, even though there are HTML and echo statements in the preceding code.

Since I won't be using the buffered text if the user is redirected, I call the ob_end_clean() function before header(), which will delete the existing buffer and stop output buffering.

Finally, the user is redirected to a loggedin.php page. The code for determining the absolute URL for redirection was explained in detail in Chapter 8.

8. Complete the ($row) conditional.

```
} else {
    echo '<p><font color="red">
    → The email address and password
    → entered do not match those on
    → file.</font></p>';
    echo '<p><font color="red">' .
    → mysql_error() . '<br />
    → <br />Query: ' . $query .
    → '</font></p>';
}
```

The $row variable could not have a value either because of a SQL/MySQL error or because an improper email address/password combination was entered. The first message here covers the second case and is what a public user should see. The second message is for your own debugging purposes and should not be part of a live application.

continues on page 448

USING OUTPUT BUFFERING

Script 11.4 *continued*

```
┌─────────────────────────────── script ───────────────────────────────┐
32       } else {
33           echo '<p><font color="red">You forgot to enter your password!</font></p>';
34           $p = FALSE;
35       }
36
37       if ($e && $p) { // If everything's OK.
38
39           /* Retrieve the user_id and first_name for
40           that email/password combination. */
41           $query = "SELECT user_id, first_name FROM users WHERE email='$e' AND password=SHA('$p')";
42           $result = @mysql_query ($query); // Run the query.
43           $row = mysql_fetch_array ($result, MYSQL_NUM); // Return a record, if applicable.
44
45           if ($row) { // A record was pulled from the database.
46
47               // Set the session data & redirect.
48               session_start();
49               $_SESSION['user_id'] = $row[0];
50               $_SESSION['first_name'] = $row[1];
51
52               ob_end_clean(); // Delete the buffer.
53
54               // Redirect the user to the loggedin.php page.
55               // Start defining the URL.
56               $url = 'http://' . $_SERVER['HTTP_HOST'] . dirname($_SERVER['PHP_SELF']);
57               // Check for a trailing slash.
58               if ((substr($url, -1) == '/') OR (substr($url, -1) == '\\') ) {
59                   $url = substr ($url, 0, -1); // Chop off the slash.
60               }
61               // Add the page.
62               $url .= '/loggedin.php';
63
64               header("Location: $url");
65               exit(); // Quit the script.
66
67           } else { // No record matched the query.
68               echo '<p><font color="red">The email address and password entered do not match those on
                 file.</font></p>'; // Public message.
69               echo '<p><font color="red">' . mysql_error() . '<br /><br />Query: ' . $query . '</font>
                 </p>';// Debugging message.
70           }
```

(script continues on next page)

9. Complete the ($e && $p) conditional, close the database connection, close the submit conditional, and close the PHP block.

```
} else {
    echo '<p><font color="red">
    → Please try again.</font>
    → </p>';
}
mysql_close();
}
?>
```

10. Make the HTML form.

```
<h2>Login</h2>
<form action="login.php"
→ method="post">
    <p>Email Address: <input type=
    → "text" name="email" size="20"
    → maxlength="40" value="<?php
    → if (isset($_POST['email']))
    → echo $_POST['email']; ?>" />
    → </p>
    <p>Password: <input type=
    → "password" name="password"
    → size="20" maxlength="20" /></p>
    <p><input type="submit" name=
    → "submit" value="Login" /></p>
    <input type="hidden" name=
    → "submitted" value="TRUE" />
</form>
```

Script 11.4 *continued*

```
71
72      } else { // Errors!
73          echo '<p><font color="red">Please
            try again.</font></p>';
74      } // End of if ($e && $p) IF.
75
76      mysql_close(); // Close the database
        connection.
77
78  } // End of the main Submit conditional.
79
80  // Display the form.
81  ?>
82  <h2>Login</h2>
83  <form action="login.php" method="post">
84      <p>Email Address: <input type="text"
        name="email" size="20" maxlength="40"
        value="<?php if (isset($_POST['email']))
        echo $_POST['email']; ?>" /> </p>
85      <p>Password: <input type="password"
        name="password" size="20" maxlength="20"
        /></p>
86      <p><input type="submit" name="submit"
        value="Login" /></p>
87      <input type="hidden" name="submitted"
        value="TRUE" />
88  </form>
89  </body>
90  </html>
91  <?php
92  ob_end_flush(); // Send everything to the
    Web browser.
93  ?>
```

Figure 11.14 If any error messages occur, they are immediately printed and the form is displayed again.

11. Complete the HTML page and flush the buffer.

```
</body>
</html>
<?php
ob_end_flush();
?>
```

The second to the last line in the script will send all of the accumulated data to the Web browser and turn off output buffering.

12. Save the file as `login.php`, upload to your Web server, and test in your Web browser (**Figure 11.14**).

For the entire process to work, a `loggedin.php` script is required, which I'll quickly write out.

To create loggedin.php:

1. Create a new PHP document in your text editor, beginning with the ob_start() function (**Script 11.5**).

```php
<?php # Script 11.5 - loggedin.php
ob_start();
?>
```

2. Create the HTML header.

```html
<!DOCTYPE html PUBLIC "-//W3C//DTD
→ XHTML 1.0 Transitional//EN"
"http://www.w3.org/TR/xhtml1/DTD/
→ xhtml1-transitional.dtd">
<html xmlns="http://www.w3.org/1999/
→ xhtml" xml:lang="en" lang="en">
<head>
  <meta http-equiv="content-type"
  → content="text/html; charset=
  → iso-8859-1" />
  <title>Logged In!</title>
</head>
<body>
```

3. Start a session and see if the user is logged in.

```php
<?php
session_start();
if (isset($_SESSION['first_name']) ) {
  echo "<p>You are now logged in,
  → {$_SESSION['first_name']}.</p>";
```

Similar to previous scripts, this page will check for the presence of a specific session variable as verification that the user is logged in. If so, they'll be greeted by name.

4. Redirect the user if they are not logged in.

```php
} else {
  ob_end_clean();
  $url = 'http://' . $_SERVER
  → ['HTTP_HOST'] . dirname($_SERVER
  → ['PHP_SELF']);
  if ((substr($url, -1) == '/') OR
  → (substr($url, -1) == '\\') ) {
    $url = substr ($url, 0, -1);
  }
  $url .= '/login.php';
  header("Location: $url");
  exit();
}
```

This code mimics that in login.php, redirecting the user back to that page should they not already be logged in.

5. Finish the page.

```php
echo '</body>
</html>';
ob_end_flush();
?>
```

continues on page 452

Script 11.5 This very simple version of `loggedin.php` makes use of output buffering and sessions.

```
1    <?php # Script 11.5 - loggedin.php
2    ob_start(); // Start output buffering.
3    ?>
4    <!DOCTYPE html PUBLIC "-//W3C//DTD XHTML 1.0 Transitional//EN"
5          "http://www.w3.org/TR/xhtml1/DTD/xhtml1-transitional.dtd">
6    <html xmlns="http://www.w3.org/1999/xhtml" xml:lang="en" lang="en">
7    <head>
8       <meta http-equiv="content-type" content="text/html; charset=iso-8859-1" />
9       <title>Logged In!</title>
10   </head>
11   <body>
12   <?php
13
14   session_start(); // Start the session.
15
16   // Greet the user by name, if possible.
17   if (isset($_SESSION['first_name']) ) {
18
19       echo "<p>You are now logged in, {$_SESSION['first_name']}.</p>";
20
21   } else { // If no session value is present, redirect the user.
22
23       ob_end_clean(); // Delete the buffer.
24
25       // Start defining the URL.
26       $url = 'http://' . $_SERVER['HTTP_HOST'] . dirname($_SERVER['PHP_SELF']);
27       // Check for a trailing slash.
28       if ((substr($url, -1) == '/') OR (substr($url, -1) == '\\') ) {
29           $url = substr ($url, 0, -1); // Chop off the slash.
30       }
31       $url .= '/login.php'; // Add the page.
32       header("Location: $url");
33       exit(); // Quit the script.
34
35   }
36
37   echo '</body>
38   </html>';
39
40   ob_end_flush(); // Send everything to the Web browser.
41   ?>
```

6. Save the page as `loggedin.php`, upload to your Web server (in the same directory as `login.php`), and test in your Web browser (**Figures 11.15** and **11.16**).

✔ Tips

- The maximum buffer size can be set in the `php.ini` file. The default is 4,096 characters.

- As of PHP 4.0.4, you can send compressed output to browsers by starting output control with `ob_start('ob_gzhandler')`, minimizing the download size of your pages. The `ob_gzhandler()` function will determine the appropriate type of compression to use (*gzip*, *deflate*, or none) depending upon what the browser can accept. Understand that compression is beneficial only on larger Web pages, and to use it, the `output_buffering` setting in the `php.ini` file must be set to *Off*.

- The `ob_get_length()` function returns the length (in number of characters) of the current buffer.

- The `ob_get_contents()` function will return the current buffer so that it may be assigned to a variable, should the need arise.

- The `ob_flush()` function—new as of PHP 4.2—will send the current contents of the buffer to the Web browser and then discard them, allowing a new buffer to be started. This function allows your scripts to maintain more moderate buffer sizes.

- The `ob_clean()` function—also new as of PHP 4.2—deletes the current contents of the buffer without stopping the buffer process.

- PHP will automatically run `ob_end_flush()` at the conclusion of a script if it is not otherwise done.

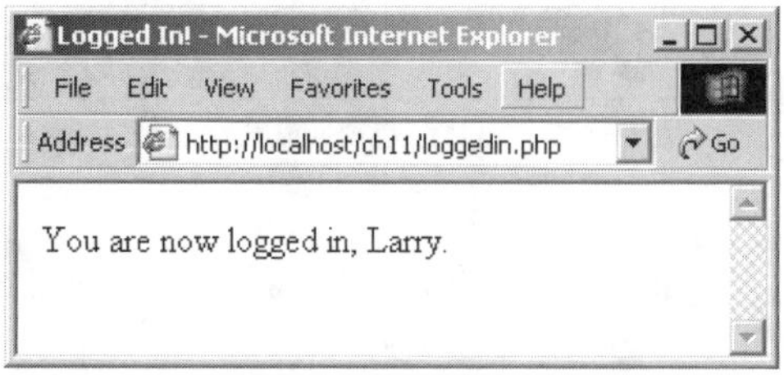

Figure 11.15 If the user is logged in, they'll be greeted by their first name.

Figure 11.16 Anyone who attempts to access the `loggedin.php` page without first logging in will be redirected back to `login.php`.

Using the Improved MySQL Extension

In Chapter 7, "Using PHP with MySQL," I introduced the standard set of PHP functions used to interact with a MySQL database. These functions have been around for years and will certainly get the job done. But new to PHP as of version 5 is the Improved MySQL Extension functions, designed to take advantage of features added in MySQL 4.1 (they specifically work with MySQL 4.1.3 and later). If your server meets these requirements, you may want to consider using these functions in your PHP applications. Generally speaking, they are both faster and more secure than the basic MySQL functions.

To start, connect to MySQL using the `mysqli_connect()` function.

```
$dbc = mysqli_connect ('localhost',
→ 'username', 'password');
```

As with the `mysql_connect()` function, this one returns a resource representing the database connection. This resource will be used as an argument in most of the other *mysqli* functions. But unlike the `mysql_connect()` function, `mysqli_connect()` will let you also specify the database to select:

```
$dbc = mysqli_connect ('localhost',
→ 'username', 'password', 'database');
```

Or you can use the `mysqli_select_db()` function:

```
mysqli_select_db($dbc, 'database');
```

If a connection problem occurred, you can call the `mysqli_connect_error()` function, which returns the connection error message.

```
mysqli_connect_error();
```

Note that this function is only for connection errors. The errors resulting from running queries can be reported by the `mysqli_error()` function:

```
mysqli_error($dbc);
```

Once you've connected to MySQL and selected a database, you run queries using the `mysqli_query()` function:

```
$result = mysqli_query($dbc, $query);
```

Notice that the syntax of this function places the database connection as the first argument and the query as the second, which is the opposite of the standard `mysql_query()` function. You'll also notice that whereas the database connection is an optional argument in most of the *mysql* functions, it's required with the Improved MySQL Extension.

To handle the results returned by a SELECT query, use `mysqli_fetch_array()` in a while loop:

```
while ($row = mysqli_fetch_array
→ ($result)) {

    // Do whatever with $row.

}
```

As with `mysql_fetch_array()`, you can add a second parameter when calling this function, dictating how the returned array should be indexed. The options are: MYSQLI_NUM, for numeric (starting at 0); MYSQLI_ASSOC, for strings (using the column names); and MYSQLI_BOTH, for both.

You can count the number of returned records with

```
$num = mysqli_num_rows($result);
```

continues on next page

And once you are finished with a query's results, you can release them and close the database connection:

```
mysqli_free_result($result);
```

```
mysqli_close($dbc);
```

These are the most important of the mysqli_* functions. There is also: mysqli_real_escape_string() for escaping problematic characters; mysqli_affected_rows(), which returns the number of rows affected by an INSERT, UPDATE, or DELETE query; a few functions related to using transactions, which will be used in Chapter 14, "Example—E-commerce"; and about two or three dozen others, all listed in the PHP manual.

As you can see, for the most part you'll use these functions exactly as you do the standard mysql_* functions. As a quick demonstration of this, I'll write a script that retrieves all of the comments stored in the *test* database. The specific table was created and the comments were added at the beginning of Chapter 10, "Web Application Security"; if you do not have a populated *comments* table, read that section first. Also, make sure that you are running PHP 5 or later with MySQL 4.1.3 or later. And if you do not know how to enable mysqli support in PHP, see Appendix A.

To use the Improved MySQL Extension:

1. Create a new PHP script in your text editor or IDE (**Script 11.6**).

   ```
   <!DOCTYPE html PUBLIC "-//W3C//DTD
   → XHTML 1.0 Transitional//EN"
   "http://www.w3.org/TR/xhtml1/DTD/
   → xhtml1-transitional.dtd">
   <html xmlns="http://www.w3.org/1999/
   → xhtml" xml:lang="en" lang="en">
   <head>
   ```

Script 11.6 The Improved MySQL Extension functions are used here to retrieve and display some records from a database.

```
1   <!DOCTYPE html PUBLIC "-//W3C//DTD XHTML
    1.0 Transitional//EN"
2          "http://www.w3.org/TR/xhtml1/DTD/
           xhtml1-transitional.dtd">
3   <html xmlns="http://www.w3.org/1999/xhtml"
    xml:lang="en" lang="en">
4   <head>
5       <meta http-equiv="content-type" content=
        "text/html; charset=iso-8859-1" />
6       <title>View Submitted Comments</title>
7   </head>
8   <body>
9   <?php # Script 11.6 - mysqli.php
10
11  // Make the connection.
12  $dbc = @mysqli_connect ('localhost',
    'username', 'password', 'test') OR die
    ('Could not connect to MySQL: ' .
    mysqli_connect_error() );
13
14  // Make the query.
15  $query = "SELECT name, comment, DATE_FORMAT
    (date_entered, '%M %D, %Y') FROM comments
    ORDER BY date_entered DESC";
16
```

(script continues on next page)

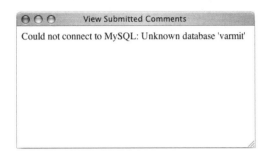

Figure 11.17 The `mysqli_connect_error()` function returns any errors that occur specifically while establishing a connection to MySQL.

```
<meta http-equiv="content-type"
→ content="text/html; charset=
→ iso-8859-1" />
<title>View Submitted Comments
→ </title>
</head>
<body>
<?php # Script 11.6 - mysqli.php
```

2. Establish a connection to the database.

```
$dbc = @mysqli_connect ('localhost',
→ 'username', 'password', 'test') OR
→ die ('Could not connect to MySQL:
→ ' . mysqli_connect_error() );
```

This function will attempt to connect to MySQL and select the *test* database. If it succeeds, the result will be assigned to the $dbc variable. If the function call fails, the die() function will terminate the execution of the script, printing the connection error in the process (**Figure 11.17**).

3. Define and execute the query.

```
$query = "SELECT name, comment,
→ DATE_FORMAT(date_entered, '%M %D,
→ %Y') FROM comments ORDER BY
→ date_entered DESC";
if ($result = @mysqli_query
→ ($dbc, $query)) {
```

The query itself is the same as one you would use if you were working with the standard MySQL functions. This one retrieves all the records from the *comments* table in descending date entered order, formatting the date in the process. The execution of the query takes place in a conditional, so that I can report on any errors if there is a problem.

continues on next page

4. Print the query results.

```
if (mysqli_num_rows($result) > 0) {
    while ($row = mysqli_fetch_array
    → ($result, MYSQLI_NUM)) {
        echo "<h3>$row[0] ($row[2])
        → </h3>
        <p>$row[1]</p><br />";
    }
} else {
    echo '<p>There are currently no
    → comments in the database.</p>';
}
```

If at least one record was returned, I'll use a `while` loop to print each record. The loop calls the `mysqli_fetch_array()` function, using the `MYSQLI_NUM` parameter so that I can refer to the returned columns using numeric indexes.

If no records were returned, a message stating such is printed.

Script 11.6 *continued*

```
17   // Run the query and handle the results.
18   if ($result = @mysqli_query($dbc, $query)) {
19
20       if (mysqli_num_rows($result) > 0) { //
         Some records returned.
21
22           // Print each record in a loop.
23           while ($row = mysqli_fetch_array
             ($result, MYSQLI_NUM)) {
24               echo "<h3>$row[0] ($row[2])</h3>
25               <p>$row[1]</p><br />";
26           }
27
28       } else { // No records returned.
29           echo '<p>There are currently no
             comments in the database.</p>';
30       }
31
32   } else { // Query didn't run properly.
33       echo '<p><font color="red">MySQL
         Error: ' . mysqli_error($dbc) .
         '<br /><br />Query: ' . $query .
         '</font></p>';// Debugging message.
34   }
35
36   // Free the result and close the
     connection.
37   mysqli_free_result($result);
38   mysqli_close($dbc);
39   ?>
40   </body>
41   </html>
```

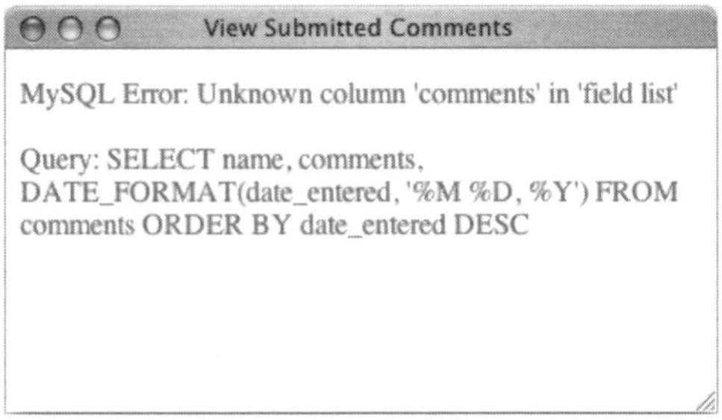

Figure 11.18 If a non-connection error occurs, the error is printed out along with the query that was being run.

Figure 11.19 The resulting page, showing all of the submitted comments (actually submitted in Chapter 10).

5. Complete the page.

```
} else {
    echo '<p><font color="red">
    → MySQL Error: ' . mysqli_error
    → ($dbc) . '<br /><br />Query: ' .
    → $query . '</font></p>';
}
mysqli_free_result($result);
mysqli_close($dbc);
?>
</body>
</html>
```

The `else` clause is invoked if there was an error in executing the query. For debugging purposes, the MySQL error will be printed along with the query being run (**Figure 11.18**).

Then the query results are freed and the database connection is closed. These are optional, but good, steps to take.

6. Save the page as `mysqli.php`, upload to your Web server, and test in your Web browser (**Figure 11.19**).

✔ Tips

■ You can use the Improved MySQL Extension in a procedural manner using functions, as I do in this example, or as an object, assuming you understand object-oriented programming. See the PHP manual for the OOP syntax.

■ Another benefit of the Improved MySQL Extension is that the `mysqli_multi_query()` function lets you execute multiple queries at one time.

New MySQL Features

Versions 4 and 4.1 of MySQL have been significant upgrades, adding many new features to the database application. Although you do not need to use all of these new features with every Web application you develop, in the right circumstances they'll make a world of difference. I'll discuss and demonstrate the most important additions here.

First up are transactions, which require the InnoDB storage engine (see Chapter 5, "Advanced SQL and MySQL," for information on the different storage engines). If you are using version 4.0 or later, you should have the InnoDB type available to you.

After that, I'll go over prepared statements. These are available as of MySQL 4.1, and you can run prepared statements through PHP using the Improved MySQL Extension, added in PHP 5.

I'll also briefly give mention to, but not go into any detail over, subqueries.

Using transactions

A *database transaction* is a sequence of queries run during a single session. For example, you might insert a record into one table, insert another record into another table, and maybe run an update. Without using transactions, each individual query takes effect immediately and cannot be undone. With transactions, you can set start and stop points and then enact or retract all of the queries as needed (for example, if one query failed, all of the queries can be undone).

Commercial interactions commonly require transactions, even something as basic as transferring $100 from my bank account to yours. What seems like a simple process is actually several steps:

◆ Confirm that I have $100 in my account.

◆ Decrease my account by $100.

◆ Increase the amount of money in your account by $100.

◆ Verify that the increase worked.

If any of the steps failed, I would want to undo all of them. For example, if the money couldn't be deposited in your account, it should be returned to mine until the entire transaction can go through.

To perform transactions with MySQL, you must use the InnoDB table type (or storage engine). To begin a new transaction in the mysql client, type

START TRANSACTION;

If you are using a version of MySQL prior to 4.0.11, you must use just BEGIN instead. Once your transaction has begun, you can now run your queries. Once you have finished, you can either enter COMMIT to enact all of the queries or ROLLBACK to undo the effect of all of the queries.

After you have either committed or rolled back the queries, the transaction is considered complete, and MySQL returns to an *autocommit* mode. This means that any queries you execute take immediate effect. To start another transaction, just type START TRANSACTION (or BEGIN).

It is important to know that certain types of queries cannot be rolled back. Specifically those that create, alter, truncate (empty) or delete tables or create or delete databases cannot be undone. Furthermore, using such a query has the effect of committing and ending the current transaction.

Finally, you should understand that transactions are particular to each connection. So one user connected through the mysql client has a different transaction than another mysql client user, both of which are different than a connected PHP script.

Figure 11.20 A new table is created within the *test* database for the purposes of demonstrating transactions.

With this in mind, I'll run through a very trivial use of transactions within the mysql client here. In Chapter 14, transactions will be run through a PHP script.

To perform transactions:

1. Connect to the mysql client and select the *test* database.

   Since this is just a demonstration, I'll use the all-purpose *test* database.

2. Create a new *accounts* table (**Figure 11.20**).

   ```
   CREATE TABLE accounts (
       id INT UNSIGNED NOT NULL
       → AUTO_INCREMENT,
       name VARCHAR(40) NOT NULL,
       balance DECIMAL(10,2) NOT NULL
       → DEFAULT 0.0,
       PRIMARY KEY (id)
   ) ENGINE=InnoDB;
   ```

   Obviously this isn't a complete table or database design. For starters, normalization would require that the user's name be separated into multiple columns, if not stored in a separate table altogether. But for demonstration purposes, this will be fine.

   The most important aspect of the table definition is its engine—InnoDB, which allows for transactions.

3. Populate the table.

   ```
   INSERT INTO accounts (name, balance)
   → VALUES ('Sarah Vowell', 5460.23),
   → ('David Sedaris', 909325.24),
   → ('Kojo Nnamdi', 892.00);
   ```

   You can use whatever names and values here that you want. The important thing to note is that MySQL will automatically commit this query, as no transaction has begun yet.

continues on next page

NEW MySQL FEATURES

4. Begin a transaction and show the current table contents (**Figure 11.21**).

```
START TRANSACTION;
SELECT * FROM accounts;
```

Again, if you are using an earlier version of MySQL you'll need to use just `BEGIN` instead of `START TRANSACTION`.

5. Subtract $100 from David Sedaris' (or any user's) account.

```
UPDATE accounts SET balance=
→ (balance-100) WHERE id=2;
```

Using an `UPDATE` query, a little math, and a `WHERE` conditional, I can subtract 100 from a balance. Although MySQL will indicate that one row was affected, the effect is not permanent until the transaction is committed.

6. Add $100 to Sarah Vowell's account.

```
UPDATE accounts SET balance=
→ (balance+100) WHERE id=1;
```

This is the opposite of Step 5, as if $100 were being transferred from the one person to the other.

7. Confirm the results (**Figure 11.22**).

```
SELECT * FROM accounts;
```

As you can see in the figure, the one balance is 100 more and the other is 100 less then they originally were (Figure 11.21).

8. Roll back the transaction.

```
ROLLBACK;
```

To demonstrate how transactions can be undone, I'll undo the effects of these queries. The `ROLLBACK` commands returns the database back to how it was prior to starting the transaction. The command also terminates the transaction, returning MySQL to its autocommit mode.

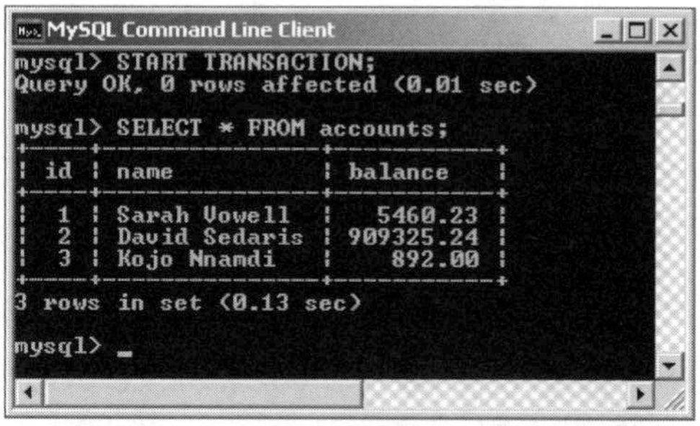

Figure 11.21 A transaction is begun and the existing table records are shown.

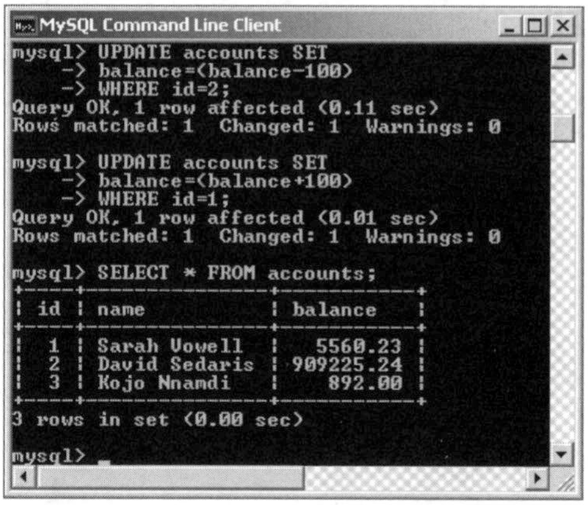

Figure 11.22 Two UPDATE queries are executed and the results are viewed.

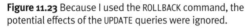

```
MySQL Command Line Client                    _□×
┌────┬──────────────┬───────────┐
│ id │ name         │ balance   │
├────┼──────────────┼───────────┤
│  1 │ Sarah Vowell │   5560.23 │
│  2 │ David Sedaris│ 909225.24 │
│  3 │ Kojo Nnandi  │    892.00 │
└────┴──────────────┴───────────┘
3 rows in set (0.00 sec)

mysql> ROLLBACK;
Query OK, 0 rows affected (0.20 sec)

mysql> SELECT * FROM accounts;
┌────┬──────────────┬───────────┐
│ id │ name         │ balance   │
├────┼──────────────┼───────────┤
│  1 │ Sarah Vowell │   5460.23 │
│  2 │ David Sedaris│ 909325.24 │
│  3 │ Kojo Nnandi  │    892.00 │
└────┴──────────────┴───────────┘
3 rows in set (0.01 sec)

mysql> _
```

Figure 11.23 Because I used the ROLLBACK command, the potential effects of the UPDATE queries were ignored.

```
MySQL Command Line Client                    _□×
mysql> START TRANSACTION;
Query OK, 0 rows affected (0.00 sec)

mysql> UPDATE accounts SET
    -> balance=(balance-100)
    -> WHERE id=2;
Query OK, 1 row affected (0.01 sec)
Rows matched: 1  Changed: 1  Warnings: 0

mysql> UPDATE accounts SET
    -> balance=(balance+100)
    -> WHERE id=1;
Query OK, 1 row affected (0.01 sec)
Rows matched: 1  Changed: 1  Warnings: 0

mysql> COMMIT;
Query OK, 0 rows affected (0.07 sec)

mysql> SELECT * FROM accounts;
┌────┬──────────────┬───────────┐
│ id │ name         │ balance   │
├────┼──────────────┼───────────┤
│  1 │ Sarah Vowell │   5560.23 │
│  2 │ David Sedaris│ 909225.24 │
│  3 │ Kojo Nnandi  │    892.00 │
└────┴──────────────┴───────────┘
3 rows in set (0.01 sec)

mysql>
```

Figure 11.24 Invoking the COMMIT command makes the transaction's effects permanent.

9. Confirm the results (**Figure 11.23**).

   SELECT * FROM accounts;

   The query should reveal the contents of the table as they original were.

10. Repeat Steps 4 through 6.

    To see what happens when the transaction is committed, the two UPDATE queries will be run again. Be certain to start the transaction first, though, or the queries will automatically take effect!

11. Commit the transaction and confirm the results (**Figure 11.24**).

    COMMIT;

    SELECT * FROM accounts;

    Once you enter COMMIT, the entire transaction is permanent, meaning that any changes are now in place. COMMIT also ends the transaction, returning MySQL to autocommit mode.

✔ Tips

- One of the great features of transactions is that they offer protection should a random event occur, such as a server crash. Either a transaction is executed in its entirety or all of the changes are ignored.

- To alter MySQL's autocommit nature, type

  SET AUTOCOMMIT=0;

  Then you do not need to type START TRANSACTION and no queries will be permanent until you type COMMIT (or use an ALTER, CREATE, etc., query).

- As of MySQL 4.0.14 and 4.1.1, you can create *savepoints* in transactions:

  SAVEPOINT *savepoint_name*;

  Then you can roll back to that point:

  ROLLBACK TO SAVEPOINT *savepoint_name*;

NEW MYSQL FEATURES

Using prepared statements

Prepared statements were added to MySQL in version 4.1. The premise behind a prepared statement is that part of a query is essentially memorized by MySQL with specific elements being defined on the fly. The benefit of prepared statements are important: greater security and better performance.

Prepared statements can be created out of any INSERT, UPDATE, DELETE, or SELECT query. In order to use them with PHP, you must use PHP's Improved MySQL Extension, available as of PHP 5. Begin by defining your query, marking *placeholders* using question marks. For the initial example, I'll assume I'm populating the *accounts* table, created in the previous section of this chapter.

```
$query = "INSERT INTO accounts
→ (name, balance) VALUES (?, ?)";
```

As you'll soon see, before the query is actually executed, the question marks will be assigned the appropriate values.

Next, prepare the statement in MySQL, assigning the results to a PHP variable.

```
$stmt = mysqli_prepare($dbc, $query);
```

At this point, MySQL will parse the query, checking for valid syntax. The speed improvement with prepared statements stems from the fact that a query needs to be parsed only once, no matter how many times it is run (presumably with different values). For this reason, the speed benefit of using prepared statements applies only when the same query is being run multiple times with different values.

Next, you *bind* PHP variables to the query's placeholders. In other words, you state that one variable should be used for one question mark, another variable for the other question mark, and so on. Continuing with the same example, you would code

```
mysqli_stmt_bind_param($stmt, "sd",
→ $name, $balance);
```

The *sd* part of the command indicates what kind of values should be expected, using the characters listed in **Table 11.3**. In this case, the query expects to receive one string (or generic type) and one decimal.

At this point, you can assign values to the PHP variables and then execute the statement.

```
$name = 'Haruki Murakami';
```

```
$balance = 45902.29;
```

```
mysqli_stmt_execute($stmt);
```

The values of $name and $balance will be used when the prepared statement is executed. To execute the statement again using different values, just repeat this last sequence.

```
$name = 'Joe Queenan';
```

```
$balance = 65487.88;
```

```
mysqli_stmt_execute($stmt);
```

To see this process in action, I'll write a script that quickly inserts several records into the *accounts* table. I'll also use the opportunity to demonstrate a couple of the other prepared statement-related functions.

Bound Value Types	
LETTER	REPRESENTS
d	decimal
i	integer
b	blob
s	all other types

Table 11.3 Use these characters to tell the mysql_stmt_bind_param() function what kinds of values to expect.

Script 11.7 In this script, prepared statements are executed using the Improved MySQL Extension functions.

```
script
1   <!DOCTYPE html PUBLIC "-//W3C//DTD XHTML
    1.0 Transitional//EN"
2         "http://www.w3.org/TR/xhtml1/DTD/
          xhtml1-transitional.dtd">
3   <html xmlns="http://www.w3.org/1999/xhtml"
    xml:lang="en" lang="en">
4   <head>
5      <meta http-equiv="content-type" content=
       "text/html; charset=iso-8859-1" />
6      <title>Prepared Statements</title>
7   </head>
8   <body>
9   <?php # Script 11.7 - prepared.php
10
11  // Make the connection.
12  $dbc = @mysqli_connect ('localhost',
    'username', 'password', 'test') OR die
    ('Could not connect to MySQL: ' .
    mysqli_connect_error() );
13
14  // Make the query.
```

(script continues on page 465)

To use prepared statements:

1. Create a new PHP script in your text editor or IDE (**Script 11.7**).

   ```
   <!DOCTYPE html PUBLIC "-//W3C//DTD
   → XHTML 1.0 Transitional//EN"
   "http://www.w3.org/TR/xhtml1/DTD/
   → xhtml1-transitional.dtd">
   <html xmlns="http://www.w3.org/1999/
   → xhtml" xml:lang="en" lang="en">
   <head>
      <meta http-equiv="content-type"
   → content="text/html; charset=
   → iso-8859-1" />
      <title>Prepared Statements</title>
   </head>
   <body>
   <?php # Script 11.7 - prepared.php
   ```

2. Connect to the *test* database.

   ```
   $dbc = @mysqli_connect ('localhost',
   → 'username', 'password', 'test') OR
   → die ('Could not connect to MySQL:
   → ' . mysqli_connect_error() );
   ```

   The *test* database, which contains the *accounts* table, will be used in this example.

continues on next page

Introducing Subqueries

Another new feature to MySQL is subqueries, which were added in version 4.1. Simply put, a subquery is a SELECT query within another query. The simplest subquery returns a single value, which can then be used in the main query.

```
SELECT * FROM table1 WHERE columnX=(SELECT MAX(columnY) FROM table2)
```

Here the subquery returns the highest value from *columnY* of *table2*. This value is then used to determine what data is selected from *table1*.

More complicated subqueries can return a row or an entire table of data, which is then used by the main query. Subqueries also have their own operators: IN, ANY, ALL, EXISTS, and NOT EXISTS.

While subqueries are a nice feature, the same result can often be achieved using a well-written join. For more information on subqueries, see the MySQL manual.

3. Define and prepare the query.

```
$query = "INSERT INTO accounts
→ (name, balance) VALUES (?, ?)";
$stmt = mysqli_prepare($dbc, $query);
```

This syntax has already been explained. The query is defined, using two place-holders for values to be assigned later. Then the mysqli_prepare() function sends this to MySQL, assigning the result to $stmt.

4. Bind the appropriate variables and create a list of values to be inserted.

```
mysqli_stmt_bind_param($stmt, "sd",
→ $name, $balance);
$data = array(
   array('Italo Calvino', 65465.99),
   array('Vladimir Nabokov', 132.74),
   array('James Joyce', 432.74),
   array('William Faulkner',
   → 841664.67),
   array('F. Scott Fitzgerald',
   → 69.23),
   array('Zora Neale Hurston',
   → 130654.44),
   array('Franz Kafka', 87.63),
   array('William Carlos Williams',
   → 9.98),
   array('Jane Austen', 1324.02),
   array('George Eliot', 49683.56)
);
```

The first line says that one string and one decimal value will be added to the pre-pared statement. The values will be found in the $name and $balance variables.

The $data array is a multidimensional list of all the values to be inserted. Using this structure, I can easily loop through each item and insert it into the database.

5. Print a caption and begin a foreach loop that executes the statements.

```
echo "<p>The query being prepared
→ is: $query</p>\n";
foreach ($data as $record) {
   $name = $record[0];
   $balance = $record[1];
   mysqli_stmt_execute($stmt);
```

The foreach loop will break each ele-ment of $data into its own array, called $record. Then the appropriate vari-ables—$name and $balance—are given their values, based upon $record. Finally, the prepared statement is executed using these values.

6. Print the results of the execution and complete the loop.

```
   echo "<p>Name: $name<br />Balance:
   → $balance<br />Result: ";
   if (mysqli_stmt_affected_rows
   → ($stmt) == 1) {
      echo 'OK';
   } else {
      echo 'FAILED ' .
      → mysqli_stmt_error($stmt);
   }
   echo '</p>';
}
```

The echo statement just prints out what values are being inserted. The successful insertion of a record is indicated using the mysqli_stmt_affected_rows() func-tion, which works as you expect it would (returning the number of affected rows). If a problem occurred, the mysqli_stmt_error() function returns the specific MySQL error message.

continues on page 466

Script 11.7 *continued*

```
15   $query = "INSERT INTO accounts (name, balance) VALUES (?, ?)";
16
17   // Prepare the statement.
18   $stmt = mysqli_prepare($dbc, $query);
19
20   // Bind the variables.
21   mysqli_stmt_bind_param($stmt, "sd", $name, $balance);
22
23   // Create an array of values to be inserted.
24   $data = array(
25      array('Italo Calvino', 65465.99),
26      array('Vladimir Nabokov', 132.74),
27      array('James Joyce', 432.74),
28      array('William Faulkner', 841664.67),
29      array('F. Scott Fitzgerald', 69.23),
30      array('Zora Neale Hurston', 130654.44),
31      array('Franz Kafka', 87.63),
32      array('William Carlos Williams', 9.98),
33      array('Jane Austen', 1324.02),
34      array('George Eliot', 49683.56)
35   );
36
37   // Print a caption.
38   echo "<p>The query being prepared is: $query</p>\n";
39
40   // Loop through the array, inserting each record.
41   foreach ($data as $record) {
42
43      // Assign the variables.
44      $name = $record[0];
45      $balance = $record[1];
46
47      // Execute the query.
48      mysqli_stmt_execute($stmt);
49
50      // Print the results.
51      echo "<p>Name: $name<br />Balance: $balance<br />Result: ";
52
53      // Print a message based upon the result.
54      if (mysqli_stmt_affected_rows($stmt) == 1) {
55         echo 'OK';
56      } else {
```

(script continues on next page)

465

7. Close the statement and the database connection.

```
mysqli_stmt_close($stmt);
mysqli_close($dbc);
```

The first function closes the prepared statement, freeing up the resources. At this point, $stmt no longer has a value. The second function closes the database connection.

8. Complete the page.

```
?>
</body>
</html>
```

9. Save the file as prepared.php, upload to your Web server, and test in your Web browser (**Figure 11.25**).

✔ Tips

■ There are two kinds of prepared statements. Here I have demonstrated *bound parameters*, where PHP variables are bound to a query. The other type is *bound results*, where the results of a query are bound to PHP variables.

■ Because of how MySQL deals with prepared statements, you don't actually need to sanctify your values using mysqli_real_escape_string() or similar functions. You should still perform basic validation in PHP, of course.

Script 11.7 *continued*

```
                            script
57          echo 'FAILED ' .
            mysqli_stmt_error($stmt);
58      }
59
60      echo '</p>';
61
62  } // End of foreach loop.
63
64  // Close the statement.
65  mysqli_stmt_close($stmt);
66
67  // Close the connection.
68  mysqli_close($dbc);
69  ?>
70  </body>
71  </html>
```

```
○ ○ ○            Prepared Statements

The query being prepared is: INSERT INTO accounts
(name, balance) VALUES (?, ?)

Name: Italo Calvino
Balance: 65465.99
Result: OK

Name: Vladimir Nabokov
Balance: 132.74
Result: OK

Name: James Joyce
Balance: 432.74
Result: OK

Name: William Faulkner
Balance: 841664.67
Result: OK

Name: F. Scott Fitzgerald
Balance: 69.23
Result: OK

Name: Zora Neale Hurston
Balance: 130654.44
Result: OK
```

Figure 11.25 Prepared statements are used to quickly insert several records.

Using PEAR

PEAR, the PHP Extension and Application Repository, is a collection of established code that programmers can incorporate into their own projects. The official Web site for PEAR is http://pear.php.net (**Figure 11.26**).

Many things I have done (or will do) in this book could be done using PEAR, including:

◆ Interacting with MySQL

◆ Controlling page caching

◆ Sending plain or HTML email

◆ Performing HTTP authentication

◆ Creating and validating HTML forms

There are many advantages to using PEAR. First of all, you can more quickly develop applications. Second, your Web sites will then be relying upon tested, established

code instead of your own (potentially buggy) work. There are really only two downsides to PEAR, in my opinion. For one, PEAR and the modules you'll want to use must be installed on a server (and the installation process—see the PEAR manual—is not as foolproof as it could be). Second, not every PEAR module is as well documented or as smooth-running as it could be.

Still, it's not difficult for the intermediate PHP programmer to use PEAR's classes, even without any formal training in object-oriented programming. As just one example of what you can do with PEAR, I'll add benchmarking to an existing script so that I can see how long various aspects of the script take to execute. In order to follow this example, you'll need to make sure that PEAR is installed, as well as the *Benchmark* class.

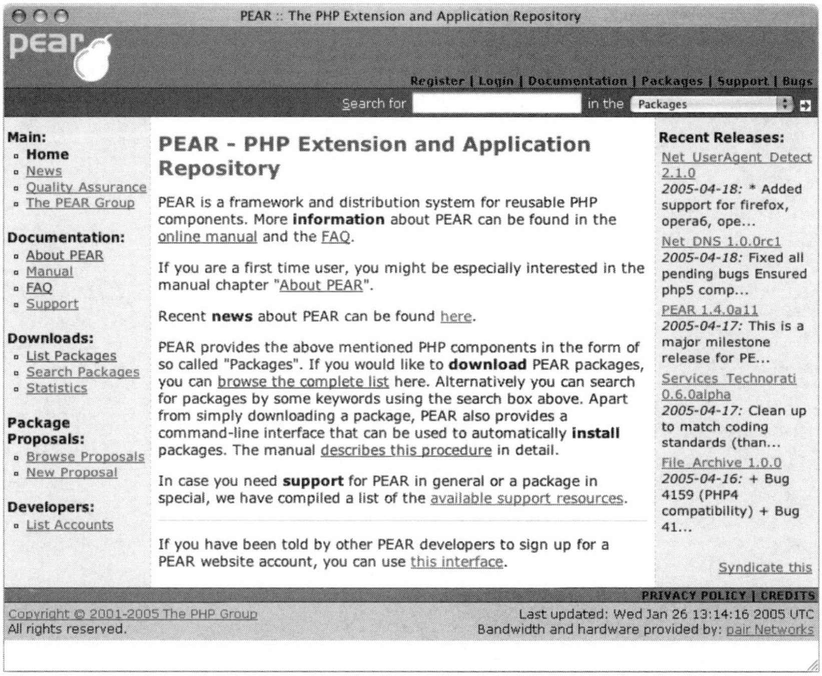

Figure 11.26 The home page for PEAR.

To benchmark a script:

1. Open mysqli.php in your text editor or IDE.

   I'm going to add benchmarking to the mysqli.php script, written earlier in the chapter. If you have not yet created this script, you can apply the concept demonstrated here to any other file.

2. At the beginning of the script, create a new timer (**Script 11.8**).

   ```
   <?php # Script 11.8 - benchmark.php
   require_once('Benchmark/Timer.php');
   $t = new Benchmark_Timer;
   $t->start();
   ?>
   ```

   To use any PEAR class, you must first require the appropriate script. Then, following the example shown in the Timer.php script (which is part of the Benchmark package), I'll create a new timer object, called $t, and start the timer.

3. After the initial HTML code, set a marker.

   ```
   $t->setMarker ('Header printed');
   ```

   First, I'll time how long it takes to print the header HTML. To do so, I set a marker using an appropriate marker name or caption with the setMarker() function (or method).

4. After connecting to the database, set another marker.

   ```
   $t->setMarker ('Connected to
   → MySQL');
   ```

   Database connections are normally big resource hogs. To time how long this took, I create another marker.

Script 11.8 Using PEAR's *Benchmark* class, I time how long various aspects of this script take.

```
1    <?php # Script 11.8 - benchmark.php
2    // Require the file and begin the process.
3    require_once('Benchmark/Timer.php');
4    $t = new Benchmark_Timer;
5    $t->start();
6    ?>
7    <!DOCTYPE html PUBLIC "-//W3C//DTD XHTML
     1.0 Transitional//EN"
8         "http://www.w3.org/TR/xhtml1/DTD/
          xhtml1-transitional.dtd">
9    <html xmlns="http://www.w3.org/1999/xhtml"
     xml:lang="en" lang="en">
10   <head>
11       <meta http-equiv="content-type" content=
         "text/html; charset=iso-8859-1" />
12       <title>View Submitted Comments</title>
13   </head>
14   <body>
15   <?php
16   // Set a marker.
17   $t->setMarker ('Header printed');
18
19   // Make the connection.
20   $dbc = @mysqli_connect ('localhost',
     'username', 'password', 'test') OR die
     ('Could not connect to MySQL: ' .
     mysqli_connect_error() );
21   $t->setMarker ('Connected to MySQL');
22
23   // Make the query.
24   $query = "SELECT name, comment, DATE_FORMAT
     (date_entered, '%M %D, %Y') FROM comments
     ORDER BY date_entered DESC";
25
26   // Run the query and handle the results.
27   if ($result = @mysqli_query($dbc, $query)) {
28       $t->setMarker ('Query has been run');
29
30       if (mysqli_num_rows($result) > 0) { //
         Some records returned.
31
```

(script continues on next page)

Script 11.8 *continued*

```
┌────────────────────────────────┐
│■□         script          □■│
├────────────────────────────────┤
32       // Print each record in a loop.
33       while ($row = mysqli_fetch_array
         ($result, MYSQLI_NUM)) {
34           echo "<h3>$row[0] ($row[2])</h3>
35           <p>$row[1]</p><br />";
36       }
37       $t->setMarker ('Finished printing
         the results');
38
39    } else { // No records returned.
40        echo '<p>There are currently no
          comments in the database.</p>';
41    }
42
43  } else { // Query didn't run properly.
44      echo '<p><font color="red">MySQL Error:
        ' . mysqli_error($dbc) . '<br /><br /
        >Query: ' . $query . '</font></p>';//
        Debugging message.
45  }
46
47  // Free the result and close the
    connection.
48  mysqli_free_result($result);
49  mysqli_close($dbc);
50  $t->setMarker ('Free and Close');
51
52  // Stop the timer and print the results.
53  $t->stop();
54  $result = $t->getProfiling();
55  foreach ($result as $element) {
56      echo "<p>{$element['name']}: {$element
        ['diff']}</p>";
57  }
58  ?>
59  </body>
60  </html>
```

5. After querying the database, make another marker.

```
$t->setMarker ('Query has been
→ run');
```

This third marker will be used to determine how long it took to define and run a query.

6. After printing all of the query results, set another marker.

```
$t->setMarker ('Finished printing
→ the results');
```

7. After closing the database connection, establish the final marker.

```
$t->setMarker ('Free and Close');
```

8. Finally, stop the timer.

```
$t->stop();
```

The stop() method of the timer will end the benchmarking process.

9. Print out the benchmark results.

```
$result = $t->getProfiling();
foreach ($result as $element) {
    echo "<p>{$element['name']}:
    → {$element['diff']}</p>";
}
```

Once you've stopped the timer, a call to the getProfiling() function will return a multidimensional array with the timing results. The easiest way to print out $result is to use a foreach loop. Within the loop, each element of the $result array is itself an array of four elements: *name* (the marker name), *time* (the time the marker was set), *diff* (the difference between this marker and the previous marker or start), and *total* (the total time elapsed since the timer was started). Using this information, I'll print out the name of each marker and the amount of time each marker took.

continues on next page

USING PEAR

10. Save the file as benchmark.php, upload to your Web server, and test in your Web browser (**Figure 11.27**).

Looking at the resulting numbers in the figure, you can see that connecting to MySQL and executing the query are the most involving steps, taking ten times as long as any other step.

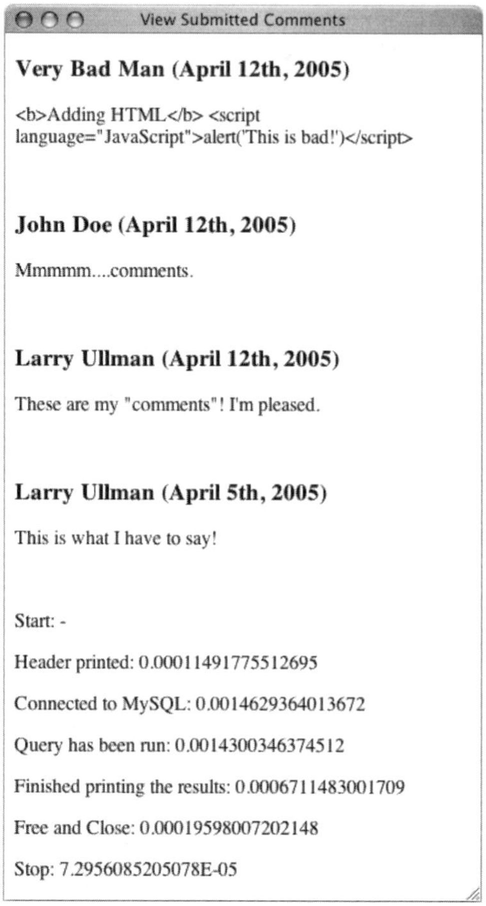

✔ Tips

- Some PEAR packages will not work on the Windows operating system because they involve Unix-specific functions.

- To see the currently available list of packages, type pear list-remote-packages in a command prompt, assuming the PEAR package manager has been installed.

- There is a subset of PEAR called PECL ("pickle," the PHP Extension Code Library) that consists of standard PEAR modules written directly in C and C++, rather than PHP, resulting in better performance.

- An important aspect of PEAR is the set of standards under which all PHP modules must be written (in terms of variable names, document structure, and so forth). Even if you will never attempt to add to the PEAR library, following these standards as a PHP programmer is well worth considering.

- The PEAR online documentation lists PEAR-specific Web sites, mailing lists, and other places to turn for support.

- If you are really interested in fine-tuning the performance of your Web applications, use the *Benchmark* class to time your scripts, and then focus on those parts that take the longest to execute (for example, the database query in this script). You can also use this class to see the speed difference between, say, using mysql_* versus mysqli_* functions, or to see the benefit of prepared statements.

View Submitted Comments

Very Bad Man (April 12th, 2005)

<b>Adding HTML</b> <script language="JavaScript">alert('This is bad!')</script>

John Doe (April 12th, 2005)

Mmmmm....comments.

Larry Ullman (April 12th, 2005)

These are my "comments"! I'm pleased.

Larry Ullman (April 5th, 2005)

This is what I have to say!

Start: -

Header printed: 0.00011491775512695

Connected to MySQL: 0.0014629364013672

Query has been run: 0.0014300346374512

Finished printing the results: 0.0006711483001709

Free and Close: 0.00019598007202148

Stop: 7.2956085205078E-05

Figure 11.27 At the bottom of the page, the result of using the Benchmark class helps reveal how long different steps of the script took to execute.

- PEAR's database abstraction class is one of its most popular tools, allowing you to develop database-independent Web applications.

A Brief Introduction to Objects and Classes

There is one last variable type that I have not discussed in this book: *objects*. Object-oriented programming (OOP) is a subject so complex that multiple chapters and even entire books are dedicated to the subject. PHP has supported objects for some time now, and version 5 of the language has taken that support to new heights.

I have omitted discussion of objects for two reasons. First, a reasonably thorough coverage of them would have meant less room for what I consider to be far more important information. And second, you can go your entire PHP programming life without ever using objects. So that the subject isn't entirely foreign to you, here's a three-second introduction:

One uses objects to encapsulate related blocks of code into one easy-to-use, easy-to-maintain *object*. You start by creating a *class*. A class is a definition of a thing, normally containing both functions (called *methods*) and variables (called *properties*). Once you've defined a class, you can create an instance of that class, which is a variable of an object type.

```
$var = new ObjectName;
```

To then call an object's method (a function), the syntax is

```
$var->functionName();
```

If you ever see this syntax, as with the PEAR example in this chapter, you'll now understand its meaning.

More advanced objects involve special functions—called *constructors*—that are called when a new instance is created and those that are invoked when an instance is deleted—called *destructors*. There is also *inheritance*, where you create a new class by expanding upon an existing class definition.

While OOP is quite powerful, it's not for faint of heart, nor should you start trying to write your own objects without a thorough understanding of the concept. And as I said, you can continue to program in PHP without ever using objects, without limiting your potential at all. Also, even the relatively novice programmer can use existing objects—like the PEAR body of code—by merely following the example syntax.

EXAMPLE— CONTENT MANAGEMENT

The first example I'll demonstrate in this book will be a content management site. The application will manage both URLs and files, which users can add, display, and access. I won't create an administrative side of the site, although I include notes at the end of the chapter as to how that would be accomplished.

Although the focus in this chapter is on a specific example, a few new functions and techniques will also be taught. The new functions include `mysql_insert_id()`, `serialize()`, `urlencode()`, `array_diff()`, and `list()`.

Creating the Template

The first step in developing this application is to create a template system to handle the HTML design. The end result (**Figure 12.1**) will use tables and some Cascading Style Sheets (CSS).

To make header.html:

1. Create a new HTML document in your text editor (**Script 12.1**).

   ```
   <!DOCTYPE html PUBLIC "-//W3C//DTD
   → XHTML 1.0 Transitional//EN"
   "http://www.w3.org/TR/xhtml1/DTD/
   → xhtml1-transitional.dtd">
   <html xmlns="http://www.w3.org/1999/
   → xhtml" xml:lang="en" lang="en">
   <head>
      <meta http-equiv="content-type"
   → content="text/html; charset=
   → iso-8859-1" />
      <title><?php echo $page_title;
   → ?></title>
   ```

   Notice that, once again, I'll use PHP to print out a page-specific title between the HTML title tags.

2. Create the CSS code.

   ```
   <style type="text/css" media=
   → "screen">
      body { background-color: #ffffff; }
      .content {
         background-color: #f5f5f5;
         padding-top: 10px;
      → padding-right: 10px;
      → padding-bottom: 10px;
      → padding-left: 10px;
         margin-top: 10px; margin-right:
      → 10px; margin-bottom: 10px;
      → margin-left: 10px;
      }
   ```

Figure 12.1 The default layout used by the application in this chapter.

Script 12.1 The header file begins the HTML layout and includes the necessary CSS code.

```
1   <!DOCTYPE html PUBLIC "-//W3C//DTD XHTML
    1.0 Transitional//EN"
2          "http://www.w3.org/TR/xhtml1/DTD/
           xhtml1-transitional.dtd">
3   <html xmlns="http://www.w3.org/1999/xhtml"
    xml:lang="en" lang="en">
4   <head>
5      <meta http-equiv="content-type" content=
       "text/html; charset=iso-8859-1" />
6      <title><?php echo $page_title; ?>
       </title>
7      <style type="text/css" media="screen">
8         body { background-color: #ffffff; }
9
10        .content {
11           background-color: #f5f5f5;
12           padding-top: 10px; padding-right:
             10px; padding-bottom: 10px;
             padding-left: 10px;
13           margin-top: 10px; margin-right:
             10px; margin-bottom: 10px;
             margin-left: 10px;
14        }
15
```

(script continues on next page)

Script 12.1 *continued*

```
                    script
16        a.navlink:link { color: #003366;
          text-decoration: none; }
17        a.navlink:visited { color: #003366;
          text-decoration: none; }
18        a.navlink:hover { color: #cccccc;
          text-decoration: none; }
19
20        td {
21           font-family: Verdana, Arial,
             Helvetica, sans-serif; font-size:
             13px;
22           vertical-align: top;
23        }
24
25        .title {
26           font-size: 24px; font-weight:
             normal; color: #ffffff;
27           margin-top: 5px; margin-bottom:
             5px; margin-left: 20px;
28           padding-top: 5px; padding-bottom:
             5px; padding-left: 20px;
29        }
30     </style>
31  </head>
32  <body>
33
34  <table width="90%" border="0" cellspacing="10"
    cellpadding="0" align="center">
35
36     <tr>
37     <td colspan="2" bgcolor="#003366">
       <p class="title">Content Management Site
       </p></td>
38     </tr>
39
```

(script continues on next page)

```
a.navlink:link { color: #003366;
→ text-decoration: none; }
a.navlink:visited { color:
→ #003366; text-decoration: none; }
a.navlink:hover { color: #cccccc;
→ text-decoration: none; }
td {
   font-family: Verdana, Arial,
→ Helvetica, sans-serif; font-size:
→ 13px;
   vertical-align: top;
}
.title {
   font-size: 24px; font-weight:
→ normal; color: #ffffff;
   margin-top: 5px; margin-bottom:
→ 5px; margin-left: 20px;
   padding-top: 5px;
→ padding-bottom: 5px
→ ; padding-left: 20px;
}
</style>
```

For this application, I'm going to use some CSS to adjust the formatting of the text. Because there's not a lot of CSS data to consider, I'll store it directly in the HEAD of the HTML code, rather than in a separate file.

3. Complete the HTML head and create the first row of the layout table.

```
</head>
<body>
<table width="90%" border="0"
→ cellspacing="10" cellpadding="0"
→ align="center">
<tr>
   <td colspan="2" bgcolor=
→ "#003366"><p class="title">
→ Content Management Site</p></td>
   </tr>
```

continues on next page

CREATING THE TEMPLATE

The basic layout of the site will be a table with three rows: the title row, another row containing the navigation links and the content, and a third row for the copyright (**Figure 12.2**).

4. Create the navigation section and begin the content cell.

```
<tr>
   <td valign="top" nowrap="nowrap">
<b><a href="index.php" class=
→ "navlink">Home</a><br />
<a href="view_urls.php" class=
→ "navlink">View URLs</a><br />
<a href="add_url.php" class=
→ "navlink">Add a URL</a><br />
<a href="view_files.php" class=
→ "navlink">View Files</a><br />
<a href="add_file.php" class=
→ "navlink">Add a File</a></b>
   </td>
<td valign="top" class="content">
   <!-- Script 12.1 - header.html -->
```

5. Save the file as header.html and upload to your Web server (into an *includes* directory).

To preview the Web document structure, see **Figure 12.3**.

Script 12.1 *continued*

```
40      <tr>
41          <td valign="top" nowrap="nowrap">
42      <b><a href="index.php" class="navlink">
        Home</a><br />
43          <a href="view_urls.php" class="navlink">
        View URLs</a><br />
44          <a href="add_url.php" class="navlink">
        Add a URL</a><br />
45          <a href="view_files.php" class="navlink">
        View Files</a><br />
46          <a href="add_file.php" class="navlink">
        Add a File</a></b>
47          </td>
48
49          <td valign="top" class="content">
50          <!-- Script 12.1 - header.html -->
```

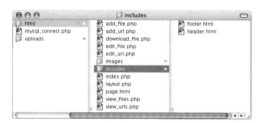

Figure 12.2 The same layout (see Figure 12.1), displayed using borders to indicate the rows and columns of the table.

Figure 12.3 The structure of the Web application, with the *html* folder as the root directory (www.address. com will point there).

Script 12.2 The footer file concludes the layout and the HTML page as a whole.

```
                        script
1   <!-- Script 12.2 - footer.html -->
2   <!-- End of Content -->
3       </td>
4     </tr>
5
6     <tr>
7       <td> </td>
8       <td align="center">&copy; 2005 Larry E.
        Ullman and DMC Insights, Inc.</td>
9     </tr>
10
11  </table>
12  </body>
13  </html>
```

To make footer.html:

1. Create a new HTML document in your text editor (**Script 12.2**).

   ```
   <!-- Script 12.2 - footer.html -->
   ```

2. Complete the middle table row.

   ```
       </td>
     </tr>
   ```

   All of the page's content is stored in the middle row, which was begun in header.html. This code will complete that row before creating the third, final row.

3. Make the bottom row and complete the HTML page.

   ```
     <tr>
       <td> </td>
       <td align="center">&copy; 2005
   → Larry E. Ullman and DMC
   → Insights, Inc.</td>
     </tr>
   </table>
   </body>
   </html>
   ```

4. Save the file as footer.html and upload to your Web server (into the *includes* directory).

Creating the Basic Pages

Before I get into the heart of the Web application (the content management itself), I need to create two more pages. One will be `index.php` and will act as the home page for the site. The second will be `mysql_connect.php`, a script that connects to MySQL and selects the database to be used (see the "Database Scheme" sidebar in the next section for more information about the database).

To make the home page:

1. Create a new PHP script in your text editor (**Script 12.3**).

   ```
   <?php # Script 12.3 - index.php
   ```

2. Set the page title and include the HTML header.

   ```
   $page_title = 'Content Management Site';
   include ('./includes/header.html');
   ?>
   ```

3. Create the content.

   ```
   <p>Spam spam spam spam spam spam
   spam spam spam spam spam spam
   spam spam spam spam spam spam
   spam spam spam spam spam spam.</p>
   <p>Spam spam spam spam spam spam
   spam spam spam spam spam spam
   spam spam spam spam spam spam
   spam spam spam spam spam spam.</p>
   ```

   Obviously, you'll want to put more useful content on your home page, but I'm using *spam* as filler (it's surprisingly filling).

4. Require the HTML footer.

   ```
   <?php
   include ('./includes/footer.html');
   ?>
   ```

Script 12.3 The application's home page (add meaningful content as needed).

```
1    <?php # Script 12.3 - index.php
2    // This is the main page for the site.
3
4    // Set the page title and include the HTML
     header.
5    $page_title = 'Content Management Site';
6    include ('./includes/header.html');
7    ?>
8
9        <p>Spam spam spam spam spam spam
10       spam spam spam spam spam spam
11       spam spam spam spam spam spam
12       spam spam spam spam spam spam.</p>
13
14       <p>Spam spam spam spam spam spam
15       spam spam spam spam spam spam
16       spam spam spam spam spam spam
17       spam spam spam spam spam spam.</p>
18
19   <?php // Include the HTML footer file.
20   include ('./includes/footer.html');
21   ?>
```

Figure 12.4 The home page.

5. Save the file as `index.php`, upload to your Web server (in the main *html* directory, see Figure 12.3), and test in a Web browser (**Figure 12.4**).

More Content Management

The content management example in this chapter deals with two specific kinds of content: files and lists of URLs. But content management systems (CMS) normally handle a third type of information: general Web content. Many CMS tools provide an interface to dynamically generate the text and/or images presented on specific pages.

I have not included such an example in this chapter because it's really not that complicated and there's only so much space. Here's the quick lowdown:

Having a Web page's content be dynamically driven is just a matter of storing text in a database table, somehow indicating what text belongs to what page on the public side. To place the text there in the first place, create a simple form with a large text area. Validate the text area upon submission and address HTML code and special characters, as warranted. The dynamic page can then pull the data out of the database and plop it into the template where appropriate. If you have multiple pages based upon the same template but using different values—say several pages of book reviews—pass the templated page the ID for the specific record in the database. This notion—passing an ID to a page—will be demonstrated with the `edit_url.php` page.

If you want to dynamically add images to a page, follow the same process as the files examples at the end of the chapter. Store the image's name in the database, store the file itself on the server, and dynamically create the HTML for the image on the public page.

To make mysql_connect.php:

1. Create a new PHP script in your text editor (**Script 12.4**).

   ```
   <?php # Script 12.4 - mysql_connect.
   → php
   ```

   This script will be identical to previous versions of it from other chapters (except perhaps for the specific username, password, and database settings). You can either create this script from scratch or modify an existing version accordingly.

2. Set the database information as constants.

   ```
   DEFINE ('DB_USER', 'username');
   DEFINE ('DB_PASSWORD', 'password');
   DEFINE ('DB_HOST', 'localhost');
   DEFINE ('DB_NAME', 'content');
   ```

   For security's sake, the MySQL user for this application should have INSERT, SELECT, UPDATE, and DELETE privileges only, and just for the *content* database.

3. Connect to MySQL and select the database.

   ```
   $dbc = @mysql_connect (DB_HOST,
   → DB_USER, DB_PASSWORD) OR die
   → ('Could not connect to MySQL: ' .
   → mysql_error() );

   @mysql_select_db (DB_NAME) OR die
   → ('Could not select the database: ' .
   → mysql_error() );
   ```

   This application will have basic error management, using the mysql_error() function (as discussed in Chapter 7, "Using PHP with MySQL"). Remember that you don't want to display MySQL errors to the general public, so you may want to use the more elaborate error handling techniques discussed in Chapter 6, "Error Handling and Debugging."

4. Define the escape_data() function.

   ```
   function escape_data ($data) {
       if (ini_get('magic_quotes_gpc')) {
           $data = stripslashes($data);
       }
       if (function_exists
   → ('mysql_real_escape_string')) {
           global $dbc;
           $data = mysql_real_escape_string
   → (trim($data), $dbc);
       } else {
           $data = mysql_escape_string
   → (trim($data));
       }
       return $data;
   }
   ```

   This function will be used to handle submitted form values, so that inserting those values into the database will not break the queries. The function is defined as it was in Chapter 8, "Web Application Development," using several savvy techniques.

   The function expects to receive one argument, assigned to $data. If Magic Quotes are on—as determined using the ini_get() function—then the stripslashes() function is applied to avoid over-escaping the data. Finally, a check is made to see if the mysql_real_escape_string() is available (it was added in PHP 4.3). If so, this function is used (and it requires a database connection, $dbc). If that function is unavailable, the older mysql_escape_string() function is called (it does not use a database connection). Finally, the well-groomed data is returned by the function.

   continues on page 482

CREATING THE BASIC PAGES

Script 12.4 This script connects to MySQL, selects the *content* database, and defines the escape_data() function, used for sanctifying submitted text.

```
1    <?php # Script 12.4 - mysql_connect.php
2
3    // This file contains the database access information.
4    // This file also establishes a connection to MySQL and selects the database.
5    // This file also defines the escape_data() function.
6
7    // Set the database access information as constants.
8    DEFINE ('DB_USER', 'username');
9    DEFINE ('DB_PASSWORD', 'password');
10   DEFINE ('DB_HOST', 'localhost');
11   DEFINE ('DB_NAME', 'content');
12
13   // Make the connection.
14   $dbc = @mysql_connect (DB_HOST, DB_USER, DB_PASSWORD) OR die ('Could not connect to MySQL: '
     . mysql_error() );
15
16   // Select the database.
17   @mysql_select_db (DB_NAME) OR die ('Could not select the database: ' . mysql_error() );
18
19   // Create a function for escaping the data.
20   function escape_data ($data) {
21
22       // Address Magic Quotes.
23       if (ini_get('magic_quotes_gpc')) {
24           $data = stripslashes($data);
25       }
26
27       // Check for mysql_real_escape_string() support.
28       if (function_exists('mysql_real_escape_string')) {
29           global $dbc; // Need the connection.
30           $data = mysql_real_escape_string (trim($data), $dbc);
31       } else {
32           $data = mysql_escape_string (trim($data));
33       }
34
35       // Return the escaped value.
36       return $data;
37
38   } // End of function.
39   ?>
```

5. Complete the PHP page.

```
?>
```

6. Save the file as `mysql_connect.php` and upload to your Web server (outside of the Web document root, see Figure 12.3).

✔ Tips

- The example in the next chapter will use more advanced error-management techniques and a modified version of this MySQL connection script.

- For more information on MySQL privileges and creating users, see Appendix A, "Installation."

Managing URLs

The next three pages to be developed will allow users to add URLs, view those already added, and edit the existing records. This section of the site relies upon three tables in the *content* database: *urls*, *url_categories*, and *url_associations*. See the "Database Scheme" sidebar for details.

Adding URLs

The `add_url.php` script will be one of the most complicated ones in the whole Web application on account of the normalized database structure. The script's form will take a URL, a URL title (or name), a description, and the categories with which it should be associated. Upon receiving the form, the URL, URL title, and description values will be added to the *urls* table. Then the primary key from that table (*url_id*) will be used along with the *url_category_id* values to add the record (or records, if multiple categories were selected) to the *url_associations* table. To refresh your memory as to the why's and how's of this process, refer back to Chapter 5, where these steps were taken within the mysql client.

To determine the *url_id* for the just-added URL, I'll use the `mysql_insert_id()` function, which I have not discussed before. Whenever a query is run on a table that contains an automatically incremented field (normally this is the primary key), MySQL will use the next logical value for that field. The `mysql_insert_id()` function will return that value.

Database Scheme

The database being used in this chapter is called *content* and was designed and created back in Chapter 5, "Advanced SQL and MySQL." At that time, three normalized tables were defined for handling URLs (the complex structure allows for a URL to be categorized under multiple types). For this chapter, I'll add an *uploads* table to manage the files. The complete structure for the database can be re-created with

```
CREATE TABLE uploads (
upload_id int(10) UNSIGNED NOT NULL AUTO_INCREMENT,
file_name VARCHAR(30) NOT NULL,
file_size INT(6) UNSIGNED NOT NULL,
file_type VARCHAR(30) NOT NULL,
description VARCHAR(100) DEFAULT NULL,
date_entered TIMESTAMP,
PRIMARY KEY (upload_id),
KEY (file_name),
KEY (date_entered)
)
CREATE TABLE urls (
url_id SMALLINT(4) UNSIGNED NOT NULL AUTO_INCREMENT,
url VARCHAR(60) NOT NULL,
title VARCHAR(60) NOT NULL,
description TINYTEXT NOT NULL,
PRIMARY KEY (url_id)
)
CREATE TABLE url_categories (
url_category_id TINYINT(3) UNSIGNED NOT NULL AUTO_INCREMENT,
category VARCHAR(20) NOT NULL,
PRIMARY KEY (url_category_id)
)
CREATE TABLE url_associations (
ua_id SMALLINT(4) UNSIGNED NOT NULL AUTO_INCREMENT,
url_id SMALLINT(4) UNSIGNED NOT NULL,
url_category_id TINYINT(3) UNSIGNED NOT NULL,
date_submitted TIMESTAMP,
approved CHAR(1) DEFAULT 'N' NOT NULL,
PRIMARY KEY (ua_id)
)
```

Remember that you can always list the tables in a database using the SQL command SHOW TABLES. To confirm the structure of a table, use DESCRIBE *tablename*.

To create add_url.php:

1. Create a new PHP document in your text editor (**Script 12.5**).

   ```
   <?php # Script 12.5 - add_url.php
   $page_title = 'Add a URL';
   include ('./includes/header.html');
   require_once ('../mysql_connect.
   → php');
   ```

   Both the form itself and the handling of the form require a database connection, so the connection script is included almost immediately. Remember to change the path of your require statement if your connection script is not stored in the directory above this file (see Figure 12.3).

2. Check if the form has been submitted.

   ```
   if (isset($_POST['submitted'])) {
   ```

   As this page will both display and handle the form, a hidden form input, named *submitted*, will be used to determine if the form needs to be handled.

3. Validate a submitted URL.

   ```
   if (eregi ('^([[:alnum:]]\-\.])+
   → (\.)([[:alnum:]]){2,4}([[:alnum:]]
   → /+=%&_\.~?\-]*)$', $_POST['url'])) {
     $u = escape_data($_POST['url']);
   } else {
     $u = FALSE;
     echo '<p><font color="red">
   → Please enter a valid URL!
   → </font></p>';
   }
   ```

   A regular expression, similar to one defined in Chapter 10, "Web Application Security," is used to validate the URL. It has been slightly modified, so that it does not look for an initial *http://*, *https://*, or *ftp://* section. If a valid URL is not submitted, or if any field is not filled out, an error message will be displayed (**Figure 12.5**).

4. Validate the URL's title and description.

   ```
   if (!empty($_POST['title'])) {
     $t = escape_data($_POST['title']);
   } else {
     $t = FALSE;
     echo '<p><font color="red">
   → Please enter a URL name/title!
   → </font></p>';
   }
   if (!empty($_POST['description'])) {
     $d = escape_data($_POST
   → ['description']);
   } else {
     $d = FALSE;
     echo '<p><font color="red">
   → Please enter a description!
   → </font></p>';
   }
   ```

   These two form inputs are just checked for a value. If they aren't empty, each value is run through the escape_data() function and assigned to a new variable. If a value is empty, an error message is displayed and the new variable is given a FALSE value.

continues on page 486

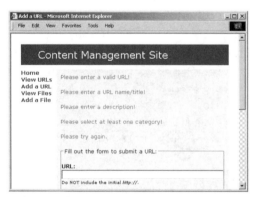

Figure 12.5 If the user fails to properly fill out the form, they'll see errors like these.

MANAGING URLs

Script 12.5 This script allows users to add URLs, associated with specific categories, to the database.

```
                             script
1    <?php # Script 12.5 - add_url.php
2    // This page allows users to add URLs to the database.
3
4    // Set the page title and include the HTML header.
5    $page_title = 'Add a URL';
6    include ('./includes/header.html');
7
8    require_once ('../mysql_connect.php'); // Connect to the database.
9
10   if (isset($_POST['submitted'])) { // Handle the form.
11
12       // Check for a URL.
13       if (eregi ('^([[:alnum:]\-\.])+(\.)([[:alnum:]]){2,4}([[:alnum:]/+=%&_\.~?\-]*)$', $_POST
         ['url'])) {
14           $u = escape_data($_POST['url']);
15       } else {
16           $u = FALSE;
17           echo '<p><font color="red">Please enter a valid URL!</font></p>';
18       }
19
20       // Check for a URL title.
21       if (!empty($_POST['title'])) {
22           $t = escape_data($_POST['title']);
23       } else {
24           $t = FALSE;
25           echo '<p><font color="red">Please enter a URL name/title!</font></p>';
26       }
27
28       // Check for a description.
29       if (!empty($_POST['description'])) {
30           $d = escape_data($_POST['description']);
31       } else {
32           $d = FALSE;
33           echo '<p><font color="red">Please enter a description!</font></p>';
34       }
35
```

(script continues on next page)

MANAGING URLS

5. Check that a category has been selected.

```
if (isset($_POST['types']) &&
→ (is_array($_POST['types']))) {
  $type = TRUE;
} else {
  $type = FALSE;
  echo '<p><font color="red">
  → Please select at least one
  → category!</font></p>';
}
```

The user will be given the option of submitting a URL in several categories, based upon the available types set in the *url_categories* table. These will be listed in a select box (**Figure 12.6**), whose name will be *types[]*. If at least one of the categories is selected, then $_POST['types'] will be set and be of an array type.

6. If everything's okay, add the URL to the *urls* table.

```
if ($u && $t && $d && $type) {
  $query = "INSERT INTO urls
  → (url, title, description) VALUES
  → ('$u', '$t', '$d')";
  $result = @mysql_query ($query);
  $uid = @mysql_insert_id();
```

Because of the structure of the database, the URL itself must be added to the *urls* table before an entry can be made into the *url_associations* table. This query will add the URL and then return the *url_id* (the auto-incremented primary key for the table), using the `mysql_insert_id()` function. This value can then be used in the second query (Step 7).

The error suppression operator (@) is used to avoid ugly error messages, which will instead be handled more gracefully later in the script.

Script 12.5 *continued*

```
                            script

36      // Check for a category.
37      if (isset($_POST['types']) && (is_array
        ($_POST['types']))) {
38          $type = TRUE;
39      } else {
40          $type = FALSE;
41          echo '<p><font color="red">
            Please select at least one category!
            </font></p>';
42      }
43
44      if ($u && $t && $d && $type) { // If
        everything's OK.
45
46          // Add the URL to the urls table.
47          $query = "INSERT INTO urls
            (url, title, description) VALUES
            ('$u', '$t', '$d')";
48          $result = @mysql_query ($query);
            // Run the query.
49          $uid = @mysql_insert_id();
            // Get the url ID.
50
51          if ($uid > 0) { // New URL has been
            added.
52
53              // Make the URL associations.
54
55              // Build the query.
56              $query = 'INSERT INTO
                url_associations (url_id,
                url_category_id, approved)
                VALUES ';
57              foreach ($_POST['types'] as $v) {
58                  $query .= "($uid, $v, 'Y'), ";
59              }
60              $query = substr ($query, 0, -2);
                // Chop off the last comma and
                space.
61
```

(script continues on page 489)

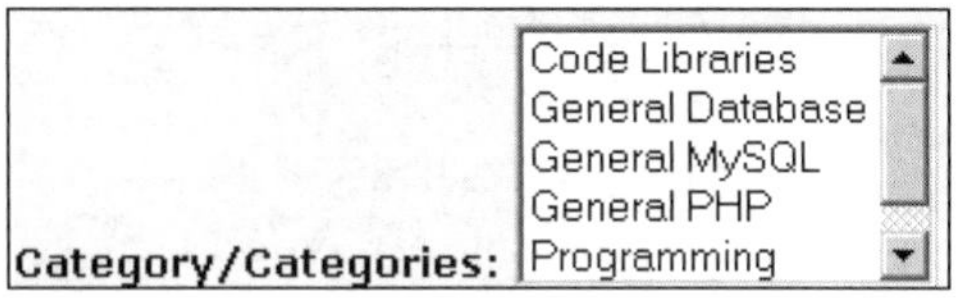

Figure 12.6 The user must select at least one category for the URL to be filed under. The select box is populated using the *url_categories* table.

7. Build the *url_associations* INSERT query.

```
if ($uid > 0) {
    $query = 'INSERT INTO
    → url_associations (url_id,
    → url_category_id, approved)
    → VALUES ';
    foreach ($_POST['types'] as $v) {
        $query .= "($uid, $v, 'Y'), ";
    }
    $query = substr ($query, 0, -2);
```

If the $uid value was retrieved, it's safe to continue with the second query (adding the record to the *url_associations* table). To do so, I begin defining the query, assigning the initial part to the $query variable. Then I loop through every chosen category, adding a record to the query for each. Finally, I use the substr() function to chop off the last two characters (the comma and the space) from the query. The resulting query will be something along the lines of INSERT INTO url_associations (url_id, url_category_id, approved) VALUES (23, 3, 'Y'), (23, 7, 'Y').

continues on next page

MANAGING URLS

8. Run the second query and report upon the results.

```
$result = @mysql_query ($query);
if (mysql_affected_rows() ==
→ count($_POST['types'])) {
    echo '<p><b>Thank you for your
    → submission!</b></p>';
    $_POST = array();
} else {
    echo '<p><font color="red">
    → Your submission could not be
    → processed due to a system error.
    → We apologize for any
    → inconvenience.</font></p>';
    echo '<p><font color="red">' .
    → mysql_error() . '<br /><br />
    → Query: ' . $query . '</font>
    → </p>';
    $query = "DELETE FROM urls WHERE
    → url_id=$uid";
    @mysql_query ($query);
}
```

After running the query, the conditional checks to see if the number of affected rows is equal to the number of selected URL categories—count($_POST['types']). If so, the user is thanked and the $_POST array is reset so that the sticky form does not reshow the values.

If a problem occurred, three things happen. First, a generic, public message is printed. Second, a debugging message, containing both the MySQL error and the query itself, is printed for your—the developer's—benefit. Finally, the URL is removed from the *urls* table because if no association could be made between the URL and a specific category (or categories), the URL itself is not needed.

9. Complete the remaining two conditionals.

```
    } else {
        echo '<p><font color="red">
        → Your submission could
        → not be processed due to a
        → system error. We apologize
        → for any inconvenience.
        → </font></p>';
        echo '<p><font color="red">' .
        → mysql_error() . '<br />
        → <br />Query: ' . $query .
        → '</font></p>';
    }
} else {
    echo '<p><font color="red">
    → Please try again.</font>
    → </p>';
}
}
```

The first else clause applies if the *urls* INSERT query does not run properly. Again, a public message and a debugging message are both included in this script, although the debugging one should never be displayed to the public at large.

The second else clause applies if the user failed to fill out the form completely.

continues on page 490

Script 12.5 *continued*

```
62          $result = @mysql_query ($query); // Run the query.
63
64          if (mysql_affected_rows() == count($_POST['types'])) { // Query ran OK.
65
66              echo '<p><b>Thank you for your submission!</b></p>';
67              $_POST = array(); // Reset values.
68
69          } else { // If second query did not run OK.
70
71              echo '<p><font color="red">Your submission could not be processed due to a system
                  error. We apologize for any inconvenience.</font></p>'; // Public message.
72              echo '<p><font color="red">' . mysql_error() . '<br /><br />Query: ' . $query . '
                  </font></p>'; // Debugging message.
73
74              // Delete the URL from the urls table.
75              $query = "DELETE FROM urls WHERE url_id=$uid";
76              @mysql_query ($query); // Run the query.
77
78          } // End of mysql_affected_rows() IF.
79
80      } else { // If first query did not run OK.
81          echo '<p><font color="red">Your submission could not be processed due to a system error.
              We apologize for any inconvenience.</font></p>'; // Public message.
82          echo '<p><font color="red">' . mysql_error() . '<br /><br />Query: ' . $query . '</font>
              </p>'; // Debugging message.
83      }
84
85  } else { // If one of the data tests failed.
86      echo '<p><font color="red">Please try again.</font></p>';
87  }
88
89 } // End of the main submitted conditional.
90 // --------- DISPLAY THE FORM ---------
```

(script continues on next page)

10. Begin defining the HTML form.

```
?>
<form action="add_url.php"
→ method="post">
    <fieldset><legend>Fill out the
    → form to submit a URL:</legend>
    <p><b>URL:</b> <input type="text"
    → name="url" size="60"
    → maxlength="60" value="<?php
    → if (isset($_POST['url']))
    → echo $_POST['url']; ?>" /><br />
    → <small>Do NOT include the
    → initial <i>http://</i>.</small>
    → </p>
    <p><b>URL Name/Title:</b>
    → <input type="text" name="title"
    → size="60" maxlength="60"
    → value="<?php if (isset($_POST
    → ['title'])) echo $_POST
    → ['title']; ?>" /></p>
    <p><b>Description:</b>
    → <textarea name="description"
    → cols="40" rows="5"><?php if
    → (isset($_POST['description']))
    → echo $_POST['description'];
    → ?></textarea></p>
```

The form itself has four inputs. The first two are text inputs, and the third is a textarea. For sake of consistency, each of these inputs uses the same name and maximum size as the corresponding field in the database.

Each input recalls the previously submitted value, in case an error occurs (**Figure 12.7**). This is accomplished by setting the value attributes of text inputs and printing a value between the textarea tags. If you have Magic Quotes enabled, you'll want to use the `strips-lashes()` function here as well.

Script 12.5 *continued*

```
        ┌─────────────── script ───────────────┐
91   ?>
92   <form action="add_url.php" method="post">
93       <fieldset><legend>Fill out the form to
         submit a URL:</legend>
94
95       <p><b>URL:</b> <input type="text"
         name="url" size="60" maxlength="60"
         value="<?php if (isset($_POST['url']))
         echo $_POST['url']; ?>" /><br /><small>
         Do NOT include the initial <i>http:
         //</i>.</small></p>
96
97       <p><b>URL Name/Title:</b> <input type=
         "text" name="title" size="60"
         maxlength="60" value="<?php if (isset
         ($_POST['title'])) echo $_POST['title'];
         ?>" /></p>
98
99       <p><b>Description:</b> <textarea
         name="description" cols="40"
         rows="5"><?php if (isset($_POST
         ['description'])) echo $_POST
         ['description']; ?></textarea></p>
100
```

(script continues on next page)

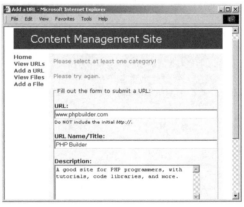

Figure 12.7 The HTML form is sticky, remembering previously entered values.

Script 12.5 *continued*

```
script
101    <p><b>Category/Categories:</b> <select
       name="types[]" multiple="multiple"
       size="5">
102    <?php // Create the pull-down menu
       information.
103    $query = "SELECT * FROM url_categories
       ORDER BY category ASC";
104    $result = @mysql_query ($query);
105    while ($row = mysql_fetch_array
       ($result, MYSQL_NUM)) {
106        echo "<option value=\"$row[0]\"";
107        // Make sticky, if necessary.
108        if (isset($_POST['types']) &&
           (in_array($row[0], $_POST
           ['types']))) {
109            echo ' selected="selected"';
110        }
111        echo ">$row[1]</option>\n";
112    }
113    ?>
114    </select></p>
115
```

(script continues on next page)

Figure 12.8 The HTML source code for the dynamically generated select menu.

Figure 12.9 The HTML source code for the dynamically generated select menu, with two values remembered (the menu is sticky).

11. Create the categories select box.

```
<p><b>Category/Categories:</b>
→ <select name="types[]"
→ multiple="multiple" size="5">
<?php
$query = "SELECT * FROM
→ url_categories ORDER BY category
→ ASC";
$result = @mysql_query ($query);
while ($row = mysql_fetch_array
→ ($result, MYSQL_NUM)) {
    echo "<option value=\"$row[0]\"";
    if (isset($_POST['types']) &&
    → (in_array($row[0], $_POST
    → ['types']))) {
        echo ' selected="selected"';
    }
    echo ">$row[1]</option>\n";
}
?>
</select></p>
```

The easiest way to allow for a URL to be associated with multiple categories is to use a select box that accepts multiple selections. The initial select tag—`<select name="types[]" multiple="multiple" size="5">`—accomplishes that. You need to also use an array as your select name (*types[]*) so that an array of values will be passed to PHP.

To populate the options, a query retrieves all of the records from the *url_categories* table. This alone will create the source code shown in **Figure 12.8**. The next hurdle is to make this menu sticky. To do so, the code `selected="selected"` needs to be added to the proper options (**Figure 12.9**). I accomplish this by checking if the `$_POST['types']` variable is set, meaning that the form has been submitted, and if the current category ID value is in `$_POST['types']`.

continues on next page

12. Complete the form and the page.

```
</fieldset>
<input type="hidden" name=
→ "submitted" value="TRUE" />
<div align="center"><input
→ type="submit" name="submit"
→ value="Submit" /></div>
</form>
<?php
mysql_close();
include ('./includes/footer.html');
?>
```

Again, the hidden input is used to determine when the form has been submitted. Finally, the database connection is closed and the footer file is included.

13. Save the file as add_url.php, upload to your Web server, and test in your Web browser (**Figure 12.10**).

✔ Tips

- If you want to deny the use of HTML in submitted values, the strip_tags() function can be used to remove all HTML and PHP tags. Refer back to Chapter 10 for more information.

- Another alteration you could make to this script would be a check ensuring that a URL is not already in the database. Theoretically, the rows in the *urls* table should all be unique.

- The mysql_insert_id() function is specific to each individual connection (interaction with a database). For this reason, you need not be concerned with the wrong value being returned even if this script were being run simultaneously by several different users.

- The mysql_insert_id() function is the PHP equivalent of MySQL's LAST_INSERT_ID() function.

Script 12.5 *continued*

```
116     </fieldset>
117     <input type="hidden" name="submitted"
        value="TRUE" />
118
119     <div align="center"><input type="submit"
        name="submit" value="Submit" /></div>
120
121 </form>
122 <?php
123 mysql_close(); // Close the database
        connection.
124 include ('./includes/footer.html');
125 ?>
```

Figure 12.10 If the URL submission process worked, a message is displayed and the form is shown again.

The list() Function

I have not yet formally discussed the list() function that's incorporated into the view_urls.php script. This function takes the values of an array and assigns them to individual variables. For example:

```
$var = array ("Larry", "Ullman");

list ($first, $last) = $var;
```

Now the $first and $last variables will have the values of *Larry* and *Ullman*, respectively.

Personally, I most frequently use list() when interacting with databases, specifically when selecting just a couple of columns of information from one row. For example:

```
$result = mysql_query ("SELECT
→ columnX, columnY FROM tablename
→ WHERE columnZ=8");

list ($x, $y) = mysql_fetch_array
→ ($result, MYSQL_NUM);
```

Rather than assigning the results of a mysql_fetch_array() call to a $row variable and then using it as an array, it is sometimes easier to create new variables using list().

Viewing submitted URLs

The script for viewing URLs will have two aspects to it: an upper portion that displays a pull-down menu of available categories and a lower portion that displays all of the links for a particular category. The first time a user accesses the page, no URLs are displayed. Once a user selects a category and submits the form, the page is displayed again, listing the URLs for that category (and the pull-down menu will still be available). This page will also provide links to edit_url.php, to be written next. Obviously this is the kind of link you would provide in order to administer a site; the ability to edit a URL would not be a publicly available feature.

To create view_urls.php:

1. Create a new PHP document in your text editor, including the requisite files (**Script 12.6**).

   ```php
   <?php # Script 12.6 - view_urls.php
   $page_title = 'View URLs';
   include ('./includes/header.html');
   require_once ('../mysql_connect.
   → php');
   ```

2. Begin the HTML form.

   ```php
   echo '<div align="center">
   <form method="get" action=
   → "view_urls.php">
   <select name="type">
   <option value="NULL">Choose a
   → Category:</option>
   ';
   ```

   Upon first arriving at the page, I'll want to show a form (**Figure 12.11**) that is just a pull-down menu and a submit button. Here, I've begun the HTML for the form. Notice that the form uses the GET method and is submitted back to this same page.

3. Retrieve all of the available URL categories, adding each to the pull-down menu.

   ```php
   $query = 'SELECT * FROM
   → url_categories ORDER BY category
   → ASC';
   $result = mysql_query ($query);
   while ($row = mysql_fetch_array
   → ($result, MYSQL_NUM)) {
     echo "<option value=\"$row[0]
     → \">$row[1]</option>
   ";
   }
   ```

   This code will retrieve every URL type from the *url_categories* table and use the returned records to create the HTML code (**Figure 12.12**) for the pull-down menu.

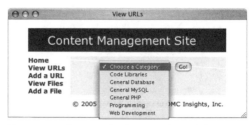

Figure 12.11 The page displays just the pull-down menu of categories when first viewed.

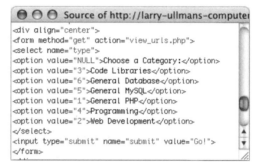

Figure 12.12 The dynamically generated HTML source code of the form.

Script 12.6 The `view_urls.php` page displays both a menu of URL categories and the URLs for a particular category. It also provides links to edit a record.

```
          script

1    <?php # Script 12.6 - view_urls.php
2    // This page displays the URLs listed in
     the database.
3
4    // Set the page title and include the HTML
     header.
5    $page_title = 'View URLs';
6    include ('./includes/header.html');
7
8    require_once ('../mysql_connect.php'); //
     Connect to the database.
9
10   // Create a form allowing the user to
     select a URL category to view.
11   echo '<div align="center">
12   <form method="get" action="view_urls.php">
13   <select name="type">
14   <option value="NULL">Choose a Category:
     </option>
15   ';
16
17   // Retrieve and display the available
     categories.
18   $query = 'SELECT * FROM url_categories
     ORDER BY category ASC';
19   $result = mysql_query ($query);
20   while ($row = mysql_fetch_array ($result,
     MYSQL_NUM)) {
21       echo "<option value=\"$row[0]\">$row[1]
         </option>
22   ";
23   }
24
25   // Complete the form.
26   echo '</select>
27   <input type="submit" name="submit"
     value="Go!">
28   </form>
29   </div>
30   ';
31
```

(script continues on page 497)

4. Complete the HTML form.

```
echo '</select>
<input type="submit" name="submit"
→ value="Go!">
</form>
</div>
';
```

5. Check if a category has been selected and retrieve the information for that category.

```
if (isset($_GET['type'])) {
    $type = (int) $_GET['type'];
} else {
    $type = 0;
}
if ($type > 0) {
    $query = "SELECT category FROM
    → url_categories WHERE
    → url_category_id=$type";
    $result = mysql_query ($query);
    list ($category) =
    → mysql_fetch_array ($result,
    → MYSQL_NUM);
    echo "<hr /><div align=\"center\">
    → <b>$category Links</b><br />
<small>(All links will open in their
→ own window. Recently added links are
→ listed first.)</small></div>\n";
```

If a category has already been selected (in which case, it will have been appended to the URL and available through the `$_GET` array), the URLs for that category should be retrieved.

The first step is to use typecasting and a conditional to ensure that `$type` is a positive integer before using it in a query. This concept was discussed in Chapter 10. Then I retrieve the name of the specific category selected using the `list()` function (see the sidebar). This value is displayed as a header for the page.

continues on next page

MANAGING URLS

6. Initialize a $first variable and query the database.

```
$first = TRUE;
$query = "SELECT u.url_id, url,
→ title, description FROM urls AS u,
→ url_associations AS ua WHERE
→ u.url_id = ua.url_id AND
→ ua.url_category_id=$type AND
→ ua.approved = 'Y' ORDER BY
→ date_submitted DESC";
$result = mysql_query ($query);
```

The $first variable will be used for two purposes. First, it will indicate that the HTML table should be started before displaying the first record. Second, it will be used to test whether or not there were any URLs returned by the query. The query itself is a JOIN on two tables, using the URL category in a WHERE condition.

7. Print out all of the returned records.

```
while ($row = mysql_fetch_array
→ ($result, MYSQL_ASSOC)) {
  if ($first) {
    echo '<table border="0"
    → width="100%" cellspacing="3"
    → cellpadding="3"
    → align="center">
<tr>
  <td align="right" width="40%">
  → <font size="+1">Link</font></td>
  <td align="left" width="50%">
  → <font size="+1">Description
  → </font></td>
  <td align="center" width=
  → "10%"> </td>
</tr>';
    $first = FALSE;
  }
  echo "  <tr>
```

```
<td align=\"right\"><a href=\
→ "http://{$row['url']}\"
→ target=\"_new\">{$row
→ ['title']}</a></td>
<td align=\"left\
→ ">{$row['description']}</td>
<td align=\"center\"><a href=\
→ "edit_url.php?uid={$row
→ ['url_id']}\">edit</a></td>
</tr>\n";
}
```

The while loop will return every record retrieved by the query. Within the while loop, each record is printed in a three-column table. The first column is the URL name, printed as a link to the actual URL. The second column is the description. And the third is an edit link, which passes the URL ID to the edit_url.php page.

Before the first record is displayed, the table and table header will be sent to the browser (**Figure 12.13**). This occurs if $first is TRUE, which it will be the first time that the loop is executed. The variable is then set to FALSE, so that the table header is not printed for each returned record.

continues on page 498

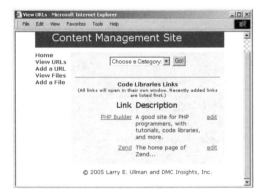

Figure 12.13 A list of URLs for a particular type.

Script 12.6 *continued*

```
         ▓▓▓▓▓▓▓▓▓▓▓▓▓▓▓▓▓▓▓▓▓▓ script ▓▓▓▓▓▓▓▓▓▓▓▓▓▓▓▓▓▓▓▓▓
32   // Retrieve the URLs for a particular category, if selected.
33   // Make sure the type is an integer.
34   if (isset($_GET['type'])) {
35       $type = (int) $_GET['type'];
36   } else {
37       $type = 0;
38   }
39
40   if ($type > 0) {
41
42       // Get the current type name.
43       $query = "SELECT category FROM url_categories WHERE url_category_id=$type";
44       $result = mysql_query ($query);
45       list ($category) = mysql_fetch_array ($result, MYSQL_NUM);
46
47       echo "<hr /><div align=\"center\"><b>$category Links</b><br />
48   <small>(All links will open in their own window. Recently added links are listed first.)
     </small></div>\n";
49
50       $first = TRUE; // Initialize the variable.
51
52       // Query the database.
53       $query = "SELECT u.url_id, url, title, description FROM urls AS u, url_associations AS ua WHERE
         u.url_id = ua.url_id AND ua.url_category_id=$type AND ua.approved = 'Y' ORDER BY
         date_submitted DESC";
54       $result = mysql_query ($query);
55
56       // Display all the URLs.
57       while ($row = mysql_fetch_array ($result, MYSQL_ASSOC)) {
58
59           // If this is the first record, create the table header.
60           if ($first) {
61               echo '<table border="0" width="100%" cellspacing="3" cellpadding="3" align="center">
62       <tr>
63         <td align="right" width="40%"><font size="+1">Link</font></td>
64         <td align="left" width="50%"><font size="+1">Description</font></td>
65         <td align="center" width="10%"> </td>
66       </tr>';
67               $first = FALSE; // One record has been returned.
68           } // End of $first IF.
69
```

(script continues on next page)

MANAGING URLS

8. Print a message if no URLs were returned and complete the main conditional.

```
if ($first) {
    echo '<div align="center">
    → There are currently no links
    → in this category.</div>';
} else {
    echo '</table>';
}
}
```

The $first variable will be set to FALSE in the while loop if any rows are returned. Therefore, if $first is still TRUE at this point, there were no records retrieved and a message should be sent saying such (**Figure 12.14**); otherwise, the table should be completed.

9. Complete the HTML page.

```
mysql_close();
include ('./includes/footer.html');
?>
```

10. Save the file as view_urls.php, upload to your Web server, and test in your Web browser.

✔ Tips

■ I have not included any MySQL-related error management in this script. The reason is that the queries are essentially static, with only one value—the URL category ID—changing. If you have problems developing this script, use the standard PHP-MySQL debugging techniques: print out queries, print out MySQL errors, run queries using the mysql client or other interfaces, etc.

■ If you want, you can apply the nl2br() function (it stands for *newline to break*) to the *description* field. This function will turn every newline character—created by pressing Return or Enter—into an (X)HTML <br /> tag.

Script 12.6 *continued*

```
70        // Display each record.
71        echo " <tr>
72            <td align=\"right\"><a href=
                \"http://{$row['url']}\" target=
                \"_new\">{$row['title']}
                </a></td>
73            <td align=\"left\">{$row
                ['description']}</td>
74            <td align=\"center\"><a href=
                \"edit_url.php?uid={$row
                ['url_id']}\">edit</a></td>
75        </tr>\n";
76
77    } // End of while loop.
78
79    // If no records were displayed...
80    if ($first) {
81        echo '<div align="center">There are
              currently no links in this category.
              </div>';
82    } else {
83        echo '</table>'; // Close the table.
84    }
85
86 } // End of $_GET['type'] conditional.
87
88 mysql_close(); // Close the database
   connection.
89 include ('./includes/footer.html');
90 ?>
```

Figure 12.14 The resulting page if a category has no associated URLs.

The serialize() and urlencode() Functions

Another previously unmentioned function to be used in this chapter is serialize(). This function can turn complex data structures into a more portable format. This function is necessary because, for example, an array cannot be inserted into a database, stored in a hidden form input, or sent in a cookie.

Serialize() takes data and creates a string that represents the original structure and value. Say you have an array defined like so:

```
$array = array("Penn", "State");
```

The serialized version of that array would be:

```
a:2:{i:0;s:4:"Penn";i:1;s:5:"State";}
```

Looking at that syntax, you can see that the data represents an array of two elements (*a:2*). The first element, indexed at *0*, is a string of four letters whose value is *Penn*. The second element, indexed at *1*, is a string of five letters whose value is *State*.

Because the serialized form of data often contains quotation marks and other problematic characters, you'll want to address those before storing the data. In this example, I will use the urlencode() function, which encodes data so that it is safe to pass from Web page to Web page (in a URL or a form).

To return data to its original format, use the unserialize() function. If you encoded the data before storing it, use the corresponding decode function—like urldecode()—*prior to* using unserialize(). You'll see all of this in action in this example. If you still don't understand any of these functions, see the PHP manual or post a message to the book's support forum.

Editing URLs

The final URL-related script will let a user edit or delete an existing URL record. The process is generally easier than one might think. First, the URL's existing information must be retrieved from the database and displayed in the form. This is essentially a sticky form, just like the add_url.php page. Added to this form is a pair of radio buttons letting the user select whether they want to edit or delete the record.

Upon form submission, the database information needs to be updated. If the URL is being deleted, DELETE queries must be run on both the *urls* and *url_associations* tables. If the URL's information is being changed, then UPDATE queries are required. For the *url_associations* table, this is a little more complex, as a URL's information could be stored in multiple rows (for multiple categories). One way to facilitate this update is by noting what the current URL categories are. To do so, I'll make use of the serialize() function (see the sidebar) in storing the current values as a hidden form input. Then the handling page will receive both the original and the new URL categories.

Finally, remember that in SQL your UPDATE and DELETE queries normally use a primary key in a WHERE clause (e.g., DELETE FROM *tablename* WHERE *pk=X*). For this reason, the edit_url.php page receives the URL's *url_id* value, through a link in view_urls.php, as $_GET['uid']. This value also needs to be stored in the form as a hidden input so that the handling script can reference it.

MANAGING URLS

499

To create the edit_url.php page:

1. Start a new PHP document in your text editor or IDE (**Script 12.7**).

```
<?php # Script 12.7 - edit_url.php
$page_title = 'Edit a URL';
include ('./includes/header.html');
```

2. Check for a valid URL ID.

```
if (isset($_GET['uid'])) {
    $uid = (int) $_GET['uid'];
} elseif (isset($_POST['uid'])) {
    $uid = (int) $_POST['uid'];
} else {
    $uid = 0;
}
if ($uid <= 0) {
    echo '<p><font color="red">
    → This page has been accessed
    → incorrectly!</font></p>';
    include ('./includes/footer.
    → html');
    exit();
}
```

This page will only work if it always has access to the URL's ID. The first conditional checks for its presence in either the $_GET or $_POST array, type-casting it to an integer in either case (just to be safe). If neither array contains a *uid* element, then $uid is set to *0*.

If $uid is not a positive number, meaning either that it wasn't received or an invalid value was received, the script should be terminated. To do so, an error message is displayed, the footer is included, and the execution of the script is halted (**Figure 12.15**).

Script 12.7 The edit_url.php page lets the user edit or delete existing URL records.

```
1   <?php # Script 12.7 - edit_url.php
2   // This page allows users to edit or delete
    existing URL records.
3
4   // Set the page title and include the HTML
    header.
5   $page_title = 'Edit a URL';
6   include ('./includes/header.html');
7
8   // Check for a URL ID.
9   if (isset($_GET['uid'])) { // Page is
    first accessed.
10      $uid = (int) $_GET['uid'];
11  } elseif (isset($_POST['uid'])) { // Form
    has been submitted.
12      $uid = (int) $_POST['uid'];
13  } else { // Big problem!
14      $uid = 0;
15  }
16
17  if ($uid <= 0) { // Do not proceed!
18      echo '<p><font color="red">This page has
        been accessed incorrectly!</font></p>';
19      include ('./includes/footer.html');
20      exit(); // Terminate execution of the
        script.
21  }
22
```

(script continues on next page)

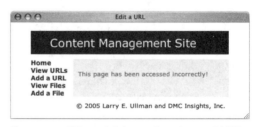

Figure 12.15 If the script does not receive a valid URL ID, this is the result.

Script 12.7 *continued*

```
23   require_once ('../mysql_connect.php'); //
     Connect to the database.
24
25   if (isset($_POST['submitted'])) { // Handle
     the form.
26
27       // Two threads: delete the record OR
         edit the record.
28
29       if ($_POST['which'] == 'delete') { //
         Delete the record.
30
31           // Delete from the urls table.
32           $query = "DELETE FROM urls WHERE
             url_id=$uid";
33           $result = mysql_query($query);
34           $affect = mysql_affected_rows();
35
36           // Delete from the url_associations
             table.
37           $query = "DELETE FROM url_
             associations WHERE url_id=$uid";
38           $result = mysql_query($query);
39           $affect += mysql_affected_rows();
40
```

(script continues on page 503)

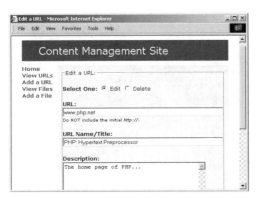

Figure 12.16 At the top of the form are two radio buttons so that the user can specify whether the record should be merely edited or removed altogether.

3. Include the database connection and see if the form has been submitted.

```
require_once ('../mysql_connect.
→ php');
if (isset($_POST['submitted'])) {
```

4. Delete the existing record, if applicable.

```
if ($_POST['which'] == 'delete') {
    $query = "DELETE FROM urls WHERE
    → url_id=$uid";
    $result = mysql_query($query);
    $affect = mysql_affected_rows();
    $query = "DELETE FROM
    → url_associations WHERE
    → url_id=$uid";
    $result = mysql_query($query);
    $affect += mysql_affected_rows();
```

The form (**Figure 12.16**) has a pair of radio buttons, allowing the user to indicate whether they are editing or deleting a record (edit is the default). This first conditional checks if the user has opted to delete the record. If so, DELETE queries need to be run on both tables, using the *url_id* in a WHERE clause. To be able to report upon the success of the queries (see Step 5), the $affect variable will store the total number of affected rows.

continues on next page

5. Report on the success of the DELETE queries and complete the page.

```
if ($affect > 0) {
    echo '<p><b>The URL has been
    → deleted!</b></p>';
} else {
    echo '<p><font color="red">
    → Your submission could not be
    → processed due to a system error.
    → We apologize for any
    → inconvenience.</font></p>';
}
include ('./includes/footer.html');
exit();
```

A bare minimum of testing is done here, just seeing if at least one row was affected by the deletion. Messages report upon the overall success. Then the footer is included and the page is terminated so that the form is not shown for a no-longer-existing record.

6. Validate all of the form fields to begin the *edit* thread.

```
} else {
    if (eregi ('^([[:alnum:]\-\.])+
    → (\.)([[:alnum:]]){2,4}([[:
    → alnum:]/+=%&_\.~?\-]*)$',
    → $_POST['url'])) {
        $u = escape_data($_POST
        → ['url']);
    } else {
        $u = FALSE;
        echo '<p><font color="red">
        → Please enter a valid URL!
        → </font></p>';
    }
```

```
if (!empty($_POST['title'])) {
    $t = escape_data($_POST
    → ['title']);
} else {
    $t = FALSE;
    echo '<p><font color="red">
    → Please enter a URL name/title!
    → </font></p>';
}
if (!empty($_POST['description'])) {
    $d = escape_data($_POST
    → ['description']);
} else {
    $d = FALSE;
    echo '<p><font color="red">
    → Please enter a description!
    → </font></p>';
}
if (isset($_POST['types']) &&
→ (is_array($_POST['types']))) {
    $type = TRUE;
} else {
    $type = FALSE;
    echo '<p><font color="red">
    → Please select at least one
    → category!</font></p>';
}
```

This else clause takes effect if $_POST['which'] is not equal to *delete*. The first steps are to validate the form data, exactly as you do in the add_url.php page.

continues on page 504

Script 12.7 *continued*

(script continues on page 505)

```
41       // Report on the success.
42       if ($affect > 0) {
43           echo '<p><b>The URL has been deleted!</b></p>';
44       } else { // No rows affected.
45           echo '<p><font color="red">Your submission could not be processed due to a system error.
             We apologize for any inconvenience.</font></p>';
46           // Print queries and use the mysql_error() function (after each mysql_query() call) to
             debug.
47       }
48
49       // Complete the page.
50       include ('./includes/footer.html');
51       exit(); // Terminate execution of the script.
52
53   } else { // Edit the URL (default action).
54
55       // Validate all of the form fields!
56
57       // Check for a URL.
58       if (eregi ('^([[:alnum:]\-\.])+(\.)([[:alnum:]]){2,4}([[:alnum:]/+=%&_\.~?\-]*)$', $_POST
         ['url'])) {
59           $u = escape_data($_POST['url']);
60       } else {
61           $u = FALSE;
62           echo '<p><font color="red">Please enter a valid URL!</font></p>';
63       }
64
65       // Check for a URL title.
66       if (!empty($_POST['title'])) {
67           $t = escape_data($_POST['title']);
68       } else {
69           $t = FALSE;
70           echo '<p><font color="red">Please enter a URL name/title!</font></p>';
71       }
72
73       // Check for a description.
74       if (!empty($_POST['description'])) {
75           $d = escape_data($_POST['description']);
76       } else {
77           $d = FALSE;
78           echo '<p><font color="red">Please enter a description!</font></p>';
```

MANAGING URLS

503

7. If the data passed all of the tests, update the record in the *urls* table.

```
if ($u && $t && $d && $type) {
    $query1 = "UPDATE urls
    → SET url='$u', title='$t',
    → description='$d' WHERE
    → url_id=$uid";
    $result1 = mysql_query($query1);
```

Updating the *urls* table is quite simple, needing only a basic UPDATE query.

8. Retrieve the original categories.

```
$exist_types = unserialize(urldecode
→ ($_POST['exist_types']));
```

In order to update the list of categories associated with a URL, I need to know what they originally were and what they are now. The original categories are stored as a hidden form input. To access them again, I reverse the serialization and encoding process. Here the $_POST['exist_types'] value is first run through urldecode() and then through unserialize(). The result will be an array of the URL's original category IDs.

9. Determine what category updates, if any, need to be made.

```
if ($_POST['types'] != $exist_types) {
    $add = array_diff($_POST['types'],
    → $exist_types);
    $delete = array_diff($exist_types,
    → $_POST['types']);
```

If the user did not change the associated categories for this URL, no updates are required. To test for this, I compare the array of original categories ($exist_types) to the array of selected categories ($_POST['types']). If they are not the same, I need to determine exactly how they differ.

To do that, I use the array_diff() function twice. This function returns an array of values that are in the first argument but not in the second. Any categories that are in $_POST['types'] but not $exist_types have been added, meaning they were additionally selected by the user. Any categories that are in $exist_types but not $_POST['types'] have been deleted, meaning they were deselected by the user.

10. Add the new category types for this URL to the database.

```
if (!empty($add)) {
    $query2 = 'INSERT INTO
    → url_associations (url_id,
    → url_category_id, approved)
    → VALUES ';
    foreach ($add as $v) {
        $query2 .= "($uid, $v, 'Y'), ";
    }
    $query2 = substr ($query2, 0, -2);
    $result2 = mysql_query ($query2);
} else {
    $result2 = TRUE;
}
```

If the user has associated this URL with new categories, I need to add them to the *url_associations* table. The process and query for doing so is exactly like that in the add_url.php page. Also, I'm using a $result2 variable to indicate the success of this specific operation. If there are no categories to be added—meaning no query was run—I set this value to TRUE.

continues on page 506

MANAGING URLs

Script 12.7 *continued*

```
┌─────────────────────────────────── script ───────────────────────────────────┐
```

```php
79      }
80
81      // Check for a category.
82      if (isset($_POST['types']) && (is_array($_POST['types']))) {
83          $type = TRUE;
84      } else {
85          $type = FALSE;
86          echo '<p><font color="red">Please select at least one category!</font></p>';
87      }
88
89      if ($u && $t && $d && $type) { // If everything's OK.
90
91          // Update the urls table.
92          $query1 = "UPDATE urls SET url='$u', title='$t', description='$d' WHERE url_id=$uid";
93          $result1 = mysql_query($query1);
94
95          // Update the url_associations table.
96          // Retrieve the old categories.
97          $exist_types = unserialize(urldecode($_POST['exist_types']));
98
99          if ($_POST['types'] != $exist_types) { // A category change was made.
100
101             // Determine the new and old categories.
102             $add = array_diff($_POST['types'], $exist_types);
103             $delete = array_diff($exist_types, $_POST['types']);
104
105             // Add new types, if needed.
106             if (!empty($add)) {
107                 $query2 = 'INSERT INTO url_associations (url_id, url_category_id, approved)
                    VALUES ';
108                 foreach ($add as $v) {
109                     $query2 .= "($uid, $v, 'Y'), ";
110                 }
111                 $query2 = substr ($query2, 0, -2); // Chop off the last comma and space.
112                 $result2 = mysql_query ($query2); // Run the query.
113             } else { // No new types.
114                 $result2 = TRUE;
115             }
116
```

(script continues on page 507)

11. Remove the old categories associated with this URL from the database.

```
if (!empty($delete)) {
  $query3 = "DELETE FROM
→ url_associations WHERE
→ (url_id=$uid) AND
→ (url_category_id IN (". implode
→ (',', $delete) . "))";
  $result3 = mysql_query($query3);
} else {
  $result3 = TRUE;
}
```

If the user deselected any categories, those records should be deleted from the *url_associations* table. Using an IN condition and PHP's implode() function, I can quickly generate a query of the form DELETE FROM url_associations WHERE (url_id=X) AND (url_category IN (A, B, C)).

Again, a flag variable ($result3) is used to track the success of this operation.

12. Report on the success of the edits.

```
} else {
  $result2 = TRUE;
  $result3 = TRUE;
}
if ($result1 && $result2 &&
→ $result3) {
  echo '<p><b>The URL has been
→ edited!</b></p>';
} else {
  echo '<p><font color="red">
→ Your submission could not be
→ processed due to a system error.
→ We apologize for any
→ inconvenience.</font></p>';
}
```

The first else clause takes effect if the selected categories haven't changed. Then I check if $result1, $result2, and $result3 are all TRUE. If so, every query ran successfully and a message is printed. If not, a generic message is printed and you'll need to do some debugging detective work to find the problem.

13. Complete all of the conditionals.

```
    } else {
      echo '<p><font color="red">
→ Please try again.</font>
      </p>';
    }
  }
}
```

The first else clause prints a message if the URL was being edited and the user omitted a field (**Figure 12.17**). The penultimate closing brace completes the edit/delete conditional. And the final closing brace completes the submission conditional.

continues on page 508

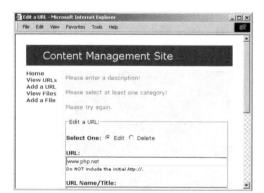

Figure 12.17 The editing process still checks, and reports upon the validity of, the form data.

Script 12.7 *continued*

```
━━━━━━━━━━━━━━━━━━━━━━ script ━━━━━━━━━━━━━━━━━━━━━━
117             // Delete old types, if necessary.
118             if (!empty($delete)) {
119                 $query3 = "DELETE FROM url_associations WHERE (url_id=$uid) AND (url_category_id
                    IN (". implode (',', $delete) . "))";
120                 $result3 = mysql_query($query3);
121             } else { // No old types.
122                 $result3 = TRUE;
123             }
124
125         } else { // No category changes being made.
126             $result2 = TRUE;
127             $result3 = TRUE;
128         }
129
130         // Report on the success.
131         if ($result1 && $result2 && $result3) {
132             echo '<p><b>The URL has been edited!</b></p>';
133         } else {
134             echo '<p><font color="red">Your submission could not be processed due to a system
                error. We apologize for any inconvenience.</font></p>';
135             // Print queries and use the mysql_error() function (after each mysql_query() call) to
                debug.
136         }
137
138     } else { // If one of the data tests failed.
139         echo '<p><font color="red">Please try again.</font></p>';
140     }
141
142   } // End of Edit/Delete if-else.
143
144 } // End of the main submitted conditional.
145
146 // --------- DISPLAY THE FORM ---------
147
```

(script continues on page 509)

MANAGING URLS

14. Retrieve the URL's current information.

```
$query = "SELECT url, title,
→ description, url_category_id
→ FROM urls LEFT JOIN
→ url_associations USING (url_id)
→ WHERE urls.url_id=$uid";
$result = mysql_query ($query);
$exist_types = array();
list($url, $title, $desc,
→ $exist_types[]) =
→ mysql_fetch_array ($result,
→ MYSQL_NUM);
while ($row = mysql_fetch_array
→ ($result, MYSQL_NUM)) {
  $exist_types[] = $row[3];
}
```

To populate the form with the current URL data, I first need to retrieve it from the database. To do so, I run a LEFT JOIN query, grabbing the *url*, *title*, and *description* from the *urls* table as well as the *url_category_id* from the *url_associations* table. The first three values I only need to retrieve once, but they'll be present in every returned row (see the results in **Figure 12.18**). Therefore, I call mysql_fetch_array() once to set the $url, the $title, and the $description variables. Then I loop through the remaining records in order to finish creating the $exist_types array. The end result will be three strings—$url, $title, and $description—and one array, $exist_types.

Because the form submissions section of the script also uses an $exist_types array, I first reset this variable with the array() function.

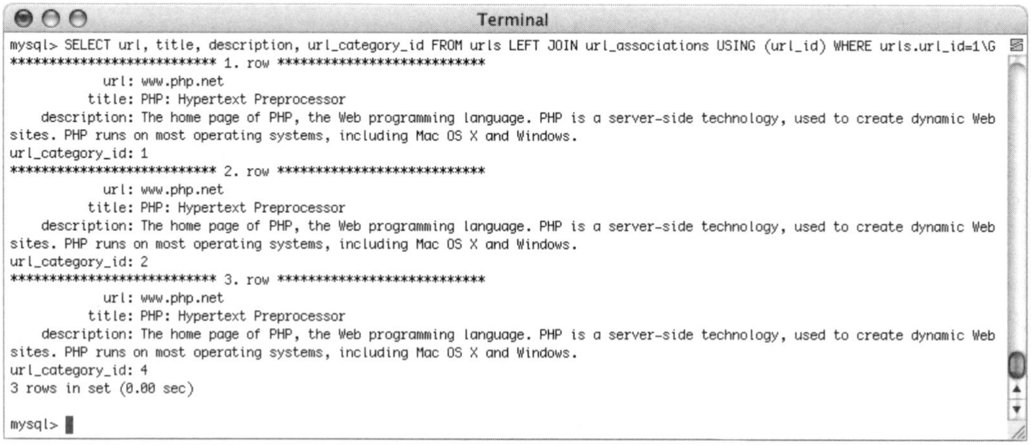

Figure 12.18 The query, executed here in the mysql client, returns all of the information I require, although some of it is redundant.

Script 12.7 *continued*

```
                    script
148  // Retrieve the URL's current information.
149  $query = "SELECT url, title, description,
     url_category_id FROM urls LEFT JOIN
     url_associations USING (url_id) WHERE
     urls.url_id=$uid";
150  $result = mysql_query ($query);
151
152  // Get all of the information for the first
     record.
153  $exist_types = array(); // Reset.
154  list($url, $title, $desc, $exist_types[]) =
     mysql_fetch_array ($result, MYSQL_NUM);
155
156  // Get the other url_category_id values.
157  while ($row = mysql_fetch_array($result,
     MYSQL_NUM)) {
158      $exist_types[] = $row[3];
159  }
160  ?>
161  <form action="edit_url.php" method="post">
162      <fieldset><legend>Edit a URL:</legend>
163
164      <p><b>Select One:</b> <input
         type="radio" name="which" value="edit"
         checked="checked" /> Edit <input type=
         "radio" name="which" value="delete"
         /> Delete</p>
165
```

(script continues on page 511)

15. Begin the HTML form.

```
?>
<form action="edit_url.php"
→ method="post">
    <fieldset><legend>Edit a URL:
    → </legend>
    <p><b>Select One:</b> <input
    → type="radio" name="which"
    → value="edit" checked="checked"
    → /> Edit <input type="radio"
    → name="which" value="delete"
    → /> Delete</p>
```

The form itself (**Figure 12.19**) will be a lot like the add_url.php form, although it does have these two radio buttons at the top.

continues on next page

Figure 12.19 The HTML form, as it looks upon first arriving (after clicking on an *edit* link in view_urls.php).

16. Continue creating the HTML form, inserting existing values as needed.

```
<p><b>URL:</b> <input type="text"
→ name="url" size="60"
→ maxlength="60" value="<?php echo
→ $url; ?>" /><br /><small>Do NOT
→ include the initial <i>http://
→ </i>.</small></p>
<p><b>URL Name/Title:</b> <input
→ type="text" name="title"
→ size="60" maxlength="60"
→ value="<?php echo $title;
→ ?>" /></p>
<p><b>Description:</b> <textarea
→ name="description" cols="40"
→ rows="5"><?php echo $desc;
→ ?></textarea></p>
```

Each of the form inputs has a preset value using the currently stored value in the database.

17. Create the categories select menu box.

```
<p><b>Category/Categories:</b>
→ <select name="types[]" multiple=
→ "multiple" size="5">
<?php
$query = "SELECT * FROM
→ url_categories ORDER BY category
→ ASC";
$result = @mysql_query ($query);
while ($row = mysql_fetch_array
→ ($result, MYSQL_NUM)) {
  echo "<option value=\"$row[0]\"";
  if (in_array($row[0],
  → $exist_types)) {
    echo ' selected="selected"';
  }
  echo ">$row[1]</option>\n";
}
 ?>
</select></p>
```

This section of code is also exactly like its predecessor in add_url.php, except that its sticky quality is based upon the $exist_types array, not $_POST['types'].

18. Add the remaining elements, including two new hidden inputs.

```
</fieldset>
<input type="hidden"
→ name="submitted" value="TRUE" />
<?php
  echo '<input type="hidden"
  → name="exist_types" value="' .
  → urlencode(serialize
  → ($exist_types)) . '" />
  <input type="hidden" name="uid"
  → value="' . $uid . '" />
  ';
?>
<div align="center"><input
→ type="submit" name="submit"
→ value="Submit" /></div>
```

continues on page 512

Script 12.7 *continued*

```
───────────────────────────────── script ─────────────────────────────────
166    <p><b>URL:</b> <input type="text" name="url" size="60" maxlength="60" value="<?php echo $url;
       ?>" /><br /><small>Do NOT include the initial <i>http://</i>.</small></p>
167
168    <p><b>URL Name/Title:</b> <input type="text" name="title" size="60" maxlength="60" value="<?php
       echo $title; ?>" /></p>
169
170    <p><b>Description:</b> <textarea name="description" cols="40" rows="5"><?php echo $desc;
       ?></textarea></p>
171
172    <p><b>Category/Categories:</b> <select name="types[]" multiple="multiple" size="5">
173    <?php // Create the pull-down menu information.
174    $query = "SELECT * FROM url_categories ORDER BY category ASC";
175    $result = @mysql_query ($query);
176    while ($row = mysql_fetch_array ($result, MYSQL_NUM)) {
177        echo "<option value=\"$row[0]\"";
178        // Make sticky, if necessary.
179        if (in_array($row[0], $exist_types)) {
180            echo ' selected="selected"';
181        }
182        echo ">$row[1]</option>\n";
183    }
184    ?>
185    </select></p>
186
187    </fieldset>
188    <input type="hidden" name="submitted" value="TRUE" />
189    <?php // Store the required hidden values.
190        echo '<input type="hidden" name="exist_types" value="' . urlencode(serialize
           ($exist_types)) . '" />
191        <input type="hidden" name="uid" value="' . $uid . '" />
192        ';
193    ?>
194    <div align="center"><input type="submit" name="submit" value="Submit" /></div>
195
196    </form>
197    <?php
198    mysql_close(); // Close the database connection.
199    include ('./includes/footer.html');
200    ?>
```

MANAGING URLS

The *exist_types* hidden form input stores an array of the currently associated URL categories. Doing so requires using both the `serialize()` and `urlencode()` functions (see the sidebar). The next hidden form input is the URL's ID, which will be needed to update or delete the records in the database. The resulting HTML source code is shown in **Figure 12.20**.

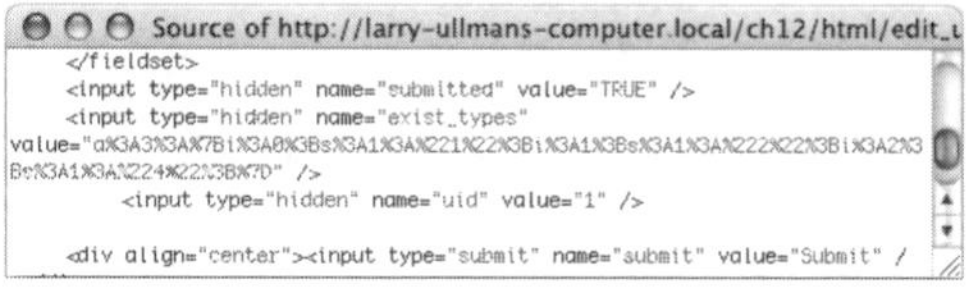

19. Complete the form and the page.

    ```
    </form>
    <?php
    mysql_close();
    include ('./includes/footer.html');
    ?>
    ```

20. Save the script as `edit_url.php`, upload to your Web server, and test in your Web browser.

✔ Tips

- For more information about the `array_diff()` or other functions used here, see the PHP manual.

- Because the `mysql_error()` function returns the error caused by the latest query associated with a connection, you must call it after each `mysql_query()` call in order to accurately debug this script. If you are confused by any of the queries, print out the query using PHP, then run it using the mysql client or other interface in order to see the results.

Figure 12.20 Two of the three hidden form inputs are populated by PHP. Both are required by the form processing side of the script.

Site Administration

Although I have not created an administrative side to this application, doing so would not be difficult. First, add an *approved* field to the *uploads* table. Then change both `add_url.php` and `add_file.php` so that *approved* is set to *N* by default. On the administrative side, create a page that retrieves all the content that has not yet been approved. To approve recently added content, run an UPDATE query on the appropriate table for that record, changing *approved* to *Y*. On the public side, change the `view_urls.php` and `view_files.php` queries so that they only select records where *approved* is equal to *Y*.

One of the benefits of this file upload system is that it's easy to correlate files on the server to those in the database (since the *upload_id* is used as the filename). If you write an administrative script to remove files from the server, you can easily delete both the record from the table and the file from the *uploads* folder using the *upload_id*.

The examples in the next chapter cover user registration and authentication. Those techniques could be coupled with this application if you wanted to protect the managed information.

Managing Files

The final segment of this Web application will manage files of any type. These scripts will allow users to upload files from their computers, which will then be stored on the server. The concept behind managing file uploads—as well as the very, very important preparation steps—was discussed in Chapter 11, "Extended Topics." This application will expand upon that basic demonstration by

◆ Storing the file's information in the database

◆ Renaming the file

◆ Providing a method of downloading the files

◆ Placing the files outside of the Web root directory, for improved security

In order to use these scripts, you'll need to do two things. First, create the *uploads* table (if you haven't already), using this SQL command (**Figure 12.21**).

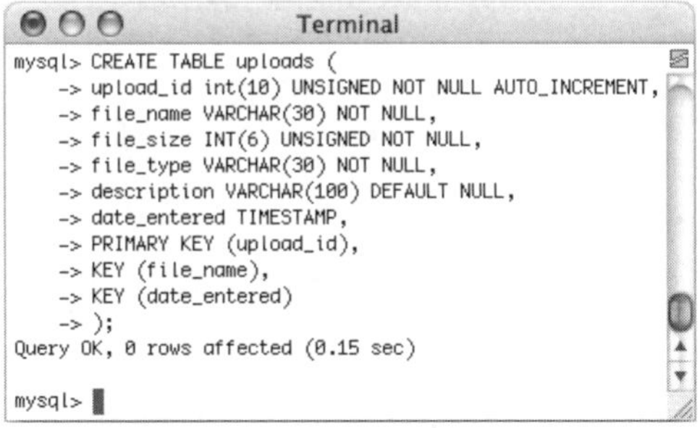

Figure 12.21 Create a new table to manage the list of uploaded files.

```
CREATE TABLE uploads (

upload_id int(10) UNSIGNED NOT NULL
→ AUTO_INCREMENT,

file_name VARCHAR(30) NOT NULL,

file_size INT(6) UNSIGNED NOT NULL,

file_type VARCHAR(30) NOT NULL,

description VARCHAR(100) DEFAULT NULL,

date_entered TIMESTAMP,

PRIMARY KEY (upload_id),

KEY (file_name),

KEY (date_entered)

)
```

Second, create an *uploads* directory, located outside of the Web directory (see Figure 12.3). Make sure that this directory has open permissions so that PHP (through the Web server) can write to it. Again, see Chapter 11 for specific instructions.

Uploading files

The page used to upload files will be rather simple, taking only a file and an optional description. To expand upon this functionality, the page will present the option of accepting up to three files. This variation will demonstrate how easy it is to manage multiple file submissions in one script.

As I mentioned, the file's information— name, type, size, and description—will be stored in the database. The file itself will be stored in the *uploads* directory and renamed using the associated *upload_id* from the *uploads* table.

To write add_file.php:

1. Create a new PHP document in your text editor (**Script 12.8**).

   ```
   <?php # Script 12.8 - add_file.php
   HTML header.
   $page_title = 'Upload a File';
   include ('./includes/header.html');
   $counter = 3;
   ```

   The $counter variable will be used to determine how many files can be uploaded in this one script.

2. Check if the form has been submitted, include the database connection, and define a for loop.

   ```
   if (isset($_POST['submitted'])) {
       require_once ('../mysql_connect.
       → php');
       for ($i = 0; $i < $counter; $i++) {
   ```

   The for loop will run the same sequence of steps for each of the potentially uploaded files. By changing the value of $counter (see Step 1), you can increase or decrease the number of allowed file uploads.

3. Check if a file has been uploaded.

   ```
   $filename = 'upload' . $i;
   $description = 'description' . $i;
   if (isset($_FILES[$filename]) &&
   → ($_FILES[$filename]['error']
   → != 4)) {
   ```

   The form's file inputs will have names like *upload0, upload1, upload2* (**Figure 12.22**). To determine if a particular file upload has been used, I first create a shorthand for the element name by combining the word *upload* with the value of $i. Then I see if $_FILES[$filename] has a value, and that it doesn't have an error value of *4*, which would mean that no file was uploaded.

   The form will also have textareas called *description0, description1*, etc., so I create a shorthand reference for those here as well.

Script 12.8 This script allows the user to upload one to three files that will then be stored on the server.

```
1   <?php # Script 12.8 - add_file.php
2   // This page allows users to upload files
    to the server.
3
4   // Set the page title and include the HTML
    header.
5   $page_title = 'Upload a File';
6   include ('./includes/header.html');
7
8   $counter = 3; // Number of files to allow
    for.
9
10  if (isset($_POST['submitted'])) { // Handle
    the form.
11
12      require_once ('../mysql_connect.php');
        // Connect to the database.
13
14      for ($i = 0; $i < $counter; $i++) { //
        Handle each uploaded file.
15
16          // Create index names to refer to the
            proper upload and description.
17          $filename = 'upload' . $i;
18          $description = 'description' . $i;
19
20          // Check for a file.
21          if (isset($_FILES[$filename]) &&
            ($_FILES[$filename]['error'] != 4)) {
22
```

(script continues on next page)

Figure 12.22 The HTML source of the page shows the different names for the dynamically generated form elements.

Script 12.8 *continued*

```
                    script
23          // Check for a description (not
            required).
24          if (!empty($_POST[$description])) {
25              $d = "'" . escape_data($_POST
                [$description]) . "'";
26          } else {
27              $d = 'NULL';
28          }
29
30          // Add the record to the database.
31          $query = "INSERT INTO uploads
            (file_name, file_size,
            file_type, description) VALUES
            ('{$_FILES[$filename]['name']}',
            {$_FILES[$filename]['size']},
            '{$_FILES[$filename]['type']}',
            $d)";
32          $result = mysql_query ($query);
33
```

(script continues on next page)

4. Validate the description.

```
if (!empty($_POST[$description])) {
    $d = "'" . escape_data($_POST
    → [$description]) . "'";
} else {
    $d = 'NULL';
}
```

As in my `add_url.php` example, I'll use a bare minimum of validation on the description input. Since this form will have no other fields to be validated, this is the only conditional required. You could also validate the size of the uploaded file to determine if it fits within the acceptable range, if you want.

One new idea here is that I want the resulting variable—`$d`—to be INSERT-able into my database as is. If there is no file description, `$d` will have a value of NULL, so that the column's value is NULL. If there is a description, `$d` will be of the format *'This is the description'*, including the single quotation marks. This should make more sense when you look at the query in the next step.

5. Insert the record into the database for this upload.

```
$query = "INSERT INTO uploads
→ (file_name, file_size, file_type,
→ description) VALUES ('{$_FILES
→ [$filename]['name']}', {$_FILES
→ [$filename]['size']}, '{$_FILES
→ [$filename]['type']}', $d)";
$result = mysql_query ($query);
```

Each uploaded file will be recorded in the database using this query. It makes use of the `$_FILES` multidimensional array, inserting the original filename, its size, and its MIME type, all of which come from the Web browser. The description is also stored.

As an added measure of security, you could run all of the `$_FILES` information through the `escape_data()` function.

continues on next page

6. Create the new filename.

```
if ($result) {
    $upload_id = mysql_insert_id();
```

The file will be stored on the server using a new name, which is much more secure than using the original user-defined name. The name of the file will be its *upload_id* from the database (retrieved by the `mysql_insert_id()` function).

7. Copy the file to its new location on the server.

```
if (move_uploaded_file($_FILES
→ [$filename]['tmp_name'], "../
→ uploads/$upload_id")) {
    echo '<p>File number ' . ($i + 1)
→ . ' has been uploaded!</p>';
} else {
    echo '<p><font color="red">
→ File number ' . ($i + 1) . '
→ could not be moved.</font></p>';
    $query = "DELETE FROM uploads
→ WHERE upload_id = $upload_id";
    $result = mysql_query($query);
}
```

I'll use the `move_uploaded_file()` function to move the temporary file to its permanent location (in the *uploads* folder with its new name). If the move worked, a message is printed indicating such. If the file could not be moved (see **Figure 12.23**), I'll delete the record from the database and print an error message.

Script 12.8 *continued*

```
34        if ($result) {
35
36            // Return the upload_id from
              the database.
37            $upload_id = mysql_insert_
              id();
38
39            // Move the file over.
40            if (move_uploaded_file
              ($_FILES[$filename]
              ['tmp_name'], "../uploads/
              $upload_id")) {
41
42                echo '<p>File number ' .
                  ($i + 1) . ' has been
                  uploaded!</p>';
43
44            } else { // File could not be
              moved.
45
46                echo '<p><font color=
                  "red">File number ' .
                  ($i + 1) . ' could not be
                  moved.</font></p>';
47
48                // Remove the record from
                  the database.
49                $query = "DELETE FROM
                  uploads WHERE upload_id =
                  $upload_id";
50                $result = mysql_query
                  ($query);
51
```

(script continues on next page)

Warning: move_uploaded_file(../uploads/7) [function.move-uploaded-file]: failed to open stream: Permission denied in **/Users/larryullman/Sites/ch12/html/add_file.php** on line **46**

Figure 12.23 If you see a permissions error like this, make sure your pathname is valid and that the permissions on the destination directory are appropriate.

Script 12.8 *continued*

```
┌──────────────────────────────────────┐
│▦          script            ▦│
├──────────────────────────────────────┤
52              // Add more detailed error
                reporting, if desired.
53
54          }
55
56      } else { // If the query did not
        run OK.
57          echo '<p><font color="red">
            Your submission could not be
            processed due to a system
            error. We apologize for any
            inconvenience.</font></p>';
58          // Print the query and invoke
            the mysql_error() function to
            debug.
59          }
60
61      } // End of if (isset($the_file)...
62
63  } // End of FOR loop.
64
65  mysql_close(); // Close the database
    connection.
66
67  } // End of the main Submit conditional.
68  ?>
69  <form enctype="multipart/form-data"
    action="add_file.php" method="post">
70
71      <fieldset><legend>Fill out the form to
        upload a file:</legend>
72      <input type="hidden" name=
        "MAX_FILE_SIZE" value="524288" />
73
```

(script continues on next page)

8. Complete the conditionals, the `for` loop, and the PHP section.

```
        } else {
            echo '<p><font color=
         → "red">Your submission
         → could not be processed
         → due to a system error.
         → We apologize for any
         → inconvenience.</font>
         → </p>';
        }
    }
}
mysql_close();
}
?>
```

9. Begin the HTML form.

```
<form enctype="multipart/form-data"
 → action="add_file.php"
 → method="post">
    <fieldset><legend>Fill out the
     → form to upload a file:</legend>
    <input type="hidden" name=
     → "MAX_FILE_SIZE" value="524288" />
```

This form will be very simple, but it contains the three necessary parts for file uploads: the form's `enctype` attribute, the `MAX_FILE_SIZE` hidden input (524,288 bytes or 512 KB), and the `file` input (three of them, actually).

continues on next page

10. Create the file and description inputs.

```php
<?php
for ($i = 0; $i < $counter; $i++) {
  echo '<p><b>File:</b> <input
→ type="file" name="upload' .
→ $i . '" /></p>
<p><b>Description:</b> <textarea
→ name="description' . $i . '"
→ cols="40" rows="5"></textarea>
→ </p><br />
';
}
?>
```

To create the inputs, I use another loop based upon the $counter variable. Within the loop, the two inputs are printed, using a unique name for each (see Figure 12.22).

Remember that you only need the one MAX_FILE_SIZE input (see Step 9), regardless of how many actual file inputs you have.

11. Complete the form and the PHP page.

```php
</fieldset>
<input type="hidden" name=
→ "submitted" value="TRUE" />
<div align="center"><input
→ type="submit" name="submit"
→ value="Submit" /></div>
</form>
<?php
include ('./includes/footer.html');
?>
```

Script 12.8 *continued*

```
74    <?php // Create the inputs.
75    for ($i = 0; $i < $counter; $i++) {
76        echo '<p><b>File:</b> <input
          type="file" name="upload' . $i . '"
          /></p>
77        <p><b>Description:</b> <textarea
          name="description' . $i . '" cols="40"
          rows="5"></textarea></p><br />
78        ';
79    }
80    ?>
81
82    </fieldset>
83    <input type="hidden" name="submitted"
      value="TRUE" />
84    <div align="center"><input type="submit"
      name="submit" value="Submit" /></div>
85
86    </form>
87    <?php
88    include ('./includes/footer.html');
89    ?>
```

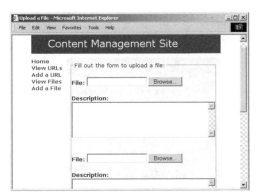

Figure 12.24 The file upload form.

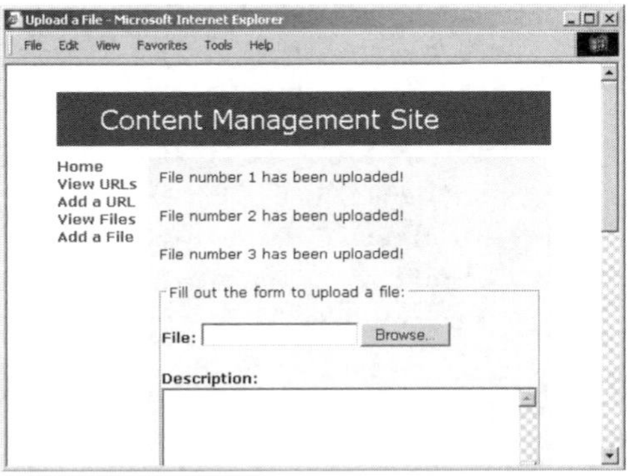

Figure 12.25 The result if the file upload worked.

12. Save the file as add_file.php, upload to your Web server, and test in your Web browser (**Figures 12.24** and **12.25**).

✔ Tips

- Once this script is ready to go live, you can suppress any future error messages by prepending the move_uploaded_file() function with @.

- Because this script uploads multiple files, you may need to adjust the post_max_size and max_execution_time settings in the php.ini file.

- The files are stored on the server *without* file extensions. This isn't a problem, though, as the files will be given their original names when the user attempts to download them.

Viewing and downloading files

The final two scripts in the application will allow users to view the uploaded files and then download them (one at a time). The viewing part is fairly obvious, but the downloading script requires extensive use of PHP's `header()` function.

To write view_files.php:

1. Create a new PHP document in your text editor (**Script 12.9**).

```php
<?php # Script 12.9 - view_files.php
$page_title = 'View Files';
include ('./includes/header.html');
require_once ('../mysql_connect.
→ php');
$first = TRUE;
```

The `$first` variable will be used as it was in the `view_urls.php` script: to create the header and indicate whether or not some files are viewable.

2. Retrieve all of the files from the database.

```php
$query = "SELECT upload_id,
→ file_name, ROUND(file_size/1024)
→ AS fs, description, DATE_FORMAT
→ (date_entered, '%M %e, %Y') AS d
→ FROM uploads ORDER BY date_entered
→ DESC";
$result = mysql_query ($query);
```

This query will return the *upload_id*, *file_name*, *description*, and a formatted date for every uploaded file, the most recently uploaded file listed first. At the same time, the query will return the file's size in kilobytes, by dividing the stored file size by 1,024 and then rounding this number off.

3. Display every record.

```php
while ($row = mysql_fetch_array
→ ($result, MYSQL_ASSOC)) {
  if ($first) {
    echo '<table border="0"
→ width="100%" cellspacing="3"
→ cellpadding="3"
→ align="center">
<tr>
  <td align="left" width="20%">
→ <font size="+1">File Name
→ </font></td>
  <td align="left" width="40%">
→ <font size="+1">Description
→ </font></td>
  <td align="center" width="20%">
→ <font size="+1">File Size
→ </font></td>
  <td align="left" width="20%">
→ <font size="+1">Upload Date
→ </font></td>
</tr>';
    $first = FALSE;
  }
  echo "  <tr>
    <td align=\"left\"><a href=
→ \"download_file.php?uid=
→ {$row['upload_id']}\">{$row
→ ['file_name']}</a></td>
    <td align=\"left\">" .
→ stripslashes($row
→ ['description']) . "</td>
    <td align=\"center\">{$row
→ ['fs']}kb</td>
    <td align=\"left\">{$row
→ ['d']}</td>
  </tr>\n";
}
```

continues on page 522

MANAGING FILES

Script 12.9 The `view_files.php` script shows the uploaded files, along with their description, size, and uploaded date.

```
1    <?php # Script 12.9 - view_files.php
2    // This page displays the files uploaded to the server.
3
4    // Set the page title and include the HTML header.
5    $page_title = 'View Files';
6    include ('./includes/header.html');
7
8    require_once ('../mysql_connect.php'); // Connect to the database.
9
10   $first = TRUE; // Initialize the variable.
11
12   // Query the database.
13   $query = "SELECT upload_id, file_name, ROUND(file_size/1024) AS fs, description, DATE_FORMAT
     (date_entered, '%M %e, %Y') AS d FROM uploads ORDER BY date_entered DESC";
14   $result = mysql_query ($query);
15
16   // Display all the URLs.
17   while ($row = mysql_fetch_array ($result, MYSQL_ASSOC)) {
18
19       // If this is the first record, create the table header.
20       if ($first) {
21           echo '<table border="0" width="100%" cellspacing="3" cellpadding="3" align="center">
22       <tr>
23           <td align="left" width="20%"><font size="+1">File Name</font></td>
24           <td align="left" width="40%"><font size="+1">Description</font></td>
25           <td align="center" width="20%"><font size="+1">File Size</font></td>
26           <td align="left" width="20%"><font size="+1">Upload Date</font></td>
27       </tr>';
28
29           $first = FALSE; // One record has been returned.
30
31       } // End of $first IF.
32
33       // Display each record.
34       echo " <tr>
35           <td align=\"left\"><a href=\"download_file.php?uid={$row['upload_id']}\">{$row['file_name']}
           </a></td>
36           <td align=\"left\">" . stripslashes($row['description']) . "</td>
37           <td align=\"center\">{$row['fs']}kb</td>
38           <td align=\"left\">{$row['d']}</td>
39       </tr>\n";
40
```

(script continues on next page)

Again, this section works much like its predecessor in `view_urls.php`. The `$first` variable is used to create a header once and then every record is printed (**Figure 12.26**). I'm using the `MYSQL_ASSOC` constant with `mysql_fetch_array()` and therefore refer to, for example, `$row['fs']`, to print out the values.

Each filename is a link to the `download_file.php` script, with the *upload_id* appended to the URL as *uid*. This value will be used by the download script to know which file to send to the Web browser.

4. Display a message if there were no files or close the table if there were.

```
if ($first) {
    echo '<div align="center">There
    → are currently no files to be
    → viewed.</div>';
} else {
    echo '</table>';
}
```

5. Complete the PHP page.

```
mysql_close();
include ('./includes/footer.html');
?>
```

6. Save the file as `view_files.php`, upload to your Web server, and test in your Web browser.

Script 12.9 *continued*

```
41   } // End of while loop.
42
43   // If no records were displayed...
44   if ($first) {
45       echo '<div align="center">There are
         currently no files to be viewed.</div>';
46   } else {
47       echo '</table>'; // Close the table.
48   }
49
50   mysql_close(); // Close the database
     connection.
51   include ('./includes/footer.html');
52   ?>
```

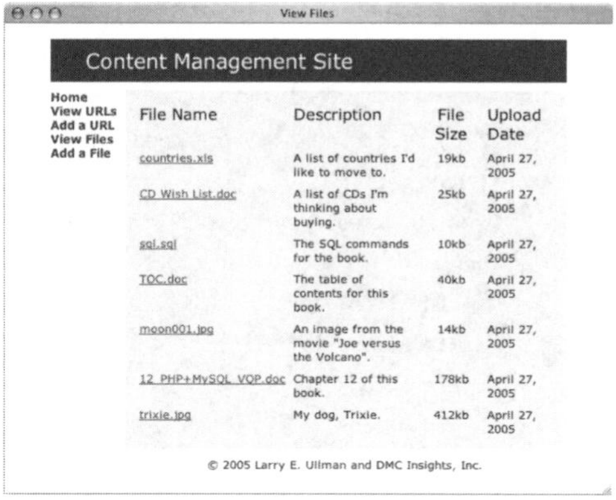

Figure 12.26 The `view_files.php` page.

Script 12.10 This script forces a file download by sending the proper headers to the Web browser.

```
1   <?php # Script 12.10 - download_file.php
2   // This pages handles file downloads
    through headers.
3
4   // Check for an upload_id.
5   if (isset($_GET['uid'])) {
6       $uid = (int) $_GET['uid'];
7   } else { // Big problem!
8       $uid = 0;
9   }
10
11  if ($uid > 0) { // OK to proceed!
12
13      require_once ('../mysql_connect.php');
        // Connect to the database.
14
15      // Get the information for this file.
16      $query = "SELECT file_name, file_type,
        file_size FROM uploads WHERE
        upload_id=$uid";
17      $result = mysql_query ($query);
18      list ($fn, $ft, $fs) =
        mysql_fetch_array ($result,
        MYSQL_NUM);
19      mysql_close(); // Close the database
        connection.
20
```

(script continues on next page)

To write download_file.php:

1. Create a new PHP document in your text editor (**Script 12.10**).

   ```
   <?php # Script 12.10 - download_
   file.php
   ```

2. Check for an *upload_id*.

   ```
   if (isset($_GET['uid'])) {
       $uid = (int) $_GET['uid'];
   } else { // Big problem!
       $uid = 0;
   }
   if ($uid > 0) {
   ```

   Before continuing, I want to ensure that the script received a valid *upload_id*, which should be a positive number. Type casting is used on the variable, as an extra precaution.

3. Retrieve the information for this file.

   ```
   require_once ('../mysql_connect.
   → php');
   $query = "SELECT file_name,
   → file_type, file_size FROM uploads
   → WHERE upload_id=$uid";
   $result = mysql_query ($query);
   list ($fn, $ft, $fs) =
   → mysql_fetch_array ($result,
   → MYSQL_NUM);
   mysql_close();
   ```

   To download the file, I'll need to know the file's name, type, and size. I retrieve all of this information from the database using $uid in my query and then the list() function.

   continues on next page

#### Chapter 12

4. Determine the file's name and location on the server.

```
$the_file = '../uploads/' . $uid;
```

For the file's name, I'm defining the entire relative path to the file. The path is *../uploads/*, plus the upload ID. Setting this as a variable here will make it easier to refer to the file later in the script.

5. Check for the existence of the file on the server.

```
if (file_exists ($the_file)) {
```

Before attempting to send the file to the Web browser, I'll confirm its existence. The `file_exists()` function returns TRUE if the file can be found on the server.

6. Send the file.

```
header ("Content-Type: $ft\n");
header ("Content-disposition:
→ attachment; filename=\"$fn\"\n");
header ("Content-Length: $fs\n");
readfile ($the_file);
```

These `header()` calls will send the file data to the Web browser, creating a download prompt (**Figure 12.27**). The first line prepares the browser to receive the file, based upon the MIME type (stored in the database when the file was uploaded). The second line sets the name of the file being downloaded, also using the original filename as it was on the user's computer. The double quotation marks around the file's name are in case there are spaces in the name.

The last `header()` function reports upon the length of the data to be sent, which was again determined when the file was uploaded. The file data itself is sent using the `readfile()` function, which reads in a file and immediately sends the content to the Web browser.

Script 12.10 *continued*

```
21    // Determine the file name on the server.
22    $the_file = '../uploads/' . $uid;
23
24    // Check if it exists.
25    if (file_exists ($the_file)) {
26
27        // Send the file.
28        header ("Content-Type: $ft\n");
29        header ("Content-disposition:
          attachment; filename=\"$fn\"\n");
30        header ("Content-Length: $fs\n");
31        readfile ($the_file);
32
```

(script continues on next page)

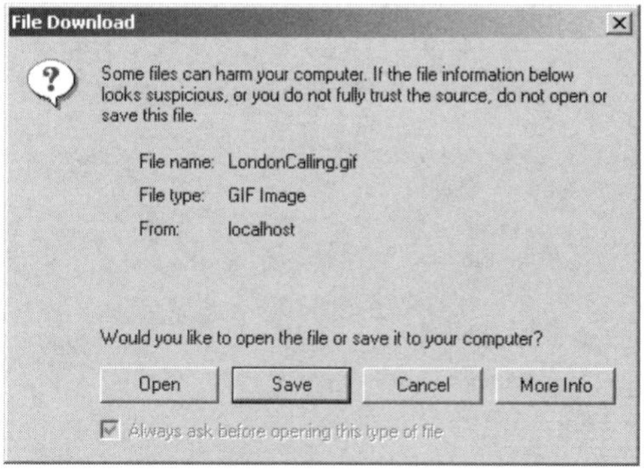

Figure 12.27 Clicking a link in the `view_files.php` page should result in this prompt (using Internet Explorer on Windows, other browsers and operating systems will behave differently).

Script 12.10 *continued*

```
┌─────────────────────────────────────┐
│░░░░░░░░░░░░░░ script ░░░░░░░░░░░░░░▣│
├─────────────────────────────────────┤
33    } else { // File doesn't exist.
34       $page_title = 'File Download';
35       include ('./includes/header.html');
36       echo '<p><font color="red">The file
         could not be located on the server.
         We apologize for any inconvenience.
         </font></p>';
37       include ('./includes/footer.html');
38    }
39
40  } else { // No valid upload ID.
41    $page_title = 'File Download';
42    include ('./includes/header.html');
43    echo '<p><font color="red">Please select
       a valid file to download.</font></p>';
44    include ('./includes/footer.html');
45  }
46  ?>
```

✔ Tips

■ Various Web browsers handle file downloads differently. You should test scripts like this one on as many browsers and platforms as possible to ensure reliable results.

■ To improve the reliability of this script, you could call the `ob_end_clean()` function prior to the `header()` lines. By doing so, you would keep other, irrelevant data, from being mixed-in with the downloaded file. You could also call the `exit()` function after `readfile()` to specifically terminate the execution of the script.

7. Complete the conditionals.

```
  } else {
      $page_title = 'File Download';
      include ('./includes/header.
      → html');
      echo '<p><font color="red">
      → The file could not be located
      → on the server. We apologize
      → for any inconvenience.
      → </font></p>';
      include ('./includes/footer.
      → html');
  }
} else {
  $page_title = 'File Download';
  include ('./includes/header.
  → html');
  echo '<p><font color="red">
  → Please select a valid file to
  → download.</font></p>';
  include ('./includes/footer.
html');
}
```

The first `else` concludes the `file_exists()` conditional. The second concludes the invalid `$uid` conditional.

8. Complete the page.

```
?>
```

Notice that this page only prints something to the Web browser if a problem occurs. If all goes well, clicking the link in `view_files.php` creates the download prompt (or immediately downloads the file, depending upon the browser), but the Web browser remains on the `view_files.php` page.

9. Save the file as `download_file.php`, upload to your Web server, and test in your Web browser (by clicking a link in `view_files.php`).

MANAGING FILES

Editing File Records

I have not included a page for editing a file record, but to do so would not be hard, particularly if you use edit_url.php as a model. For starters, you'll need to provide the edit_file.php page with the *upload_id*, presumably linked from view_files.php (as view_urls.php linked to edit_url.php). On edit_file.php, you would then validate the *upload_id* in exactly the same way (confirming that it is a positive integer).

For the form itself, start with the edit and delete radio buttons. Then retrieve all of the current file information and print most of it in the browser, showing the current file's name, size, and upload date. Create a new file input (just one) and a description textarea, preset with the current description (from the database).

When handling the form, first see if the file should be deleted. If so, run a DELETE query on the table (using the *upload_id* in a WHERE clause) and then remove the actual file using unlink().

If the file's record is being edited, check if a new file has been submitted. If so, update all of the file's information in the table and then move the upload to its final destination, using the exact same filename—specifically, the upload ID. This will have the effect of replacing the old file. If a new file was not uploaded, meaning that just the description was edited, then you only need to update that particular column in the database.

Example—
User Registration

The second example in the book—a user registration system—is one of the more common uses of PHP and MySQL. Most of the scripts developed here have been introduced and explained in previous chapters, although this chapter will place them all within the same context, using a consistent programming theory.

Users will be able to register, log in, log out, change their password, and reset their password (should it be forgotten). A feature added in this edition of the book will be the requirement that users activate their account—by clicking a link in an email—before they can log in. Once the user has logged in, sessions will be used to limit access to pages and track the user.

As in the preceding chapter, the focus here will be on the public side of things (never fear: Chapter 14, "Example—E-Commerce," includes some administration). Of course, I'll include notes at the end of the chapter discussing what you might do to add administrative features. Along the way you'll also see recommendations as to how this application could easily be expanded or modified.

Creating the Templates

The application in this chapter will use a new template design. This template makes extensive use of Cascading Style Sheets (CSS), creating a clean look without the need for images. It has tested well on all current browsers and will appear as unformatted text on browsers that don't support CSS 2 (including text browsers like Lynx). The intended layout for this site (**Figure 13.1**) is derived from one freely provided by BlueRobot (www.bluerobot.com), a good, albeit outdated, source for basic CSS templates.

To begin, I'll write two template files: header.html and footer.html. As in the Chapter 9, "Cookies and Sessions," examples, the footer file will display certain links depending upon whether or not the user is logged in, determined by checking for the existence of a session variable. Further, the header file will begin sessions and output buffering, while the footer file will end output buffering. (See Chapter 11, "Extended Topics," for more information on output control.)

To make header.html:

1. Create a new document in your text editor (**Script 13.1**).

   ```
   <?php # Script 13.1 - header.html
   ```

2. Begin output buffering and start a session.

   ```
   ob_start();
   session_start();
   ```

   I'll be using output buffering for this application, so that I need not worry about error messages when I use HTTP headers, redirect the user, or send cookies. Every page will make use of sessions as well (it's safe to place the session_start() call after ob_start(), since nothing has been sent to the Web browser yet).

Since every public page will use both of these techniques, placing these lines in the header.html file saves me the hassle of placing them in every single page (and makes it easier to edit later, if necessary).

3. Check for a $page_title variable and close the PHP section.

   ```
   if (!isset($page_title)) {
       $page_title = 'User Registration
       → System';
   }
   ?>
   ```

   As in the other times I've used a template system, the page's title—which appears at the top of the browser window—will be set on a page-by-page basis. This conditional checks if the $page_title variable has a value and, if it doesn't, sets it to a default string. This is a nice, but optional, check to include in the header.

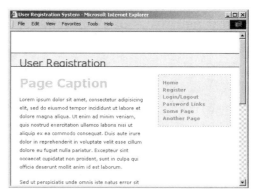

Figure 13.1 The basic appearance of this Web application.

Script 13.1 The header file begins the HTML, starts the session, and turns on output buffering.

```
                    script
1    <?php # Script 13.1 - header.html
2    // This page begins the HTML header for the
     site.
3
4    // Start output buffering.
5    ob_start();
6    // Initialize a session.
7    session_start();
8
9    // Check for a $page_title value.
10   if (!isset($page_title)) {
11       $page_title = 'User Registration
         System';
12   }
13   ?>
14   <!DOCTYPE html PUBLIC "-//W3C//DTD XHTML
     1.0 Transitional//EN"
15           "http://www.w3.org/TR/xhtml1/DTD/
             xhtml1-transitional.dtd">
16   <html xmlns="http://www.w3.org/1999/xhtml"
     xml:lang="en" lang="en">
17   <head>
18       <meta http-equiv="content-type" content=
         "text/html; charset=iso-8859-1" />
19       <title><?php echo $page_title; ?>
         </title>
20   <style type="text/css" media="screen">
     @import "./includes/layout.css";</style>
21   </head>
22   <body>
23   <div id="Header">User Registration</div>
24   <div id="Content">
25   <!-- End of Header -->
```

4. Create the HTML head.

```
<!DOCTYPE html PUBLIC "-//W3C//DTD
→ XHTML 1.0 Transitional//EN"
"http://www.w3.org/TR/xhtml1/DTD/
→ xhtml1-transitional.dtd">
<html xmlns="http://www.w3.org/1999/
→ xhtml" xml:lang="en" lang="en">
<head>
    <meta http-equiv="content-type"
    → content="text/html; charset=
    → iso-8859-1" />
    <title><?php echo $page_title;
    → ?></title>
<style type="text/css" media=
→ "screen">@import "./includes/
→ layout.css";</style>
</head>
```

The PHP $page_title variable is printed out between the title tags here. Then, the CSS document is included. It will be called layout.css and stored in a directory called *includes*. You can download the file from the book's Web site (on the Scripts page).

5. Begin the HTML body.

```
<body>
<div id="Header">User Registration
→ </div>
<div id="Content">
```

The body creates the banner across the top of the page and then starts the content part of the Web page (up until *Page Caption* in Figure 13.1).

6. Save the file as header.html.

CREATING THE TEMPLATES

529

To make footer.html:

1. Create a new document in your text editor (**Script 13.2**).

   ```
   </div>
   <div id="Menu">
   <a href="index.php">Home</a><br />
   ```

2. Use PHP to dynamically display the appropriate links.

   ```
   <?php # Script 13.2 - footer.html
   if (isset($_SESSION['user_id']) AND
   → (substr($_SERVER['PHP_SELF'], -10)
   → != 'logout.php')) {
       echo '<a href="logout.php">Logout
   → </a><br />
   <a href="change_password.php">Change
   → Password</a><br />
   ';
   } else {
       echo '<a href="register.php">
   → Register</a><br />
   <a href="login.php">Login</a><br />
   <a href="forgot_password.php">
   → Forgot Password</a><br />
   ';
   }
   ?>
   ```

   If the user is logged in (which means that $_SESSION['user_id'] is set and this isn't the logout page), the user will see links to log out and to change their password. Otherwise, the user will see links to log in and reset a forgotten password.

Script 13.2 The footer file concludes the HTML, displaying links based upon the user status (logged in or not), and flushes the output to the Web browser.

```
1   <!-- End of Content -->
2   </div>
3
4   <div id="Menu">
5   <a href="index.php">Home</a><br />
6   <?php # Script 13.2 - footer.html
7   // This page completes the HTML template.
8
9   // Display links based upon the login
    status.
10  // Show LOGIN links if this is the LOGOUT
    page.
11  if (isset($_SESSION['user_id']) AND
    (substr($_SERVER['PHP_SELF'], -10)
    != 'logout.php')) {
12      echo '<a href="logout.php">Logout
        </a><br />
13  <a href="change_password.php">Change
    Password</a><br />
14  ';
15  } else { //  Not logged in.
16      echo '<a href="register.php">
        Register</a><br />
17  <a href="login.php">Login</a><br />
18  <a href="forgot_password.php">Forgot
    Password</a><br />
19  ';
20  }
21  ?>
22  <a href="#">Some Page</a><br />
23  <a href="#">Another Page</a><br />
24  </div>
25  </body>
26  </html>
27  <?php // Flush the buffered output.
28  ob_end_flush();
29  ?>
```

Figure 13.2 The directory structure of the site on the Web server, assuming *html* is the document root (where www.address.com points).

3. Complete the HTML.

```
<a href="#">Some Page</a><br />
<a href="#">Another Page</a><br />
</div>
</body>
</html>
```

I've included two dummy links for other pages to be added.

4. Flush the buffer to the Web browser.

```
<?php
ob_end_flush();
?>
```

The footer file will send the accumulated buffer to the Web browser, completing the output buffering begun in the header script.

5. Save the file as footer.html and upload, along with header.html and layout.css (from the book's supporting Web site), to your Web server, placing all three in the *includes* directory (**Figure 13.2**).

CREATING THE TEMPLATES

531

Writing the Configuration Scripts

This Web site will make use of two configuration-type scripts. One, `config.inc.php`, will manage errors and could be used for other purposes, such as defining functions and establishing constants. The other, `mysql_connect.php`, will store all of the database-related information.

Making a configuration file

The sole purpose of the configuration file will be to establish the error-management policy for the site. The technique involved—creating your own error handling function—was covered in Chapter 6, "Error Handling and Debugging." In this chapter I'll modify the original version in a couple of ways.

During the development stages, I'll want every error reported in the most detailed way (**Figure 13.3**). Along with the specific error message, all of the existing variables will be shown, as will the current date and time. This will be formatted so that it fits within the site's template (in other words, there will be a dedicated error formatting style defined in the CSS file).

During the production, or live, stage of the site, I'll want to handle errors more gracefully (**Figure 13.4**). At that time, the detailed error messages will not be printed in the Web browser, but instead sent to an email address. Because certain errors (called notices) may or may not be indicative of a problem (see Chapter 6), such errors will be reported in an email but ignored in the Web browser.

Figure 13.3 During the development stages of the Web site, I want all errors to be made as obvious and as informative as possible.

Figure 13.4 If errors occur while a site is live, the user will only see a message like this (but a detailed error message will be emailed to the administrator).

Script 13.3 This configuration script dictates how errors are handled.

```
                    script
1    <?php # Script 13.3 - config.inc.php
2
3    // This script determines how errors are
     handled.
4
5    // Flag variable for site status:
6    $live = FALSE;
7
8    // Error log email address:
9    $email = 'InsertRealAddressHere';
10
11   // Create the error handler.
12   function my_error_handler ($e_number,
     $e_message, $e_file, $e_line, $e_vars) {
13
14      global $live, $email;
15
16      // Build the error message.
17      $message = "An error occurred in script
        '$e_file' on line $e_line: \n<br />
        $e_message\n<br />";
18
```

(script continues on next page)

To write config.inc:

1. Create a new document in your text editor (**Script 13.3**).

```
<?php # Script 13.3 - config.inc.php
```

2. Define the required variables.

```
$live = FALSE;
$email = 'InsertRealAddressHere';
```

The $live variable is the most important one. If it is FALSE, detailed error messages are sent to the Web browser (Figure 13.3). Once the site goes live, this variable should be set to TRUE so that detailed error messages are never revealed to the Web user (Figure 13.4). The $email variable is where the error messages will be sent when the site is live. You would obviously use your own e-mail address for this value.

3. Begin defining the error-handling function.

```
function my_error_handler
→ ($e_number, $e_message, $e_file,
→ $e_line, $e_vars) {
    global $live, $email;
    $message = "An error occurred in
    → script '$e_file' on line $e_line:
    → \n<br />$e_message\n<br />";
```

The function definition begins like the one in Chapter 6. It expects to receive five arguments: the error number, the error message, the script in which the error occurred, the line number on which PHP thinks the error occurred, and an array of variables that exist.

Next, I make the two variables defined earlier accessible by invoking the global statement. Then I begin defining my $message variable.

continues on next page

WRITING THE CONFIGURATION SCRIPTS

4. Add the current date and time.

```
$message .= "Date/Time: " .
→ date('n-j-Y H:i:s') . "\n<br />";
```

To make the error reporting more useful, I'll include the current date and time in the message. A newline character and an HTML <br /> tag are included to make the resulting display more legible.

5. Append all of the existing variables.

```
$message .= "<pre>" . print_r
→ ($e_vars, 1) . "</pre>\n<br />";
```

The $e_vars variable is an array of all variables that exist at the time of the error, along with their values. I can use the print_r() function to append the contents of $e_vars onto $message. To make it easier to read this section of the message in the Web browser, I use the HTML <pre> tags.

6. Handle the error according to the value of $live.

```
if ($live) {
    error_log ($message, 1, $email);
    if ($e_number != E_NOTICE) {
        echo '<div id="Error">A system
        → error occurred. We apologize
        → for the inconvenience.
        → </div><br />';
    }
} else {
    echo '<div id="Error">' .
    → $message . '</div><br />';
}
```

Script 13.3 *continued*

```
19    // Add the date and time.
20    $message .= "Date/Time: " . date('n-j-Y
      H:i:s') . "\n<br />";
21
22    // Append $e_vars to the $message.
23    $message .= "<pre>" . print_r ($e_vars,
      1) . "</pre>\n<br />";
24
25    if ($live) { // Don't show the specific
      error.
26
27        error_log ($message, 1, $email);
          // Send email.
28
29        // Only print an error message if the
          error isn't a notice.
30        if ($e_number != E_NOTICE) {
31            echo '<div id="Error">
              A system error occurred.
              We apologize for the
              inconvenience.</div><br />';
32        }
33
34    } else { // Development (print the
      error).
35        echo '<div id="Error">' . $message .
          '</div><br />';
36    }
37
38    } // End of my_error_handler() definition.
39
40    // Use my error handler.
41    set_error_handler ('my_error_handler');
42    ?>
```

As I mentioned earlier, if the site is live, the detailed message should be sent in an email and the Web user should only see a generic message. To take this one step further, the generic message will not be printed if the error is of a specific type: `E_NOTICE`. Such errors occur for things like referring to a variable that does not exist, which may or may not be a problem. To avoid potentially inundating the user with error messages, I check if `$e_number` is not equal to `E_NOTICE`, which is a constant defined in PHP (see the PHP manual).

If the site isn't live, the entire error message is printed, for any type of error message. In both cases, I surround the message with `<div id="Error">`, which will format the message per the rules defined in my CSS file.

7. Complete the function definition and tell PHP to use your error handler.

```
}
set_error_handler ('my_error_
→ handler');
?>
```

You have to use the `set_error_handler()` function to tell PHP to use your own function for errors.

8. Save the file as `config.inc.php`, and upload to the Web server, placing it in the *includes* directory.

Making the database script

The second configuration-type script will be `mysql_connect.php`, a variation on the database connection file used multiple times in the book already. Its primary purpose is to connect to MySQL and select the database. The script will also define the `escape_data()` function, which is used to process all form data before using it in a SQL query.

If a problem occurs, this page will make use of the error-handling tools established in `config.inc.php`. To do so, I'll use the `trigger_error()` function. This function lets you tell PHP that an error occurred. Of course PHP will handle that error using the `my_error_hanlder()` function, as established in the configuration script.

Database Permissions

As a security matter, this Web application should use its own specific MySQL user and password. Instead of accessing the database as a generic Web user or as the root user (a very, very bad idea), establish a new username and password with access only to the database here (*sitename*).

The MySQL user should have permission to insert, update, and select records but nothing more. By creating a new user with very particular permissions, the potential security risk is minimized should that access information be compromised.

To write mysql_connect.php:

1. Create a new document in your text editor (**Script 13.4**).

   ```
   <?php # Script 13.4 - mysql_connect.
   → php
   ```

2. Set the database access information.

   ```
   DEFINE ('DB_USER', 'username');
   DEFINE ('DB_PASSWORD', 'password');
   DEFINE ('DB_HOST', 'localhost');
   DEFINE ('DB_NAME', 'sitename');
   ```

3. Attempt to connect to MySQL and select the database.

   ```
   if ($dbc = mysql_connect (DB_HOST,
   → DB_USER, DB_PASSWORD)) {
      if (!mysql_select_db (DB_NAME)) {
   ```

   In previous scripts, these two steps each took place in a single line. In those scripts, if the function didn't return the proper result, the die() function was called. Since I will be using my own error-handling function and not simply killing the script, I'll rewrite these steps as conditionals.

4. Handle any errors if the database could not be selected.

   ```
      trigger_error("Could not select
   → the database!\n<br />MySQL
   → Error: " . mysql_error());
      include ('./includes/footer.html');
      exit();
   }
   ```

   If the script could not select the database, I want to send the error message to the my_error_handler() function. By doing so, I can ensure that the error is handled according to the currently set management technique (live stage versus development). Instead of calling my_error_handler() directly, I use trigger_error(), whose first argument is the error message.

Script 13.4 The database connection script creates a function for escaping data and manages MySQL-related errors.

```
1    <?php # Script 13.4 - mysql_connect.php
2
3    // This file contains the database access
     information.
4    // This file also establishes a connection
     to MySQL and selects the database.
5
6    // Set the database access information as
     constants.
7    DEFINE ('DB_USER', 'username');
8    DEFINE ('DB_PASSWORD', 'password');
9    DEFINE ('DB_HOST', 'localhost');
10   DEFINE ('DB_NAME', 'sitename');
11
12   if ($dbc = mysql_connect (DB_HOST, DB_USER,
     DB_PASSWORD)) { // Make the connnection.
13
14      if (!mysql_select_db (DB_NAME)) { // If
        it can't select the database.
15
16         // Handle the error.
17         trigger_error("Could not select
           the database!\n<br />MySQL Error:
           " . mysql_error());
18
19         // Print a message to the user,
           include the footer, and kill the
           script.
20         include ('./includes/footer.html');
21         exit();
22
23      } // End of mysql_select_db IF.
24
25   } else { // If it couldn't connect to MySQL.
26
27      // Print a message to the user, include
        the footer, and kill the script.
28      trigger_error("Could not connect to
        MySQL!\n<br />MySQL Error: " .
        mysql_error());
```

(script continues on page 538)

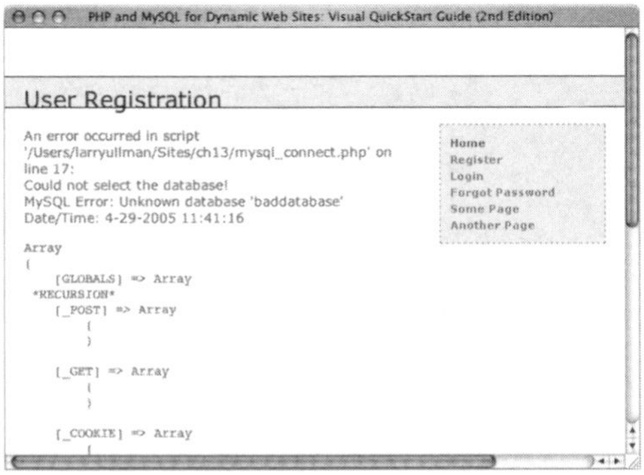

Figure 13.5 A database selection error occurring during the development of the site.

Because an inability to select the database will most likely undermine the functionality of the script, I'll also include the footer file to complete the HTML page and terminate the script. **Figure 13.5** shows the end result if a problem occurs during the development stage.

5. Repeat the process if a connection could not be established.

```
} else {
   trigger_error("Could not connect
   → to MySQL!\n<br />MySQL Error: " .
   → mysql_error());
   include ('./includes/footer.
   → html');
   exit();
}
```

These lines are permutations of the ones in Step 4 and will be executed if the script could not connect to MySQL. As in that example, the `mysql_error()` function is used as part of the error message.

6. Create the `escape_data()` function.

```
function escape_data ($data) {
   if (ini_get('magic_quotes_gpc')) {
      $data = stripslashes($data);
   }
   if (function_exists('mysql_real_
   → escape_string')) {
      global $dbc;
      $data = mysql_real_escape_
      → string (trim($data), $dbc);
   } else {
      $data = mysql_escape_string
      → (trim($data));
   }
   return $data;
}
```

continues on next page

For an explanation of this syntax, see the original version in Chapter 8, "Web Application Development."

7. Complete the PHP code.

```
?>
```

8. Save the file as `mysql_connect.php`, and upload to the Web server, outside of the Web document directory.

✔ Tips

■ On the one hand, it might make sense to place the contents of both configuration files in one script for ease of reference. Unfortunately, doing so would add unnecessary overhead (namely, connecting to and selecting the database) to scripts that don't require a database connection (e.g., `index.php`).

■ For the error management file, I used `.inc.php` as the extension, indicating that the script is both an included file but also a PHP script. For the MySQL connection page, I just used `.php`, as it's clear from the file's name what the script does. These are minor, irrelevant distinctions, but I would strongly advocate that both files end with `.php`, for security purposes.

Script 13.4 *continued*

```
29     include ('./includes/footer.html');
30     exit();
31
32  } // End of $dbc IF.
33
34  // Create a function for escaping the data.
35  function escape_data ($data) {
36
37      // Address Magic Quotes.
38      if (ini_get('magic_quotes_gpc')) {
39          $data = stripslashes($data);
40      }
41
42      // Check for mysql_real_escape_string()
        support.
43      if (function_exists('mysql_real_escape_
        string')) {
44          global $dbc; // Need the connection.
45          $data = mysql_real_escape_string
            (trim($data), $dbc);
46      } else {
47          $data = mysql_escape_string
            (trim($data));
48      }
49
50      // Return the escaped value.
51      return $data;
52
53  } // End of function.
54  ?>
```

Script 13.5 The script for the site's home page, which will greet a logged in user by name.

```
1    <?php # Script 13.5 - index.php
2    // This is the main page for the site.
3
4    // Include the configuration file for error
     management and such.
5    require_once ('./includes/config.inc.
     php');
6
7    // Set the page title and include the HTML
     header.
8    $page_title = 'PHP and MySQL for Dynamic
     Web Sites: Visual QuickStart Guide (2nd
     Edition)';
9    include ('./includes/header.html');
10
11   // Welcome the user (by name if they are
     logged in).
12   echo '<h1>Welcome';
13   if (isset($_SESSION['first_name'])) {
14       echo ", {$_SESSION['first_name']}!";
15   }
16   echo '</h1>';
17   ?>
18   <p>Spam spam spam spam spam spam
19   spam spam spam spam spam spam
20   spam spam spam spam spam spam
21   spam spam spam spam spam spam.</p>
22   <p>Spam spam spam spam spam spam
23   spam spam spam spam spam spam
24   spam spam spam spam spam spam
25   spam spam spam spam spam spam.</p>
26
27   <?php // Include the HTML footer file.
28   include ('./includes/footer.html');
29   ?>
```

Creating the Home Page

The home page for the site, called `index.php`, will be a model for the other pages on the public side. It will require the configuration file (for error management) and the header and footer files to create the HTML design. This page will also welcome the user by name, assuming the user is logged in.

To write index.php:

1. Create a new document in your text editor (**Script 13.5**).

   `<?php # Script 13.5 - index.php`

2. Include the configuration file, set the page title, and include the HTML header.

   `require_once ('./includes/config.`
   `→ inc.php');`

   `$page_title = 'PHP and MySQL for`
   `→ Dynamic Web Sites: Visual`
   `→ QuickStart Guide (2nd Edition)';`

   `include ('./includes/header.html');`

   The script includes the configuration file first so that everything that happens afterward will be handled using the error-management processes established therein. Then the `header.html` file is included, which will start output buffering, begin the session, and create the initial part of the HTML layout.

   continues on next page

3. Greet the user and complete the PHP code.

```
echo '<h1>Welcome';
if (isset($_SESSION['first_name'])) {
    echo ", {$_SESSION['first_name']
    → }!";
}
echo '</h1>';
?>
```

The *Welcome* message will be printed to all users. If a `$_SESSION['first_name']` variable is set, the user's first name will also be printed. So the end result will be either just *Welcome* (**Figure 13.6**) or *Welcome, Name!* (**Figure 13.7**).

4. Create the content for the page.

```
<p>Spam spam spam spam spam spam
spam spam spam spam spam spam
spam spam spam spam spam spam
spam spam spam spam spam spam.</p>
<p>Spam spam spam spam spam spam
spam spam spam spam spam spam
spam spam spam spam spam spam
spam spam spam spam spam spam.</p>
```

5. Include the HTML footer.

```
<?php
include ('./includes/footer.html');
?>
```

The footer file will complete the HTML layout (primarily the menu bar on the right side of the page) and conclude the output buffering.

6. Save the file as `index.php`, upload to the Web server, and test in a Web browser.

✔ Tip

■ If you compare the list of links in Figures 13.6 and 13.7, you'll see how the conditional in `footer.html` changes the list of options.

Figure 13.6 If the user is not logged in, this is the home page they will see.

Figure 13.7 If the user is logged in, the index page will greet the user by name.

The Database Scheme

The database being used by this application was first created back in Chapter 4, "Introduction to SQL and MySQL," and has been modified since then. The database currently consists of only one table, *users*. To create the table as it should be defined for this chapter, use this SQL command:

```
CREATE TABLE users (

user_id INT unsigned NOT NULL
→ auto_increment,

email varchar(40) NOT NULL,

pass CHAR(40) NOT NULL,

first_name varchar(15) NOT NULL,

last_name varchar(30) NOT NULL,

active CHAR(32),

registration_date datetime NOT NULL,

PRIMARY KEY (user_id),

UNIQUE KEY (email),

KEY (email, pass)

)
```

Most of the table's structure should be familiar to you by now. One new addition is the *active* column, which will be used to indicate whether a user has activated their account (by clicking a link in the registration email) or not. It will either store the 32-character-long activation code or have a NULL value.

A unique index is placed on the *email* field, and another index is placed on the combination of the *email* and *pass* fields. These two fields will be used together during the login query, so indexing them as one makes sense.

Registration

The registration script was first started in Chapter 7, "Using PHP with MySQL." It has since been improved upon in many ways. This version of register.php will do the following:

◆ Both display and handle the form

◆ Validate the submitted data using regular expressions

◆ Redisplay the form with the values remembered if a problem occurs (the form will be *sticky*)

◆ Process the submitted data using the escape_data() function from the mysql_connect.php script

◆ Ensure a unique email address

◆ Send an email containing an activation link

To write register.php:

1. Create a new document in your text editor (**Script 13.6**).

   ```
   <?php # Script 13.6 - register.php
   ```

2. Include the configuration file and the HTML header.

   ```
   require_once ('./includes/config.
   → inc.php');
   $page_title = 'Register';
   include ('./includes/header.html');
   ```

3. Create the conditional that checks for the form submission and then include the database connection script.

   ```
   if (isset($_POST['submitted'])) {
       require_once ('../mysql_connect.
       → php');
   ```

   Make sure that your `mysql_connect.php` page defines the `escape_data()` function and selects the right database (*sitename*).

4. Validate the first and last names.

   ```
   if (eregi ('^[[:alpha:]]\.\' \-]
   → {2,15}$', stripslashes(trim($_POST
   → ['first_name'])))) {
       $fn = escape_data($_POST
       → ['first_name']);
   } else {
       $fn = FALSE;
       echo '<p><font color="red"
       → size="+1">Please enter your
       → first name!</font></p>';
   }
   if (eregi ('^[[:alpha:]]\.\' \-]
   → {2,30}$', stripslashes(trim($_POST
   → ['last_name'])))) {
       $ln = escape_data($_POST
       → ['last_name']);
   } else {
       $ln = FALSE;
       echo '<p><font color="red"
       → size="+1">Please enter your last
       → name!</font></p>';
   }
   ```

Script 13.6 The registration script uses regular expressions for security and a sticky form for user convenience. It sends an email to the user upon a successful registration.

```
1    <?php # Script 13.6 - register.php
2    // This is the registration page for the site.
3
4    // Include the configuration file for error
     management and such.
5    require_once ('./includes/config.inc.php');
6
7    // Set the page title and include the HTML
     header.
8    $page_title = 'Register';
9    include ('./includes/header.html');
10
11   if (isset($_POST['submitted'])) { // Handle
     the form.
12
13       require_once ('../mysql_connect.php');
         // Connect to the database.
14
15       // Check for a first name.
16       if (eregi ('^[[:alpha:]]\.\' \-]
         {2,15}$', stripslashes(trim($_POST
         ['first_name'])))) {
17           $fn = escape_data($_POST
             ['first_name']);
18       } else {
19           $fn = FALSE;
20           echo '<p><font color="red"
             size="+1">Please enter your first
             name!</font></p>';
21       }
22
23       // Check for a last name.
24       if (eregi ('^[[:alpha:]]\.\' \-]
         {2,30}$', stripslashes(trim($_POST
         ['last_name'])))) {
25           $ln = escape_data($_POST
             ['last_name']);
26       } else {
27           $ln = FALSE;
28           echo '<p><font color="red"
             size="+1">Please enter your last
             name!</font></p>';
29       }
30
```

(script continues on page 545)

REGISTRATION

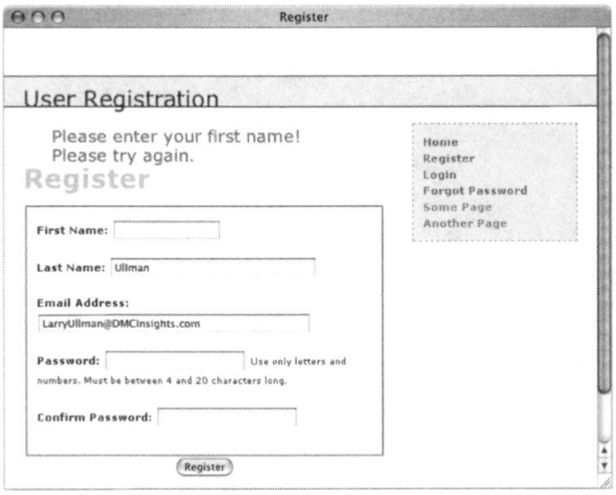

Figure 13.8 If the first name value does not pass the regular expression test, an error message is printed.

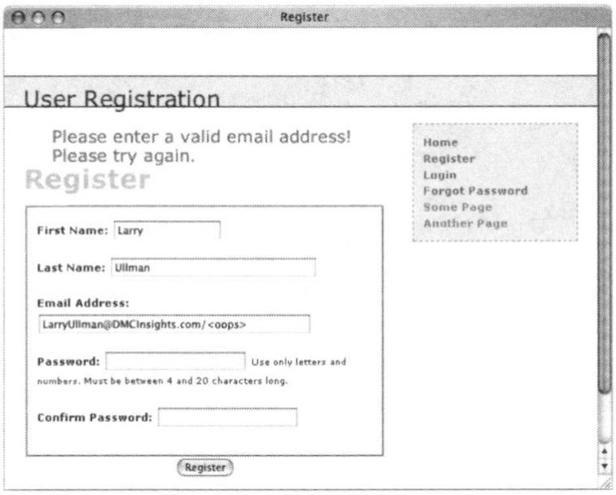

Figure 13.9 The submitted email address must be of the proper format.

The form will be validated using regular expressions, discussed in Chapter 10, "Web Application Security." For the first name value, the assumption is that it will contain only letters, a period (as in an initial), an apostrophe, a space, and the dash. Further, I expect the value to be within the range of 2 to 15 characters long.

If this condition is met, the `$fn` variable is assigned the value of the `escape_data()` version of the submitted value; otherwise, `$fn` will be false and an error message is printed (**Figure 13.8**).

The same process is used to validate the last name, although that regular expression allows for a longer length.

Using regular expressions to validate all of the form data may be overkill, but I wanted to demonstrate more sample regular expression patterns.

5. Validate the email address (**Figure 13.9**).

```
if (eregi ('^[[:alnum:]][a-z0-9_\.
→\-]*@[a-z0-9\.\-]+\.[a-z]
→{2,4}$', stripslashes(trim($_POST
→['email'])))) {
    $e = escape_data($_POST['email']);
} else {
    $e = FALSE;
    echo '<p><font color="red"
    →size="+1">Please enter a valid
    →email address!</font></p>';
}
```

The pattern for the email address was described in Chapter 10 and works rather well in my experience. In all of the validation routines, I make sure to validate a trimmed version of the variable, with the slashes stripped to avoid problems with Magic Quotes.

continues on next page

REGISTRATION

6. Validate the passwords (**Figures 13.10** and **13.11**).

```
if (eregi ('^[[:alnum:]]{4,20}$',
→ stripslashes(trim($_POST
→ ['password1']))))  {
    if ($_POST['password1'] == $_POST
    → ['password2']) {
        $p = escape_data($_POST
        → ['password1']);
    } else {
        $p = FALSE;
        echo '<p><font color="red"
        → size="+1">Your password did
        → not match the confirmed
        → password!</font></p>';
    }
} else {
    $p = FALSE;
    echo '<p><font color="red"
    → size="+1">Please enter a valid
    → password!</font></p>';
}
```

The password must be between 4 and 20 characters long and contain only letters and numbers. Furthermore, the first password (*password1*) must match the confirmed password (*password2*).

7. If every test was passed, check for a unique email address.

```
if ($fn && $ln && $e && $p) {
    $query = "SELECT user_id FROM
    → users WHERE email='$e'";
    $result = mysql_query ($query) or
    → trigger_error("Query: $query\n
    → <br />MySQL Error: " . mysql_
    → error());
```

continues on page 546

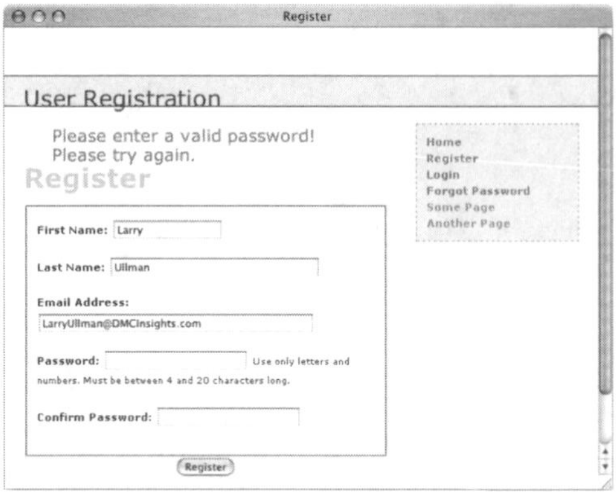

Figure 13.10 The passwords are checked for the proper format, length, and...

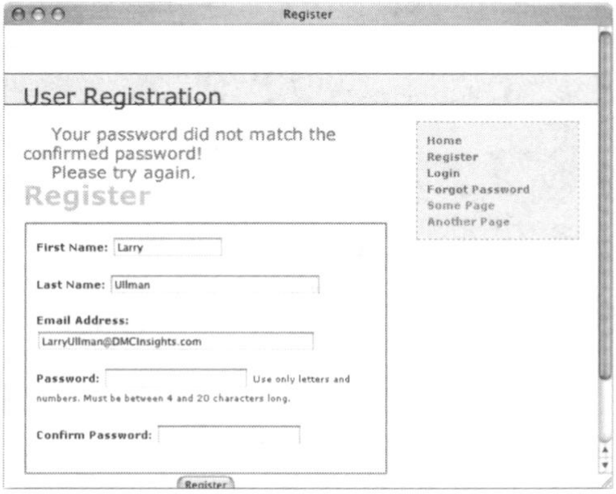

Figure 13.11 ...that the password value matches the confirmed password value.

REGISTRATION

Script 13.6 *continued*

```
                                        script
31    // Check for an email address.
32    if (eregi ('^[[:alnum:]][a-z0-9_\.\-]*@[a-z0-9\.\-]+\.[a-z]{2,4}$', stripslashes(trim($_POST
      ['email'])))) {
33        $e = escape_data($_POST['email']);
34    } else {
35        $e = FALSE;
36        echo '<p><font color="red" size="+1">Please enter a valid email address!</font></p>';
37    }
38
39    // Check for a password and match against the confirmed password.
40    if (eregi ('^[[:alnum:]]{4,20}$', stripslashes(trim($_POST['password1'])))) {
41        if ($_POST['password1'] == $_POST['password2']) {
42            $p = escape_data($_POST['password1']);
43        } else {
44            $p = FALSE;
45            echo '<p><font color="red" size="+1">Your password did not match the confirmed password!
              </font></p>';
46        }
47    } else {
48        $p = FALSE;
49        echo '<p><font color="red" size="+1">Please enter a valid password!</font></p>';
50    }
51
52    if ($fn && $ln && $e && $p) { // If everything's OK.
53
54        // Make sure the email address is available.
55        $query = "SELECT user_id FROM users WHERE email='$e'";
56        $result = mysql_query ($query) or trigger_error("Query: $query\n<br />MySQL Error: " .
          mysql_error());
57
58        if (mysql_num_rows($result) == 0) { // Available.
59
60            // Create the activation code.
61            $a = md5(uniqid(rand(), true));
62
63            // Add the user.
64            $query = "INSERT INTO users (email, pass, first_name, last_name, active,
              registration_date) VALUES ('$e', SHA('$p'), '$fn', '$ln', '$a', NOW() )";
65            $result = mysql_query ($query) or trigger_error("Query: $query\n<br />MySQL Error: " .
              mysql_error());
66
```

(script continues on page 547)

If the form passed every test, this conditional will be TRUE. Then I must search the database to see if the submitted email address is currently being used, since that column's value must be unique across each record. As with the MySQL connection script, if a query doesn't run, I'll call the trigger_error() function to invoke my self-defined error reporting function. The specific error message will include both the query being run and the MySQL error (**Figure 13.12**), so that the problem can easily be debugged.

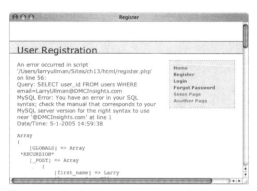

Figure 13.12 If a MySQL query error occurs, it should be easier to debug thanks to this informative error message.

8. If the email address is unused, register the user.

```
if (mysql_num_rows($result) == 0) {
    $a = md5(uniqid(rand(), true));
    $query = "INSERT INTO users
    → (email, pass, first_name,
    → last_name, active, registration_
    → date) VALUES ('$e', SHA('$p'),
    → '$fn', '$ln', '$a', NOW() )";
    $result = mysql_query ($query) or
    → trigger_error("Query: $query\n
    → <br />MySQL Error: " .
    → mysql_error());
```

The query itself is rather simple, but it does require the creation of an activation code. To accomplish that, I use the same code as I did in Chapter 10 for generating a unique 32-character string.

The MySQL SHA() function is used to encrypt the password.

Script 13.6 *continued*

	script	
67	`if (mysql_affected_rows() == 1) {`
	`// If it ran OK.`
68	
69	`// Send the email.`
70	`$body = "Thank you for`
	`registering at the User`
	`Registration site. To activate`
	`your account, please click on`
	`this link:\n\n";`
71	`$body .= "http://www.`
	`whateveraddressyouwanthere`
	`.com/activate.php?x=" .`
	`mysql_insert_id() . "&y=$a";`
72	`mail($_POST['email'],`
	`'Registration Confirmation',`
	`$body);`
73	
74	`// Finish the page.`
75	`echo '<h3>Thank you for`
	`registering! A confirmation`
	`email has been sent to your`
	`address. Please click on the`
	`link in that email in order to`
	`activate your account.</h3>';`
76	`include ('./includes/footer.`
	`html'); // Include the HTML`
	`footer.`
77	`exit();`
78	
79	`} else { // If it did not run OK.`
80	`echo '<p><font color="red"`
	`size="+1">You could not be`
	`registered due to a system`
	`error. We apologize for any`
	`inconvenience.</font></p>';`
81	`}`
82	

(script continues on page 549)

9. Send an email or print an error message, reflecting the success of the registration.

```
if (mysql_affected_rows() == 1) {
    $body = "Thank you for registering
→ at the User Registration site.
→ To activate your account, please
→ click on this link:\n\n";
    $body .= "http://www.
→ whateveraddressyouwanthere.com/
→ activate.php?x=" . mysql_insert_
→ id() . "&y=$a";
    mail($_POST['email'],
→ 'Registration Confirmation',
→ $body);
    echo '<h3>Thank you for
→ registering! A confirmation
→ email has been sent to your
→ address. Please click on the
→ link in that email in order to
→ activate your account.</h3>';
    include ('./includes/footer.html');
    exit();
} else {
    echo '<p><font color="red"
→ size="+1">You could not be
→ registered due to a system
→ error. We apologize for any
→ inconvenience.</font></p>';
}
```

continues on next page

With this registration process, the important thing is that the confirmation mail gets sent to the user, because they will not be able to log in until after they've activated their account. This email should contain a link to the activation page, `activate.php` (you'll need to change the domain name so that it's accurate). The link also passes two values along in the URL. The first, generically called *x*, will be the user's ID from the database. The second, *y*, is the activation code. The URL, then, will be something like *http://www.domainname.com/activate.php?x=22&y=901e09ef25bf6e3ef95c93088450b008*.

A thank-you message is printed out upon successful registration, along with the activation instructions (**Figure 13.13**).

If the query failed for some reason, an error message is printed to the browser (although the live version of the site should never have a problem at this juncture).

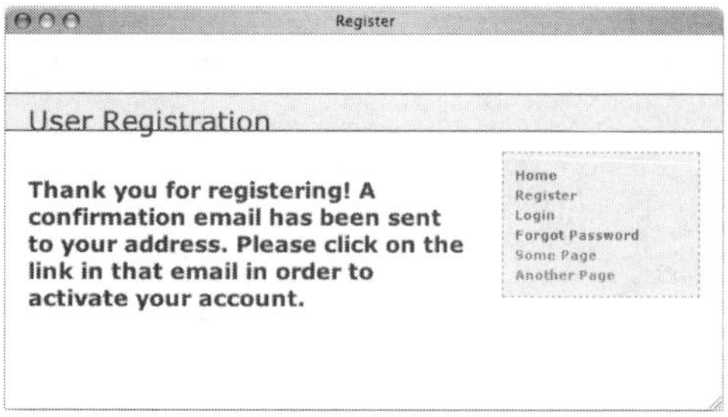

Figure 13.13 The resulting page after a user has been successfully registered.

Script 13.6 *continued*

```
                    script
83        } else { // The email address is not
          available.
84            echo '<p><font color="red"
              size="+1">That email address has
              already been registered. If you
              have forgotten your password, use
              the link to have your password
              sent to you.</font></p>';
85        }
86
87        } else { // If one of the data tests
          failed.
88            echo '<p><font color="red"
              size="+1">Please try again.</font>
              </p>';
89        }
90
91        mysql_close(); // Close the database
          connection.
92
93   } // End of the main Submit conditional.
94   ?>
95
```

(script continues on page 551)

Figure 13.14 If an email address has already been registered, the user is told as much.

10. Complete the conditionals and the PHP code.

```
        } else {
            echo '<p><font color="red"
            → size="+1">That email
            → address has already been
            → registered. If you have
            → forgotten your password,
            → use the link to have your
            → password sent to you.
            → </font></p>';
        }
    } else {
        echo '<p><font color="red"
        → size="+1">Please try again.
        → </font></p>';
    }
    mysql_close();
}
?>
```

The first else is executed if a person attempts to register with an email address that has already been used (**Figure 13.14**). The second else applies when the submitted data fails one of the validation routines (see Figures 13.9 through 13.11).

continues on next page

11. Display the HTML form (**Figure 13.15**).

```
<h1>Register</h1>

<form action="register.php"
→ method="post">

  <fieldset>

  <p><b>First Name:</b> <input
→ type="text" name="first_name"
→ size="15" maxlength="15" value=
→ "<?php if (isset($_POST['first_
→ name'])) echo $_POST['first_
→ name']; ?>" /></p>

  <p><b>Last Name:</b> <input
→ type="text" name="last_name"
→ size="30" maxlength="30" value=
→ "<?php if (isset($_POST['last_
→ name'])) echo $_POST['last_
→ name']; ?>" /></p>

  <p><b>Email Address:</b> <input
→ type="text" name="email"
→ size="40" maxlength="40" value=
→ "<?php if (isset($_POST
→ ['email'])) echo $_POST
→ ['email']; ?>" /> </p>

  <p><b>Password:</b> <input
→ type="password" name="password1"
→ size="20" maxlength="20" />
→ <small>Use only letters and
→ numbers. Must be between 4 and
→ 20 characters long.</small></p>

  <p><b>Confirm Password:</b>
→ <input type="password"
→ name="password2" size="20"
→ maxlength="20" /></p>

  </fieldset>

  <div align="center"><input type=
→ "submit" name="submit" value=
→ "Register" /></div>

  <input type="hidden" name=
→ "submitted" value="TRUE" />

</form>
```

12. Include the HTML footer.

```
<?php
include ('./includes/footer.html');
?>
```

13. Save the file as register.php, upload to your Web server, and test in your Web browser.

✔ Tips

■ Because every column in the *users* table cannot be NULL (except for *active*), I require that each input be correctly filled out. If a table had an optional field, you should still confirm that it is of the right type if submitted, but not require it.

■ Except for encrypted fields (such as the password), the maximum length of the form inputs and regular expressions should correspond to the maximum length of the column in the database.

■ If Magic Quotes GPC (*GET, POST, COOKIE*) is turned on, the sticky part of the form should strip the slashes from the values before printing them. For example:

```
<?php if (isset($_POST['first_
name'])) echo stripslashes($_
POST['first_name']); ?>
```

Figure 13.15 The registration form as it appears when the user first arrives.

Script 13.6 *continued*

```
                                    script

96    <h1>Register</h1>
97    <form action="register.php" method="post">
98       <fieldset>
99
100      <p><b>First Name:</b> <input type="text" name="first_name" size="15" maxlength="15" value="<?php
         if (isset($_POST['first_name'])) echo $_POST['first_name']; ?>" /></p>
101
102      <p><b>Last Name:</b> <input type="text" name="last_name" size="30" maxlength="30" value="<?php
         if (isset($_POST['last_name'])) echo $_POST['last_name']; ?>" /></p>
103
104      <p><b>Email Address:</b> <input type="text" name="email" size="40" maxlength="40" value="<?php
         if (isset($_POST['email'])) echo $_POST['email']; ?>" /> </p>
105
106      <p><b>Password:</b> <input type="password" name="password1" size="20" maxlength="20" />
         <small>Use only letters and numbers. Must be between 4 and 20 characters long.</small></p>
107
108      <p><b>Confirm Password:</b> <input type="password" name="password2" size="20" maxlength="20"
         /></p>
109      </fieldset>
110
111      <div align="center"><input type="submit" name="submit" value="Register" /></div>
112      <input type="hidden" name="submitted" value="TRUE" />
113
114   </form>
115
116   <?php // Include the HTML footer.
117   include ('./includes/footer.html');
118   ?>
```

Activating an Account

A new feature I've added to this registration example in this edition of the book is the activation process. When a person registers, an activation code will be associated with their account. This will also be sent as a link in the registration confirmation email.

The user then has to click the link in the email, which will take them to the site's activation page. The link will pass to the activation script the user's ID number and the activation code. If these two values match those in the database, the activation code will be removed from the record, indicating an active account. The login page, developed next, will allow only users who have activated their account to log in.

To create the activation page:

1. Begin a new PHP script in your text editor or IDE (**Script 13.7**).

   ```
   <?php # Script 13.7 - activate.php
   require_once ('./includes/config.
   → inc.php');
   $page_title = 'Activate Your Account';
   include ('./includes/header.html');
   ```

2. Validate the values that should be received by the page.

   ```
   if (isset($_GET['x'])) {
       $x = (int) $_GET['x'];
   } else {
       $x = 0;
   }
   if (isset($_GET['y'])) {
       $y = $_GET['y'];
   } else {
       $y = 0;
   }
   ```

   As I mentioned, if the user clicks the link in the registration confirmation email,

they'll pass two values to this page: the user ID and the activation code. I first check for the presence of x (the user's ID); if it is there, I type-cast it as an integer, just in case. For y (the activation code), I just check for its existence. In either case, if the value is not present, then the variable is set to 0.

3. If $x and $y have the correct values, activate the user.

   ```
   if ( ($x > 0) && (strlen($y) == 32)) {
       require_once ('../mysql_connect.
       → php');
       $query = "UPDATE users SET active=
       → NULL WHERE (user_id=$x AND
       → active='" . escape_data($y) . "')
       → LIMIT 1";
   $result = mysql_query ($query) or
   → trigger_error("Query: $query\n
   → <br />MySQL Error: " . mysql_
   → error());
   ```

   The conditional checks that $x is a positive integer and that $y is 32 characters long, which is the length of the string returned by the md5() function in register.php. If both conditions are TRUE, an UPDATE query is run. This query removes the activation code from the user's record by setting the *active* column to NULL.

4. Report upon the success of the query.

   ```
   if (mysql_affected_rows() == 1) {
       echo "<h3>Your account is now
       → active. You may now log in.
       → </h3>";
   } else {
       echo '<p><font color="red"
       → size="+1">Your account could not
       → be activated. Please re-check
       → the link or contact the system
       → administrator.</font></p>';
   }
   ```

continues on page 554

Script 13.7 To activate an account, the user must come to this page, passing it their user ID number and activation code.

```
1    <?php # Script 13.7 - activate.php
2    // This page activates the user's account.
3
4    // Include the configuration file for error management and such.
5    require_once ('./includes/config.inc.php');
6
7    // Set the page title and include the HTML header.
8    $page_title = 'Activate Your Account';
9    include ('./includes/header.html');
10
11   // Validate $_GET['x'] and $_GET['y'].
12   if (isset($_GET['x'])) {
13       $x = (int) $_GET['x'];
14   } else {
15       $x = 0;
16   }
17   if (isset($_GET['y'])) {
18       $y = $_GET['y'];
19   } else {
20       $y = 0;
21   }
22
23   // If $x and $y aren't correct, redirect the user.
24   if ( ($x > 0) && (strlen($y) == 32)) {
25
26       require_once ('../mysql_connect.php'); // Connect to the database.
27       $query = "UPDATE users SET active=NULL WHERE (user_id=$x AND active='" .
         escape_data($y) . "') LIMIT 1";
28       $result = mysql_query ($query) or trigger_error("Query: $query\n<br />MySQL Error: " .
         mysql_error());
29
30       // Print a customized message.
31       if (mysql_affected_rows() == 1) {
32           echo "<h3>Your account is now active. You may now log in.</h3>";
33       } else {
34           echo '<p><font color="red" size="+1">Your account could not be activated. Please re-check the
           link or contact the system administrator.</font></p>';
35       }
36
37       mysql_close();
38
39   } else { // Redirect.
40
```

(script continues on page 555)

If one row was affected by the query, then the user's account is now active and a message says as much (**Figure 13.16**). If no rows are affected, the user is notified of the problem (**Figure 13.17**). This would most likely happen if someone tried to fake the *x* and *y* values or if there's a problem in following the link from the email to the Web browser.

5. Complete the main conditional.

```
    mysql_close();
} else {
    $url = 'http://' . $_SERVER
➝ ['HTTP_HOST'] . dirname($_SERVER
➝ ['PHP_SELF']);
    if ((substr($url, -1) == '/') OR
➝ (substr($url, -1) == '\\') ) {
        $url = substr ($url, 0, -1);
    }
    $url .= '/index.php';
    ob_end_clean();
    header("Location: $url");
    exit();
}
```

The else clause takes effect if $x and $y are not of the proper value and length. In such a case, the user is just redirected to the index page.

6. Complete the page.

```
include ('./includes/footer.html');
?>
```

7. Save the file as activate.php, upload to your Web server, and test by clicking the link in the registration email (**Figure 13.18**).

Figure 13.16 If the database could be updated using the provided user ID and activation code, the user is notified that their account is now active.

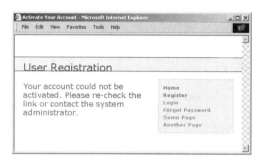

Figure 13.17 If an account is not activated by the query, the user is told of the problem.

Figure 13.18 The registration confirmation email includes a link to activate the account.

Script 13.7 *continued*

```
41      // Start defining the URL.
42      $url = 'http://' . $_SERVER['HTTP_HOST']
        . dirname($_SERVER['PHP_SELF']);
43      // Check for a trailing slash.
44      if ((substr($url, -1) == '/') OR (substr
        ($url, -1) == '\\') ) {
45          $url = substr ($url, 0, -1); // Chop
            off the slash.
46      }
47      // Add the page.
48      $url .= '/index.php';
49
50      ob_end_clean(); // Delete the buffer.
51      header("Location: $url");
52      exit(); // Quit the script.
53
54  } // End of main IF-ELSE.
55
56  include ('./includes/footer.html');
57  ?>
```

✔ Tips

■ I specifically use the vague x and y as the names in the URL for security purposes. While someone may figure out that the one is an ID number and the other is a code, it's sometimes best not to be explicit about such things.

■ You may want to add a *From* parameter to your mail() call in register.php so that you can indicate who sent the confirmation email.

ACTIVATING AN ACCOUNT

Logging In and Logging Out

In Chapter 9, I wrote many versions of the login.php and logout.php scripts, using variations on cookies and sessions. Here I'll develop standardized versions of both that adhere to the same practices as the whole application. The login query itself is slightly different here in that it also checks that the *active* column has a NULL value, which means that the user has activated their account.

To write login.php:

1. Create a new document in your text editor (**Script 13.8**).

   ```
   <?php # Script 13.8 - login.php
   ```

2. Require the configuration file and the HTML header.

   ```
   require_once ('./includes/config.
   → inc.php');
   $page_title = 'Login';
   include ('./includes/header.html');
   ```

3. Check if the form has been submitted, require the database connection, and validate the submitted data.

   ```
   if (isset($_POST['submitted'])) {
     require_once ('../mysql_connect.
     → php');
     if (!empty($_POST['email'])) {
       $e = escape_data($_POST
       → ['email']);
     } else {
       echo '<p><font color="red"
       → size="+1">You forgot to enter
       → your email address!</font>
       → </p>';
       $e = FALSE;
     }
     if (!empty($_POST['pass'])) {
       $p = escape_data($_POST
       → ['pass']);
   ```

Script 13.8 The login form will redirect the user to the home page after registering the first name and user ID values in a session

```
1    <?php # Script 13.8 - login.php
2    // This is the login page for the site.
3
4    // Include the configuration file for error
     management and such.
5    require_once ('./includes/config.inc.php');
6
7    // Set the page title and include the HTML
     header.
8    $page_title = 'Login';
9    include ('./includes/header.html');
10
11   if (isset($_POST['submitted'])) { // Check
     if the form has been submitted.
12
13      require_once ('../mysql_connect.php');
        // Connect to the database.
14
15      // Validate the email address.
16      if (!empty($_POST['email'])) {
17         $e = escape_data($_POST['email']);
18      } else {
19         echo '<p><font color="red"
           size="+1">You forgot to enter your
           email address!</font></p>';
20         $e = FALSE;
21      }
22
23      // Validate the password.
24      if (!empty($_POST['pass'])) {
25         $p = escape_data($_POST['pass']);
26      } else {
27         $p = FALSE;
28         echo '<p><font color="red"
           size="+1">You forgot to enter your
           password!</font></p>';
29      }
30
```

(script continues on page 558)

Figure 13.19 The login form checks only if values were entered, without using regular expressions.

```
} else {
    $p = FALSE;
    echo '<p><font color="red"
    → size="+1">You forgot to enter
    → your password!</font></p>';
}
```

I could certainly validate the submitted data using regular expressions; however, that level of testing is unwarranted and will slow down the login process. If, for example, the user enters *12345* as their email address, then the login query will not return a match anyway. Therefore, it's unnecessary to apply a regular expression first.

If the user does not enter any values into the form, error messages will be printed (**Figure 13.19**).

4. If both validation routines were passed, retrieve the user information.

```
if ($e && $p) {
    $query = "SELECT user_id, first_
    → name FROM users WHERE (email=
    → '$e' AND pass=SHA('$p')) AND
    → active IS NULL";
    $result = mysql_query ($query) or
    → trigger_error("Query: $query\n
    → <br />MySQL Error: " . mysql_
    → error());
```

The query will attempt to retrieve the user ID and first name for the record whose email address and password match those submitted. The MySQL query uses the SHA() function on the *pass* column, as the password is encrypted using that function in the first place. The query also checks that the *active* column has a NULL value, meaning that the user has successfully accessed the activate. php page.

continues on next page

5. If a match was made in the database, log the user in and redirect them.

```
if (@mysql_num_rows($result) == 1) {
$row = mysql_fetch_array ($result,
→MYSQL_NUM);
   mysql_free_result($result);
   mysql_close();
   $_SESSION['first_name'] = $row[1];
   $_SESSION['user_id'] = $row[0];
   $url = 'http://' . $_SERVER
→['HTTP_HOST'] . dirname($_SERVER
→['PHP_SELF']);
   if ((substr($url, -1) == '/') OR
→(substr($url, -1) == '\\') ) {
      $url = substr ($url, 0, -1);
   }
   $url .= '/index.php';
   ob_end_clean();
   header("Location: $url");
   exit();
```

The login process consists of storing the retrieved values in the session (which was already started in header.html) and then redirecting the user to the home page. The ob_end_clean() function will delete the existing buffer (the output buffering is also begun in header.html), since it will not be used. The redirection code is in accordance with the preferred method, as described in Chapter 8.

6. Complete the conditionals and close the database connection.

```
   } else {
      echo '<p><font color="red"
→size="+1">Either the email
→address and password
→entered do not match those
→on file or you have not yet
→activated your account.
→</font></p>';
   }
```

Script 13.8 *continued*

```
                         script

31    if ($e && $p) { // If everything's OK.
32
33        // Query the database.
34        $query = "SELECT user_id,
          first_name FROM users WHERE
          (email='$e' AND pass=SHA('$p')) AND
          active IS NULL";
35        $result = mysql_query ($query) or
          trigger_error("Query: $query\n<br />
          MySQL Error: " . mysql_error());
36
37        if (@mysql_num_rows($result) == 1) {
          // A match was made.
38
39            // Register the values &
              redirect.
40            $row = mysql_fetch_array
              ($result, MYSQL_NUM);
41            mysql_free_result($result);
42            mysql_close(); // Close the
              database connection.
43            $_SESSION['first_name'] =
              $row[1];
44            $_SESSION['user_id'] = $row[0];
45
46            // Start defining the URL.
47            $url = 'http://' . $_SERVER
              ['HTTP_HOST'] . dirname($_SERVER
              ['PHP_SELF']);
48            // Check for a trailing slash.
49            if ((substr($url, -1) == '/') OR
              (substr($url, -1) == '\\') ) {
50                $url = substr ($url, 0, -1);
                  // Chop off the slash.
51            }
52            // Add the page.
53            $url .= '/index.php';
54
55            ob_end_clean(); // Delete the
              buffer.
56            header("Location: $url");
57            exit(); // Quit the script.
58
```

(script continues on page 561)

Figure 13.20 An error message is displayed if the submitted username and password do not match any registered values or if the account has not yet been activated.

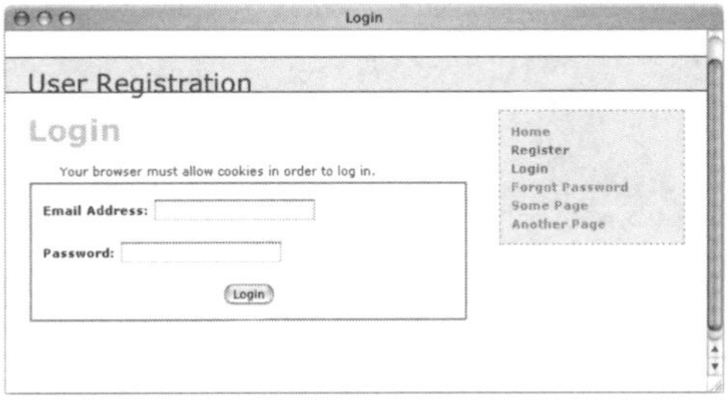

Figure 13.21 The login form.

```
    } else {
        echo '<p><font color="red"
➝ size="+1">Please try again.
➝ </font></p>';
    }
    mysql_close();
}
?>
```

The error message (**Figure 13.20**) indicates that the login process could fail for two possible reasons. One is that the submitted email address and password do not match those on file. The other reason is that the user has not yet activated their account.

7. Display the HTML login form (**Figure 13.21**).

```
<h1>Login</h1>
<p>Your browser must allow cookies
➝ in order to log in.</p>
<form action="login.php"
➝ method="post">
    <fieldset>
    <p><b>Email Address:</b> <input
➝ type="text" name="email"
➝ size="20" maxlength="40"
➝ value="<?php if (isset($_POST
➝ ['email'])) echo $_POST
➝ ['email']; ?>" /></p>
    <p><b>Password:</b> <input
➝ type="password" name="pass"
➝ size="20" maxlength="20" /></p>
    <div align="center"><input
➝ type="submit" name="submit"
➝ value="Login" /></div>
    <input type="hidden" name=
➝ "submitted" value="TRUE" />
    </fieldset>
</form>
```

continues on next page

LOGGING IN AND LOGGING OUT

The login form, like the registration form, will submit the data back to itself. It also remembers the submitted email address, should there be a problem and the form is displayed again.

Notice that I add a message informing the user that cookies must be enabled to use the site (if a user does not allow cookies, the user will never get access to the logged-in user pages).

8. Include the HTML footer.

```php
<?php
include ('./includes/footer.html');
?>
```

9. Save the file as login.php, upload to your Web server, and test in your Web browser (**Figure 13.22**).

Figure 13.22 Upon successfully logging in, the user will be redirected to the home page, where they will be greeted by name.

Script 13.8 *continued*

```
                                           script
59          } else { // No match was made.
60              echo '<p><font color="red" size="+1">Either the email address and password entered do not
                match those on file or you have not yet activated your account.</font></p>';
61          }
62
63      } else { // If everything wasn't OK.
64          echo '<p><font color="red" size="+1">Please try again.</font></p>';
65      }
66
67      mysql_close(); // Close the database connection.
68
69  } // End of SUBMIT conditional.
70  ?>
71
72  <h1>Login</h1>
73  <p>Your browser must allow cookies in order to log in.</p>
74  <form action="login.php" method="post">
75      <fieldset>
76      <p><b>Email Address:</b> <input type="text" name="email" size="20" maxlength="40" value="<?php
        if (isset($_POST['email'])) echo $_POST['email']; ?>" /></p>
77      <p><b>Password:</b> <input type="password" name="pass" size="20" maxlength="20" /></p>
78      <div align="center"><input type="submit" name="submit" value="Login" /></div>
79      <input type="hidden" name="submitted" value="TRUE" />
80      </fieldset>
81  </form>
82
83  <?php // Include the HTML footer.
84  include ('./includes/footer.html');
85  ?>
```

To write logout.php:

1. Create a new document in your text editor and include the necessary files (**Script 13.9**).

```
<?php # Script 13.9 - logout.php
require_once ('./includes/config.
→ inc.php');
$page_title = 'Logout';
include ('./includes/header.html');
```

2. Redirect the user if they are not logged in.

```
if (!isset($_SESSION['first_name'])) {
   $url = 'http://' . $_SERVER
   → ['HTTP_HOST'] . dirname($_SERVER
   → ['PHP_SELF']);
   if ((substr($url, -1) == '/') OR
   → (substr($url, -1) == '\\') ) {
      $url = substr ($url, 0, -1);
   }
   $url .= '/index.php';
   ob_end_clean();
   header("Location: $url");
   exit();
```

If the user is not currently logged in (determined by checking for a $_SESSION['first_name'] variable), the user will be redirected to the home page.

3. Log out the user if they are currently logged in.

```
} else {
   $_SESSION = array();
   session_destroy();
   setcookie (session_name(), '',
   → time()-300, '/', '', 0);
}
```

To log the user out, the session values will be reset, the session data will be destroyed on the server, and the session cookie will be deleted. These lines of code were first used and described in Chapter 9.

4. Print a logged-out message and complete the PHP page.

```
echo "<h3>You are now logged out.
→ </h3>";
include ('./includes/footer.html');
?>
```

5. Save the file as logout.php, upload to your Web server, and test in your Web browser (**Figure 13.23**).

✔ Tips

■ If you added a loggedin field to the *users* table, you could set this to 1 when a user logs in, and then be able to count how many people are currently online at any given moment. Set the value to 0 when the user logs out.

■ By adding a last_login DATETIME field to the *users* table, you could update it when a user logs in. Then you would know the last time a person accessed the site and have an alternative method for counting how many users are currently logged in (say, everyone that logged in within the past so many minutes).

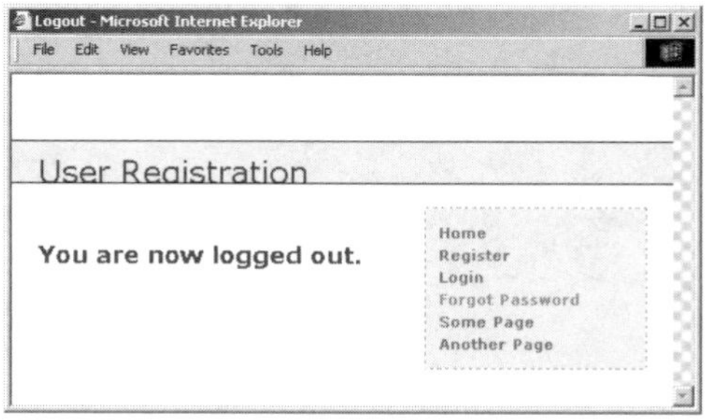

Figure 13.23 The results of successfully logging out.

Script 13.9 The logout form destroys all of the session information, including the cookie.

```
script
1    <?php # Script 13.9 - logout.php
2    // This is the logout page for the site.
3
4    // Include the configuration file for error management and such.
5    require_once ('./includes/config.inc.php');
6
7    // Set the page title and include the HTML header.
8    $page_title = 'Logout';
9    include ('./includes/header.html');
10
11   // If no first_name variable exists, redirect the user.
12   if (!isset($_SESSION['first_name'])) {
13
14       // Start defining the URL.
15       $url = 'http://' . $_SERVER['HTTP_HOST'] . dirname($_SERVER['PHP_SELF']);
16       // Check for a trailing slash.
17       if ((substr($url, -1) == '/') OR (substr($url, -1) == '\\') ) {
18           $url = substr ($url, 0, -1); // Chop off the slash.
19       }
20       // Add the page.
21       $url .= '/index.php';
22
23       ob_end_clean(); // Delete the buffer.
24       header("Location: $url");
25       exit(); // Quit the script.
26
27   } else { // Logout the user.
28
29       $_SESSION = array(); // Destroy the variables.
30       session_destroy(); // Destroy the session itself.
31       setcookie (session_name(), '', time()-300, '/', '', 0); // Destroy the cookie.
32
33   }
34
35   // Print a customized message.
36   echo "<h3>You are now logged out.</h3>";
37
38   include ('./includes/footer.html');
39   ?>
```

Password Management

The final aspect of the public side of this site is the management of passwords. There are two processes to consider: resetting a forgotten password and changing an existing one.

Resetting a password

It inevitably happens that people forget their login passwords for Web sites, so having a contingency plan for these occasions is important. One option would be to have the user email the administrator when this occurs, but administering a site is difficult enough without this extra hassle. Thus, I will make a script whose purpose is to reset a forgotten password.

Because the passwords stored in the database are encrypted using MySQL's SHA() function, there's no way to retrieve an unencrypted version. The alternative is to create a new, random password and change the existing password to this value. Rather than just display the new password in the Web browser (that would be terribly insecure), it will be emailed to the address with which the user registered.

To write forgot_password.php:

1. Create a new document in your text editor and include the necessary files (**Script 13.10**).

```
<?php # Script 13.10 -
→ forgot_password.php
require_once ('./includes/config.
→ inc.php');
$page_title = 'Forgot Your Password';
include ('./includes/header.html');
```

2. Check if the form has been submitted and validate the email address.

```
if (isset($_POST['submitted'])) {
    require_once ('../mysql_connect.
    → php');
```

```
if (empty($_POST['email'])) {
    $uid = FALSE;
    echo '<p><font color="red"
    → size="+1">You forgot to enter
    → your email address!</font>
    → </p>';
} else {
    $query = "SELECT user_id FROM
    → users WHERE email='". escape_
    → data($_POST['email']) . "'";
    $result = mysql_query ($query)
    → or trigger_error("Query:
    → $query\n<br />MySQL Error: " .
    → mysql_error());
    if (mysql_num_rows($result)
    → == 1) {
        list($uid) = mysql_fetch_
        → array ($result, MYSQL_NUM);
    } else {
        echo '<p><font color="red"
        → size="+1">The submitted
        → email address does not
        → match those on file!</font>
        → </p>';
        $uid = FALSE;
    }
}
```

continues on page 566

Script 13.10 The forgot_password.php script allows users to reset their password without administrative assistance.

```
                                      script

1    <?php # Script 13.10 - forgot_password.php
2    // This page allows a user to reset their password, if forgotten.
3
4    // Include the configuration file for error management and such.
5    require_once ('./includes/config.inc.php');
6
7    // Set the page title and include the HTML header.
8    $page_title = 'Forgot Your Password';
9    include ('./includes/header.html');
10
11   if (isset($_POST['submitted'])) { // Handle the form.
12
13       require_once ('../mysql_connect.php'); // Connect to the database.
14
15       if (empty($_POST['email'])) { // Validate the email address.
16           $uid = FALSE;
17           echo '<p><font color="red" size="+1">You forgot to enter your email address!</font></p>';
18       } else {
19
20           // Check for the existence of that email address.
21           $query = "SELECT user_id FROM users WHERE email='". escape_data($_POST['email']) . "'";
22           $result = mysql_query ($query) or trigger_error("Query: $query\n<br />MySQL Error: " .
             mysql_error());
23           if (mysql_num_rows($result) == 1) {
24
25               // Retrieve the user ID.
26               list($uid) = mysql_fetch_array ($result, MYSQL_NUM);
27
28           } else {
29               echo '<p><font color="red" size="+1">The submitted email address does not match those on
                 file!</font></p>';
30               $uid = FALSE;
31           }
32
33       }
34
```

(script continues on page 567)

This form will take an email address input and update the password for that record. The first step is to validate that an email address was entered (there's no need for the extra overhead of a regular expression). Second, an attempt is made to retrieve the user ID for that email address in the database. If no such record could be found, an error message is displayed (**Figure 13.24**). I'll be using $uid (user ID) as my flag variable, as I'll need this value in order to update the password in the database.

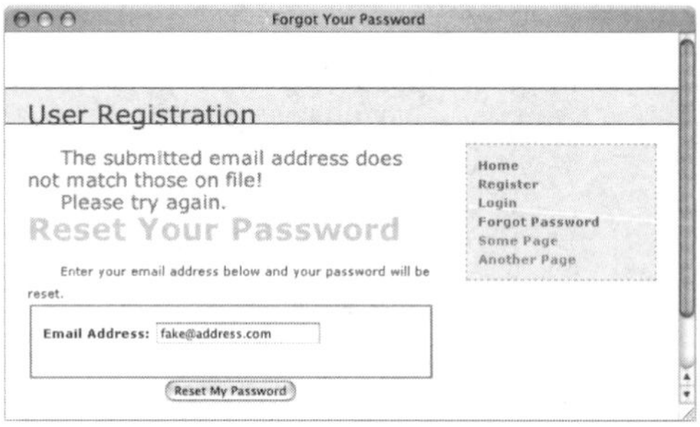

3. Create a new, random password.

```
if ($uid) {
    $p = substr ( md5(uniqid(rand
    →(),1)), 3, 10);
```

To create a new, random password, I'll make use of four PHP functions. The first is uniqid(), which will return a unique identifier. It is fed the arguments rand() and 1, which makes the returned string more random. This returned value is then sent through the md5() function, which calculates the MD5 hash of a string. At this stage, a hashed version of the unique ID is returned, which ends up being a string 32 characters long.

From this string, the password is determined by pulling out 10 characters starting with the third one, using the substr() function. All in all, this code will return a very random and meaningless 10-character string (containing both letters and numbers) to be used as the temporary password.

Figure 13.24 If the user entered an email address that is not found in the database, an error message is shown.

Figure 13.25 The resulting page after successfully resetting a password.

Script 13.10 *continued*

```
                    script
35    if ($uid) { // If everything's OK.
36
37        // Create a new, random password.
38        $p = substr ( md5(uniqid
          (rand(),1)), 3, 10);
39
40        // Make the query.
41        $query = "UPDATE users SET pass=
          SHA('$p') WHERE user_id=$uid";
42        $result = mysql_query ($query) or
          trigger_error("Query: $query\n<br />
          MySQL Error: " . mysql_error());
43        if (mysql_affected_rows() == 1) {
          // If it ran OK.
44
45            // Send an email.
46            $body = "Your password to log
              into SITENAME has been
              temporarily changed to '$p'.
              Please log in using this password
              and your username. At that time
              you may change your password to
              something more familiar.";
47            mail ($_POST['email'], 'Your
              temporary password.', $body,
              'From: admin@sitename.com');
48            echo '<h3>Your password has been
              changed. You will receive the
              new, temporary password at
              the email address with which you
              registered. Once you have logged
              in with this password, you may
              change it by clicking on the
              "Change Password" link.</h3>';
49            mysql_close(); // Close the
              database connection.
50            include ('./includes/footer.
              html'); // Include the HTML
              footer.
51            exit();
52
53        } else { // If it did not run OK.
54
```

(script continues on page 569)

4. Update the password in the database.

```
$query = "UPDATE users SET pass=SHA
→ ('$p') WHERE user_id=$uid";
$result = mysql_query ($query) or
→ trigger_error("Query: $query\n
→ <br />MySQL Error: " .
→ mysql_error());
if (mysql_affected_rows() == 1) {
    $body = "Your password to log
    → into SITENAME has been
    → temporarily changed to '$p'.
    → Please log in using this
    → password and your username.
    → At that time you may change your
    → password to something more
    → familiar.";
    mail ($_POST['email'], 'Your
    → temporary password.', $body,
    → 'From: admin@sitename.com');
    echo '<h3>Your password has been
    → changed. You will receive the
    → new, temporary password at the
    → email address with which you
    → registered. Once you have logged
    → in with this password, you may
    → change it by clicking on the
    → "Change Password" link.</h3>';
    mysql_close();
    include ('./includes/footer.
    → html');
    exit();
```

Using the user ID (the primary key for the table) that was retrieved earlier, the password for this particular user is updated to the SHA() version of $p, the random password. Then an email is sent to the user and a message is printed (**Figure 13.25**).

continues on next page

5. Complete the conditionals and the PHP code.

```
        } else {
            echo '<p><font color="red"
            → size="+1">Your password
            → could not be changed due to
            → a system error. We
            → apologize for any
            → inconvenience.</font></p>';
        }
    } else {
        echo '<p><font color="red"
        → size="+1">Please try again.
        → </font></p>';
    }
    mysql_close();
}
?>
```

6. Make the HTML form (**Figure 13.26**).

```
<h1>Reset Your Password</h1>
<p>Enter your email address below
→ and your password will be reset.
→ </p>
<form action="forgot_password.php"
→ method="post">
  <fieldset>
  <p><b>Email Address:</b> <input
  → type="text" name="email"
  → size="20" maxlength="40"
  → value="<?php if (isset($_POST
  → ['email'])) echo $_POST
  → ['email']; ?>" /></p>
  </fieldset>
  <div align="center"><input type=
  → "submit" name="submit" value=
  → "Reset My Password" /></div>
  <input type="hidden" name=
  → "submitted" value="TRUE" />
</form>
```

Figure 13.26 The simple form for resetting a password.

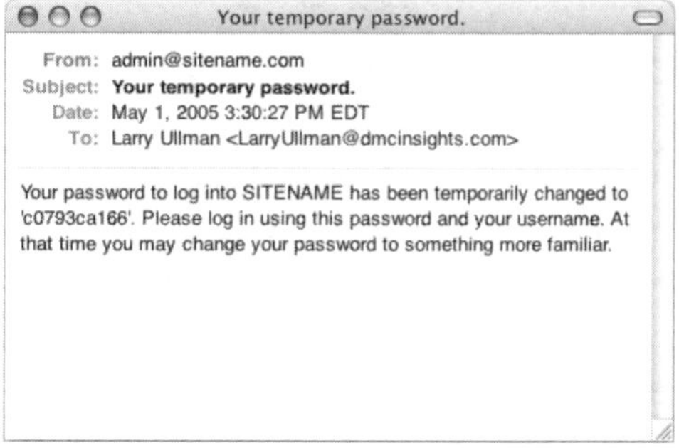

Figure 13.27 The email message received after resetting a password.

Script 13.10 *continued*

```
         ┌──────────── script ────────────┐
55             echo '<p><font color="red"
               size="+1">Your password could not
               be changed due to a system
               error. We apologize for any
               inconvenience.</font></p>';
56
57         }
58
59     } else { // Failed the validation test.
60         echo '<p><font color="red" size=
           "+1">Please try again.</font></p>';
61     }
62
63     mysql_close(); // Close the database
       connection.
64
65 } // End of the main Submit conditional.
66
67 ?>
68
69 <h1>Reset Your Password</h1>
70 <p>Enter your email address below and your
   password will be reset.</p>
71 <form action="forgot_password.php"
   method="post">
72     <fieldset>
73     <p><b>Email Address:</b> <input
       type="text" name="email" size="20"
       maxlength="40" value="<?php
       if (isset($_POST['email'])) echo $_POST
       ['email']; ?>" /></p>
74     </fieldset>
75     <div align="center"><input type="submit"
       name="submit" value="Reset My Password"
       /></div>
76     <input type="hidden" name="submitted"
       value="TRUE" />
77 </form>
78
79 <?php
80 include ('./includes/footer.html');
81 ?>
```

The form takes only one input, the email address. If there is a problem when the form has been submitted (see Figure 13.24), the submitted email address value will be shown again.

7. Include the HTML footer.

```
<?php
include ('./includes/footer.html');
?>
```

8. Save the file as forgot_password.php, upload to your Web server, and test in your Web browser.

9. Check your email to see the resulting message after a successful password reset (**Figure 13.27**).

Changing a password

The change_password.php script was initially written in Chapter 7 (called just password. php), as an example of an UDPATE query. The one developed here will be very similar in functionality but will differ in that only users who are logged in will be able to access it. Therefore, the form will only need to accept the new password and a confirmation of it (the user's existing password and email address will have already been confirmed by the login page).

To write change_password.php:

1. Create a new document in your text editor and include the necessary files (**Script 13.11**).

```php
<?php # Script 13.11 -
→ change_password.php
require_once ('./includes/config.
→ inc.php');
$page_title = 'Change Your Password';
include ('./includes/header.html');
```

2. Check that the user is logged in.

```php
if (!isset($_SESSION['first_name'])) {
  $url = 'http://' . $_SERVER
→ ['HTTP_HOST'] . dirname($_SERVER
→ ['PHP_SELF']);
  if ((substr($url, -1) == '/') OR
→ (substr($url, -1) == '\\') ) {
    $url = substr ($url, 0, -1);
  }
  $url .= '/index.php';
  ob_end_clean();
  header("Location: $url");
  exit();
```

The assumption will be that this page is accessed only by logged-in users. To enforce this idea, the script checks for the existence of the $_SESSION['first_name'] variable. If it is not set, then the user will be redirected.

3. Check if the form has been submitted and include the MySQL connection.

```php
} else {
  if (isset($_POST['submitted'])) {
    require_once ('../mysql_
→ connect.php');
```

The key to understanding how this script functions is that there are three possible scenarios: the user is not logged in (and therefore redirected), the user is logged in and viewing the form, and the user is logged in and has submitted the form.

This else clause takes effect if the user is logged in, in which case the script then needs to determine if the form has been submitted or not.

4. Validate the submitted password.

```php
if (eregi ('^[[:alnum:]]{4,20}$',
→ stripslashes(trim($_POST
→ ['password1'])))) {
  if ($_POST['password1'] == $_POST
→ ['password2']) {
    $p = escape_data($_POST
→ ['password1']);
  } else {
    $p = FALSE;
    echo '<p><font color="red"
→ size="+1">Your password did
→ not match the confirmed
→ password!</font></p>';
  }
} else {
  $p = FALSE;
  echo '<p><font color="red"
→ size="+1">Please enter a valid
→ password!</font></p>';
}
```

continues on page 572

Script 13.11 With this page, users can change an existing password (if they are logged in).

```
1    <?php # Script 13.11 - change_password.php
2    // This page allows a logged-in user to change their password.
3
4    // Include the configuration file for error management and such.
5    require_once ('./includes/config.inc.php');
6
7    // Set the page title and include the HTML header.
8    $page_title = 'Change Your Password';
9    include ('./includes/header.html');
10
11   // If no first_name variable exists, redirect the user.
12   if (!isset($_SESSION['first_name'])) {
13
14       // Start defining the URL.
15       $url = 'http://' . $_SERVER['HTTP_HOST'] . dirname($_SERVER['PHP_SELF']);
16       // Check for a trailing slash.
17       if ((substr($url, -1) == '/') OR (substr($url, -1) == '\\') ) {
18           $url = substr ($url, 0, -1); // Chop off the slash.
19       }
20       // Add the page.
21       $url .= '/index.php';
22
23       ob_end_clean(); // Delete the buffer.
24       header("Location: $url");
25       exit(); // Quit the script.
26
27   } else {
28
29       if (isset($_POST['submitted'])) { // Handle the form.
30
31           require_once ('../mysql_connect.php'); // Connect to the database.
32
33           // Check for a new password and match against the confirmed password.
34           if (eregi ('^[[:alnum:]]{4,20}$', stripslashes(trim($_POST['password1'])))) {
35               if ($_POST['password1'] == $_POST['password2']) {
36                   $p = escape_data($_POST['password1']);
37               } else {
38                   $p = FALSE;
39                   echo '<p><font color="red" size="+1">Your password did not match the confirmed
                      password!</font></p>';
40               }
```

(script continues on page 573)

The new password should be validated using the same tests as those in the registration process. Error messages will be displayed if problems are found (**Figure 13.28**).

5. Update the password.

```
if ($p) {
    $query = "UPDATE users SET pass=
    → SHA('$p') WHERE user_id=
    → {$_SESSION['user_id']}";
    $result = mysql_query ($query) or
    → trigger_error("Query: $query\n
    → <br />MySQL Error: " .
    → mysql_error());
    if (mysql_affected_rows() == 1) {
        echo '<h3>Your password has
        → been changed.</h3>';
        mysql_close();
        include ('./includes/footer.
        → html');
        exit();
    } else {
        echo '<p><font color="red"
        → size="+1">Your password
        → could not be changed due to a
        → system error. We apologize for
        → any inconvenience.</font>
        → </p>';
    }
```

Using the user's ID—stored in the session when the user logged in—the password field can be updated in the database. If the update worked, a confirmation message is printed to the Web browser (**Figure 13.29**).

6. Close the database connection and complete the conditionals and the PHP code.

```
    } else {
        echo '<p><font color="red"
        → size="+1">Please try again.
        → </font></p>';
    }
    mysql_close();
}
?>
```

continues on page 574

Figure 13.28 As in the registration process, the user's new password must pass the validation routines, otherwise they will see error messages.

Figure 13.29 The script has successfully changed the user's password.

PASSWORD MANAGEMENT

Script 13.11 *continued*

```
                                          script
41        } else {
42            $p = FALSE;
43            echo '<p><font color="red" size="+1">Please enter a valid password!</font></p>';
44        }
45
46        if ($p) { // If everything's OK.
47
48            // Make the query.
49            $query = "UPDATE users SET pass=SHA('$p') WHERE user_id={$_SESSION['user_id']}";
50            $result = mysql_query ($query) or trigger_error("Query: $query\n<br />MySQL Error: " .
              mysql_error());
51            if (mysql_affected_rows() == 1) { // If it ran OK.
52
53                // Send an email, if desired.
54                echo '<h3>Your password has been changed.</h3>';
55                mysql_close(); // Close the database connection.
56                include ('./includes/footer.html'); // Include the HTML footer.
57                exit();
58
59            } else { // If it did not run OK.
60
61                // Send a message to the error log, if desired.
62                echo '<p><font color="red" size="+1">Your password could not be changed due to a system
                  error. We apologize for any inconvenience.</font></p>';
63
64            }
65
66        } else { // Failed the validation test.
67            echo '<p><font color="red" size="+1">Please try again.</font></p>';
68        }
69
70        mysql_close(); // Close the database connection.
71
72    } // End of the main Submit conditional.
73
74    ?>
75
```

(script continues on page 575)

PASSWORD MANAGEMENT

7. Create the HTML form (**Figure 13.30**).

```
<h1>Change Your Password</h1>
<form action="change_password.php"
→ method="post">
  <fieldset>
  <p><b>New Password:</b> <input
  → type="password" name="password1"
  → size="20" maxlength="20" />
  → <small>Use only letters and
  → numbers. Must be between 4 and
  → 20 characters long.</small></p>
  <p><b>Confirm New Password:</b>
  → <input type="password"
  → name="password2" size="20"
  → maxlength="20" /></p>
  </fieldset>
  <div align="center"><input type=
  → "submit" name="submit" value=
  → "Change My Password" /></div>
  <input type="hidden" name=
  → "submitted" value="TRUE" />
</form>
```

This form takes two inputs: the new password and a confirmation of it. A description of the proper format is given as well.

Since password inputs in HTML forms cannot be given preset values, there's no reason to set them using PHP (to make the form sticky).

8. Complete the HTML page.

```
<?php
}
include ('./includes/footer.html');
?>
```

9. Save the file as change_password.php, upload to your Web server, and test in your Web browser.

✔ Tips

■ Once this script has been completed, users can reset their password with the previous script and then log in using the temporary, random password. After logging in, users can change their password back to something more memorable with this page.

■ The mysql_affected_rows() function will return 0 if an UPDATE query does not actually alter the value of any column in a record. For this reason, if users attempt to change their password but use their current password as the new one, this page will do nothing. Hopefully, this limitation should not be a problem, but you can rewrite the messages and error handling to allow for this possibility.

■ Because the site's authentication does not rely upon the user's password from page to page (in other words, the password is not checked on each subsequent page after logging in), changing a password will not require the user to log back in.

Figure 13.30 The *Change Your Password* form.

Script 13.11 *continued*

```
                              script

76      <h1>Change Your Password</h1>
77      <form action="change_password.php" method="post">
78        <fieldset>
79        <p><b>New Password:</b> <input type="password" name="password1" size="20" maxlength="20"
          /> <small>Use only letters and numbers. Must be between 4 and 20 characters long.</small></p>
80        <p><b>Confirm New Password:</b> <input type="password" name="password2" size="20"
          maxlength="20" /></p>
81        </fieldset>
82        <div align="center"><input type="submit" name="submit" value="Change My Password" /></div>
83        <input type="hidden" name="submitted" value="TRUE" />
84      </form>
85
86  <?php
87  } // End of the !isset($_SESSION['first_name']) ELSE.
88  include ('./includes/footer.html');
89  ?>
```

Site Administration

For this application, how the site administration works depends upon what you want it to do. For starters, you could add an *administrator* column to the users table (an unsigned TINYINT), indicating which users are administrators (*1* for administrators, *0* for common users). Then, when you logged in as an administrator, different links could appear.

One additional page you would probably want would be a view_users.php script, like the one created in Chapter 7 and modified in Chapter 8. You could use this to link to an edit_user.php page, which would allow you to manually activate an account or change a person's password. You could also delete a user using such a page.

EXAMPLE— E-COMMERCE

In this, the final chapter of the book, I'll develop one last Web application, an e-commerce site. Despite the recent economic slump and the devaluation of Web sites, e-commerce still plays a vital role on the Internet and is a prominent use of PHP and MySQL.

In this example, I'll design a site for the purpose of selling prints of art. Unfortunately, to write and explain the entire application would require a book in itself. Furthermore, some aspects of e-commerce—like how you handle the money—are extremely particular to each individual site. Trying to demonstrate such a process would be a waste of space. With these restrictions in mind, the focus in this chapter is on the core functionality of an e-commerce site: populating a catalog as an administrator, displaying products to the public, creating a shopping cart, and storing orders in a database.

From a technological standpoint, this application will use the Improved MySQL Extension functions, which require that you are using PHP 5 with MySQL 4.1.3 or later. These functions were introduced in Chapter 11, "Extended Topics," but haven't otherwise been fully used to this point. If the server you are using does not meet these requirements, you will need to make the necessary modifications to the PHP scripts. For the most part, this is a matter of replacing mysqli_*something*() with mysql_*something*(), as well as making minor modifications to the order of the function's arguments. Throughout this chapter I will repeatedly add reminders as to what changes will be required if you are using the older software.

Creating the Database

The e-commerce site in this example will use the simply named *ecommerce* database. It was marginally used in Chapter 11, but without the structure it will have here. I'll explain each table's role prior to creating the database in MySQL.

With any type of e-commerce application there are three broad kinds of data to be stored: the product information (what is being sold), the customer information (who is making purchases), and the order information (what was purchased and by whom). Going through the normalization process (see Chapter 5, "Advanced SQL and MySQL"), I've come up with five tables (**Figure 14.1**).

The first two tables store all of the products being sold. As I said before, the site will be selling artistic prints. The *artists* table (**Table 14.1**) stores the information for the artists whose work is being sold. This table contains just a minimum of information (the artists' first, middle, and last names), but you could easily add the artists' birth and death dates, biographical data, and so forth. The *prints* table (**Table 14.2**) is the main products table for the site. It stores the print names, prices, and other relevant details. It is linked to the *artists* table using the *artist_id*.

The *customers* table (**Table 14.3**) does exactly what you'd expect: it records the personal information for each client. At the least, it reflects the person's first name, last name, email address, password, and shipping address, as well as the date they registered. Presumably the combination of the email address and password would allow the user to log in, shop, and access their account. Since it's fairly obvious what information this table would store, I'll define it with only the three essential columns for now.

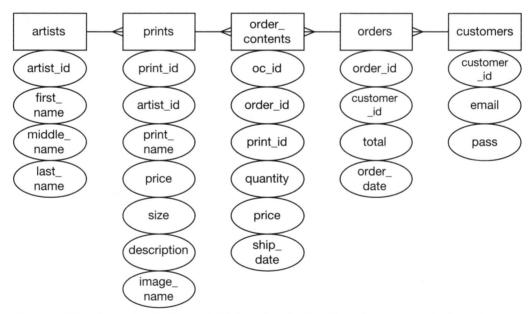

Figure 14.1 This entity-relationship diagram (ERD) shows how the five tables in the *ecommerce* database relate to one another.

The artists Table

Column	Type
artist_id	INT(3) UNSIGNED NOT NULL
first_name	VARCHAR(20) default NULL
middle_name	VARCHAR(20) default NULL
last_name	VARCHAR(30) NOT NULL

Table 14.1 The *artists* table will be used to link artist names to each individual print (see Table 14.2).

The prints Table

Column	Type
print_id	INT(4) UNSIGNED NOT NULL
artist_id	INT(3) UNSIGNED NOT NULL
print_name	VARCHAR(60) NOT NULL
price	DECIMAL(6,2) NOT NULL
size	VARCHAR(60) default NULL
description	VARCHAR(255) default NULL
image_name	VARCHAR(30) NOT NULL

Table 14.2 The *prints* table is the equivalent of a products table in other e-commerce applications. Items listed in the *prints* table will be purchased by the customer.

The customers Table

Column	Type
customer_id	INT(5) UNSIGNED NOT NULL
email	VARCHAR(40) NOT NULL
pass	CHAR(40) NOT NULL

Table 14.3 The *customers* table is being defined in the most minimal way for the purposes of this chapter's example. Expand its definition to suit your application's needs.

The orders Table

Column	Type
order_id	INT(10) UNSIGNED NOT NULL
customer_id	INT(5) UNSIGNED NOT NULL
total	DECIMAL(10,2) NOT NULL
order_date	TIMESTAMP NOT NULL

Table 14.4 The *orders* table will record the customer's ID, the order total, and the date of the order.

The final two tables store all of the order information. There are any number of ways you could do this, but I've chosen to store general order information—the total, the date, and the customer's ID—in an *orders* table (**Table 14.4**). This table could also have separate columns reflecting the shipping cost, the amount of sales tax, any discounts that applied, and so on. The *order_contents* table (**Table 14.5**) will store the actual items that were sold, including the quantity and price. The *order_contents* table is essentially a middleman, used to avoid the many-to-many relationship between *prints* and *orders* (each print can be in multiple orders, and each order can have multiple prints).

In order to be able to use transactions (see Chapter 11), the two order tables will use the InnoDB storage engine. The others will use the default MyISAM type. See Chapter 5 for more information on the available storage engines (table types).

The order_contents Table

Column	Type
oc_id	INT(10) UNSIGNED NOT NULL
order_id	INT(10) UNSIGNED NOT NULL
print_id	INT(4) UNSIGNED NOT NULL
quantity	TINYINT UNSIGNED NOT NULL DEFAULT 1
price	DECIMAL(6,2) NOT NULL
ship_date	DATETIME DEFAULT NULL

Table 14.5 The *order_contents* table stores the specific items in an order.

To create the database:

1. Log in to the mysql client and create the *ecommerce* database, if it doesn't already exist.

    CREATE DATABASE ecommerce;

    USE ecommerce;

    For these steps, you can use either the mysql client or another tool like phpMyAdmin.

2. Create the *artists* table (**Figure 14.2**).

    CREATE TABLE artists (

    artist_id INT(3) UNSIGNED NOT NULL
    → AUTO_INCREMENT,

    first_name VARCHAR(20) default NULL,

    middle_name VARCHAR(20) default NULL,

    last_name VARCHAR(30) NOT NULL,

    PRIMARY KEY (artist_id),

    KEY full_name (last_name, first_name)

) ENGINE=MyISAM;

    This table stores just four pieces of information for each artist. Of these, only *last_name* is required (is defined as NOT NULL), as there are single-named artists (e.g., Christo). I've added definitions for the indexes (or keys) as well. The primary key is the *artist_id*, and an index is placed on the combination of the first and last name, which may be used in an ORDER BY clause.

3. Create the *prints* table (**Figure 14.3**).

    CREATE TABLE prints (

    print_id INT(4) UNSIGNED NOT NULL
    → AUTO_INCREMENT,

    artist_id INT(3) UNSIGNED NOT NULL,

    print_name VARCHAR(60) NOT NULL,

    price decimal(6,2) NOT NULL,

    size VARCHAR(60) default NULL,

    description VARCHAR(255) default NULL,

    image_name VARCHAR(30) NOT NULL,

    PRIMARY KEY (print_id),

    KEY artist_id (artist_id),

    KEY print_name (print_name),

    KEY price (price)

) ENGINE=MyISAM;

All of the columns in the *prints* table are required except for the *size* and *description*. I've also set indexes on the *artist_id*, *print_name*, and *price* fields, each of which may be used in queries. You could add to this table an *in_stock* field, to indicate the availability of products.

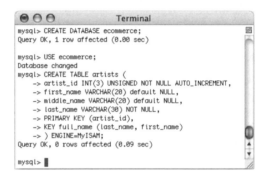

Figure 14.2 Making the first table.

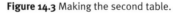

Figure 14.3 Making the second table.

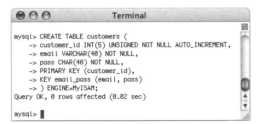

Figure 14.4 Creating a basic version of the *customers* table.

```
mysql> CREATE TABLE orders (
    -> order_id INT(10) UNSIGNED NOT NULL AUTO_INCREMENT,
    -> customer_id INT(5) UNSIGNED NOT NULL,
    -> total decimal(10,2) NOT NULL,
    -> order_date TIMESTAMP,
    -> PRIMARY KEY (order_id),
    -> KEY customer_id (customer_id),
    -> KEY order_date (order_date)
    -> ) ENGINE=InnoDB;
Query OK, 0 rows affected (0.41 sec)

mysql>
```

Figure 14.5 Making the *orders* table.

4. Create the *customers* table (**Figure 14.4**).

```
CREATE TABLE customers (
customer_id INT(5) UNSIGNED NOT NULL
→ AUTO_INCREMENT,
email VARCHAR(40) NOT NULL,
pass CHAR(40) NOT NULL,
PRIMARY KEY (customer_id),
KEY email_pass (email, pass)
) ENGINE=MyISAM;
```

This is the code used to create the *customers* table. You could throw in the other appropriate fields (name, address, phone number, the registration date, etc.). As I won't be dealing with those values—or user management at all—in this chapter, I've omitted them.

5. Create the *orders* table (**Figure 14.5**).

```
CREATE TABLE orders (
order_id INT(10) UNSIGNED NOT NULL
→ AUTO_INCREMENT,
customer_id INT(5) UNSIGNED NOT NULL,
total decimal(10,2) NOT NULL,
order_date TIMESTAMP,
PRIMARY KEY (order_id),
KEY customer_id (customer_id),
KEY order_date (order_date)
) ENGINE=InnoDB;
```

All of the *orders* fields are required, and three indexes have been created. Notice that a foreign key column here, like *customer_id*, is of the same exact type as its corresponding primary key (*customer_id* in the *customers* table). The *order_date* field will store the date and time an order was entered. Being defined as a TIMESTAMP, it will automatically be given the current value when a record is inserted.

Finally, because I'll want to use transactions with the *orders* and *order_contents* tables, both will use the InnoDB storage engine.

continues on next page

CREATING THE DATABASE

6. Create the *order_contents* table (**Figure 14.6**).

```
CREATE TABLE order_contents (
oc_id INT(10) UNSIGNED NOT NULL
→ AUTO_INCREMENT,
order_id INT(10) UNSIGNED NOT NULL,
print_id INT(4) UNSIGNED NOT NULL,
quantity TINYINT UNSIGNED NOT NULL
→ DEFAULT 1,
price decimal(6,2) NOT NULL,
ship_date DATETIME default NULL,
PRIMARY KEY (oc_id),
KEY order_id (order_id),
KEY print_id (print_id),
KEY ship_date (ship_date)
) ENGINE=InnoDB;
```

In order to have a normalized database structure, I've separated out each order into its general information—the customer, the order date, and the total amount—and its specific information—the actual items ordered and in what quantity. The table has foreign keys to the *orders* and *prints* tables. The *quantity* has a set default value of 1. The *ship_date* is defined as a DATETIME, so that it can have a NULL value, meaning that the item has not yet shipped. Again, this table must use the InnoDB storage engine in order to be part of a transaction.

You may be curious why I'm storing the price in this table when that information is already present in the *prints* table. The reason is simply this: the price of a product may change. The *prints* table indicates the current price of an item; the *order_contents* table indicates the price at which an item was purchased.

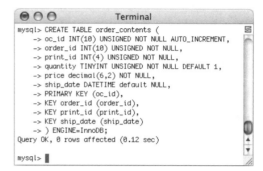

Figure 14.6 Making the final table for the *ecommerce* database.

✔ Tips

- Depending upon what a site is selling, it would have different tables in place of *artists* and *prints*. The most important attribute of any e-commerce database is that there is a products table that lists the individual items being sold with a product ID associated with each. So a large, red polo shirt would have one ID, which is different than a large, blue polo shirt's ID, which is different than a medium, blue polo shirt's ID. Unique, individual product identifiers let you track orders and product quantities.

- If you wanted to store multiple addresses for users—home, billing, friends, etc.—create a separate addresses table. In this table store all of that information, including the address type, and link those records back to the customers table using the customer ID as a primary-foreign key.

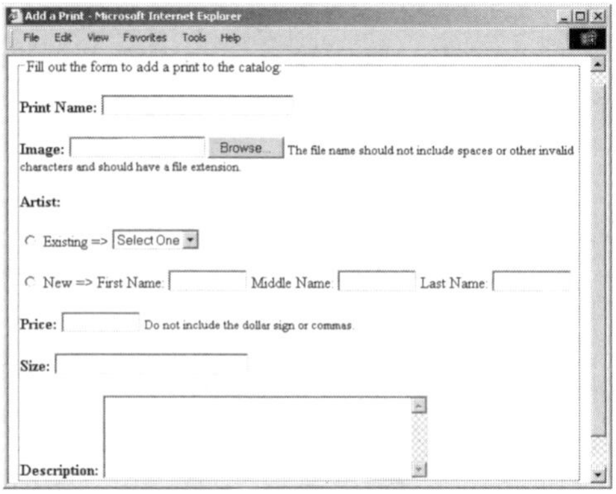

Figure 14.7 The HTML form for adding prints to the catalog.

Security

With respect to an e-commerce site, there are three broad security considerations. The first is how the data is stored on the server. You need to protect the MySQL database itself (by setting appropriate access permissions) and the directory where session information is stored (see Chapter 9, "Cookies and Sessions," for what setting must be changed).

The second security consideration has to do with protecting access to sensitive information. The administrative side of the site, which would have the ability to view orders and customer records, must be safeguarded to the highest level.

The third factor is protecting the data during transition. By the time the customer gets to the checkout process (where credit card and shipping information comes in), secure transactions must be used. To do so entails establishing a Secure Sockets Layer (SSL) on your server with a valid certificate and then changing to an *https://* URL. Also be aware of what information is being sent via e-mail, since those messages are frequently not transmitted through secure avenues.

The Administrative Side

The first script I'll write will be for the purpose of adding products (specifically a print) to the database. The page will allow the administrator to select the artist by name or enter a new one, upload an image, and enter the details for the print (**Figure 14.7**). The image will be stored on the server, and the print's record inserted into the database. But since this—and pretty much every script in this chapter—will require a connection to the MySQL database, I'll write a connection script first.

As I stated in the introduction to this chapter, I'll be using the Improved MySQL Extension functions, first demonstrated in Chapter 11. These functions require that you have

- PHP 5 or greater

- MySQL 4.1.3 or greater

- Improved MySQL Extension support enabled in PHP

In case you don't meet all of these criteria or if you would just prefer to use the standard MySQL functions, I'll include the alternative code in these first two examples. You'll see it commented out in the scripts, but it won't be present in the step-by-step sequences. You can also always refer back to the examples in Chapter 7, "Using PHP with MySQL," for the proper syntax (or use the PHP manual, of course).

To keep a complicated process more simple, none of the examples in this chapter will use the kind of error management techniques you would want on a live site. When you're ready to make an actual e-commerce application, incorporate the error management ideas discussed elsewhere in the book (like that developed in Chapter 13, "Example—User Registration").

To create mysql_connect.php:

1. Create a new PHP document (**Script 14.1**).

   ```
   <?php # Script 14.1 - mysql_connect.
   → php
   ```

2. Define the database connection constants.

   ```
   define ('DB_USER', 'username');
   define ('DB_PASSWORD', 'password');
   define ('DB_HOST', 'localhost');
   define ('DB_NAME', 'ecommerce');
   ```

   Naturally you will need to use a username/password/hostname combination that has access to your MySQL database.

3. Connect to MySQL and select the database.

   ```
   $dbc = mysqli_connect (DB_HOST,
   → DB_USER, DB_PASSWORD, DB_NAME) OR
   → die ('Could not connect to MySQL:
   → ' . mysqli_connect_error() );
   ```

   Although you may want to use more advanced error-management techniques, for the sake of brevity and development, I'll use the die() function if a connection error occurs.

   Again, this code uses the mysqli_* functions. See the commented-out code in the script to see how the standard mysql_* functions connect to MySQL and select the database.

4. Define the escape_data() function and complete the PHP page.

   ```
   function escape_data ($data) {
      if (ini_get('magic_quotes_gpc')) {
         $data = stripslashes($data);
      }
      global $dbc;
      $data = mysqli_real_escape_string
      → ($dbc, trim($data));
      return $data;
   }
   ```

This function is defined much as it has been in the past. The function takes a string of data as its lone argument. It then checks to see if Magic Quotes is enabled. If so, the slashes are stripped from the data to avoid over-escaping the string. Next, the database connection is made available via the global statement and the string is run through the mysqli_real_escape_string() function. Finally, the processed string is returned by the function.

5. Complete the PHP script and upload to your Web server (outside of the Web document root).

   ```
   ?>
   ```

   The structure for this site will be exactly like that in the previous two examples, keeping security in mind as much as possible. For a visual representation of the layout, see **Figure 14.8**.

Figure 14.8 The site structure for this Web application. The MySQL connection script and the *uploads* directory (where images will be stored) are not within the Web directory (they aren't available via *http://*) .

Script 14.1 The `mysql_connect.php` script connects to the database, using the Improved MySQL Extension functions, and defines a function for handling data.

```
1    <?php # Script 14.1 - mysql_connect.php
2
3    // This file contains the database access information for the database.
4    // This file also establishes a connection to MySQL and selects the database.
5
6    // Set the database access information as constants.
7    define ('DB_USER', 'username');
8    define ('DB_PASSWORD', 'password');
9    define ('DB_HOST', 'localhost');
10   define ('DB_NAME', 'ecommerce');
11
12   // Make the connnection and then select the database.
13
14   // Improved MySQL Version:
15   $dbc = mysqli_connect (DB_HOST, DB_USER, DB_PASSWORD, DB_NAME) OR die ('Could not connect to
     MySQL: ' . mysqli_connect_error() );
16
17   /* Standard MySQL Version:
18   $dbc = mysql_connect (DB_HOST, DB_USER, DB_PASSWORD) OR die ('Could not connect to MySQL: ' .
     mysql_error() );
19   mysql_select_db (DB_NAME) OR die ('Could not select the database: ' . mysql_error() );
20   */
21
22   // Create a function for escaping the data.
23   function escape_data ($data) {
24
25       // Address Magic Quotes.
26       if (ini_get('magic_quotes_gpc')) {
27           $data = stripslashes($data);
28       }
29
30       // Improved MySQL Version:
31       global $dbc;
32       $data = mysqli_real_escape_string($dbc, trim($data));
33
34       /* Standard MySQL Version:
35       // Check for mysql_real_escape_string() support.
36       if (function_exists('mysql_real_escape_string')) {
37           global $dbc; // Need the connection.
38           $data = mysql_real_escape_string (trim($data), $dbc);
39       } else {
40           $data = mysql_escape_string (trim($data));
41       } */
42
43       // Return the escaped value.
44       return $data;
45
46   } // End of function.
47   ?>
```

To create add_print.php:

1. Create a new PHP document, beginning with the HTML head (**Script 14.2**).

```
<!DOCTYPE html PUBLIC "-//W3C//DTD
→ XHTML 1.0 Transitional//EN"
"http://www.w3.org/TR/xhtml1/DTD/
→ xhtml1-transitional.dtd">
<html xmlns="http://www.w3.org/1999/
→ xhtml" xml:lang="en" lang="en">
<head>
   <meta http-equiv="content-type"
   → content="text/html; charset=
   → iso-8859-1" />
   <title>Add a Print</title>
</head>
<body>
<?php # Script 14.2 - add_print.php
```

Normally, I would create a template system for the administrative side, but since I'll be writing only this one administrative script in this chapter, I'll do without.

2. Include the database connection script and check if the form has been submitted.

```
require_once ('../../mysql_connect.
→ php');
if (isset($_POST['submitted'])) {
```

The administration folder will be located inside of the main (*html*) folder and is therefore two directories above the connection script. Keep your directory structure (Figure 14.8) in mind when including files.

Script 14.2 This administration page adds products to the database. It handles a file upload, inserts the new print into the *prints* table, and even allows for a new artist to be submitted.

```
1   <!DOCTYPE html PUBLIC "-//W3C//DTD XHTML
    1.0 Transitional//EN"
2        "http://www.w3.org/TR/xhtml1/DTD/
         xhtml1-transitional.dtd">
3   <html xmlns="http://www.w3.org/1999/xhtml"
    xml:lang="en" lang="en">
4   <head>
5      <meta http-equiv="content-type" content=
       "text/html; charset=iso-8859-1" />
6      <title>Add a Print</title>
7   </head>
8   <body>
9   <?php # Script 14.2 - add_print.php
10  // This page allows the administrator to
    add a print (product).
11
12  require_once ('../../mysql_connect.php');
    // Connect to the database.
13
14  if (isset($_POST['submitted'])) { // Check
    if the form has been submitted.
15
16     // Validate the print_name, image,
       artist (existing or first_name,
       last_name, middle_name), size, price,
       and description.
17
18     // Check for a print name.
19     if (!empty($_POST['print_name'])) {
20         $pn = escape_data($_POST
           ['print_name']);
21     } else {
22         $pn = FALSE;
23         echo '<p><font color="red">Please
           enter the print\'s name!</font>
           </p>';
24     }
25
```

(script continues on page 588)

Figure 14.9 If the print's name is not submitted, the record will not be added to the database.

3. Validate the print's name.

```
if (!empty($_POST['print_name'])) {
    $pn = escape_data($_POST['print_
    → name']);
} else {
    $pn = FALSE;
    echo '<p><font color="red">
    → Please enter the print\'s name!
    → </font></p>';
}
```

This is one of the required fields in the *prints* table and should be checked for a value. I could also choose to use regular expressions here, but I'm assuming that the site's administrator will not want to undermine the integrity of the application. If no value is entered, an error message is printed (**Figure 14.9**).

continues on next page

4. Handle the image file, if one was selected.

```
if (is_uploaded_file ($_
FILES['image']['tmp_name'])) {
  if (move_uploaded_file($_FILES
→ ['image']['tmp_name'], "../../
→ uploads/{$_FILES['image']
→ ['name']}")) {
    echo '<p>The file has been
→ uploaded!</p>';
  } else {
    echo '<p><font color="red">
→ The file could not be moved.
→ </font></p>';
    $i = FALSE;
  }
  $i = $_FILES['image']['name'];
} else {
  $i = FALSE;
}
```

When I demonstrated the techniques for handling file uploads with PHP (in Chapter 11), I mentioned the is_uploaded_file() function. It returns TRUE if a file was uploaded and FALSE if not. If a file was uploaded, the script will attempt to move the file over to the *uploads* directory. Messages are printed (**Figure 14.10**) indicating its success in doing so.

Finally, the $i variable will be set to either the name of the file or an empty string.

This is one area of the script that could be easily improved. You could do what I did in Chapter 12, "Example—Content Management," and rename the print using the print's ID from the database. You could also validate that the image is of the right size and type. To keep an already busy script more manageable, I'm assuming that the administrator will use this page properly.

Script 14.2 *continued*

```
        script
26    // Check for an image.
27    if (is_uploaded_file ($_FILES
      ['image']['tmp_name'])) {
28      if (move_uploaded_file($_FILES
        ['image']['tmp_name'], "../../
        uploads/{$_FILES['image']
        ['name']}")) { // Move the file over.
29
30        echo '<p>The file has been
          uploaded!</p>';
31
32      } else { // Couldn't move the file
        over.
33        echo '<p><font color="red">
          The file could not be moved.
          </font></p>';
34        $i = FALSE;
35      }
36      $i = $_FILES['image']['name'];
37    } else {
38      $i = FALSE;
39    }
40
```

(script continues on next page)

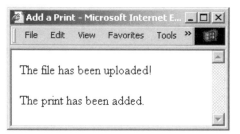

Figure 14.10 The result if a file was selected for the print's image and it was successfully uploaded.

THE ADMINISTRATIVE SIDE

Script 14.2 *continued*

```
script
41      // Check for a size (not required).
42      if (!empty($_POST['size'])) {
43          $s = escape_data($_POST['size']);
44      } else {
45          $s = '<i>Size information not
            available.</i>';
46      }
47
48      // Check for a price.
49      if (is_numeric($_POST['price'])) {
50          $p = (float) $_POST['price'];
51      } else {
52          $p = FALSE;
53          echo '<p><font color="red">Please
            enter the print\'s price!</font>
            </p>';
54      }
55
56      // Check for a description (not
        required).
57      if (!empty($_POST['description'])) {
58          $d = escape_data($_POST
            ['description']);
59      } else {
60          $d = '<i>No description available.
            </i>';
61      }
62
```

(script continues on page 591)

Figure 14.11 The print's price is checked for an appropriate value and type.

5. Validate the size, price, and description inputs.

```
if (!empty($_POST['size'])) {
    $s = escape_data($_POST['size']);
} else {
    $s = '<i>Size information not
    → available.</i>';
}
if (is_numeric($_POST['price'])) {
    $p = (float) $_POST['price'];
} else {
    $p = FALSE;
    echo '<p><font color="red">
    → Please enter the print\'s price!
    → </font></p>';
}
if (!empty($_POST['description'])) {
    $d = escape_data($_POST
    → ['description']);
} else {
    $d = '<i>No description available.
    → </i>';
}
```

The size and description values are optional, but the price is not. As a basic validity test, I ensure that the submitted price is a number (it should be a decimal) using the is_numeric() function. If the value is numeric, I type-cast it as a floating-point number just to be safe. An error message will be printed if no price or an invalid price is entered (**Figure 14.11**).

If the size and description inputs are not used, I'll set the $s and $d variables to default messages. These default messages will then be displayed on the public side.

continues on next page

THE ADMINISTRATIVE SIDE

6. Check if a new artist is being entered.

```
if ($_POST['artist'] == 'new') {
  $query = 'INSERT INTO artists
  → (first_name, middle_name,
  → last_name) VALUES (';
```

To enter the print's artist, the administrator will have two choices (**Figure 14.12**): select an existing artist (from the records in the *artists* table) using a pull-down menu or enter the name of a new artist. If a new artist is being entered, the record will have to be inserted into the *artists* table before the print is added to the *prints* table. Here, I have begun the appropriate query for adding an artist.

7. Finish assembling the query.

```
if (!empty($_POST['first_name'])) {
  $query .= "'" . escape_data
  → ($_POST['first_name']) . "', ";
} else {
  $query .= 'NULL, ';
}
if (!empty($_POST['middle_name'])) {
  $query .= "'" . escape_data
  → ($_POST['middle_name']) . "', ";
} else {
  $query .= 'NULL, ';
}
if (!empty($_POST['last_name'])) {
  $query .= "'" . escape_data
  → ($_POST['last_name']) . "')";
  $result = mysqli_query
  → ($dbc, $query);
  $a = mysqli_insert_id($dbc);
} else {
  $a = FALSE;
  echo '<p><font color="red">
  → Please enter the artist\'s name!
  → </font></p>';
}
```

The artist's first and middle names are optional fields, whereas the last name is not (since there are artists referred to by only one name). Depending upon whether the inputs have a value, either the first and middle names will be added to the query or NULL will be. The final query created by this process will be like INSERT...VALUES (NULL, NULL, 'Christo') or INSERT...VALUES ('John', 'Singer', 'Sargeant'). Because the last name is a required field, an error message is printed if it's omitted for a new artist record (**Figure 14.13**).

If the new artist was added to the database, the artist's ID will be retrieved (for use in the print's INSERT query) using the mysqli_insert_id() function.

continues on page 592

Figure 14.12 The administrator can select an existing artist from the database or choose to submit a new one.

Figure 14.13 If a new artist is being used, the artist's last name must be entered, at the least.

THE ADMINISTRATIVE SIDE

Script 14.2 *continued*

```
                                    script
63     // Validate the artist.
64     if ($_POST['artist'] == 'new') {
65
66         // If it's a new artist, add the artist to the database.
67         $query = 'INSERT INTO artists (first_name, middle_name, last_name) VALUES (';
68
69         if (!empty($_POST['first_name'])) {
70             $query .= "'" . escape_data($_POST['first_name']) . "', ";
71         } else {
72             $query .= 'NULL, ';
73         }
74
75         if (!empty($_POST['middle_name'])) {
76             $query .= "'" . escape_data($_POST['middle_name']) . "', ";
77         } else {
78             $query .= 'NULL, ';
79         }
80
81         // Check for a last_name.
82         if (!empty($_POST['last_name'])) {
83             $query .= "'" . escape_data($_POST['last_name']) . "')";
84
85             // Improved MySQL Version:
86             $result = mysqli_query($dbc, $query);
87             $a = mysqli_insert_id($dbc);
88
89             /* Standard MySQL Version:
90             $result = mysql_query ($query); // Run the query.
91             $a = mysql_insert_id(); // Get the artist ID.
92             */
93
94         } else { // No last name value.
95             $a = FALSE;
96             echo '<p><font color="red">Please enter the artist\'s name!</font></p>';
97         }
98
```

(script continues on page 593)

8. Complete the artist conditional.

```
} elseif ( ($_POST['artist']
→ == 'existing') && ($_POST
→ ['existing'] > 0)) {
  $a = (int) $_POST['existing'];
} else {
  $a = FALSE;
  echo '<p><font color="red">
  → Please enter or select the
  → print\'s artist!</font></p>';
}
```

If the administrator opted to use an existing artist, then a check is made that an artist was selected from the pull-down menu. If this condition failed, then an error message is printed (**Figure 14.14**).

9. Insert the record into the database.

```
if ($pn && $p && $a && $i) {
  $query = "INSERT INTO prints
  → (artist_id, print_name, price,
  → size, description, image_name)
  → VALUES ($a, '$pn', $p, '$s',
  → '$d', '$i')";
  if ($result = mysqli_query
  → ($dbc, $query)) {
    echo '<p>The print has been
    → added.</p>';
  } else {
    echo '<p><font color="red">
    → Your submission could not be
    → processed due to a system
    → error.</font></p>';
  }
```

If the four required fields (*print_name*, *price*, *artist_id*, and *image_name*) have proper values, the print will be added to the database. Messages will be sent to the Web browser indicating the success of running the query (**Figure 14.15**).

If you are using the older MySQL functions, you'll need to change the code accordingly. And if you encounter MySQL errors, use the standard debugging methods: printing out the query, using mysqli_error() or mysql_error(), and so on.

10. Complete the conditionals.

```
} else {
  echo '<p><font color="red">
  → Please click "back" and try
  → again.</font></p>';
}
} else {
?>
```

The first else statement applies when one of the four validation tests fails. The second else will be used to display the form if it has not been submitted.

continues on page 594

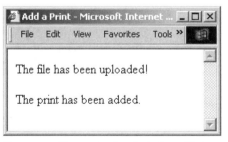

Figure 14.14 If no artist is entered or selected, an error message is printed.

Figure 14.15 The result of a print being added to the catalog.

Script 14.2 *continued*

```
┌─────────────────────────────── script ───────────────────────────────┐
99   } elseif ( ($_POST['artist'] == 'existing') && ($_POST['existing'] > 0)) { // Existing
     artist.
100      $a = (int) $_POST['existing'];
101  } else { // No artist selected.
102      $a = FALSE;
103      echo '<p><font color="red">Please enter or select the print\'s artist!</font></p>';
104  }
105
106  if ($pn && $p && $a && $i) { // If everything's OK.
107
108      // Add the print to the database.
109      $query = "INSERT INTO prints (artist_id, print_name, price, size, description, image_name)
         VALUES ($a, '$pn', $p, '$s', '$d', '$i')";
110      if ($result = mysqli_query ($dbc, $query)) { // Worked.
111          echo '<p>The print has been added.</p>';
112      } else { // If the query did not run OK.
113          echo '<p><font color="red">Your submission could not be processed due to a system error.
             </font></p>';
114      }
115
116  } else { // Failed a test.
117          echo '<p><font color="red">Please click "back" and try again.</font></p>';
118  }
119
120  } else { // Display the form.
121      ?>
122
```

(script continues on page 595)

11. Begin creating the HTML form.

```
<form enctype="multipart/
→ form-data" action="add_print.php"
→ method="post">
    <input type="hidden" name=
    → "MAX_FILE_SIZE" value="524288" />
    <fieldset><legend>Fill out the
    → form to add a print to the
    → catalog:</legend>
    <p><b>Print Name:</b> <input
    → type="text" name="print_name"
    → size="30" maxlength="60" /></p>
    <p><b>Image:</b> <input
    → type="file" name="image" />
    → <small>The file name should not
    → include spaces or other invalid
    → characters and should have a
    → file extension.</small></p>
```

Because this form will allow a user to upload a file, I must include the enctype in the form tag and the MAX_FILE_SIZE hidden input.

12. Create the artist pull-down menu.

```
<p><b>Artist:</b>
<p><input type="radio"
→ name="artist" value="existing"
→ /> Existing =>
<select name="existing"><option>
→ Select One</option>
<?php
$query = "SELECT artist_id,
→ CONCAT_WS(' ', first_name,
→ middle_name, last_name) AS name
→ FROM artists ORDER BY last_name,
→ first_name ASC";
$result = mysqli_query
→ ($dbc, $query);
```

```
while ($row = mysqli_fetch_array
→ ($result, MYSQLI_ASSOC)) {
    echo "<option value=\"{$row
    → ['artist_id']}\">{$row
    → ['name']}</option>\n";
}
mysqli_close($dbc);
?>
</select></p>
```

The artist pull-down menu will be dynamically generated (**Figure 14.16**) from the records stored in the *artists* table using this PHP code. It's prefaced by a radio button so that the administrator can select an existing artist or enter a new one (see Step 13). The MySQL CONCAT_WS() function—short for *concatenate with separator*—is used to retrieve the artist's entire name as one value. If you are confused by the query's syntax, run it in the mysql client or other interface to see the results.

continues on page 596

Figure 14.16 The PHP-generated HTML source code for the artists portion of the form.

Script 14.2 *continued*

```
│ ▣                              script                              ▣ │
123    <form enctype="multipart/form-data" action="add_print.php" method="post">

124

125        <input type="hidden" name="MAX_FILE_SIZE" value="524288" />

126

127        <fieldset><legend>Fill out the form to add a print to the catalog:</legend>

128

129        <p><b>Print Name:</b> <input type="text" name="print_name" size="30" maxlength="60" /></p>

130

131        <p><b>Image:</b> <input type="file" name="image" /> <small>The file name should not
           include spaces or other invalid characters and should have a file extension.</small></p>

132

133        <p><b>Artist:</b>
134        <p><input type="radio" name="artist" value="existing" /> Existing =>
135        <select name="existing"><option>Select One</option>
136        <?php // Retrieve all the artists and add to the pull-down menu.
137        $query = "SELECT artist_id, CONCAT_WS(' ', first_name, middle_name, last_name) AS name
           FROM artists ORDER BY last_name, first_name ASC";
138        $result = mysqli_query ($dbc, $query);
139        while ($row = mysqli_fetch_array ($result, MYSQLI_ASSOC)) {
140            echo "<option value=\"{$row['artist_id']}\">{$row['name']}</option>\n";
141        }
142        mysqli_close($dbc); // Close the database connection.
143        ?>
144        </select></p>
```

(script continues on next page)

13. Create the inputs for adding a new artist.

```
<p>
<input type="radio" name="artist"
→ value="new" /> New =>
First Name: <input type="text"
→ name="first_name" size="10"
→ maxlength="20" />
Middle Name: <input type="text"
→ name="middle_name" size="10"
→ maxlength="20" />
Last Name: <input type="text"
→ name="last_name" size="10"
→ maxlength="30" />
</p>
```

Rather than create a separate form for adding artists to the database, the administrator will have the option of doing so directly here. The PHP code that handles the form (described earlier) will create a new database record using the new artist information.

14. Complete the HTML form.

```
<p><b>Price:</b> <input
→ type="text" name="price"
→ size="10" maxlength="10" />
→ <small>Do not include the dollar
→ sign or commas.</small></p>
<p><b>Size:</b> <input
→ type="text" name="size" size="30"
→ maxlength="60" /></p>
<p><b>Description:</b> <textarea
→ name="description" cols="40"
→ rows="5"></textarea></p>
</fieldset>
<div align="center"><input
→ type="submit" name="submit"
→ value="Submit" /></div>
<input type="hidden" name=
→ "submitted" value="TRUE" />
</form>
```

Script 14.2 *continued*

```
|■□        script        ▣|
145        <p>
146        <input type="radio" name="artist"
           value="new" /> New =>
147        First Name: <input type="text"
           name="first_name" size="10"
           maxlength="20" />
148        Middle Name: <input type="text"
           name="middle_name" size="10"
           maxlength="20" />
149        Last Name: <input type="text"
           name="last_name" size="10"
           maxlength="30" />
150        </p>
151
152        <p><b>Price:</b> <input type="text"
           name="price" size="10"
           maxlength="10" /> <small>Do not
           include the dollar sign or commas.
           </small></p>
153
154        <p><b>Size:</b> <input type="text"
           name="size" size="30" maxlength="60"
           /></p>
155
156        <p><b>Description:</b> <textarea
           name="description" cols="40"
           rows="5"></textarea></p>
157
158        </fieldset>
159
160        <div align="center"><input
           type="submit" name="submit"
           value="Submit" /></div>
161        <input type="hidden"
           name="submitted" value="TRUE" />
162
163    </form>
164    <?php
165    } // End of main conditional.
166    ?>
167    </body>
168    </html>
```

15. Complete the PHP conditional and the HTML page.

```
<?php
}
?>
</body>
</html>
```

This last bit of PHP code—the curly brace—completes the `else` part of the conditional (that displays the form if it hasn't been submitted).

16. Save the file as `add_print.php`.

17. Create the necessary directories on your server.

This administrative page will require the creation of two new directories. One, which I'll call *4dm1n* (see Figure 14.8), will house the administrative files themselves. The second, *uploads*, should be placed below the Web document directory and have its privileges changed so that PHP can move files into it. See Chapter 11 for more information on this.

continues on next page

18. Upload `add_print.php` to your Web server (into the administration folder) and test in your Web browser (**Figures 14.17** and **14.18**).

✔ Tips

■ This is actually the most complicated script in this entire chapter. The complexity arises from the artists option (use an existing one or add a new one). To simplify this aspect of the application, you could create one form for adding artists to the database and a separate one for adding prints (the separate `add_print. php` page would therefore only allow the selection of an existing artist).

■ Although I did not do so here for the sake of brevity, I would recommend that separate MySQL users be created for the administrative and the public sides. The admin user would need SELECT, INSERT, UPDATE, and DELETE privileges, while the public one would need only SELECT and INSERT.

■ The administrative pages should be protected in the most secure way possible. This could entail HTTP authentication using Apache, a login system using sessions or cookies, or even placing the admin pages on another, possibly offline, server (so the site could be remotely managed from just one location).

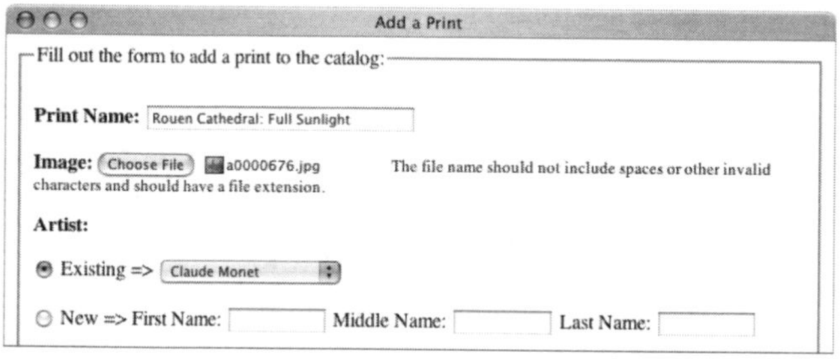

Figure 14.17 Here I'm adding a print using an existing artist.

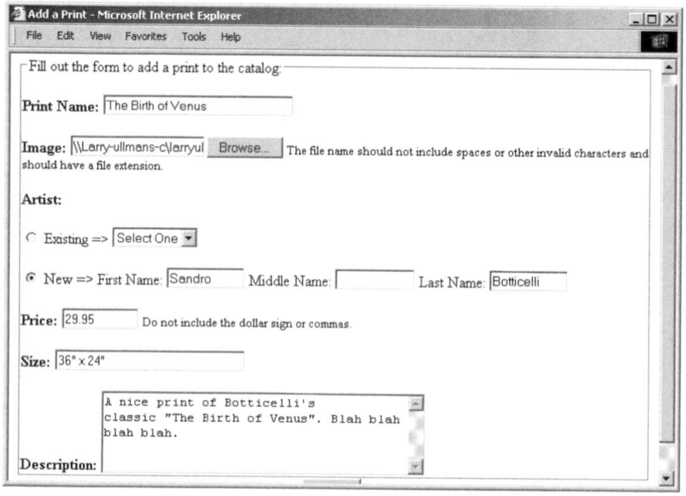

Figure 14.18 In this example, I'm adding a print for a new artist.

Script 14.3 The header file creates the initial HTML and begins the PHP session.

```
1    <?php # Script 14.3 - header.html
2    // This page begins the session, the HTML
     page, and the layout table.
3
4    session_start(); // Start a session.
5    ?>
6    <!DOCTYPE html PUBLIC "-//W3C//DTD XHTML
     1.0 Transitional//EN"
7         "http://www.w3.org/TR/xhtml1/DTD/
          xhtml1-transitional.dtd">
8    <html xmlns="http://www.w3.org/1999/xhtml"
     xml:lang="en" lang="en">
9    <head>
10     <meta http-equiv="content-type" content=
       "text/html; charset=iso-8859-1" />
11     <title><?php echo $page_title; ?>
       </title>
12   </head>
13   <body>
```

(script continues on next page)

Creating the Public Template

Before I get into the heart of the public side, I'll need to create the requisite HTML header and footer files. I'll whip through these quickly, since the techniques involved should be familiar territory by this point in the book.

To make header.html:

1. Create a new PHP document in your text editor (**Script 14.3**).

   ```
   <?php # Script 14.3 - header.html
   ```

2. Begin the session.

   ```
   session_start();
   ?>
   ```

   It's very important that the user's session is maintained across every page, so I'll start the session in the header file. If the session was lost on a single page, then a new session would begin on subsequent pages, and the user's history—the contents of the shopping cart—would be gone.

3. Create the HTML head.

   ```
   <!DOCTYPE html PUBLIC "-//W3C//DTD
   → XHTML 1.0 Transitional//EN"
   "http://www.w3.org/TR/xhtml1/DTD/
   → xhtml1-transitional.dtd">
   <html xmlns="http://www.w3.org/1999/
   → xhtml" xml:lang="en" lang="en">
   <head>
       <meta http-equiv="content-type"
       → content="text/html; charset=
       → iso-8859-1" />
       <title><?php echo $page_title;
       → ?></title>
   </head>
   <body>
   ```

   As with all the other versions of this script, the page's title will be set as a PHP variable and printed out within the title tags.

continues on next page

4. Create the top row of the table.

```
<table cellspacing="0"
→ cellpadding="0" border="0"
→ align="center" width="600">
  <tr>
    <td align="center" colspan="3">
    → <img src="images/title.jpg"
    → width="600" height="61"
    → border="0" alt="title"
    → /></td>
  </tr>
  <tr>
    <td><a href="index.php">
    → <img src="images/home.jpg"
    → width="200" height="39"
    → border="0" alt="home page"
    → /></a></td>
    <td><a href="browse_prints.php">
    <img src="images/prints.jpg"
    → width="200" height="39"
    → border="0" alt="view the
    → prints" /></a></td>
    <td><a href="view_cart.php">
    → <img src="images/cart.jpg"
    → width="200" height="39"
    → border="0" alt="view your
    → cart" /></a></td>
  </tr>
```

This layout will use images to create the links for the public pages (**Figure 14.19**).

5. Start the middle row.

```
<tr>
  <td align="left" colspan="3"
  → bgcolor="#ffffcc"><br />
```

All of each individual page's content will go in the middle row, so the header file begins this row and the footer file will close it.

6. Save the file as header.html and upload to your Web server (create an *includes* directory in which to store it).

Script 14.3 *continued*

```
14   <table cellspacing="0" cellpadding="0"
       border="0" align="center" width="600">
15       <tr>
16           <td align="center" colspan="3">
               <img src="images/title.jpg"
               width="600" height="61" border="0"
               alt="title" /></td>
17       </tr>
18       <tr>
19           <td><a href="index.php">
               <img src="images/home.jpg"
               width="200" height="39" border="0"
               alt="home page" /></a></td>
20           <td><a href="browse_prints.php">
               <img src="images/prints.jpg"
               width="200" height="39" border="0"
               alt="view the prints" /></a></td>
21           <td><a href="view_cart.php">
               <img src="images/cart.jpg"
               width="200" height="39" border="0"
               alt="view your cart" /></a></td>
22       </tr>
23       <tr>
24           <td align="left" colspan="3"
               bgcolor="#ffffcc"><br />
25   <!-- Content starts here! -->
```

Figure 14.19 The banner created by the header file.

Script 14.4 The footer file closes the HTML, creating a copyright message in the process.

```
1    <!-- Script 14.4 - footer.html -->
2    <!-- Content starts here! -->
3          <br /></td>
4       </tr>
5       <tr>
6          <td align="center" colspan="3"
          bgcolor="#669966"><font
          color="#ffffff">&copy; Copyright...
          </font></td>
7       </tr>
8    </table>
9    </body>
10   </html>
```

Figure 14.20 The copyright row created by the footer file.

To make footer.html:

1. Create a new HTML document in your text editor (**Script 14.4**).

   ```
   <!-- Script 14.4 - footer.html -->
   ```

2. Complete the middle row, create the bottom row, and complete the HTML (**Figure 14.20**).

   ```
         <br /></td>
      </tr>
      <tr>
         <td align="center" colspan="3"
       → bgcolor="#669966"><font color=
       → "#ffffff">&copy; Copyright...
       → </font></td>
      </tr>
   </table>
   </body>
   </html>
   ```

3. Save the file as footer.html and upload to your Web server (also in the *includes* directory).

To make index.php:

1. Create a new PHP document in your text editor (**Script 14.5**).

```
<?php # Script 14.5 - index.php
$page_title = 'Make an Impression!';
include ('./includes/header.html');
?>
```

2. Create the page's content.

```
<p>Welcome to our site....please
→ use the links above...blah, blah,
→ blah.</p>
<p>Welcome to our site....please
→ use the links above...blah, blah,
→ blah.</p>
```

Obviously a real e-commerce site would have some actual content on the main page. You could put lists of recently added items here (if you added a *date_entered* column to the *prints* table), highlight specials, or do whatever.

3. Complete the HTML page.

```
<?php
include ('./includes/footer.html');
?>
```

4. Save the file as index.php, upload to your Web server, and test in your Web browser (**Figure 14.21**).

✔ Tips

■ The images used in this example are available for download through the book's companion Web site: www. DMCInsights.com/phpmysql2.

The images are available on the Extras page and as part of the downloadable files found on the Scripts page.

■ Since sessions are key to the functionality of this application, review the information presented in Chapter 9 or in the PHP manual to understand all of the session considerations.

Script 14.5 The script for the site's home page.

```
1    <?php # Script 14.5 - index.php
2    // This is the main page for the site.
3
4    // Set the page title and include the HTML
     header.
5    $page_title = 'Make an Impression!';
6    include ('./includes/header.html');
7    ?>
8
9    <p>Welcome to our site....please use the
     links above...blah, blah, blah.</p>
10   <p>Welcome to our site....please use the
     links above...blah, blah, blah.</p>
11
12   <?php // Include the HTML footer file.
13   include ('./includes/footer.html');
14   ?>
```

Figure 14.21 The public home page for the e-commerce site.

The Product Catalog

For customers to be able to purchase products, they'll need to view them first. To this end, I'll create two scripts for accessing the product catalog. The first, `browse_prints.php`, will display a list of the available prints. If a particular artist has been selected, only that artist's work will be shown; otherwise, every print will be listed.

The second script, `view_print.php`, will be used to display the information for a single print, including the image. On this page customers will find an *Add to Cart* link, so that the print may be added to the shopping cart. Because the print's image is stored outside of the Web root directory, `view_print.php` will use a separate script—very similar to `download_file.php` from Chapter 12, "Example—Content Management"—for the purpose of displaying the image.

Searching the Product Catalog

The structure of this database makes for a fairly easy search capability, should you desire to add it. As it stands, there are only three logical fields to use for search purposes: the print's name, its description, and the artist's last name. A `LIKE` query could be run on these using the following syntax:

```
SELECT…WHERE prints.description LIKE
→ '%keyword%' OR prints.print_name
→ LIKE '%keyword%' …
```

Another option would be to create an advanced search, wherein the user selects whether to search the artist's name or the print's name (similar to what the Internet Movie Database, `www.imdb.com`, does with people versus movie titles).

Finally, you could make use of MySQL's full-text search capability to return results in their order of relevance.

To make browse_prints.php:

1. Create a new PHP document in your text editor (**Script 14.6**).

```
<?php # Script 13.6 - browse_prints.
→ php
$page_title = 'Browse the Prints';
include ('./includes/header.html');
require_once ('../mysql_connect.
→ php');
```

2. Build the query.

```
if (isset($_GET['aid'])) {
  $aid = (int) $_GET['aid'];
  if ($aid > 0) {
    $query = "SELECT artists.
    → artist_id, CONCAT_WS(' ',
    → first_name, middle_name,
    → last_name) AS name, print_
    → name, price, description,
    → print_id FROM artists, prints
    → WHERE artists.artist_id =
    → prints.artist_id AND prints.
    → artist_id =$aid ORDER BY
    → prints.print_name";
  } else {
    $query = "SELECT artists.
    → artist_id, CONCAT_WS(' ',
    → first_name, middle_name,
    → last_name) AS name, print_
    → name, price, description,
    → print_id FROM artists, prints
    → WHERE artists.artist_id =
    → prints.artist_id ORDER BY
    → artists.last_name ASC,
    → prints.print_name ASC";
  }
} else {
  $query = "SELECT artists.
  → artist_id, CONCAT_WS(' ',
  → first_name, middle_name, last_
  → name) AS name, print_name,
  → price, description, print_id
  → FROM artists, prints WHERE
```

```
  → artists.artist_id = prints.
  → artist_id ORDER BY artists.
  → last_name ASC, prints.print_name
  → ASC";
}
```

The query is a standard join across the *artists* and *prints* tables (to retrieve the artist name information with each print's information). The first time the page is viewed, every print by every artist will be returned. If a user clicks one artist's name, the user will be returned back to this page, but now the URL will be, for example, *browse_prints.php?aid=529*. In that case, the clause AND prints.art-ist_id = $aid is added to the query and the ORDER BY is slightly modified so that just that artist's works are displayed.

So the two different roles of this script—showing every print or just those for an individual artist—are defined by this conditional, while the rest of the script works the same in either case.

For security purposes, I use type casting on the author ID and make sure that it's a positive integer prior to using it in a query.

3. Create the table head.

```
echo '<table border="0" width="90%"
→ cellspacing="3" cellpadding="3"
→ align="center">
<tr>
<td align="left" width="20%">
→ <b>Artist</b></td>
<td align="left" width="20%">
→ <b>Print Name</b></td>
<td align="left" width="40%">
→ <b>Description</b></td>
<td align="right" width="20%">
→ <b>Price</b></td>
</tr>';
```

continues on page 606

Script 14.6 The `browse_prints.php` script displays every print in the catalog or every print for a particular artist, depending upon the presence of $_GET['aid'].

```
script

1    <?php # Script 14.6 - browse_prints.php
2    // This page displays the available prints (products).
3
4    // Set the page title and include the HTML header.
5    $page_title = 'Browse the Prints';
6    include ('./includes/header.html');
7
8    require_once ('../mysql_connect.php'); // Connect to the database.
9
10   // Are we looking at a particular artist?
11   if (isset($_GET['aid'])) {
12       $aid = (int) $_GET['aid'];
13       if ($aid > 0) {
14           $query = "SELECT artists.artist_id, CONCAT_WS(' ', first_name, middle_name, last_name)
             AS name, print_name, price, description, print_id FROM artists, prints WHERE artists.
             artist_id = prints.artist_id AND prints.artist_id =$aid ORDER BY prints.print_name";
15       } else {
16           $query = "SELECT artists.artist_id, CONCAT_WS(' ', first_name, middle_name, last_name)
             AS name, print_name, price, description, print_id FROM artists, prints WHERE artists.
             artist_id = prints.artist_id ORDER BY artists.last_name ASC, prints.print_name ASC";
17       }
18   } else {
19       $query = "SELECT artists.artist_id, CONCAT_WS(' ', first_name, middle_name, last_name)
         AS name, print_name, price, description, print_id FROM artists, prints WHERE artists.
         artist_id = prints.artist_id ORDER BY artists.last_name ASC, prints.print_name ASC";
20   }
21
22   // Create the table head.
23   echo '<table border="0" width="90%" cellspacing="3" cellpadding="3" align="center">
24   <tr>
25   <td align="left" width="20%"><b>Artist</b></td>
26   <td align="left" width="20%"><b>Print Name</b></td>
27   <td align="left" width="40%"><b>Description</b></td>
28   <td align="right" width="20%"><b>Price</b></td>
29   </tr>';
30
```

(script continues on next page)

4. Display every returned record.

```
$result = mysqli_query ($dbc, $query);
while ($row = mysqli_fetch_array
→ ($result, MYSQLI_ASSOC)) {
  echo "  <tr>
      <td align=\"left\"><a href=\
      → "browse_prints.
php?aid={$row['artist_id']}\">{$row
→ ['name']}</a></td>
      <td align=\"left\"><a href=\
      → "view_print.php?pid={$row
      → ['print_id']}\">{$row
      → ['print_name']}</td>
      <td align=\"left\">{$row
      → ['description']}</td>
      <td align=\"right\">\${$row
      → ['price']}</td>
    </tr>\n";
}
```

Script 14.6 *continued*

```
31   // Display all the prints, linked to URLs.
32   $result = mysqli_query ($dbc, $query);
33   while ($row = mysqli_fetch_array
     ($result, MYSQLI_ASSOC)) {
34
35      // Display each record.
36      echo " <tr>
37          <td align=\"left\"><a href=\
            "browse_prints.php?aid={$row
            ['artist_id']}\">{$row['name']}
            </a></td>
38          <td align=\"left\"><a href=\
            "view_print.php?pid={$row['print_
            id']}\">{$row['print_name']}</td>
39          <td align=\"left\">{$row
            ['description']}</td>
40          <td align=\"right\">\${$row
            ['price']}</td>
41      </tr>\n";
42
43   } // End of while loop.
44
45   echo '</table>'; // Close the table.
46
47   mysqli_close($dbc); // Close the database
     connection.
48   include ('./includes/footer.html');
49   ?>
```

```
<tr>
    <td align="left"><a href="browse_prints.php?aid=10">Edgar Degas</a></td>
    <td align="left"><a href="view_print.php?pid=5">The Millinery Shop</a></td>
    <td align="left"><i>No description available.</i></td>
    <td align="right">$30.50</td>
</tr>
<tr>
    <td align="left"><a href="browse_prints.php?aid=6">Claude Monet</a></td>
    <td align="left"><a href="view_print.php?pid=2">Rouen Cathedral: Full Sunlight</a></td>
    <td align="left">One in Monet's "Roeun Cathedral" series. And blah and blah and blah blah blah.</td>
    <td align="right">$52.00</td>
</tr>
<tr>
    <td align="left"><a href="browse_prints.php?aid=4">Georges Seurat</a></td>
    <td align="left"><a href="view_print.php?pid=3">A Sunday on La Grande Jatte</a></td>
    <td align="left">Seurat's masterpiece and a classic of the Pointillism movement.</td>
    <td align="right">$45.50</td>
</tr>
<tr>
    <td align="left"><a href="browse_prints.php?aid=4">Georges Seurat</a></td>
    <td align="left"><a href="view_print.php?pid=4">Tree</a></td>
    <td align="left">Seurat's sketch shows the trees which will later appear in "A Sunday on La Grande Jatte".</td>
    <td align="right">$22.30</td>
</tr>
```

Figure 14.22 The source code for the page reveals how the artist and print IDs are appended to the links.

I want the page to display the artist's full name, the print name, the description, and the price for each returned record. Further, the artist's name should be linked back to this page (with the artist's ID appended to the URL), and the print name should be linked to `view_print.php` (with the print ID appended to the URL). **Figure 14.22** shows some of the resulting HTML source code.

Remember that if you are not using the Improved MySQL Extension functions, you'll need to change your function calls here.

5. Close the table, the database connection, and the HTML page.

```
echo '</table>';
mysqli_close($dbc);
include ('./includes/footer.html');
?>
```

6. Save the file as `browse_prints.php`, upload to your Web server, and test in your Web browser (**Figures 14.23** and **14.24**).

✔ Tips

■ You could easily take the dynamically generated pull-down menu from `add_print.php` and use it as a navigational tool on the public side. Set the form's action attribute to `browse_print.php`, change the name of the pull-down menu to *aid*, use the `get` method, and when users select an artist and click Submit, they'll be taken to, for example, *browse_print.php?aid=5*.

■ Although I did not do so here, you could paginate the returned results using the technique described in Chapter 8, "Web Application Development" (see the `view_users.php` script).

■ Another feature you could add to this page is the option to choose how the prints are displayed. By adding links to the column headings (e.g., to *browse_prints.php?order=price*), you could change the `ORDER BY` in the query and therefore the resulting display. Again, this idea was demonstrated in Chapter 8.

Figure 14.23 The current product listing, created by `browse_prints.php`.

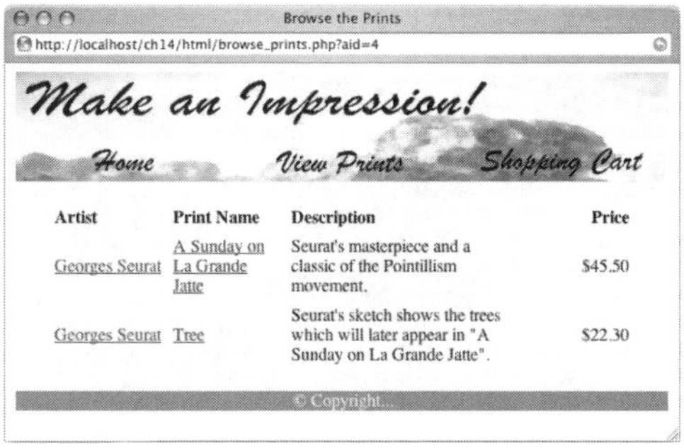

Figure 14.24 If a particular artist is selected (by clicking on the artist's name), the page displays works only by that artist.

To make view_print.php:

1. Create a new PHP document in your text editor (**Script 14.7**).

   ```php
   <?php # Script 14.7 - view_print.php
   $problem = FALSE;
   ```

   I'll use the $problem variable to track whether or not a problem occurred on this page.

2. Validate that a print ID has been passed to this page.

   ```php
   if (isset($_GET['pid'])) {
   ```

   This script won't work if it does not receive a valid print ID, so I check for the ID's existence first.

3. Retrieve the information from the database.

   ```php
   $pid = (int) $_GET['pid'];
   require_once ('../mysql_connect.
   → php');
   $query = "SELECT CONCAT_WS(' ',
   → first_name, middle_name, last_name)
   → AS name, print_name, price,
   → description, size, image_name
   → FROM artists, prints WHERE artists.
   → artist_id = prints.artist_id AND
   → prints.print_id = $pid";
   $result = mysqli_query ($dbc, $query);
   ```

   The query is a join like the one in browse_prints.php, but it selects only the information for a particular print. I'm type-casting the print ID as an integer prior to using it in the query for security purposes (so that a malicious user doesn't try to break my query using invalid $_GET['pid'] values).

Script 14.7 The view_print.php script shows the details for a particular print. It also includes a link to add the product to the customer's shopping cart.

```
script
1   <?php # Script 14.7 - view_print.php
2   // This page displays the details for a
    particular print.
3
4   $problem = FALSE; // Assume no problem.
5
6   if (isset($_GET['pid'])) { // Make sure
    there's a print ID.
7
8       $pid = (int) $_GET['pid'];
9
10      require_once ('../mysql_connect.php');
        // Connect to the database.
11
12      $query = "SELECT CONCAT_WS(' ',
        first_name, middle_name, last_name)
        AS name, print_name, price,
        description, size, image_name FROM
        artists, prints WHERE artists.
        artist_id = prints.artist_id AND
        prints.print_id = $pid";
13      $result = mysqli_query ($dbc, $query);
14
```

(script continues on next page)

Script 14.7 *continued*

```
15      if (mysqli_num_rows($result) == 1)
        { // Good to go!

16

17          // Fetch the information.
18          $row = mysqli_fetch_array ($result,
            MYSQLI_ASSOC);

19

20          // Start the HTML page.
21          $page_title = $row['print_name'];
22          include ('./includes/header.html');

23

24          // Display a header.
25          echo "<div align=\"center\">
26          <b>{$row['print_name']}</b> by
27          {$row['name']}
28          <br />{$row['size']}
29          <br />\${$row['price']}
30          <a href=\"add_cart.php?pid=$pid\">
            Add to Cart</a>
31          </div><br />";

32

33          // Get the image information and
            display the image.
```

(script continues on next page)

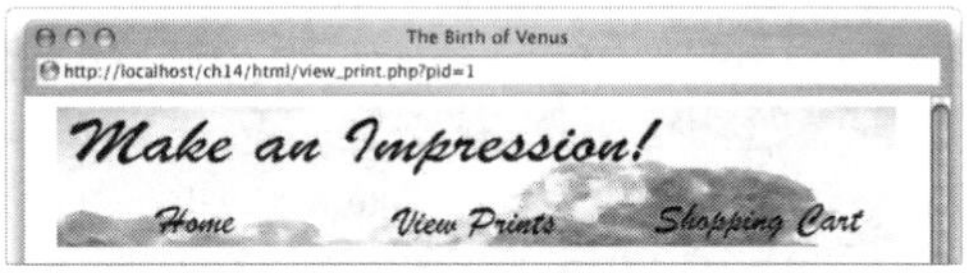

Figure 14.25 The browser page title will be the name of the print being viewed (like *The Birth of Venus* here).

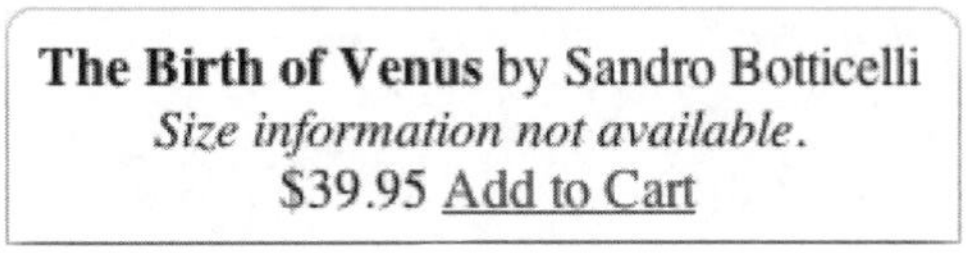

Figure 14.26 The print information and a link to buy it are displayed at the top of the page.

4. If a record was returned, retrieve the information, set the page title, and include the HTML header.

```
if (mysqli_num_rows($result) == 1) {
$row = mysqli_fetch_array ($result,
→ MYSQLI_ASSOC);
    $page_title = $row['print_name'];
    include ('./includes/header.html');
```

The browser window's title (**Figure 14.25**) will be the name of the print.

5. Begin displaying the print information.

```
echo "<div align=\"center\">
    <b>{$row['print_name']}</b> by
    {$row['name']}
    <br />{$row['size']}
    <br />\${$row['price']}
    <a href=\"add_cart.php?pid=
    → $pid\">Add to Cart</a>
    </div><br />";
```

The header for the print will be the print's name (in bold), followed by the artist's name, the size of the print, and its price. Finally, a link is displayed giving the customer the option of adding this print to the shopping cart (**Figure 14.26**). The shopping cart link is to the add_cart.php script, passing it the print ID.

continues on next page

6. Display the image and description.

```
if ($image = @getimagesize
→ ("../uploads/{$row['image_name']
→ }")) {
    echo "<div align=\"center\">
    → <img src=\"show_image.php?
    → image={$row['image_name']}\"
    → $image[3] alt=\"{$row
    → ['print_name']}\" />";
} else {
    echo "<div align=\"center\">No
    → image available.";
}
echo "<br />{$row['description']}
→ </div>";
```

This section of the script will first attempt to retrieve the image's dimensions by using the `getimagesize()` function. If it is successful in doing so, the image itself will be displayed. This process is a little unusual in that the source for the image calls the `show_image.php` page. This script, to be written next, retrieves and displays the `$_GET['image']` passed to it.

If the script could not retrieve the image information (because the image is not on the server or no image was uploaded), a message is displayed instead.

Finally, the print's description is added (**Figure 14.27**).

7. Complete the two main conditionals.

```
    } else {
        $problem = TRUE;
    }
    mysqli_close($dbc);
} else {
    $problem = TRUE;
}
```

```
                                    script
34          if ($image = @getimagesize
            ("../uploads/{$row['image_
            name']}")) {
35              echo "<div align=\"center\">
                <img src=\"show_image.php
                ?image={$row['image_name']}\"
                $image[3] alt=\"{$row['print_
                name']}\" />";
36          } else {
37              echo "<div align=\"center\">
                No image available.";
38          }
39          echo "<br />{$row['description']}
            </div>";
40
```

(script continues on next page)

Botticelli's classic painting. Blah blah blah blah blah.

Figure 14.27 The print's image followed by its description.

THE PRODUCT CATALOG

Script 14.7 *continued*

```
┌────────────────────────────────────┐
│ ▣          script            ▣ │
├────────────────────────────────────┤
41      } else { // No record returned from the
        database.
42          $problem = TRUE;
43      }
44
45      mysqli_close($dbc); // Close the
        database connection.
46
47  } else { // No print ID.
48      $problem = TRUE;
49  }
50
51  if ($problem) { // Show an error message.
52      $page_title = 'Error';
53      include ('./includes/header.html');
54      echo '<div align="center">This page has
        been accessed in error!</div>';
55  }
56
57  // Complete the page.
58  include ('./includes/footer.html');
59  ?>
```

- Depending upon the Magic Quotes setting of your PHP installation, you may or may not need to make use of the `stripslashes()` function when displaying the print information in this and the previous script.

The first `else` clause is in case one record is not returned by the query. The second is in case no print ID is passed to this page. Under both circumstances the `$problem` variable is set to `TRUE`, which will be used by the script in the next step.

8. If a problem occurred, display an error message,

```
if ($problem) {
    $page_title = 'Error';
    include ('./includes/header.html');
    echo '<div align="center">
    → This page has been accessed in
    → error!</div>';
}
```

If the print's information could not be retrieved from the database for whatever reason, an error should be displayed. Because the HTML header would not have already been included if a problem occurred, it must be included here first.

9. Complete the page.

```
include ('./includes/footer.html');
?>
```

10. Save the file as `view_print.php` and upload to your Web server.

✔ Tips

- Many e-commerce sites use an image for the *Add to Cart* link. To do so in this example, replace the text *Add to Cart* (within the `<a>` link tag) with the code for the image to be used. The important consideration is that the `add_cart.php` page gets passed the product ID number.

- If you want to show the availability of a product, add an *in_stock* field to the *prints* table. Then display an *Add to Cart* link or *Product Currently Out of Stock* message according to the value in this column for that print.

To write show_image.php:

1. Create a new PHP document in your text editor (**Script 14.8**).

   ```
   <?php # Script 14.8 - show_image.php
   ```

2. Check for an image name.

   ```
   if (isset($_GET['image'])) {
   ```

   Before continuing, I want to ensure that the script received a valid image name, which should be part of the HTML *src* attribute for each print (**Figure 14.28**) in view_print.php.

3. Check that the image is a file on the server.

   ```
   $image = "../uploads/{$_GET
   → ['image']}";
   if (file_exists ($image) && (is_file
   → ($image))) {
      $name = $_GET['image'];
   ```

   Before attempting to send the image to the Web browser, I want to make sure that it exists and that it is a file (as opposed to a directory). If so, I create a new variable called $name that will be used when the image is sent to the Web browser.

   As a security measure, I hard-code the image's full path as a combination of *../uploads* and the received image name. Even if someone were to attempt to use this page to see */path/to/secret/file*, this script would look for *../uploads//path/to/secret/file* (including the double-slash), which is safe. You could also validate the MIME type (*image/jpg*, *image/gif*) of the file here.

Script 14.8 This script is called by view_print.php (Script 14.7) and displays the image stored in the *uploads* directory.

```
1   <?php # Script 14.8 - show_image.php
2   // This pages retrieves and shows an image.
3
4   // Check for an image name.
5   if (isset($_GET['image'])) {
6
7      // Full image path:
8      $image = "../uploads/{$_GET['image']}";
9
10     // Check that the image exists and is
       a file.
11     if (file_exists ($image) && (is_file
       ($image))) {
12        $name = $_GET['image'];
13     } else {
14        $image = './images/unavailable.gif';
15        $name = 'unavailable.gif';
16     }
17
18  } else { // No image name.
19     $image = './images/unavailable.gif';
20     $name = 'unavailable.gif';
21  }
22
23  // Get the image information.
24  $ft = mime_content_type($image);
25  $fs = filesize($image);
26
27  // Send the file.
28  header ("Content-Type: $ft\n");
29  header ("Content-disposition: inline;
       filename=\"$name\"\n");
30  header ("Content-Length: $fs\n");
31  readfile ($image);
32
33  ?>
```

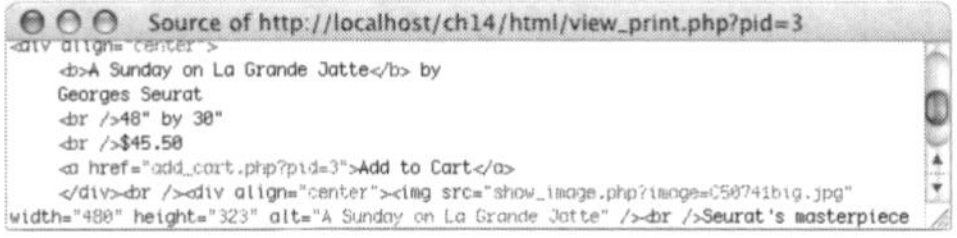

Figure 14.28 The HTML source of the `view_print.php` page shows how the *src* attribute of the `img` tag calls the `show_image.php` script.

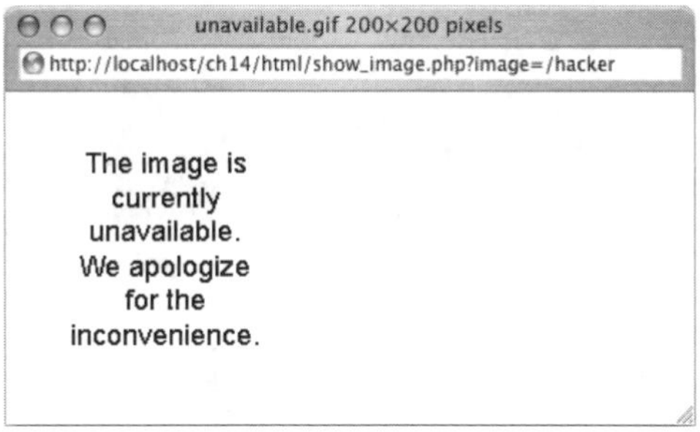

Figure 14.29 If the page cannot access a valid print image, this default image will be displayed.

4. Complete the two validation conditionals.

```
    } else {
        $image = './images/unavailable.
        → gif';
        $name = 'unavailable.gif';
    }
} else {
    $image = './images/unavailable.
    → gif';
    $name = 'unavailable.gif';
}
```

If the image doesn't exist or isn't a file, the first `else` clause comes into effect. If no image name was passed to this script, the second `else` clause applies. In either case, a default image will be used (**Figure 14.29**).

5. Retrieve the image information.

```
$ft = mime_content_type($image);
$fs = filesize($image);
```

To download the file, I'll need to know the file's type and size. I retrieve this information using the `mime_content_type()` and `filesize()` functions. The first one was added in PHP 4.3 but needs to be enabled on Windows in order to work.

continues on next page

6. Send the file.

```
header ("Content-Type: $ft\n");
header ("Content-disposition:
→ inline; filename=\"$name\"\n");
header ("Content-Length: $fs\n");
readfile ($image);
```

These `header()` calls will send the file data to the Web browser, much as they did in Chapter 12. The key difference between that example and this one is that the *Content-disposition* is now set as *inline*, as opposed to *attachment*. Because of this distinction, the sent file (the image) will be displayed in the browser, whereas previously the browser was prompted to download the file to the user's computer.

To revisit the overall syntax, the first line prepares the browser to receive the file, based upon the MIME type. The second line sets the name of the file being sent.

The last `header()` function indicates how much data is to be expected. The file data itself is sent using the `readfile()` function, which reads in a file and immediately sends the content to the Web browser.

7. Complete the page.

```
?>
```

Notice that this page contains no HTML. It only sends an image file to the Web browser.

8. Save the file as `show_image.php`, upload to your Web server, and test in your Web browser by viewing any print (**Figure 14.30**).

Figure 14.30 The `view_print.php` page, where the print's image is retrieved and shown thanks to `show_image.php`.

✔ Tip

■ If the `view_print.php` page does not show the image for some reason, you'll need to debug the problem by running the `show_image.php` directly in your Web browser. View the HTML source of `view_print.php` and find the value of the `img` tag's *src* attribute. Then use this as your URL (in other words, go to `http://localhost/show_image.php?image=BirthOfVenus.jpeg`). If an error occurred, running `show_image.php` is the best way to find it.

Sample $_SESSION['cart'] Values		
(INDEX)	QUANTITY	PRICE
2	1	54.00
568	2	22.95
37	1	33.50

Table 14.6 The $_SESSION['cart'] variable will be a multidimensional array. Each array element will use the print ID for its index. Each array value will be an array of two elements: the quantity of that print ordered and the price of that print.

Enabling mime_content_type()

This function will work on Windows, but only after you do a little configuring of PHP. The full instructions for configuring PHP are in Appendix A, "Installation," but what you'll need to do is...

In your php.ini file, enable the Mime Magic extension by removing the semicolon in this line:

```
; extension=php_mime_magic.dll
```

Then restart your Web server and you should be good to go! Again, if you don't understand the configuration process, see the detailed instructions in the first appendix.

The Shopping Cart

Once you have created a product catalog, as I have now, the actual shopping cart itself can be surprisingly simple. The method I've chosen to use in this example is to record the product IDs, prices, and quantities in a session. Knowing these three things will allow the scripts to calculate totals and do everything else required.

These next two examples will provide all the necessary functionality for the shopping cart. The first script, add_cart.php, will add items to the shopping cart. The second, view_cart. php, will both display the contents of the cart and allow the customer to update it.

Adding items

The add_cart.php script will take one argument—the ID of the print being purchased—and will use this to update the cart. The cart itself is a session variable, meaning it's accessed through the $_SESSION['cart'] variable. The cart will be a multidimensional array whose keys will be product IDs. The values of the array elements will themselves be arrays: one element for the quantity and another for the price (**Table 14.6**).

To create add_cart.php:

1. Create a new PHP document in your text editor (**Script 14.9**).

```
<?php # Script 14.9 - add_cart.php
```

2. Include the page header and check that a print was selected.

```
$page_title = 'Add to Cart';
include ('./includes/header.html');
if (isset ($_GET['pid'])) {
```

As with the view_print.php script, I do not want to proceed with this script if no print ID has been received.

3. Determine if a copy of this print has already been selected.

```
$pid = (int) $_GET['pid'];
if (isset($_SESSION['cart'][$pid])) {
    $_SESSION['cart'][$pid]['quantity'
    → ]++;
    echo '<p>Another copy of the print
    → has been added to your shopping
    → cart.</p>';
```

Before adding the current print to the shopping cart (by setting its quantity to 1), I need to check if a copy is already in the cart. For example, if the customer selected print #519 and then decided to order another, the cart should now contain two copies of the print. So I first check if the cart has a value for the current print ID. If so, the quantity is determined by adding 1 to that value and a message is displayed (**Figure 14.31**).

Script 14.9 This script adds products to the shopping cart by referencing the product (or print) ID.

```
1   <?php # Script 14.9 - add_cart.php
2   // This page adds prints to the shopping
    cart.
3
4   // Set the page title and include the HTML
    header.
5   $page_title = 'Add to Cart';
6   include ('./includes/header.html');
7
8   if (isset ($_GET['pid'])) { // Check for a
    print ID.
9
10      $pid = (int) $_GET['pid'];
11
12      // Check if the cart already contains
        one of these prints, increment the
        quantity.
13      if (isset($_SESSION['cart'][$pid])) {
14
15          $_SESSION['cart'][$pid]['quantity']
            ++; // Add another.
16
17          // Display a message.
18          echo '<p>Another copy of the print
            has been added to your shopping cart.
            </p>';
19
20      } else { // New product to the cart,
        get the price information.
21
22          require_once ('../mysql_connect.
            php'); // Connect to the database.
23
24          $query = "SELECT price FROM prints
            WHERE prints.print_id = $pid";
25          $result = mysqli_query ($dbc,
            $query);
26
27          if (mysqli_num_rows($result) == 1)
            { // Valid print ID.
28
```

(script continues on page 618)

Figure 14.31 The result after clicking an *Add to Cart* link for an item that was already present in the shopping cart.

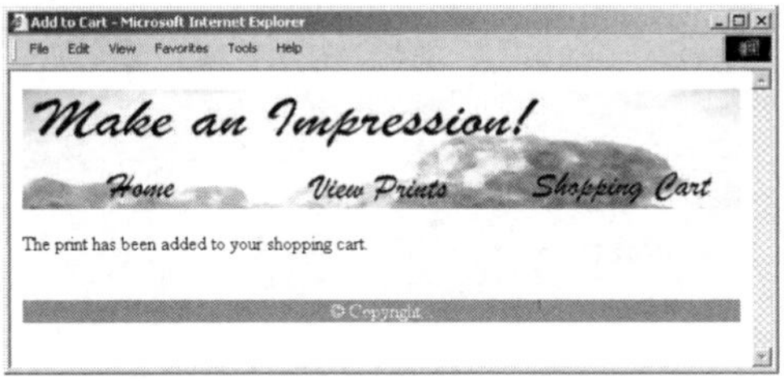

Figure 14.32 The result after adding a new item to the shopping cart.

4. Add the new product to the cart.

```
} else {
  require_once ('../mysql_connect.
  → php');
  $query = "SELECT price FROM prints
  → WHERE prints.print_id = $pid";
  $result = mysqli_query ($dbc,
  → $query);
  if (mysqli_num_rows($result)
  → == 1) {
    list($price) = mysqli_fetch_
    → array ($result, MYSQLI_NUM);
    $_SESSION['cart'][$pid] =
    → array ('quantity' => 1,
    → 'price' => $price);
    echo '<p>The print has been
    → added to your shopping cart.
    → </p>';
```

If the product is not currently in the cart, this else clause comes into play. Here, the print's price is retrieved from the database using the print ID. If the price is successfully retrieved, a new element is added to the $_SESSION['cart'] multidimensional array.

Since each element in the $_SESSION ['cart'] cart array is itself an array, I use the array() function to set the quantity and price. A simple message is then displayed (**Figure 14.32**).

continues on next page

THE SHOPPING CART

617

5. Complete the conditionals.

```
        } else {
            echo '<div align="center">
            → This page has been accessed
            → in error!</div>';
        }
        mysqli_close($dbc);
    }
} else {
    echo '<div align="center">
    → This page has been accessed in
    → error!</div>';
}
```

The first else applies if no price could be retrieved from the database, meaning that the submitted print ID is invalid. The second else applies if no print ID is received by this page at all.

6. Include the HTML footer and complete the PHP page.

```
include ('./includes/footer.html');
?>
```

7. Save the file as add_cart.php, upload to your Web server, and test in your Web browser (by clicking an *Add to Cart* link).

✔ Tips

■ If you would rather display the contents of the cart after something's been added, you could combine the functionality of this script with that of view_cart.php, written next.

■ Similarly, you could easily copy the technique used in view_print.php to this script so that it would display the details of the product just added.

Script 14.9 *continued*

```
       script
29        // Fetch the information.
30        list($price) = mysqli_fetch_
          array ($result, MYSQLI_NUM);
31
32        // Add to the cart.
33        $_SESSION['cart'][$pid] = array
          ('quantity' => 1, 'price' =>
          $price);
34
35        // Display a message.
36        echo '<p>The print has been added
          to your shopping cart.</p>';
37
38     } else { // Not a valid print ID.
39        echo '<div align="center">This
          page has been accessed in error!
          </div>';
40     }
41
42     mysqli_close($dbc);
43
44   } // End of isset($_SESSION
     ['cart'][$pid] conditional.
45
46 } else { // No print ID.
47   echo '<div align="center">This page has
     been accessed in error!</div>';
48 }
49
50 include ('./includes/footer.html');
51 ?>
```

THE SHOPPING CART

Script 14.10 The `view_cart.php` script both displays the contents of the shopping cart and allows the user to update the cart's contents.

```
1    <?php # Script 14.10 - view_cart.php
2    // This page displays the contents of the
     shopping cart.
3    // This page also lets the user update the
     contents of the cart.
4
5    // Set the page title and include the HTML
     header.
6    $page_title = 'View Your Shopping Cart';
7    include ('./includes/header.html');
8
9    // Check if the form has been submitted (to
     update the cart).
10   if (isset($_POST['submitted'])) { //
     Check if the form has been submitted.
11
12       // Change any quantities.
13       foreach ($_POST['qty'] as $k => $v) {
14
15           // Must be integers!
16           $pid = (int) $k;
17           $qty = (int) $v;
18
19           if ( $qty == 0 ) { // Delete.
20               unset ($_SESSION['cart'][$pid]);
21           } elseif ( $qty > 0 ) { // Change
             quantity.
22               $_SESSION['cart'][$pid]
                 ['quantity'] = $qty;
23           }
24
25       } // End of FOREACH.
26   } // End of SUBMITTED IF.
27
```

(script continues on page 621)

Viewing the shopping cart

The `view_cart.php` script will be more complicated than `add_cart.php` because it serves two purposes. First, it will display the contents of the cart in detail. Second, it will give the customer the option of updating the cart by changing the quantities of the items therein (or deleting an item by making its quantity 0). To fulfill both roles, I'll display the cart's contents as a form and have the page submit the form back to itself.

Finally, this page will link to a `checkout.php` script, intended as the first step in the checkout process.

To create view_cart.php:

1. Create a new PHP document in your text editor (**Script 14.10**).

   ```
   <?php # Script 14.10 - view_cart.php
   $page_title = 'View Your Shopping
   → Cart';
   include ('./includes/header.html');
   ```

2. Update the cart if the form has been submitted.

   ```
   if (isset($_POST['submitted'])) {
       foreach ($_POST['qty'] as $k =>
       → $v) {
           $pid = (int) $k;
           $qty = (int) $v;
           if ( $qty == 0 ) {
               unset ($_SESSION['cart']
               → [$pid]);
           } elseif ( $qty > 0 ) {
               $_SESSION['cart'][$pid]
               → ['quantity'] = $qty;
           }
       }
   }
   ```

continues on next page

THE SHOPPING CART

If the form has been submitted, then the script needs to update the shopping cart to reflect the entered quantities. These quantities will come in as an array called $_POST['qty'] whose index is the print ID and whose value is the new quantity (see **Figure 14.33** for the HTML source code of the form). If the new quantity is 0, then that item should be removed from the cart by unsetting it. If the new quantity is not 0 but is a positive number, then the cart is updated to reflect this.

If the quantity is not a number greater than or equal to 0, then no change will be made to the cart. This will prevent a user from entering a negative number, creating a negative balance due, and getting a refund.

3. Determine if the shopping cart is empty.

```
$empty = TRUE;
if (isset ($_SESSION['cart'])) {
   foreach ($_SESSION['cart'] as $key
→ => $value) {
      if (isset($value)) {
         $empty = FALSE;
         break;
      }
   }
}
```

Because the contents of the shopping cart may have just changed (if the form was submitted), I need to check that it's not empty before attempting to display it. To do so, I first check that the cart session variable is set (which means that at least one product has been added to it, even if that product has since been removed). Then I loop through the cart, testing each item for a quantity. If at least one item has a quantity, then the cart is not empty. To save the hassle of having to access every potential quantity, the first time that a quantity is found, the loop will be exited using break.

```
<form action="view_cart.php" method="post">
   <tr>
      <td align="left">Edgar Degas</td>
      <td align="left">The Millinery Shop</td>
      <td align="right">$30.50</td>
      <td align="center"><input type="text" size="3" name="qty[5]" value="2" /></td>
      <td align="right">$61.00</td>
   </tr>
   <tr>
      <td align="left">Claude Monet</td>
      <td align="left">Rouen Cathedral: Full Sunlight</td>
      <td align="right">$52.00</td>
      <td align="center"><input type="text" size="3" name="qty[2]" value="1" /></td>
      <td align="right">$52.00</td>
   </tr>
   <tr>
      <td align="left">Georges Seurat</td>
      <td align="left">A Sunday on La Grande Jatte</td>
      <td align="right">$45.50</td>
      <td align="center"><input type="text" size="3" name="qty[3]" value="3" /></td>
      <td align="right">$136.50</td>
   </tr>
```

Figure 14.33 The HTML source code of the view shopping cart form shows how the quantity fields reflect both the product ID and the quantity of that print in the cart.

Script 14.10 *continued*

```
                    script
28   // Check if the shopping cart is empty.
29   $empty = TRUE;
30   if (isset ($_SESSION['cart'])) {
31       foreach ($_SESSION['cart'] as $key =>
         $value) {
32           if (isset($value)) {
33               $empty = FALSE;
34               break; // Leave the loop.
35           }
36       } // End of FOREACH.
37   } // End of ISSET IF.
38
39   // Display the cart if it's not empty.
40   if (!$empty) {
41
42       require_once ('../mysql_connect.php');
         // Connect to the database.
43
44       // Retrieve all of the information for
         the prints in the cart.
45       $query = "SELECT print_id, CONCAT_WS
         (' ', first_name, middle_name,
         last_name) AS name, print_name FROM
         artists, prints WHERE artists.
         artist_id = prints.artist_id AND
         prints.print_id IN (";
46       foreach ($_SESSION['cart'] as $pid =>
         $value) {
47           $query .= $pid . ',';
48       }
49       $query = substr ($query, 0, -1) . ')
         ORDER BY artists.last_name ASC';
50       $result = mysqli_query ($dbc, $query);
51
```

(script continues on next page)

4. If the cart is not empty, create the query to display its contents.

```
if (!$empty) {
    require_once ('../mysql_connect.
    → php');
    $query = "SELECT print_id,
    → CONCAT_WS(' ', first_name,
    → middle_name, last_name) AS name,
    → print_name FROM artists, prints
    → WHERE artists.artist_id =
    → prints.artist_id AND prints.
    → print_id IN (";
    foreach ($_SESSION['cart'] as $pid
    → => $value) {
        $query .= $pid . ',';
    }
    $query = substr ($query, 0, -1)
    → . ') ORDER BY artists.last_name
    → ASC';
    $result = mysqli_query ($dbc,
    → $query);
```

The query is a join similar to one I've used many times in this chapter. One addition is the use of the IN SQL clause. Instead of just retrieving the information for one print (as in the view_print.php example), I'll want to retrieve all the information for every print in the shopping cart. To do so, I use a list of print IDs in a query like SELECT… print_id IN (519, 42, 427)…. I could have also used SELECT… WHERE print_id=519 OR print_id=42 or print_id=427…, but that's unnecessarily long-winded.

continues on next page

THE SHOPPING CART

5. Create the table and begin the HTML form.

```
echo '<table border="0" width="90%"
→ cellspacing="3" cellpadding="3"
→ align="center">
<tr>
   <td align="left" width="30%">
   → <b>Artist</b></td>

   <td align="left" width="30%">
   → <b>Print Name</b></td>

   <td align="right" width="10%">
   → <b>Price</b></td>

   <td align="center" width="10%">
   → <b>Qty</b></td>

   <td align="right" width="10%">
   → <b>Total Price</b></td>
</tr>
<form action="view_cart.php"
→ method="post">
';
```

Script 14.10 *continued*

```
52      // Create a table and a form.
53      echo '<table border="0" width="90%"
        cellspacing="3" cellpadding="3"
        align="center">
54      <tr>
55         <td align="left" width="30%">
           <b>Artist</b></td>
56         <td align="left" width="30%">
           <b>Print Name</b></td>
57         <td align="right" width="10%">
           <b>Price</b></td>
58         <td align="center" width="10%">
           <b>Qty</b></td>
59         <td align="right" width="10%">
           <b>Total Price</b></td>
60      </tr>
61  <form action="view_cart.php" method="post">
62  ';
63
64      // Print each item.
65      $total = 0; // Total cost of the order.
66      while ($row = mysqli_fetch_array
        ($result, MYSQLI_ASSOC)) {
67
68          // Calculate the total and sub-
            totals.
69          $subtotal = $_SESSION['cart'][$row
            ['print_id']]['quantity'] *
            $_SESSION['cart'][$row
            ['print_id']]['price'];
70          $total += $subtotal;
71
72          // Print the row.
73          echo " <tr>
74          <td align=\"left\">{$row['name']}
            </td>
75          <td align=\"left\">{$row['print_
            name']}</td>
76          <td align=\"right\">\${$_SESSION
            ['cart'][$row['print_id']]
            ['price']}</td>
```

continues on page 624

Figure 14.34 The shopping cart displayed as a form where the specific quantities can be changed.

6. Print out the returned records (**Figure 14.34**).

```
$total = 0;
while ($row = mysqli_fetch_array
→ ($result, MYSQLI_ASSOC)) {
    $subtotal = $_SESSION['cart']
    → [$row['print_id']]['quantity']
    → * $_SESSION['cart'][$row
    → ['print_id']]['price'];
    $total += $subtotal;
    echo "  <tr>
    <td align=\"left\">{$row
    → ['name']}</td>
    <td align=\"left\">{$row
    → ['print_name']}</td>
    <td align=\"right\">\${$_SESSION
    → ['cart'][$row['print_id']]
    → ['price']}</td>
    <td align=\"center\"><input
    → type=\"text\" size=\"3\"
    → name=\"qty[{$row['print_id']}]\"
    → value=\"{$_SESSION['cart'][$row
    → ['print_id']]['quantity']}\"
    → /></td>
    <td align=\"right\">$" . number_
    → format ($subtotal, 2) . "</td>
</tr>\n";
}
```

When displaying the cart, I will also want to calculate the order total, so I initialize a $total variable first. Then for each returned row (which represents one print), I multiply the price of that item times the quantity to determine the subtotal (the syntax of this is a bit complex because of the multidimensional $_SESSION['cart'] array). This subtotal is added to the $total variable.

Each record is also printed out as a row in the table, with the quantity displayed as a text input type whose value is preset (based upon the quantity value in the session).

continues on next page

7. Close the database connection, then complete the table and the form.

```
mysqli_close($dbc);
echo '  <tr>
    <td colspan="4" align="right">
  → <b>Total:<b></td>
    <td align="right">$' . number_
  → format ($total, 2) . '</td>
  </tr>
  </table><div align="center"><input
  → type="submit" name="submit"
  → value="Update My Cart" />
  <input type="hidden" name=
  → "submitted" value="TRUE" />
  </form><br /><br /><a href=
  → "checkout.php"><font size="+2">
  → Checkout</font></a></div>';
```

The running order total is displayed in the final row of the table, using the number_format() function for formatting.

8. Finish the main conditional and the PHP page.

```
} else {
    echo '<p>Your cart is currently
  → empty.</p>';
}
include ('./includes/footer.html');
?>
```

Script 14.10 *continued*

```
77         <td align=\"center\"><input type=\
           "text\" size=\"3\" name=\"qty
           [{$row['print_id']}]\" value=
           \"{$_SESSION['cart'][$row['print_
           id']]['quantity']}\" /></td>
78         <td align=\"right\">$" . number_
           format ($subtotal, 2) . "</td>
79     </tr>\n";
80     } // End of the WHILE loop.
81
82     mysqli_close($dbc); // Close the
       database connection.
83
84     // Print the footer, close the table,
       and the form.
85     echo '  <tr>
86         <td colspan="4" align="right"><b>
           Total:<b></td>
87         <td align="right">$' . number_format
           ($total, 2) . '</td>
88     </tr>
89     </table><div align="center"><input
       type="submit" name="submit"
       value="Update My Cart" />
90     <input type="hidden" name="submitted"
       value="TRUE" />
91 </form><br /><br /><a href="checkout.php">
   <font size="+2">Checkout</font></a></div>';
92
93 } else {
94     echo '<p>Your cart is currently empty.
       </p>';
95 }
96
97 include ('./includes/footer.html');
98 ?>
```

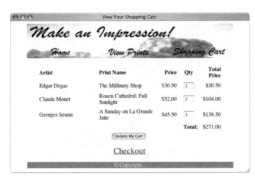

Figure 14.35 If I make changes to any quantities and click *Update My Cart*, the shopping cart and order total are updated (compare with Figure 14.34).

Figure 14.36 I removed everything in the shopping cart by setting the quantities to 0.

9. Save the file as view_cart.php, upload to your Web server, and test in your Web browser (**Figures 14.35** and **14.36**).

You can remove an item from the cart by setting its quantity to 0 (a note should be added to the page so that the customer knows this).

✔ Tips

■ On more complex Web applications, I would be inclined to write a function strictly for the purpose of displaying a cart's contents (since several pages might do so).

■ The key to a secure e-commerce application is to watch how data is being sent and used. For example, it would be far less secure to place a product's price in the URL where it could easily be changed.

Recording the Orders

After displaying all the products as a catalog, and after the user has filled up their shopping cart, there are three final steps:

◆ Checking the user out

◆ Recording the order in the database

◆ Fulfilling the order

Ironically, the most important part—checking out (i.e., taking the customer's money)—could not be adequately demonstrated in a book, as it's so particular to each individual site. So what I've done instead is given an overview of that process in the sidebar.

Similarly, the act of fulfilling the order is beyond the scope of the book. For physical products, this means that the order will need to be packaged and shipped. Then the order in the database would be marked as shipped by noting the shipping date. This concept shouldn't be too hard for you to grasp.

What I can adequately show in this chapter is how the order information would be stored in the database. To ensure that the order is completely and correctly entered into both the *orders* and *order_contents* tables, I'll use transactions (introduced in Chapter 11).

This script, submit_order.php, represents the final step the customer would see in the e-commerce process. Because the steps preceding this script have been skipped in this book, a little doctoring of the process is required.

To create submit_order.php:

1. Create a new PHP document in your text editor or IDE (**Script 14.11**).

   ```
   <?php # Script 14.11 - submit_order.
   → php
   $page_title = 'Order Confirmation';
   include ('./includes/header.html');
   ```

2. Create two temporary variables.

   ```
   $customer = 1;
   $total = 178.93;
   ```

   To enter the orders into the database, this page needs two additional pieces of information: the customer's identification number (which is the *customer_id* from the *customers* table) and the total of the order. The first would presumably be determined when the customer logged in (it would probably be stored in the session). The second value may also be stored in a session (after tax and shipping are factored in) or may be received by this page from the billing process. But as I don't have immediate access to either value (having skipped those steps), I'll create these two variables to fake it.

3. Include the database connection and turn off MySQL's autocommit mode.

   ```
   require_once ('../mysql_connect.
   → php');
   mysqli_autocommit($dbc, FALSE);
   ```

   The mysqli_autocommit() function can turn MySQL's autocommit feature on or off. Since I'll want to use a transaction to ensure that the entire order is entered properly, I'll turn off autocommit first. If you have any questions about transactions, see Chapter 11 or the MySQL manual.

   continues on page 628

Script 14.11 The final script in the e-commerce application records the order information in the database. It uses transactions to ensure that the whole order gets submitted properly.

```
script

1    <?php # Script 14.11 - submit_order.php
2    // This page inserts the order information into the table.
3    // This page would come after the billing process.
4    // This page assumes that the billing process worked (the money has been taken).
5
6    // Set the page title and include the HTML header.
7    $page_title = 'Order Confirmation';
8    include ('./includes/header.html');
9
10   // Assume that the customer is logged in and that this page has access to the customer's ID.
11   $customer = 1; // Temporary.
12
13   // Assume that this page receives the order total.
14   $total = 178.93; // Temporary.
15
16   require_once ('../mysql_connect.php'); // Connect to the database.
17
18   // Turn autocommit off.
19   mysqli_autocommit($dbc, FALSE);
20
21   // Add the order to the orders table.
22   $query = "INSERT INTO orders (customer_id, total) VALUES ($customer, $total)";
23   $result = mysqli_query($dbc, $query);
24   if (mysqli_affected_rows($dbc) == 1) {
25
26      // Need the order ID.
27      $oid = mysqli_insert_id($dbc);
28
29      // Insert the specific order contents into the database.
30      $query = "INSERT INTO order_contents (order_id, print_id, quantity, price) VALUES ";
31      foreach ($_SESSION['cart'] as $pid => $value) {
32         $query .= "($oid, $pid, {$value['quantity']}, {$value['price']}), ";
33      }
34      $query = substr($query, 0, -2); // Chop off last two characters.
35      $result = mysqli_query($dbc, $query);
36
```

(script continues on page 629)

4. Add the order to the *orders* table.

```
$query = "INSERT INTO orders
→ (customer_id, total) VALUES
→ ($customer, $total)";
$result = mysqli_query($dbc, $query);
if (mysqli_affected_rows($dbc)
→ == 1) {
```

This query is very simple, entering only the customer's ID number and the total amount of the order into the *orders* table. The *order_date* field in the table will automatically be set to the current date and time, as it's a TIMESTAMP column.

5. Retrieve the order ID and insert the order contents into the database.

```
$oid = mysqli_insert_id($dbc);
$query = "INSERT INTO order_
→ contents (order_id, print_id,
→ quantity, price) VALUES ";
foreach ($_SESSION['cart'] as $pid
→ => $value) {
  $query .= "($oid, $pid, {$value
  → ['quantity']}, {$value['price']}
  → ), ";
}
$query = substr($query, 0, -2);
$result = mysqli_query($dbc, $query);
```

The *order_id* value from the *orders* table is needed in the *order_contents* table to relate the two. This value, the *print_id*, the quantity ordered, and the price are all entered as individual records in the *order_contents* table. By looping through the shopping cart, as I did in view_cart. php, I can dynamically build up a query.

If you have any problems with this or the other queries in this script, use your standard MySQL debugging techniques: print out the query using PHP, print out the MySQL error, and run the query using another interface, like the mysql client.

6. Report on the success of the transaction.

```
if (mysqli_affected_rows($dbc)
→ == count($_SESSION['cart'])) {
  mysqli_commit($dbc);
  mysqli_close($dbc);
  unset($_SESSION['cart']);
  echo '<p>Thank you for your order.
  → You will be notified when the
  → items ship.</p>';
```

The conditional checks to see if as many records were entered into the database as exist in the shopping cart. In short: did each product get inserted into the *order_contents* table? If so, then the transaction is complete and can be committed. Then the shopping cart is emptied and the user is thanked. Logically you'd want to send a confirmation email to the customer here as well.

7. Handle any MySQL problems.

```
} else {
  mysqli_rollback($dbc);
  mysqli_close($dbc);
  echo '<p>Your order could not be
  → processed due to a system
  → error. You will be contacted
  → in order to have the problem
  → fixed. We apologize for the
  → inconvenience.</p>';
}
} else {
  mysqli_rollback($dbc);
  mysqli_close($dbc);
  echo '<p>Your order could not be
  → processed due to a system error.
  → You will be contacted in order
  → to have the problem fixed. We
  → apologize for the inconvenience.
  → </p>';
}
```

continues on page 630

Script 14.11 *continued*

```
┌──────────────────────────────────── script ────────────────────────────────────┐
37    // Report on the success.
38    if (mysqli_affected_rows($dbc) == count($_SESSION['cart'])) { // Whohoo!
39
40        // Commit the transaction.
41        mysqli_commit($dbc);
42        mysqli_close($dbc);
43
44        // Clear the cart.
45        unset($_SESSION['cart']);
46
47        // Message to the customer.
48        echo '<p>Thank you for your order. You will be notified when the items ship.</p>';
49
50        // Send emails and do whatever else.
51
52    } else { // Rollback and report the problem.
53
54        mysqli_rollback($dbc);
55        mysqli_close($dbc);
56
57        echo '<p>Your order could not be processed due to a system error. You will be contacted in
          order to have the problem fixed. We apologize for the inconvenience.</p>';
58        // Send the order information to the administrator.
59
60    }
61
62    } else { // Rollback and report the problem.
63
64        mysqli_rollback($dbc);
65        mysqli_close($dbc);
66
67        echo '<p>Your order could not be processed due to a system error. You will be contacted in order
          to have the problem fixed. We apologize for the inconvenience.</p>';
68        // Send the order information to the administrator.
69
70    }
71
72    include ('./includes/footer.html');
73    ?>
```

RECORDING THE ORDERS

The first else clause applies if the correct number of records were not inserted into the *order_contents* table. The second else clause applies if the original *orders* table query fails. In either case, the entire transaction should be undone, so the mysqli_rollback() function is called.

If a problem occurs at this point of the process, it's rather serious because the customer has been charged but no record of their order has made it into the database. This shouldn't happen, but just in case, you should write all the data to a text file and/or email all of it to the site's administrator or do *something* that will create a record of this order. If you don't, you'll have some very irate customers on your hands.

8. Complete the page.

```
include ('./includes/footer.html');
?>
```

9. Save the file as submit_order.php, upload to your Web server, and test in your Web browser (**Figure 14.37**).

Because there's no direct link to this script, you'll need to fill up your shopping cart and then manually change the URL in the Web browser to http://*your.domain.here*/submit_order.php.

✔ Tips

■ On a live, working site, you should assign the $customer and $total variables real values for this script to work.

■ For testing purposes, you could also change the *Checkout* link on view_cart.php so that it points to submit_order.php. Then you could more easily go from the one step to the other.

Figure 14.37 The customer's order is now complete, after entering all of the data into the database.

■ PHP has the ability to work directly with some common credit card processing systems (e.g., Cybercash or Verisign). See the PHP manual for more information.

■ If you'd like to learn more about e-commerce or see variations on this process, a quick search on the Web will turn up various examples and tutorials for making e-commerce applications with PHP.

The Checkout Process

The checkout process (which I will not discuss in detail) involves three steps:

1. Confirm the order.

2. Confirm/submit the billing and shipping information.

3. Process the billing information.

Steps 1 and 2 should be easy enough for intermediate programmers to complete on their own by now. In all likelihood, most of the data in Step 2 would come from the *customers* table, after the user has registered and logged in.

Step 3 is the trickiest one and could not be adequately addressed in any book. The particulars of this step vary greatly depending upon how the billing is being handled and by whom. To make it more complex, the laws are different depending upon whether the product being sold is to be shipped later or is immediately delivered (like access to a Web site or a downloadable file).

Most small to medium-sized e-commerce sites use a third party to handle the financial transactions. Normally this involves sending the billing information, the order total, and a store number (a reference to the e-commerce site itself) to another Web site. This site will handle the actual billing process, debiting the customer and crediting the store. Then a result code will be sent back to the e-commerce site, which would be programmed to react accordingly. In such cases, the third-party handling the billing will provide the developer with the appropriate code and instructions to interface with their system.

RECORDING THE ORDERS

INSTALLATION

When I first started writing about PHP and MySQL it never crossed my mind that so many readers would actually install the software themselves. Of course, this was before the existence of Windows 2000 and Mac OS X, and before the increased desktop usage of Unix (and specifically Linux) operating systems.

Between the advent of newer operating systems—Mac OS X is essentially Unix, and Windows XP is built upon Windows NT—and easy-to-run installers, it has become very easy for even the beginner developer to turn their home computer into a Web server. And the price of PHP and MySQL—free!—literally can't be beat.

As I mention in the introduction to the book, there are three technical requirements: MySQL (the database application), PHP (the scripting language), and the Web serving application (that send requested pages to the browser). In this appendix I will describe the installation of these tools on two different platforms—Windows and Macintosh—which should cover most readers. (My assumption has always been that if you know enough to be running some version of Unix, you probably already know how to install software like PHP and MySQL.)

After covering installation, I discuss related issues that will be of importance to almost every user. First, I introduce how to create users in MySQL. Next, I demonstrate how to test your PHP and MySQL installation, showing techniques you'll want to use when you begin working on any server for the first time. Finally, you'll learn how to configure PHP to change how it runs.

Installation on Windows

Windows users have a plethora of options for installing the required applications. Microsoft has produced two different Web servers—IIS (Internet Information Services) and PWS (Personal Web Server)—and you can also use the freeware Xitami, among others. For consistency's sake, and because it's arguably the best Web server available, I'll show how to install Apache.

As for MySQL, it will run on most Windows operating systems (specifically those that are 32-bit, such as Windows 95, 98, ME, NT, 2000, and XP). For my example here, I'll be installing the latest release of MySQL, along with Apache and PHP, on Windows 2000, but the installation process should be similar for most versions of Windows. But first, two quick notes....

You should be aware that MySQL often makes significant changes to its software and installers with each major or minor new release. If the installation process differs from that in the book, see the MySQL manual for the latest, corresponding instructions. This may also be an issue with PHP, but those changes are normally less frequent or dramatic.

Second, while you can follow these instructions and manually install all the requisite software, there is another alternative. You can find online several different free all-in-one packages that will install Apache, PHP, MySQL—and sometimes extras like phpMyAdmin—in one fell swoop. The downside is that if an installation problem occurs, it may be harder to debug.

To install MySQL on Windows:

1. Download the recommended Generally Available (GA) release of the MySQL database server from `http://dev.mysql.com/downloads/`.

   MySQL will indicate the recommended version of their software, which will be a stable version of the latest release. As of the time of this writing, this is version 4.1.11.

   On the downloads page, you'll want to download the Windows Essentials version (**Figure A.1**).

2. On your computer, double-click the downloaded file in order to begin the installation process.

   The file downloaded from MySQL's Web site will be of the type MSI, a common Windows installer.

Windows downloads (platform notes)

The different packages for Microsoft Windows are explained in the article "The all-new MySQL Server Windows Installer". **Note:** When upgrading from versions of MySQL prior to 4.1.5, you must uninstall the existing version before installing a new version. Later versions may be upgraded with the installer without uninstalling.

Windows Essentials (x86)	4.1.11 14.1M	Pick a mirror
	MD5: dc331c3a3c9b151d3840dd2b4c47cd49	Signature
Windows (x86)	4.1.11 35.1M	Pick a mirror
	MD5: b4b9d56bbf8139197f9c730c96c48595	Signature
Without installer (unzip in C:\)	4.1.11 36.2M	Pick a mirror
	MD5: 6330f744f8c15cd9c3f6c70c023cc563	Signature

Figure A.1 From MySQL's Web site, grab the Windows Essentials installer for the latest recommended version of MySQL.

Figure A.2 Select an installation type.

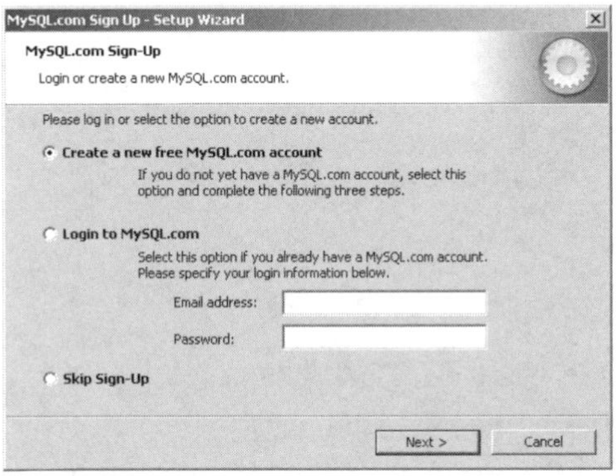

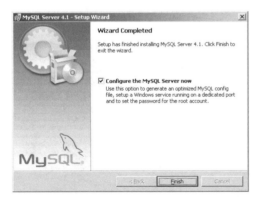

Figure A.3 Sign up for a MySQL.com account to use some of MySQL's support options.

3. Select the installation type: Typical, Complete, or Custom (**Figure A.2**).

Naturally, the Typical installation should be fine for most users.

4. Click your way through the installation process and, if you want, sign up for a MySQL.com account (**Figure A.3**).

You don't have to sign up, but doing so has its benefits. For starters, an account lets you post at `forums.mysql.com` (a support forum), subscribe to MySQL newsletters, and the like.

5. Opt for configuring the MySQL Server now when prompted (**Figure A.4**) and click Finish.

The installation process is now complete, which means you should set up how the MySQL server runs. The installer will take you over to the configuration wizard for this purpose.

continues on next page

Figure A.4 After finishing the installation, you can be taken directly to the configuration wizard.

6. Select whether you want to perform a Detailed or Standard configuration (**Figure A.5**).

Most users will probably want to go with Standard here (although Detailed is the default).

7. Set the basic MySQL settings (**Figure A.6**).

With the Standard configuration, there are just a few choices. You should opt for installing MySQL as a Windows service, and have it launch the server automatically so that it's always running. You should also choose to include MySQL's bin directory in the Windows PATH, which will make it easier to run MySQL applications from the command line.

8. Define the security settings (**Figure A.7**).

The choices you make here are very important. For starters, enter a good root user's password. The root user has unlimited access to MySQL, so this password should be secure and one you won't forget.

Besides that, I would recommend that you not enable root access from remote machines or create an anonymous account. Both are security risks.

9. Click your way through the rest of the configuration process.

✔ Tips

■ Once you've created the root MySQL user, you can create other, day-to-day users, with the information provided later in this chapter.

■ The MySQL configuration wizard can be used to configure a new installation or to reconfigure an existing MySQL installation.

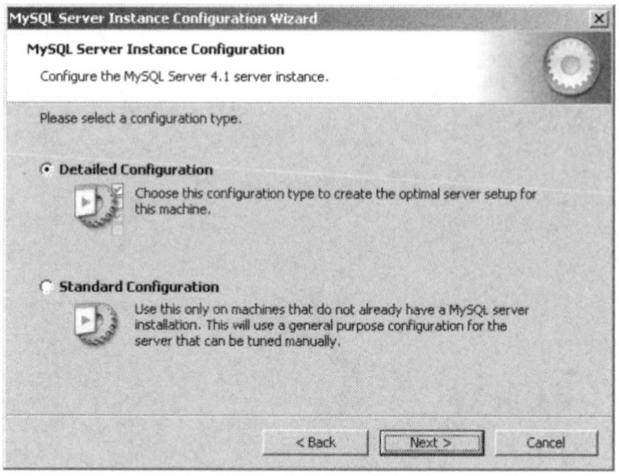

Figure A.5 Select what type of configuration to perform: Detailed or Standard.

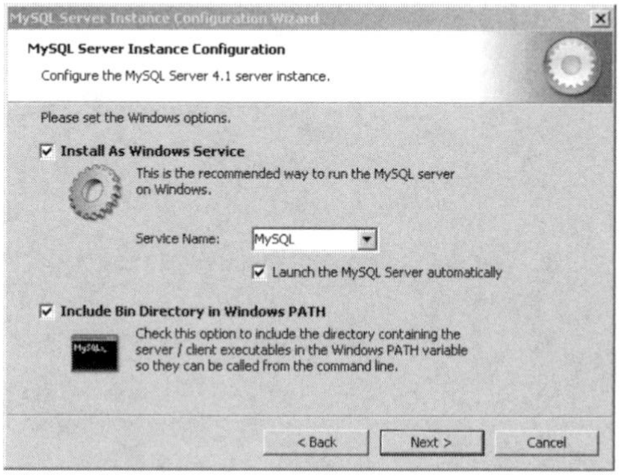

Figure A.6 Configure MySQL so that it always runs.

Figure A.7 The security settings are the most critical part of the configuration process.

To install Apache with PHP:

1. Download the latest version of Apache from `http://httpd.apache.org`.

   Apache is available is two versions: 1 and 2. Although 2 is the latest, there are issues when it comes to using it with PHP (it's complicated), and Apache 1 is still an excellent product. In short, I would advise that you go with the latest version of Apache 1. This is 1.3.33 at the time of this writing.

   Apache for Windows is available as a simple executable file.

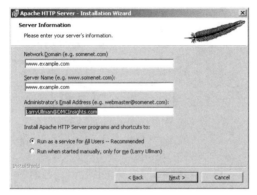

Figure A.8 If you are developing sites on your own computer, you can enter whatever values you want here.

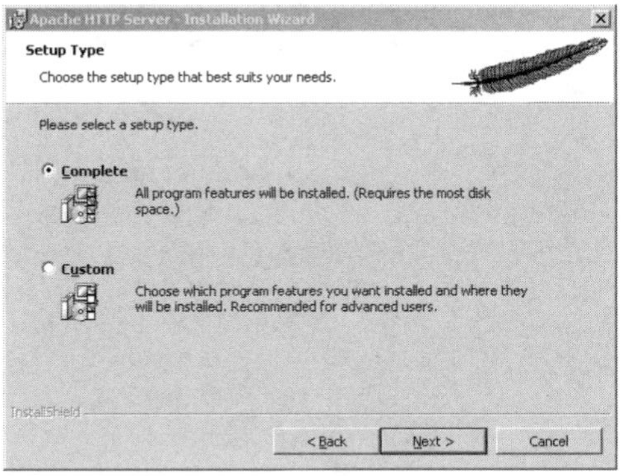

Figure A.9 Select a Complete installation of Apache.

2. On your computer, double-click the installer that you downloaded to begin the download process.

3. Follow through the wizard.

   The installer will go through several steps, including agreeing to the license. When it comes time to entire the server information (**Figure A.8**), you can enter pretty much whatever (assuming you won't actually be hosting live Web sites). You should, though, opt to run Apache as a service for all users.

4. Select the Complete installation type (**Figure A.9**).

5. Finish the Apache installation.

   To complete the setup, select the destination folder (the default is `C:\Program Files\Apache Group`, which should be fine) and click Next. Then click Install to complete the actual installation process.

6. Click Finish once the installer is done.

7. Download the latest version of PHP from `www.php.net`.

   You should download the Windows Zip package. At the time of this writing, the latest version was 5.0.4.

8. On your computer, extract the downloaded file to a permanent directory.

   You'll need to unzip the downloaded files. You can put its contents pretty much anywhere, but `C:\php` makes sense. Do not use spaces in the directory path, as that can cause some servers to crash.

   continues on next page

INSTALLATION ON WINDOWS

9. Copy the `php5ts.dll` file to Apache's `bin` directory.

In order for Apache to use PHP, it needs access to this DLL file. You can copy (or move) it from the PHP directory to Apache's `bin` directory, which is `C:\Program Files\Apache Group\bin` by default.

10. Copy `php.ini-dist` to the Window's directory and rename it `php.ini`.

The `php.ini` file controls how PHP behaves. The Zip package comes with a couple of examples of this file, `php.ini-dist` being one of them. You should copy or move this to your Windows directory, which may be `C:\WINNT` or `C:\Windows` or the like, depending upon your specific operating system. Rename the file `php.ini`.

11. From the Start menu, select Programs > Apache HTTP Server > Configure Apache Server > Edit the Apache httpd. conf Configuration File.

Now you'll need to tell Apache to use PHP for certain files. To do so, you'll need to edit Apache's configuration file (`httpd.conf`). Fortunately, the Apache installer creates a Start menu shortcut for this purpose, which should open the file in Notepad or another text editor.

12. At the end of the LoadModule section, add (**Figure A.10**)

```
LoadModule php5_module "c:/php/php5apache.dll"
```

This step and the next one tell Apache to load the PHP module.

13. At the end of the AddModule section add

```
AddModule mod_php5.c
```

14. Find where it says `<IfModule mod_mime.c>` and add (**Figure A.11**)

```
AddType application/x-httpd-php .php
AddType application/x-httpd-php-source .phps
```

The first line tells Apache to handle files with a `.php` extension as a PHP file. The second says that `.phps` files are PHP source code.

15. Add `index.php` as a directory index.

Find the line that begins with `DirectoryIndex` and change it to read

```
DirectoryIndex index.html index.php
```

This lets `index.php` be a main file in a directory (so that Apache will serve up `www.sitename.com/index.php` if the user just types in `www.sitename.com`).

16. Restart Apache (**Figure A.12**).

To restart Apache you must:

A) Select Start > Run.

B) Enter `cmd` at the Run prompt to bring up the command prompt.

C) Type `NET STOP APACHE` to stop the currently running Apache.

D) Type `NET START Apache` to start Apache again.

17. See the instructions later in the chapter for testing your installation.

✔ Tips

■ See the configuration section at the end of this chapter to learn how to configure PHP by editing the `php.ini` file.

■ If you have problems with the installation, refer to the PHP manual, specifically checking out the user-submitted comments.

```
# Note: The order in which modules are loaded is important.  Don't change
# the order below without expert advice.
#
# Example:
# LoadModule foo_module modules/mod_foo.so
#
#LoadModule vhost_alias_module modules/mod_vhost_alias.so
#LoadModule mime_magic_module modules/mod_mime_magic.so
#LoadModule status_module modules/mod_status.so
#LoadModule info_module modules/mod_info.so
#LoadModule speling_module modules/mod_speling.so
#LoadModule rewrite_module modules/mod_rewrite.so
#LoadModule anon_auth_module modules/mod_auth_anon.so
#LoadModule dbm_auth_module modules/mod_auth_dbm.so
#LoadModule digest_auth_module modules/mod_auth_digest.so
#LoadModule digest_module modules/mod_digest.so
#LoadModule proxy_module modules/mod_proxy.so
#LoadModule cern_meta_module modules/mod_cern_meta.so
#LoadModule expires_module modules/mod_expires.so
#LoadModule headers_module modules/mod_headers.so
#LoadModule usertrack_module modules/mod_usertrack.so
#LoadModule unique_id_module modules/mod_unique_id.so
LoadModule php5_module  "c:/php/php5apache.dll"
```

Figure A.10 Manually edit Apache's configuration file in order to enable PHP.

```
#
# TypesConfig describes where the mime.types file (or equivalent) is
# to be found.
#
<IfModule mod_mime.c>
    TypesConfig conf/mime.types
    AddType application/x-httpd-php .php
    AddType application/x-httpd-php-source .phps
</IfModule>
```

Figure A.11 Don't forget to add the two new MIME types to Apache's configuration.

```
C:\WINNT\system32\cmd.exe                                    _ □ ×
C:\Documents and Settings\Larry Ullman>NET STOP APACHE
The Apache service is stopping......
The Apache service was stopped successfully.

C:\Documents and Settings\Larry Ullman>NET START APACHE
The Apache service is starting..
The Apache service was started successfully.

C:\Documents and Settings\Larry Ullman>
```

Figure A.12 You have to restart Apache for any configuration changes to take effect.

Installation on Mac OS X

The Macintosh was always a user-friendly computer, frequently used by Web developers for graphic design and HTML coding. Now, thanks to OS X, the Macintosh is a programmer's computer as well.

OS X, in version 10.4 (aka Tiger) at the time of this writing, has a Unix base with a glorious Macintosh interface. The Unix aspect of the operating system—predicated upon Free BSD—allows the use of standard Unix tools, such as PHP, MySQL, and Apache, with remarkable ease. In fact, Tiger comes with Apache and PHP already installed (but the latter is not enabled by default).

Like any other Unix technology, you can download the source code for these packages and manually build them (I've done it myself many a time, and it's not too strenuous). However, I would recommend you take the easy way out and use Marc Liyanage's precompiled systems, available at www. entropy.ch/software/macosx. Marc—who ought to receive an award for the amount of OS X–specific work he does—provides up-to-date, easy-to-use installers for many different technologies. In this appendix, I'll install MySQL using the package provided by MySQL and PHP using Marc's precompiled module. The instructions will demonstrate this process using Mac OS X 10.3 (Panther), but the steps will be similar with Tiger or Jaguar (10.2).

As an aside, these instructions are particular to Mac OS X, the basic version of the operating system. Mac OS X server has Apache, PHP, and MySQL preinstalled.

To install and start MySQL:

1. In your Web browser, go to `http://dev.mysql.com/downloads/`.

   This page displays all of the available MySQL products. You'll want to select the Generally Available (GA) release of the MySQL database server. This will be marked as *recommend*.

2. In the resulting page, scroll down to the Mac OS X section and click the Standard Installer package for your version of Mac OS X (**Figure A.13**).

   You will then be asked to select a mirror, and then the download will begin.

3. On your computer, double-click the downloaded file to mount it.

   The downloaded file is a disk image that must then be mounted. The Disk Utility application will automatically do this once you double-click the `.dmg` file.

4. Open the disk image and double-click the *mysql-standard...* package (**Figure A.14**) to begin the installation process.

5. Follow through the installation process.

   There are a few, very obvious steps, like agreeing to the license and selecting a destination disk (**Figure A.15**). Behind the scenes, the package will install all of the necessary files into the `/usr/local/mysql-<version>` directory. It will also create a symbolic link from `/usr/local/mysql` to this directory so that the MySQL files can be more easily accessed. Any existing MySQL files are backed up to `/usr/local/mysql.bak`, including any existing data. Finally, the installer runs the `mysql_install_db` script, which creates the *mysql* and *test* databases (the former being required for users and permissions).

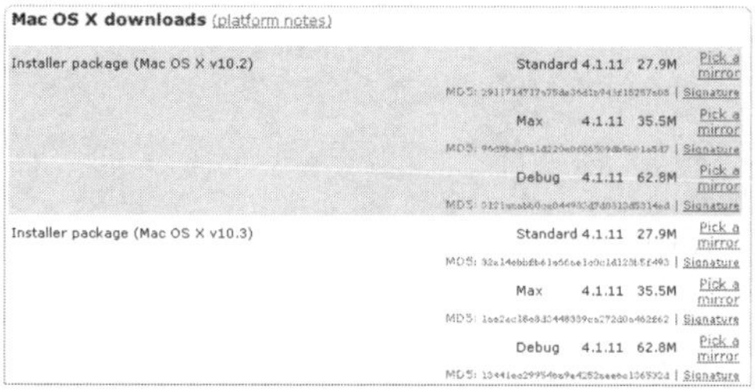

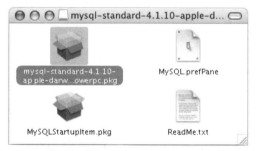

Figure A.13 Be certain to download the *Standard Installer package* version of MySQL for Mac OS X.

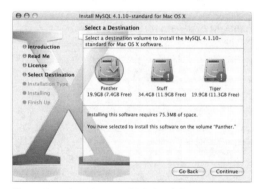

Figure A.14 The mounted disk image contains several files. I have highlighted the actual installer in this image.

Figure A.15 If you have multiple hard drives or partitions, install MySQL on the one with your operating system.

Figure A.16 Install the MySQL preferences pane for yourself or for all users.

Figure A.17 The MySQL preferences pane can be used to control the MySQL database server.

6. Install the MySQL preference pane by double-clicking the MySQL.prefPane file in the disk image (see Figure A.14).

   These next steps will install a System Preferences pane so that you can easily start and stop MySQL.

7. At the prompt (**Figure A.16**), decide for whom the pane should be installed.

8. Open System Preferences and click MySQL, under Other.

   The new MySQL preferences pane will be available the next time you open the System Preferences. If System Preferences was open when you installed the MySQL pane, you'll need to quit and reopen System Preferences.

9. Use the new pane to start and stop the MySQL server (**Figure A.17**).

✔ Tips

- See the "MySQL Permissions" section later in this appendix for guidelines on creating users.

- If upgrading MySQL from a previous version, be certain to stop the existing MySQL server before installing the new version.

To install PHP:

1. In your Web browser, head over to www.entropy.ch/software/macosx/php.

2. Download the appropriate version of PHP for your operating system (**Figure A.18**). This will download the PHP installer to your computer.

3. On your computer, double-click the downloaded file in order to mount it.

4. Double-click the PHP package in the mounted image (**Figure A.19**) to begin the installation process.

5. Follow through the installer.

   The installer is really easy to use. You'll need to click Continue a couple of times, select a destination disk (this should be the same hard disk or partition that also has your operating system), and enter the administrative password.

✔ Tips

- See the "Testing Your Installation" section later in this appendix for guidelines on confirming the results of installing PHP and MySQL.

- Apple's software updates will frequently alter your PHP installation because they may replace the existing httpd.conf file or PHP module.

- Aaron Faby also provides many free installers for OS X at www.server-logistics.com.

- It is recommended that you not replace or significantly alter the Apache installation, as it's so integral to the operating system as a whole.

- Another alternative is to use the all-in-one installer available at http://wserverxkit.sourceforge.net. It will install MySQL, PHP, Apache, and even phpMyAdmin.

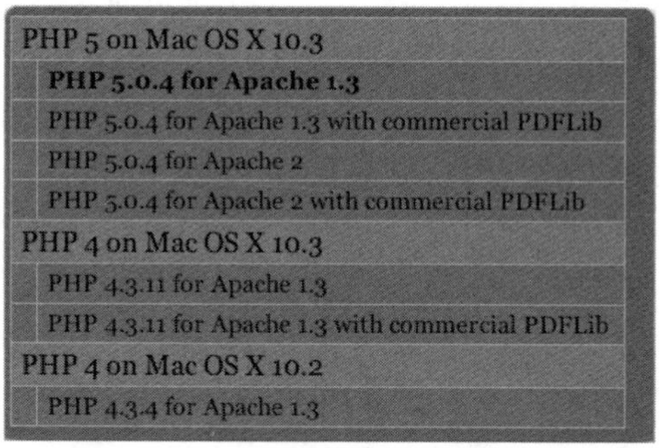

Figure A.18 There are several different PHP installers available at www.entropy.ch.

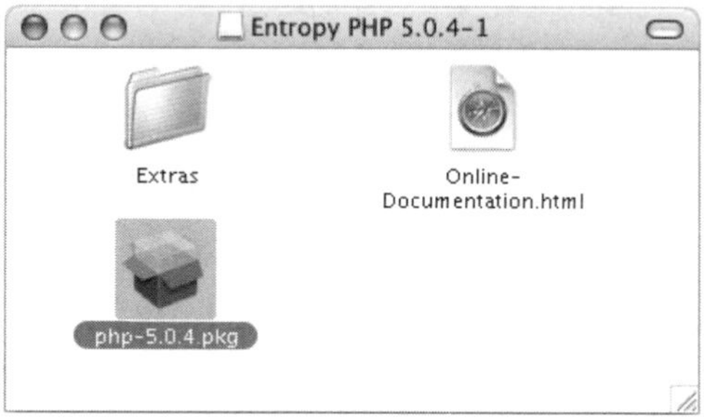

Figure A.19 The PHP installer for Mac OS X.

MySQL Permissions

Once MySQL has been successfully installed, you should immediately set a password for the root user. Until you have done so, anyone can access your databases and have administrative-level privileges. Windows users who followed the steps earlier for installing MySQL can skip this step, since the root user was created when the MySQL configuration wizard was run.

Once you've established the root user's password, you can begin establishing the users who will regularly access the database (for example, from PHP scripts). It is very insecure to use the root user for general purposes, so everyone should create some new MySQL users for regular use.

Setting the root user password

The mysqladmin utility, as the name might imply, is used to perform administrative-level tasks on your database. These include stopping MySQL, setting the root user's password, and more. (Some of the things you can do with mysqladmin can also be accomplished more directly within the mysql client, though.)

One of the first uses of mysqladmin is to assign a password to the root user. When MySQL is installed, there is no such value established. This is certainly a security risk that ought to be remedied before you begin to use the server. Just to clarify, your databases can have several users, just as your operating system might. The MySQL users are different from the operating system users, even if they share a common name. Therefore, the MySQL root user is a different entity than the operating system's root user, having different powers and even different passwords (preferably but not necessarily).

Most important, understand that the MySQL server must be running for you to use mysqladmin.

Again, if you ran the MySQL configuration wizard on Windows, you have already established a root user's password and can skip ahead to the next sequence of steps.

To assign a password to the root user:

1. Log on to your system from a command-line interface.

For Mac OS X and Linux users, this is just a matter of opening the Terminal application. For Windows users, you'll need to choose Start > Run, then enter cmd, and click OK.

2. Move to the mysql/bin or just mysql directory, depending upon your operating system.

cd /usr/local/mysql (Unix or Mac OS X)

or

cd C:\mysql\bin (Windows)

On some operating systems, you cannot access the mysqladmin utility directly. Therefore, you should go to one directory below it. On Windows you can head immediately into the bin directory.

3. Enter the following, replacing *thepassword* with the password you want to use (**Figure A.20**):

bin/mysqladmin -u root password
→ 'thepassword' (Unix or Mac OS X)

or

mysqladmin -u root password
→ 'thepassword' (Windows)

Keep in mind that passwords within MySQL are case-sensitive, so *Kazan* and *kazan* are not interchangeable. The term *password* that precedes the actual quoted password tells MySQL to encrypt that string.

If you see an error with this step, you could also try one of the following:

./bin/mysqladmin -u root password
→ 'thepassword'

or

/path/to/bin/mysqladmin -u root
→ password 'thepassword'

Figure A.20 Establishing a password for the root user.

MySQL Privileges

PRIVILEGE	ALLOWS
SELECT	Read rows from tables.
INSERT	Add new rows of data to tables.
UPDATE	Alter existing data in tables.
DELETE	Remove existing data from tables.
INDEX	Create and drop indexes in tables.
ALTER	Modify the structure of a table.
CREATE	Create new tables or databases.
DROP	Delete existing tables or databases.
RELOAD	Reload the grant tables (and therefore enact user changes).
SHUTDOWN	Stop the MySQL server.
PROCESS	View and stop existing MySQL processes.
FILE	Import data into tables from text files.
GRANT	Create new users.
REVOKE	Remove the permissions of users.

Table A.1 The list of privileges that can be assigned to MySQL users.

Creating users and privileges

After you have MySQL successfully up and running, and after you've established a password for the root user, it's time to begin adding other users. To improve the security of your applications, you should always create new users for accessing your databases, rather than continue to use the root user at all times.

The MySQL privileges system was designed to restrict access to only certain commands on specific databases by individual users. This technology is how a Web host, for example, can securely have several users accessing several databases, without concern. Each user within the MySQL system can have specific capabilities on specific databases from specific hosts (computers). The root user—the MySQL root user, not the system's—has the most power and is used for creating subusers, although subusers can be given rootlike powers (inadvisably so).

When a user attempts to do something with the MySQL server, MySQL will first check to see if the user has the permission to connect to the server at all (based upon the username, the user's password, and the information in the user table of the mysql database). Second, MySQL will check to see if the user has the permission to run the specific SQL statement on the specific databases—for example, to select data, insert data, or create a new table. To determine this, MySQL uses the *db*, *host*, *user*, *tables_priv*, and *columns_priv* tables, again from the *mysql* database. **Table A.1** lists the various privileges that can be set on a user-by-user basis.

continues on next page

MySQL Permissions

There are a handful of ways to set users and privileges within MySQL, but I prefer to do it manually, using the mysql client and the GRANT command. The syntax goes like this:

```
GRANT privileges ON database.* TO
→ username IDENTIFIED BY 'password'
```

For the *privileges* aspect of this statement, you can list specific privileges from the list in Table A.1, or you can allow for all of them using ALL (which is not prudent). The *database*.* part of the statement specifies which database and tables the user can work on. You can name specific tables using the *database*.*tablename* syntax or allow for every database with *.* (again, not prudent). Finally, you can specify the username and a password.

The username has a maximum length of 16 characters. When creating a username, be sure to avoid spaces (use the underscore instead) and note that usernames are case-sensitive. The password has no length limit but is also case-sensitive. The passwords will be encrypted within the mysql database, meaning they cannot be recovered in a plain text format. Omitting the IDENTIFIED BY 'password' clause results in that user not being required to enter a password (which, once again, should be avoided).

Finally, there is the option of limiting users to particular hostnames. The hostname is either the name of the computer on which the MySQL server is running (*localhost* being the most common value here) or the name of the computer from which the user will be accessing the server. This can even be an IP address, should you choose. To specify a particular host, change your statement to

```
GRANT privileges ON database.* TO
→ username@hostname IDENTIFIED BY
→ 'password'
```

To allow for any host, use the hostname wildcard character (%).

```
GRANT privileges ON database.* TO
→ username@'%' IDENTIFIED BY 'password'
```

As an example of this process, I will create a new user with specific privileges for a database called *sitename*. The following instructions will require using the mysql client or a similar interface to MySQL. I discuss how to access this tool in detail in Chapter 4, "Introduction to SQL and MySQL."

To create new users:

1. Log in to the mysql client as the MySQL root user.

   If you are using Windows, the MySQL installer created a shortcut to the mysql client under Programs > MySQL. If you are using Mac OS X or Unix, you'll need to use a Terminal application and type

   ```
   /usr/local/mysql/bin/mysql -u root -p
   ```

   If MySQL was not installed in that directory, you'll need to change your pathname accordingly.

   If you don't feel like messing with all of this, you can use phpMyAdmin or any of the other interface tools listed in Appendix C, "Resources."

2. Create the *sitename* database, if it does not already exist.

   ```
   CREATE DATABASE sitename;
   ```

   Creating a database is quite easy, using the preceding syntax. This is also discussed in Chapter 4.

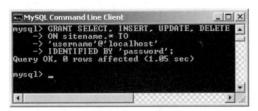

Figure A.21 CREATING A USER THAT CAN PERFORM BASIC TASKS ON ONE DATABASE.

Figure A.22 THE FLUSH PRIVILEGES COMMAND MUST BE RUN FOR THE USER CHANGES TO TAKE EFFECT.

3. Create a user that has basic-level privileges on the *sitename* database (**Figure A.21**).

```
GRANT SELECT, INSERT, UPDATE, DELETE ON
→ sitename.* TO 'username'@'localhost'
→ IDENTIFIED BY 'password';
```

The generic *username* user can browse through records (SELECT from tables) and add (INSERT), modify (UPDATE), or DELETE them. The user can only connect from *localhost* (from the same computer) and can only access the *sitename* database.

4. Apply the changes (**Figure A.22**).

```
FLUSH PRIVILEGES;
```

The changes just made will not take effect until you have told MySQL to reset the list of acceptable users and privileges, which is what this command will do. Forgetting this step and then being unable to access the database using the newly created users is a common mistake.

✔ TIPS

- Any database whose name begins with *test_* can be accessed by any user who has permission to connect to MySQL. Therefore, be careful not to create databases named this way unless it truly is experimental.

- There is an even more manual way to create new users: by running INSERT commands on the *user* and other *mysql* database tables. This is only for the more experienced users who fully comprehend the relationships among the *user*, *db*, and other *mysql* tables.

MySQL Permissions

Testing Your Installation

Now that you've installed everything and created the necessary MySQL users, you should test the installation. I'll create two quick PHP scripts for this purpose. In all likelihood, if an error occurred during one of the processes, you would already know it by now, but these steps will allow you to perform tests on your (or any other server) before getting into complicated PHP programming.

The first script being run is phpinfo.php. It both tests if PHP is enabled and shows a ton of information about the PHP installation. As simple as this script is, it is one of the most important scripts PHP developers ever write because it provides so much valuable knowledge.

The second script will serve two purposes. It will first see if support for MySQL has been enabled. If not, you'll need to see the next section of this chapter to change that. The script will also test if the MySQL user has permission to connect to a specific MySQL database.

To test PHP:

1. Create the following PHP document in a text editor (**Script A.1**).

   ```
   <?php
   phpinfo();
   ?>
   ```

   The phpinfo() function returns the configuration information for a PHP installation in a table. It's the perfect tool to test that PHP is working properly.

   You can use almost any application to create your PHP script as long as it can save the file in a plain text format.

2. Save the file as phpinfo.php.

   You need to be certain that the file's extension is just .php. Be careful when using Notepad on Windows, as it will secretly appended .txt. Similarly, TextEdit on Mac OS X wants to save everything as .rtf.

3. Place the file in the proper directory on your server.

   What the proper directory is depends upon your operating system and your Web server. If you are using a hosted site, check with the hosting company (although it should be fairly obvious once you FTP into the site). For Windows users who installed Apache, the directory is called **htdocs** and is within the Apache directory (C:\Program Files\Apache Group\Apache by default). For Mac OS X users, the proper directory is called Sites, found within your Home folder.

4. Test in your Web browser (**Figure A.23**).

   Run this script in your Web browser by going to http://*your.url.here*/phpinfo.php. On your own computer, this may be something like http://localhost/phpinfo.php or http://localhost/~*username*/phpinfo.php, where ~*username* is your short username (Mac OS X).

Script A.1 The phpinfo.php script tests and reports upon the PHP installation.

```
1   <?php
2   phpinfo();
3   ?>
```

Figure A.23 The information for this server's PHP configuration.

Script A.2 The `mysql_test.php` script tests for MySQL support in PHP and if the proper MySQL user privileges have been set.

```
         script
1    <?php
2    echo mysql_connect ('localhost',
     'username', 'password');
3    ?>
```

```
○ ○ ○    http://localhost/mysql_test.php

Resource id #2
```

Figure A.24 The PHP script was able to connect to the MySQL server.

```
○ ○ ○    http://localhost/mysql_test.php

Warning: mysql_connect() [function.mysql-connect]:
Access denied for user 'username'@'localhost' (using
password: YES) in
/Users/larryullman/Sites/mysql_test.php on line 2
```

Figure A.25 The script was not able to connect to the MySQL server.

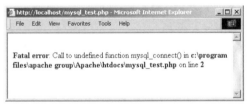

```
http://localhost/mysql_test.php - Microsoft Internet Explorer   _□×
 File   Edit   View   Favorites   Tools   Help

Fatal error: Call to undefined function mysql_connect() in c:\program
files\apache group\Apache\htdocs\mysql_test.php on line 2
```

Figure A.26 The script was not able to connect to the MySQL server because PHP does not have MySQL support enabled.

■ If a PHP script cannot connect to a MySQL server, it is normally because of a permissions issue. Double-check the username, password, and host being used, and be absolutely certain to flush the MySQL privileges.

To test PHP and MySQL:

1. Create a new PHP document in your text editor (**Script A.2**).

```
<?php
echo mysql_connect ('localhost',
→ 'username', 'password');
?>
```

This script will attempt to connect to the MySQL server using the username and password just established in this appendix. The results of this connection will be printed to the browser using the echo() statement.

2. Save the file as `mysql_test.php`, upload to your server, and test in your Web browser (**Figure A.24**).

If the script was able to connect, it will print something like *Resource id #2*. If it could not connect, you should see an error message like that in **Figure A.25**. Most likely this indicates a problem with the MySQL user's privileges (see the previous section of this chapter).

If you see an error like in **Figure A.26**, this means that PHP does not have MySQL support enabled. See the next section of this chapter for the solution.

✔ Tips

■ For security reasons, you should not leave the `phpinfo.php` and `mysql_test.php` scripts on a live server because they give away too much information.

■ If you run a PHP script in your Web browser and it attempts to download the file, then your Web server is not recognizing that file extension as PHP. Check your Apache (or other Web server) configuration to correct this.

■ PHP scripts must always be run from a URL starting with *http://*. They cannot be run directly off a hard drive (as if you had opened it in your browser).

TESTING YOUR INSTALLATION

649

Configuring PHP

If you have installed PHP on your own computer, then you also have the ability to configure how PHP runs. Changing PHP's behavior is very simple and will most likely be required at some point in time. Just a few of the things you'll want to consider adjusting are

◆ Whether or not *display_errors* is on

◆ The default level of error reporting

◆ The Magic Quotes settings

◆ Support for MySQL and the Improved MySQL Extension functions

What each of these means—if you don't already know—is covered in the book's chapters and in the PHP manual. But for starters, I would highly recommend that you make sure that *display_errors* is on.

The short version of the configuration process is: edit the php.ini file and then restart the Web server. But because many different problems can arise, I'll cover configuration in more detail. If you are looking to enable support for an extension, like the MySQL functions, the configuration is more complicated (see the sidebar).

Enabling Extension Support

Many PHP configuration options can be altered by just editing the php.ini file. But enabling (or disabling) an extension—in other words, adding support for extended functionality—requires more effort. To enable support for an extension for just a single PHP page, you can use the dl() function. To enable support for an extension for all PHP scripts requires a bit of work. Unfortunately, for Unix and Mac OS X users, you'll need to rebuild PHP with support for this new extension. Windows users have it easier:

First, edit the php.ini file (see the steps in this section), removing the semicolon before the extension you want to enable. For example, to enable MySQL support, you'll need to find the line that says

```
;extension=php_mysql.dll
```

and remove that semicolon.

Next, find the line that sets the *extension_dir* and adjust this for your PHP installation. Assuming you installed PHP into C:\php, then your php.ini file should say

```
extension_dir = "C:/php/ext"
```

or

```
extension_dir = "C:\\php\\ext"
```

This tells PHP where to find the extension. (The two backslashes are required because a single backslash has special meaning in PHP.)

Save the php.ini file and restart your Web server. If the restart process indicates an error finding the extension, double-check to make sure that the extension exists in the *extension_dir* and that your pathnames are correct.

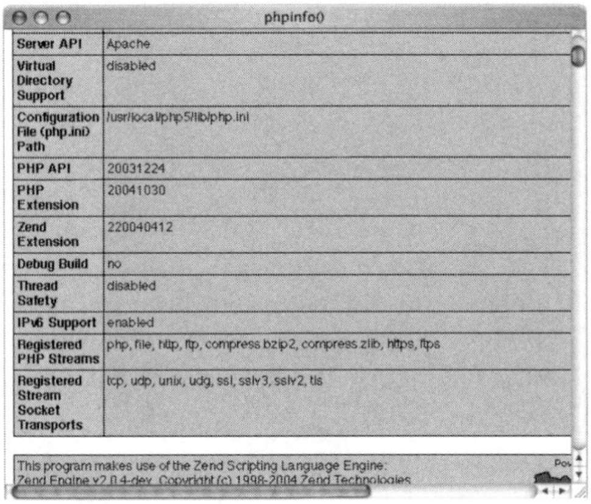

Figure A.27 The Configuration File value tells you which php.ini file is used for configuration purposes.

To configure PHP:

1. Run a phpinfo() script (see the previous section) in your Web browser.

2. In the resulting page, look for the line that says "Configuration File (php.ini) Path" (**Figure A.27**).

   It should be about six rows down in the table.

3. Note the location of your php.ini file.

   This is the active file PHP is using. Your server may have multiple php.ini files on it, but this is the one that counts.

   If you don't have a php.ini file on your server (if the value is blank in the phpinfo.php script), create one by following these steps:

   A) Download the complete source code from www.php.net/downloads.php.

   B) Extract the source so that you now have a folder of files.

   C) Find the php.ini-dist file, located within the main folder.

   D) Rename this file as php.ini and move it to the proper directory (where PHP thinks the php.ini file should be).

4. Open the php.ini file in any text editor.

   If you are using Mac OS X, you do not have easy access to the php.ini directory. You can either use the Terminal to access the file, open it using BBEdit's *Open Hidden* option, or use something like TinkerTool to show hidden files in the Finder.

   If you go to the directory listed and there's no php.ini file there, follow the sequence in Step 3 to create one.

   continues on next page

CONFIGURING PHP

5. Make any changes you want, keeping in mind the following:

▲ Comments are marked using a semi-colon. Anything after the semicolon is ignored.

▲ Instructions on what most of the settings mean are included in the file.

▲ The top of the file lists general information with examples. Do not change these values! Change the settings where they appear later in the file.

▲ For safety purposes, don't change any original settings. Just comment them out (by preceding the line with a semicolon) and then add the new, modified line afterward.

▲ Add a comment (using the semicolon) to mark what changes you made and when. For example:

```
; register_globals = Off
register_globals = On ; Added by
→ LEU 4/8/2005
```

6. Save the file.

7. Restart the Web server (Apache, IIS, Xitami, etc.).

You do not have to restart the entire computer, just the Web serving application (Apache, IIS, etc.). How you do this depends upon the application being used, the operating system, and the installation method. Windows users can follow the instructions at the end of the Windows installation sequence. Mac OS X users can stop and then start Personal Web Sharing (under System Preferences > Sharing). Unix users can normally just enter `apachectl graceful` in a Terminal window.

8. Rerun the `phpinfo.php` script to make sure the changes took effect.

✔ Tips

■ Any changes to PHP's (or Apache's) configuration file do not take effect until you restart Apache. Always make sure that you restart the Web server to enact changes!

■ Editing the wrong `php.ini` file is a common mistake. This is why I recommend that you run a `phpinfo.php` script to see which `php.ini` file PHP is using.

REFERENCE

Even after writing several books on PHP and MySQL, there are still many things that I can never quite remember. Whether it's the proper syntax of a function, the formatting parameters used by date(), or the correct regular expression character, it's best to have the correct syntax at hand, rather than wildly making guesses.

For this reason, I've placed some of the most necessary references in this one location. This appendix consists primarily of tables (most of which have appeared elsewhere in the book) but also contains a wee bit of new information.

PHP

By no means could this appendix replace the value of the PHP manual, but the tables and information listed here might save you a trip online to view it. In this section you'll find lists of

◆ Operators, comparators, and their precedence

◆ Date- and time-formatting parameters and functions

◆ Regular expression characters and classes

◆ And more!

Operators and comparators

Many of PHP's operators and comparators (symbols used to make comparisons) are self-evident. Still, to be explicit, I've listed most of them in **Table B.1**. Along with these, don't forget about the variations on the assignment operators: .=, +=, -=, *=, and /=.

Table B.2 places most of Table B.1 in order of precedence, from highest (at the top) to lowest. You can memorize this list when writing complex statements or use parentheses to always guarantee the order in which operators will be evaluated.

PHP Operators

SYMBOL	MEANING	TYPE
=	is assigned the value of	assignment
==	is equal to	comparison
!=	is not equal to	comparison
<	less than	comparison
>	greater than	comparison
<=	less than or equal to	comparison
>=	greater than or equal to	comparison
!	is not	logical
&&	and	logical
and	and	logical
||	or	logical
or	or	logical
xor	or not	logical
+	addition	arithmetic
-	subtraction	arithmetic
*	multiplication	arithmetic
/	division	arithmetic
%	modulus	arithmetic
.	concatenation	miscellaneous
++	increment by 1	arithmetic
--	decrement by 1	arithmetic

Table B.1 PHP's characters for performing operations or making comparisons.

Operator Precedence

OPERATOR
! ++ --
* / %
+ - .
< <= > >=
== != ===
&&
||
= += -= *= /= .= %=
and
xor

Table B.2 The precedence given to PHP's operators and comparators, from most important (at the top) to least.

PHP

Date() Function Formatting

CHARACTER	MEANING	EXAMPLE
Y	year as 4 digits	2005
y	year as 2 digits	05
n	month as 1 or 2 digits	2
m	month as 2 digits	02
F	month	February
M	month as 3 letters	Feb
j	day of the month as 1 or 2 digits	8
d	day of the month as 2 digits	08
l (lowercase L)	day of the week	Monday
D	day of the week as 3 letters	Mon
w	day of the week as a single digit	0 (Sunday)
z	day of the year: 0 to 365	
t	number of days in the given month	31
g	hour, 12-hour format as 1 or 2 digits	6
G	hour, 24-hour format as 1 or 2 digits	18
h	hour, 12-hour format as 2 digits	06
H	hour, 24-hour format as 2 digits	18
i	minutes	45
s	seconds	18
a	am or pm	am
A	AM or PM	PM

Table B.3 These are the formatting parameters to use with the date() function.

The getdate() Array

KEY	MEANING	EXAMPLE
year	year	2005
mon	month	12
month	month name	December
mday	day of the month	25
weekday	day of the week	Tuesday
hours	hours	11
minutes	minutes	56
seconds	seconds	47

Table B.4 The array returned by the getdate() function.

Date and time

After years of programming in PHP, what I still frequently must look up are the formatting parameters used with the date() function. I have recorded most of these in **Table B.3**. You'll find them in year, month, day, hour, minute, second order, since listing them alphabetically makes it harder to find the formatting you want (check the manual for comparison).

As a reminder, the syntax for using the date function is

```
date (format, timestamp)
```

The function takes the format as a quoted string and can also take an optional timestamp (as an integer). The date() function will return a string value. For example,

```
echo date ("F j, Y"); // May 3, 2005
```

The getdate() function, discussed in Chapter 3, "Creating Dynamic Web Sites," returns an array of information for a particular date. The keys and values stored in the array are displayed in **Table B.4**.

```
$date_array = getdate();
```

This function also takes an optional timestamp.

Regular expressions

In Chapter 10, "Web Application Security," I discussed regular expressions as a means to validate user-submitted form data. Here is a repeat of the three tables listed in that section, with some minor alterations (**Tables B.5**, **B.6**, and **B.7**). These characters are used to establish patterns that will be matched using the ereg(), eregi(), ereg_replace(), and eregi_replace() functions.

Metacharacters

CHARACTER	MEANING
^	Indicates the beginning of a string
$	Indicates the end of a string
.	Any single character
|	Alternatives (or)
\	Escapes the following character
()	Used for making groups
[]	Used for defining classes

Table B.5 These characters have special meanings for regular expressions, although not within classes.

Quantifiers

CHARACTER	MEANING
?	0 or 1
*	0 or more
+	1 or more
{x}	exactly *x* occurrences
{x, y}	between *x* and *y* (inclusive)
{x,}	at least *x* occurrences

Table B.6 Use these symbols to specify quantities in your regular expressions.

Character Classes

CLASS	MEANING
[a-z]	Any lowercase letter
[a-zA-Z]	Any letter
[0-9]	Any number
[\f\r\t\n\v]	Any white space
[aeiou]	Any vowel
[[:alnum:]]	Any letter or number
[[:alpha:]]	Any letter (same as [a-zA-Z])
[[:blank:]]	Any tabs or spaces
[[:digit:]]	Any number (same as [0-9])
[[:lower:]]	Any lowercase letter
[[:upper:]]	Any uppercase letter
[[:punct:]]	Punctuation characters (. , ; : -)
[[:space:]]	Any white space

Table B.7 These classes are shorthand for common character sets.

The getimagesize() Array

ELEMENT	VALUE	EXAMPLE
0	image's width in pixels	423
1	image's height in pixels	368
2	image's type	2 (representing JPG)
3	appropriate HTML img data	height="xx" width="yy"

Table B.8 The getimagesize() function returns an array with these keys and values.

The $_FILES Array

INDEX	MEANING
name	The original name of the file (as it was on the user's computer)
type	The MIME type of the file, as provided by the browser
size	The size of the uploaded file in bytes
tmp_name	The temporary filename of the uploaded file as it was stored on the server
error	The error code associated with any problem in uploading

Table B.9 When uploading files, use the $_FILES array to access them.

Other references

The last set of PHP references I'll include are a grab bag of ideas discussed throughout the book. **Table B.8** lists the key-value pairs returned by the getimagesize() function. The most frequently used value is indexed at 3, which is a string used to create the HTML code for the height and width of the image. The third element in the array is a numeric representation of the image type where *1* means GIF, *2* is JPG, *3* PNG, *4* SWF (Shockwave Format), *5* PSD (Photoshop), *6* BMP (Bitmap), *7* and *8*, TIFF (two different types), and so on.

Finally, **Table B.9** displays the contents of the $_FILES array, used when uploading files through the Web browser.

PHP

MySQL

Selecting the proper column type for your tables is key to a successful database. **Table B.10** lists the different string, number, and other types you can use, along with how much space they will take up on the server's hard drive. When choosing a type for each column, you should use the most efficient (i.e., the most size-frugal) data type given what the largest value of the column could be.

MySQL Data Types

TYPE	SIZE	DESCRIPTION
CHAR[Length]	*Length* bytes	A fixed-length field from 0 to 255 characters long
VARCHAR[Length]	String length + 1 bytes	A variable-length field from 0 to 255 characters long
TINYTEXT	String length + 1 bytes	A string with a maximum length of 255 characters
TEXT	String length + 2 bytes	A string with a maximum length of 65,535 characters
MEDIUMTEXT	String length + 3 bytes	A string with a maximum length of 16,777,215 characters
LONGTEXT	String length + 4 bytes	A string with a maximum length of 4,294,967,295 characters
TINYINT[Length]	1 byte	Range of –128 to 127 or 0 to 255 unsigned
SMALLINT[Length]	2 bytes	Range of –32,768 to 32,767 or 0 to 65,535 unsigned
MEDIUMINT[Length]	3 bytes	Range of –8,388,608 to 8,388,607 or 0 to 16,777,215 unsigned
INT[Length]	4 bytes	Range of –2,147,483,648 to 2,147,483,647 or 0 to 4,294,967,295 unsigned
BIGINT[Length]	8 bytes	Range of –9,223,372,036,854,775,808 to 9,223,372,036,854,775,807 or 0 to 18,446,744,073,709,551,615 unsigned
FLOAT	4 bytes	A small number with a floating decimal point
DOUBLE [Length, Decimals]	8 bytes	A large number with a floating decimal point
DECIMAL [Length, Decimals]	Length + 1 or Length + 2 bytes	A DOUBLE stored as a string, allowing for a fixed decimal point
DATE	3 bytes	In the format of YYYY-MM-DD
DATETIME	8 bytes	In the format of YYYY-MM-DD HH:MM:SS
TIMESTAMP	4 bytes	In the format of YYYYMMDDHHMMSS; acceptable range ends in the year 2037
TIME	3 bytes	In the format of HH:MM:SS
YEAR	1 byte	In the format of either YY or YYYY
ENUM	1 or 2 bytes	Short for *enumeration*, which means that each column can have one of several possible values
SET	1, 2, 3, 4, or 8 bytes	Like ENUM except that each column can have more than one of several possible values
TINYBLOB	String length + 1 byte	A binary file with a maximum length of 255 characters
BLOB	String length + 2 bytes	A binary file with a maximum length of 65,535 characters
MEDIUMBLOB	String length + 3 bytes	A binary file with a maximum length of 16,777,215 characters
LONGBLOB	String length + 4 bytes	A binary file with a maximum length of 4,294,967,295 characters

Table B.10 The list of available types for column definitions in a MySQL table.

MySQL Operators and Comparators

OPERATOR	MEANING
+	addition
-	subtraction
*	multiplication
/	division
%	modulus
=	equals
<	less than
>	greater than
<=	less than or equal to
>=	greater than or equal to
!=	not equal to
IS NOT NULL	has a value
IS NULL	does not have a value
BETWEEN	within a range
NOT BETWEEN	outside of a range
OR (also ||)	where one of two conditionals is true
AND (also &&)	where both conditionals are true
NOT (also !)	where the condition is not true
LIKE	where the value matches a string
NOT LIKE	where the value does not match a string
%	multiple wildcard character (used with LIKE and NOT LIKE)
_	single wildcard character (used with LIKE and NOT LIKE)
REGEXP	where the value matches a pattern
NOT REGEXP	where the value does not match a pattern

Table B.11 The symbols and terms to use for performing operations and comparisons on a MySQL table.

Boolean Mode Operators

OPERATOR	MEANING
+	Must be present in every match
-	Must not be present in any match
~	Lowers a ranking if present
*	Wildcard
<	Decrease a word's importance
>	Increase a word's importance
" "	Must match the exact phrase
()	Create subexpressions

Table B.12 Use these operators to fine-tune your FULLTEXT searches.

When it comes to defining columns, remember that any column type can be NULL or NOT NULL, integers can be UNSIGNED, and any number can be ZEROFILL. An integer column can also be designated as AUTO_INCREMENT if it is set as the primary key for that table.

Table B.11 shows most of the operators and comparators used in SQL queries on a MySQL database. Most of these are part of the SQL standard and will also work with any database application.

Table B.12 lists the special characters used in BOOLEAN mode in FULL TEXT searches. For example:

```
SELECT * FROM tablename WHERE

MATCH(column) AGAINST('+database -mysql'
→ IN BOOLEAN MODE)
```

I talked about FULL TEXT searches and BOOLEAN mode in Chapter 5, "Advanced SQL and MySQL."

Table B.13 has the most basic SQL terms listed, most of which were discussed in Chapter 4, "Introduction to SQL and MySQL," and Chapter 5.

SQL Terminology

TERM	USAGE
ALTER	Change the structure of a table.
CREATE	Create a table or database.
DELETE	Delete rows from a table.
DESCRIBE	Reveal the structure of a table.
DROP	Delete entire tables or databases.
INSERT	Add a row to a table.
SELECT	Retrieve information from a database.
SHOW	Retrieve information about the structure of a database or table.
TRUNCATE	Delete and redefine a table.
UPDATE	Modify a database entry.

Table B.13 SQL has surprisingly few terms but can still do very complex procedures.

PHP

MySQL Functions

Preformatting the results returned by a query makes your data more usable and can cut down on the amount of programming interface required (i.e., how much work you have to do in PHP). To format query results, you make use of MySQL's built-in functions, first introduced in Chapter 4. **Table B.14** shows those used on strings. **Table B.15** has most, but not all, of the number-based functions.

Text Functions

FUNCTION	USAGE	PURPOSE
CONCAT()	CONCAT(x, y, ...)	Creates a new string of the form *xy*.
LENGTH()	LENGTH(column)	Returns the length of the value stored in the column.
LEFT()	LEFT(column, x)	Returns the leftmost *x* characters from a column's value.
RIGHT()	RIGHT(column, x)	Returns the rightmost *x* characters from a column's value.
TRIM()	TRIM(column)	Trims excess spaces from the beginning and end of the stored value.
UPPER()	UPPER(column)	Capitalizes the entire stored string.
LOWER()	LOWER(column)	Turns the stored string into an all-lowercase format.
SUBSTRING()	SUBSTRING (column, start, length)	Returns *length* characters from *column* beginning with *start* (indexed from 0).

Table B.14 These MySQL functions can be used to manipulate string values.

Numeric Functions

FUNCTION	USAGE	PURPOSE
ABS()	ABS(x)	Returns the absolute value of *x*.
CEILING()	CEILING(x)	Returns the next-highest integer based upon the value of *x*.
FLOOR()	FLOOR(x)	Returns the integer value of *x*.
FORMAT()	FORMAT(x, y)	Returns *x* formatted as a number with *y* decimal places and commas inserted every three spaces.
MOD()	MOD(x, y)	Returns the remainder of dividing *x* by *y* (either or both can be a column).
RAND()	RAND()	Returns a random number between 0 and 1.0.
ROUND()	ROUND(x, y)	Returns the number *x* rounded to *y* decimal places.
SIGN()	SIGN(x)	Returns a value indicating whether a number is negative (–1), zero (0), or positive (+1).
SQRT()	SQRT(x)	Calculates the square root of *x*.

Table B.15 These MySQL functions perform calculations, formatting, and other treatments on numbers.

PHP

Grouping Functions

FUNCTION	PURPOSE
AVG()	Returns the average value of the column.
COUNT()	Counts the number of rows.
COUNT(DISTINCT)	Counts the number of distinct column values.
MIN()	Returns the smallest value from the column.
MAX()	Returns the largest value from the column.
SUM()	Returns the sum of all the values in the column.

Table B.16 The grouping functions are frequently, but not always, used with an SQL GROUP BY clause.

Table B.16 lists the aggregate or grouping functions. **Table B.17** is the catchall for miscellaneous functions. Most every function can be applied either to the value retrieved from a column or to a manually entered one:

```
SELECT ROUND(column, 2) FROM tablename
```

```
SELECT ROUND(3.142857, 2)
```

Date and time

Depending upon where a date or time value originates, either PHP or MySQL may be used to format the returned value. I earlier listed the parameters for formatting dates in PHP with the date() function and mentioned PHP's getdate() function. **Table B.18** lists some of MySQL's date- and time-related functions. **Table B.19** has the formatting to use with DATE_FORMAT() and TIME_FORMAT().

Other Functions

FUNCTION	USAGE	PURPOSE
CONCAT_WS()	CONCAT_WS ('-', column1, column2)	Combines the elements with the one common separator.
DATABASE()	DATABASE()	Returns the name of the database currently being used.
ENCODE()	ENCODE('string', 'salt')	Returns an encrypted version of *string*, which can be decrypted.
ENCRYPT()	ENCRYPT('string', 'salt')	Returns an encrypted version of *string* using *salt* (requires the Unix crypt library).
DECODE()	DECODE('string', 'salt')	Returns a decrypted version of *string*.
LAST_INSERT_ID()	LAST_INSERT_ID()	Returns the previous auto-incremented value.
SHA()	SHA('string')	Returns an encrypted version of *string*.
USER()	USER()	Returns the name of the user of the current session.

Table B.17 This table shows functions that handle encryption and other miscellaneous tasks.

PHP

Date and Time Functions

FUNCTION	USAGE	PURPOSE
HOUR()	HOUR(column)	Returns just the hour value of a stored date.
MINUTE()	MINUTE(column)	Returns just the minute value of a stored date.
SECOND()	SECOND(column)	Returns just the second value of a stored date.
DAYNAME()	DAYNAME(column)	Returns the name of the day for a date value.
DAYOFMONTH()	DAYOFMONTH(column)	Returns just the numerical day value of a stored date.
MONTHNAME()	MONTHNAME(column)	Returns the name of the month in a date value.
MONTH()	MONTH(column)	Returns just the numerical month value of a stored date.
YEAR()	YEAR(column)	Returns just the year value of a stored date.
ADDDATE()	ADDDATE(column, INTERVAL x type)	Returns the value of x units added to column.
SUBDATE()	SUBDATE(column, INTERVAL x type)	Returns the value of x units subtracted from column.
CURDATE()	CURDATE()	Returns the current date.
CURTIME()	CURTIME()	Returns the current time.
NOW()	NOW()	Returns the current date and time.
UNIX_TIMESTAMP()	UNIX_TIMESTAMP(date)	Returns the number of seconds since the epoch until the current moment or until the date specified.

Table B.18 MySQL's functions for working with date and time values.

DATE_FORMAT() and TIME_FORMAT() Parameters

TERM	USAGE	EXAMPLE
%e	Day of the month	1-31
%d	Day of the month, two-digit	01-31
%D	Day with suffix	1st-31st
%W	Weekday name	Sunday-Saturday
%a	Abbreviated weekday name	Sun-Sat
%c	Month number	1-12
%m	Month number, two-digit	01-12
%M	Month name	January-December
%b	Month name, abbreviated	Jan-Dec
%Y	Year	2002
%y	Year	02
%l (lowercase L)	Hour	1-12
%h	Hour, two digit	01-12
%k	Hour, 24-hour clock	0-23
%H	Hour, 24-hour clock, two-digit	00-23
%i	Minutes	00-59
%S	Seconds	00-59
%r	Time	8:17:02 PM
%T	Time, 24-hour clock	20:17:02
%p	AM or PM	AM or PM

Table B.19 The parameters used by the DATE_FORMAT() and TIME_FORMAT() functions.

PHP

RESOURCES

This book was written with a specific purpose in mind: teaching how to develop dynamic Web sites using PHP and MySQL. In the course of the material, some secondary subjects were mentioned (e.g., JavaScript and Cascading Style Sheets), and some primary subjects were glossed over. The resources listed in this appendix should help fill in the gaps and round out the information presented.

Besides the included resources, I'd recommend familiarizing yourself with the companion Web site to this text. By pointing your browser to `www.DMCInsights.com/phpmysql2`, you'll find

◆ More Web links (over 350 at last count)

◆ Sample scripts not demonstrated in this book

◆ Extra tutorials and information

◆ A support forum for questions and issues arising from this book

◆ An errata page, listing printing errors (which unfortunately do happen)

All of the resources listed in this chapter are items I have come across that may be useful to the average reader. Referencing something here does not constitute an endorsement, nor does it imply that each of these is the best possible resource or tool for your needs. And, as the Web is an ever-changing place, some of these sites may shut down, and new, possibly better, ones will arrive.

Finally, I should state in advance that I only list Web resources here (even the two magazines mentioned are available for download). Naturally there are oodles of books available on many of the topics I mention in this appendix. Just offhand, I can think of several on PHP, MySQL, and related subjects that I've written, and this book's publisher (Peachpit Press, `www.peachpit.com`) has put out many excellent titles on CSS, JavaScript, HTML, and the like.

PHP

If you have not done so already, you should immediately acquire some version of the PHP manual before beginning to work with the language. The manual is available from the official PHP site—see `www.php.net/docs.php` (**Figure C.1**)—as well as a number of other locations. You can download the manual in over a dozen languages in any of these formats. The official Web site also has an annotated version of the manual available at `www.php.net/manual/en`, where other users have added helpful notes and comments that may solve some of the problems you encounter when using a particular function.

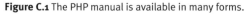

Figure C.1 The PHP manual is available in many forms.

✔ Tips

- You can quickly access the manual page for any particular function by going to the URL `www.php.net/function_name`.

- The popularity of PHP is such that there are now two magazines on the subject. One is *php|architect*, `www.phparch.com` (**Figure C.2**), and the other is the *International PHP Magazine*, `www.phpmag.net`. Both are available in a downloadable PDF format.

Figure C.2 The *php|architect* magazine is a popular publication for PHP programmers, available in both digital and print formats.

PHP Web sites

I'll mention just a few of the many very useful Web sites you can turn to when programming in PHP, and then leave it up to you to decide which ones you like the best. Most of these also contain links to other PHP-related sites.

The first, and most obvious, site to bookmark is PHP.net, `www.php.net`, the official site for PHP.

Next, you should familiarize yourself with Zend.com, `www.zend.com` (**Figure C.3**), the home page for the creators of the Zend Engine (the heart of PHP 4 and 5). The site

Figure C.3 For PHP developers, the next-best thing to the PHP home page is Zend.com.

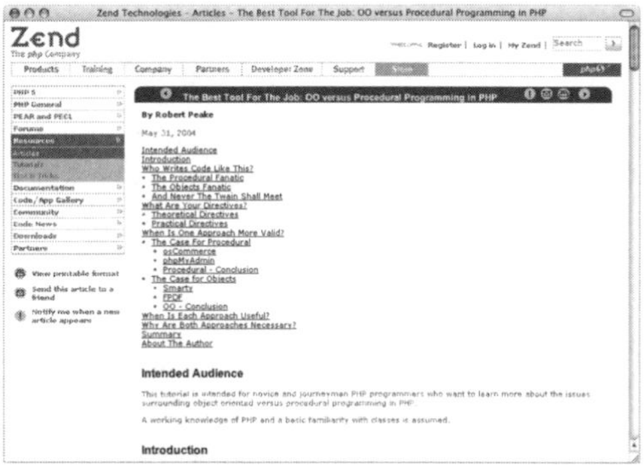

Figure C.4 One of the many articles you'll find at Zend.com is this introduction to OOP.

Figure C.5 PEAR has its own thought-out rules for coding standards.

contains numerous downloads plus a wealth of other resources, straight from the masters, so to speak.

For information on specific topics, PHPBuilder, `www.phpbuilder.com`, is a great place to turn. The site has dozens of articles explaining how to do particular tasks using PHP and often MySQL.

WeberDev.com, `www.weberdev.com`, is a mixed bag of PHP and MySQL resources. There's an area of beginner guides, a section for finding work, and plenty of articles, code samples, and the like.

I did not cover one particular variable type in this book: objects. PHP does have support for object-oriented programming, which has been increased in PHP 5. As you improve upon your programming skills, and especially as you build a strong code library, being able to create and utilize objects can improve your programming speed and minimize run-time errors. You can find several good tutorials online regarding objects in PHP. You may also want to read this article at Zend.com, `www.zend.com/zend/art/oo-proc.php` (**Figure C.4**), which discusses object-oriented versus procedural programming. (Procedural programming is what this book uses.)

One final Web reference I'll mention is the PHP Coding Standard. The standard is a document making recommendations for programming in PHP in terms of proper format and syntax for variable names, control structures, and so forth. While you shouldn't feel obligated to abide by these rules, there are some solid and well-thought-out recommendations that can help minimize errors as you program. Unfortunately the PHP Coding Standard's URL changes with some frequency, so find the latest version by doing a search on "PHP Coding Standard".

✔ Tip

■ Another source for coding standards can be found in the documentation for PEAR, `http://pear.php.net` (**Figure C.5**).

PHP

Newsgroups and mailing lists

If you have access to newsgroups, you can use these as a great sounding board for ideas, as well as a place to get your most difficult questions answered. Of course you can always give back to the group by offering your own expertise to those in need.

The largest English-language PHP newsgroup is `comp.lang.php`. You may be able to access `comp.lang.php` through your ISP or via a pay-for-use Usenet organization. There are newsgroups available in languages other than English, too.

The PHP Web site lists the available mailing lists you can sign up for at `www.php.net/mailing-lists.php` (**Figure C.6**).

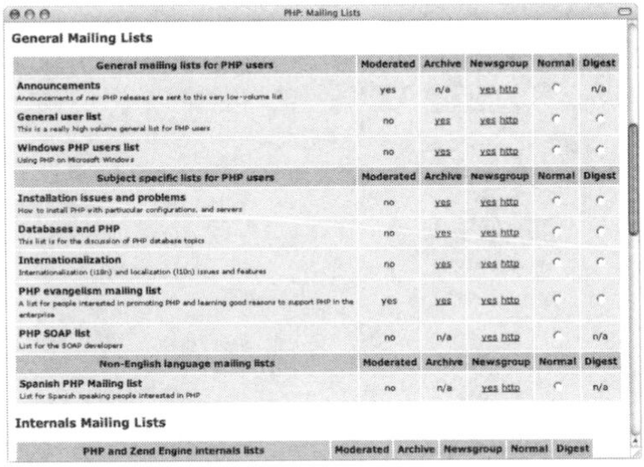

Code Repositories

There's no shortage of code libraries online these days. Due to the generous (and often showy) nature of PHP programmers, many sites have scores of PHP code, organized and available for download. The best online code repositories are

◆ HotScripts.com, `www.hotscripts.com`

◆ PX: the PHP code exchange, `http://px.sklar.com` (**Figure C.7**)

◆ The PHP Resource Index, `http://php.resourceindex.com/Complete_Scripts/` (**Figure C.8**)

◆ The PHP Classes Repository, `www.php-classes.org`

Whether you are looking for a quick fix to a problem or want to see what other developers have done, these sites are worth a gander.

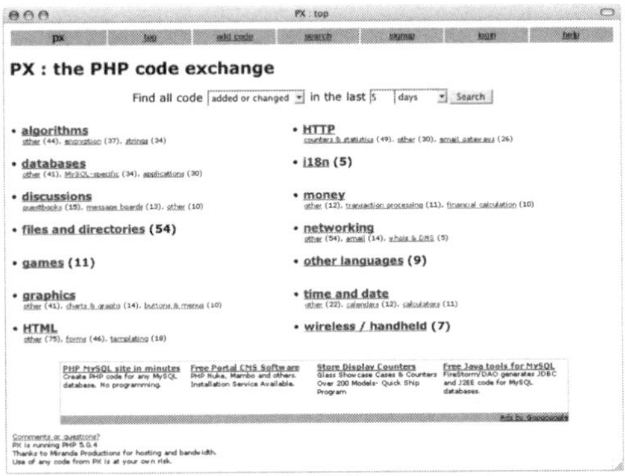

Figure C.6 There are dozens of PHP mailing lists that you can sign up for.

Figure C.7 PX provides PHP code in many different categories.

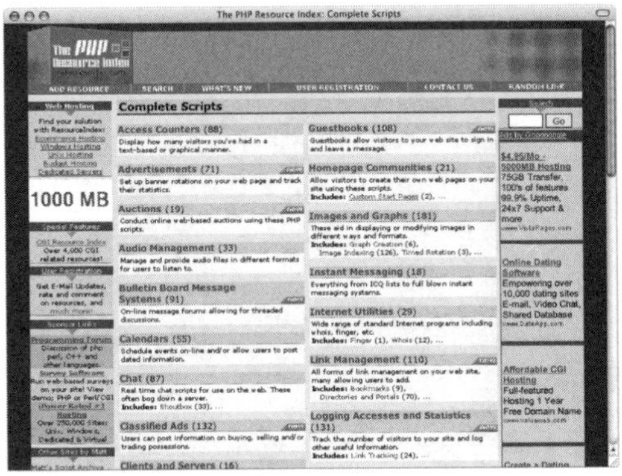

Figure C.8 The PHP Resource Index has a lot of useful information, including hundreds of PHP scripts.

PHP

✔ Tips

- You can also find code examples at `Zend.com`, `PHPBuilder.com`, and many other general PHP Web sites.

- Of course you can always find PHP scripts by doing a search using Google or other search engines.

- The references listed in this appendix—and many more—can be found on the links page of the book's supporting Web site.

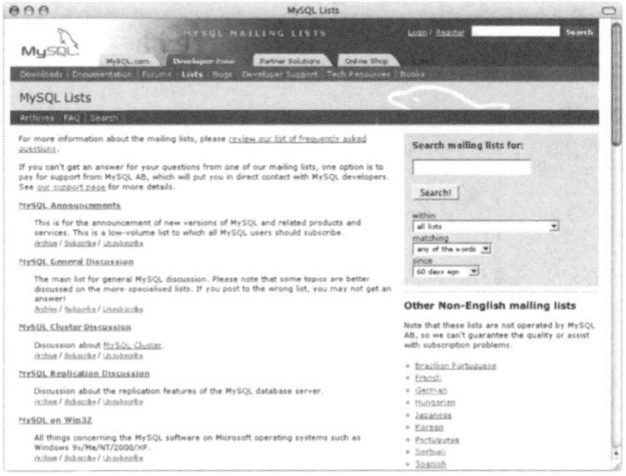

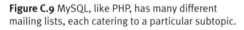

Figure C.9 MySQL, like PHP, has many different mailing lists, each catering to a particular subtopic.

MySQL

The absolutely very first resource you should consider is the MySQL manual, available through the company's Web site (`www.mysql.com`) in many different forms. The main online version has the added advantage of being searchable, while another online version includes user-submitted comments that are occasionally helpful. I also keep a copy of the manual on my hard drive for whichever version of MySQL I am running (since the manual reflects the current version of MySQL, it's smart to retain older copies).

Once you've performed an exhaustive search through the MySQL manual, you can consider turning to one of several MySQL-dedicated mailing lists (there are no official MySQL newsgroups). Each list focuses on a different area related to MySQL:

- Announcements
- General
- Java
- Windows
- ODBC
- C++
- Perl

All of these but the announcements are available in a digest form so that you can receive two large emails per day rather than dozens of individual ones. Plus these lists are available in other languages. For more information, see `http://lists.mysql.com` (**Figure C.9**).

continues on next page

MySQL

From the lists page, you can perform searches through the mailing list archives. Doing a quick search there before posting a question to a mailing list (and presumably after you've scoured the MySQL manual) will save you time and the potential flaming from the list members.

For MySQL debugging assistance, check out the list of MySQL Gotchas, `http://sql-info.de/mysql/gotchas.html`. This page covers oddities you may encounter while using a MySQL database.

MySQL tools

For interacting with MySQL, I generally use either the mysql client or phpMyAdmin, `www.phpmyadmin.net`, but these are not your only choices. There are quality open source and commercial applications available for any platform. I'll mention a smattering of them here.

To start, MySQL AB, the company behind MySQL, has created a GUI application called the Query Browser. It's freely available for Windows and Linux (`www.mysql.com/products/query-browser`).

MYdbPAL, `www.it-map.com/html/mydbpal_.html`, is a highly regarded—and free!—tool for Windows. With it you can design and administer your databases. Webyog, `www.webyog.com/sqlyog/index.php`, provides similar functionality and is available in both free and cost versions.

The free (personal edition) dbSuite, `www.dbsuite.de/dbsuiteAdminTool.html` (**Figure C.10**), runs on both Windows (2000/XP) and Mac OS X. It provides a method for administering and creating databases, as well as an alternative way of running queries. Mac OS X users can also use the free CocoaMySQL, `http://cocoamysql.sourceforge.net`, or YourSQL, `www.mludi.net/YourSQL` (**Figure C.11**).

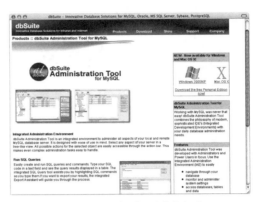

Figure C.10 The very professional dbSuite is a graphical alternative to working with MySQL through a command-line interface.

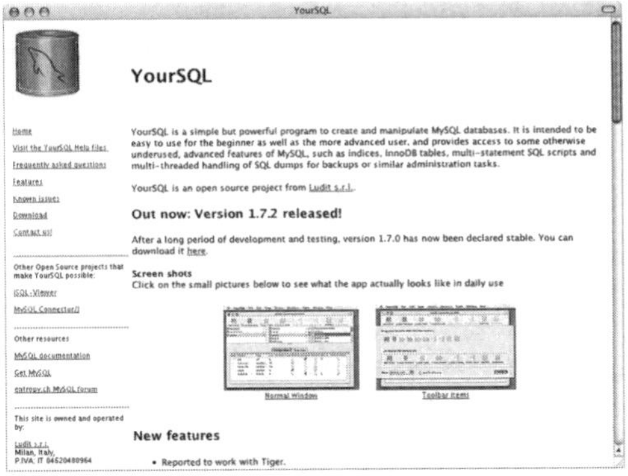

Figure C.11 YourSQL is a popular application for interacting with MySQL on Mac OS X.

MySQL

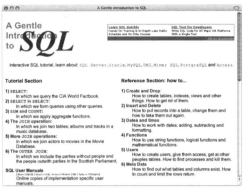

Figure C.12 A Gentle Introduction to SQL is a great beginner's guide to the language.

Figure C.13 The W3 Schools' Web site has a lot of useful information on SQL, HTML, CSS, and more.

SQL

Since SQL is used by MySQL and other databases, you can find an endless supply of resources for this language. While generic SQL references will not necessarily show you how to get the most out of a MySQL database, they should teach you the fundamentals. A few online SQL references include

◆ A Gentle Introduction to SQL, `www.sql-zoo.net` (**Figure C.12**)

◆ SQL Course, `www.sqlcourse.com`

◆ SQL Course 2, `www.sqlcourse2.com`

◆ W3Schools.com, `www.w3schools.com/sql/default.asp` (**Figure C.13**)

◆ SQL.org, `www.sql.org`, a portal for most everything involved with databases

SQL

Security

Web server, operating system, and PHP security are all topics that could merit their own book. Unfortunately, outdated information is detrimental when it comes to security. Thus, the best way to stay in touch with the relevant security issues of the day is to track the following Web sites:

◆ PHP Security Consortium, `www.phpsec.org` (**Figure C.14**), focuses primarily on PHP-related security issues. There are articles on specific topics, a security guide, and links to other resources.

◆ A Study in Scarlet, `www.securereality.com.au/studyinscarlet.txt`, is a paper presented by Shaun Clowes that discusses a number of PHP-specific security issues. Although outdated, some fundamental ideas are discussed.

◆ The W3C's Security Resources, `www.w3.org/Security/`, is the World Wide Web Consortium's compendium of pertinent Web security information.

◆ OWASP, `www.owasp.org` (**Figure C.15**), is the Open Web Application Security Project. Although it's not PHP-specific, there's plenty of good information and tools to be found here.

◆ The MySQL documentation includes its own specific section on security at `http://dev.mysql.com/doc/mysql/en/security.html`.

I'll also add that MySQL, as of version 4.0, has the ability to use SSL (Secure Sockets Layer) to connect to a database over a safer connection. The manual further describes how to use SSH to do the same. Both are worth considering wherever secure data transmission is critical.

Figure C.14 The PHP Security Consortium is a good starting point for improving your security knowledge.

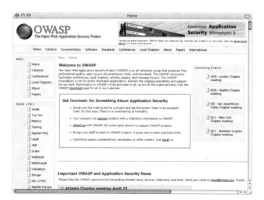

Figure C.15 For general Web security knowledge and advice, turn to OWASP.

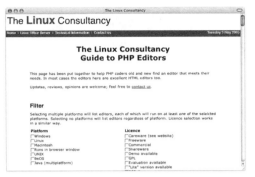

Figure C.16 If you need to find a new PHP text editor, this is the place to turn.

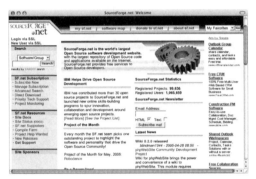

Figure C.17 SourceForge is the home to nearly 100,000 open source projects.

Figure C.18 The hip and useful Spoono.

Other Resources

There are a number of Web links worth knowing that do not fit conveniently into one of the other categories in this chapter (or otherwise do not merit their own category). Some of these links pertain to general Web development, and a number are specifically related to the technologies discussed in this book. Again, check the companion Web site for more current, descriptive, and complete listings.

For your software needs, you might consider turning to the Linux Consultancy's list of PHP Editors, www.thelinuxconsultancy. co.uk/phpeditors.php (**Figure C.16**). They have noted practically every possible text editor you could use for PHP development. Readers can also submit reviews of a particular application and see what platforms are supported and at what cost.

General

SourceForge, www.sourceforge.net, claims to be the world's largest repository of open source applications (and there's good cause to believe that). Thousands of different technologies are developed through and hosted by SourceForge (**Figure C.17**).

Web development

Developer Shed, www.devshed.com, is a general Web development site that includes articles discussing the various programming languages and technologies you are likely to use. These include PHP, Apache, and security.

WebMonkey, www.webmonkey.com, is very similar to DevShed, although it is broader in scope.

Spoono, www.spoono.com (**Figure C.18**), covers many aspects of developing Web sites, from graphic design to programming to HTML and JavaScript.

(X)HTML

The obvious resource for HTML concerns is the World Wide Web Consortium's home page, www.w3.org (**Figure C.19**), as they supervise the language. The site has loads of information but can be too technical. After that, you should also consider some of the resources I've previously listed, including W3Schools.com, WebMonkey.com, and DevShed.com.

There are several HTML-validation applications available online, which are free to use. These will tell you—even with PHP-generated pages—if a page has any problems. The two best free validators are the W3C's (http://validator.w3.org) and WebXACT (http://webxact.watchfire.com). The former focuses on adherence to standards, while the later is geared toward accessibility.

UseIt.com, www.useit.com, is Jakob Nielsen's Web site for discussing Web usability. Nielsen, who has written books on the subject, presents numerous do's and don'ts for Web development (**Figure C.20**).

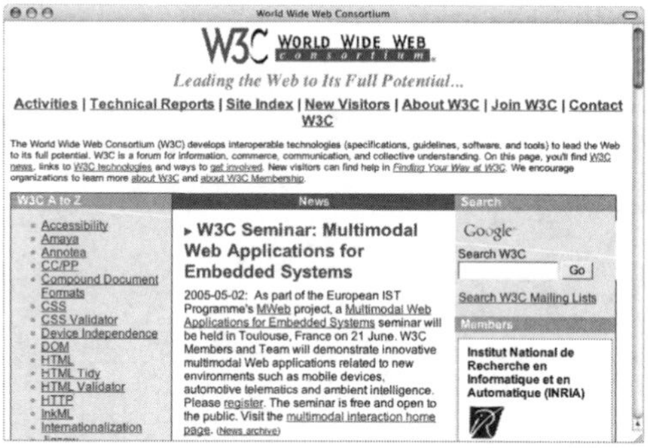

Figure C.19 The W3C site lists all HTML specifications.

Figure C.20 Jakob Nielsen is one of the leaders of Web usability ideology.

CSS

I use CSS (Cascading Style Sheets) in a couple of this book's examples but did not have the space to discuss the concept in detail. One of the great things about CSS is that you can use any number of freely available templates for your projects without a complete knowledge of how CSS works. Start by perusing and using the templates available at these sites:

◆ GordonMac.com, `www.gordonmac.com/downloads/html/`

◆ css Zen Garden, `www.csszengarden.com`

◆ Open Directory, `http://dmoz.org/Computers/Data_Formats/Style_Sheets/CSS/Examples/Layout/`

Once you've piqued your interest, begin *really* learning CSS online at

◆ CSS Panic Guide, `www.thenoodleincident.com/tutorials/css/index.html`

◆ A List Apart, `www.alistapart.com`

◆ Glish, `http://glish.com/css/`

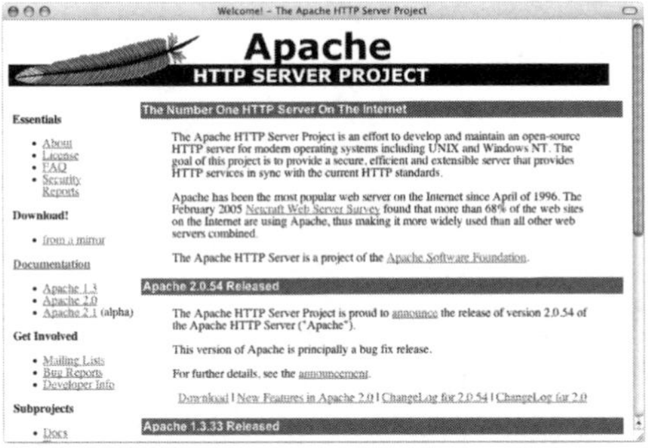

Figure C.21 The home page for the Apache Web server.

JavaScript

In my opinion, JavaScript resources on the Web tend to be inconsistent. You'll frequently need to peruse several just to find the information you are looking for. When the need arises, I recommend starting with

◆ `www.javascript.com`

◆ `http://javascript.internet.com`

As always, you may have the best luck by performing searches using Google, Yahoo!, or the like.

Apache Web server

Because the Apache Web server is the most popular server in use, especially on non-Windows operating systems, it's no surprise that there are several Web sites dedicated to the software. After you've read everything at Apache's home page, `http://httpd.apache.org` (**Figure C.21**), go to Apache Week, `www.apacheweek.com`, and Apache Today, `www.apachetoday.com`.

INDEX